EMERGENT
METHODS
IN SOCIAL
RESEARCH

D1563205

We dedicate this work to Matilda White Riley, for her inspiration, dedication, and vision of a holistic approach to our understanding of methods, and to David Rosen for inspiring all those around him to think way beyond the borders of the box.

EMERGENT
METHODS
IN SOCIAL
RESEARCH

EDITED BY

SHARLENE NAGY HESSE-BIBER
BOSTON COLLEGE

PATRICIA LEAVY
STONEHILL COLLEGE

SAGE Publications
Thousand Oaks ▪ London ▪ New Delhi

For information:

Sage Publications, Inc.
2455 Teller Road
Thousand Oaks, California 91320
E-mail: order@sagepub.com

Sage Publications Ltd.
1 Oliver's Yard
55 City Road
London EC1Y 1SP
United Kingdom

Sage Publications India Pvt. Ltd.
B-42, Panchsheel Enclave
Post Box 4109
New Delhi 110 017 India

Printed in the United States of America.

This book is printed on acid-free paper.

Library of Congress Cataloging-in-Publication Data

Emergent methods in social research / Sharlene Nagy Hesse-Biber, Patricia Leavy, [editors].
   p. cm.
Includes bibliographical references and index.
ISBN 1-4129-0917-1 (cloth : alk. paper) — ISBN 1-4129-0918-X (pbk.: alk. paper)
   1. Social sciences—Research—Methodology. I. Hesse-Biber, Sharlene Nagy. II. Leavy, Patricia, 1975—.
H61.E437 2006
300.72—dc22

                                            2005024323

06   07   08   09   10   9   8   7   6   5   4   3   2   1

Acquiring Editor:	Lisa Cuevas Shaw
Project Editor:	Jenn Reese
Typesetter:	C&M Digitals (P) Ltd.
Cover Artist:	Victoria Lee Croasdell

Contents

Acknowledgments   vii

**Introduction: Emergent Methods in
Social Research Within and Across Disciplines**   ix

1. Skirting a Pleated Text: De-Disciplining
   an Academic Life   1
   Laurel Richardson

2. Getting Connected: How Sociologists
   Can Access the High Tech Élite   13
   Trond Arne Undheim

3. A Sociologist Among Economists: Some Thoughts
   on Methods, Positionality, and Subjectivity   43
   Sarah Babb

4. Ethnography and Conversation Analysis:
   What Is the Context of an Utterance?   55
   Douglas W. Maynard

5. Creativity Within Qualitative Research
   on Families: New Ideas for Old Methods   95
   Sharon A. Deacon

6. Sampling Human Experience in Naturalistic Settings   109
   Tamlin Conner and Eliza Bliss-Moreau

7. Feminist Visualization: Re-envisioning
   GIS as a Method in Feminist Geographic Research   131
   Mei-Po Kwan

8. Practical Strategies for Combining Qualitative and
   Quantitative Methods: Applications to Health Research   165
   David L. Morgan

9. Performing Autoethnography: An Embodied
    Methodological Praxis   183
        Tami Spry

10. Exposed Methodology: The Body as a Deconstructive Practice   213
        Wanda S. Pillow

11. Ethnodrama: Performed Research—Limitations and Potential   235
        Jim Mienczakowski

12. On the *Listening Guide*: A Voice-Centered Relational Method 253
        Carol Gilligan, Renée Spencer,
        M. Katherine Weinberg, and Tatiana Bertsch

13. Friendship as Method   273
        Lisa M. Tillmann-Healy

14. Gender Imago   295
        Niza Yanay and Nitza Berkovitch

15. The Personal Is Political: Using Daily Diaries
    to Examine Everyday Prejudice-Related Experiences   313
        Lauri L. Hyers, Janet K. Swim, and Robyn K. Mallett

16. Feminist Media Ethnography in India:
    Exploring Power, Gender, and Culture in the Field   337
        Radhika Parameswaran

Conclusion: "Coming at Things Differently":
The Need for Emergent Methods   375

Index   383

About the Editors   405

About the Contributors   407

Acknowledgments

In the work toward this book, we appreciate the help of a number of people who supported the endeavor. Thank you to the many scholars who have contributed to our theoretical and practical understanding of emergent methods. In this vein we extend our appreciation to the contributors in this book who are the pioneers of new ways of knowing. We are very grateful to our students at Boston College and Stonehill College, particularly those in our qualitative research methods courses, for their inspiration and support. We would like to express a heartfelt thank you and our deep gratitude to Stonehill students Laura MacFee and Paul Sacco for their unfailing support during all aspects of putting this book together. Paul and Laura, we thank you for your help editing, formatting, proofing, and so much more, including your positive and supportive personalities. We would also like to thank Stonehill students Kathryn Maloney, Lisa Hastings, and Alyssa Voss for their proofreading work.

Sharlene Nagy Hesse-Biber is especially grateful to her husband, Michael, and daughters, Sarah Alexandra and Julia Ariel, for their patience, love, and understanding during all phases of the preparation of this book. Sharlene dedicates this work to Matilda White Riley, her first research methods mentor, who inspired her to think holistically about theory and methods.

Patricia Leavy is deeply grateful to her family and friends for their help, support, patience, inspiration, and humor during the preparation of this book. Patricia thanks her remarkable daughter, Madeline Claire, for teaching her new ways to think, see, and feel each and every day. Patricia dedicates this work, with love, to David Rosen for inspiring all those around him to think way beyond the borders of the box.

We want to acknowledge the enthusiastic support we received from the staff at Sage Publications. In particular, we extend a spirited thank you to Alison Mudditt, Lisa Cuevas, and Karen Wong.

Sage and the authors would also like to thank the following individuals for their contributions:

Nancy C. Larson
Arizona State University

Jon'a F. Meyer
Rutgers University (Camden)

Diana R. Grant
Sonoma State

Introduction

Emergent Methods in Social Research Within and Across Disciplines

The goal of this volume is to introduce "state of the art" social research methods that address the growing methods-theory gap within and across the disciplines. The social justice movements of the 1960s, in particular the civil rights movement and the women's movement, as well as an increasing global economic arena, challenged our traditional modes of thinking about the nature of the individual and society. Much of traditional research has been entrenched in a positivist paradigm, one that assumes a unified truth with the goal of testing knowledge and providing little room for exploration and interpretation of multiple perspectives. New theoretical contributions from feminist standpoint theory (Harding, 2004; Smith, 2004), postcolonial theory (Mohanty, 1988, 1999; Spivak, 1990), postmodernism (Nicholson & Seidman, 1999), ethnic studies (Perez, 1999), queer studies (Calvin, 2000), and critical theory and critical race theory (Wing, 2000) destabilized traditional forms of knowledge building by asking *new* questions that expose the power dynamics of knowledge building and by unearthing previously subjugated knowledge regarding the interconnections between race, gender, sexuality, class, and nationality. These diverse theoretical perspectives often cross disciplinary boundaries with the goal of creating new spaces for dialogue around issues of social justice and oppression. To compound matters, some research methods texts emphasize the learning of skills by taking a cookbook approach, spending little time discussing the links between theory and methods (see Seiler, 2004). A recent review of a methods textbook, in fact, states that the strength of the book lies in how "light" it is on theory:

The author has taken a cookbook approach to the discipline and provides a considerable amount of forms and checklists to support that approach. . . . For students who are unfamiliar with market research methodologies, this book would serve as a comprehensive guide to conducting that research. As such, one should not be disappointed that the book is heavily weighted toward practical applications and light on theoretical issues in qualitative research. After all, the purpose of the book is not to expand or explore the theoretical concepts surrounding qualitative methods but to provide data to support meaningful brand marketing. (Villella, 2002)

Yet, as sociologist Robert Merton noted early on, theory and methods are integral parts to the research endeavor:

Nor is it enough to say that research and theory must be married if sociology is to bear legitimate fruit. They must not only exchange solemn vows—they must know how to carry on from there. Their reciprocal roles must be clearly defined. (Merton, 1967, p. 171)

Even when theoretical concerns are addressed within the social sciences, Merton notes that much of the early training in the social sciences disciplines, like sociology, relied more on "knowing how to test a battery of hypotheses" than on "knowing the theory from which to derive hypotheses to be tested" (Merton, 1967, pp. 140–141). Sociologist Norman Denzin suggests that researchers who link theory with methods often tend to rely on "middle-range" theories (see Merton, 1967) that serve to shed light on "special areas" of research inquiry, with few ideas that lead to more general theoretical areas that have a wider applicability:

. . . the tendency to develop within limited boundaries theories resting on special methodologies—what Merton (1967) terms "middle-range sociology"—and while it brings theory and method closer together, a specific commitment to the special areas of inquiry seriously limits the far-ranging value of general theory. To read of a tightly integrated theory of small-group interaction is pleasing because it is theory but disappointing because it is not developed from a more abstract set of formulations. Small-group theory exists hand in hand with theories of the family, of political sociology, of delinquency, and so on, but seldom do these specialized theories with their localized methods come together in one large and more general theory. (Denzin, 1989, p. 3)

Beyond the issue of delinking theory from method, there is the movement toward specialization in research methods as well. The specific intent is to master one research method. Denzin remarks on the lack of innovation in the use of methods among researchers who often stick with one "tried and true" method that is often situated in their own discipline:

> Other sociologists have tended to use methods with little thought for either their theoretical implications or their differing ability to shed light on theory. Many sociologists now use only one method in their studies—thereby eschewing the potential value of other methodologies. Small-group theorists rely nearly entirely upon the experiment, while family sociologists primarily use the survey technique, and students of organizations overemphasize field strategies such as participant observation. This tendency has given rise to a rather parochial, specialty-bound use of research methods. (Denzin, 1989, p. 3)

While a range of new methods is beginning to develop across and within the disciplines, they remain dispersed and marginalized, resulting in a widening of the gap between new theoretical questions and the methods needed to answer them. The gap is also fostered by the paucity of training programs in emerging methods in the social science curriculum, and the continuing divide between qualitative and quantitative methods (see Denzin & Lincoln, 1994). While there is a lessening of this divide (Teddlie & Tashakkori, 2003), there is still controversy in terms of how each of these methods should be integrated, with some researchers taking up a renewed interest in mixed-methods research designs as a way of providing new tools for resolving the widening gap between theory and methods in the research process.

What Are Emergent Methods?

Emergent research methods are the logical conclusion to paradigm shifts, major developments in theory, and new conceptions of knowledge and the knowledge-building process. As researchers continue to explore new ways of thinking about and framing knowledge construction, so, too, do they develop new ways of building knowledge, accessing data, and generating theory. In this sense, new methods and methodologies are theory driven and question driven. Emergent methods often arise in order to answer research questions that traditional methods may not adequately address. Evolving theoretical paradigms in the disciplines have opened up the possibilities of the development of innovative methods to get at new theoretical perspectives. Early on, noted philosopher Thomas Kuhn in his work *The Structure of Scientific Revolutions* (1970) argues that science at any one point in time is characterized by a particular paradigm, or way of thinking. Knowledge is filtered through the particular model or paradigm or set of paradigms currently dominant within a particular field. Paradigms provide a conceptual framework through which to view the world. They are models within which the basic concepts and ideas of a particular discipline are understood. What is regarded as legitimate knowledge—ideas such as who can know and what can be known—is filtered through particular disciplinary ways of knowing, or the paradigms within which scientific work proceeds. One of Kuhn's key points regarding why one paradigm wins out over another is that knowledge building is primarily political in nature—often it is irrational and subjective phenomena that affect the development of science. The paradigm that emerges victorious is the one that has the most converts—it need not have the greater explanatory power.

Emergent methods are conscious of the link between epistemology (a view on how knowledge is constructed), methodology (the theoretical question[s] that informs our research and how it is carried out), and method (the specific tools used to carry out research). Emergent methods are particularly useful in getting at issues of power and authority in the research process, from question formulation to carrying out and writing up research findings. We can think of these methods as hybrid in the sense that they often borrow and adapt methods from their own disciplines or can cross disciplinary boundaries to create new tools and an concepts or refashion tools or concepts that exist in order to answer complex and often novel questions. Emergent methods can consist of both qualitative and quantitative methods or a combination of both.

To work with an emergent method may require the researcher to engage at the borders of traditional methods and sometimes work from a multidisciplinary or even interdisciplinary position. Emergent methods disrupt traditional ways of knowing, such as positivism, in order to create rich new meanings. Adopting an interdisciplinary perspective is often a process in which one becomes both an insider and an outsider—taking on a multitude of different standpoints and negotiating these identities simultaneously. This is aptly expressed by Trinh T. Minh-ha's concept of multiple subjectivities:

> Working right at the limits of several categories and approaches means that one is neither entirely inside or outside. One has to push one's work as far as one can go: to the borderlines, where one never stops, walking on the edges, incurring constantly the risk of falling off one side or the other side of the limit while undoing, redoing, modifying this limit. (Minh-ha, 1991, p. 218)

Working with emergent methods calls forth a reassessment of one's standpoint as a researcher by raising questions of disciplinary location:

- How tightly bound am I to my own discipline—its concepts, methods, and so forth?
- If I experience role conflict or tension in trying to occupy multidisciplinary positions, how are these issues resolved?
- Do I conduct research as a disciplinary insider, an outsider, or both?
- If I adopt the standpoint of outsider, am I overly identified with the other's viewpoint?
- If I adopt the role of insider, do I allow myself to take risks, to challenge my disciplinary standpoint?

Emergent Methods in Ethnographic Research

Some of the chapters in this book challenge social researchers to question traditional forms of knowledge construction within ethnography. Theoretical insights from feminism, poststructuralism, and critical race theory, as well as postcolonial theory, challenge ethnographic researchers to build bridges that link new research questions with innovative ethnographic methods that can address issues of power, authority, and representation in the research process. Laurel Richardson's "Skirting a Pleated Text: De-Disciplining an Academic Life" talks about the need for de-disciplining ourselves. Being tightly entrenched in one's own discipline can limit the types of questions (story lines) a researcher asks by a "suppression in their own voices" (Chapter 1, this volume). Laurel Richardson's chapter provides new theoretical insights through studying her own academic struggles so that what she writes is true to her self-experience. Her poststructural perspective sees knowledge building as "contextually situated, local, and partial" (Chapter 1). Positivism and its reliance on the tenet of objectivity requires the researcher to distance herself from knowledge production; however, for Richardson there is no "truth" out there waiting to be discovered. She does not place her values, attitudes, and feelings in abeyance by suppressing her own voice in service of obtaining "truth." Power and authority are ever present in the types of questions all researchers ask; whether visible or not, the researcher is present within the research context. Yet, Richardson is torn about how she can write about her own academic experience while remaining true to these traditional positivistic requirements of knowledge building. She crosses disciplinary boundaries, borrowing methods of writing that are autobiographical. Her writing becomes the telling of a series of stories that she calls

a pleated text, traditional and experimental papers written over a period of 10 years folded between what I call "writing-stories"—about the contexts in which I wrote those papers. The pleats can be spread open at any point, folded back, unfurled. (Chapter 1)

These texts form the basis of her book *Fields of Play: Constructing an Academic Life* (Richardson, 1997).

Richardson's interaction with feminist poststructuralist theories calls forth experimental writing practices to convey her story. She notes, "Experimenting with textual form, I wrote sociology as drama, responsive readings, narrative poetry, pagan ritual, lyrical poetry, prose poems, humor, and autobiography" (Chapter 1). Richardson pushes on the boundaries of traditional modes of representing knowledge building not "to reject social scientific writing, but rather to enlarge the field through other representation forms" (Chapter 1).

Trond Arne Undheim's chapter, "Getting Connected: How Sociologists Can Access the High Tech Élite," stresses the importance of "studying up." Studies of elites are not standard practices within the social sciences. Elites occupy key positions within society, wielding power and control while often remaining invisible. They protect their privacy through multiple ways of preventing access to them that range from unlisted phone numbers to employing a staff to screen their calls and contacts. Undheim provides some important suggestions for how to access and conduct interviews with elites. He provides specific examples from the research literature on elites and by drawing on his own study of high-tech elites in the United States, Italy, and Norway. He suggests new techniques for accessing elites as well as practical suggestions for reworking the traditional interview method, with its emphasis on "asymmetrical exchange." He employs a range of "improvisational" techniques borrowed from journalism and psychology as well as criminology. The journalistic style "is intuitive, quick, active. . . . Journalists are used to working through acquaintances, contacts, friends, and secretaries." A "therapeutic" mode of inquiry stresses the importance of "identity and trust," especially within the interview process. He also urges researchers to place themselves in the role of detective. Detective work requires "an investigative, methodic, and curious type who dedicates him/herself to solve mysteries and problems" (Chapter 2, this volume).

Sociologist Sarah Babb's chapter, "A Sociologist Among Economists: Some Thoughts on Methods, Positionality, and Subjectivity," talks about the nuts and bolts of studying economic elites. She is interested in understanding how U.S.-trained economists managed to "take over the Mexican government," (Chapter 3, this volume) specifically through their influence on Mexican economic policies. She provides a behind-the-scenes account of her own journey from question formulation to the carrying out of her research using a range of content-analytic and interview methods that she reshapes in order to get at subjugated knowledge of a powerful elite that spans many decades. In fact, she herself notes, "I find myself asking whether there is a name for the kind of research that I did. I ultimately think the best way to describe my research was that I used everything I could get my hands on" (Chapter 3). She also shares her trials and tribulations as a novice researcher who is gathering data for her doctorate and how her own position as a white female researcher interfaces with the realities of the research setting. She notes, in fact, that her gender turned out to be an asset among the primarily male elites she interviewed:

> As a woman in her late twenties, I appeared non-threatening, and often found myself the recipient of "gentlemanly" treatment—being taken out to lunch, having doors held open for me, and so on. (Chapter 3)

She notes, however, the importance of personal networks within the setting that provided entry into this elite circle.

Employing emergent methods, notes Babb, requires a great deal of self-esteem and social support:

> As one slowly collects the patches that are to be assembled into the quilt, it seems impossible to imagine how it will all fit together. The task seems doubly impossible when one compares one's own activities to those of researchers engaged in methods that are more straightforward—to the historian in his archives, or the demographer at her computer terminal. (Chapter 3)

Emergent Methods Across the Disciplines: A Sampling of Innovative Techniques

Sociologist Douglas W. Maynard's chapter, "Ethnography and Conversation Analysis: What Is the Context of an Utterance?" examines how ethnographers and conversation analysts, through combining both these approaches, can enhance their understanding of social interaction. Ethnography relies on participant observation and interviews to capture the everyday goings-on within natural settings. Conversation analysts are interested in capturing the fine details of conversations—for example, the specific sequence of words and behaviors of those who interact in a natural setting. Douglas W. Maynard provides us with a unique example of how to use both these approaches by analyzing an in-depth conversation on how "bad news" is delivered by pediatricians in a clinical setting to parents who will learn for the first time that their young son is mentally retarded. He argues that ethnographic accounts gathered through interviews help the conversation analysis and provide the researcher with "access to inner experience and its relation to behavior and conduct" (Chapter 4, this volume). Maynard notes that ethnographic data can enable the researcher to discover patterns in how bad news is delivered within and across a variety of clinical settings as well as the range of responses recipients of bad news have. However, what is missing, notes Maynard, is our understanding of how the delivery of bad news concerns how experience is lived in real time. What specific interaction is produced in the giving and receiving of bad news? How is conversation sequenced and organized? Maynard feels that the extent to which these methods are integrated within any natural setting resides along a continuum of affinity and nonaffinity that is explained in his chapter.

Psychologist Sharon Deacon provides a unique emergent technique to enhance "old methods." In her chapter, "Creativity Within Qualitative Research on Families: New Ideas for Old Methods," she suggests a variety of "active" methods that can be used to involve research participants in the research process to understand the lived experiences of her respondents. She advocates the use of multimedia techniques such as photography and videography, and crosses disciplinary boundaries by drawing on ideas from the arts (sculpting, photography, drawing, and role-playing) and the humanities (through writing exercises and the use of metaphors and time lines). She provides the researcher with ideas about how to employ each of these active methods in her family research projects. She cautions researchers to carefully consider whether these methods would enhance the process of data gathering or detract from it. A consideration of the population being studied is crucial; some methods may not be appropriate for certain groups, such as children. There is also the concern that researchers who are unfamiliar with the application of these methods may do more harm than good if respondents perceive the researcher as uncomfortable in the practice of these new tools.

Psychologists Tamlin Conner and Eliza Bliss-Moreau's chapter, "Sampling Human Experience in Naturalistic Settings," provides an excellent example of how social researchers can employ innovative techniques to enhance our understanding of human experience. They take up the question of how the social sciences can measure the experience of their respondents, given that experience itself is characterized by a "temporal quality" and subject to "revision in memory." They discuss the history and technique of "experience sampling," which provides respondents a new way to report their inner feelings, thoughts, and behaviors within the context of their daily routines. They provide a detailed example of how this technique can be used in social research. Experience sampling uses a variety of technological devices to sample and record human experience in naturalistic settings. The authors discuss both the strengths and drawbacks of this method. An important strength of the technique is that experience is captured throughout the day and occurs within a natural setting, as opposed to a laboratory setting that may introduce bias into the measurement of experience. Experience sampling provides important answers to questions such as the following:

- How does experience change throughout a given period?
- Do some experiences covary with one another?
- What impact, if any, do some experiences have on others?
- How does an individual's experience vary within and between different settings, genders, and so forth?
- Do some social contexts promote specific experiences (when one is alone versus within a group)?

There are drawbacks to using such an approach, however. Experience gathered in a naturalistic setting may not get at the specific experiences the researcher is interested in measuring. If you are, for example, interested in how conflict and coping are measured, the researcher may run into trouble getting enough examples of this occurrence in a natural setting.

Those who practice experience sampling are still left with answering issues of cause and effect:

- What does it mean to say there is a relationship between sadness and specific context (being alone or with specific individuals)?
- What is the cause and effect of sadness?

Experience sampling that uses technology (palm devices and/or computers) makes some projects expensive to carry out and may place high compliance demands on respondents throughout their daily routines. More intimate experiences may be difficult to capture altogether. Another important issue is how one's experience actually translates into behavior. What determines action beyond experience?

Geographer Mei-Po Kwan's chapter, "Feminist Visualization: Re-envisioning GIS as a Method in Feminist Geographic Research," illuminates how new theoretical perspectives can serve as a catalyst toward the creation of new methods. Mei-Po Kwan is a feminist geographer who challenges traditional knowledge building in the field of geographic research. Kwan's work helps to highlight the lack of attention to women's concerns in the field of geographic research, which often renders women invisible while promoting and preserving the interests of the dominant group. She argues that visualization and vision are crucial forms of knowledge building. Kwan further asserts that the lens of traditional geography is inherently disembodied and masculinist, one that often assumes "a God's eye view." She argues that all visualization is a view from somewhere and, through her feminist geographer's lens, she calls forth new methods for promoting visual technologies that take into account the range of differences within the social reality in terms of gender, race, class, sexuality, and so on. She advocates for alternative cartographic practices such as the "countermaps" that more adequately represent oppressed groups' maps and destabilize dominant representations of reality.

Feminist visualization requires the geographer to practice reflexivity in her research endeavors. Drawing on the work of several feminist geographers (Rose, 2001), Kwan provides the reader with several checklists for accomplishing reflexivity when applying this method. The first practice is to be mindful "at the site of production," where the researcher reflects on how she practices "meaning making." A second site at which to be mindful is the image itself, where the geographer looks not only for presence but also for absence. This is a reflection on the power and authority of the image to marginalize and/or privilege groups and issues. The third checklist practice is to reflect on how the images are perceived by an audience:

- Does the image favor a point of view?
- Is the audience encouraged to question or renegotiate this image?

She argues that feminist geographers have an important contribution to make to their field, yet their ideas and concerns remain separated from mainstream geographic practices. She notes feminist geographers, in fact, practice visualization differently: with an attention to "proximity and compression" instead of "vast space in which the viewer's position is hard to infer" (Kwan, Chapter 7, this volume). The goal of feminist visualization is not to represent "truth" but to explore how individuals experience their world across the multiple categories of race, class, gender, sexuality, and so on. She provides excellent examples of how a feminist geographical perspective crosses disciplinary lines. She relates the example of how one researcher studies the impact of the local geographical context on women's labor market outcome by combining geographic visualization techniques with a vast number of qualitative methods, such as looking at the nearness of female-dominated jobs to women's homes. The juxtaposition of qualitative and geographic methods helps unearth the important spatial dimensions of the gendering of occupations. In a similar way, geographical analysis can be combined with epidemiological analysis. She notes that studies of breast cancer rates by community provide crucial information to environmental advocates who are studying the relationship between toxic waste and the rise in the incidence of breast cancer. She also notes how certain qualitative materials, for example, respondents' hand-drawn maps and sketches, can provide a much richer context for interpreting traditional geographical images from the point of view of the "other." For example, geographic images that trace the everyday lives of women from different racial/ethnic and class backgrounds can enrich our understanding of the lives of diverse women.

Sociologist David Morgan introduces a set of mixed-methods strategies for combining qualitative and quantitative methods. Mixed-methods designs are particularly suited for accessing subjugated knowledge through providing a voice to those whose viewpoints may be left out of the research process. Morgan suggests four mixed-methods research designs that depend on the sequencing (time ordering) as well as relative importance (priority) of each method.

The Body

Over the past three decades, the body—our physical, fleshy, corporeal reality—has gained attention in feminist and postmodern theory, which has necessitated the development of emergent methods and methodologies. The feminist and postmodern scholars who have paid particular attention to the body have long explained the importance of embodiment. In this tradition, all social actors are embodied actors—our experience, vision, and standpoint are embodied. We know and experience social reality from our embodied standpoints within the society. One cannot separate knowledge, action, and experience from our embodied vantage points within the culture. In particular, scholars have examined how, in a hierarchical society, our bodies are sexed, gendered, racialized, and classed. Given the surge of interest in embodiment, and the theoretical implications of this direction in thought, it is congruent that researchers would begin to develop new methods and methodologies aimed at accessing the knowledge of corporeality.

Elizabeth Grosz (1994) has been at the cutting edge of developing theory about corporeality. Grosz distinguishes between two approaches to theorizing the body: (a) the inscribed body and (b) the lived body.

The inscribed body serves as a site of meaning—where social meanings are constructed and resisted. In other words, the body is marked by our social historical context (Grosz, 1994, p. 61). Drawing on the work of Michel Foucault (1977) and Susan Bordo (1989), Grosz explains, "The body is not outside of history, for it is produced through and in history" (Grosz, 1994, p. 148).

When Grosz explains that the body is a site of meaning situated in a sociohistorical context, she is remarking on the process by which cultural norms and values are inscribed on the body. There can be "subtle" or "violent" inscriptions (1994, p. 141). For example, our bodies become gendered and racialized; these inscriptions may be subtle, but they are culturally bound and cumulative in effect (p. 141). The way we sex or gender or racialize the body is not natural or ahistorical but rather embedded in existing relations of power (pp. 141–142): "Inscriptions on the subject's body coagulate corporeal signifiers into signs, producing all the effects of meaning, representation, depth, within or subtending our social order" (1994, p. 141).

Because our bodies serve as a site of meaning making within our culture, they also serve as a site of scholarly investigation. Inscription is only one of the ways our bodies come to matter.[1]

The lived body refers to people's experiential knowledge, that which is linked to their physicality. Grosz is heavily influenced by Merleau-Ponty (1962), who rejects the Cartesian mind-body dichotomy and argues we must look at the "necessary interconnectedness" of the mind and body (Grosz, 1994, p. 86). Under this framework, the body is not conceptualized as an object but rather as the "condition and context" through which individuals have relations to objects and through which we give and receive information (p. 86). Therefore, the body is an instrument through which meaning is generated. We have knowledge about our bodies by living in them: "It is an embodied subject that occupies a perspective on objects" (p. 90).

Given the nature of embodiment, researchers can access important knowledge through merging the mind and body and examining the "lived body," or experience had through the body. Merleau-Ponty (1962) located experience between the mind and body, thus necessitating a link between the two if human experience is to be understood. Grosz explains as follows:

> Perception is, as it were, midway between mind and body and requires the functioning of both . . . experience is always necessarily embodied, corporeally constituted, located in and as the subject's incarnation. Experience can only be understood between mind and body—or across them—in their lived conjunction. (1994, pp. 94–95)

In order to access experiential knowledge, researchers must, then, find ways to access "enfleshed knowledge" (Spry, Chapter 9, this volume) and integrate the mind and body in their research.

Paying critical attention to the body can literally and metaphorically transform and inform research practices. If we develop research questions and enter the research process with a focus on the body and bodily experience and/or inscription, we are influenced in many ways, including what we look at, how we look, what we ask, and what aspects of social reality we represent. Moreover, if we are attentive to the body, we, as writers of social experience, can explore how the body works in narrating individual and collective stories.

Wanda Pillow (Chapter 10, this volume) discovered the centrality of the body in her research once she had begun data collection. She was conducting research on pregnant teenagers and their experiences. Once she began the research process, she realized that feminist, critical, postmodern, and qualitative research theories had not properly prepared her for the physicality of her research experiences. The body, the changing body, the experience of the pregnant body, structural responses to girls' changing bodies, and the perceptions of others toward girls' pregnant bodies became central to her research. In fact, without focusing on the body, it would not have been possible to understand much of the experience of this population. Accordingly, Pillow modified her research to focus on the bodies and bodily experiences of the girls she was studying. In other words, she developed a *body-centered methodology* in direct response to her research question and research needs— she developed a new approach to her ethnographic work based on the failure of traditional methodologies to access the information she was seeking. In her chapter, she discusses her research process and how a shift to the body allowed her to ask and answer research questions that would otherwise be impossible to address. Likewise, she was able to access knowledge that would otherwise remain invisible. For another topical example, consider how the study of body image among diverse populations also changes dramatically when bodily experience and the inscribed body (gendered and racialized body) become central sites of investigation. This emergent method provides researchers with a way to ask and answer a host of new research questions and revisit research topics studied in the past while shining a light on previously unseen aspects of that reality.

Autoethnographic Performance and Ethnodrama: Integrating Mind and Body

Drawing on scholarship regarding embodiment, researchers are also developing methods that explicitly integrate the mind and body in the research process. This movement in research methodology is also linked to developments in postmodern theory that have inspired researchers to consider, on a meaningful level, the way in which they represent their research. Some scholars have drawn on creative and artistic ways of representing their research, including performance-based approaches. The combination of this theoretical direction and a desire to access bodily knowledge through merging mind and body has given birth to a new range of performance-driven methods, which are not only about using performance as representation, but also about using performance as a method of data collection and interpretation. At the intersection of these theoretical and methodological commitments, autoethnographic performance has emerged as a distinct research method.

Autoethnographic performance is a method that works at the intersection of the intellectual and the bodily, blurring these traditionally binary categorizations. Specifically, this method merges text (the autoethnographic narrative) and the body (the performative aspects of research). First we will explain traditional autoethnographic research and then we will review this new method.

Autoethnography developed out of a tradition of qualitative researchers using autobiographical data in both direct and indirect ways in their research. For example, field researchers often keep a journal, ethics diary, or reflective diary where they document their thoughts, feelings, emotions, impressions, and so forth (Tenni, Smyth, & Boucher, 2003, p. 2). In this way, autobiographical data is often a part of the qualitative research process. Building on this tradition and grounding itself in the practice of oral history, autoethnographies developed as an extension and permutation of the oral history method. Generally, autoethnography is a method of oral history in which the researcher becomes his or her own subject. With this method, researchers use their own thoughts, feelings, and experiences as a means of understanding the social world, or some aspect of it. "*Autoethnography* refers to writing about the personal and its relationship to culture. It is an autobiographical genre of writing and research that displays multiple layers of consciousness" (Ellis, 2004, p. 37, quoting Dumont, 1978).

Ellis (2004) expands on this definition in order to illustrate the richness of this method and the representational possibilities, which, as you will see, include performance:

> "What is autoethnography?" you might ask. My brief answer: research, writing, story, and method that connect the autobiographical and personal to the cultural, social, and political. Autoethnographic forms feature concrete action, emotion, embodiment, self-consciousness, and introspection portrayed in dialogue, scenes, characterization, and plot. Thus, autoethnography claims the conventions of literary writing. (p. xix)

The method can help a researcher raise his or her self-consciousness and is, by nature, a highly reflexive practice. Additionally, this method contains personal and political emancipatory possibilities (Spry, Chapter 9). The narrative that emerges is autobiographical but situated within a cultural backdrop. An autoethnographic text develops from a researcher's embodied position and is thus a bodily, as well as intellectual, production (Chapter 9). Furthermore, because researchers engaged in autoethnographic research often record their emotional experiences during the research project (for example, feeling pain during the process may be a marker that something important is being explored), the method is by nature bodily as well as intellectual:

> The engagement with what is going on for us must be physical, emotional and intellectual. It is with the physical and emotional in particular, that we often get the first clue that something is happening and may be worthy of exploration. So our annoyance, discomfort, restlessness, sadness, excitement, triumph, tense neck, scratchy eyes or feeling of serenity is also data that alert us to something. This process may cause some degree of distress so having supports in place (such as a supervisor, colleague or support group) is important. (Tenni, Smyth, & Boucher, 2003, p. 3)

Under this method, knowledge is, then, in a very real sense, constructed at the junction of the mind and body. The emergence of autoethnographic performance as a method in its own right is then not surprising.

Autoethnographic performance is a new method that operates at the intersection of oral history, ethnography, autoethnography, and theater. Autoethnographic performance captures both the "autobiographic impulse" and the "ethnographic moment" (Chapter 9). When using this method, Spry urges us to ask, How do we witness our own constructions of reality? Furthermore, given that this is an embodied methodology, the act of performance allows researchers to "re-inhabit" their bodies as a part of the knowledge-building process (Chapter 9). One of the guiding ideas in autoethnographic performance is that there is a "purposeful dialogue" between the reader and author—those who read and participate in the performative aspects of the research are moved both intellectually and emotionally (Chapter 9). This allows those who learn from these narratives to access both intellectual and carnal, emotive, bodily knowledge. Thus this method validates the multiple ways in which people come to know, and sees these varied ways as dialectical as opposed to binary.

In addition to autoethnographic performance, researchers across disciplines have created other methods that draw on theater in an effort to merge the mind and body into the research endeavor. One such method is called *ethnodrama*. Ethnodramatic research bridges theater and scholarly research. This research method developed as the theater community and research community came together to develop "a theory with practice" (Mienczakowski, Chapter 11, this volume). Again, we can see that theoretical developments directly influence the construction of new research practices.

Ethnodramatic research is a collective enterprise between the researcher and research participants. This method draws on early documentary-style dramas and the kind of "verbatim theater" traditionally used in oral history methods (in which the oral history transcript is recited as is; Chapter 11). In ethnodrama, the dramatic scripts and performance pieces develop with research informants controlling the text and its representation. The audience provides an ongoing validation process and modifications are continually made to both the script and the performance of the script. In this vein, all participants in the project are in a struggle to create social meaning and, moreover, to share meaning. The focus on ongoing validation and the cocreation of social meaning poses a challenge to traditional ethnographic writing, in which the researcher is positioned as the authority. Ethnodramatic performances are about "the present moment" and are thus fluid, and emerging social meaning is open for modification (Chapter 11). The idea is to cocreate "plausible" accounts of social reality (Chapter 11). Proponents of this method cite both the educational and the emancipatory possibilities that are also present in autoethnographic performance. Mienczakowski says the method offers "emotional enlightenment" (Chapter 11).

The power of this method to allow for the coconstruction of meaning, and to build knowledge and share social meaning in a fluid manner, makes it a valuable method in many disciplines. As such, this method is used in health research, health training, education, the social sciences, and multimethod approaches and applied research across the disciplines. Within the social sciences, this method, or a modification of it, can be used to create dramatized narratives out of interview, oral history, ethnographic, or autoethnographic data. The effectiveness of this method within such diverse kinds of research indicates that some emergent research practices are not discipline specific but rather malleable methods that can be adapted to fit a variety of research questions and research purposes.

Listening as Method

Communication has been the focal point for many kinds of research practices, including intensive interview and oral history interview. Typically, qualitative researchers interested in the coconstruction of meaning have worked in collaboration with their research participants to create narratives. These methods of inquiry require active listening on the part of the researcher. Now, our understanding of how listening can serve knowledge building is being expanded.

Psychologist Carol Gilligan developed the "listening guide" as a method of psychological analysis. This method involves a series of steps called "sequential listenings" and constitutes a systematic way researchers can use listening as a method of inquiry. This method developed in the discipline of psychology as a way to access the "inner world" of participants, a central component in psychological research. This method of psychological analysis draws on voice, resonance, and relationship—these are seen as "ports of entry into the human psyche" (Chapter 12, this volume). As seen in the body-related methods we've already reviewed, this research method is also influenced by scholarship on embodiment. Psychologists who practice this method explain that voice is also embodied. Voice exists in a cultural context, in relation to self, and in relation to others (Chapter 12). Additionally, voice is based on a shared set of assumptions. In practice, this method requires a deep level of participation on the part of the researcher—this kind of listening is active, engaged, and consistent. As you will see in the listening guide reading, things a researcher might listen to or for include the following: Who is speaking? To whom is one speaking? In what cultural framework is one speaking?

The scholars who have developed this method have built on the idea of following the lead of the person speaking and are influenced by prominent scholars in psychology and psychoanalysis including Breuer, Freud, and Piaget. Although this method developed in psychology, it has the potential to be used more broadly across the social sciences. In fact, this emergent method is influenced not only by psychological theory and research but also by literary theory. Across the disciplines, qualitative methods are being created for interpreting narratives as part and parcel of meaning making.

Friendship as Method

As we just discussed, using listening as a research technique requires active participation on the part of the researcher, who coconstructs knowledge with his or her research participants. This method thus draws on some of the main tenets of the qualitative paradigm. Some of the body- and performance-driven methods we discussed earlier also draw on qualitative conceptions of research as a collaborative endeavor of shared meaning construction. These principles and the traditional practice of ethnography, particularly anthropological ethnography, have come together and coalesced into a new method of inquiry: friendship.

Tillmann-Healy developed friendship as a qualitative method and a particular form of fieldwork. There is a clear methodological link between the process of field research and the course of friendship. Commonalities between these two processes include gaining entry, role negotiation, relational dialectics, development over time, and being engaged in the world of another (Chapter 13, this volume). In addition to being a specific method of ethnography, this method is also conceptually close to in-depth interview, where reciprocity is integral to narrative construction. This method has emerged out of the interpretive tradition, which emphasizes understanding, phenomenology, feminism, queer theory, and critiques of positivism (Chapter 13). Additionally, the method shares aspects of participatory action research. As you can see, friendship as a form of field research crosses disciplinary boundaries and operates at the intersection of multiple disciplinary traditions. The method is also similar to an anthropological approach to field research, where a research project develops organically in a natural environment. In other words, in anthropology, fieldwork is situated in the normal context of the people being studied and thus in the normal context of relationships and friendships (Chapter 13).

Field research is one of the oldest and most respected qualitative methods of inquiry. With that said, if you understand traditional ethnography, then you already understand some of the assumptions underlying the friendship method: reciprocity, interaction, investment, and understanding. However, in traditional ethnography, the researcher goes into a setting that is natural to the participants, gathers data (partly through forming relationships in the field), and leaves the field and generates "knowledge" out of his or her field notes and so forth. Friendship as a method differs in that the researcher is looking for *intersubjective meanings*. Moreover, as in natural friendships, the researcher gives as much as he or she gets. There is a deep and genuine level of investment in the lives of the participants. Key components of this method include vulnerability, compassion, and giving (Chapter 13). In other words, the method is guided by and grounded within an "ethic of friendship," which demands giving and reciprocity at a high level (Chapter 13). This method challenges traditional practices of ethics within the research process. In addition to providing a new method that draws on the traditional methods of ethnography and in-depth interview, friendship as method also extends forward our cross-disciplinary conversation about ethics throughout research practice.

Friendship as method is not the only emergent method that draws on ideals of reciprocity and meaningful relationships. Scholars interested in reflexive practice and accessing silenced knowledge are also looking for new ways to generate intersubjective meanings. Feminists are among those pioneering new methods of inquiry.

Emergent Feminist Research Practices: Writing-in-Response, Daily Diary Research, and Feminist Media Ethnography

In recent years, writing has emerged as a research method. Laurel Richardson pioneered writing as a method of inquiry or knowing by focusing on the way writing fosters a researcher's own voice and can function as a process of discovery. Merging writing as method and the reciprocity of friendship, *writing-in-response* has developed as a new research tool. But this method also developed with a feminist sensibility. Long interested in accessing subjugated knowledges, feminists have developed approaches to research that "get at" the experiences and experiential knowledge of those typically marginalized within the research process. As seen in the Maynard reading, there are some methods emerging aimed at accessing experience. There are also methods developing that problematize experience. Yanay and Berkovitch created the writing-in-response method as a way of problematizing experience and reflexively exploring ideas and theories collaboratively across disciplinary boundaries.

Niza Yanay and Nitza Berkovitch developed writing-in-response almost on the fly. Initially, each scholar was scheduled to give a lecture (on their own topics); however, after the first speaker presented, the second speaker modified her talk in order to respond to issues raised by the first speaker. In essence, this resulted in an unplanned "speaking-in-response" method of knowledge building. From this experience came writing-in-response as a form of dialogue where knowledge develops through an interactive process between the parties involved. Yanay and Berkovitch achieved writing-in-response by using personal electronic correspondence. This method can be conceptualized as a particular "genre" of correspondence and dialogue. The participating parties are coperformers in the knowledge-building process. Differing from autoethnography, writing as method, and other forms of reflexive writing, when using this method, the audience that will respond to the narrative is not imagined (the people who could potentially read and respond to the piece), but the responder is known and immediately engaged in the process. As you'll see in "Gender Imago" (Chapter 14), the authors talk about the intimacy of letters versus the immediacy of speaking. Also seen in their exploration of feminist theory and reflexive engagement with their experiences and feelings about their experiences, this method unravels the tension between theory and experience and allows scholars to explore the junctures and, sometimes, disjunctures between theory and personal experience. This may be particularly appealing to scholars working from critical, feminist, and queer studies, and other theoretical perspectives committed to reflexivity and attentive to relations of power.

Daily diary research is another new research method that draws on writing, except with this method, it is the research participants who engage in the writing. Hyers, Swim, and Mallett (Chapter 15, this volume) have developed the daily diary method as an alternative way qualitative researchers can get at people's daily experiences. Many qualitative research methods, such as ethnography and various types of interview, aim at yielding information about people's daily experiences, and so Hyers, Swim, and Mallett developed a new writing-driven method to get at this kind of information. This is an example of creating a new way to ask a certain set of research questions, and, as we will see, the new method allows for new insight.

In diary research, participants employ a method of participant observation in which the participants are true collaborators. Participants record their thoughts, feelings, observations, and behaviors in a diary. This kind of diary is very different from the personal diaries with which you may be familiar. Personal diaries are usually written as an ongoing narrative and are meant to be kept private. The diary writing in diary research is meant to be used for knowledge-building purposes, and the writing is more directed and purposeful than typical diary narration. The research diary can be structured in many different ways and can include open-ended and closed-ended response formats. The researcher can predetermine categories of events that the person will write about. Likewise, the researcher can schedule entry times (such as a particular time each day) or may leave the entry schedule to participants (who may choose to write only when something of note occurs). In sum, the diary structure can vary to fit a range of research purposes. This method can also be employed from a range of epistemological positions. Hyers, Swim, and Mallett illustrate the fit between this method and the tenets of feminist standpoint theory, which posits that the only way to know the social world is by accessing the vantage points of those groups differentially located within the society (such as women) who have unique knowledge. In addition to being employed from multiple epistemological positions, diary research can be used to study a range of topics that center on getting at people's daily experiences. When used from a feminist perspective, daily diary research can be used to access subjugated knowledge.

For example, Hyers, Swim, and Mallett explain that this method is well suited for the study of everyday discrimination. Because racial or gender discrimination is so insidious, the best way to understand the routine experience of prejudice and discrimination is to record daily experiences. In this regard, daily diary research may have a strong advantage over other qualitative methods that rely on recall and memory. Those methods, such as interviewing, may miss important data regarding the daily experience of discrimination, as participants may forget certain instances and their thoughts, feelings, and observations at the time of incident. In this way, an emergent method not only addresses the same kinds of issues that other traditional methods address but also may be a real tool to get at knowledge that would otherwise remain invisible. There are other emergent feminist methods that also aim at accessing oppressed knowledge.

Feminist media ethnography is a new, hybrid method being used by feminists who are interested in the relationship between power and research. Feminist media ethnographies are necessarily situated within discourses of power (Parameswaran, Chapter 16, this volume). The emergence of this unique method of inquiry has its roots in a larger challenge posed by feminists.

As Kamala Visweswaran (1994, 2003) explains, androcentric bias has historically influenced the practice of ethnography and the selection of "classic ethnographies" to the point that, despite the breadth of ethnographic work conducted by female anthropologists, the purported "significant" ethnographic work has all been conducted by male researchers. Female ethnographers have had their work marginalized within the research and academic communities. As such, Visweswaran (1994) suggested the development of a *feminist ethnography*. Such a practice would, perhaps, focus on the relationships women have to other women, including the power differences between women (Visweswaran, 2003, p. 76). Furthermore, feminist ethnography might examine the "processes of identification (and lack thereof) that inform description" (p. 74). In this way, women would be included in all facets of ethnographic work, and the work itself would draw on the tenets of feminism (such as attention to power, reducing hierarchical divisions, and accounting for subjectivity or standpoint). Drawing on the notion of a feminist ethnography, Parameswaran details a specific form of feminist ethnography: feminist media ethnography.

As we have already seen, many emergent research methods draw on or somehow modify traditional ethnography in order to address new questions from new epistemological and theoretical vantage points. This is true of ethnodrama and friendship as method in particular. Feminist media ethnography is influenced by multiple theoretical frameworks, including postmodernism, postcolonial theory, and feminist theory. This method also draws on postmodern and feminist approaches to anthropology and the interdisciplinary work being done in cultural studies. Moreover, researchers in a variety of fields can use this method. Feminist media ethnography can be adapted to answer research questions in anthropology, geography, literary studies, sociology, and women's studies and, in this way, draws on multiple disciplines and crosses disciplinary borders.

You may be wondering how this form of ethnography differs from traditional ethnography, other than adhering to feminist principles (such as accessing subjugated knowledge). As explained in the selection by Radhika Parameswaran, when using feminist media ethnography, the researcher has multiple roles in the field in relation to his or her research participants. This method, like the body-centered methods discussed earlier, challenges binary conceptualizations of ethnography in practice. For example, a researcher practicing feminist media ethnography doesn't buy into the insider/outsider dualism but rather occupies multiple roles that are themselves fluid, and is thus likely to be both insider and outsider, to varying degrees, at the same and different times within the research process. In addition to resisting binary thinking, this method is highly reflexive, requiring the researcher to examine his or her positionality (which may, too, be dynamic) within the research process. A part of this examination is an acute attention to power and the discourses of power that bear on the knowledge-building process.

Conclusion

Research methods are not fixed entities: They are fluid, can bend and be combined to create tools for newly emerging issues and to unearth previously subjugated knowledge. Emergent methods are often driven by new epistemologies on knowledge production, which in turn create new research questions (methodologies) that often require an innovation in methods. The chapters in this book stress how important it is *not* to delink these processes from one another, as is often done in the teaching of research methods.

This book also highlights how each researcher needs to examine his or her own research practices. Focusing on our own positionality within the research process helps to break down the idea that research is the "view from nowhere." We are also reminded of the many ways our own agendas impact the research process at all points in our research—from the selection of the research problem to the selection of method and the ways in which we analyze and interpret our findings—which is crucial for creating authenticity in the research process. Representation is part of a process and is imbued with power and authority.

There is also a need to be mindful of dualistic thinking that can grab hold of our research and of how we need to be open to the development of new concepts and measures. These chapters underscore the importance of looking beyond our own disciplines so that we might imagine how we might expand our disciplinary visions in order to revision, a process that Laurel Richardson calls "de-disciplining" ourselves as researchers.

The authors of this volume push on the boundaries of traditional knowledge building by venturing out of their methods comfort zone and using their creativity, intellect, and social skills to create new tools or refashion old ones in the service of answering complex questions that arise from a range of newly emerging theoretical perspectives.

Note

1. Here we are influenced by the title of Judith Butler's book *Bodies That Matter*.

References

Bordo, S. (1989). Anorexia nervosa: Psychopathology as the crystallization of culture. In I. Diamond & L. Quinby (Eds.), *Feminism and Foucault: Reflections on resistance*. Boston: Northeastern University Press.

Calvin, T. (Ed.). (2000). Straight with a twist: Queer theory and the subject of homosexuality. Urbana: University of Illinois Press.

Denzin, N. (1989). *The research act: A theoretical introduction to sociological methods* (3rd ed.). Englewood Cliffs, NJ: Prentice Hall.

Denzin, N. K., & Lincoln, Y. S. (Eds.). (1994). Handbook of qualitative research. Thousand Oaks, CA: Sage.

Dumont, J. (1978). *The headman and I: Ambiguity and ambivalence in the field-working experience*. Austin: University of Texas Press.

Ellis, C. (2004). *The ethnographic I: The methodological novel about autoethnography*. Walnut Creek, CA: AltaMira Press.

Foucault, M. (1977). *Discipline and punish: The birth of the prison* (A. Sheridan, Trans.). London: Allen Lane.

Foucault, M. (1979). *Discipline and punish: The birth of the prison* (A. Sheridan, Trans.). New York: Vintage Books.

Foucault, M. (1981). *The history of sexuality, vol.1: An introduction*. Harmondsworth, Middlesex, UK: Penguin.

Grosz, E. (1994). *Volatile bodies: Toward a corporeal feminism*. Bloomington: Indiana University Press.

Harding, S. (2004). Rethinking standpoint epistemology: What is "strong objectivity"? In S. Hesse-Biber & M. Yaiser (Eds.), *Feminist perspectives on social research* (pp. 39–64). New York: Oxford University Press

Kuhn, T. (1970). *The structure of scientific revolutions* (2nd ed.). Chicago: University of Chicago Press.

Merleau-Ponty, M. (1962). *Phenomenology of perception*. (C. Smith, Trans.). London: Routledge and Kegan Paul.

Merton, R. K. (1967). *On theoretical sociology*. New York: Free Press.

Minh-ha, T. T. (1991). *Framer framed*. New York: Routledge.

Mohanty, C. (1988). Under Western eyes: Feminist scholarship and colonial discourses. *Feminist Review, 30*, 61–88.

Mohanty, C. (1992). Feminist encounters: Locating the politics of experience. In M. Barrett & A. Phillips (Eds.), *Destabilizing theory: Contemporary feminist debates* (pp. 74–92). Stanford, CA: Stanford University Press.

Mohanty, C. (1999). Women workers and capitalist scripts: Ideologies of domination, common interests, and the politics of solidarity. In S. Hesse-Biber, C. Gilmartin, & R. Lydenberg (Eds.), *Feminist approaches to theory and methodology* (pp. 362–388). New York: Oxford University Press.

Nicholson, L., & Seidman, S. (Eds.). (1999). *Social postmodernism: Beyond identity politics*. Cambridge, UK: Cambridge University Press.

Perez, E. (1999). *The decolonial imaginary: Writing Chicanos into history.* Bloomington: Indiana University Press.

Richardson, L. (1997). *Fields of play: Constructing an academic life.* New Brunswick, NJ: Rutgers University Press.

Rose, G. (2001). *Visual methodologies: An introduction to the interpretation of visual materials.* London: Sage.

Seiler, M. (2004). *Performing financial studies: A methodological cookbook.* New York: Prentice Hall.

Smith, D. (2004). Women's perspective as a radical critique of sociology. In S. Hesse-Biber & M. Yaiser (Eds.), *Feminist perspectives on social research* (pp. 27–38). New York: Oxford University Press.

Spivak, G. C. (1990). *The postcolonial critic: Interviews, strategies, dialogue.* New York: Routledge.

Teddlie, C., & Tashakkori, A. (2003). Major issues and controversies in the use of mixed methods in the social and behavioral sciences. In A. Tashakkori & C. Teddlie (Eds.), *Handbook of mixed methods in social and behavioral research* (pp. 3–50). Thousand Oaks, CA: Sage.

Tenni, C., Smyth, A., & Boucher, C. (2003). The researcher as autobiographer: Analyzing data written about oneself. *Qualitative Report, 8*(1), 1–12.

Tillmann-Healy, L. (2003). Friendship as method. *Qualitative Inquiry, 9*(5), 729–749.

Villella, O. (2002, June). Review note: H. Mariampolski (2001): Qualitative market research: A comprehensive guide. *Forum: Qualitative Sozialforschung / Forum: Qualitative Social Research, 3*(4). Retrieved November 27, 2004, from http://www.qualitative-research.net/fqs-texte/4–02/4–02review-villella-e.htm

Visweswaran, K. (1994). *Fictions of feminist ethnography.* Minneapolis: University of Minnesota Press.

Wing, A. K. (Ed.). (2000). *Global critical race feminism: An international reader.* New York: New York University Press.

1

Skirting a Pleated Text

De-Disciplining an Academic Life

Laurel Richardson

Fields of Play: Constructing an Academic Life (Richardson, 1997) is the story of a woman's struggles in academia in the context of contemporary intellectual debates about entrenched authority, disciplinary boundaries, writing genres, and the ethics and politics of social scientific inquiry and presentation. The woman is myself, the story, an embodiment of these issues. I hope the story resonates with those who are struggling to make sense of their lives in academia.

I believe that writing is both a theoretical and a practical process through which we can (a) reveal epistemological assumptions, (b) discover grounds for questioning received scripts and hegemonic ideals—both those within the academy and those incorporated within ourselves, (c) find ways to change those scripts, (d) connect to others and form community, and (e) nurture our emergent selves.

Applying my theoretical understandings to sociological writing, I asked, How do the specific circumstances in which we write affect what we write? How does what we write affect who we become? In answering these questions, I found that if I were to write the Self into being that I wanted to be, I would have to "de-discipline" my academic life.

What practices support our writing and develop a care for the self despite conflict and marginalization? What is (are) the ethical subject's relation(s) to research practices? And what about the integration of academic interests, social concerns, emotional needs, and spiritual connectedness?

Fields of Play explores these issues through what I call a pleated text, traditional and experimental papers written over a period of 10 years folded between what I call "writing-stories"—about the contexts in which I wrote those papers. The pleats can be spread open at any point, folded back, unfurled.

Framing academic essays in writing-stories displaced the boundaries between the genres of selected writings and autobiography, "repositioning them as convergent genres that, when intertwined, create new ways of reading/writing." These ways are more congruent with poststructural understandings of how knowledge is contextually situated, local, and partial. At the beginning, the book, the writing-story, is a personal story, framing the academic work. As the book progresses, distinctions between the "personal" and the "academic" become less clear. The last essay, "Vespers," stands in a section by itself, simultaneously a writing-story and a sociology-story, though I do not name a single sociological concept. In the genre of convergence, neither "work" nor "Self" is denied.

The present chapter is a (very) partial-story about the construction of *Fields of Play* and how writing it has changed me. I skirt around the text but enter one of its pleats: departmental politics as one context for writing and as a site of discipline. I provide three examples of departmental politics: (a) an excerpt from a writing-story about my own department; (b) the first act of a surrealist drama about a surreal, yet real, sociology department; and (c) an excerpt from a multivoiced text, which builds community across departments and academic status. The three examples span a decade. They are not a narrative of progress.

We are restrained and limited by the kinds of cultural stories available to us. Carolyn Heilbrun (1998) suggests that we do not imitate lives, we live "story lines." To the extent that our lives are tied to our disciplines, our ability to construct ourselves in other stories will depend on how the discipline can be deconstructed. The social scientific disciplines' story line includes telling writers to suppress their own voices, adopt the all-knowing, all-powerful voice of the academy, and keep their mouths shut about academic in-house politics. But contemporary philosophical thought raises problems that exceed and undermine that academic story line. We are always present in our texts, no matter how we try to suppress ourselves. We are always writing in particular contexts—contexts that affect what and how we write and who we become. Power relationships are always present.

"Authority"

I began *Fields of Play* with a writing-story called "Authority." Here is an excerpt:

> I begin this collection, and my reflections on it, at the time when I found a different way of "playing the field," of exploring its boundaries and possibilities, and my life within it. This was the mid-1980s. No more children living at home; no major medical or family crises; a husband who liked to cook; friends; completion of a major research project and book tour; academic sinecure; and severe marginalization within my sociology department, which relieved me of committee work and of caring about outcomes. For the first time in my adult life, I had free time, playtime, time I could ethically and practically call "mine."
>
> Like a medieval warlord who executes or banishes all who might pose a threat to his absolute authority, my newly appointed department chair deposed the three other contenders for the position, all men, from their "fiefdoms," their committee chairships. He stonewalled written complaints or queries. He prohibited public disagreement by eliminating discussion at faculty meetings. He abolished one of the two committees I chaired, the "Planning Committee," a site of open dialogue. He restricted the departmental Affirmative Action Committee's province, which I also chaired, to undergraduate enrollments. I publicly disagreed with him on his new affirmative action policy. Then, at the first university Affirmative Action Awards dinner, where I was being honored, surrounded by top university administration, my face making a face, repulsed, I shrugged his arm off from around my shoulder.
>
> The chair hired a consultant, a well-known functionalist, to review faculty vitae. The consultant declared me "promising"—the chair told me as one might tell a student, not the full professor I was—but the consultant had also declared "gender research" a "fad." The chair advised me to return to medical sociology, a field I was "in" during a one-year postdoctorate, ten years earlier. Research it, teach it, he advised, teach it now, at the graduate level. He may have already had me down to do it. He discarded ten years of my research, teaching, and service, it seemed. I told him I strongly disagreed with his plans for my academic future. Perhaps it was only coincidental that sometime later that same year at the annual departmental banquet, hitherto a lighthearted gathering of colleagues and friends, the visiting consultant, now hired as an after-dinner speaker, lectured for an hour about why people, in the interests of smooth institutional functioning, should yield to authority.
>
> I was on quarter break, out of town, when the department chair's secretary called to tell me that the chair had added an extra undergraduate course to my

teaching schedule for the next quarter, a week away. My stomach cramped in severe pain. No, I said, I absolutely will not accept this assignment. I was adamant, unyielding. I telephoned the new dean, a sociologist and putative feminist, who would soon be elevated to provost. Her "best advice" to me—on this and subsequent matters—was to "roll over." I refused. She then taught the course herself, in my place. Rather than pull rank on the chair, a man, she modeled "rolling over." It was a course on the sociology of women.

I felt no gratitude to her. I had wanted protection, for my colleagues as well as for myself, from a chair's punitive and arbitrary actions. Instead, she presented herself in my place, as the sacrificial lamb. The clear message, it seemed to me, was that if she, the dean of the college, was willing to sacrifice herself, so should we all. Her action legitimated the chair's right to do anything he wanted.

My new chair was empowered to micromanage all aspects of "his" department's life, even to the point of dictating a senior colleague's intellectual life. Any refusal to "roll over" precipitated punitive action in salary, in what one could teach and when, in virtual exile to Coventry. Thus in the mid-1980s, I experienced what has, by the mid-1990s, become an experience common to faculty members of American colleges and universities: "Total Quality Management" in pursuit of "Excellence."

Many departmental colleagues understood that, like the chair's previously conquered opponents, I had become dangerous to associate with, dangerous to even know. In their minds I had brought it upon myself, which of course I had. As I write these paragraphs, my stomach swells and hurts just as it did then. (Richardson, 1997, pp. 9–11)

In the mid-1980s, not only did departmental life surprise me; so, too, did the theoretical concepts of feminist poststructuralism—reflexivity, authority, authorship, subjectivity, power, language, ethics, and representation. Soon, I was challenging the grounds of my own and others' authority and raising ethical questions about my own practices as a sociologist.

Experimenting with textual form, I wrote sociology as drama, responsive readings, narrative poetry, pagan ritual, lyrical poetry, prose poems, humor, and autobiography. Experimenting with content, I wrote about narrative, science writing, literary devices, fact/fiction, and ethics. Experimenting with voice, I coauthored with a fiction writer, played second theorist to a junior scholar, turned colleagues' words into dramas. Experimenting with frame, I invited others into my texts, eliding the oral and the written, constructing performance pieces, creating theater. Troubled with the ethical issues of doing research "on" others, I wrote about my own life. I did unto myself as I had done unto others. And, troubled by academic institutions, I began to discover more agreeable pedagogical and writing practices and alternative community-building sites.

I experimented with three interrelated questions: (a) How does the way we are supposed to write up our findings become an unexamined trope in our claims to authoritative knowledge? (b) What might we learn about our "data" if we stage it in different writing formats? and (c) What other audiences might we be able to reach if we step outside the conventions of social scientific writing?

My intentions then—and now—have never been to dismiss social scientific writing, but rather to examine it. My intentions then—and now—have never been to reject social scientific writing, but rather to enlarge the field through other representational forms.

By the mid-1980s, I could no longer write in science's omniscient Voice from Nowhere. Responding to the long-suppressed poet within, I wrote up an in-depth interview with an unwed mother, "Louisa May," as a five-page poem, adhering to both social scientific and literary protocols. A poem as "findings" was not well received at my sociology meetings; I was accused of fabricating Louisa May and/or of being her, among other things. To deal with the assault, I wrote a realist drama about it from my (very accurate, non-fabricated, easily-checked-for-reliability) "field notes" taken at the meeting. In 1993, with the assault warming up in my home department, I decided to write a surreal drama—"Educational Birds"—about my life in academia. Surreal seemed appropriately isomorphic to the real.

ACT I FROM THE ETHNODRAMA "EDUCATIONAL BIRDS"

(Scene One: It is a chilly September afternoon in a sociology department chair's office. The walls are catacomb drab; there are no mementos, pictures, or plants in the room. Seated at one end of a large conference table are two women: a department chair with her back to the windows, and full Professor Z. looking out to the silent gray day.)

CHAIR: I've been reading your work, because of salary reviews—

PROFESSOR Z.:   —

CHAIR: You write very well.

PROFESSOR Z.:   —

CHAIR: But is it Sociology?

PROFESSOR Z.:   —

(Scene Two: On leaving the department office, Professor Z. sees Visiting Professor M. at the drinking fountain. The pipes are lead. The university says it's not a problem if you let the water run. Professor M. is letting the water run into his coffee maker. His hair is flat, plastering his head; he's heavy-looking, somber, wearing worn blue pants and a stretched-out dun cardigan, hanging loosely to his mid-thighs. Not the eager Harvard man hired a year ago.)

PROFESSOR Z.:   Looks like you've acclimated.

(Scene Three: It is an overcast November noon at the Faculty Club. Pictures of deceased faculty, men in drab suits, line the room; wrought-iron bars secure the windows. Professor Z. and assistant Professor Q., whose five-author paper "Longitudinal Effects of East to Midwest Migration on Employment Outcomes: A Log-Linear Analysis" has made her a member of the salary committee, are having lunch.)

ASSISTANT PROFESSOR Q.:   Everyone says, "You write very well."

PROFESSOR Z.:   Is that a compliment?

ASSISTANT PROFESSOR Q.:   "But is it Sociology?"

(Scene Four: A cold and dismal January afternoon in the sociology seminar room. During one of the department's "reconstruction" phases, the oak conference table was disassembled and the legs lost. Without a leg to stand on, it lies, in pieces, at the far end of the room next to discarded computer equipment. The wallpaper is flaking away like mummy wrappings. Assembled are the new graduate students, the graduate chair, and the department chair. The new students are being taught how to teach.)

NEW GRADUATE STUDENT: *(Addressing the department chair)* Can you tell us about the worst undergraduate sociology class you ever took?

DEPARTMENT CHAIR: Yes. The worst course was one where the professor read a poem.

GRADUATE STUDENTS: —

DEPARTMENT CHAIR: What a waste of time! (Richardson, 1997, p. 197)

The story of a life is less than the actual life, because the story told is selective, partial, contextually constructed, and because the life is not yet over. But the story of a life is also more than the life, the contours and meanings allegorically extending to others, others seeing themselves, knowing themselves through another's life story, re-visioning their own, arriving where they started, and knowing "the place for the first time."

My fears for this "place"—academia—had grown over the course of writing the book. Over the decade, academia had become increasingly inhospitable to those who would change it and to those who are most vulnerable—graduate students. In the penultimate paper in *Fields,* I wanted to link the embodiedness of scholarship across generations, disciplines, and theoretical positions. I wanted the book to include the voices of graduate students in different sociology departments, to link my story with their stories, to write a new collective story. I wrote "Are You My Alma Mater?" as the vehicle.

"Are You My Alma Mater?"

New mines have been set. As in real war fields, the young, inexperienced, and adventurous are the most vulnerable to detonations. Graduate students. Four examples have passed over my desk in the past two weeks. On a feminist e-mail list came this request from a first-year graduate student:

> My department has been having a series of "feminist epistemology" debates . . . The anger/hostility/backlash/defensiveness in some of the faculty and the increasing alienation and marginalization of feminist (and students pursuing critical race theory) students is troublesome to me (one of the disenchanted grad students). When I raised my concern, it was suggested that I organize the next seminar. While I am not altogether sure this is a responsibility I want, I am wondering if any of you have had successful . . . forums which address hostilities within the discipline/departments yet does not increase those hostilities or place less powerful people (untenured faculty or graduate students) at greater risk . . . Please reply to me privately.

When I asked the student for permission to quote her e-mail, she asked for anonymity:

> It drives me crazy that I have to be afraid to even speak, but it is realistic. Actually, even posting to [the listserv] made me nervous, but I can't think of other ways of accessing resources beyond my pathetic institution.

Another graduate student, Eric Mykhalovsky (1996), writes about what happened to him when he used an autobiographical perspective in the practice of sociology. Changing his "I" to "you," he writes in *Qualitative Sociology,*

During a phone call "home" you hear that your application for doctoral studies has been rejected. Your stomach drops. You are in shock, disbelief. When doing your M.A. you were talked about as a "top" student. . . . Later you receive a fax giving an "official account" of your rejection. Your disapproval, it seems, was based on reviewers' reservations with the writing samples submitted as part of your application. One evaluator, in particular, considered your article, "Table Talk," to be a "self-indulgent, informal biography—lacking in accountability to its subject matter." You feel a sense of self-betrayal. You suspected "Table Talk" might have had something to do with the rejection. It was an experimental piece, not like other sociological writing—YOU SHOULD HAVE KNOWN BETTER!

Slowly self-indulgence as assessment slips over the text to name you. You begin to doubt yourself—are you really self-indulgent? The committee's rejection of your autobiographical text soon feels, in a very painful way, a rejection of you. All the while you buy into the admission committee's implicit assessment of your work as not properly sociological. (pp. 133–134)

Third, in a personal letter requesting advice on whether to apply to my university, a lesbian graduate student from another university recounts,

I cannot do the research I want to and stay here. The department wants to monitor how many lesbians they let in because they're afraid that gender will be taken over by lesbians. I'll be allowed to do gender here if I do it as part of the "social stratification" concentration, but not if I want to write about lesbian identity construction or work from a queer studies perspective.

And fourth, there are documents on my desk pertaining to a required graduate seminar, in a famous department, on how to teach sociology. In that seminar, according to the documents, a non-American student of color questioned the white male professor's Eurocentrism. Following a heated dispute, the professor provided a statistical count of the racial distribution of students in undergraduate classes—80 percent are white. The professor, then, putatively said that instructors cannot afford to alienate students by teaching multiculturalism; that professors are uncomfortable teaching multiculturalism "crap"; that the student raising these issues could "go to hell"; and that white heterosexual males were being discriminated against. When the student of color complained to the department administrators, they proposed he "voluntarily" withdraw from the class. The department administrators (including another new chair) later attended the seminar, supported the syllabus, and sidestepped discussion of the race-based issues. The professor apologized to the seminar for breaking his own code of proper behavior in the classroom, but he apparently had not grasped the import of postcolonialism. He was modeling his teaching model.

As a result, at least one graduate student has chosen to go elsewhere for the Ph.D. The student sent an e-mail to all faculty, staff, and graduate students to avert "idle speculation" regarding the reasons for departure:

It has disgusted, saddened and enraged me that this department has chosen to ignore and avoid the serious occurrences of racism going on within it. Instead of admitting to these problems and dealing with them, the department has used its institutional power to scapegoat, marginalize and penalize individuals who dare to challenge its racist structure. Then those in power go back to their computer screens to study race as a dummy variable, not even realizing that a sociological process called *racism* is happening in their midst. . . . Students are advised to study social movements, not participate in them. . . . [H]ere racism is not considered real sociology, as evidenced by students having to start "extracurricular" groups to do reading on postmodernist or Afrocentric thought.

I am leaving because, while I respect, learn and appreciate the importance of things like demography and statistics, the same appreciation and respect is not offered here to other areas of sociology which are very influential in the field, and institutional power is used to prevent students from learning about them.

I sincerely hope that the prospect of losing more talented students, especially those who are students of color (who are not leaving because they "can't handle it [statistics courses],") will compel this department to reevaluate its capacity to serve its students of diverse backgrounds and interests more effectively. My career just didn't have time to wait for all that to happen.

Feminist epistemology, autobiographical sociology, queer studies, and Afrocentric and postcolonial perspectives are apparently so dangerous that the graduate students who have been exposed to these plagues must be quarantined, invalidated, or expelled from the university nest. Graduate students are "terminated" lest they reproduce themselves. (Richardson, 1997, pp. 208–213)

As I pause in the writing of this paper, wondering what to write next, the UPS man delivers an advance shipment copy of *Fields of Play*. The production editor's note says, "Congratulations" and "Thanks for all your cooperation along the way; I hope you're as pleased as we are with the final result."

The final result for the production editor is the book, I think. But what is it for me? What have been the consequences of the book's feminist-poststructuralist practices? How have I changed?

For starters, I have taken early retirement from my "home" sociology department. I have left it physically and emotionally. As a shaman might say, I have called my spirit back; the place no longer has power over me. I go into the building and do not feel alienated. Sometimes, I sing while I am there.

Leaving my department, however, has not meant leaving the sociological perspective, the academy, or professional associations. I teach qualitative methods to Ph.D. students in the Cultural Studies program in Educational Policy and Leadership at Ohio State University. There, I find a positive commitment to qualitative research among the faculty and the graduate students. I visit universities and colleges, teach, lecture, present at conferences, write handbook chapters and sociology articles, edit a feminist reader, and serve on editorial boards. My professional life is full and nurturing, having let go of that which I did not value.

Indeed, I have let many things go.

In 1985, while working on a book that I was tired of working on, I cross-stitched into a sampler the aphorism: "I finish what I start." I put the sampler over my computer so I could read the affirmation over and over again, and I finished the book, as I have most things I start. My persistence has been a point of pride.

But, now, as I apply poststructural understandings of temporality to my life and work, my ideas of "start" and "finish" have changed. When does a project start? When is it finished? Says who? Now, I find I can put projects aside, perhaps never to return to them purposively, but never to be away from them either; they remain as traces in that which I do.

The sampler I have moved to the living room; metaphorically, that seems apt. In its place on the wall, I have a picture of my flapper mother wearing a kid leather cloche and fox coat, holding my sister—then 7 months; now 70 years. When does a project start? When is it finished?

And my writing. Oh, how I value my writing time. I understand autobiographical writing as a feminist practice. It is how I both center myself and connect to others. The last essay in *Fields of Play,* "Vespers," is an account of how an experience at a vespers service when I was 8 shaped my relationships to my parents and to my academic work; it is a forgiveness story. Others have told me it resonates with their lives. A new essay, "Paradigms Lost" (in press), recounts a car accident and a coma. It is a recovery story. Only now— 25 years after the accident—am I able to tell that story, and only, I think, because I have accepted writing as a process of discovery, and writing autobiographically as a feminist-sociological praxis. "Jeopardy" and "Meta-Jeopardy" (in press) narrativize some of my experiences with parenting and grandparenting. In the next few years, I plan to write more of these essays, structured rhizomatically, the way my life is experienced—lines of flight; whirling, whirling skirts of pleated texts. A surprisingly surprising de-disciplined life . . .

Acknowledgments

An earlier version of this chapter was presented to the American Educational Research Association (AERA), Chicago, Illinois, March 24, 1997, and was published in *Qualitative Inquiry, 3,* 295–303 (1997). I thank Ernest Lockridge for his careful reading of this text and Sage Publications for permission to reprint it here.

References

Heilbrun, C. (1988). *Writing a woman's life.* New York: W. W. Norton.

Mykhalovsky, E. (1996). Reconsidering table talk: Critical thoughts on the relationship between sociology, autobiography, and self-indulgence. *Qualitative Sociology, 19*(1): 131–51.

Richardson, L. (1997). *Fields of play: Constructing an academic life.* New Brunswick, NJ: Rutgers University Press.

Richardson, L. (in press). Meta-jeopardy. *Qualitative Inquiry.*

Richardson, L. (in press). Paradigms lost. *Symbolic Interaction.*

2

Getting Connected

How Sociologists Can Access the High Tech Élite

Trond Arne Undheim

Élite studies have been relatively neglected in the qualitative methods literature (Coleman, 1996, p. 336; Hertz & Imber, 1995). As a consequence, the interview methods literature in the social sciences does not adequately address the issue of access to élite interviews. Nor does it address the élite interview process itself (Breakwell, Hammond, & Fife-Schaw, 1995; Brenner, Brown, & Canter, 1985; Crabtree & Miller, 1992; Fog, 1994; Fowler & Mangione, 1990; McCracken, 1988; Stewart & Cash, 1997; Sudman & Bradburn, 1982; Weiss, 1994). Despite its élite sample (scientists, engineers, policy-makers) the science and technology studies (STS) community (Undheim, 2002) suffers from the same lack of attention to access, with Traweek (1995) as a notable exception. The author discusses the small literature on qualitative élite studies (Hertz & Imber, 1995; Walford, 1994) as well as contributions on élite interviewing (Burgess,

1988; Cassell, 1988; Dexter, 1970; Moyser, 1988; Spector, 1980; Thomas, 1995). Practical consultation for interview practice is also given. Seeing access as an ongoing, precarious process, the author recommends improvisation by ways of a threefold journalistic, therapeutic, and investigative modus operandi. The author draws on a study of the situated nature of high tech practices and is based on interview experience with knowledge workers, experts, and high tech CEOs in the United States, Italy, and Norway. As well, he brings experiences from a previous study of regional innovation in Norway and Great Britain (Thorvik & Undheim, 1998).

É lites are people who occupy, by heritage, merit or circumstances, a key place in power networks both online and offline. Often associated with power, privilege and position, the élite might not as such constitute, or embody readily observable traits, or group itself in a way that is easily categorized. Rather, the élite way of influence is sometimes better described in retrospect, by analyzing how actor-networks were mobilized. Actually, élite impact is often quite invisible, and the most influential might not look like they are. This, of course, is also due to the prevalent élite strategy of staying behind the scenes while deploying a multi-faceted power game. Here, online élites play a particular role, immersed as it were in *cyberpower* (Jordan, 2000), largely invisible to most of us, yet arguably quite effective also in manipulating real-life events (Nye, 2002).

In the following, I will discuss how élites can be found, accessed, and interviewed, starting out with an analysis of the science and technology studies (STS) community as well as some classic approaches to interviewing found in the existing literature. Scholars who study the interplay of technical, scientific and social aspects of reality (STS) are critical towards taken-for-granted assumptions about how society is configured. Rather, they prefer to show the precise *construction* of actor-networks by tracing the impact of technological determinism, identifying actors and their *place-making*, that is, the ongoing sense making, cooperation, and exchange online and offline (Undheim, 2002).

Since science and technology is widely regarded as housing élites, I will start there. While a substantial part of the science and technology studies (STS) literature investigates people and settings that we normally would classify and regard as élite, relatively little is written about how these groups and settings were accessed. However, access to high-energy physics labs, molecular biologists, or NASA scientists, is not self-evident. In fact, we should assume that there must have been many barriers before access was obtained, restrictions that were encountered underway, and many missed attempts at access that are not reported. This makes access a more interesting phenomenon, a feature of STS research in need of more sustained reflection.

In addition, within STS there has been little explicit discussion about what characterizes the relationship between researcher and informant as crucial moments in the research act, with exception for Hess' (2001) recent claim about the co-production of knowledge between scholars and informants in STS ethnography. I will not speculate at length about the reasons for this neglect, but the fact that STS is an emerging subject, especially compared to the groups it attempts to study, and the very practice they uphold— 'Science'—may have something to do with it. Élite studies are irrevocably immersed in issues of power, domination, and authority, but also in issues of exchange, reciprocity, and altruism. Knorr-Cetina's (1999) experience is that 'it can't do any harm' often is the best legitimating voice of leading figures when trying to explain the presence of sociologists in their labs:

> [. . .] many thanks to Pierre Darriulat, who, at an early stage was the first to allow us in [the particle collider experiment UA2 at CERN in Geneva]—even though, as he told me at the first contact over the phone, he did not think this research would lead anywhere, he believed that UA2 was an open environment and that it should depend on participants what they did with us. (Knorr-Cetina, 1999, p. vii)

Researchers need access to people, settings, materials, and documents. Access implies inside knowledge, and is a precarious, ongoing, and renegotiable process (Johnson, 1975). Traweek (1995) is a case in point. She investigates the powers at play when a young, female researcher ventures into high-energy physics labs in the US, Japan, Switzerland, and France. Sometimes ironic, other times bitterly laconic, Traweek (1995, p. 48) recounts how she, in fact, learned about science, access and sexual dynamics:

> I learned that wearing my miniskirts to the lab reduced the physicists responses to one [. . .] Thirty years and fifty pounds later I found that in Japan I was assigned [the role of] *obachan* [. . .] This might be translated as auntie.

Traweek (1995) compares access work to the characters at play in *My Fair Lady* (Shaw, 1941); Eliza, Henry Higgins, Mrs. Higgins, and Colonel Pickering. In fact, Henry Higgins uses all of them to build his 'voice over,' to give voice to 'Science.' While Traweek clearly identifies with Eliza, the seduced girl who must re-learn to speak (Traweek, 1995, p. 39), the girlish attitude could also lead straight into Henry Higgins' 'innocent' scientific experiment, or in fact to claiming to be a technical device—"I am a detector"

(Traweek, 1995, p. 39). Studying up, to Traweek, is also about watching access relations among her research subjects. In order to counter their empire-building male counterparts, the Japanese women physicists the[y] studied had devised networking strategies to get business donations of expensive equipment. Traweek (1995, p. 49) also highlights how Japanese high-energy physicists use *bachigai*, outsider positions, *gaiatsu*, foreign pressure, and *kokusaika*, the concern about Japan's identity in global politics, to build support for new labs like the Japanese National Laboratory.

But while many STS people may have followed Laura Nader's (1972) anthropological plea to 'study-up,' Traweek (1995) seems quite alone reflecting about what studying-up means as a strategy of inquiry. In the anthropology community at large access is embedded in discussions of establishing rapport in the field. In the classic accounts of Goffman (1961) and Garfinkel (1967), as well as in Hannerz (1969), Van Maanen (1988), and Clifford and Marcus (1986) we find extensive descriptions of 'entering the field.' Ethnographically oriented studies or handbooks like Marshall and Rossman (1995), or Hammersley and Atkinson (1983) also discuss the topic. However, most of these accounts do not take in the 'élite' problematic as such. Typically, anthropologists find people 'very curious and very friendly' (Rainbird, 1990, p. 89).

By strategy of inquiry, I intend the skills, assumptions, enactments, and material practices of the researcher (Denzin & Lincoln, 2000, p. 371). I invite the reader to reflect on what happens when interviews are embedded in power asymmetry. This is meant as an effort to identify some methodological issues related to élite interviewing, pragmatic as well as principal, in order to invite a more sustained reflection on such matters. Even if ethnographic approaches may have the STS ideal, given the importance attached to so-called laboratory studies (Knorr-Cetina, 1995), there is little doubt that interviews loom large among the research techniques applied by STS researchers.

Many scholars today argue élite influence on society is growing because of globalization, high tech, and the emphasis on knowledge and expertise (Castells, 1996; Giddens, 1991; Knorr-Cetina, 1999). Accessing this emerging high tech élite poses an additional challenge to social scientists. STS is potentially at the center of this debate, because of its ongoing access to scientists, engineers, technologists, and other professional and élite groups.

The Interview in Social Science Methodology

The scarcity of STS contributions that explicitly address methodological issues may well be understandable when we notice the abundance of methodological contributions in the social sciences at large. Still, the relevance and validity of the standard fare for STS type of studies should be addressed. The interview is a good starting point.

Most research strategy includes the use of interviews in some form. The literature on interviews is vast and diverse (Breakwell, Hammond, & Fife-Schaw, 1995; Brenner, Brown, & Cantor, 1985; Crabtree & Miller, 1992; Fog, 1994; Fowler & Mangione, 1990; Holstein & Gubrium, 1995; Kahn & Cannel, 1957; McCracken, 1988; Mishler, 1986; Seidmann, 1991; Spradley, 1979; Stewart & Cash, 1997; Sudman & Bradburn, 1982; Weiss, 1994).

However, interviews with the élite present an additional challenge. Here, access must be negotiated against the rigidity of public or corporate bureau-cracy, being aware of how governments, policy-makers, or institutions see interviews as potential threats to the public 'brand' (Aaker, 1996) or subjec-tive reality constructs of the institution itself and its members. Actually, Spencer (1982, p. 25) found élite members of the US Military Academy West Point were honestly committed to the military 'mission,' but were wary that an interview might threaten their career and their identity. Likewise, the exchange itself might not be viewed as balanced. After all, the value of con-tributing to social science is highly symbolic, and seldom contains direct, tangible exchanges that contribute to the interviewee's status or well being (Kahn & Cannel, 1968, p. 149). Thirdly, the legitimacy of the researcher might be in question (Spencer, 1982, p. 24). Leaders ask what right researchers have to intrude in 'their organization.'

Social scientists too rarely study up (Ostrander, 1993, p. 7), maybe because it has been assumed to be easier to 'study up' than 'study down' (Lofland & Lofland, 1995, p. 25). At least, discussions of such methods are scarce, and some claim it has been neglected in the literature (Coleman, 1996, p. 336; Hertz & Imber, 1995). Conceptual confusion might complicate the matter. While Nader (1972) instigated the debate using the term 'studying-up' to describe non-natives, westerners, and élites, discussions on this issue are now found under several headings. Some of these are: 'access' (Chandler, 1990, p. 124), 'negotiating entry,' 'getting in' (Lofland & Lofland, 1995, p. 31), 'reciprocity' (Rossman & Rallis, 1998, p. 105), 'trust relations' (Johnson, 1975), 'sampling' (Lee, 1993), 'studying-up' (Cassel, 1988; Nader, 1972), 'gatekeepers' (Broadhead & Rist, 1976; Hammersley & Atkinson, 1983, p. 38), 'élite oral history' (Seldon & Pappworth, 1983), 'researching sensitive topics' (Lee, 1993), or 'participant observation' (Jorgensen, 1989). However, while some of these volumes deal explicitly with interviewing élites, none are exhaustive in their understanding of the matter.

What types of élites do social scientists study? A short list of élite mono-graphs will do some justice to this question. For instance, we find public figures (Spector, 1980), female leaders (Puwar, 1997), surgeons (Bosk, 1979), national defence intellectuals (Cohn, 1987), nuclear weapons researchers (Gusterson, 1996), physicists (Knorr-Cetina, 1999; Traweek, 1995), upper-class women (Ostrander, 1984), and top business executives (Thomas, 1995). Élite typology is complex and will not be discussed in detail. See Moyser and Wagstaffe (1987) for a useful introduction.

Élite studies have been important in the social sciences at least since Mills' (1956) classic study, but qualitative interviews are not so much discussed in this regard. While the literature is not abundant, a handful of monographs, edited books, articles and book-chapters deal with access to élite interviews or observation (Cassell, 1988; Coleman, 1996; Dexter, 1970; Gronning, 1997; Moyser, 1988, Moyser & Wagstaffe, 1987; Ostrander, 1993; Spector, 1980; Spencer, 1982; Thomas, 1995; Winkler, 1987). Most scholars agree access is time-consuming and entails coping with rejection and scepticism by both formal and informal organizational gatekeepers that constrain fieldwork and interviews (Jackall, 1998; Smith, 2001; Thomas, 1995). However, the issue of access to high tech knowledge workers, CEOs, and managers in particular is not so much discussed. Notably, there is little practical advice on how to do such studies if you do not happen to be 'connected' to a Business School, or have academic or public credentials that ensure access almost everywhere. Exceptions are Brannen (1987), Galaskiewitz (1987), Hoffmann (1980), Thomas (1995) and Winkler (1987) who underline the importance of inside connections, persistence, social skills, and improvisation.

Winkler (1987, p. 135) states access always involves face-to-face negotiation, and demands time, effort and risk on [the] part of the researcher. His best strategy was to arrange 'group discussion' with drinks at a business venue just after the close of the business day. One reason for success was that the élites are anxious about their status and seek confirmation in such events. Second, the practice of inviting others you have not met, and going to business events to 'network' made the turn-up rate quite astounding.

Access has been particularly tied to discussions of research ethics, and with good reason. Where access is problematic, there is always an ethical issue involved. The research community has responsibility towards the subjects or institutions under scrutiny, towards society (potentially threatening information), and towards the researcher. For example, when doing research on deviant groups, particularly hazardous settings exist, and situations might arise (Lee, 1993, p. 9). For instance, Friedman's (1990) covert work as a Hollywood actor, a High School substitute, and a religious school supervisor brought about several ethical and personal issues; he got 'false' friends, was bored because of routine work and low status, and was challenged on his truthfulness and sincerity in religious matters. Although some advocate avoiding the traditional protecting measures of confidentiality and anonymity when writing about public figures (Spector, 1980, p. 99), this poses ethical issues. Mainstream research ethics advice, however, is to be 'truthful, but vague' about your objectives (Taylor & Bogdan, 1984), and keep anonymity. For a thorough and thoughtful discussion of ethics in covert research, see Lofland and Lofland (1995).

Even though qualitative research is well suited to study élites, this research tradition is most frequently associated with studies of marginal or powerless groups. This may be inherited from the Chicago School tradition (Lee, 1993, p. 12). Studies of deviant groups, outsiders (Becker, 1966), gang-members (Whyte, 1943), and delinquents (Shaw, 1930) have set the dominating strategy of inquiry. In effect, this tradition meant that the powerful were neglected in favor of the powerless (Smith, 1988).

After the Chicago School decline, interviews for some time became the domain of empiricist survey research. In the United States, these were led by Lazarsfeld (1962) and Merton (1947). Here, quantification and statistical sophistication were key strategies. What Lazarsfeld (1944) called 'open ended interviews' were supplying measures, in that they do not set fixed answers in terms of which a respondent must reply. Such interviews had their major use in (a) clarifying the meaning of a respondent's answer, (b) singling out the decisive aspect of an opinion, (c) deciding what has influenced an opinion, (d) determining complex attitude patterns, (e) interpreting motivations, and drives and (f) clarifying statistical relationships (Lazarsfeld, 1944). With the empirical tradition, 'interview error' became a methodological topic (Sudman & Bradburn, 1982). The inheritance from that time is found in textbooks and articles on qualitative methods, as well. For instance, in the *International Encyclopedia of the Social Sciences,* Kahn and Cannel (1968, p. 149) wrote:

> [. . .] the research interview has been defined as a conversation with a purpose [and] may be defined as a two-person conversation that is initiated by the interviewer for the specific purpose of obtaining information that is relevant to research. [. . .] In the research interview the respondent is led to restrict his discussion to the questions posed.

Clearly, this is a quite rigid, quantitatively inspired expression of the research interview. Subheadings like 'the interview like measurement' (p. 150), [express] a clear positivist mindset. Here, the conception of a strict 'interview guide' is still strong and interviewing is a research technique rather than a mode of inquiry.

The 1970s–1990s brought about a resurgence of qualitative inquiry. Glaser and Strauss (1968) outlined 'grounded theory,' an approach where research design, theory, and method are deliberately 'stumbled upon' because of the richness of 'data' when you approach your research setting with an open mind. Nevertheless, they have since developed rigorous rules of coding procedures. Also, Garfinkel's (1967) ethnomethodology, and Goffman's interaction analysis (1961) brought attention to the value of unfocused face-to-face meetings.

The early 1980s brought feminist methodology. Oakley (1981, p. 55) states that a feminist approach is needed when interviewing women. In her account, interviewing women is a cozy, friendly and sisterly exchange of information. Similarly, other feminist accounts discuss empathy, trust, and ethics (Finch, 1984). In the 1980s, the long, in-depth interviews were again in fashion, and McCracken (1988) is the most cited guide from this era. He states interview studies begin with literature reviews, continue with an examination of your own associations and cultural categories, and end in the final questionnaire which will consist in a set of biographical questions followed by a series of question areas. Each of these will have a set of grand-tour questions with floating prompts underway. It will also consist in planned prompting in the form of 'contrast,' 'category,' 'special incident,' and 'auto-driving' questions. The 'rough guide' specifies topics, but the interview itself is negotiated (McCracken, 1988, p. 37). However, the empiricist advice from survey research still holds the stances: "To avoid bias, the interviewing must be done nondirectively," and "questions must never be asked in a leading or directive manner as this exerts pressure on informants to answer in particular ways" (Brenner et al., 1985, p. 151).

In reaction to this, a narrative tradition also has emerged (Mishler, 1986). When we conduct interviews, states Mishler (1986), we are *pattern makers* more than we are *pattern finders*. In historical scholarship, too, this trend is prevalent. Élite oral history, Seldon and Pappworth (1983, pp. 36–52) maintain, gives facts not recorded in documents, like the spirit in which a document was written, insight into the personalities of leaders, clarifications of factual conclusions, underlying assumptions and motives, but also atmosphere and color. In fact, the interview relationship itself might be personally enriching.

The 1990s, finally, is a decade of consolidation for qualitative interview methods. By now, interview studies have gained acceptance in more mainstream American academic journals, and the qualitative versus quantitative controversy is put to rest, at least for the moment. Sensitive research topics (Lee, 1993) receive major attention, and feminist scholarship is in vogue. There is no need to hide that intensive interviewing seeks to discover the informant's *experience* of a particular topic or situation (Lofland & Lofland, 1995, p. 18).

But experiences are more mixed. For instance, Cotterill (1992) incorporates issues of friendship, openness, and power. Feminists stress the need to 'learn to listen' (Anderson & Jack, 1991, p. 11). Still, in the literature we find that 'difficult people' to interview still tend to be workers, women (Faimberg, 1996; Kaul, 1999), people with learning difficulties (Booth & Booth, 1994, p. 415), children, and the elderly (Breakwell, Hammond, & Fife-Schaw, 1995, p. 236). Depth interviewing is seen as a means of giving 'vulnerable subjects' voice in the making of their own history. There is the fear of forcing or manipulating individuals into discussing topics they do not want to talk about (Anderson & Jack, 1991, p. 13).

Similarly, the importance of an improved discourse on élite interviewing may be emphasized with reference to the increased interest in networks and knowledge workers (Castells, 1996, p. 198). This emerging network élite consists of 'switchers,' initiators of networks with a huge amount of what Granovetter (1973) labeled "weak ties." These are potential social relationships that extend your networks exponentially in an important direction. In the words of Malcolm Gladwell of the *New Yorker Magazine,* switchers 'stand at the intersection of different worlds, connecting people, creating opportunities, and spreading ideas' (Gladwell, 1999, p. 52). Also called the digerati (Brochmann, 1995), they include the traditional élite like politicians, experts of all sorts, scientists, businessmen, famous people, musicians, and artists. The new aspect is that they are intrinsically connected to the new, growing businesses in information and communication technology. These may be the people we are looking for in future élite studies. The question is how to approach them; how to make them give us a timeslot in their incredibly busy schedule. And once we have accomplished this: how to get something useful out of the interview itself. The importance of being able to access this élite is growing. However, this emerging high tech élite may be more difficult to research than the scientists and engineers of traditional STS research because of their more intimate relationship with politics and business and because of the symbolic importance attached to being busy and unavailable to people outside of their networks. So how may we get to interview them?

In the following, I will try to describe a set of strategies of access. This is based on experience from previous and ongoing research that have necessitated access to the high tech élite, like CEOs, scientists and policy-makers in the United States, Norway, Italy, and Great Britain. This experience emphasizes the need for a reflexive approach, but also a particular daring, directness and inventiveness. In this respect, we may learn from other professions that are interested in the same group of people, or at least from their 'spirit.' This is necessary in order to transcend the technical, neo-positivist attitude that still characterizes a lot of interview methodology.

Shifting Modes of Inquiry

The interview appears to be a situation of asymmetrical exchange. The researcher receives information, without giving the informant anything back. To remedy this situation, it is suggested that the researcher may pay her debt by acting as a public voice of the informant group or use the information as a source of suggesting improvements. However, this perception overlooks the possibility that there may be other rewards in being interviewed. It may be a change to present one's views or [argue] one's own version of events. It may even be interesting, since many interviews also offer opportunities for the exchange of points of views or experiences.

To understand these implicit advantages of being interviewed, we may draw upon experiences and images from other types of interviews than the research interview. I will argue that it is advantageous to the approach to high tech élites that we at least consider in a metaphorical manner what interviewing may mean when performed by other professions. In the following, I will briefly explore three such mindsets or modes of inquiry: the "journalistic," the "therapeutic" and the "investigative." The use of quotation marks is meant to underline that this is not a study of what journalists, therapists or detectives really do. Rather, I use some commonplace ideas of their roles as a way of exploring different ways of doing interview research in relation to the high tech élite. The aim is for the interviewer to manage a three-fold framework both when negotiating access and when performing the interview (which calls for maintaining, re-negotiating, or even improving access).

The "Journalistic" Mode

Sociology and journalism have for long had a dubious relationship. Especially the Chicago school, in particular Robert Park, was close both in method and writing-style (Lindner, 1996). More aggressively, Douglas (1976) argues for an investigative, rugged, combative style of inquiry modeled on investigative journalism. Thus, there are several reasons why social science should reflect on how journalists operate. Some journalists do more than 10,000 interviews in their career, a number very few social scientists aspire to. While you could make the case that journalistic interviews have a different purpose and go after different things or claim research interviews go deeper, we find there are numerous lessons across these boundaries. Moreover, journalists are already out there doing interviews, affecting the ways political or other élites understand the interview situation (Puwar, 1997, p. 1; Williams, 1980, p. 310).

The journalistic approach is intuitive, quick, active, and the journalist is not afraid to ask, even to ask twice. The journalist often takes keynotes during the interview, instead of, or in addition to listening to the tape-recorded version. This is both quicker and more apt for catching the core issues. Then you might not need to write out the entire text, and you only have to listen to parts of it—and you save a lot of time.

Journalists are used to working through acquaintances, contacts, friends, and secretaries. As a researcher you might gain from mastering social situations to the extent that you can fire away questions, be ready to jot down a few lines, be happy with a few comments, and do interviews on the spot, in elevators, or on the move. As Ostrander (1993, p. 25) points out, taking advantage of chance meetings or one's own social contacts may be as important as careful planning. In short, the key informant approach is the treatment you get from journalists. They do not care that you are a researcher. They want the facts now. That is in five minutes. While this is a source of tension for both groups, they can learn from each other. Journalists have the type of active knowledge seeking that Castells (1996) claims characterizes contemporary society, where information flows freely, quickly, and often through the virtual grapevine. If you want to get something out of your empirical attitude, you might not have the luxury of waiting for people to call you. I will illustrate this with an account of how I snowball sample recruited, accessed, and employed a journalistic, improvisational mindset.

I have said that using informants is a key, both to acquire an interview (get access), and to know what to look for once you have got it (maintaining access). Key informants are people with special knowledge about your subject, or access to data you cannot get to, or that you need to familiarize yourself with. You can call them up many times, check information, acquire new contacts, or ask additional questions. Some informal contact with key informants is useful, and entails less work than people you have consciously found, called-up, arranged an interview with, and where the transcript is written out. You may combine these loose types of interaction with more standard research interviews.

But how do you choose these particular key informants? In my project on the telecommunications industry, one informant came as a result of a phone call to the Regional Information Director. On my questions about the Telenor *Nomade* campaign, she directed me to several different people working at Telenor Mobile, who were responsible for the general marketing campaigns. The people I sought were not there, but the secretary told me that a person who now had left the firm really was the person responsible for the idea itself. I asked for his number, and called him repeatedly, with no luck. But after a few days he suddenly called me back, and I could hear by his voice that he was ready for a phone interview here and now, not a planned encounter next week that would take him even more energy.

I then dropped everything and improvised an interview, still in the middle of constructing an interview guide, and somewhat unprepared. After 20 minutes, however, he had given me several interesting reflections as well as several good hints about new informants. This is the real sense of the term "snowball sample." It is also the journalistic approach. With my traditional 'researcher' mindset I would be crippled and would have asked him to call me back when I was prepared. But social science is a creative venture not to be controlled by rational planning alone. We need to improvise and make use of Mills' (1959) *sociological imagination*. If you cannot improvise, most data is out of reach. After all, data is somewhat ephemeral.

Hans-Wilhelm Steinfeld, 48, is a Norwegian journalist who has lived 12 years in Moscow. Respected for his accomplishments as a reporter, but also for his temper and powerful presence, he has done hundreds of interviews, both for TV and for radio. A former correspondent to Russia, he explains his approach in this way:

> In the Secret Services there is the principle of the Pilot fish; you attach yourself to somebody you think can become something. In the case of Gorbatchev [whom he has interviewed ca. 40 times] and Jeltsin it was this principle that counted, in combination with the old axiom from Russian plan economy: "Good planning can not compete with pure luck[2]."

Steinfeld's luck was to live 12 of the most turbulent years of Eastern Europe in Russia. His dissertation brought him to Northern Caucasus, where he met the local party leader Mikhail Sergejevitz Gorbatchev: "I had no idea, then, how strategic my acquaintance would become," Steinfeld states.

Apart from a talent in meeting the right people, networking skills also include some down-to-earth methods that could be used by anyone. For instance, it is always important to remember who and what you represent, and employ that in different ways that [suit] the occasion. Big is not always beautiful. Reminding us of Traweek's (1995) experience as 'Eliza,' Steinfeld remembers one particular occasion of power dynamics, access and improvisation:

> I always had the privilege of representing the Norwegian Broadcasting Corporation. It is small, but respected. In the middle of May of 1980 there was a meeting between the American and Soviet foreign ministers in Vienna. Kevin O'Ryan from BBC and I went against the current, ignored the announced American press conference and placed ourselves outside of Hofburg castle to try for Andrej Gromyko. I approached Gromyko by pointing to my colleague, asking whether BBC and Norwegian TV could get a question. Gromyko looked

aggressively at my BBC-colleague and said in English: 'Oh yes? BBC—the organization that knows everything in the world and maybe a bit more than everything?' I quickly pointed to myself and asked whether or not little, innocent NRK from Oslo then could ask instead, and we got a six-minute interview.

Now, what can we learn from this story? Many who refuse an interview are in reality afraid of not having enough interesting things to say to you. Contrary to what it might seem like, if you are famous or have a privileged position, you might never get them 'on the hook.' And when you do, what they say will be influenced by who you are. For this reason, famous scholars who have a public image are unfit for interviewing most of the time.

Secondly, Steinfeld cleverly uses the authority of the other person, then twists it to his advantage when he finds out this does not work. This is a move that could be described as re-translation of a discourse (Latour, 1987). The discourse was about big broadcasting having high thoughts about its own role. Steinfeld turns this around, using Gromyko's own logic.

The "Therapeutic" Mode

Establishing rapport is about gaining trust, whether or not this is spelled out. Previous research points out that identity and trust play a key role in getting access (Johnson, 1975; Lee, 1993). Hoffmann's (1980) respondent discovered that he knew a member of Hoffman's family. Insider status was thus granted, and considerable new insight on the recruitment of Boards of Directors was provided. We might not always be that lucky, but being aware of how identity plays into the process is still a key. In fact, the interview is a rare occasion for high tech leaders to open up, share thoughts and profit from the human touch and undivided attention that the interviewer provides. As the modern proverb goes, "It is lonely at the top." Even a leader might not have room for such self-exploration in his daily life. Often s/he finds being interviewed quite fulfilling (Coleman, 1996, p. 339). Feminists like Oakley (1981, 2000), Fog (1985) and Kaul (1999) share such a perspective, as do systemic therapists like Andersen (1991), White (1991) and Anderson (1997) who value relationships and narrations over early diagnosis, since research subjectivity is the condition, not the qualitative bias of interview practice. Actually, the interview should be a collaborative relationship between equals where meaning emerges (Anderson, 1997). But to achieve it, we need to learn to listen:

> Women often mute their own thoughts and feelings when they try to describe their lives in the familiar and publicly acceptable terms of prevailing concepts and conventions. (Anderson & Jack, 1991, p. 11)

Therapeutic mode, however, does much more than helping the access to the 'muted' channel of woman's subjectivity. What we want to do, sometimes, is to grasp the situation. We want to react by intuition, discover by uncovering layers, much like the psychotherapist. We need to be observant. Maybe we even need to experience, in order to understand, as would be the phenomenological claim at this point.

We may share the urge to understand how the actor has experienced important life-events. We do not share the interest in resolving those problems, if they cannot be remedied by that particular encounter (Kahn & Cannel, 1968, p. 149). That is to say, unless we really have a lot of time and want to enter a fieldwork informant relationship to this person, in the way that Whyte (1943) was able to befriend his main informant Doc.

Psychoanalyst Haydee Faimberg (1996, p. 668) recommends listening to how the patient has listened to the interpretation. She then assigns new meaning to what he said, beyond what he thought he was saying, a move she calls "listening to listening." Therapeutic mode can be manipulative, smart, and cynical, but also calm and empathetic. The strong point of therapeutic mode is the way it makes you understand the interview relationship.

Many interviews become easy after you "get going." Why? Because you let people talk about themselves. If you manage to find a topic that's [dear] to your subject, you practically just have to steer the interview in your direction. This is what McCracken (1988) describes as "grand tour questions." Only that you sometimes have to dig for a while to find it, it does not come prepared from your guide.

In a previous experience with interviewing CEOs (Thorvik & Undheim, 1998), we often found ourselves being totally fascinated and immersed in the world of the other. Sometimes this is necessary, in order to 'get the whole story.' Instead of the promised ten minutes, we often got an hour's interview, just by showing up two people, and by giving exclusive attention. One example is our interview with an industrialist in Leksvika, an industrial township quite far off of Trondheim, Norway. We were impressed with what this person and his father had built up through the years, and made no secret about it. We overtly expressed our fascination with this 'industrial adventure'—an informant term we adopted. As a result, he took the time to give us anecdotes, and detailed insights that went way out of his prepared schedule. He felt flattered, and gave us the interview in appreciation. The interview became the backbone of our reflection from then on. It embodied the social entrepreneurial spirit we had been looking for.

On another occasion, I drove for two-and-a-half hours each way to interview the *Fylkesmann* of Nord-Trondelag County. In her otherwise busy schedule, we had three hours together. She said it straight out: "If you come such a long way, you must think this is important. Then I do, too."

The point about the therapeutic mindset is easily interpreted as unethical because it appears to be manipulative. Thus, we need to be careful with this metaphor and the kind of manipulative practice it may suggest. However, it is important to consider the fact that an interview may be an opportunity for a kind of exchange of views and an expression of altruism that may make people feel important and even comfortable, relaxed and at ease. To overlook this fact may make us unable to understand the rationale for giving us access in the first place.

The "Investigative" Mode

Already Sanders (1976) wrote about the sociologist as detective. Sharing the fascination for physical evidence and physical features with the STS scholar, the detective is an investigative, methodic and curious type who dedicates him/herself to solve mysteries and problems. Supposedly, s/he investigates to resolve other people's mysteries, but as detective novelists reveal, detectives are most of all fascinated by solving them. The detective wants to find out "what really happened," but in doing so, s/he is always testing theories (Sanders, 1976, p. 3).

Sociologists need to learn from historians, journalists and detectives how to tell a story, how to give an account of the turn of events. It is what people want to hear, anyway, and it is what they will remember. Giving a believable account of the turn of events is important. Especially when interviewing politicians who have their own political agenda, even in interviews: "one never knows if one has managed to access how things really are . . . one might receive filtered, quick sound bites, that are clichéd responses" (Puwar, 1997, p. 4). This is an occasion where the best detective novels can teach sociology a lesson. In the introduction to Dashiell Hammett's detective novel *The Continental Op*[3], Steven Marcus reveals the essentials of this powerful method:

> The Op interviews the person or persons most immediately accessible. They may be innocent or guilty—it doesn't matter; it is an indifferent circumstance. Guilty or innocent, they provide the Op with an account of what they know, of what they assert really happened. The Op begins to investigate; he compares these accounts with others that he gathers; he snoops about; he does research; he shadows people, arranges confrontations between those who want to avoid one another, and so on. What he soon discovers is that the "reality" that anyone involved will swear to is in fact itself a construction, a fabrication, a fiction, a faked and alternative reality—and that it has been gotten together before he ever arrived on the scene. And the Op's work therefore is to deconstruct, decompose,

deplot and defictionalize that "reality" and to construct or reconstruct out of it a true fiction, i.e., an account of what "really" happened. (Marcus, 1974, p. xix)

We need to learn to use investigative mode to find out what exactly is going on in our field. We need to find the 'story line,' the exact turn of events. What is the real agenda here? (Obviously, by 'real' I do not mean to retort to the pattern-finding agenda, only to direct attention to the empirical threads the interviewer could follow). Who is hiding what from whom? Am I getting the right information? Who is holding something back? What is going on backstage?

For instance, in a study of Norwegian and Italian telecom carriers, I had one employee tell me: "it seems you are some sort of industrial spy. You cannot come to see our secrets. Are you crazy?" This person was some sort of a social scientist, but worked for Telecom Italia. So, they did not want me to run to their competitor.

A little later, when presenting my research topic to a Norwegian telecom employee, I knew that they were giving me the tourist explanation. So I experienced that he did not think I was interested, or capable of grasping the real issues at hand. The result was that they did not come up in the interview. In the end, if I had not been able to change his perception of me, and my ambitions, I would have to read it out from the context. Or, worse, I would have to come back. But many times, these things never catch my attention. If I forget to take the 'investigative' mindset, I risk taking everything I am told at face value.

What the investigative mode consists of is a detailed inquiry. Without resorting to extreme Sherlock Holmesian methods, this means doing what otherwise is known as a cognitive interview. Cognitive interviews cover police interrogations, military briefs, lawyer interviews with clients, testimonials, in short, all type of interrogatives. This can, of course be done to children, adolescents, adults, elderly, celebrities, élites or novices. Cognitive interview is a powerful perspective because it points to the fact that events are very soon 'forgotten,' or hidden behind the many layers of imaginative reconstruction, so familiar to anyone who has tried to get the 'truth' out of someone.

The cognitive interview was devised to improve eyewitnesses' memory by using mnemonic strategies which ask witnesses to think about what happened and encourage them to make as many retrieval attempts as possible (Campos & Alonso Quecuty, 1999, p. 47). In the legal context, obviously, the elicitation of complete and accurate statements from witnesses and victims is essential.

Although the police generally receives too little training, and should be informed by both laboratory and field methods from psychology in assessing and documenting eyewitness accounts, a lot can be learned from the police approach as such. Directness, authoritative behavior, and clear, short questions are all characteristics that could be applied with luck in other interview contexts. One study of cognitive interview techniques surveying 96 trained and 65 untrained police officers found trained officers were significantly more likely to use instructions to mentally reinstate context, use different orders, change perspectives and imagery. Frequently used techniques were to establish rapport, to report everything, to encourage concentration, to witness compatible questioning, and to give mental reinstatement of context (Kebbell, Milne, & Wagstaff, 1999).

Mixing Mindsets

Having sketched three mindsets, we should not fail to mention that these may overlap quite naturally, and that previous studies have documented the hybrid practices of the investigative journalist (Guba, 1981; Smith, 1992). Actually, the ideal would be to manage all of them at the same time, switching between them, or adapting as you go along. Here, again, the merit of my threefold distinction is to underline how the journalistic mindset catches the ephemeral nature of things on-the-go, the investigative mindset digs deeper, is suspicious and penetrates commonplace, faulty, or concealing behavior, while the therapeutic mindset repairs aggressiveness by treating the interview as [an] honest human exchange. This way, more, better, and meaningful interviews occur quite naturally and might release tension and contribute to deeper understanding of the human condition on the part of both interviewer and interviewee.

Accessing Élite Settings

There is a notable difference between expert and élite interviews. Experts are often narrow-minded specialists, whereas élites are more generalists as ideal types. This demands a different approach. Among other things, the preparation for the interview is different. To experts you might need to show your familiarity with technical jargon, in order for them to take you seriously. To élites, who might be equally clever, or influential, a general grasp of the issues, and showing you have an overview can be equally in demand.

Now, these strategies could be combined with network technology. The opportunities of getting access to interviews could be summed up as improved communication tools and increased communication through the use of new, mobile media (Internet, e-mail, cellphones). The potential is, at first sight, that getting in touch with the élite becomes easier since availability is increased.

Another advantage is psychological. Actually, some claim physical presence is higher valued in a network society, since the interview thus becomes a very real situation in the midst of mediated or virtual communication. But since élites protect themselves, they might be further away than before, just accessible to the 'insiders' (secretaries, family, friends, and colleagues). Increased mobility means people are difficult to find in their offices. Busy people also switch e-mail accounts often. Also, the diffusion of technology might make everyone else catch up with you and your 'advanced' access methods.

Looking at the interviewer as a "journalist," a "therapist" or a "detective" could be done all at once. We need to be able to switch perspectives during the interview. They serve as complimentary mindsets.

Knowing why you will not get hold of a person is part of the research agenda. There has to be a reason why you are not deemed important, or why a certain source will not speak. STS has been concerned with this, but has not spelled it out as a methodology. Who you get access to, and also whom you think you might get access to, of course, will set limits to your research agenda. It limits you in significant ways, and it puts discursive frames to your thinking. Sometimes this is a threat to the treatment of the topic. Often, this is the case in qualitative studies in political science. Not every professor who is interested in US foreign policy gets access to the President.

Studying regional development (Thorvik & Undheim, 1998) we interviewed 80 people from the power élite in the region of Trondelag, Norway, as well as national actors. Our sample included mayors, politicians, cabinet members, business leaders, bankers, industrialists and University professors. The sample choice reflected our desire to explore the reasons for pessimism on regional economic possibilities in one of Norway's most resourceful regions, for instance home of the largest private research institution of Northern Europe, Sintef, as well as the Norwegian University of Science and Technology. Getting an interview took from one to five weeks at most. We phoned up several times, faxed interview proposals, followed up, and did so several times, if necessary. Our proposal consisted in a brief description of our project and of ourselves. Most of all we made sure to point out why it would be so important to us that this particular person took the time to talk with us. To each person we had a different strategy. We always worked in a team of two, so I had to synchronize what I said to what my partner had said earlier.

Sometimes we did not take "no" for an answer, and said we needed to speak with this person. We could also play 'good guy/bad guy.' I would try to express how thankful we would be if we could get a confirmation now, he would call the day after, saying we had no more time, and needed to speak with our guy in person—now. Only one person refused to talk to us, and this was the Minister of Industry. His aggressive and some would say ill-informed comments formed the background of our research agenda—the public view of our region's potential for growth and prosperity. His secretary maintained it was appropriate to talk to someone on a subsidiary level. We did not think so, but even persistent efforts to convince his secretary did not produce results. It is very likely that he was not prepared to defend his comments, and did not want more fuzz about the whole affair.

Intellectual craftsmanship is a lifestyle, an attitude towards your intellectual projects that has no off-hours: "the most admirable thinkers within the scholarly community you have chosen to join do not split their work from their lives" (Mills, 1959, p. 211). Getting access also means allowing yourself to get exposed to the problem, getting inspiration, getting into it. Mills (1959, p. 211) wrote:

> You do not really have to study a topic you are working on; for as I have said, once you are into it, it's everywhere. You are sensible to its themes; you see and hear them everywhere in your experience, especially, it always seems to me, in apparently unrelated areas. Even the mass media, especially bad movies and cheap novels and picture magazines and night radio, are disclosed in fresh importance to you.

Working in this way, as journalists or entrepreneurs, we get new ideas frequently, and are able to act upon them. Now, let us take a look at the issue Spencer (1982) and Mills (1956) raised; sociologists need to access élites more forcefully and intelligently.

Borrowing Power from the Powerful

While previous research suggests using social ties, own status, and personal contacts (Hoffmann, 1980, p. 47), sometimes your own personal authority is not enough to secure access. Access might also be denied because your agenda seems threatening (Moyser, 1988, p. 119). To alleviate these problems, various strategies exist. Spencer (1982, p. 29) suggests two strategies in order to access the Military Academy at West Point; either to try to make an influential person pave the way, or become a journalist. Likewise, Lofland and Lofland (1995, p. 60) recommend the use of allies both to get in and to ensure continued access. Let us study a variation of this theme that contains using other people's authority as a benchmark of your own importance. The following is an excerpt of a phone conversation I had in March 1999:

> "I am writing a Ph.D. on ICT-based companies and their view on societal development," I start out, hopefully. "In this context I would much like an interview

with Morten Lundal . . ." The quick response pulls me back in the chair: "I think I can tell you immediately that he has no time for that . . . we get a lot of these inquiries, you know!" Telenor Nextel CEO Morten Lundal apparently has a fierce secretary. Refusing to give up, however, I blast back: "But I think he will look at it differently . . . I have chosen Nextel, Mobile and Corporate communication, [two Telenor subsidiaries, as well as the main corporate office] and I have an interview with VP Technology [name] on Friday." A short pause makes me hold my breath, but then it comes, surprisingly: Yes [that is something else] where did you say you called from? I will notify you, so if you don't hear anything, call back around three.

The secretary changed opinion of me when I mentioned some powerful people. What I really did was to transform the discussion by claiming allies (Latour, 1987). In Latour's (1987) terminology I was going from weaker to stronger rhetoric. To students, graduate students, younger researchers and the like, these methods are vital, in order to bypass the important corporate veil of secretaries and other gatekeepers. What are the appropriate techniques for getting through this filter?

The most important advice is to try to find some commonalties between you and the high tech CEO or engineer you want to interview. (1) Draw on pre-existing contacts (élites, friends-of élites, family connections, school affiliation, or religious community). When face-to-face, or on the phone you may refer to a common context, like "we met at . . .," even though the contact was ephemeral. (2) Your presentation needs to be brief and "self-important." There is no need for academic language, just get straight to the facts. (3) Be creative with e-mail. In my attempts to get in touch with CEOs, I often sent out five e-mails for each response, out of which only one became an interview. (4) With or without e-mail, proposals can be sent directly to powerful people if you know their exact name, address, and use prominent letterheads, for instance from your university affiliation. (5) Especially with e-mail and Internet, you can afford easy, cheap and quick follow-ups. Here, secretaries are [the] key. Once you have got your feet inside the door, their responsibility is to take care of your inquiry. They will go to great lengths not to miss appointments. (6) With e-mail you may obtain quick response time. I sometimes got interviews in a matter of minutes. But the e-mail pitch must be succinct, crisp, and clear. You need to praise, explain, impress, and respect all parties involved. (7) Tell the secretary that you are currently talking to a lot of important people, and that you thought it would be fair to give your boss a chance to voice his opinion on this, as well. (8) Gatekeepers are sometimes more important than CEOs. Make 'friends' with the secretary, be polite, smile, or come visit. (9) Attend, or better organize gatherings, 'business meetings' and cocktail luncheons. You can arrange with guest speakers, or speak yourself. But beware, Winkler (1987) warns of the costs of the expected alcoholic and gastronomic bribery. (10) Lastly, be persistent, and do not give up. They will give in if you take the time. This happened several times with me. Once, after 15 phonecalls, 3 faxes, and 3 e-mails by two team-members, we finally got through. The secretary admitted she got 'tired' of us, and had to ask her boss at last.

When gatekeepers try to keep you out, they do not state their real reasons. Such as: (a) "I don't know who you are." Therefore it is important to present yourself using the right "code," whatever that might be. Believe me, it is worth finding this out. (b) "I don't have anything to say." The fear of having nothing to say could also apply to élites, but especially to experts whom you might want to ask questions outside of their expertise. Here, make sure you are not posing a threat. Encourage them by toning down the knowledge needed to be helpful to you. In fact, you might think it is important to find out why s/he is 'silent' on this matter. (c) "I don't see what's in it for me." You must then change your approach and maybe give out different types of 'candy.' You might not have monetary rewards (this might actually have worked with rich people, who are notorious for being [misers]), but do not mind that, since it is ethically questionable. Rather, you should here somehow manage to appeal to the therapeutic relief of a good conversation. Maybe, you can suggest joining him or her in their sailing boat? Or, you might ask to see their mansion that you have heard so much about, or just say that you would not mind doing the interview in the taxi to and from the airport.

From Access to Information

Once you sit with your élite sample, Jorgensen (1989, p. 86) rightfully says you should try to ask several types of questions. (1) Grand-tour questions that give an overview, and [get] the interviewee going, hopefully for half an hour, (2) mini-tour questions that go in more detail, (3) example questions for illustration, (4) experience questions (what actually happened), and (5) native-language-questions to clarify insider terms. However, a main challenge may be in the creation of a productive setting of the interview. Access is not just about being able to meet, but also to get answers to your questions.

The interview itself could be seen as a process with three elements: the opening, the grand tour, and the follow-up. The opening mainly calls for the "therapeutic" mindset, because of the sensitivity and social intelligence necessary to grasp the situation, and create the right social setting for the interview. The grand tour, where you want to get long answers, calls for all three mindset[s] ("journalistic," "therapeutic," and "investigative") because you may need to vary your mode of inquiry. The follow-up, in turn, is the task suited for the "detective." She or he wants to make sure all the facts are on the table.

The literature rightfully claims the opening of the interview is important. You have to establish the right atmosphere. While some advocate "admitting you are nervous" (Maaloe, 1996, p. 191), I would consider that the situation may call for making a joke, talking about the weather, hobbies, commenting on the office you are in, or something of that sort. As I was walking into the room at the beginning of my interview with a CEO in a large industrial corporation, I caught that the CEO and his secretary were discussing whether the weather was good for repairing his sailing boat. I quickly hooked on to this conversation as I passed through the secretary's room and into his office. I started talking about the joy of sailing and about how relaxing it must be to work outdoors, getting away from the hectic life in the office. This won his appeal, and both of us were at ease with the situation from then on. Two-thirds into the interview, I felt confident enough to raise critical questions about his role in the corporation. This also went ok. The interview situation calls for confidence, calmness and control—but also for improvisation. The Norwegian journalist Steinfeld explains: "If I improvise during an interview, it is the rule rather than the exception." Of course, the way you improvise depends upon your personality, experience and current state of mind. Are you confident, are you rested and calm, or eager, stressed, and nervous? McCracken (1988) points out that you need to use yourself as an instrument in the research process. As Oakley (1981, p. 41) states: " . . . the goal of finding out about people through interviewing is best achieved when . . . the interviewer is prepared to invest her own personal identity in the relationship."

Thinking like journalists, we would be more direct. As Steinfeld, the Norwegian journalist explains: "The first question is often just a formality. I use it to warm up the interview object if time and frames allow it. Then I try to catch him, partly through following up important thing said, or by surprising and contradictory contra-questions if the chance comes up. I try to avoid being rhetorical because rhetorical questions do best without answers. Often the answers can, should and do become corrective. I partly "hunt" the temperature in an interview to stimulate engagement among the viewers. But when it is important, the technique is to stimulate the interview object to explain herself or himself richer, for instance let the power holder express herself or himself in detail about a pressed situation."

Another move is to establish links between your and their worlds. In her interviews with women MP's in England, Puwar (1997, p. 2) found it useful to use her background from Coventry. The MP had her first constituency there, and had taught Puwar's nephew. Mentioning this created a powerful bond that lasted long after the interview.

The interview gives a double challenge. It challenges you, and it challenges the person you are interviewing. You need to be on the edge, risking something, risking to be asking naive questions, to be passive since you are mostly listening. You need to be provocative, to inspire to open up, to stimulate discussion, reflection and interest. You need to show you find his or her thoughts on this issue important. If you interview a scientist, the interview is not at all a nice "conversation with a purpose," as Kahn and Cannel (1957, p. 149) claimed long ago. It is about challenging status quo. It is about discovering structures by opening up new layers in people's thinking, opening black boxes.

What kind of competence should you display when interviewing the high tech élite? Traditionally, the literature claims the ideal position is that of an "accepted novice" (Maaloe, 1996, p. 146). Most interview textbooks claim you should pretend you do not know anything about the issue in case. You should open up, allowing others to use the words of their own. Actually, in my experience the opposite is true. The élite resists interviewers with little or no knowledge about what they are doing. In fact, it is better to "show off" some of your knowledge, and then discover that you get some respect. While it might be true that a foreigner has certain advantages when it comes to fieldwork because she or he is not viewed as a threat (Maaloe, 1996, p. 146), the general advice of appearing like a novice is of questionable value. You risk [losing] respect, getting little or no time to talk, and you might be unable to steer the interview in the direction you want.

The interview is a reflective process where your informant might learn as much as you. A good interviewer participates in the reflection, and leads your informants further when they feel they do not have more to say (Lie, 1998, p. 53). A good interviewer uses his social intelligence (Gardner, 1993), his intrapersonal and interpersonal skills, and his emotional intelligence (Goleman, 1995). Most of all, what matters, is to give exclusive attention. Nothing else is as flattering as that. Nothing will make the other person open up to you like careful but active listening. Listening, then, becomes a form of activity (Faimberg, 1996).

Final Remarks

The issue of getting access has been relatively neglected in STS, maybe because STS scholars do not see the problem. But even researchers who are lucky enough to obtain access do well in reflecting on their own role. Johnson (1975) states access is a precarious, ongoing, and implicit bargaining process. The importance of inside connections, persistence, social skills, and improvisation suggested in the literature (Brannen, 1987; Galaskiewitz, 1987;

Hoffmann, 1980; Thomas, 1995; Winkler, 1987) can be appreciated by ways of detailed empirical examples. Trust, respect, reciprocity, professional prestige or even self-esteem comes into play.

Human encounters cannot and should not be completely planned out. After all, what we are after is subjective meanings, the discovery of hidden, surprising, boring, or shocking 'realities' inherent in the research setting. If we partly accept Johnson's (1975) paradox (that the knowledge needed to access a setting can only be known once inside that setting), imaginative, playful choices will outdo rational, planned ones.

With recent advances in technology (Castells, 1996), gaining access has at once become both easier and more difficult. Easier because new access-points like e-mail have evolved; more difficult because the powerful always find ways to protect their time.

The more general issue raised in this article is the appropriate role of the researcher. Where are the limits to what we can do without compromising our integrity as researchers? How much power do we have as a profession? How does this vary within the research community, across disciplines, and with different professional status (undergrads, grad-students, post-docs, researchers, or tenured professors)? How do personality, training, and sense of experimentation come into play? The most important lesson, in the end, is to be pragmatic about method. Apart from upholding research ethics, the other question is what method works?

What works will depend upon the setting, the mindset of the researcher (which we have tried to enlarge with the 'investigative,' 'therapeutic' and 'journalistic' *modus operandi*) and the status, position and culture of the researcher. In this vein, the article could be read as a reflection on the mindset of a relatively young, Scandinavian, male social scientist. Most of the available interview literature is written by older, tenured professors who are US or UK based. That may make a difference?

Ever so often, handbooks on interview methods just assume we are all the same and have the same needs. But this is not so. This, evidently, also poses a problem with my article, where various issues are ignored or bracketed, both for brevity and for lack of attention to all aspects of access. Notably, cultural dimensions are not described in any detail. Thus, there are plenty of opportunities for future research.

Notes

1. The author thanks Professor Knut H. Sørensen, Norwegian University of Science and Technology, Professor Raymond Lee at Royal Holloway University of

London, Professor Claude Fischer, University of Berkeley, California, as well as an anonymous reviewer for substantial comments on this article. Also, thanks to the Norwegian Research Council, who made this project possible through their research grant under the SKIKT-program.

2. Mail-interview with Hans-Wilhelm Steinfeld, 15.03.99.

3. Op is abbreviation for operation or the operative team, and is often used in military or police intelligence jargon.

References

Aaker, D. A. (1996). *Building strong brands*. New York: The Free Press.

Andersen, T. (1991). *The reflecting team: Dialogues and dialogues about the dialogues*. New York: Norton.

Anderson, H. (1997). *Conversation, language, and possibilities: A postmodern approach to therapy*. New York: Basic Books.

Anderson, K., & Jack, D. C. (1991). Learning to listen. In S. B. Gluck & D. Patai (Eds.), *Women's words: The feminist practice of oral history* (pp. 11–26). New York: Routledge.

Becker, H. S. (1966). *Outsiders: Studies in the sociology of deviance*. New York: Free Press.

Booth, T., & Booth, W. (1994). The use of depth interviewing with vulnerable subjects—lessons from a research study of parents with learning-difficulties. *Social Science and Medicine, 39*(3), 415–424.

Bosk, C. L. (1979). *Forgive and remember: Managing medical failure*. Chicago: University of Chicago Press.

Brannen, P. (1987). Working on directors: Some methodological issues. In G. Moyser & M. Wagstaffe (Eds.), *Research methods for élite studies* (pp. 166–180). London: Allen and Unwin.

Breakwell, G. M., Hammond, S., & Fife-Schaw, C. (1995). *Research methods in psychology*. London: Sage.

Broadhead, R., & Rist, R. (1976). Gatekeepers and the social control of social research. *Social Problems, 21*, 52–64.

Brochmann, J. (Ed.). (1995). *The third culture*. New York: Simon and Schuster.

Brenner, M. C., Brown, J., & Canter, D. (1985). *The research interview: Uses and approaches*. London: Academic Press.

Burgess, R. G. (Ed.). (1982). *Field Research: A sourcebook and field manual*. London: George Allen and Unwin.

Campos, L., & Alonso Quecuty, M. L. (1999). The cognitive interview: Much more than simply try again. *Psychology, Crime and Law, 5*, 1–2.

Cassell, J. (1988). The relationship of observer to observed when studying up. In R. G. Burgess (Ed.), *Studies in qualitative methodology* (Vol. 1, pp. 89–108). Greenwich: JAI Press.

Castells, M. (1996). *The rise of the network society*. London: Blackwell.

Chandler, J. (1990). Researching and the relevance of gender. In R. G. Burgess (Ed.), *Studies in qualitative methodology* (Vol. 2, pp. 119–140). Greenwich: Jai Press.

Clifford, J., & Marcus, G. E. (Eds.). (1986). *Writing culture: The poetics and politics of ethnography.* Berkeley: University of California Press.

Cohn, C. (1987). Sex and death in the rational world of defence intellectuals. *Signs: Journal of Women in Culture and Society, 12*(4), 687–718.

Coleman, S. (1996). Obstacles and opportunities in access to professional work organizations for long-term fieldwork: The case of Japanese laboratories. *Human Organization, 55*(3), 334–343.

Cotterill, P. (1992). Interviewing women: Issues of friendship, vulnerability, and power. *Women's Studies International Forum, 15*(5/6), 593–606.

Crabtree, B. F., & Miller, W. L. (1992). *Doing qualitative research: Vol. 3. Research methods for primary care.* Newbury Park, CA: Sage.

Denzin, N. K., & Lincoln, Y. S. (2000). *Handbook of qualitative research* (2nd ed.). Thousand Oaks, CA: Sage Publications.

Dexter, L. A. (1970). *Élite and specialized interviewing.* Evanston, IL: Northwestern University Press.

Douglas, J. D. (1976). *Investigative social research.* Beverly Hills, CA: Sage.

Faimberg, H. (1996). Listening to listening. *International Review of Psycho-analysis, 77*(4), 667–677.

Finch, J. (1984). 'It's great to have someone to talk to': The ethics and politics of interviewing women. In C. Bell & H. Roberts (Eds.), *Social researching: Politics, problems, practice* (pp. 70–87). London: Routledge and Kegan Paul.

Fog, J. (1985). Om den folsomme fornuft og den fornuftige følsomhed: Psykoterapi som erkendelsesparadigme, *Psyke and Logos, 6*(1), 59–84.

Fog, J. (1994). *Med samtalen som utgangspunkt. Det kvalitative forskningsinterview.* København: Akademiske Forlag A/S.

Fowler, Jr., F. J., & Mangione, T. W. (1990). *Standardized survey interviewing: Minimizing interviewer-related error.* Newbury Park, CA: Sage.

Friedman, N. L. (1990). Conventional covert ethnographic research by a worker. In R. Burgess (Ed.), *Studies in qualitative methodology* (Vol. 2, pp. 189–204). Greenwich: Jai Press.

Galaskiewicz, J. (1987). The study of a business élite and corporate philanthropy in a United States metropolitan area. In G. Moyser & M. Wagstaffe (Eds.), *Research methods for élite studies* (pp.147–165). London: Allen and Unwin.

Garfinkel, H. (1967). *Studies in ethnomethodology.* Englewood Cliffs: Prentice-Hall.

Gardner, H. (1993). *Multiple intelligences: The theory in practice.* New York: Basic Books.

Giddens, A. (1991). *Modernity and self-identity.* Stanford, CA: Stanford University Press.

Gladwell, M. (1999, January). Six degrees of Lois Weisberg. *The New Yorker, 11,* 52–63.

Glaser, B. G., & Strauss, A. L. (1968). *The discovery of grounded theory: Strategies for qualitative research.* London: Weidenfeld and Nicolson.

Goffman, E. (1961). *Asylums.* New York: Doubleday.

Goleman, D. (1995). *Emotional intelligence.* New York: Bantam Books.

Granovetter, M. (1973). The strength of weak ties. *American Journal of Sociology, 78,* 1360–1380.

Grønning, T. (1997). Accessing large corporations: Research ethics and gatekeeper-relations in the case of researching a Japanese-invested factory. *Sociological Research Online, 2*(4). Retrieved July 2, 2002, from http://www.socresonline.org.uk/socresonline/2/4/9.html

Guba, E. G. (1981). Investigative reporting. In N. L. Smith (Ed.), *Metaphors for evaluation: Sources of new methods* (pp. 67–86). Beverly Hills, CA: Sage.

Gusterson, H. (1996). Nuclear rites: A weapons laboratory at the end of the cold war. Berkeley: University of California Press.

Hammersley, M., & Atkinson, P. (1983). *Ethnography.* London: Routledge.

Hannerz, U. (1969). *Soulside: Inquiries into ghetto culture and community.* New York: Colombia University Press.

Hertz, R., & Imber, J. B. (1995). *Studying élites using qualitative methods.* London: Sage.

Hess, D. (2001). Ethnography and the development of science and technology studies. In P. Atkinson, A. Coffey, S. Delamont, J. Lofland, & L. Lofland (Eds.), *Handbook of ethnography* (pp. 220–233). London: Sage.

Hoffmann, J. E. (1980). Problems of access in the study of social élites and Boards of Directors. In W. B. Shaffir, R. A. Stebbins, & A. Turowetz (Eds.), *Fieldwork experience: Qualitative approaches to social research* (pp. 45–56). New York: St. Martin's Press.

Holstein, J. A., & Gubrium, J. F. (1995). *The active interview.* Thousand Oaks, CA: Sage.

Jackall, R. (1988). *Moral mazes: The world of corporate managers.* New York: Oxford University Press.

Johnson, J. (1975). *Doing field research.* New York: Free Press.

Jorgensen, D. L. (1989). *Participant observation. A methodology for human studies.* Newbury Park, CA: Sage Publications.

Jordan, T. (2000). *Cyberpower.* New York: Routledge.

Kahn, R. L., & Cannel, C. (1957). *The dynamics of interviewing.* New York: Wiley.

Kahn, R. L., & Cannel, C. (1968). Interviewing: Social research. In D. L. Sils (Ed.), *International encyclopedia of the social sciences* (pp. 149–161). London: Macmillan Company.

Kaul, H. (1999). *Å intervjue voksne.* Paper presented at the workshop on *Tegn, Tale og Betydning,* Trondheim, 15–17. April.

Kebbel, M. R., Milne, R., & Wagstaff, G. F. (1999). The cognitive interview: A survey of its forensic effectiveness. *Psychology, Crime and Law, 5*(1–2), 101–115.

Knorr-Cetina, K. (1995). Laboratory studies. The cultural approach to the study of science. In S. Jasanoff, G. E. Markle, J. C. Peterson, & T. Pinch (Eds.), *Handbook of science and technology studies* (pp. 140–166). Thousand Oaks, CA: Sage.

Knorr-Cetina, K. (1999). *Epistemic cultures.* Cambridge: Harvard University Press.

Latour, B. (1987). *Science in action*. Milton Keynes: Open University Press.

Lazarsfeld, P. F. (1944). The controversy over detailed interviews. An offer for negotiation. *Public Opinion Quarterly,8*, 38–60.

Lazarsfeld, P. F. (1962). The sociology of empirical social research. *American Sociological Review, 17*, 757–767.

Lee, R. M. (1993). *Doing research on sensitive topics*. London: Sage.

Lie, M. (1998). *Computer dialogues: Technology, gender and change*. Trondheim: Norway: Center for Feminist Studies, NTNU.

Lindner, R. (1996). *The reportage of urban culture: Robert Park and the Chicago School*. Cambridge: Cambridge University Press.

Lofland, J., & Lofland, L. H. (1995). *Analyzing social settings* (3rd ed.). Belmont, CA: Wadsworth.

Marshall, C., & Rossman, G. B. (1995). *Designing qualitative research* (2nd ed.). London: Sage.

McCracken, G. (1988). *The long interview*. London: Sage.

Maaløe, E. (1996). *Case-studier af og om mennesker i organisationer*. København: Akademisk forlag.

Marcus, S. (1974). Introduction. In D. Hammett, *The continental op* (pp. i-xxix). New York: Vintage Books.

Merton, R. K. (1947). Selected properties of field work in the planned community. *American Sociological Review, 12*, 304–312.

Mills C. W. (1956). *The power élite*. New York: Oxford University Press.

Mills, C. W. (1959). *The sociological imagination*. New York: Grove Press.

Mishler, E. G. (1986). *Research interviewing: Context and narrative*. Cambridge: Harvard University Press.

Moyser, G. (1988). Non-standardized interviewing in élite research. In R. Burgess (Ed.), *Studies in qualitative methodology* (Vol. 1, pp. 109–136). Greenwich: JAI Press.

Moyser, G., & Wagstaffe, M. (Eds.). (1987). Studying élites: Theoretical and methodological issues. In G. Moyser & M. Wagstaffe (Eds.), *Research methods for élite studies* (pp. 1–24). London: Allen and Unwin.

Nader, L. (1972). Up the anthropologist: Perspectives gained from studying up. In D. Hymes (Ed.), *Reinventing anthropology*. New York: Pantheon.

Nye, J. (2002). *Bound to lead*. Oxford: Oxford University Press.

Oakley, A. (1981). Interviewing women: A contradiction in terms. In H. Roberts (Ed.), *Doing feminist research* (pp. 30–61). London: Routledge.

Oakley, A. (2000). *Experiments in knowing: Gender and method in the social sciences*. New York: The New Press.

Ostrander, S. A. (1984). *Women of the upper class*. Philadelphia: Temple University Press.

Ostrander, S. A. (1993). Surely you're not in this just to be helpful: Access, rapport, and interviews in three studies of élites. *Journal of Contemporary Ethnography, 22*(1), 1–27.

Puwar, N. (1997). Interviewing women MPs. *Sociological Research Online*, 2(1). Retrieved July 4, 2002, from http://www.socresonline.org.uk/socresonline/2/1/4.html

Rainbird, H. (1990). Expectations and revelations: Examining conflict in the Andes. In R. G. Burgess (Ed.), *Studies in qualitative methodology* (Vol. 2, pp. 77–98). Greenwich: Jai Press.

Rossman, G. B., & Rallis, S. F. (1998). *Learning in the field*. Thousand Oaks: Sage.

Sanders, W. B. (1976). *The sociologist as detective: An introduction to research methods*. New York: Praeger Publishers.

Seidmann, I. E. (1991). *Interviewing as qualitative research*. New York: Teachers College Press.

Seldon, A., & Pappworth, J. (1983). *By word of mouth: Élite oral history*. New York: Methuen.

Shaw, C. R. (1930). *The Jack Roller: A Delinquent boy's own story*. Chicago: University of Chicago Press.

Shaw, G. B. (1941). *Pygmalion: A romance in five acts*. Harmondsworth: Penguin.

Smith, D. (1988). *The Chicago School: A liberal critique of capitalism*. London: Macmillan.

Smith, N. L. (Ed.). (1992). *Varieties of investigative evaluation*. San Francisco: Jossey-Bass.

Smith, V. (2001). Ethnographies of work, work of ethnographers. In P. Atkinson, A. Coffey, S. Delamont, J. Lofland, & L. Lofland (Eds.), *Handbook of ethnography* (pp. 220–233). London: Sage.

Spector, M. (1980). Learning to study public figures. In W. B. Shaffir, R. A. Stebbins, & A. Turowetz (Eds.), *Fieldwork experience: Qualitative approaches to social research* (pp. 45–56). New York: St. Martin's Press.

Spencer, G. (1982). Methodological issues in the study of bureaucratic élites: A case study of West Point. In R. G. Burgess (Ed.), *Field research: A sourcebook and field manual* (pp. 23–30). London: George Allen and Unwin.

Spradley, J. P. (1979). *The ethnographic interview*. New York: Holt, Rinehard, and Winston.

Stewart, C. J., & Cash, Jr., W. B. (1997). *Interviewing: Principles and practices* (8th ed.). Boston: McGraw Hill.

Sudman, S., & Bradburn, N. M. (1983). *Asking questions. A practical guide to questionnaire design*. London: Jossey-Bass Publishers.

Taylor, S. J., & Bogdan, R. (1984). *Introduction to qualitative research*. New York: Wiley.

Thomas, R. J. (1995). Interviewing important people in big companies. In R. Hertz & J. B. Imber (Eds.), *Studying élites using qualitative methods* (pp. 3–17). London: Sage.

Thorvik, K., & Undheim, T. A. (1998). *Trøndelag 2030: Status og muligheter i et internasjonalt perspektiv*. Trondheim: Leiv Eriksson Vekstsenter.

Traweek, S. (1995). When Eliza Doolittle studies 'enry 'iggins. In S. Aronwitz, B. R. Martinsons, & M. Menser (Eds.), *Technoscience and cyber culture: A cultural study* (pp. 37–55). London: Routledge.

Undheim, T. A. (2002). What the Net can't do: The everyday practice of Internet, globalization, and mobility. (Ph.D. dissertation). *STS Report 55/02,* NTNU, Norway: Center for Technology and Society.

Van Maanen, J. (1988). *Tales of the field: On writing ethnography.* Chicago: University of Chicago Press.

Walford, G. (Ed.). (1994). *Researching the powerful in education.* London: UCL Press.

Weiss, R. S. (1994). *Learning from strangers.* New York: The Free Press.

White, M., & Epston, D. (1990). *Narrative means to therapeutic ends.* New York: Norton.

Whyte, W. F. (1943). *Street corner society.* Chicago: Chicago University Press.

Williams, P. M. (1980). Interviewing politicians: The life of Hugh Gaitskell. *Political Quarterly, 18*(3), 303–316.

Winkler, J. (1987). The fly on the wall of the inner sanctum: Observing company directors at work. In G. Moyser & M. Wagstaffe (Eds.), *Research methods for élite studies* (pp. 129–146). London: Allen and Unwin.

3

A Sociologist Among Economists

Some Thoughts on Methods, Positionality, and Subjectivity

Sarah Babb

I arrived in Mexico City in the summer of 1995 with a vague area of interest rather than a clear hypothesis. I was generally interested in how U.S.-trained economists had come to be so influential in the Mexican government, and how changing economic ideas had contributed to Mexico's move to free-market economic policies. The topic was timely. For more than a decade, technocrats with advanced degrees from American universities had been liberalizing the Mexican economy. Universally praised by the international business press, these technocrats had suddenly fallen out of favor, with the sudden, sharp devaluation of the peso at the beginning of that year, which was followed by a tremendous economic crisis.

Early on, I decided that my original "take" on these issues would be to study the historical evolution of the Mexican economics profession over the course of the 20th century. My doctoral dissertation, which was the basis for what later became the book *Managing Mexico: Economists from Nationalism to Neoliberalism* (Princeton University Press, 2001) ended up drawing on a quirky smorgasbord of methods, including primary and secondary historical sources, interviews with key insiders, an analysis of the career trajectories of graduates from Mexico's top economics program

(ITAM), an analysis of trends in public and private higher education in Mexico based on government data, and a content analysis of 287 undergraduate economics theses. In this essay, I re-create the story of how I arrived at these methods, and my experiences in deploying them. In the first section, I discuss how I arrived at my particular combination of historical methods and sources. In the second section, I discuss how I negotiated the dilemmas of my own position vis-à-vis my subjects.

Negotiating Historical Methods

Historical sociology is not a method in itself, but rather encompasses the "study of the past to find out how societies work and change" (Smith, 1991, p. 3). It therefore encompasses a myriad of topics and a variety of methodological approaches. Sociologists looking to make broad historical generalizations about more than one national case tend to rely heavily on the synthesis of secondary sources, because it is usually not feasible to find and analyze primary sources for long spans of time and multiple national contexts. Perhaps the most famous example of this sort of research is Barrington Moore's *Social Origins of Dictatorship and Democracy*, which examines historical origins of political regimes in the United States, France, England, Germany, China, and Japan (Moore, 1966).

Because I was only looking at a single case, I did not wish to confine myself to synthesizing secondary literature, particularly as the existing literature on the topic in which I was interested was extremely sparse. However, analyzing primary documents presents historical sociologists with a dilemma: when one chooses to adopt the methods of historians, it becomes much more difficult to draw the larger theoretical conclusions favored by sociologists. None of my dissertation committee members was a Latin Americanist, and none of them was interested in Mexican economists as a topic of study per se; they wanted me to tell a story that had implications that could be of relevance to nonspecialists—about the relationship between the state and professions, how policies change, how external pressures shape organizations, and so on. This meant that I could not afford to lose sight of the forest for the trees. I vividly recall conversations that I had with a historian friend in Mexico City, who failed to understand how I could possibly be doing serious research, because I was only willing to spend a week or two looking for archival documents on Mexican technocrats in the 1930s, and subsequently moved on to other decades, sources, and subjects!

Of course, I was interested in many other decades, and I wanted to link a story about economists over these multiple decades to a larger story about the evolution of the Mexican economy and society. In other words, I wanted to synthesize multiple levels of theoretical analysis—I wanted to be "close to" original, micro-level data, while preserving my ability to draw macro-level conclusions. Historical sociologists interested in striking this balance arrive at different mixtures of primary and secondary materials. On the one hand, John Markoff's magnum opus on the French Revolution, *The Abolition of Feudalism,* relies very heavily on coded *cahiers de doléance,* lists of grievances that were presented to the Estates General upon the disintegration of the old regime (Markoff, 1996). Viviana Zelizer's *Pricing the Priceless Child* is a cultural analysis of changing attitudes toward childhood in the 19th and 20th centuries in the United States; although it makes significant use of secondary sources, the core of the book is made up of excerpts from the popular press, the reports of government and public service organizations, and other miscellaneous cultural artifacts from the periods covered by the study (Zelizer, 1985). Toward the other end of the spectrum, my dissertation advisor's book *City of Capital* draws on share-trading records of the East India Company to show how political party affiliation influenced economic behavior in England in the 1700s, but sets these findings within a context of many chapters synthesizing secondary literature (Carruthers, 1996). Vivek Chibber's recent study of postwar economic policy in India and Korea is mostly a synthesis of secondary sources; however, Chibber is able to offer a new and heterodox account of why the two national cases turned out so differently through skillful mining of archival resources, including Indian government documents and collections of private papers (Chibber, 2003).

A significant problem for historical sociologists interested in working with primary materials is finding documents that allow for analysis of trends over significant spans of time. To take a contrasting example, my historian friend in Mexico was writing his doctoral dissertation on the life and ideas of a famous figure of the Mexican revolution. His job was to locate the archives where information on this individual's life was located, and to systematically mine these sources. My task, in contrast, was to find information that was at once shallower and wider, spanning from the 1920s through the 1990s. Ideally, I needed documents spanning the entire period that were both consistent and comparable. They also needed to be analyzable in a way that did not bog me down in a swamp of details about any single period or historical figure.

Thus, I needed to find historical documents that were consistent enough to be comparable over time. Institutions that endure over time, such as newspapers, governments, and universities, tend to produce this sort of document, and are thus a boon to historical sociologists. For example, Tilly, Tilly, & Tilly's (1975) famous work on cycles of protest from 1830 to 1930 relies on the sampling of newspaper articles to document how many, where, when, and what kinds of protests occurred. Unlike these authors, however, I was particularly interested in trends in *ideas* over time. In particular, I wanted to look at the ideas emanating from the two most important economics programs in Mexico: Mexico's first economics program at the Autonomous National University (UNAM), and its currently most influential economics program at the Autonomous Technological Institute of Mexico (ITAM). Whereas the UNAM has the reputation for being a hotbed of leftist ideology, the ITAM is known for being a center for the training of American-style economics, where students go on to receive American Ph.D.s in economics and to achieve top positions within the Mexican government. Three of Mexico's finance ministers over the past 20 years have been ITAM graduates.

It occurred to me that the most direct way to look at how these economics programs changed over time was to examine the syllabi of required courses and to use the works listed on the syllabi as a way of gauging where the programs "stood" on matters of economic policy. However, it soon became apparent that the syllabi that would have allowed for such an analysis did not exist. In hindsight, I suppose I should not have been surprised by this; after all, universities in the United States do not generally hold on to syllabi from past undergraduate courses, and there was no reason to expect Mexican universities to be any different. A sociologist at the Colegio de México, Francisco Zapata, offered me an extremely useful tip that was to extricate me from this dead end. "Why don't you go look at the economics theses?" he offered. "They're all just sitting there at the university libraries."

The suggestion that I look at undergraduate economics theses requires further explanation. Unlike American undergraduate programs, which allow students to explore courses outside their major, and which last only four years, Mexican programs specialize in a single discipline, last five years, and typically result in the writing of an undergraduate thesis; thus, it is something like an undergraduate and graduate education combined. When I went to the library of the Faculty of Economics at the National University, I discovered that the theses were a treasure trove of information just waiting to be mined: they spanned from the late 1920s through the present, their rhetoric was rich, they exhibited fascinating differences over time, and the authors they cited and methods they used were evocative of what it meant to be "an economist" in Mexico at different historical periods. I became even more excited when I ventured into the economics library at the ITAM, where the more recent theses were perfect replications (in Spanish) of mainstream American economics.

I was to spend many hours in the libraries of these two universities with my laptop, taking notes and developing a coding system for content analysis. Content analysis is a method for analyzing the message characteristics of documents systematically—or, to put it somewhat differently, any method in which the meaning of documents is analyzed in a way that attempts to be duplicable and comparable (see Gamson, 1992; Neuendorf, 2002). Conventional historians are known for synthetic interpretations of primary sources that are often unique—personal letters, the Declaration of Independence, and so on. In contrast, content analysts *count* message elements in documents belonging to the same category (e.g., newspaper articles, history textbooks), according to a predetermined coding scheme. Content analysis allows researchers to make generalizations about the overall content of a set of documents in ways that are easily comparable across groups of documents.

Content analysis can be particularly powerful for analyzing systems of meaning comparatively and historically, because it theoretically allows the researcher to track more subtle differences or changes over time than might come to light using more impressionistic methods. For example, content analysis might allow us to state that a random sample of 1000 issues from three major newspapers from 1965 through 1975 show a steady increase in the mention of the issue of women's rights; it might also allow us to say that the *New York Times* was consistently more sympathetic to the cause than the *Washington Post*. Because I was interested in changes in economic thought over time and across economics programs, content analysis seemed like the ideal method to use. The content-analytic approach I ultimately adopted was to thoroughly read the introduction and conclusion of each thesis, where main theoretical points and citations were made, and skim the middle for methodological approaches. I coded each thesis for theoretical citations, methodology, and various rhetorical features—most important, position on government intervention in the economy. I also copied juicy quotes verbatim to use as illustrations of general trends.

However, the theses did not speak for themselves. As I continued to code and analyze them, I was plagued by multiple unanswered questions. Why, for example, was there a sudden escalation in the citation of University of Chicago authors in the ITAM theses during the 1970s? Did this indicate a deliberate institutional alliance between the ITAM and the University of Chicago economics program, as had occurred with Chile's Catholic University in earlier decades? How, then, could I explain the subsequent decline in Chicago citations in the 1980s and 1990s—when neoliberalism in Mexico came into its own? At a more macro level, how did the differences that I observed over time and across programs fit into a larger story about Mexican economics and the role of economists in policymaking?

These were questions that could not be answered by any amount of content analysis: the micro-level data could not tell me about the macro-level context. Thus, as my research progressed, I found myself drawing on many other sources. Some of these sources were secondary—histories of the

Mexican political system, economic histories, Roderic Camp's invaluable and exhaustive historical studies of Mexican political elites, and official institutional histories of the National University. In addition to secondary sources, informants were a crucial resource that allowed me to tell a larger story about the data contained in the theses. People directly involved in the institutions and processes that I was studying answered my questions both directly, in interviews, and indirectly, through facilitating access to other sources of data. In retrospect, I believe that I did the research for this book just in time: in just the past 5 years, a number of my key informants have passed away.

Fortunately, I had an abundance of connections, because a year prior to coming with a Fulbright to do my dissertation research, I had spent a year studying at the Colegio de México with a grant from the Social Science Research Council's Pre-Dissertation program (which unfortunately no longer exists). This enabled me both to become comfortably fluent in Spanish and to make many friends and contacts in Mexico City, who provided both wonderful social support and a link to sources of information.

Sometimes the help my informants provided was unexpected. Because I was a personal friend of several UNAM economics graduates, I was given access to an unpublicized collection of political documents from the radical student movement that had so heavily influenced the UNAM economics program in the late 1960s and 1970s. Through another UNAM personal contact, I was introduced to the (then) rector of the UNAM economics program, who gave me access to a recent study on the career trajectories of UNAM economics graduates, which I immediately photocopied and incorporated into my study. Because I knew an ITAM professor personally, I was able to establish a series of connections that led me to the ITAM's Alumni Society, which maintained a database of graduates that included information about current employment and graduate training. Coding these thousand-odd cases (with names removed to protect confidentiality) was extremely tedious, but it helped me to answer a number of important questions. Most important, it showed me that although ITAM graduates with American Ph.D.s had high-profile positions within the Mexican government, most ITAM graduates had neither foreign graduate degrees nor fancy government jobs: The modal ITAM graduate held a BA and was working for the private sector.

My study benefited tremendously from the fact that it was, for the most part, relatively *contemporary* history, which enabled me to talk to people who had lived through and made the history that I was investigating. Over time, my initial group of informants expanded, as connections spawned further connections. The most important of these informants was Víctor Urquidi, a Mexican economist who began working at the Mexican Central Bank as a very young man in the 1940s, and who remained an active participant in debates about Mexican economic policy until his recent death in 2004. Of all my informants, Víctor was the one who provided the most key pieces of information, as well as the most connections to other informants. Víctor was simultaneously a subject, a lunch companion and friend, a provider of personal contacts, and an academic advisor who read my dissertation from cover to cover with extraordinary speed.

Over the course of my research, I conducted 53 interviews with informants, who provided me with two different kinds of information. The first was a sort of "thick description" of the periods and institutional contexts with which they were familiar, which gave me glimpses into the larger meanings of the events I was documenting. What did it feel like to be in the Mexican Central Bank in the 1940s? What were some of the internal disputes and divisions over the reform of the ITAM's economics curriculum in the 1960s? The second kind of information was key pieces of data that enabled me to "fill in the blanks," answering questions on which my documents were silent. For example, from interviewing ITAM professors, I was able to discover that the sudden increase in Chicago citations at the ITAM was not due to a larger institutional commitment to Chicago thinking, but rather because the director of the economics program at the time happened to be a Chicago graduate; as soon as the directorship changed, the disproportionate weight of Chicago citations disappeared. From interviewing an official of the government scholarship agency, I was able to discover that the reason there seemed to be hardly any Mexican Ph.D.s from more leftist American economics programs (e.g., the University of Massachusetts, the New School) was that these programs were not on the "List of Excellence" that qualified them for government scholarship assistance.

Because interviews with informants were so important to making sense of my topic, I found myself confronting some issues more typically faced by ethnographers than historians. My own characteristics—as an American, as a student, as a young woman, and so on—were at risk of influencing the way my informants responded to me, and impeding my access to information. In the following section, I discuss how these dilemmas of "positionality" played out, as well as how I managed the issues of my own subjectivity and bias.

Negotiating Positionality and Subjectivity

Although interviews were indispensable to my research, I cannot claim that this study represented *ethnography* in the serious sense of the term. Rather, my interviews mostly assumed the form of incomplete oral histories, in which individuals recounted parts of their lives and careers. Nevertheless, some of the issues that I encountered in gathering information through interviews were common to ethnographers. A researcher's own ascribed and achieved characteristics influence the way their subjects respond to them in the field, as well as the way they analyze the social language and behavior they encounter. As Reinharz (1997) points out, researchers in the field do not simply play roles; they bring multiple "selves" to the process of investigation. These multiple selves should not be viewed merely as hindrances to "objective" research, to be shed whenever possible in favor of a more scientific role; they are tools that can be mobilized as a way of making connections to the people whom we investigate.

The most obvious characteristics of mine that might have influenced my subjects' responses were my culture and nationality. Over the centuries, Mexico has been invaded by the U.S. many times; this history, combined with ongoing American influence over Mexican policies, has contributed to a strong sense of nationalism that often merges into anti-Americanism. My overwhelming sense, however, was that my being a U.S. national was more of an advantage than a burden. When dealing with U.S.-trained economists, my nationality was, of course, an advantage. More generally, however, I think that my respectful attitude, combined with the fact that I was showing a flattering interest in people's lives and careers, as sufficient to overcome any anti-American prejudice that I might have encountered.

I also believe that my gender was a tremendous asset in helping to get my informants, the vast majority of whom were men, to open up to me. As a woman in her late twenties, I appeared nonthreatening, and often found myself the recipient of "gentlemanly" treatment—being taken out to lunch, having doors held open for me, and so on. In Mexican culture, as in American culture, there is an established gender dynamic in conversation: The female role is to ask eager questions about a man's life, and the man, flattered by the focus of female attention, holds forth at great length. Thus, what I was doing was following the steps of a well-understood cultural dance. Had I been conducting equivalent research in China, for example, I wonder whether I would have had the same experience.

Perhaps the most significant obstacle I faced in my research was that I was, in many cases, "studying up"—interviewing elites, who were either formerly or currently in positions of power. How would these individuals react to a humble and impoverished graduate student's pleas for information? Here, I found that social networks were essential. This was one of the areas in which Víctor Urquidi's assistance was absolutely crucial, because he had a tremendous network of personal connections to economists, businessmen, and government officials. I recall that in some cases, he would even have his secretary call on my behalf to make appointments for me. Once launched in this way,

I was able to establish contacts with more individuals sympathetic to my research, who were then able to help connect me to more interviewees, in snowball fashion. At the time, I owned a single suit, bought for me by my mother, which received considerable use, and which still hangs in my closet—for sentimental reasons, as it is now out of fashion!

Moreover, there was an important characteristic that I shared in common with many of my informants, which undoubtedly helped enhance communication: namely, that I was a Ph.D. student studying academics. This not only made it easier to converse, but also, I believe, served as a hermeneutic bridge—I did not feel like an outsider studying "the Other." This was particularly the case with informants who had studied in the United States, but with almost all my informants, the points of common understanding were manifold: theories of social change and development, course requirements, scholarships, examinations, grading, and so on.

Where the interpretation of my findings was concerned, my most significant problem was not overcoming my own subjectivity, but finding an appropriate subjectivity to begin with. In other words, what I needed was a "voice" through which to make sense of my findings and tell a story about them. Finding a voice is particularly fraught with difficulty in situations where researchers are examining topics around which there is great political controversy (see Michalowski, 1997). "Going native" was described by European colonialists as the process of conforming to the uniform social and cultural pattern of those among whom one lives. But the "natives" among whom I was living were far from uniform in their points of view. My topic lay directly on top of a deep political fault line dividing Mexicans who endorsed the market-liberalizing model favored by Washington, and those who thought that the model was the most recent incarnation of Yankee imperialism. The former camp had won control of the Mexican government, and economists belonging to this tendency were in a dominant position within the profession; meanwhile, economists associated with the latter position were marginalized from policy debates. As I was interpreting and telling a story about my findings, I could simply not fail to take some kind of position on these issues—but what would that position be?

On the one hand, I was skeptical of the neoliberal claim that removing government interference with markets was the holy grail of development success. On the other hand, I did not feel particularly aligned with the economists who had come out of the student movements of the 1960s and 1970s—now mostly teaching at public universities like the UNAM. Many remained committed to the tenets of orthodox Marxism and dependency theory. Although I was sympathetic to these theoretical tendencies (as a professor, I teach both in my classes), I could also understand the criticism leveled against the UNAM: that it failed to prepare its graduates for jobs in the world; during the late 1960s and 1970s, practical topics such as mathematics had been de-emphasized, and the program had adopted a new program of studies in which students were required to take seven semesters of Marxist theory. It seemed to me that for all their virtues as critical tools, both orthodox Marxism and dependency theory were deficient in their ability to create a positive policy program—short of socialist revolution, which seemed a rather remote possibility. In large measure, it seemed to me that this tendency within Mexican economics was marginal to policy by definition.

I did ultimately end up "going native." However, the group of natives to whom I became identified belonged neither to the former group nor to the latter group described above. Through getting to know Víctor better, I became aware that there had been an older generation of economists and policymakers who Raymond Vernon (1963) described as *técnicos*—hard-headed pragmatists who presided over the so-called Mexican Miracle of the 1950s and 1960s, when the economy grew at an average rate of 6% per year. Within this group, there were some political differences, with some falling to the right and others farther to the left wing of the spectrum. Some of them were self-taught; a handful of them had foreign graduate degrees. What they shared in common, however, was a lack of theoretical dogmatism of any sort—including the dogma of market liberalization.

While I was aware of the faults of Mexico's postwar development model, it seemed to me that the point of view of Víctor and others belonging to this group provided a strong position from which to evaluate and criticize the reigning neoliberal model. Thus, not only did I bring multiple "selves" to my research, but I also found myself actively constructing a new "self" as my research progressed (see Reinharz, 1997). I emerged from this experience permanently changed, and I imagine that my "Mexican developmentalist self" will influence my work throughout the rest of my career.

Some Final Thoughts

As I conclude this piece for a book on emergent methods, I find myself asking whether there is a name for the kind of research that I did. I ultimately think the best way to describe my research was that I used everything I could get my hands on. I am not the first historical sociologist to proceed in this way. I was fortunate to have been in an ideal position to triangulate data from historical documents with oral-historical accounts from individuals who had participated in that history. Because I was in a land of strong institutions—universities, state agencies, archives, and so on—I was able to glue my story together with rich historical accounts and descriptive statistics. A similar study would doubtless be possible in the United States or Korea; it would be far more difficult to put together in a place like El Salvador or Mozambique.

I also believe that researchers engaged in this study need either to have exceptionally high self-esteem or to have exceptionally strong external support. As one slowly collects the patches that are to be assembled into the quilt, it seems impossible to imagine how it will all fit together. The task seems doubly impossible when one compares one's own activities to those of researchers engaged in methods that are more straightforward—to the historian in his archives or the demographer at her computer terminal. I had many moments of despair, when it seemed arrogant to have attempted such an ambitious and unorthodox task. Evidence of my hubris, it seemed to me, was that I was constantly cutting, pasting, and rewriting—tearing apart what I had built, rebuilding it, and then tearing it down again once more. I was fortunate to have had extremely supportive and responsive committee members, who continually told me that I was doing something worthwhile and interesting.

References

Babb, S. (2001). *Managing Mexico: Economists from nationalism to neoliberalism.* Princeton, NJ: Princeton University Press.

Carruthers, B. (1996). *City of capital: Politics and markets in the English financial revolution.* Princeton, NJ: Princeton University Press.

Chibber, V. (2003). *Locked in place: State-building and late industrialization in India.* Princeton, NJ: Princeton University Press.

Gamson, W. A. (1992). *Talking politics.* Cambridge, UK: Cambridge University Press.

Markoff, J. (1996). *The abolition of feudalism: Peasants, lords, and legislators in the French Revolution.* University Park: Pennsylvania State University Press.

Michalowski, R. J. (1997). Ethnography and anxiety: Field work and reflexivity in the vortex of U.S.-Cuban relations. In R. Hertz (Ed.), *Reflexivity and voice* (pp. 45–69). Thousand Oaks, CA: Sage.

Moore, B. (1966). *Social origins of dictatorship and democracy: Lord and peasant in the making of the modern world.* Boston: Beacon Press.

Neuendorf, K. A. (2002). *The content analysis guidebook.* Thousand Oaks, CA: Sage.

Reinharz, S. (1997). Who am I? The need for a variety of selves within the field. In R. Hertz (Ed.), *Reflexivity and voice* (pp. 3–20). Thousand Oaks, CA: Sage.

Smith, D. (1991). *The rise of historical sociology.* Philadelphia: Temple University Press.

Tilly, C., Tilly, L., & Tilly, R. (1975). *The rebellious century: 1830–1930.* Cambridge, MA: Harvard University Press.

Vernon, R. (1963). *The dilemma of Mexico's development: The roles of the private and public sectors.* Cambridge, MA: Cambridge University Press.

Zelizer, V. (1985). *Pricing the priceless child: The changing social value of children.* New York: Basic Books.

4

Ethnography and Conversation Analysis

What Is the Context of an Utterance?

Douglas W. Maynard

A s this book makes clear, investigators who wish to examine social phenomena in an immediate way—that is, without the technologies of the survey or other measuring instruments, coding, counting, and quantifying—have an increasing number of choices. The two choices I examine in this chapter are conversation analysis and ethnography. Conversation analysis (CA) investigates how utterances, by virtue of the sequences in which they appear, perform recognizable social actions. Traditional ethnography depends on interview and participant observation to capture facets of members' life world, and would seem compatible with CA, which uses audio and video capture of interaction in its natural settings. Doing CA involves scrutiny of recordings and detailed transcripts and would seem to be a more intense kind of observation, potentially adding to ethnographic strategies. Or, from the other direction, we could say that ethnography enhances the CA style of close inspection of talk. We will see, however, that the combined use of ethnography and CA involves a number of theoretical and methodological issues and that these issues are important to consider when employing the two methodologies together. In particular, if one is examining conversational interaction, a question is whether and how ethnography can provide access to the context in which talk and its constituent utterances reside.

The substantive matter in this chapter is the conveyance of "bad news" between parties in various kinds of social settings. In previous research (Maynard, 1996, 2003) using ethnographic and other narrative data, I have shown that discrete strategies for presenting the news affect recipients' realization of the news in different ways. As might be expected, both *stalling* and *bluntness* heighten the possibility of misapprehension, whereas the strategy of *forecasting* enhances understanding and apprehension of the news. Even a simple preannouncement, such as "I have some bad news," helps to prepare a recipient for the forthcoming announcement. Essentially, forecasting works well because it has two facets to it. On the one hand, a deliverer who forecasts is giving some preindication to a recipient of what is to come. On the other hand, the recipient, having been signaled, can estimate and predict what the news will be, can anticipate what is going to be said. Indeed, a regular pattern when news is forecasted is for recipients to venture a guess or candidate announcement and for the deliverer to simply confirm it. Here is one example:

> I have a friend who had a brother who was in a lot of trouble all the time over a period of a year. And I got a call from my friend and she said, "Have you talked to Mary?" and she sounded upset. And I said "no" and she sounded so upset, immediately in my brain it turned into *uh oh what's going on*. And she said, "It's Davy." And immediately I said, "Is he dead?" And she said, "Yeah." . . . But like I knew it before she said it. It was really strange because it was almost as if the conversation was just a play, because I knew what was going to happen and I just went through the ritual of the conversation. (Maynard, 2003, p. 45)

In this case, the forecasting ("Have you talked to Mary?" "It's Davy") and the way it leads to the recipient's guess ("Is he dead?") seems rather inadvertent, although at other times it is a more purposeful strategy.

With a collection of narratives about bad news, identifying the strategies of delivery (whether they are done purposefully or not) and examining patterns of receipt will inevitably bring up a difficulty. It is that fitting the peculiarities of circumstance into one or the other of the analytically derived types of delivery (forecasting, stalling, being blunt) is often not easy to do. For example, when a clinician stalls in telling parents diagnostic news, it can aggravate a tendency on the part of parents to deny and normalize. Normalization, in turn, produces expectations on the part of potential recipients:

> The child was a twin, whose sister was stillborn. After the birth, the parents were told, "The other baby's fine," and the mother "didn't realize that anything could still go wrong." The baby was hard to feed, but the mother "thought it was just because she was a preemie." When the baby was 6 months old, the mother began to realize that her daughter "was not holding things like other babies" but again attributed the slowness to her prematurity. When, at the baby's regular 6-month checkup, the pediatrician suggested the possibility of cerebral palsy, the mother "just broke down completely in his office." She said that she "just couldn't believe it." (Darling, 1979, p. 139)

Even though we do not know the pediatrician's exact manner of delivering the bad news, the indications are that he was gently suggestive in a forecasting manner rather than boldly forthright in presenting the diagnosis (he "suggested the possibility of cerebral palsy"). Nevertheless, in the context of an initial stall ("the other baby's fine") and the mother's resultant normalizing beliefs about her child, the disclosure appears to have been experienced as entirely blunt. In a way, the bluntness of an informing is not an innate property of the deliverer's manner but is relative to the contingently ordered time delay in which the delivery ultimately occurs and to the set of convictions or beliefs a potential recipient holds during this period.

Accordingly, whether any verbal form of delivery exhibits features of forecasting, stalling, or bluntness is dependent on what participants know; what they expect; and how they hide, provide, and discern cues about their worlds of habitation. Consider how even the most terse verbal message can be part of a situational contexture that is utterly communicative to a recipient. A husband who was waiting for his wife to arrive home at a local airport after a brief trip knew that her return involved one change of planes in Denver. While awaiting her arrival, he heard the phone ring, and answered the phone, according to his own account, with a "casual hello."

> The caller sighed heavily and said (without reciprocating my hello), "I'm in Denver." I immediately identified the caller as my wife, and I knew from her sigh, the tone of her voice, her lack of reciprocity, and the violation of the mutually understood expectation that she wouldn't call before I picked her up at the airport that she had bad news. She informed me that her plane had been late and this led to her missing her connecting flight by three minutes. (Maynard, 2003, p. 59)

Here, the utterance "I'm in Denver" merely reports the caller's location. As a report, it does not name the type of news it projects. Nevertheless, the narrator, operating in a context of mutual expectation regarding phone communication between his wife and himself, knows immediately "that she had bad news."

The upshot is that, instead of regarding these strategies as literal descriptions of complex modes of communication, behavior, and relationship, a better approach may be to regard them in the way that ethnomethodology regards talk. All utterances are indexical expressions: How a participant understands an utterance depends on the relation of that utterance to such things as the person speaking it and the time or place of its production (Garfinkel, 1967, pp. 4–5). In other words, for their meaning, utterances depend on their context; the character of a message is related to the particularity of circumstances in which it is embedded. The question is, of what does context consist? How is one to analyze context? One answer is, use ethnography because, by way of interview and observation, it gives wider access to the social setting than does the talk itself. For me, however, there is a different answer. An utterance's context is the organized sequence of turns in which it appears. This is not to discount the role of ethnography but it is to say that the analyst draws on a much more immediate and local sense of an utterance's context than ethnography provides. For example, to the extent possible, analytic interpretations of what someone says must be grounded internally to the conversation—in participants' own, turn-by-turn, displayed understandings and practice-based orientations rather than less technical observations (note taking, for instance) or interview-based narratives about such interaction.

Of course, this principled, or strong, version of CA methodology cannot work in relation to every feature of interaction. An investigator takes for granted or ignores some features in order to "focus" analytically on a particular phenomenon or "activity type" (Drew & Heritage, 1992; Levinson, 1979). My own inquiry, dealing with the actions of delivering and receiving bad and good news as these actions traverse an array of social settings, is activity focused in this very sense. I explain how, rather than investigating a particular setting where news deliveries occur, I came to examine these deliveries generically in various environments, assuming or using background features without analytic explication. However, whereas CA, in its methodologically strong version, eschews ethnographic description because it draws on resources that are external to the participants' ongoing or real-time situated talk, my research, primarily based on audio and video recordings of interaction, also has been heavily ethnographic. It therefore trenchantly raises the question of how to integrate the ethnographic data with the mechanically recorded data and conversation analysis of news delivery activities.

To put the matter succinctly, I regard ethnography as an ineluctable resource for analysis, using it in a relationship with CA that is one of limited affinity. This is different from other approaches in which the relationship between the analysis of recorded interaction and ethnography is one of mutual affinity, and ethnography and CA or discourse analysis are more freely interwoven. The issues involved in this contrast between limited and mutual affinity are complex, and I probe them more fully after discussing the activity focus of my study.

Collecting Data to Analyze an Activity Rather Than a Setting

I became interested in the phenomena of bad and good news when a colleague, Professor Bonnie Svarstad of the University of Wisconsin School of Pharmacy, had completed her own coding studies of discourse data—tape recordings and transcripts—from a developmental disabilities clinic (Lipton & Svarstad, 1977; Svarstad & Lipton, 1977) and offered these data to me. As I began to read transcripts and listen to the recordings with as few preconceived ideas as possible,[1] it soon emerged that a dramatic and difficult event was occurring. The tapes exhibited what I call a *noetic crisis* (Maynard, 2003, p. 12), or breakdown in the taken-for-granted social world as clinicians convey diagnostic bad news to families. Clinicians talked quickly, hesitated, used euphemism, backtracked, and engaged other tactics indicating that relaying a diagnosis was no simple naming or labeling matter (Gill & Maynard, 1995). Parents responded with questions, silence, stoical statements, or emotional outbursts, or in other ways that mirrored and entered into the clinicians' presentational difficulties.

Although I began by listening to someone else's tape recordings, the project soon took on an expansive life of its own and developed into a traditional field study. After working with these audiotapes, I obtained a grant from the National Institutes of Health to expand my investigation by observing, interviewing, and videotaping in a local center for developmental disabilities. In this center full-time for one year and part-time for another, I watched the operations of the clinic, participated in meetings, talked to professionals and family members, and took copious notes on the diagnostic process, in addition to recording examinations and diagnostic informing interviews. My idea was that the study of other clinical processes (Marlaire & Maynard, 1990; Maynard & Marlaire, 1992), complemented by ethnographic inquiry, including observations and interviews, would enhance my analysis of the delivery and reception of diagnostic news. I know that my ethnographic inquiries did augment analysis of the informing interviews, but I also made a decision that studying the delivery of *diagnostic* news in the medical environment would benefit by inquiry into the delivery of *news* in more casual conversational interaction. In other words, my study should concentrate not just on the clinic as a setting for the presentation of a diagnosis but also on the relation of practices involved in clinical presentations to the conversational undergirding on which those practices build. As an *activity,* the delivery of bad news occurs in many social worlds, and to understand that activity in its fullness and in relation to generic devices for its delivery, data are needed that sample its variety.

Along with expanding my investigation to include ordinary conversation, I made another decision. Following the Sacks, Schegloff, and Jefferson (1974) strategy of collecting data across settings, I wanted to sample diagnostic news deliveries in other kinds of clinics besides the developmental disabilities one. This comparative approach[2] differs from previous ethnographic research on bad news, which tends to be occupationally and substantively confined. Investigators, in studying professionals (clergy, law enforcement personnel, medical practitioners), not only slight participants giving news to one another in more private and ordinary conversational encounters. Substantively, they also concentrate on one particular topic—such as death, cancer, developmental disabilities, or legal entailment. Subsequent to my presence in the developmental disabilities clinic, I gathered data in a department of internal medicine at a Midwestern university teaching hospital, at a clinic for HIV-antibody testing in an urban setting, and in the oncology clinic and hospital ward of another university teaching hospital in the eastern United States.

All my endeavors to assemble comparative clinical data involved observation and interview in addition to the focal aim of taping a multiplicity of diagnostic announcements. My most intensive field study was at the HIV-antibody testing clinic, which was mostly staffed by volunteers. This meant that I could and did become a working member of the setting, and I spent time at the intake desk, being trained as a counselor, and doing HIV prevention instruction with individual clients. As an ethnographer, I wrote copious notes about my experiences and observations in each setting to which I gained access, and gathered two kinds of narrative data: (a) about participants' views of bad or good news that they experienced in the particular setting and (b) about their previous experiences with bad or good news. Placing this information together with stories from students in my classes and from journalistic and research literatures returns us to the original issue. With taped real-time interactions as well as field research and narrative data in hand, how do we handle the research evidence? Granting primacy to recorded talk and social interaction, as I do, what is the context of utterances occurring within this interaction? What is the relation between CA and ethnography?

Affinities Between Conversation Analysis and Ethnography

Ethnographers are often much more expansive than conversation analysts in what they consider the context of talk to be, and they muster their observations and interviews to describe features of the distant social environment (sometimes referred to as "social structure") thought to be relevant to understanding given utterances. Consequently, ethnographers sometimes criticize CA for its almost exclusive use of recorded interactions, eschewal of field methods, and willed neglect of social structure. However, the ethnographic proposal—what I call the "contextual critique"—that CA needs to turn its attention away from local organization and appreciate the provenance of such organization in external structure, would mean distorting the phenomena of everyday life and the social experience of participants. Conversation analysts question whether ethnographers have a systematic enough way of connecting social structure to talk.

What is needed, I believe, is for each perspective—ethnography and CA—to have a deeper appreciation of the other. Conversation analysts have not explicated their use of ethnography and could benefit from reflective consideration of field methods and the copious ethnographic literature. At the same time, ethnographers need to appreciate the CA rejoinder to their contextual critique, which helps in specifying why using ethnography in a limited way to inform CA is desirable. Limited use of ethnography provides *analytic control* over the interpretive statements that an investigator proposes and prevents *data loss* that derives from premature decisions about what interactional detail is of critical importance to the study.

Mutual Affinity

The number of ethnographic investigators who combine traditional methods of participant observation and open-ended interviewing with a more or less heavy use of tape recordings is very large,[3] in part because of the technological advantages (Grimshaw, 1989, pp. 58–64; Sacks, 1984). Researchers in the fields of communications (Hopper, 1990/1991; Nelson, 1994), discourse analysis (Jonathon Potter, 1997; van Dijk, 1985), linguistically-oriented anthropology (Duranti, 1997, pp. 98–99; Erickson & Schulz, 1982; M. H. Goodwin, 1990; J. J. Gumperz, 1982), pragmatics (Levinson, 1983), and sociology (Corsaro, 1982; Grimshaw, 1989; Gubrium & Holstein, 1997; Jimerson, 1998; Miller, 1994; Silverman, 1993; Spencer, 1994) use recordings along with ethnographic methods, sometimes as a supplement to participant observation and interview and sometimes without prioritizing either approach. As opposed to the "primary or exclusive" use of tape-recorded material, for example, Emerson, Fretz, and Shaw (1995) propose that such usage is *"one way among others* for closely examining the meaning events and experiences have for those studied" (p. 77, emphasis added).

An extended argument for mutual affinity is to be found in Gubrium and Holstein (1997), who advocate combining ethnographic *naturalism* with ethnomethodological *social constructionism*. In naturalistic inquiry, the stress is on immersion in the social worlds of prison, mental illness, medical settings, street life, schools, and communities. As demonstrated in such classics as Whyte's *Street Corner Society* (1943), Liebow's *Tally's Corner* (1967), and Anderson's *A Place on the Corner* (1976), the attempt is made to secure the *substance* of life in these worlds by capturing members' own words, modes of expression, descriptions of experience, and the like. Social constructionism, which includes the methods of CA, involves a shift of attention from an ethnographic insider's depiction of substance to the *how* of social life—the methods implicit in talk and interaction whereby social actors sustain the substantive sense that life has. This distinction between grasping substance and studying the methods or practices for the achievement of meaning highlights a shift investigators can make as they probe a given setting. Here, then, is a clear statement of mutual affinity. In my own research using both recordings and ethnography, however, a difficulty is knowing when or how to make the transition between capturing everyday substance through ethnographic naturalism and breaking down that substance into the methodic practices for its achievement. I will specify strategies for making this transition when I discuss limited affinity.

The "Contextual Critique" of Conversation Analysis

Before explicating the notion of limited affinity, other ground needs to be cleared. A point of contention between those who advocate for a mutual affinity between ethnography and CA and those who, like me, suggest a more limited approach is whether studying conversation, performing *sequential analysis*,[4] and confining investigation mostly to recordings and transcripts is by itself adequate social science. Indeed, some conversation analysts, particularly those who concentrate on "ordinary" conversation as opposed to that which occurs in institutional settings, eschew ethnography altogether. Such eschewal gives rise to criticism of CA's close attention to what have been called the "autonomous"-seeming structures (Corsaro, 1981, pp. 12–16; Duranti, 1988; Zimmerman, 1988) of sequential organization of talk. Without explication of the *larger* context of that talk, CA misses the forest for the trees. In Bourdieu's (1977) words, ethnomethodologists and conversation analysts operate with the "occasionalist illusion" that the essence of interaction is entirely contained within it. Other sociologists (Burawoy, 1991, pp. 271–276; Cicourel, 1987; Grimshaw, 1989; Mehan, 1991; Miller, 1994) have developed this critique, as have discourse analysts (Coulthard, 1977; Stubbs, 1983) and linguistic anthropologists. The student of Thai language and society Michael Moerman suggests that CA has a preoccupation with the "dry bones" of talk and is "bloodless" and "impersonal" with regard to "richly experienced human reality" (1988, pp. x–xi). Against Moerman, Pomerantz (1990/1991) observes that he invokes notions of members' "orientations" and "concerns" and implies that ethnographers have privileged access to these features of conduct. Pomerantz, along with Potter (1998), suggests approaching these "mental" concepts as social and occasioned rather than as static backdrops to behavior. However, making the case for a "culturally-contexted conversation analysis," Moerman (1988, p. 57) writes, "Sequential analysis delineates the structure of social interaction and thus provides the loci of actions. Ethnography can provide the meanings and material conditions of the scenes in which the actions occur" (p. 57).

Less trenchantly but similarly, Hanks (1996), in speaking to linguistic traditions, argues that spoken interactions contain elements of both transcendent formal structures of language and more contingent, local, and momentary developments. CA, being confined to the proximate realm, disregards the "broader social backdrop" (p. 218) of everyday interactions. While recognizing that "the surrounding discourse in which any expression is embedded is its first tie to context," there are "larger scale discursive formations" in need of analytic appreciation (pp. 185, 223).

Judging by the convergence of many fine scholars on the contextual critique of CA, the impulse to grasp the large, or wide, social backdrop to a particular spoken activity is strongly felt. As strong as it is, however, where the impulse leads is not at all clear. Goodwin and Duranti (1992, p. 2) argue, for example, that "it does not seem possible at the present time to give a single, precise, technical definition of context, and eventually we might have to accept that such a definition may not be possible." Indeed, when advocating for context, investigators do not often specify what is meant by "broader" or "larger scale" social structures and organizations or precisely how to incorporate features of context residing outside of and purportedly influencing direct interaction and talk. Hanks (1996, pp. 217–222) points to Goffman's (1974, 1979) frame-analytic "participation frameworks," Gumperz's (1982) "contextualization cues," and Lave and Wenger's (1991) "communities of practice" as notions helpful to the involvement of social environments in the dissection of conversational interaction.[5] Although these notions are intuitively appealing and are employed pervasively in many studies that fit in the *ethnography of speaking* tradition (Hymes, 1974), a close look suggests they nevertheless are like what Blumer (1956) once called "sensitizing concepts" and do not theoretically or methodologically provide a disciplined approach to capturing their referents in the expansive social arenas to which they point.[6] In short, as Schegloff (1987, p. 221) argues, investigators have treated "contexts" (frameworks, cues, communities) as utterly transparent, when they may be anything but.

Response to the Contextual Critique

The impulse to grasp wider contexts surrounding an utterance points toward obtaining more ethnographic information and data. Without proper analytic control of contextual information, however, paradoxically, investigators may lose data in which the local orderliness or important facets of social organization actually reside.

Analytic Control. The burden for investigators is to provide a methodological apparatus—what Kaufmann (1944) describes as inquiry-specific rules of scientific procedure—for decisions about what to include from the wider-than-sequential context or broader social environment surrounding an utterance or other piece of interaction. In much very fine ethnography, I do not find rules of procedure for incorporating the analysis of social structure. Consequently, like other conversation analysts, I have come to rely on terms that Schegloff (1987, 1991) raises about "micro and macro" sociology and "talk and social structure." In examining utterances and interaction, two questions to be posed about larger or broader structures, categories, or organizations are (a) whether such categories are *relevant* to participants and, if so, (b) whether they are *procedurally consequential* in the sense that participants display, in their talk and interaction, an orientation to them. Considerations of relevance point to the many possible ways in which the "same" participant can be identified. Against the positivist solution of defining relevance according to sociodemographic categories that may have theoretical provenance or are statistically significant in their correlation with attitudes and beliefs, Schegloff (1987) proposes a concrete approach. Investigators' characterizations of participants should be grounded in actual displays of participants themselves using such characterizations to perform and understand their actions. Furthermore, if social structure and other abstract aspects of "context" are real to the participants, they will be procedurally consequential, as reflected in speech exchange systems (turn-taking)[7] and other features of talk, such as repair (Schegloff, Jefferson, & Sacks, 1977). In CA, *repair* refers to mechanisms for dealing with troubles or problems in speaking, hearing, or understanding the talk in progress—what someone has just said—and these mechanisms may be encouraged or suppressed in specific environments. In the survey interview, for example, certain mechanisms for repair are suppressed on behalf of attempting to achieve standardization (Moore & Maynard, 2002).

Data Loss. Instead of providing methodological criteria for analyzing context, investigators often rely on those sensitizing concepts that are more or less theoretically sophisticated but otherwise ungrounded vernacular depictions of interactions. Consider further the work of Bourdieu (1977, pp. 4–6), who eloquently criticizes "objectivist knowledge" for its ignorance of "practical knowledge of the social world," opposes abstract rule-oriented theories of social action, incorporates real time as a feature to be appreciated about social life, and thereby assimilates an extraordinary amount of complexity and detail in his analysis of everyday social and cultural phenomena. The ground seems well plowed for inquiries alive to all manifestations of ordinary conduct that contingently develop in the course of actual talk and social interaction. Not so, however, for, according to Bourdieu, actors are situated according to a "habitus" and system of "dispositions" that derive from social structure—the material conditions of class relations—and thereby provide the forms that interaction takes (pp. 78–81). Whereas the implications are clear, the mechanism is not; social structure is somehow operating behind the backs of participants. Indeed, when Bourdieu says, "'interpersonal' relations are never, except in appearance, *individual-to-individual* relationships and . . . the truth of the interaction is never entirely contained in the interaction" (p. 81), it could simply imply that, as Grimshaw (1989, p. 83) puts it, "Life is complex." Any strip of interaction, because it is complex, could be accorded "alternative interpretations," and it is difficult to adjudicate among them. But Bourdieu is up to other things. He means that nothing is autonomous in the domain of language use; anything and everything interactionally is related to habitus and its class conditioning.[8] As against the "occasionalist illusion," this smacks of a "social-structural illusion," the idea that there is no time out from participants' potential placement according to race, gender, class, and a society's other structural positionings.

Conversation analysts subscribe to a different sensibility—that many social behaviors are ordered according to local principles that are impervious to effects from social structure. Not always or everywhere, for conversation analysts neither dispute the importance of class and other social structural concepts nor argue with studies documenting, for instance, the distribution of language styles according to class or ethnic backgrounds of people (Schegloff, 1997, p. 413), as in the pioneering work of Labov (1972a; 1972b), Gumperz (1982), and other sociolinguists, most recently Baugh (1999). In fact, there is a growing number of CA studies in which speech practices are an independent variable predicting bureaucratic decisions (Boyd, 1998) or are a dependent variable affected by specific historical, social, or interactional circumstances (Clayman & Heritage, 2002; Heritage & Stivers, 1999; Lavin & Maynard, 2001).

When, however, investigators assume that vernacular, categorical, or typological references to a setting or its participants are pervasively relevant and that the social structures and institutions embodied by such references are omnirelevant in their influence on talk and social interaction, it may mean losing analytic grip on the phenomena that participants themselves regard as prominent. This is because a consequence of working with vernacular terms, categories, and types is to discard or subsume particular, discrete circumstances of real-time talk and social interaction. As Schegloff (1991, pp. 60–61) puts it,

> The vernacular characterization "absorbs" the details of the talk as an unnoticed "of course" in such a "formulated-as-institutional" setting, and does not prompt one to note and explicate how the talk enacts "doing being in that setting." . . . If the focus of inquiry is the organization of conduct, the details of action, the practices of talk, then every opportunity should be pressed to enhance our understanding of any available detail about those topics. Invoking social structure at the outset can systematically distract from, even blind us to, details of those domains of event in the world.

In the upcoming section on limited affinity, I discuss problems with this strong version of CA strategy and its eschewal of ethnography. The present point is that ethnographic insistence on the relevance of larger and wider institutional structures can result in a loss of interactionally consequential particulars, for attention shifts from concrete utterances in the fullness of their detail and as the embodiment of actual social actions to embrace narrative or other general accounts concerning social surroundings.

If anything has emerged from ethnomethodological and CA inquiry in recent decades, it is that participants in real social worlds *do* show orientations to the most immediate, embodied, pragmatic contexts of any given utterance. Analysts in these traditions are concerned to grasp the small-scale practices, impervious to prior theorizing and impossible to imagine, in which such orientations appear. Not only in complete utterances and turns, but also in hesitations, false starts, breathing, silences, speech tokens, prosodic manipulations, and other minutia of interaction, participants accomplish socially big things by virtue of the adjacent and sequential positioning of utterances, turns, and minutia. Among the big things they achieve, independently from possible accretions of social structure, is *intersubjectivity*— mutual understanding and conjoint orientation, which make actual concerted activity possible in the real social world.

Limited Affinity

The notion of limited affinity implies precise ways in which ethnography complements CA. I will discuss three uses to which conversation analysts put ethnography: (a) in descriptions of settings and identities of parties; (b) in explications of terms, phrases, or courses of action unfamiliar to an investigator or reader; and (c) in explanations of "curious" patterns that prior sequential analysis may reveal.

Describing Settings and Identities. A problem with the strong version of CA strategy is its recommendation that especially in analyzing talk in institutional (medical, legal, business, etc.) settings, we need to attend to how participants "do being in that setting" (Schegloff, 1991, pp. 60–61). As Garfinkel (1967, p. 32) remarks, *every* feature of a setting, without exception, is the managed accomplishment of members' practical actions. This implies that in a clinic, for example, participants' identities as doctor and patient are an outcome of work that makes those identities visible. However, an analyst necessarily may need to disattend to aspects of identity work to concentrate on other activities as also central to the setting. Without choosing which features and activities to concentrate on analytically in a setting, and which features therefore to describe ethnographically in the background, investigators are faced with an enormously complicated task in which all prominent features of a setting—all "doings"—require inquiry.

Explicating Unfamiliar Terms, Phrases, or Courses of Action. A second type of limited affinity between CA and ethnography highlights meanings that participants take for granted but that are not transparent either for an analyst or a reader of a conversational extract. Conversation and discourse analysts' tendency to work in their own language communities, Duranti (1997, pp. 267–277) argues, obscures the extent to which ethnographic knowledge of taken-for-granted expressions is necessary for the detailed analysis of conversational structure. It is a point well taken, for ethnographic knowledge—an insider's understanding of terms, phrases, and courses of action—is something that CA regularly draws on when displaying and analyzing a particular excerpt (Maynard, 2003, pp. 74–75). Ethnography may be necessary not only for comprehending relatively casual references in recorded conversations, but especially for learning the definition of technical nomenclature in such institutional settings as medicine (Cicourel, 1987). An analyst of doctor-patient interaction may have to learn about medical procedures or phrases to understand what is being said in a particular sequence and may need to define such procedures or phrases for readers.

Explaining "Curious" Patterns That Prior Sequential Analysis May Reveal. A third type of limited affinity between ethnography and CA situates the investigator in a setting in a more traditional field-study sense, and involves the use of observation and interview to capture or confirm in abstract terms what a conversation analytic inquiry may propose about concrete interactional organization in the setting's talk. Participants' vernacular descriptions, captured when the investigator interviews them, may help make sense of patterns that sequential analysis suggests but cannot fully explain. In our study of HIV and AIDS counseling, we found that counselors, despite official recommendations about tailoring "safer sex" teachings to the needs of individual clients, often gave clients information that appeared to be irrelevant to them personally. That is, counselors may introduce a panorama of recommendations that meet with passive and silent responses, and sometimes open contestation, from clients (Kinnell & Maynard, 1996). In CA terms, counselors regularly initiate advice-giving talk that is unsuccessful in occasioning uptake from clients.[9] A reason for recommendations being ill fitted to clients, discovered through ethnographic participation in the setting, is that counselors are taught not only to minister to individual clients (if they can) but also to assume that clients would relay to their wider community of friends and acquaintances information that may be personally irrelevant. Hence the apparent insensitivity to clients' own needs, evident in the sequencing of counselor-client interaction, is at least partially responsive to a perceived "institutional mandate" (Drew & Heritage, 1992, pp. 22–23; Maynard, 1984, p. 12) to effect social change in communities where HIV is highly prevalent.

Another example of the explanatory use of ethnography comes from our research in an oncology clinic. A patient who had been dealing with gall bladder cancer for a year had just undergone an unsuccessful operation to remove more of the tumor. Subsequently, the physician needed to tell this patient that the cancer was no longer treatable, and that, although he would be released from the hospital, he was at the end stage of the disease and life process. All that could be medically provided was palliative care. Inspection and analysis of the natural interaction as captured on the videotape revealed no mention of imminent dying and death. Instead, we observed the physician, at a particular juncture in the conversation, broaching the topic of hospice, the patient and his partner collaboratively shifting the topic from hospice to a nursing home where the patient could go upon discharge from the hospital, and the conversation thereby developing contingently in ways that avoided discussion of hospice. Through his references to hospice, we described the oncologist as somewhat unsuccessfully alluding to the patient's dying. And because allusive talk purposely avoids explicit formulation, it was helpful to consult what the oncologist said to me in an interview about this encounter: "Sometimes I use the discussion of hospice, not so much because it's important to me that the patient accept a home hospice program, but . . . to get the conversation really directed where you want it to go, which is on death and dying issues" (Lutfey & Maynard, 1998, p. 325). Only with the ethnographic information was it possible to verify that the physician, when broaching the hospice topic, was working to inform the patient that the latter was soon going to die. Although use of ethnography in this fashion may be close to what Gubrium and Holstein (1997), Moerman (1988), and others recommend for enriching conversation analytic inquiry, it bears repeating that ethnography is a post hoc way of explaining the existence of interactional practices, particularly when *prior* sequential analysis reveals curious-seeming patterns.

Building Additional Affinities Between Conversation Analysis and Ethnography

Bad and good news represent naturally occurring breaches in the structure of everyday life. Locating such breaches does not, however, solve the problem of how to study their constituent features and the practices by which participants, faced with having to suspend their ordinary stance of belief, effortlessly reassemble a known-in-common world. Participants in episodes of disclosure can provide post hoc accounts that provide initial access to the practices and methods of worldly suspension and reassembly. However, in part because of the problem that indexical expressions present—fitting the detail of actual modes for conveying news into strategic types—the bigger sociological prize exists in knowing how to handle analytically the contingently formed, real-time particularities of participants' conduct together. An ethnomethodological proposal is that in these particularities—in the *detail* of participants' conduct—resides an orderliness associated with practices, methods, or procedures of minute but socially consequential mundane behavior. To be found in these practices and methods is the participants' world as it is or comes to be known-in-common and newly taken for granted.

It can even be said that, because it contains and is the product of concerted actions, *detail itself is a type of context,* and its incorporation analytically involves going deeper into the concreteness of a setting, even if it does not broaden the investigation abstractly. Wanting to capture this depth, I employ ethnomethodology and CA because, in theoretical and methodological ways, they enable systematic and rigorous attention to the fullness of participants' spoken sociality and its generic structuring. I use ethnography in a limited affinity with CA to (a) refer to settings and participants according to institutional or other identities and categories, (b) describe courses of action related to a focal episode and unfamiliar terms within it, and (c) explain curious sequential patterns.

Although I have so far stressed the *limited* affinity between CA and ethnography, to differentiate my methodology from that of those who pose *mutual* affinity, the operative word in both combinations is still *affinity.* An implication is that more linkages can be developed between CA and ethnography. Where I have said that ethnography is of manifest use to CA, the reverse also can be true: CA can be employed on behalf of ethnographic inquiry. One example is Duneier's (1999) study of the remarks that street vendors direct toward women passersby. In a coauthored methodological discussion about this research, and in a manner similar to Gubrium and Holstein (1997, Chapter 7), Duneier and Molotch (1999, pp. 1269–1270) suggest that, instead of taking the *unmotivated* CA stance toward interactional detail, such research can in fact be *motivated* by substantive concerns. Recording and analyzing street conversations reveals practices through which male vendors work to open conversations with female passersby and the unreciprocated efforts of the women to close these conversations. Recordings and "applied" CA of them are used to "enrich the more conventional sociological ethnography" (Duneier, & Molotch, 1999, p. 1272). Conversation analysts themselves have used the CA approach in an ethnographic and applied way, as in our probing the use of the concept of "justice" in a jury deliberation (Maynard & Manzo, 1993), in Heritage and Lindström's (1998) analysis of the phenomenology of shared experiences between a new mother and her British health visitor, and in other studies.

Another bridge to be built between CA and ethnography involves *extended* social activities. My research on singular episodes of bad and good news does not address the ways in which, over long periods of time, participants progressively adjust to some altered social world. When medical personnel first tell them that they have some chronic illness, for instance, patients may not know how to react:

Ron Rosato recounted, "I said, 'Well, what is this problem?' And they put me in a hospital and took a lot of tests, and they said, 'Everything is fine, Ron, but— so we've come up with multiple sclerosis, a possible multiple sclerosis.' I said, 'What is that?' and they said, 'You'll learn about it.' And I did." (Charmaz, 1991, p. 18)

In learning about a diagnosis, recipients like Ron Rosato progressively alter their response to the initial news delivery and experience further announcements about the condition. Analysis of the full process as a duration would require something along the lines of what Corsaro (1996) calls "longitudinal ethnography."

A longitudinal approach to bad and good news would allow us to map how the social worlds of participants undergo metamorphosis in and through paced, incremental announcements, as when someone who has suffered disease or accident gets better or worse, or alternates between the two and staying the same, across days, weeks, months, or longer periods. There is also the task that chronically ill persons face as they inform others about their diagnosis over time (Charmaz, 1991).[10] Using CA, longitudinal designs can encompass the activity of news delivery and receipt as an enduring process. Along these lines, Beach (2001, 2002, 2003) has collected telephone calls from a family wherein the wife and mother was diagnosed with cancer and ultimately died. Family members were dispersed and, over the phone, kept one another informed of the outcome of therapeutic interventions, tests, and other matters related to the progress of her illness. Beach's work with this data is a kind of longitudinal CA.

Besides applying CA to enhance substantive ethnographic investigations and to develop longitudinal studies of interactional activities, still other rigorous linkages between CA and traditional ethnography can be built. The affinities between CA and ethnography—limited, mutual, and others— continue to be explored.[11]

Coda: In the Clinic

CA research constrains the use of ethnography when it attempts to grasp the context of an utterance by positing connections to "wider" social structures, because it would embody an abstracting movement away from interactional detail. I will illustrate how analytic control and data loss affect proposals about what happens substantively in the social world by reviewing a portion of the ethnographic literature on bad news, along with an example of a diagnostic "informing" interview.

One of the first recordings I came across in the developmental disabilities clinic data I was given involves 7-year-old Donald Riccio (pseudonym), whom the clinic diagnosed as "mildly" mentally retarded.[12] The informing interview took place after Donald was referred to the clinic because of speech and other difficulties at school. Two pediatricians were at the interview—Dr. Davidson was the one who evaluated Donald and performed the diagnosis, and Dr. Andrew introduced herself as the physician who would be responsible for seeing Donald at the clinic for subsequent visits. Dr. Andrew does not speak in the excerpt below. Immediately after introductions, Dr. Davidson began the diagnostic news delivery (see Appendix for transcribing conventions).

(1) DD #11

```
 1   Dr. D:   I think- you know I'm sure you're anxious about (1.0) toda:y

 2            and I know this has been a re:all:y hard year for you.

 3                 (0.4)

 4   Dr. D:   .hhh and I think you've really done an extraordinary job (0.4)

 5            in (0.8) dealing with something that's very hard for any human

 6            being or any parent.

 7                 (0.8)

 8   Dr. D:   And you know Mrs. Riccio and I can talk as parents as well as

 9            .hhh

10   Mrs. R:  True

11   Dr. D:   uh my being a professional.

12                 (0.6)

13   Dr. D:   It's hard when there's something not all right with a child.

14                 (1.0)

15   Dr. D:   .hhhhh very hard.

16                 (1.0)

17   Dr. D:   And I admire both of you really and (0.8) an' (2.2) as hard as

18            it is (0.4) seeing that there is something that is the matter
```

```
19          with Donald, he's not like other kids (0.2) he is slow, he is

20          retarded.

21               (0.2)

22  Mrs. R:  HE IS NOT RETAR[DED!   ]

23  Mr. R:                  [Ellen.]

24  Mrs. R:  HE IS NOT RETARDED!=

25  Mr. R:   =Ellen.

26               (0.3)

27  Mr. R:   Uh plea:s::e

28  Mrs. R:  NO::!

29  Mr. R:   May- look- (0.6) it's their way of:: I'oh'know.

30  Mrs. R:  hhhhh HE'S NOT RETAR:(ghh)DED! ((sobbing))

31               (2.5)

32  Dr. D:   He can learn and he is lear[ning]

33  Mrs. R:                             [hhhh]

34  Mr. R:   Yes [he is learning ]          [I-   ]

35  Dr. D:       [and he's making] good prog[ress.]

36  Mrs. R:      [.hhhhhhhhhhhhhhh]
```

At lines 19–20, Dr. Davidson proposes the diagnosis of retardation, in a straightforward way that an interview-based study by Clark and LaBeff (1982) would characterize, in comparison with *oblique, elaborate, nonverbal,* or *conditional* methods, as *direct.* The mother, Mrs. Riccio, "breaks down" (Darling, 1979) when she hears this suggestion. By contrast, the father's stance toward the diagnosis is not clear; he addresses his wife and not the clinician. Now, to account for the news delivery and the parents' reactions, potentially we can go in two different directions. One is toward a relatively abstract understanding of the interaction, based on what can be gleaned ethnographically about the backgrounds of participants. The other direction, confining ourselves mostly to the recording and using ethnography in a limited way, is to pursue detail and to be concrete about the practical organization of the encounter.

Ethnographic Abstraction

The tendency in past qualitative studies of bad news has been to glean further ethnographic information about the setting and the identities of the parties. Ethnographers, in fact, have an admirable record of letting no stone go unturned to garner facts about a particular research site, the biographies and demographic identities of participants—ages, ethnicities, genders, socio-economic classes, occupational categories—and the cultures to which they belong because of these identities. Such effort is particularly evident in McClenahen and Lofland's (1976, pp. 255–257) finding that when bearers (U.S. marshals) and recipients (ordinary citizens) of bad news differ in terms of race, class, and education, there is less "emotional involvement." Deputies use such "distancing" tactics as employing "more foreboding and formal settings of delivery." Similarly, according to Glaser and Strauss (1965, p. 146), physicians take into account a family's ethnicity, religion, and educational level in determining whether and how much news to convey about a patient's dying. And Clark and LaBeff (1982), in their study of death telling, state *conditions* for how professionals convey the news. "The lack of well-defined, normative guidelines for such deliveries," they argue, " . . . requires the deliverers to construct various tactics influenced by situation and structural factors, including occupation, setting, characteristics of the deceased, and the type of death" (p. 379). In these accounts, then, authors describe modes of delivery in typological terms and correlate these modes with other abstractions about attributes of the setting and traits of the parties involved.

With this approach, we would be interested in information that Svarstad and Lipton (1977) obtained by interviewing the parents extensively both before and after the informing interview from which the previous excerpt is taken. The Riccio family, by way of the Hollingshead Index of Social Position, was found to be in the lower social class. They were white and of Italian extraction, Catholic in religion, and the parents both had high school educations. The father worked for a utility company, servicing air conditioners, whereas the mother was a homemaker with three other children besides Donald. This information implies several things, in keeping with previous ethnographic research. The family is a "traditional" one, with a stay-at-home mother and a father who works at a "blue-collar" outside job. Both pediatricians (with MDs) are women, which, in the early 1970s, when the interview was recorded, meant that they had very nontraditional occupational roles, and relatively high-paying ones at that. Accordingly, these educational, class, occupational, and gender role differences between family and clinicians imply a great deal of social distance. Furthermore, such social distance may be a basis for the direct delivery of diagnosis, because professionals are less caring about how their recipients will react when they do not share the same social background (Glaser & Strauss, 1965, pp. 122–123) and are more likely to be more "cold" and "heartless" (Clark & LaBeff, 1982, pp. 371–372), possibly to achieve clarity at the expense of shocking recipients (Clark & LaBeff, 1986, p. 257; Glaser & Strauss, 1965, p. 125). Based on our ethnographic background information, then, a reasonable proposal is that the pediatrician evokes the mother's strong and emotional reaction to be starkly clear about the diagnosis and because of structural distance from her recipients. As for the father's reaction to the news, the literature has not said much about how or why the partner of one recipient may respond differently.

It needs to be granted that despite the suggestions from ethnographers of bad news about the importance of participants' backgrounds, field researchers often warn against imposing exogenous categories on their data. There is, however, an impetus in some ethnography, especially in studies of bad news, as well as in research advocating for a mutual affinity between recordings and ethnography, to attend to such backgrounds and categories when dealing with interactional data. For instance, van Dijk (1999), describing the position of critical discourse analysis (CDA), remarks, "There is no hesitation in examining text and context separately, and once a feature of context has been observed, postulated or otherwise identified, CDA may be used to explore whether and how such a feature affects, or is affected by, structures of text and talk" (p. 460).[13]

I think it is tenable to state that a "feature of context" is affected by structures of text and talk; the difficulty is in going the other direction. Statements about the influence of external or exogenous factors tend to be based on the observer's often-laborious effort to gather demographic or historical information rather than equally rigorous demonstrations *from* the interactional data. In the literature on bad news, most enlightening about the empirical and analytical difficulties are Glaser and Strauss (1965), reflecting on their own previous statements proposing how social factors affect the presentation of bad news:

> The relationship of social factors such as ethnic status, social class, language, religion, and education to properties of disclosure to the family (particularly if, when, and how disclosure occurs) is an important research problem. The research should also develop the intervening interaction process that links the relationship of a social factor to a kind of disclosure. (p. 146)

Schegloff's notions of relevance and procedural consequentiality seem to be the exacting terms that Glaser and Strauss are calling for, a way of exerting analytic control over what may be said about the processual "links" between social factors and disclosure practices. What are the connections? Are the social factors ones to which the participants themselves are demonstrably attuned or are they a selection that the analyst has made on theoretical or other independent grounds? Why just these social structural factors and not others? How is analytic control to be exerted so that the social factors of importance in the experience of participants are validly part of the interaction? And beside analytic control lies the issue of data loss: preoccupation with social distance between clinicians and parents based on knowledge of background factors means that we disattend to much of the detail exhibited in the interaction in favor of inferences about interactionally unseen structural influences.

Detail, Concreteness, and the Organization of Practices

The other direction to go when asking questions about how clinicians present and parents handle diagnostic news is to adhere more closely to the interactional stream of data and to use ethnography in a limited way. In introducing the transcript, I characterized the setting as a developmental disabilities clinic and identified the participants as "pediatricians" and "parents" (mother, father). I also provided the level of Donald's mental retardation, assuming the reader's familiarity with this broad term, but also giving the official classification. These limited ethnographic descriptions and clarifications allow for *focusing* on the central *activity* of delivering and receiving the diagnosis. Other ethnographic information (concerning the ethnic, class, and educational backgrounds) comes into analysis only if the participants themselves display an orientation to it (Emerson et al., 1995, pp. 12–16). In other words, most of the time Dr. Davidson can be heard to be speaking as a pediatrician, and Mr. and Mrs. Riccio as parents. That matter is relatively straightforward. What that means, and where and when the participants talk or listen to one another under other auspices is not so straightforward.

Rather than dwell on the abstract identities of the participants, a conversation analytic strategy is to examine the full sequential context of the diagnostic news delivery, which starts with Dr. Davidson moving from introductions (not on transcript) with an assertion recognizing the parents' anxiety and "really hard year" (lines 1–2).

(2) DD #11 (first part)

```
 1  Dr. D:  I think- you know I'm sure you're anxious about (1.0) toda:y

 2          and I know this has been a re:all:y hard year for you.

 3              (0.4)

 4  Dr. D:  .hhh and I think you've really done an extraordinary job (0.4)

 5          in (0.8) dealing with something that's very hard for any human

 6          being or any parent.

 7              (0.8)

 8  Dr. D:  And you know Mrs. Riccio and I can talk as parents as well as

 9          .hhh

10  Mrs. R: True

11  Dr. D:  uh my being a professional.

12              (0.6)

13  Dr. D:  It's hard when there's something not all right with a child.

14              (1.0)

15  Dr. D:  .hhhhh very hard.

16              (1.0)

17  Dr. D:  And I admire both of you really and (0.8) an' (2.2) as hard as

18          it is (0.4) seeing that there is something that is the matter

19          with Donald, he's not like other kids (0.2) he is slow, he is

20          retarded.
```

Following a silence (line 3), Dr. Davidson also compliments them (lines 4–6) on their "dealing" with a vaguely formulated "something that's very hard. . . ." This may operate as what Goodwin (1996) calls a "prospective indexical," anticipating the diagnosis to come; the turn also meets with silence (line 7). Then, Dr. Davidson suggests that she "can talk" with Mrs. Riccio as a "parent" (lines 8–9), a suggestion with which Mrs. Riccio agrees (line 10), as Dr. Davidson goes on to say "as well as .hhh uh my being a professional" (line 11). Following another silence (line 12), Dr. Davidson again claims to recognize how "hard" things may be, referring once more to "something" and adding the phrase "not all right with a child" (line 13). This is a *litotes,* a rhetorical form of negation that, by its inexplicitness, permits alluding to or hinting at a delicate matter that so far remains unnamed (Bergmann, 1992, pp. 148–151). Yet another silence occurs (line 14), after which the pediatrician emphasizes the difficulty ("*very* hard," line 15). A longer silence develops here (line 16), followed by Dr. Davidson announcing her admiration of the parents (line 17) and producing a stronger version of the "something" phrase (lines 18–19). And the stress on "is" in "something that *is* the matter with Donald," may reinforce how the phrase in its positive characterization provides a contrast with the previous negative phrase, or litotes. Still, it alludes to rather than names what the "matter" is.

From this point, Dr. Davidson moves into the official diagnosis of retardation, this movement involving another litotes for comparative declaration (Donald is "*not* like other kids," line 19) and a vernacular assessment ("he *is* slow," line 19) that leads into Dr. Davidson, through an assertive format, *predicating the diagnosis as an attribute of the person* (Maynard, 2004): "he is retarded."[14] Until now, contrary to our ethnographically abstract depiction of this interaction, Dr. Davidson has been very cautious, alluding several times to "something" that is "very hard," "not all right," and "the matter," in approaching an announcement of the official diagnosis. Her practices during this approach include claiming recognition of their plight by repeating four times how "hard" they have had it, complimenting the parents on the job they have done, and proposing the relevance of a relationship ("parents")[15] outside the professional-client one, in a way that nevertheless recognizes the latter as primary. Consequently, rather than the analyst needing to make inferences about the relevance of participants' backgrounds (social factors), Dr. Davidson herself formulates such relevance. Putting these practices together, and considering them as *proposals of affiliation,* it would be difficult to sustain an argument that this is a fully "cold" or "heartless" and socially distanced presentation on the part of the clinician.

However, the only device that procures any uptake from the parents is Dr. Davidson's invoking of the "parents" identity. Silences meet the actions of complimenting and recognizing the parents' "hard" challenges,

and resistance is exhibited to Dr. Davidson's affiliative proposals. Because
most of Dr. Davidson's attempts at affiliation appear to fail, the environment for delivery of bad diagnostic news is not a fully auspicious one.
Arriving at the term "retarded" (line 20), Dr. Davidson stops talking, and,
following a 0.2 second silence, Mrs. Riccio receipts the diagnosis with a
series of loudly oppositional turns (lines 22, 24, 28, and 30), and she ends
up sobbing (line 30):

(3) DD #11 (continued)

```
20  Dr. D:        . . . he is slow, he is retarded.

21                      (0.2)

22  Mrs. R:      HE IS NOT RETAR[DED!   ]

23  Mr. R:                    [Ellen.]

24  Mrs. R:      HE IS NOT RETARDED!=

25  Mr. R:       =Ellen.

26                      (0.3)

27  Mr. R:       Uh plea:s::e

28  Mrs. R:      NO::!

29  Mr. R:       May- look- (0.6) it's their way of::

                 I'oh'know.

30  Mrs. R:      hhhhh HE'S NOT RETAR:(ghh)DED! ((sobbing))

31                      (2.5)

32  Dr. D:       He can learn and he is lear[ning]

33  Mrs. R:                                 [hhhh]

34  Mr. R:       Yes [he is learning ]        [I-  ]

35  Dr. D:           [and he's making] good prog[ress.]

36  Mrs. R:           [.hhhhhhhhhhhhhhh]
```

As Mrs. Riccio vigorously displays her disagreement, Mr. Riccio addresses
Mrs. Riccio by her first name (lines 23, 25), produces a plea (line 27), and
after her strong rejection ("NO::," line 28), appears to refer to the diagnosis
as the clinic's "way of . . ." but then abandons the effort with a knowledge
disclaimer ("I 'oh 'know," line 29). Mr. Riccio, accordingly, does not himself
exhibit a reaction to the diagnosis. Subsequent to Mrs. Riccio's sobbing
rejection of the diagnosis (line 30), there is a substantial silence (line 31),

whereupon Dr. Davidson engages a *good news exit* from the bad news, suggesting that Donald "can learn" and "is learning" (line 32). Mr. Riccio agrees with this (line 34), as Dr. Davidson continues with the assessment of Donald as "making good progress" (line 35). Mr. Riccio's line 34 utterance is the second instance of his aligning with what the pediatrician has to say. Meanwhile, at lines 33 and 36, Mrs. Riccio is audibly sighing in overlap with her husband's and the pediatrician's talk.

A Puzzle: Contrasting Parental Reactions to a Forceful Presentation of Diagnosis

Although the detailed analysis of recorded interaction gives a finer appreciation of the pediatrician's work to mitigate the impact of the clinic's bad news, we also see that that work is not fully successful. However, this analysis demonstrates that if social distance is maintained between Dr. Davidson and the parents, it is partly a function of their resistance to her overtures rather than residing in her manner of presentation to them, as if her different social status was a causal factor in her approach. Of course, she does forge ahead in a relatively blunt way to present the parents with the diagnosis of mental retardation. Is there more that can be said about this strategy? And how do we analyze the quite different ways these parents receive the news?

Social Structure or Psychology or Natural Periodicity. If we were to draw on previous literature, we would be on thin ground, because it does not say much about how recipients reply to bad news announcements in the environment of and in relation to the announcement itself. Discussions of social structural effects in the bad news literature are about the strategies *deliverers* choose for giving the bad news. When ethnographers discuss responsiveness, they mostly concentrate on psychological effects. We know that when coroners' deputies tell surviving spouses and other relatives about someone's death, these messengers report that a prominent reaction is some expression of *grief* (Charmaz, 1975, pp. 307–309). Likewise, experts in the area of developmental disabilities see parents experiencing this emotion, or "sorrow," because a diagnosis means loss of the "fantasized normal child" (Olshansky, 1962; Wikler, Wasow, & Hatfield, 1981). Grief and sorrow are consistent with the noetic crisis implicated in hearing about a changed social world. Thus, where Mrs. Riccio may have presupposed the essential competence of her son, the clinic's diagnosis suggests a different version of him, and consequently a new social world for her as mother and for the family. The radical loss of an assumed former world, as Katz (1999, p. 197) suggests, may call forth her crying as an embodied idiom that replaces speech when the latter is inadequate to one's experience. However, previous descriptions of grieving mostly invoke the psychological impact of bad news, do not discuss where and how *in interaction* these emotions are expressed, and do not account for other kinds of reactions, such as silence and withholding and assuagement of his wife's response on the order of Mr. Riccio's actions after the news delivery.

Glaser and Strauss (1965, pp. 121–135) provide the most comprehensive analysis of reactions to bad news, arguing that they occur as a series of *stages*. First is depression, which is followed by acceptance or denial. Denial, in prolonging the adjustment to bad news, may eventuate in acceptance. Each of these stages can be described in behavioral terms, acceptance being characterized by *preparations* for handling the announced condition, whereas denial *blocks communication*. In these terms, Mrs. Riccio appears to be blocking communication and Mr. Riccio to be accepting and preparing to deal with his son's retardation. These parents, accordingly, would be seen to be at different stages in the response process, but this process in either case represents a trajectory occasioned by the delivery of an official diagnosis but otherwise psychologically independent of it. That is, the description of stages mostly detaches them from their concrete relations to the diagnostic presentation and posits a natural progression with its own periodicity.

CA and Ethnography. So a puzzle remains. In this episode, how are the delivery of diagnosis and the parents' differential responsiveness to be understood concretely and interactionally, rather than in abstract relation to social structure or psychology or natural periodicity? What more can we say about the pediatrician's affiliative-but-blunt mode of delivering the diagnosis? About the mother's crying and the father's relatively restrained response? My answers to these questions are more fully developed elsewhere (Maynard, 2003), but two matters can be mentioned briefly.

One matter involves my third form of limited affinity—explaining a curious pattern in the talk by way of observation and interview. I did not collect the developmental disabilities data from which the episodes with the Riccio family derive, but I can draw on my ethnographic experience in an HIV-testing clinic to propose that Dr. Davidson's blunt approach may have been a *purposeful* device to provoke an emotional reaction. Counselors at the HIV clinic deliver bad news that a client is HIV positive in a straightforward and assertive manner similar to Dr. Davidson's bluntness about Donald's diagnosis of mental retardation. In the HIV clinic, although this confrontational style was apparent in the recordings I obtained, why the counselors employed such a style was not evident from the tapes. My ethnographic inquiry revealed that, as one counselor put it, it was important to "crack the emotional nut," because this is what moves clients forward in the therapeutic and remedial process. Whereas the predominant pattern in interaction is for bad news to be *shrouded* and only good news to be *exposed,* these counselors disregarded this asymmetry. One counselor at the clinic, if unsuccessful during early parts of a session in evoking an emotional response from an HIV-positive client, would hug him at the apparent end of the session:

> Some people who go into a stoic mode and [say] "I've expected this, it's okay, I've dealt with it, da ta da ta da," once you get into a hug situation they decompensate a little bit, they start crying, and I can really find out more information about where they're really at. And then the real interviewing begins. You know, so initially it's the ending of the interview but many times it's just the start. (Maynard, 2003, p. 196)

Like the HIV counselors, if Dr. Davidson saw Mrs. Riccio as in denial or otherwise emotionally contained, and thereby inhibiting therapeutic progress for herself as well as Donald, this pediatrician may have fully meant to garner the mother's emotive reaction.

The other matter related to our interactional puzzle concerns the parents' differential responses and points toward further sequential analysis to understand how ordered these responses are. Diagnostic news deliveries often occasion the pair of reactions Mr. and Mrs. Riccio exhibit—hers of crying or flooding out and his of restraint or stoicism. That is, while each parent's reaction is capable of description in psychological terms, they are also deeply socially organized. Here is a different example:

> A 40-year-old woman had extensive Hodgkin's disease which was fully explained to her and her husband by the medical registrar. "I sat there and I could see him talking but I couldn't take anything in. When I got home I burst into tears, but afterwards I calmed down and my husband explained all that had been said." (Souhami, 1978, p. 936)

Here, an individual conducts herself to be stoic at first and emotionally expressive later, according to the setting in which she is embedded. At other times, as with the Riccios, the stoic and emotional responses may be spread across bodies, so to speak—one spouse breaks down, whereas the other exhibits great restraint.

Conclusion

Ethnographic data, including narratives about everyday life, can be helpful in providing access to inner experience and its relation to behavior and conduct. Using ethnography, it is possible to discern patterns for the delivery of bad news, for instance, and their effects on recipients' realization of the news. However, whether gathered by observation or interview, narrative data glosses what participants undergo and produce as part of their *lived* experience as they organize such experience in real time through ongoing talk and social interaction. An aspect of glossing is the production of typologies that neglect the problem of indexical expressions. For any close appreciation of the order in these expressions and in actual lived experience, an endeavor such as CA is an important resource. Among the advantages it offers is the analysis of interaction involving conversational sequences as a context in which utterances appear and from which they derive their character as social actions.

If only to identify participants or to describe the background to some focal episode, however, integrating CA and ethnography is inevitable. In addition, investigators may elect to pursue such integration in various ways. Some take a stance that there is a mutual affinity between these endeavors, as when CA enhances ethnography, or CA is used in a longitudinal way, or CA complements the ethnomethodological study of work settings. I have proposed a more limited affinity, which foregrounds the study of *activities* rather than particular *settings*. In any case, doing CA while also carrying out ethnography, and vice versa, can enhance an investigator's overall project.

Notes

1. My lack of familiarity with developmental disabilities facilitated this approach, which has parallels with the ethnographic strategy of "hanging out" (Dingwall, 1997, p. 53) in a setting to experience the people and the social situation, avoiding prior questions and letting the situation pose its own questions. Although I was far from being physically in the setting, and could not attain the kind of "immersion" that ethnographers seek (Emerson, Fretz, & Shaw, 1995, p. 22), I was present indirectly by way of what I could hear and read as real-time conversations on the tapes and transcripts.

2. My strategy for collecting data has parallels with what Glaser and Strauss (1967, Chapter V) call the "constant comparative method," which enables obtaining diverse instances of a phenomenon in order to develop an analysis that confronts the full complexity of that phenomenon.

3. Some ethnographers (P. Atkinson, 1990; Clough, 1992; Denzin, 1991; Richardson, 1991; van Maanen, 1995), including other contributors to this book, have supplemented traditional field methods with postmodern forms of inquiry, including various kinds and combinations of rhetorical, textual, discourse, and cinematic analyses.

4. Sequential analysis involves dealing with utterances in relation to immediately preceding or succeeding turns of talk. "Adjacency pairs," such as greeting-greeting, question-answer, invitation-reply, and other two-turn couplets, are examples of tightly organized sequences. For a detailed description of adjacency pairs, see Schegloff and Sacks (1973, pp. 295–296); for more general discussion of sequential analysis, see Heritage (1984, pp. 245–246).

5. Of these, participation frameworks, or ways in which speakers and recipients adopt different "footings," or stances, in relation to utterances, have been most closely integrated with conversation analytic studies. See, for example, Clayman (1988), Goodwin (1986), Goodwin (1990), Houtkoop-Steenstra (2000), and Maynard (1984, 1989).

6. For more thorough discussion of Goffman's frame analysis and Gumperz's contextualization cues, see Corsaro (1981) and Maynard and Whalen (1995). Cicourel (1974) and Corsaro (1982) advocate the strategy of *triangulation,* in which research subjects are asked to view videotapes of their own or others' interactions and to offer interpretations. This strategy adds to a project's interpretive base and helps to disambiguate obscure terms or phrases, but does not provide criteria for determining how social structure or other facets of context affect the course of interaction. For a wide-ranging discussion of the issues involved in social structure and interaction, see Wilson (1991).

7. See Heritage and Greatbatch's (1991) general discussion of how turn-taking characteristics constitute talk as an institutional form of interaction. Their specific focus is the news interview; also see Atkinson and Drew (1979) for a treatment of courtroom turn-taking, Boden (1994) on turn-taking in business meetings, and Manzo (1996) on turn-taking in jury deliberations. Drew and Heritage (1992) have systematized Schegloff's (1987) recommendations regarding procedural consequentiality to include, as sites of talk-in-interaction where this consequentiality may be expressed, lexical choice, turn design, sequence organization, overall structural organization, and "social epistemology" and "relations" (professional cautiousness, asymmetries in talk, and other matters).

8. By and large, Bourdieu does not study interaction, and I am taking his remarks about cultural categories, which are cognitive entities, and applying these remarks to the realm of interaction. For example, in *Distinction,* Bourdieu (1984, pp. 467–468) discusses "taste" in art and other aesthetic domains as a classification system, driven by specific material interests according to actors' class position. Actors construct the social world but do so from "internalized embodied schemes" or "cognitive structures" that, "having been constituted in the course of collective history," operate to determine practices that enter into the apprehension of an everyday commonsense world.

9. See also the research of Heritage and Sefi (1992). They identify a "dilemma" that faces home health visitors in Britain, who are purveyors of advice that is frequently not well received by first-time mothers. The dilemma involves a "ticket of entry" problem, or how to justify their visits to homes. Heritage and Sefi describe this dilemma through ethnographic characterizations of the health visitor role and mothers' perceptions of it. The dilemma involves health visitors' need to make themselves useful in a situation where what they have to offer may not be needed or wanted.

10. Also see Gubrium's (1975) study of a nursing home and how the news of a death is disseminated (despite efforts of staff to contain it) from the dead person's room to staff, to other residents on the floor, and, finally, throughout the entire home. On a different tack (a study in a work setting), but still relatively longitudinal, M. H. Goodwin (1996) examines how personnel transmit the news of a landed plane to different divisions and areas of an airport (and the prosodic manipulations necessary to convey messages in a multifocused setting).

11. See, for example, Lavin (2002) and Lutfey (2000). Particularly important for developing the CA-ethnography relation, per the discussion in ten Have (1999, pp. 57–60) are studies of work settings (Heath & Luff, 2000; Luff, Hindmarsh, & Heath, 2000). And see Peräkylä's (1997, pp. 203–205) proposals about how CA, in researching institutional settings, can incorporate the analysis of different "layers of the organization of interaction."

12. In the classification system for mental retardation, "mild" covers those with IQs of 50–70; Donald was tested at 54. "Moderate" retardation covers the 35–49 IQ range, "severe" refers to those in the 20–34 span, and "profound" is used for individuals with IQ scores below 20.

13. The remarks of van Dijk are part of an editorial lead-in to an exchange published in *Text* between Billig (1999) and Schegloff (1999) regarding CDA and CA. For additional discussion of CDA and CA, see Wetherell (1998) and Schegloff (1998). For a broader statement regarding CDA, see Fairclough and Wodak (1997). And for an effort to integrate a critical, Foucaudian discourse analysis with a conversation-analytic understanding of the organization of "troubles talk" (Jefferson, 1988), see Miller and Silverman (1995).

14. See also Peräkylä (1998) on what he calls "plain assertions" for delivering diagnostic news in primary care health settings.

15. Because this utterance (line 8) is addressed to "Mrs. Riccio," Dr. Davidson may be suggesting the relevance of their identities as "mothers" and not just as "parents."

APPENDIX

Transcribing Conventions

1. Overlapping speech

A: Oh you do? R[eally   ]
B: [Um hmmm]

Left hand brackets mark a point of overlap, while right hand brackets indicate where overlapping talk ends.

2. Silences

A: I'm not use ta that.
   (1.4)
B: Yeah me neither.

Numbers in parentheses indicate elapsed time in tenths of seconds.

3. Missing speech

A: Are they?
B: Yes because . . .

Ellipses indicate where part of an utterance is left out of the transcript.

4. Sound stretching

B: I did oka::y.

Colon(s) indicate the prior sound is prolonged. More colons, more stretching.

5. Volume

A: That's where I REALLY
   want to go.

Capital letters indicate increased volume.

6. Emphasis

A: I do not want it.

Underline indicates increased emphasis.

7. Breathing

A: You didn't have to worry
   about having the .hh hhh
   curtains closed.

The "h" indicates audible breathing. The more "h's" the longer the breath. A period placed before it indicates inbreath; no period indicates outbreath.

8. Laugh tokens

A: Tha(h)t was really neat.

The "h" within a word or sound indicates explosive aspirations; e.g., laughter, breathlessness, etc.

9. Explanatory material

A: Well ((cough)) I   Materials in double parentheses
    don't know   indicate audible phenomena other
                             than actual verbalization.

10. Candidate hearing

B: (Is that right?) (   ) Materials in single parentheses
                             indicate that transcribers were
                             not sure about spoken words.
                             If no words are in parentheses,
                             the talk was indecipherable.

11. Intonation.

A: It was unbelievable.   A period indicates fall in tone,
    I ↑had a three point   a comma indicates continuing
    six? I ¬think.   intonation, a question mark
B: You did.   indicates increased tone. Up
                             arrows (↑) or down arrows (¬)
                             indicate marked rising and
                             falling shifts in intonation
                             immediately prior to the rise or
                             fall.

12. Sound cut off

A: This- this is true   Dashes indicate an abrupt cutoff
                             of sound.

13. Soft volume

A: °Yes.° That's true.   Material between degree signs is
                             spoken more quietly than
                             surrounding talk.

14. Latching

A: I am absolutely   Equal signs indicate where there
    sure.=   is no gap or interval between
B: =You are.   adjacent utterances.

                             Equal signs also link different
A: This is one thing   parts of a speaker's utterance
    [that I=   when that utterance carries over
B: [Yes?   to another transcript line.

A: =really want to do.

15. Speech pacing

A: What is it?   Part of an utterance delivered
B: >I ain't tellin< you   at a pace faster than
                             surrounding talk is enclosed
                             between "greater than" and "less
                             than" signs.

Source: Adapted from Gail Jefferson, "Error Correction as an Interactional Resource," *Language in Society*, 2:181–199, 1974.

References

Anderson, E. (1976). *A place on the corner.* Chicago: University of Chicago Press.

Atkinson, J. M., & Drew, P. (1979). *Order in court: The organisation of verbal interaction in judicial settings.* London: MacMillan.

Atkinson, P. (1990). *The ethnographic imagination: Textual constructions of reality.* Newbury Park, CA: Sage.

Baugh, J. (1999). *Out of the mouths of slaves.* Austin: University of Texas Press.

Beach, W. A. (2001). Stability and ambiguity: Managing uncertain moments when updating news about Mom's cancer. *Text, 21,* 221–250.

Beach, W. A. (2002). Between dad and son: Initiating, delivering, and assimilating bad cancer news. *Health Communication, 14,* 271–298.

Beach, W. A. (2003). Managing optimism. In P. Glenn, C. D. LeBaron, & J. Mandelbaum (Eds.), *Studies in language and social interaction: In honor of Robert Hopper* (pp. 175–194). Mahwah, NJ: Lawrence Erlbaum.

Bergmann, J. R. (1992). Veiled morality: Notes on discretion in psychiatry. In P. Drew & J. Heritage (Eds.), *Talk at work: Interaction in institutional settings* (pp. 137–162). Cambridge, UK: Cambridge University Press.

Billig, M. (1999). Whose terms? Whose ordinariness? Rhetoric and ideology in conversation analysis. *Discourse & Society, 10,* 543–582.

Blumer, H. (1956). Sociological analysis and the "variable." *American Sociological Review, 21,* 683–690.

Boden, D. (1994). *The business of talk.* Cambridge, UK: Polity Press.

Bourdieu, P. (1977). *Outline of a theory of practice.* Cambridge, UK: Cambridge University Press.

Bourdieu, P. (1984). *Distinction: A social critique of the judgment of taste.* Cambridge, MA: Harvard University Press.

Boyd, E. (1998). Bureaucratic authority in the "company of equals": The interactional management of medical peer review. *American Sociological Review, 63,* 200–224.

Burawoy, M. (1991). The extended case method. In M. Burawoy, A. Burton, A. A. Ferguson, K. J. Fox, J. Gamson, N. Gartrell, et al. (Eds.), *Ethnography unbound: Power and resistance in the modern metropolis* (pp. 271–287). Berkeley: University of California Press.

Charmaz, K. (1975). The coroner's strategies for announcing death. *Urban Life, 4,* 296–316.

Charmaz, K. (1991). *Good days, bad days: The self in chronic illness and time.* New Brunswick, NJ: Rutgers University Press.

Cicourel, A. V. (1974). *Cognitive sociology: Language and meaning in social interaction.* New York: Free Press.

Cicourel, A. V. (1987). The interpenetration of communicative contexts: Examples from medical encounters. *Social Psychology Quarterly, 50,* 217–226.

Clark, R. E., & LaBeff, E. E. (1982). Death telling: Managing the delivery of bad news. *Journal of Health and Social Behavior, 23,* 366–380.

Clark, R. E., & LaBeff, E. E. (1986). Ending intimate relationships: Strategies of breaking off. *Sociological Spectrum, 6,* 245–267.

Clayman, S. E. (1988). Displaying neutrality in television news interviews. *Social Problems, 35,* 474–492.

Clayman, S. E., & Heritage, J. (2002). Questioning presidents: Journalistic deference and adversarialness in the press conferences of Eisenhower and Reagan. *Journal of Communication, 52,* 749–775.

Clough, P. T. (1992). *The end(s) of ethnography.* Thousand Oaks, CA: Sage.

Corsaro, W. A. (1981). Communicative processes in studies of social organization: Sociological approaches to discourse analysis. *Text, 1,* 5–63.

Corsaro, W. A. (1982). Something old and something new: The importance of prior ethnography in the collection and analysis of audio-visual data. *Sociological Methods and Research, 11,* 145–166.

Corsaro, W. A. (1996). Transitions in early childhood: The promise of comparative, longitudinal ethnography. In R. Jessor, A. Colby, & R. A. Shweder (Eds.), *Ethnography and human development: Context and meaning in social inquiry* (pp. 419–456). Chicago: University of Chicago Press.

Coulthard, M. (1977). *An introduction to discourse analysis.* London: Longman.

Darling, R. B. (1979). *Families against society: A study of reactions to children with birth defects.* Beverly Hills, CA: Sage.

Denzin, N. K. (1991). *Images of postmodern society.* London: Sage.

Dingwall, R. (1997). Accounts, interviews and observations. In G. Miller & R. Dingwall (Eds.), *Context & method in qualitative research* (pp. 51–65). London: Sage.

Drew, P., & Heritage, J. (1992). Analyzing talk at work: An introduction. In P. Drew & J. Heritage (Eds.), *Talk at work* (pp. 3–65). Cambridge, UK: Cambridge University Press.

Duneier, M. (1999). *Sidewalk.* New York: Farrar, Straus & Giroux.

Duneier, M., & Molotch, H. (1999). Talking city trouble: Interactional vandalism, social inequality, and the "urban interaction problem." *American Journal of Sociology, 104,* 1263–1295.

Duranti, A. (1988). The ethnography of speaking: Toward a linguistics of the praxis. In F. Newmeyer (Ed.), *Linguistics: The Cambridge survey* (Vol. 4, pp. 210–228). Cambridge, UK: Cambridge University Press.

Duranti, A. (1997). *Linguistic anthropology.* New York: Cambridge University Press.

Emerson, R. M., Fretz, R. I., & Shaw, L. L. (1995). *Writing ethnographic field notes.* Chicago: University of Chicago Press.

Erickson, F., & Schulz, J. (1982). *The counselor as gatekeeper: Social interaction in interviews.* New York: Academic Press.

Fairclough, N., & Wodak, R. (1997). Critical discourse analysis. In T. A. v. Dijk (Ed.), *Discourse as social interaction* (pp. 258–284). London: Sage.

Garfinkel, H. (1967). *Studies in ethnomethodology.* Englewood Cliffs, NJ: Prentice-Hall.

Gill, V. T., & Maynard, D. W. (1995). On "labeling" in actual interaction: Delivering and receiving diagnoses of developmental disabilities. *Social Problems, 42,* 11–37.

Glaser, B. G., & Strauss, A. L. (1965). *Awareness of dying.* Chicago: Aldine.

Glaser, B. G., & Strauss, A. L. (1967). *The discovery of grounded theory: Strategies for qualitative research.* Chicago: Aldine.

Goffman, E. (1974). *Frame analysis: An essay on the organization of experience.* New York: Harper & Row.

Goffman, E. (1979). Footing. *Semiotica,* 1–29.

Goodwin, C. (1986). Audience diversity, participation, and interpretation. *Text, 6,* 283–316.

Goodwin, C. (1996). Transparent vision. In E. Ochs, E. A. Schegloff, & S. A. Thompson (Eds.), *Interaction and grammar* (pp. 370–404). Cambridge, UK: Cambridge University Press.

Goodwin, C., & Duranti, A. (1992). Rethinking context: An introduction. In A. Duranti & C. Goodwin (Eds.), *Rethinking context: Language as an interactive phenomenon* (pp. 1–42). Cambridge, UK: Cambridge University Press.

Goodwin, M. H. (1990). *He-said-she-said: Talk as social organization among Black children.* Bloomington: Indiana University Press.

Goodwin, M. H. (1996). Informings and announcements in their environment. In E. Couper-Kuhlen & M. Selting (Eds.), *Prosody in conversation: Interactional studies* (pp. 436–461). Cambridge, UK: Cambridge University Press.

Grimshaw, A. (1989). Collegial discourse: Professional conversation among peers. Norwood, NJ: Ablex.

Gubrium, J. F. (1975). *Living and dying at Murray Manor.* New York: St. Martin's Press.

Gubrium, J. F., & Holstein, J. A. (1997). *The new language of qualitative method.* New York: Oxford University Press.

Gumperz, J. (1982). *Language and social identity.* Cambridge, UK: Cambridge University Press.

Gumperz, J. J. (1982). *Discourse strategies.* Cambridge, UK: Cambridge University Press.

Hanks, W. F. (1996). *Language and communicative practices.* Boulder, CO: Westview Press.

Heath, C., & Luff, P. (2000). *Technology in action.* Cambridge, UK: Cambridge University Press.

Heritage, J. (1984). *Garfinkel and ethnomethodology.* Cambridge, UK: Polity Press.

Heritage, J., & Greatbatch, D. (1991). On the institutional character of institutional talk: The case of news interviews. In D. Boden & D. H. Zimmerman (Eds.), *Talk and social structure* (pp. 93–137). Cambridge, UK: Polity Press.

Heritage, J., & Lindström, A. (1998). Motherhood, medicine, and morality: Scenes from a medical encounter. *Research on Language and Social Interaction, 31,* 397–438.

Heritage, J., & Sefi, S. (1992). Dilemmas of advice: Aspects of the delivery and reception of advice in interactions between health visitors and first time mothers. In P. Drew & J. Heritage (Eds.), *Talk at work* (pp. 359–417). Cambridge, UK: Cambridge University Press.

Heritage, J., & Stivers, T. (1999). Online commentary in acute medical visits: A method of shaping patient expectations. *Social Science and Medicine, 49,* 1501–1517.

Hopper, R. (1990/1991). Ethnography and conversation analysis after *Talking Culture. Research on Language and Social Interaction, 24,* 161–170.

Houtkoop-Steenstra, H. (2000). *Interaction and the standardized survey interview: The living questionnaire.* Cambridge, UK: Cambridge University Press.

Hymes, D. (1974). *Foundations in sociolinguistics: An ethnographic approach.* Philadelphia: University of Pennsylvania Press.

Jefferson, G. (1988). On the sequential organization of troubles-talk in ordinary conversation. *Social Problems, 35,* 418–441.

Jimerson, J. B. (1998). "Who has next?" The symbolic, rational, and methodical use of norms in pickup basketball. *Social Psychology Quarterly, 2,* 136–156.

Katz, J. (1999). *How emotions work.* Chicago: University of Chicago Press.

Kaufmann, F. (1944). *Methodology of the social sciences.* New York: Oxford University Press.

Kinnell, A. M. K., & Maynard, D. W. (1996). The delivery and receipt of safer sex advice in pretest counseling sessions for HIV and AIDS. *Journal of Contemporary Ethnography, 24,* 405–437.

Labov, W. (1972a). *Language in the inner city: Studies in the Black English vernacular.* Philadelphia: University of Pennsylvania Press.

Labov, W. (1972b). *Sociolinguistic patterns.* Philadelphia: University of Pennsylvania Press.

Lave, J., & Wenger, E. (1991). *Situated learning: Legitimate peripheral participation.* Cambridge, UK: Cambridge University Press.

Lavin, D. (2002). *Building a case and getting out: Inmate strategies for obtaining parole.* Unpublished doctoral dissertation, Indiana University, Bloomington.

Lavin, D., & Maynard, D. W. (2001). Standardization vs. rapport: Respondent laughter and interviewer reaction during telephone surveys. *American Sociological Review, 66,* 453–479.

Levinson, S. C. (1979). Activity types and language. *Linguistics, 17,* 356–399.

Levinson, S. C. (1983). *Pragmatics.* Cambridge, UK: Cambridge University Press.

Liebow, E. (1967). *Tally's corner.* Boston: Little, Brown.

Lipton, H. L., & Svarstad, B. L. (1977). Sources of variation in clinicians' communication to parents about mental retardation. *American Journal of Mental Deficiency, 82,* 155–161.

Luff, P., Hindmarsh, J., & Heath, C. (2000). *Workplace studies: Recovering work practice and informing system design.* Cambridge, UK: Cambridge University Press.

Lutfey, K. (2000). *Social dimensions of noncompliance with medical treatment regimens: The case of diabetes.* Unpublished doctoral dissertation, Indiana University, Bloomington.

Lutfey, K., & Maynard, D. W. (1998). Bad news in oncology: How physician and patient talk about death and dying without using those words. *Social Psychology Quarterly, 61,* 321–341.

Manzo, J. (1996). Taking turns and taking sides: Opening scenes from two jury deliberations. *Social Psychology Quarterly, 59,* 107–125.

Marlaire, C. L., & Maynard, D. W. (1990). Standardized testing as an interactional phenomenon. *Sociology of Education, 63,* 83–101.

Maynard, D. W. (1984). *Inside plea bargaining: The language of negotiation.* New York: Plenum Press.

Maynard, D. W. (1989). On the ethnography and analysis of discourse in institutional settings. In J. A. Holstein & G. Miller (Eds.), *New Perspectives on Social Problems.* Greenwich, CT: JAI Press.

Maynard, D. W. (1996). On "realization" in everyday life: The forecasting of bad news as a social relation. *American Sociological Review, 61,* 109–131.

Maynard, D. W. (2003). *Bad news, good news: Conversational order in everyday talk and clinical settings.* Chicago: University of Chicago Press.

Maynard, D. W. (2004). On predicating a diagnosis as an attribute of a person. *Discourse Studies, 6,* 53–76.

Maynard, D. W., & Manzo, J. (1993). On the sociology of justice: Theoretical notes from an actual jury deliberation. *Sociological Theory, 11,* 171–193.

Maynard, D. W., & Marlaire, C. L. (1992). Good reasons for bad testing performance: The interactional substrate of educational exams. *Qualitative Sociology, 15,* 177–202.

Maynard, D. W., & Whalen, M. R. (1995). Language, action, and social interaction. In K. Cook, G. Fine, & J. House (Eds.), *Sociological Perspectives in Social Psychology* (Vol. 1, pp. 49–75). Boston: Allyn & Bacon.

McClenahen, L., & Lofland, J. (1976). Bearing bad news: Tactics of the deputy U.S. marshal. *Sociology of Work and Occupations, 3,* 251–272.

Mehan, H. (1991). The school's work of sorting students. In D. Boden & D. H. Zimmerman (Eds.), *Talk and social structure* (pp. 71–90). Cambridge, UK: Polity Press.

Miller, G. (1994). Toward ethnographies of institutional discourse: Proposal and suggestions. *Journal of Contemporary Ethnography, 23,* 280–306.

Miller, G., & Silverman, D. (1995). Troubles talk and counseling discourse: A comparative study. *The Sociological Quarterly, 36,* 725–747.

Moerman, M. (1988). *Talking culture: Ethnography and conversation analysis.* Philadelphia: University of Pennsylvania Press.

Moore, R. J., & Maynard, D. W. (2002). Achieving understanding in the standardized survey interview: Repair sequences. In D. W. Maynard, H. Houtkoop, N. C. Schaeffer, & H. v. d. Zouwen (Eds.), *Standardization and tacit knowledge: Interaction and practice in the survey interview* (pp. 281–311). New York: Wiley Press.

Nelson, C. K. (1994). Ethnomethodological positions on the use of ethnographic data in conversation analytic research. *Journal of Contemporary Ethnography, 23,* 307–329.

Olshansky, S. (1962). Chronic sorrow: A response to having a mentally defective child. *Social Casework, 43,* 191–194.

Peräkylä, A. (1997). Reliability and validity in research based on tapes and transcripts. In D. Silverman (Ed.), *Qualitative research: Theory, method and practice* (pp. 201–220). London: Sage.

Peräkylä, A. (1998). Authority and accountability: The delivery of diagnosis in primary health care. *Social Psychology Quarterly, 61,* 301–320.

Pomerantz, A. (1990/1991). Mental concepts in the analysis of social action. *Research on Language and Social Interaction, 24,* 299–310.

Potter, J. (1997). Discourse analysis as a way of analysing naturally occurring talk. In D. Silverman (Ed.), *Qualitative research: Theory, method and practice* (pp. 144–160). London: Sage.

Potter, J. (1998). Cognition as context (whose cognition?). *Research on Language and Social Interaction, 31,* 29–44.

Richardson, L. (1991). Postmodern social theory: Representational practices. *Sociological Theory, 9,* 173–179.

Sacks, H. (1984). Notes on methodology. In J. M. Atkinson & J. Heritage (Eds.), *Structures of social action* (pp. 21–27). Cambridge, UK: Cambridge University Press.

Sacks, H., Schegloff, E. A., & Jefferson, G. (1974). A simplest systematics for the organization of turn-taking for conversation. *Language, 50,* 696–735.

Schegloff, E. A. (1987). Between macro and micro: Contexts and other connections. In J. Alexander, R. M. B. Giesen, & N. Smelser (Eds.), *The micro-macro link* (pp. 207–234). Berkeley: University of California Press.

Schegloff, E. A. (1991). Reflections on talk and social structure. In D. Boden & D. H. Zimmerman (Eds.), *Talk and social structure* (pp. 44–70). Berkeley: University of California Press.

Schegloff, E. A. (1997). Discourse, pragmatics, conversation analysis. *Discourse Studies, 1,* 405–435.

Schegloff, E. A. (1998). Reply to Wetherell. *Discourse & Society, 9,* 413–416.

Schegloff, E. A. (1999). "Schegloff's texts" as "Billig's data": A critical reply. *Discourse & Society, 10,* 558–572.

Schegloff, E. A., Jefferson, G., & Sacks, H. (1977). The preference for self-correction in the organization of repair in conversation. *Language, 53,* 361–382.

Schegloff, E. A., & Sacks, H. (1973). Opening up closings. *Semiotica, 8,* 289–327.

Silverman, D. (1993). *Interpreting qualitative data: Methods for analysing talk, text, and interaction.* London: Sage.

Souhami, R. L. (1978, October 28). Teaching what to say about cancer. *The Lancet,* 935–936.

Spencer, J. W. (1994). Mutual relevance of ethnography and discourse. *Journal of Contemporary Ethnography, 23,* 267–279.

Stubbs, M. (1983). *Discourse analysis: The sociolinguistic analysis of natural language.* Oxford, UK: Blackwell.

Svarstad, B. L., & Lipton, H. L. (1977). Informing parents about mental retardation: A study of professional communication and parent acceptance. *Social Science and Medicine, 11,* 645–651.

ten Have, P. (1999). *Doing conversation analysis*. London: Sage.

van Dijk, T. (Ed.). (1985). *Handbook of discourse analysis, volumes 1–4*. London: Academic Press.

van Dijk, T. (1999). Critical discourse analysis and conversation analysis. *Discourse & Society, 10*, 459–460.

van Maanen, J. (Ed.). (1995). *Representation in ethnography*. Thousand Oaks, CA: Sage.

Wetherell, M. (1998). Positioning and interpretative repertoires: Conversation analysis and post-structuralism in dialogue. *Discourse & Society, 9*, 387–412.

Whyte, W. F. (1943). *Street corner society*. Chicago: University of Chicago Press.

Wikler, L., Wasow, M., & Hatfield, E. (1981). Chronic sorrow revisited: Parent vs. professional depiction of the adjustment of parents of mentally retarded children. *American Journal of Orthopsychiatry, 51*, 63–70.

Wilson, T. (1991). Social structure and the sequential organization of interaction. In D. Boden & D. Zimmerman (Eds.), *Talk and social structure* (pp. 22–43). Cambridge, UK: Polity Press.

Zimmerman, D. H. (1988). On conversation: The conversation analytic perspective. In *Communication Yearbook II* (pp. 406–432). Newbury Park, CA: Sage.

5

Creativity Within Qualitative Research on Families

New Ideas for Old Methods

Sharon A. Deacon

Q ualitative researchers are continually searching for research methods that engage their participants in the data collection process. When researching living, dynamic systems such as families, researchers need to find methods that can encapsulate the multi-dimensionality of the human experience. The purpose of this paper is to acquaint researchers with some creative and active methods they can use not only to involve their participants in the research process, but also to more fully learn about and experience the perceptions, feelings, and life events of their participants. The methods discussed include sculpting, photography and videography, art and drawing, role-playing, writing exercises, metaphors, and timelines.

From Deacon, S. A., "Creativity with Qualitative Research on Families: New Ideas for Old Methods," in *Qualitative Report, 4*(3), copyright © 2000, reprinted with permission.

Introduction

Most people either love or hate research; they are either energized by the idea of gathering data and stories and analyzing findings or think it is too reductionistic and separated from real life. In many cases and for many people, research has become routinized to the point that it involves "standard procedures" (Patton, 1997). The same methods are being used in the same ways with the same analyses. I believe that there is much room for innovation and creativity in the research process and I have chosen to start by integrating new methods into the process.

Family researchers today are likely to consider using both quantitative and qualitative methods in their research designs (Sprenkle & Moon, 1996). Yet, they are not as likely to consider creating a new method with which to gather data. However, therapists are constantly creating new qualitative methods for family assessment; a primary aspect of research on families (Goldman, 1990, 1992). Through a research project focused on qualitative evaluation of HIV/AIDS prevention programs, I, along with colleagues, had the opportunity to devise some creative ideas for doing qualitative research. Actually, the methods I describe are not really "new," but rather it is their use in qualitative research that is less widely known.

The purpose of this paper [is] to acquaint readers with some of the more actively creative methods they can use to collect qualitative data. I will discuss how to gather information from research participants through the use of sculpting, art and drawing, metaphors, writing exercises, timelines, and photography and videography. The intent behind this paper is to stimulate the creativity of qualitative researchers, to make research more engaging and exciting for everyone involved, and to place high value on the stories and feedback of research participants.

The Underlying Research Philosophy

Research methods should flow logically from the questions one asks (Patton, 1997). The way we do research should be a reflection of the issues and values embedded in our area of interest (Whitmore, 1994). At the same time, many researchers support multiple methods that capture the various dimensions of description and change. Our research traditions, by and large, privilege either numbers or words and focus on the use of numerical measurement instruments or interviews for data collection. More active and tangible methods for data collection (e.g., videos, photography, artwork) are rare in both quantitative and qualitative research literatures. Yet, more active methods of data collection may be a better fit for those studying dynamic, living systems, such as families and human service programs. Why not use more multi-dimensional methods to study these multi-dimensional systems? Further, some populations (such as children, adolescents, those with limited verbal or writing skills, etc.) may be able to better respond to methods that match their active, continually developing context.

The methods below serve to accomplish the goal of making research with human systems more multi-dimensional. Further, these methods were derived with a participatory research philosophy in mind. The methods attempt to reduce the level of the researcher-participant hierarchy and create partnerships between all those involved in the research (Piercy & Thomas, 1999). The purpose behind many of these methods is to find ways to make living systems actually come alive; not only to hear, but to see the stories behind the participants' perceptions and experiences; not only to observe, but to actually become a part of that which we as researchers are studying.

At the same time, data gathering can be more naturalistic (such as with observations) or more manipulated (such as with structured interviews). The activities below also represent both sides of this continuum. For example, with videography, participants may be freer to express themselves in whatever way they normally would. However, with writing exercises and incomplete prompts, researchers limit participants to a particular focus and means of expression. Therefore, the creative methods below are not intended as completely naturalistic, but rather represent a similar range of means with which researchers can control the data they gather.

Rigorous research need not be limited to systematic designs and analyses but can be broadened to absorption in the actual gathering of data. We change as researchers by merely studying and interacting with our participants and the data we gather (Rosenblatt, 1995). We are the research instruments (Patton, 1990). Thus, in using these more active methods of data collection, it is also the responsibility of the researcher to analyze and include his/her own experiences and perceptions in the data analyses and report (whether it is through triangulation, member checks, audits, etc.). Active and creative research that is engaging and ever changing can be sound research.

Finally, many of the methods described below can stand on their own as the main means for gathering data. However, researchers can also use them as additions to more formal data gathering (such as structured interviews) or in various combinations. By using multiple data collection methods, researchers triangulate their data, allowing them to analyze a question or topic from multiple angles, sources, and varieties of expression (Lincoln & Guba, 1985; Patton, 1990). This [in] turn can increase the trustworthiness of the data and findings—the degree to which others can have confidence in the authenticity, believability, and applicability of the findings (Lincoln & Guba, 1985). Thus, in broadening the ways we collect data and using multiple data sources and collection methods, we are also increasing our avenues to build trustworthiness within our research.

Creative Means to Gather Data

Readers can use the means described below in basic or applied research, program evaluations, and needs assessments. Furthermore, many of these activities can take place in interviews or focus groups and can be used in case studies and archival analyses. I have chosen to focus the methods primarily on research with families; however, researchers can adapt these methods to almost any topic or research question.

Sculpting

Family therapists have used sculpting to assess relationships, roles, and functioning in families as a way to gather data about clients (Constantine, 1978). Family sculptures are physical representations (using actual people) or in vivo statues that depict how someone perceives a specific group or system (such as a family, program staff, or business). In a standard sculpture, one person ("the sculptor") directs the others to assume postures that depict how he/she sees them at a particular point in time (Duhl, Kantor, & Duhl, 1973). Sculptors use closeness and space, body posture, facial expressions, and props to show their perception of each person's (e.g., family member's) relationship with the others. For example, a parent might sculpt a rebellious son far apart from the rest of the family, sticking his tongue out at them and making faces. An involved, peacekeeping employer might have her arms reaching out to her employees. Whatever the situation, researchers can ask people in a specific group to sculpt one another in order to get a better picture of how they relate to and perceive each other. To gather historical information or future predictions, the researcher can ask various research participants to sculpt the group at some time in the past (perhaps a time of crisis or at a significant event), in the present, and at some point in the future. Family therapists, such as Gehring and Schultheiss (1987) encourage participants to use dolls, sticks, and chess pieces instead of humans to make sculptures which allows all participants to create their own sculptures simultaneously.

There are also special kinds of sculptures. In a linear sculpture, participants place themselves along an imaginary line on the floor, which represents their feelings about some bipolar dimension of some issue or topic (Constantine,

1978). Researchers can ask participants to physically place themselves along a continuum of power (from "high" to "low") to assess their agency in a given system. Researchers can also use continua of personal traits such as cheerfulness, respectfulness of others, willingness to follow rules, helpfulness, talker-listener, etc. In a recent program evaluation, I asked the staff of an agency to rate their superiors on leadership qualities (e.g., collaborative, respectful, flexibility). The staff was surprised to see that they all perceived one leader in a very negative way, as they all continually congregated on the same area of the line. This empowered the staff, as a group, to discuss their concerns with the superior. As an evaluator, I was able to develop hypotheses about where improvements could be made in the agency to promote a more positive atmosphere among the staff and leadership.

Researchers can learn about participants' opinions and attitudes by asking them to physically place themselves along a continuum (an imaginary line on the floor) of "agree-disagree" according to a series of value-laden statements. For example, researchers can make statements such as: "This family cooperates with each other"; "The staff communicates well"; "The rules in this organization are fair"; or "The children in this family have little say in what happens to the family." I encourage readers to consult Constantine (1978) for additional types of sculptures (such as polar sculptures, boundary sculptures, relationship sculptures, and typological sculptures) that researchers can use to actively involve participants in the data collection process while gathering valuable information at the same time.

Art/Drawing

In qualitative research, we often think of verbal dialogue or observation as the optimal means in which to collect data. But as the saying goes, sometimes a picture can be worth a thousand words. I have discovered that people's drawings, whether literal depictions or abstract symbolisms, can be data that provide quality information in a fun and creative manner.

You can actively engage research participants in the data collection process by asking them to draw their perceptions, feelings, or a situation instead of using verbal description. If you are interested in the context in which they live, you might ask them to draw a picture of their house or neighborhood or a map of their city (Coppersmith, 1980; Moelino, Anggal, & Piercy, in press). For example, in an effort to understand the street life of rural Indonesian at-risk youth, Moelino, Anggal, and Piercy (in press) asked the youth to create maps of their neighborhoods and indicate what activities (prostitution, drug deals, etc.) took place where. If you want to know about people's perceptions of their family's history, you might have them draw a picture of their family

or create a family tree labeling family members according to certain characteristics (e.g., history of depression, substance abusers, ethnicity, educational
level, etc.). You can also gather information about research participants' perceptions of some event by asking them to draw something symbolic that represents the event to them. For example, when I asked a group of participants
to draw a reflection of their work with HIV/AIDS prevention, one woman
drew a bridge to symbolize the path of education from "uninformed" to "safe
and educated."

Qualitative researchers might also be interested in interactional processes.
Researchers can use drawings as enactments, that is, activities in which they
observe participants working together, and take note of communication style,
conflict resolution, teamwork, roles, rules of interactions, etc. Adapting the
art therapy exercises used by Wadeson (1972), researchers could ask a specific group of participants to draw a joint picture (of anything) without
talking to one another (to assess nonverbal communication and conflict resolution skills), individual self-portraits which each gives to the other to edit
and complete (to understand each person's perceptions of self and another),
an individual abstract of the relationship (to assess views of the relationship),
a mural which reflects all of their experiences separately yet as a whole, or
scribbles/free drawings (as data about interests, feelings, ideas).

In addition to drawings, researchers can gather information through activities such as painting, clay sculpting, or other creative constructions. Research
participants may choose to paint instead of draw, or even create a setting
or symbol with clay. They might use clay to physically represent a map
or neighborhood or to create a three-dimensional representation of their
thoughts or feelings about a specific topic. In one research study, the researcher
asked participants to create life-size collages or representations of their lives,
which others could view through an actual window (the director set-up a
temporary wall with windows set in it ten feet back from the wall where the
participants displayed their collages). The participants were then able to
describe their lives by creating a scene with various media and pictures and
then supplementing their creation with their own reactions and words.
Furthermore, observers were also able to react to the scenes and share their
own stories and meanings about what they saw. Literally, others were able to
interact with the collages and various dialogues took place.

With all of the above examples, my hope is to inspire readers to find ways
in which research participants can use their creativity and actively engage in
sharing information through drawing and art. Additionally, art and drawing
are expressive ways that children can provide information to researchers
and serve as participants in the research (Kwiatkowska, 1978; Willmuth &
Boedy, 1979). Further, not only is art a way to gather information, but it can

be an actual therapeutic or interventive experience for research participants. Art is a way to capture participants' experiences in vivo, rather than through words alone.

Metaphors

Similar to drawings, research participants can use metaphors to describe their experiences, feelings, or specific events. Metaphors allow people to describe one thing using an analogy of another (Cade, 1982). When researchers ask participants to describe something in metaphors, participants have more freedom to use their creativity and own experiences to reflect on the specific topic; they leave established mental sets to think of the topic in a new and varied way (Cade, 1982). Language develops different meaning as words become more vivid and we capture moods and interpretations in metaphors. In essence, we create verbal pictures through metaphors, while at the same time making room for new insights on an old topic (Confer, 1987; Kopp, 1995).

There are a variety of metaphors a researcher can elicit. The researcher, for example, can ask participants to describe themselves, each other, or certain events as colors, styles of music or specific song titles, television shows or characters, fairy tales, movies, household objects, foods, shapes, modes of transportation, sounds, book titles, toys, games, or articles of clothing. The researcher can then ask participants about why they chose their metaphors and what they symbolize. For example, a researcher studying the grieving process might ask participants to describe their grief as if it were some kind of moving object or cycle. To study adolescents' perceptions of their parents, the researcher could ask them to describe their families in terms of a popular song, style of music, or book. In a meeting of AIDS service workers, I asked each person to describe their work in terms of a television show or movie. One participant moved the group to tears as she described her work [on] the show *Touched By an Angel*. She popped in and out of people's lives always hoping to have made a difference, but knowing that their fate was not up to her. This person's creative example had a synergistic effect as others in the group started discussing the difficulties and rewards of their work in relation to media analogies. I, as the researcher, gathered abundant information about the personal experiences of these individuals through their metaphors. For any research, metaphors can be an engaging, vivid way to gather information that is meaningful to both the researcher and participants.

Writing Exercises

When we think of using writing as a method of qualitative research, we usually think of open-ended questions on a survey. However, there are other writing activities researchers can use that are not ordinary or monotonous to gather information from participants. Researchers can ask participants to keep journals of their daily activities or feelings, and then use these journals as one way to understand and describe participants and their lives (Symon, 1998). Researchers can also request that participants keep logs of certain activities, memories, or dreams as a way to gather information.

Incomplete prompts are words or beginnings of sentences or stories ("prompts") that researchers can ask participants to finish with their own ideas. With incomplete sentences, researchers ask participants to fill in their thoughts for a list of unfinished sentences that relate to the topic of study. For example, "When I was in the hospital, I felt . . ."; "The hardest time in my life was . . ."; "The turning point was when . . . ." Researchers can also give participants topics to write on or titles for stories and then ask participants to use their creative writing skills to write the story. In studying rural farm families, a researcher might ask the family to write a story on "The challenges of farm life that most people never realize." Or, to study reactions to a devastating flood, a researcher might ask participants to tell a story titled, "Lessons for Recovering." Finally, researchers can ask participants to write about headlines in newspapers that reflect current events ("The Future Direction of Our Community," "One Family's Reaction to the Tragedy"), or classified ads for specific desires ("Perfect Parent Wanted: Qualifications: . . . ," "Perfect Job . . . ," etc.). In a focus group with children going through various family crises, I asked each child to tell me about himself or herself by creating the front page of their local newspaper and writing the headlines and stories of their lives. The children enjoyed the process and were very open to describing the crises that were happening in their families as "news events," while I gathered much information about the children's perceptions of their family crises and current events.

Writing is one way for participants to tell their stories (Gilbert, 1993; Oskowitz & Meulenberg-Buskens, 1997). One of the greatest benefits of writing exercises is that research participants actually give the researcher their stories and words in an exact form. The words are directly from the participants and reflect their stories. On the downside, participants must be willing and able to write down their stories and take the time to develop them.

Timelines

Often qualitative researchers are interested in changes over time, history, and developmental processes. Timelines are one way that researchers can document such events. Together with participants, researchers can create timelines of specific family histories, program histories, historical developments and events, and contextual factors contributing to change. One human services program tracked its history and development by creating a timeline on the wall of the major events that occurred in the program. The employees tacked up news releases, program brochures, pictures of meetings, minutes, etc. as they occurred chronologically. They were then able to actually see where periods of progress occurred and analyze periods of "quiet." They could discuss the successes and shortcomings of the program's development as they actually viewed it through time.

Duhl (1981) discusses the use of a chronological chart to track major family events and compare family members' reactions to them. Researchers can gather information about births, deaths, marriages, divorces, job history, education, relocations, immigrations, etc. It is important in any research to understand the context in which the events or topics we are studying occur. Timelines are simple and easy ways to organize this information and analyze the impact of context on current life.

Videography & Photography

When we use qualitative research as a means to really understand some event or peoples' lives, we are trying to create a vivid picture in others' minds that reflects that which we are studying. What better way to show others what/who we study than by actually *showing* them? Photographs and videos can be excellent ways to disseminate qualitative data. Researchers can take videos or pictures of the settings they are studying, the people involved (with their permission of course), the events that occur, and the situations they experience. Television proves this: what makes more of an impact, hearing about children suffering in other countries or seeing their faces and the environments in which they live? Researchers might choose to take photographs of a family throughout their day, depicting the daily goings-on of the family, or they might collect photos of weddings in an effort to describe the cultural traditions around this family milestone. That is the heart of qualitative data, actually "seeing" the big picture.

In conjunction with a participatory philosophy, researchers can ask participants to create videos or photo albums that depict their lives or specific events. In a project in Indonesia, youths created a video to teach others about their high-risk environments related to HIV/AIDS (Moelino, Anggal, & Piercy, in press). This video gave researchers abundant data about the lives of these youths on the streets. Other researchers have used photographs and video clips in presentations to funding agencies and agency boards as a way to acquaint them with the populations and problems under study.

Psychodrama & Role-Plays

Researchers can use psychodrama and role-plays to enact specific interactions and events. Within psychodrama, people express their thoughts and feelings in spontaneous and dramatic ways through the use of role-playing (Blatner, 1973; Greenberg, 1974; Moreno, 1964). For example, researchers can ask participants to re-enact a specific event or interaction that they describe as life-changing or pivotal in relation to the issue they are studying. In a study of family rituals at bedtime, a researcher could ask families to role-play their usual behaviors. Researchers can assess the perceptions of different participants by asking them to direct the interaction as they each see it and then discuss how each of their experiences is different.

Researchers who study families can ask them to re-enact holidays, a typical day, dinner table interactions, daily rituals, a vacation, or any other event that might provide a window into the dynamics of the family (Leveton, 1992). Researchers can assess how the family communicates, who maintains the power, how members attract or repel each other, who gets the attention, who does what, how problems begin, and what meaning the family attaches to various interactions.

With a group of adolescents, my colleague and I transformed the typical focus group into a "talk-show." We assigned one youth the role of "host" and gave him a list of particular topics and questions to ask the guest "experts" panel and audience. Others then volunteered to be the "expert" guests whom the host interviewed about the topic we were studying. The remainder of the youth served as audience members, raising their hands to comment on questions and react to the opinions of the "experts." While this looked like a role-play, we were able to gather important information about real life for these youths.

Although role-plays and dramas can seem fake and contrived, they can also give researchers information that is only attainable through direct observation of an event (or re-created event). Further, when researchers watch role-plays they can generate questions about specific interactions that they can then inquire about later.

Analyzing, Interpreting, & Presenting the Data

The data that is produced and gathered through these active methods can be analyzed and interpreted as data collected through most other means. The researcher analyzes the created products and the participants' interpretations, reflections, and reactions to them for themes, categories, quotes, etc. For example, the researcher might analyze the commonalities and distinctions between the family sculptures of various adolescents. Or, if studying the familial traditions around weddings, the researcher might analyze wedding photographs or videos for common interactions, rituals, or events. Finally, to analyze drawings, a researcher might look for ways to categorize the drawings or objects in the drawings (by color, by amount of detail, by the subject in the drawing, by the mood of the drawing, by various sizes of people in the drawings, etc.) and then use constant comparison to compare the different meanings participants attributed to their drawings.

The key is that the researcher also needs to be overt about his/her own interpretations of the products (artwork, photographs, sculptures, and so on) and should clarify his/her own reactions from those of the participants. At the same time, since the researcher and participants can actively engage in these processes together, it is important to include the researcher's perceptions and experiences as data that has influenced and co-created the results.

In reports and presentations, researchers can then use these "tangible results" as examples of the research findings. With permission of the participants, researchers can actually show their audiences what they studied and the data they gathered. Researchers and their audiences can physically interact with the data and react to it, creating more data and dialogue about the topic of interest.

Limitations

The methods I discussed above are not meant to be used in every context and for every research purpose. Rather, they are ways to broaden the context of data gathering in order to make the process interesting and engaging for all involved. Clearly, researchers need to assess whether these methods would enhance the process or limit or detract from it, according to the issue and population they are studying. For example, with families with children, such methods might make the process seem less monotonous and more interesting. However, people who feel self-conscious or shy or studies focused on highly sensitive topics (such as sexual abuse) may not lend themselves as well to such methods as sculpture, role-playing, or artwork. Further, if the researcher is unfamiliar or uncomfortable with the method, the participants will detect this and the researcher and research may lose credibility. In sum, these methods can enliven the research process when they are used effectively and with good reason.

Conclusion

Qualitative research can be systematic and rigorous and still be innovative, creative, and actively dynamic. Researchers can integrate the methods I discuss in this paper in interviews, focus groups, or case studies, or simply use these methods on their own. The goal is to make research engaging for everyone involved, while at the same time capturing the real experiences of dynamic, multi-dimensional, living systems such as families.

References

Blatner, A. (1973). *Acting-in: Practical applications of psychodramatic methods.* New York: Springer.

Cade, B. W. (1982). Some uses of metaphor. *Australian Journal of Family Therapy, 3*(3): 135–140.

Confer, W. N. (1987). *Intuitive psychotherapy: The role of creative therapeutic intervention.* New York: Human Sciences Press, Inc.

Constantine, L. L. (1978). Family sculpture and relationship mapping techniques. *Journal of Marriage and Family Counseling, 4:* 13–23.

Coppersmith, E. (1980). The family floor plan: A tool for training, assessment, and intervention in family therapy. *Journal of Marital and Family Therapy, 6:* 141–145.

Duhl, F. J. (1981). The use of the chronological chart in general systems family therapy. *Journal of Marital and Family Therapy, 7:* 361–373.

Duhl, F., Kantor, D., & Duhl, B. (1973). Learning space and action in family therapy. In D. Bloch (Ed.), *Techniques of family psychotherapy: A primer.* New York: Grune & Stratton.

Gehring, T. M., & Schultheiss, R. B. (1987). Family measurement techniques. *American Journal of Family Therapy, 15:* 261–264.

Gilbert, N. (Ed.) (1993). *Researching social life.* London, England, UK: Sage.

Goldman, L. (1990). Qualitative assessment. *Counseling Psychologist, 18*(2): 205–213.

Goldman, L. (1992). Qualitative assessment: An approach for counselors. *Journal of Counseling and Development, 70:* 616–621.

Greenberg, I. A. (1974). *Psychodrama: Theory and therapy.* New York: Behavior Publications.

Kwiatkowska, H. Y. (1978). *Family therapy and evaluation through art.* Springfield, IL: Thomas.

Kopp, R. R. (1995). *Metaphor therapy.* New York: Brunner/Mazel.

Leveton, E. (1992). *A clinician's guide to psychodrama* (2nd ed.). New York: Springer.

Lincoln, Y., & Guba, E. (1985). *Naturalistic inquiry.* Newbury Park, CA: Sage.

Moelino, L., Anggal, W., Piercy, F. (in press). HIV/AIDS-risk for underserved Indonesian youth: A multi-phase participatory action-reflection-action study. *Journal of HIV/AIDS Prevention & Education for Adolescents & Children.*

Moreno, J. (1964). *Psychodrama: Volume 1* (3rd ed.). New York: Beacon House.

Oskowitz, B., & Meulenberg-Buskens, I. (1997). Preparing researchers for a qualitative investigation of a particularly sensitive nature: Reflections from the field. *South African Journal of Psychology, 27*(2): 83–88.

Patton, M. Q. (1990). *Qualitative evaluation and research methods.* Thousand Oaks, CA: Sage.

Patton, M. Q. (1997). *Utilization-focused evaluation.* Thousand Oaks, CA: Sage.

Piercy, F., & Thomas, V. (1998). Participatory evaluation research: An introduction for family therapists. *Journal of Marital and Family Therapy, 24*(2): 165–176.

Rosenblatt, P. (1995). Ethics of qualitative interviewing with grieving families. *Death Studies, 19:* 139–155.

Sprenkle, D., & Moon, S. (1996). *Family therapy research: A handbook of methods.* New York: Guilford.

Symon, G. (1998). Qualitative research diaries. In G. Symon & C. Cassell (Eds.), *Qualitative methods and analysis in organizational research: A practical guide* (pp. 94–117). London, England, UK: Sage Publications Ltd.

Wadeson, H. (1972). Conjoint marital art therapy techniques. *Psychiatry, 35:* 89–98.

Whitmore, E. (1994). To tell the truth: Working with oppressed groups in participatory approaches to inquiry. In P. Reason (Ed.), *Participation in human inquiry* (pp. 82–98). Thousand Oaks, CA: Sage.

Willmuth, M., & Boedy, D. L. (1979). The verbal diagnostic and art therapy combined: An extended evaluation procedure with family groups. *Art Psychotherapy, 6:* 11–18.

6

Sampling Human Experience in Naturalistic Settings

Tamlin Conner and Eliza Bliss-Moreau

T he topic of subjective experience—what people subjectively think, feel, and perceive—has interested philosophers, scientists, and laypeople alike. No matter what our role, as scientist or friend, we gain access to the subjective experience of others through the questions we ask and the answers people give. In the social sciences, this interest translates into the regular use of questionnaires, wherein people typically describe how they feel or behave "in general" (e.g., "How happy are you generally?") or how they felt or behaved in the past (e.g., "How happy were you over *this past month?*"). While these global and retrospective assessments serve a purpose, they fail to adequately capture the rich contextualized representations of what people actually feel and think in daily life. Such limitations, coupled with advances in technology, have led to the emergence of a newer class of procedures, collectively called *experience sampling methods*. These methods allow people to report on their subjective experiences *in situ,* as they go about their daily lives.

Sampling Human Experience

Experience sampling methods refer to a collection of procedures that share three qualities—they allow people to report on experiences *in natural settings, in real time* (not later from memory), and *on repeated time occasions*. For example, in a typical experience sampling method (ESM) study, people are asked questions about their experiences (e.g., "How happy do you feel right now?") as they go about their daily activities. This process can be accomplished in several ways: (a) through the use of a computerized device (e.g., personal data assistant, called a "PDA") that audibly signals participants throughout the day to answer questions displayed on the device, (b) through the use of paper booklets that participants complete at scheduled times or at random times (if pagers or programmable watches are used as signaling devices), or (c) through other emergent means such as logging onto websites or phoning in reports.

Brief History of Experience Sampling Methods

Naturalistic sampling methods have been around since the early years of social science (for a more detailed history, see Wheeler & Reis, 1991). Among the early pioneers of this methodology were sociologists Sorokin and Berger (1939), who gathered detailed accounts of how men and women spent their time in daily life, and psychologists Wessman and Ricks (1966), who investigated the links between daily mood fluctuations and depression in female college students. The 1970s and early 1980s saw the development of modern-day ESM, as paper-and-pencil diaries were combined with audible beepers to allow for the spontaneous sampling of subjective experience (Csikszentmihalyi, Larson, & Prescott, 1977; Hormuth, 1986; Hurlburt, 1979; Klinger, 1978; Larson & Csikszentmihalyi, 1978, 1983). With this technology, the term *experience sampling method* was coined (Larson & Csikszentmihalyi, 1983).

When first introduced, ESM referred to a particular technique involving the *random signaling* of participants during the day to answer questions about their experience (with a pager). Today, the term ESM is often used more broadly to refer to any procedure in which people report their experiences in naturalistic contexts over time, whether in response to a random signal, at fixed times during the day (e.g., at 10:00 a.m., 2:00 p.m., and 4:00 p.m.), or after specified events (e.g., a conflict, meal, or cigarette). Some people use the term ESM in the strict sense (to refer to random signaling), and others use it more in the general sense, as we do in this chapter. Note that ESM is also referred to as *diary methods* (Bolger, Davis, & Rafaeli, 2003), *event-sampling methods* (Reis & Gable, 2000), *thought sampling* (Hurlburt, 1997), and *ecological momentary assessment* (Stone & Shiffman, 1994). This last term, ecological momentary assessment, is used in the medical sciences to refer to procedures that incorporate the ambulatory monitoring of physical states (e.g., blood pressure or heart rate) along with self-reports.

Uses of Experience Sampling Methods

ESM and related procedures have been used to investigate a broad range of phenomena across many domains of science. One of the earliest and most well developed applications of ESM has been for the study of emotional experience (e.g., Larson, Csikszentmihalyi, & Graef, 1980; Wessman & Ricks, 1966). By asking respondents to report on their emotions over an extended period of time, social and personality psychologists have gained considerable insight into the ebb and flow of daily emotional experiences. ESM research has revealed diurnal (Clark, Watson, & Leeka, 1989) and weekly patterns in mood (Larsen & Kasimatis, 1990; Stone, Neale, & Shiffman, 1993), as well as individual differences in mood variability (e.g., Eid & Diener, 1999; Fleeson, 2001; Penner, Shiffman, Paty, & Fritzsche, 1994) and in the entrainment of mood to normative cycles (Larsen & Kasimatis, 1990). These differences, in turn, correlate with important factors such as psychological vulnerability (i.e., greater mood variability is associated with higher neuroticism, Eid & Diener, 1999) and personality traits (i.e., extraverts are less entrained to weekly mood cycles; Larsen & Kasimatis, 1990). ESM research has also revealed that individuals differ in the degree of overlap between emotional states normally considered to be distinct (Feldman, 1995). Some people appear to distinguish between feelings of anxiety and feelings of depression in their daily lives, whereas others do not make such distinctions. This individual difference has implications for the comorbidity of anxiety and depression.

Indeed, ESM research has played an important role in clinical research. Researchers have used ESM to study how people cope with life's daily stressors (e.g., Stone, Neale, & Shiffman, 1993), the beneficial effects of being mindful (Brown & Ryan, 2003), and the characteristics of being in "flow" (Csikszentmihalyi & Csikszentmihalyi, 1988). ESM research has revealed the experiences of individuals suffering from depression (Swendsen, 1998; Wang et al., 2004) and other mental illnesses, including psychosis (Myin-Germeys, Delespaul, & van Os, 2003). For example, ESM research has shown that individuals vulnerable to psychosis are more emotionally reactive in daily life compared to nonvulnerable controls (Myin-Germeys, van Os, Schwartz, Stone, & Delespaul, 2001). Remarkably, ESM research has been used to study people diagnosed with schizophrenia (de Vries, 1992), showing how they feel better in smaller social groups and worse when alone (de Vries & Delespaul, 1989)—findings with clear, practical implications.

In health-related research, studies using ESM have given practitioners a unique window into the correlates and predictors of illness and wellness (for a review, see Stone, Shiffman, & de Vries, 1999). ESM research has been used to study the experiences of asthma sufferers (e.g., Smyth, Soefer, Hurewitz, Kliment, & Stone, 1999), individuals with chronic arthritic pain (e.g., Stone, Broderick, Porter, & Kaell, 1997), smokers who are trying to quit (e.g., Shiffman, Engberg, Paty, & Perz, 1997), and middle-income Americans and their drinking behaviors (e.g., Mohr et al., 2001), to name a select few. Recent technological advances in ambulatory physiological monitoring have also made it possible to track physiological activity along with subjective experience. Researchers have measured heart rate and blood pressure as people go about their daily activities (Goldstein, Jamner, & Shapiro, 1992; Jamner, Shapiro, Goldstein, & Hug, 1991; Kamarck, Peterman, & Raynor, 1998; Kamarck et al., 1998). They have also measured stress hormones via salivary cortisol to show that cortisol levels are higher for individuals who perceive and cope with stress less effectively (van Eck, Berkhof, Nicolson, & Sulon, 1996; see also Ockenfels, Porter, Smyth, & Kirschbaum, 1995).

ESM research is also used in sociology and business-related fields. Continuing the tradition of Sorokin and Berger, sociologists have employed ESM and related methodologies for investigating how time is budgeted (for an ESM-sociology discussion, see Juster, Hiromi, & Stafford, 2003). ESM research is also gaining ground in organizational research (Beal & Weiss, 2003), where it is used to track experiential factors that contribute to job satisfaction (Weiss, Nicholas, & Daus, 1999) and economic decision-making practices (Seo, 2004).

Rationale for Using Experience Sampling Methods

There are several reasons why ESM is emerging as a vital method in the social sciences.

First, ESM research enables measurement of subjective experiences in *naturalistic settings,* providing a window into people's experiences as they go about their daily lives. This setting contrasts markedly with many standard ways of assessing subjective experience, wherein people are asked to recall their experiences from memory or to fill out questionnaires in the lab, sometimes under experimental conditions designed to approximate real life. Consider the value of naturalistic reporting contexts for relationships research. Using ESM, researchers have gained considerable insight into how couples seek out and respond to each other emotionally. Researchers have asked couples to report on how they feel and what they do in response to conflict over a period of time. Analyses have revealed the systematic factors that promote feelings of intimacy between partners (Laurenceau, Barrett, & Pietromonaco, 1998) and the processes by which partners affect each other emotionally under times of stress (Thompson & Bolger, 1999; for other examples see Gable, Reis, & Downey, 2003; and Larson & Almeida, 1999).

Second, ESM research captures experiences as they occur in real time, not recalled later from memory or reported in global terms. In the past, it was thought that real-time, retrospective, and global self-reports should all correspond—that a person who is happy in her daily life will also accurately recall these happy feelings and report being a happy person "in general." But we now know that these self-reports reflect different types of knowledge and will not necessarily correspond (Robinson & Clore, 2002). Real-time reports capture immediate subjective states that fluctuate in response to changing events and conditions, and constitute a form of *episodic knowledge*. In contrast, global reports capture enduring beliefs about experiences and constitute a form of *semantic knowledge*. Retrospective reports fall somewhere in between, reflecting a blend of what actually happened with what we believe probably happened. In the past, the mistake has been to use global and retrospective reports as proxies for episodic experience.

In fact, there are several interesting types of memory biases that strongly call into question the use of retrospective self-reports for obtaining accurate reports of experiences as they originally occurred. First, we humans are not terribly good at accurately summarizing our past experiences over time. If we are asked to report how much pain we experienced *over the course of a week,* for example, our summaries tend to be overinfluenced by the most intense relevant experiences ("the peak") and to a lesser extent by what happened most recently ("the end"), whereas underinfluenced by the duration of the experience ("duration neglect"; Fredrickson & Kahneman, 1993). Not only are we poor summarizers, but also we tend to fill in our memory gaps with our theories about ourselves. For example, memory for emotional experiences is often biased by people's beliefs about their own emotionality (Barrett, 1997; Larsen, 1992), which can be influenced by gender stereotypes (Barrett, Robin, Pietromonaco, & Eyssell, 1998). As a result, when men and women recall how they felt over the past few weeks, women typically recall having more intense moods than do men, in line with gender stereotypes that women are the more "emotional sex." Yet, remarkably, when men and women report their moods in the moment with ESM, they tend to show similarly intense moods (Barrett et al., 1998; for a review, see Robinson & Clore, 2002). Patterns like these also emerge in the retrospective reports of individuals from different cultures. For example, the cultural stereotype of the "happy American" has been shown to positively bias American college students' retrospections of well-being compared to students from Asian countries (Oishi, 2002). Again, few differences were found in actual well-being reported using ESM.

Last, ESM research yields an incredibly rich data set, giving researchers considerable *flexibility in data analysis.* Multiple observations are generated per person, which allow for intraindividual, or *idiographic,* analyses (i.e., the analysis of behavioral patterns for each person in a study). For example, with ESM, it is possible to examine how each person changes over time or how he or she reacts to changing conditions and contexts. Such analyses can reveal the rich contextual nature of human experience. If individuals vary in these patterns, investigators can test whether other person-level factors (demographic characteristics, personality traits, or any other relevant variables, typically measured separately from ESM) might account for the heterogeneity. In this way, ESM data are ideally suited to multilevel modeling procedures, where observations are the lower-level data "nested" within individuals as the upper-level data (for descriptions, see Nezlek, 2001; Reis & Gable, 2000). Data can also be analyzed using sophisticated time-series procedures to reveal systematic temporal patterns (for a description, see West & Hepworth, 1991).

Disadvantages/Caveats in Using Experience Sampling Methods

Despite the many strengths of ESM, there are a number of disadvantages that should be highlighted. First, research using ESM is primarily *correlational in nature.* Experiences and situations are measured rather than manipulated, and so ESM can only provide insight into the co-relations between variables (e.g., feelings of greater control tend to correspond with feelings of well-being), not the causal relations between variables (e.g., feelings of control cause feelings of well-being). Furthermore, ESM research depends on the natural incidence of particular events or experiences. If researchers are studying the relation between conflict and coping, for example, then they will need to determine whether there will be enough situations of conflict that naturally occur in order to warrant sampling.

ESM studies are also extremely *resource intensive.* Implementing such a study has the potential of being financially costly, demanding of participants, and challenging for the research team. Furthermore, available resources will likely dictate the sampling platform (i.e., whether one uses computerized or paper-and-pencil instruments) as well as the sample size of the study (see the "Design and Implement ESM" section below).

Another issue to consider is *measurement reactivity.* ESM studies are unique in that they require people to actively attend to and verbalize their experiences repeatedly over time (often as much as 10 times per day over several weeks). This raises the question about whether the repeated self-monitoring of experience influences the very experience being measured. In general, evidence for reactivity is weak and/or mixed, although, admittedly, understanding of reactivity is very limited at this point. For example, one study examined trends over time as participants reported on their alcohol consumption, smoking, and sexual activities, among other behaviors (Gillmore et al., 2001). Analysis of trends showed overall decreased reporting of drinking, smoking, and sex, suggesting that sampling may sometimes lead participants to begin limiting risky behavior (presumably because they become aware of how much they partake in risky behavior). These effects, however, are not consistent (at least for drinking; Hufford, Shields, Shiffman, Paty, & Balabanis, 2002; Litt, Cooney, & Morse, 1998) and it is unclear whether participants simply began to underreport their risky behaviors due to social desirability. Fewer studies have examined reactivity for more subjective experiences like emotion or pain, where we might expect that asking people to attend to and document these experiences might make them unnaturalistically aware. In all likelihood, reactivity depends on several factors, including how well an individual can verbalize the experience being probed. To the extent that one is used to attending and labeling particular experiences (e.g., one's emotional state), sampling may simply mimic normal conditions and should not be a problem.

Finally, it should be noted that ESM studies are *not necessarily the "gold standard"* of self-report measures. While it is often crucial to measure experiences in a situated fashion, these moment-by-moment reports of experience may not *always* be the best measurement choice—it depends on the research question. Experience sampling captures the representation of experience as it occurs, or close to its occurrence, within the context of a person's everyday life (episodic experience—i.e., "How happy are you *right now?*"). These procedures do not reveal how a person organizes and retains representations of experience once the events have passed—that knowledge, distortions and all, can be important, too. Recent research suggests that people make important decisions about their future based on how they remember their experiences, not necessarily what *actually* happened in the moment. For example, memories of pain experienced during a medical procedure, more so than actual pain felt during the procedure, have been shown to predict important decisions about whether to undergo follow-up colonoscopies (Redelmeier, Katz, & Kahneman, 2003), and retrospective reports of enjoyment during a vacation, more so than people's actual reported enjoyment during the vacation, have been shown to predict whether people would seek to go on a similar trip in the future (Wirtz, Kruger, Scollon, & Diener, 2003). These same effects might hold for other types of investigations and so it is important to consider what types of representations of experience are important (momentary versus retrospective versus global).

How to Design and Implement ESM

This section presents guidelines for designing and implementing an ESM study. We also encourage readers to look at other useful primers (e.g., Bolger, Davis, & Rafaeli, 2003; Conner, Barrett, Bliss-Moreau, Lebo, & Kaschub, 2003; Csikszentmihalyi, Hektner, & Schmidt, in press; Reis & Gable, 2000; Stone, Shiffman, & de Vries, 1999; Wheeler & Reis, 1991). In general, the first step is to assess one's resources—how much money and human power can be dedicated to the project. We break these resources into three types: platform implementation, subject remuneration, and the strength of the research team.

Assess Resources

Resources for Platform Implementation. ESM studies can be implemented in two main ways (computerized vs. paper and pencil), which differ in cost. Computerized sampling is the most financially costly, but it can provide the greatest flexibility in experimental design as well as greater assurance that participants comply with the sampling procedure. Computerized sampling methods use palmtop computers, personal data assistants (PDAs), or mobile phones (Collins, Kashdan, & Gollnisch, 2003) outfitted with specialized software that enables participants to report on behaviors and experiences throughout the day (for a discussion of computerized ESM, see Barrett & Barrett, 2001; Conner et al., 2003; Shiffman, 2000). Participants carry around these devices and then report on their experiences when cued by the device or when they initiate the report themselves. The basic costs associated with computerized experience sampling are the price of the computerized units (roughly $100 for a decent PDA × 50 = $5,000), batteries and protective cases ($500–$1,000), as well as a potential cost for sampling software (free to very costly; see the "Software and Equipment" section below).

For all the costs associated with computerized ESM, there are considerable benefits. Many types of sampling procedures are "time-based" (Bolger, Davis, & Rafaeli, 2003) and rest on the assumption that respondents will complete their reports at certain times or immediately in response to a random audible signal. Computerized methods control these timing elements to ensure that respondents complete their reports at the appropriate times and not later from memory. Computerized procedures also allow for flexibility in how the questions are presented. Questions may be presented sequentially or randomly to minimize response sets and order effects. These procedures also reduce human error associated with data management because data can be transferred directly from the PDA to a master computer without being entered by hand. And, finally, computerized procedures also provide the ability to record additional information, like response latencies to each question, which are not attainable with paper-and-pencil reports. In research, it can be useful to know how quickly a person was able to answer a question about his or her subjective experience.

Paper-and-pencil measures are a cost-effective alternative when resources are tight or when computerized procedures are ill suited for the study population (i.e., the elderly, subjects in higher crime areas where a PDA would be a safety risk). Questionnaire sheets, booklets, or any type of rating form (e.g., the Rochester Interaction Record; Nezlek, Wheeler, & Reis, 1983) can be designed and given to participants to fill out during the day (for additional guidelines on using paper-and-pencil measures, see Bolger, Davis, & Rafaeli, 2003; and also Green, Rafaeli, Bolger, Shrout, & Reis, in press). These paper-and-pencil measures are often used in combination with electronic pagers (e.g., Czikszentmihalyi & Larson, 1987) or programmable watches (e.g., de Vries, Dijkman-Caes, & Delespaul, 1990), which act as random signaling devices. The advantages of paper-and-pencil methods include reduced cost and lower overhead in terms of equipment. Paper-and-pencil methods also allow for open-ended responses, which makes them good for qualitative analyses. The disadvantages include the inability to randomize item content and greater risk of "non-compliant" responding (Stone, Shiffman, Schwartz, Broderick, & Hufford, 2002). Noncompliance can occur if people forget to fill out their reports at designated times; if they fill them out at the wrong times; or worse, if they complete multiple reports later from memory. Fortunately, compliance can be improved dramatically by establishing good working relationships with participants (see Green et al., in press). So, although rapport with participants is crucial for all ESM studies, it is especially critical for studies using a paper-and-pencil platform.

Resources for Participant Remuneration. Another consideration is the availability of resources to remunerate participants for their time. Compared with other empirical methods, ESM studies are relatively taxing to participants because they require a significant time and energy commitment. Adequate remuneration entices respondents to sign up for a study and deters attrition. Depending on the population, a complex remuneration structure comprising multiple incentives can work well, starting with participant payment. At the time of publication, the average rate of pay for college students was approximately $20 a week. To maintain participants' motivation throughout the duration of long studies, researchers also provide smaller remunerations on a weekly basis (e.g., movie passes) and hold drawings for smaller prizes (e.g., $25 gift certificates to restaurants, university sweatshirts, tickets to events). At the end of the study, researchers also sometimes hold drawings for a "grand prize" (e.g., for a PDA). Participants earn weekly remunerations and raffle tickets by coming to their regularly scheduled meeting with their research assistant. If the study is being run in a psychology department with a research requirement, research credits can also be used. Another form of incentive is to emphasize to participants their contributions to science. This helps participants to understand (validly, we believe) how important their participation is and that they are performing a much-valued social function.

Resources of the Research Team. A strong and potentially large research team is particularly important for successful ESM studies. Research assistants work closely with participants over the course of the study and strive to develop a relationship of mutual understanding. Research assistants must undergo extensive training (particularly in the case of computerized ESM) so that they are able to independently troubleshoot problems when problems arise. Research assistants should also pilot the procedure (e.g., carry around the device for a week) so they can understand what it is like to be a participant. Also, because ESM research generates large volumes of data, it is important that research assistants be well trained and comfortable with managing such data sets.

Determine Sampling Protocol and Parameters

Another important design consideration is the type of *sampling protocol* and the *length of the sampling period*. There are three types of sampling protocols (see Reis & Gable, 2000, for an in-depth discussion of these protocols). The first type of sampling protocol is signal-contingent sampling, in which participants report on their experiences at random times following a signal. Signal-contingent protocols typically ask participants to answer questions about their experience at that particular moment (i.e., How are you feeling *right now?*) and so this protocol is well suited to investigating target behaviors that are ongoing and likely to be occurring at the time of a given signal (e.g., mood). Signal-contingent protocols typically use between 4 and 12 signals each day, and the signals are usually delivered "randomly within equal intervals." This means that for a study sampling eight times a day between the hours of 10:00 a.m. and 10:00 p.m., the first signal would come randomly between 10:00 and 11:30 a.m., the second signal would come randomly between 11:30 a.m. and 1:00 p.m., and so on, because there are eight 1½ hour intervals between 10:00 a.m. and 10:00 p.m. This ensures that the unpredicted signals are distributed throughout the day. The unpredictable nature of the signals combined with the immediacy of the reporting is advantageous when studying experiences that are highly susceptible to memory bias or possibly affected by mental preparation; however, because of their randomness and frequency, signal-contingent procedures are the most burdensome for participants.

The second type of sampling protocol is interval-contingent sampling, in which participants report on their experiences at fixed times (i.e., specific hours during the day; morning, afternoon, and evening; or daily at night). Interval-contingent protocols generate strong time-series data because time points are fixed for all participants, so comparisons of responses can be made within and between individuals across specific times. Interval-contingent sampling is also great for measuring experiences that are less susceptible to memory bias (i.e., concrete, countable events). Participants can be asked to report on experiences or behaviors that occurred since the last time they made their report (e.g., "How many cigarettes have you smoked today?"). Interval-contingent protocols are the least burdensome to participants because reports are made at standardized times and so participants can configure their schedules around these reports. This regularity can be a drawback for the measurement of certain experiences (e.g., stress) because it allows participants to mentally prepare to report on their experiences (e.g., calming themselves down prior to making a report).

The third type of sampling protocol is event-contingent sampling, in which participants report on their experiences in response to specific events defined by the researcher (e.g., following an interpersonal conflict or a meal). Such protocols are well suited for assessing experiences and behaviors surrounding specific rare events, such as unprotected sex, which may not be occurring if one is sampled randomly or at set times. While event-contingent protocols are typically less demanding of participants than signal-contingent protocols, they require that participants be able to identify the contingent event, which can sometimes require training. Also note that compliance is an issue because it is impossible to ensure that participants respond immediately following the target event. Even computerized procedures cannot ensure compliance with event-contingent sampling.

The other major design considerations are the length of the sampling period and the number of sampling moments per day. These factors vary considerably within published studies. Although normative estimates are hard to come by, the average length of an ESM study (using a signal-contingent procedure) is between 1 and 2 weeks, averaging 8 to 12 signals per day, yielding 56 to 168 observations (see Reis & Gable, 2000). There are several things to consider in making these decisions, the first being the naturalistic incidence of target events and states. For interval- and signal-contingent procedures, observations should be frequent enough during each day to capture important fluctuations in experience but not so frequent that they inconvenience participants without any incremental gain (Reis & Gable, 2000). Second, researchers should consider the total number of observations needed for a stable estimate of the phenomena. A multilevel power analysis should be run (Snijders & Bosker, 1999) to determine how many sampling moments are required for a stable estimate, assuming that the goal of the experiment is to model both within and between subject variance components. And, for event-contingent procedures, the sampling period should be long enough to accommodate the targeted numbers of observations per person. A fourth consideration is the burden to participants. Delespaul (1992) advises against sampling more than six times per day over longer sampling periods (i.e., 3 weeks plus) unless the reports are especially short (i.e., 2 minutes or less) and additional incentives are provided. Barrett (2004) has had success sampling 10 times daily over 4- and 6-week intervals by keeping the question time short (i.e., 2 minutes) and by adding weekly incentives (i.e., movie tickets, weekly lotteries). The last consideration is the anticipated response rate (the average number of signals/moments to which participants respond). Response rates tend to be highest (95% and above) for interval-contingent procedures using paper-and-pencil instruments that are completed either once or twice daily. On the other hand, response rates tend to be the lowest for signal-contingent procedures using computerized devices that signal multiple times per day (e.g., 50–70%; responding to 5–7 of 10 signals per day on average). If participants respond to only 50–75% of the trials, lengthening the sampling period will allow one to reach the target number of observations.

Choose Software and Equipment

If you decide to run a computerized ESM study, the next step is to choose the software and purchase equipment. A more detailed description of software and equipment considerations can be found in Conner et al. (2003). The choice of software depends on the requirements of your study, and the software will dictate the equipment that is needed. Researchers should conduct a Web search of sampling software, because new software is continually being developed and existing software changes rapidly. For basic studies involving the presentation of a set number of items in a signal-, interval-, or event-contingent protocol, researchers can use a prepackaged, user-configurable program such as ESP (the Experience Sampling Program, Barrett & Barrett, 2001). ESP is a free, open-source software program that researchers can download from the Web, configure with little or no programming knowledge, and install onto either palmtop computers (running the Windows CE operating system) or PDAs (running the Palm operating system). The software comes with a step-by-step manual and is easy to use. For a complete listing of features, see the online manual (http://www.experience-sampling.org). Other existing freeware options include iESP (see http://seattleweb.intel-research.net/projects/esm/iESP.html), and the Purdue Momentary Assessment Tool (PMAT, http://www.mfri.purdue.edu/pages/PMAT/). If advanced features are needed, there are several other options. Researchers can use commercial software, hire an independent programmer, or employ a specialized consulting company that will design and implement specialized software. Consulting services are expensive, however, as many are geared toward supporting larger, government-funded studies.

After selecting the software, equipment comes next. In our experience, there are several important factors in deciding which portable sampling devices to purchase. First, the devices must be compatible with the software. Typically, this requires making sure the devices run on the same operating system for which the software was designed (e.g., Palm versus Windows). A second factor is the cost and quality of the devices. With each year, lower-cost PDAs are becoming increasingly available, but devices do vary in quality. It is important to research the different models to determine which brand and model best balances cost and quality. Also consider the size of the screen, the brightness and resolution, and the sound of the audible signal. Year-long warranties and excellent customer service help, too.

A Few Additional Tips

Prior to running any computerized ESM study, we strongly advise purchasing a single "test PDA" before purchasing the entire fleet. Install the software, configure it according to desired parameters, and see how it works. If all is well, then purchase the rest of your fleet. To cut down on costs, also consider purchasing a smaller fleet of devices and then running participants in waves. For example, a fleet of 40 would allow you to collect data for 120 participants in three waves of 40. Another useful tip is to initially purchase about 20% more units up front. This will save costs in the long run because after one or two studies, units will no longer be under warranty and they will start to break down. Researchers can replenish their fleet with units known to be compatible with the current software.

Once the equipment has been purchased and the software installed and configured on the fleet, it is crucial to pilot test a sample of the devices. Our research assistants typically pilot a PDA for at least a week to provide feedback on their experiences. Pilot testers can tell you whether items need clarification, whether the audible tone was loud enough, and if they needed more time to answer the initial prompt. For example, in one study, we extended the time participants had to respond to the initial prompt to 2½ minutes based on their feedback. Pilot testing also helps estimate response rates. If motivated research assistants only respond to 60% of the prompts, then consider a louder tone or extending the sampling period by a few days to yield enough observations per person.

Implement the Study

ESM studies present several challenges in terms of implementation. These include recruiting participants, maintaining their motivation, ensuring compliance with the study protocol, and maintaining the integrity of the equipment.

Recruitment. ESM research necessitates high levels of commitment on the part of the participants, so oftentimes extra steps must be taken to recruit interested participants. With college populations, researchers often use banners and flyers posted in high-visibility areas (e.g., a central walking path on campus, dorms) that try to pique students' interest with an interesting question. For example, Reis and Gable (2000) report recruiting with questions like "How many hours a day do people spend socializing?" (p. 207). We also find it effective to include the amount of money we offer as remuneration. For example, "Need money? Learn more about yourself, and earn $50 in the process." Ads can also be placed for nonstudent participants in local newspapers.

Maintaining Motivation. Not only must participants be willing to start a study, but also they must be committed to completing it. ESM studies can be fairly time intensive, and so maintaining participant interest and motivation is crucially important. Again, one of the most important factors in maintaining motivation is a positive working relationship between the researcher and the participant (Green et al., in press). Participants will adhere to the policies and practices of the study, or disregard them entirely, largely in response to a research assistant's attitude. Participants should feel important, that researchers are responsive to their needs (via attentive contact and positive reinforcement), and that they are doing something meaningful with their time. Participants who feel positive about the study and who feel a greater sense of responsibility to their research assistant are less likely to cancel appointments and breach study protocols. Also, as discussed earlier, a complex remuneration system also helps, especially a system with multiple incentives (e.g., prizes, drawings).

Increasing Compliance. The success of an ESM study also depends on the conscientiousness, or compliance, of participants—that they respond when they are asked to respond, as honestly as they can, and not in a random fashion. Again, a positive relationship between the researcher and the participant is extremely important. Also important is for participants to be very clear about the study procedures. Participants should be walked through the ESM procedure and given the opportunity to ask questions and get comfortable with the procedure. Another way to boost performance is to provide clear, immediate feedback to participants regarding their response rates. Feedback about response rates can dramatically increase the amount of usable data by making participants aware if they need to be more watchful in making their reports.

Maintaining Equipment. Damage and wear of equipment is an inevitable part of running a computerized ESM study, but some steps can be taken to minimize such damage. PDAs can be carried around in protective cases and their screens covered with either Teflon-based car wax or a protective plastic sheet to prevent scratching. And, using top-of-the-line batteries will extend the lifetime of the units because they are less likely to corrode. Top-of-the-line batteries will also prevent fewer data disasters (e.g., when batteries die and data stored are permanently erased).

Prepare, Clean, and Analyze Data

ESM research yields volumes of data that must be entered, organized, and readied prior to any statistical analysis. Consider an ESM study with 100 participants. If each participant answers 20 items at 100 observation points, this study could potentially yield 200,000 data points. With paper-and-pencil sampling procedures, all data must be entered manually by hand—a lengthy and error-prone process, but certainly achievable. Computerized ESM bypasses this step because data are retrieved directly from the portable devices through a simple "hotsync" procedure to a desktop computer. This process eliminates manual data entry; however, careful steps must be taken not to inadvertently override or erase files. Once the data are entered, they are typically compiled and cleaned prior to analysis. Data are compiled by moving the data from individual files into one large file, arranged in the way best suited to statistical analysis. We typically use a univariate set-up so that each row contains the answers for one sampling moment for each person (suitable for the Hierarchical Linear Modeling program; Raudenbush, Bryk, & Congdon, 2005). Each participant has the same number of rows (some of which contain missing data), and participants' data are stacked on top of each other, starting with Participant 1. Once the data are compiled, they are then cleaned. Data derived from computerized ESM are checked for duplicate or missing records and the data entered from paper-and-pencil sampling are checked for data entry errors. Also, with computerized data, trials with extremely fast reaction times typically indicate participant error (i.e., inadvertently tapping the screen twice for the previous item) and should be excluded from analysis and documented in the write-up.

After being compiled and cleaned, the data are ready to be analyzed. There are innumerable ways to analyze such a rich data set. We recommend several excellent texts, each of which describes statistical procedures in detail, including multilevel modeling procedures (Bolger, Davis, & Rafaeli, 2003; Kenny, Bolger, & Kashy, 2002; Kenny, Kashy, & Bolger, 1998; Nezlek, 2001; Reis & Gable, 2000).

Conclusion

Emergent methods have the power to stimulate theory and research in the social sciences. Once introduced and refined, these methods reveal original directions in research, allowing investigators to ask and answer questions otherwise unconsidered. In the spirit of this idea, we have reviewed the theory and practice of experience sampling methods as useful tools in the social sciences. Although experience sampling should not be undertaken lightly without consideration of rationale and resources, these methods are becoming increasingly feasible with gains in technology and a growing body of methodological guidelines. We hope this chapter serves as a helpful resource.

References

Barrett, L. F. (1997). The relationships among momentary emotion experiences, personality descriptions, and retrospective ratings of emotion. *Personality and Social Psychology Bulletin, 23*(10), 1100–1110.

Barrett, L. F. (2004). Feelings or words? Understanding the content in self-report ratings of emotional experience. *Journal of Personality and Social Psychology, 87*, 266–281.

Barrett, L. F., & Barrett, D. J. (2001). An introduction to computerized experience sampling in psychology. *Social Science Computer Review, 19*(2), 175–185.

Barrett, L. F., Robin, L., Pietromonaco, P. R., & Eyssell, K. M. (1998). Are women the "more emotional" sex? Evidence from emotional experiences in social context. *Cognition and Emotion, 12*(4), 555–578.

Beal, D. J., & Weiss, H. M. (2003). Methods of ecological momentary assessment in organizational research. *Organizational Research Methods, 6*(4), 440–464.

Bolger, N., Davis, A., & Rafaeli, E. (2003). Diary methods: Capturing life as it is lived. *Annual Review of Psychology, 54,* 579–616.

Brown, K. W., & Ryan, R. M. (2003). The benefits of being present: Mindfulness and its role in psychological well-being. *Journal of Personality and Social Psychology, 84*(4), 822–848.

Clark, L. A., Watson, D., & Leeka, J. (1989). Diurnal variation in the positive affects. *Motivation and Emotion, 13*(3), 205–234.

Collins, R. L., Kashdan, T. B., & Gollnisch, G. (2003). The feasibility of using cellular phones to collect ecological momentary assessment data: Application to alcohol consumption. *Experimental and Clinical Psychopharmacology, 11*(1), 73–78.

Conner, T., Barrett, L. F., Bliss-Moreau, E., Lebo, K., & Kaschub, C. (2003). A practical guide to experience-sampling procedures. *Journal of Happiness Studies, 4*(1), 53–78.

Csikszentmihalyi, M., & Csikszentmihalyi, I. S. (1988). *Optimal experience: Psychological studies of flow in consciousness.* New York: Cambridge University Press.

Csikszentmihalyi, M., Hektner, J., & Schmidt, J. (in press). *Measuring the quality of everyday life: The ESM handbook.* Thousand Oaks, CA: Sage.

Csikszentmihalyi, M., & Larson, R. (1987). Validity and reliability of the experience-sampling method. *Journal of Nervous and Mental Disease* [Special issue: Mental disorders in their natural settings: The application of time allocation and experience-sampling techniques in psychiatry], *175*(9), 526–536.

Csikszentmihalyi, M., Larson, R., & Prescott, S. (1977). The ecology of adolescent experience. *Journal of Youth and Adolescence, 6,* 281–294.

de Vries, M. W. (Ed.). (1992). *The experience of psychopathology: Investigating mental disorders in their natural settings.* Cambridge, UK: Cambridge University Press.

de Vries, M. W., & Delespaul, P. A. (1989). Time, context, and subjective experiences in schizophrenia. *Schizophrenia Bulletin, 15*(2), 233–244.

de Vries, M., Dijkman-Caes, C., & Delespaul, P. (1990). The sampling of experience: A method of measuring the co-occurrence of anxiety and depression in daily life. In J. D. Maser & C. R. Cloninger (Eds.), *Comorbidity of mood and anxiety disorders* (pp. 707—726). Washington, DC: American Psychiatric Press.

Delespaul, P. A. E. G. (1992). Technical note: Devices and time-sampling procedures. In M. W. de Vries (Ed.), *The experience of psychopathology: Investigating mental disorders in their natural settings* (pp. xvii, 363–373). New York: Cambridge University Press.

Eid, M., & Diener, E. (1999). Intraindividual variability in affect: Reliability, validity, and personality correlates. *Journal of Personality and Social Psychology, 76*(4), 662–676.

Feldman, L. A. (1995). Valence focus and arousal focus: Individual differences in the structure of affective experience. *Journal of Personality and Social Psychology, 69*, 153–166.

Fleeson, W. (2001). Toward a structure- and process-integrated view of personality: Traits as density distributions of states. *Journal of Personality and Social Psychology, 80*(6), 1011–1027.

Fredrickson, B. L., & Kahneman, D. (1993). Duration neglect in retrospective evaluations of affective episodes. *Journal of Personality and Social Psychology, 65*(1), 45–55.

Gable, S. L., Reis, H. T., & Downey, G. (2003). He said, she said: A quasi-signal detection analysis of daily interactions between close relationship partners. *Psychological Science, 14*(2), 100–105.

Gillmore, M. R., Gaylord, J., Hartway, J., Hoppe, M. J., Morrison, D. M., & Leigh, B. C. (2001). Daily data collection of sexual and other health-related behaviors. *Journal of Sex Research, 38*(1), 35–42.

Goldstein, I. B., Jamner, L. D., & Shapiro, D. (1992). Ambulatory blood pressure and heart rate in healthy male paramedics during a workday and a nonworkday. *Health Psychology, 11*(1), 48–54.

Green, A. S., Rafaeli, E., Bolger, N., Shrout, P. E., & Reis, H. T. (in press). Paper or plastic? Data equivalence in paper and electronic diaries. *Psychological Methods.*

Hormuth, S. E. (1986). The sampling of experiences in situ. *Journal of Personality, 54*, 262–293.

Hufford, M. R., Shields, A. L., Shiffman, S., Paty, J., & Balabanis, M. (2002). Reactivity to ecological momentary assessment: An example using undergraduate problem drinkers. *Psychology of Addictive Behaviors, 16*(3), 205–211.

Hurlburt, R. T. (1979). Random sampling of cognitions and behavior. *Journal of Research in Personality, 13*(1), 103–111.

Hurlburt, R. T. (1997). Randomly sampling thinking in the natural environment. *Journal of Consulting and Clinical Psychology, 65*(6), 941–949.

Jamner, L. D., Shapiro, D., Goldstein, I. B., & Hug, R. (1991). Ambulatory blood pressure and heart rate in paramedics: Effects of cynical hostility and defensiveness. *Psychosomatic Medicine, 53*(4), 393–406.

Juster, F. T., Hiromi, O., & Stafford, F. P. (2003). An assessment of alternative measures of time use. *Sociological Methodology, 33*(1), 19–54.

Kamarck, T. W., Peterman, A. H., & Raynor, D. A. (1998). The effects of the social environment on stress-related cardiovascular activation: Current findings, prospects, and implications. *Annals of Behavioral Medicine* [Special issue: Social psychophysiology of cardiovascular response: Implications for the study of reactivity, risk, and disease], *20*(4), 247–256.

Kamarck, T. W., Shiffman, S. M., Smithline, L., Goodie, J. L., Paty, J. A., & Gnys, M. (1998). Effects of task strain, social conflict, and emotional activation on ambulatory cardiovascular activity: Daily life consequences of recurring stress in a multiethnic adult sample. *Health Psychology, 17*(1), 17–29.

Kenny, D. A., Bolger, N., & Kashy, D. A. (2002). Traditional methods for estimating multilevel models. In D. S. Moskowitz & S. L. Hershberger (Eds.), *Modeling intraindividual variability with repeated measures data: Methods and applications* (Multivariate applications book series, pp. 1–24). Mahwah, NJ: Lawrence Erlbaum.

Kenny, D. A., Kashy, D. A., & Bolger, N. (1998). Data analysis in social psychology. In D. T. Gilbert, S. T. Fiske, et al. (Eds.), *The handbook of social psychology* (Vol. 1, 4th ed., pp. 233–265). New York: McGraw-Hill.

Klinger, E. (1978). Dimensions of thought and imagery in normal waking states. *Journal of Altered States of Consciousness, 4*(2), 97–113.

Larsen, R. J. (1992). Neuroticism and selective encoding and recall of symptoms: Evidence from a combined concurrent and retrospective study. *Journal of Personality and Social Psychology, 62*(3), 480–488.

Larsen, R. J., & Kasimatis, M. (1990). Individual differences in entrainment of mood to the weekly calendar. *Journal of Personality and Social Psychology, 58*(1), 164–171.

Larson, R. W., & Almeida, D. M. (1999). Emotional transmission in the daily lives of families: A new paradigm for studying family process. *Journal of Marriage and the Family, 61*(1), 5–20.

Larson, R. W., & Csikszentmihalyi, M. (1978). Experiential correlates of time alone in adolescence. *Journal of Personality, 46*(4), 677–693.

Larson, R. W., & Csikszentmihalyi, M. (1983). The experience sampling method. *New Directions for Methodology of Social and Behavioral Science, 15*, 41–56.

Larson, R. W., Csikszentmihalyi, M., & Graef, R. (1980). Mood variability and the psychosocial adjustment of adolescents. *Journal of Youth and Adolescence, 9*(6), 469–490.

Laurenceau, J. P., Barrett, L. F., & Pietromonaco, P. R. (1998). Intimacy as an interpersonal process: The importance of self-disclosure, partner disclosure, and perceived partner responsiveness in interpersonal exchanges. *Journal of Personality and Social Psychology, 74*(5), 1238–1251.

Litt, M. D., Cooney, N. L., & Morse, P. (1998). Ecological momentary assessment (EMA) with alcoholics: Methodological problems and potential solutions. *Health Psychology, 17*, 48–52.

Mohr, C. D., Armeli, S., Tennen, H., Carney, M. A., Affleck, G., & Hromi, A. (2001). Daily interpersonal experiences, context, and alcohol consumption: Crying in your beer and toasting good times. *Journal of Personality and Social Psychology, 80*(3), 489–500.

Myin-Germeys, I., Delespaul, P., & van Os, J. (2003). The experience sampling method in psychosis research. *Current Opinion in Psychiatry, 16*(12), 33–38.

Myin-Germeys, I., van Os, J., Schwartz, J. E., Stone, A. A., & Delespaul, P. A. (2001). Emotional reactivity to daily life stress in psychosis. *Archives of General Psychiatry, 58*(12), 1137–1144.

Nezlek, J. B. (2001). Multilevel random coefficient analyses of event and interval contingent data in social and personality psychology research. *Personality and Social Psychology Bulletin, 27*, 771–785.

Nezlek, J. B., Wheeler, L., & Reis, H. T. (1983). Studies of social participation. *New Directions for Methodology of Social and Behavioral Science, 15*, 57–73.

Ockenfels, M. C., Porter, L., Smyth, J., & Kirschbaum, C. (1995). Effect of chronic stress associated with unemployment on salivary cortisol: Overall cortisol levels, diurnal rhythm, and acute stress reactivity. *Psychosomatic Medicine, 57*(5), 460–467.

Oishi, S. (2002). The experiencing and remembering of well-being: A cross-cultural analysis. *Personality and Social Psychology Bulletin, 28*(10), 1398–1406.

Penner, L. A., Shiffman, S., Paty, J. A., & Fritzsche, B. A. (1994). Individual differences in intraperson variability in mood. *Journal of Personality and Social Psychology, 66*(4), 712–721.

Raudenbush, S. W., Bryk, A. S., & Congdon, R. (2005). *HLM 6: Hierarchical linear and non-linear modeling.* Lincolnwood, IL: Scientific Software International.

Redelmeier, D. A., Katz, J., & Kahneman, D. (2003). Memories of colonoscopy: A randomized trial. *Pain, 104*(1), 187–194.

Reis, H. T., & Gable, S. L. (2000). Event sampling and other methods for studying daily experience. In H. T. Reis & C. M. Judd (Eds.), *Handbook of research methods in social and personality psychology* (pp. 190–222). New York: Cambridge University Press.

Robinson, M. D., & Clore, G. L. (2002). Belief and feeling: Evidence for an accessibility model of emotional self-report. *Psychological Bulletin, 128*(6), 934–960.

Seo, M. G. (2004, August). *The effect of affective experience on the direction, intensity, and persistence of task behavior.* Paper presented at the meeting of the Academy of Management, New Orleans, LA.

Shiffman, S. (2000). Real-time self-report of momentary states in the natural environment: Computerized ecological momentary assessment. In A. A. Stone, J. S. Turkkan, C. A. Cachrach, J. B. Jobe, H. S. Kurtzman, & V. S. Cain (Eds.), *The science of self-report: Implications for research and practice* (pp. 277–296). Mahwah, NJ: Lawrence Erlbaum.

Shiffman, S., Engberg, J. B., Paty, J. A., & Perz, W. G. (1997). A day at a time: Predicting smoking lapse from daily urge. *Journal of Abnormal Psychology, 106*(1), 104–116.

Smyth, J. M., Soefer, M. H., Hurewitz, A., Kliment, A., & Stone, A. A. (1999). Daily psychosocial factors predict levels and diurnal cycles of asthma symptomatology and peak flow. *Journal of Behavioral Medicine, 22*(2), 179–193.

Snijders, T., & Bosker, R. (1999). *Multilevel analysis: An introduction to basic and advanced multilevel modeling,* London: Sage.

Sorokin, P. A., & Berger, C. F. (1939). *Time-budgets of human behavior.* Oxford, UK: Harvard University Press.

Stone, A. A., Broderick, J. E., Porter, L. S., & Kaell, A. T. (1997). The experience of rheumatoid arthritis pain and fatigue: Examining momentary reports and correlates over one week. *Arthritis Care and Research, 10*(3), 185–193.

Stone, A. A., Neale, J. M., & Shiffman, S. (1993). Daily assessments of stress and coping and their association with mood. *Annals of Behavioral Medicine, 15*(1), 8–16.

Stone, A. A., & Shiffman, S. (1994). Ecological momentary assessment (EMA) in behavioral medicine. *Annals of Behavioral Medicine, 16,* 199–202.

Stone, A. A., Shiffman, S. S., & de Vries, M. W. (1999). Ecological momentary assessment. In D. Kahneman & E. Diener (Eds.), *Well-being: The foundations of hedonic psychology* (pp. 26–39). New York: Russell Sage Foundation.

Stone, A. A., Shiffman, S., Schwartz, J. E., Broderick, J. E., & Hufford, M. R. (2002). Patient non-compliance with paper diaries. *British Medical Journal, 324*(7347), 1193–1194.

Swendsen, J. D. (1998). The helplessness-hopelessness theory and daily mood experience: An idiographic and cross-situational perspective. *Journal of Personality and Social Psychology, 74*(5), 1398–1408.

Thompson, A., & Bolger, N. (1999). Emotional transmission in couples under stress. *Journal of Marriage and the Family, 61*(1), 38–48.

van Eck, M. M., Berkhof, H., Nicolson, N., & Sulon, J. (1996). The effects of perceived stress, traits, mood states and stressful daily events on salivary control. *Psychosomatic Medicine, 58*(5), 447–458.

Wang, P. S., Beck, A. L., Berglund, P., McKenas, D. K., Pronk, N. P., Simon, G. E., et al. (2004). Effects of major depression on moment-in-time work performance. *American Journal of Psychiatry, 161*, 1885–1891.

Weiss, H. M., Nicholas, J. P., & Daus, C. S. (1999). An examination of the joint effects of affective experiences and job beliefs on job satisfaction and variations in affective experiences over time. *Organizational Behavior and Human Decision Processes, 78*(1), 1–24.

Wessman, A. E., & Ricks, D. F. (1966). *Mood and personality*. Oxford, UK: Holt, Rinehart, & Winston.

West, S. G., & Hepworth, J. T. (1991). Statistical issues in the study of temporal data: Daily experiences. *Journal of Personality, 59*, 609–662.

Wheeler, L., & Reis, H. T. (1991). Self-recording of everyday life events: Origins, types, and uses. *Journal of Personality* [Special issue: Personality and daily experience], *59*(3), 339–354.

Wirtz, D., Kruger, J., Scollon, C. N., & Diener, E. (2003). What to do on spring break? The role of predicted, on-line, and remembered experience in future choice. *Psychological Science, 14*(5), 520–524.

7

Feminist Visualization

Re-envisioning GIS as a Method in Feminist Geographic Research

Mei-Po Kwan

Richly evocative figures exist for feminist visualizations of the world as witty agent . . . We just live here and try to strike up non-innocent conversations by means of our prosthetic devices, including our visualization technologies. (Haraway, 1991, p. 199)

The critical discourse on geographic information systems (GIS) in the past decade or so has raised important questions about the value of GIS in human geographic research. While many maintain that the development and use of GIS constitute a scientific pursuit capable of producing objective knowledge of the world, others criticize GIS for its inadequate representation of space and subjectivity, its positivist epistemology, its instrumental rationality, its technique-driven and data-led methods, and its role as surveillance

From Kwan, M., "Feminist Visualization: Re-envisioning GIS as a Method in Feminist Geographic Research," in the *Annals of the Association of American Geographers*, 92(4), 2002, pp. 645–661. Reprinted with permission of Blackwell Publishing, Ltd.

or military technology deployed by the state. The debate between GIS researchers and critics in the 1990s, however, does not seem to have affected GIS practices in geographic research in significant ways (Schuurman, 2000; Kwan, 2002b, 2002c).

By this I do not mean that there has been a lack of response from GIS scientists and practitioners. On the contrary, both GIS researchers and critics have been involved in major research initiatives that attempt to address the limitations of GIS and its negative impacts on society—from issues of ontology, representation, and scale to the social and political implications of GIS for various social groups (e.g., Sheppard & Poiker, 1995; Burrough & Frank, 1996; Quattrochi & Goodchild, 1997; Obermeyer, 1998; Egenhofer, et al., 1999; Good-child, et al., 1999; Mark, et al., 1999; Sheppard, et al., 1999; Winter, 2001). Among recent studies, research on public-participation GIS (PPGIS) has made significant progress beyond the antagonism in the early phase of the critical discourse (Harris & Weiner, 1998; Craig, Harris, & Weiner, 2002). This literature has addressed issues such as the simultaneous empowering and marginalizing effect of GIS in local politics, representations of multiple realities and local knowledges, and the scale-dependence of power-knowledge in GIS (e.g., Elwood & Leitner, 1998; Weiner & Harris, 1999; Sieber, 2000; Elwood, 2001; Ghose, 2001; Aitken, 2002; Weiner, Harris, & Craig, 2002).

Insights from this literature, however, have yet to bear significantly upon GIS practices in geographic research at large and on the relationship between GIS and critical geographies in particular. Despite several calls for the integration of GIS practices with critical social theories (e.g., Sui, 1994; Miller, 1995; Yapa, 1998; Johnston, 1999), development in critical GIS practice in geographic research has been quite limited to date. GIS and critical geographies remain two separate, if not overtly antagonistic, worlds. Nadine Schuurman and Geraldine Pratt (2002, [p.] 292) aptly describe the situation as "the binary split of two solitudes." In a similar vein, Susan Hanson (2002) and Sara McLafferty (2002) argue that GIS and feminist geography are unconnected and uncommunicative and that the possibility that both may have the potential to enrich each other has been ignored. The critical discourse on GIS in the 1990s has stimulated much debate and critical reflection on GIS technology and methods, but it does not seem to have led to the kind of changes for which critics have called (Kwan, 2002b, 2002c). Critical engagement that seeks to conceive and materialize the critical potential of GIS for geographic research is still sorely needed.

In this article, I explore the possibilities for this kind of critical engagement through revisiting some of the central arguments in the critical discourse from feminist perspectives.[1] I examine whether GIS methods are inherently incompatible with feminist epistemologies through interrogating their connection with positivist scientific practices and visualization technologies. Bearing in mind the limitations of current GIS, I explore several ways in which GIS methods may be used to enrich feminist geographic research. Further, I reflect upon critical issues pertinent to the use of GIS-enabled visualization as a geographical method and describe feminist visualization as a possible critical GIS practice in feminist research. I suggest that GIS can be re-envisioned and used in feminist geography in ways that are congenial to feminist epistemologies and politics. These alternative practices represent a new kind of critical engagement with GIS that is grounded on the critical agency of the GIS user/researcher.

Feminist Geography and GIS

Feminist geography has witnessed tremendous growth in the last two decades. It is a highly diverse and innovative subfield of geography, with practitioners from a variety of epistemological and methodological perspectives (e.g., Jones, Nast, & Roberts, 1997; McDowell & Sharp, 1997; Moss, 2002b). While at least three broad strands of feminist geography can be identified in the literature (McDowell, 1993a, 1993b; Mattingly & Falconer-Al-Hindi, 1995; Moss, 1995; Pratt, 2000), the most active of these in recent years is arguably what Pratt (2000) describes as feminist geographies of difference—a strand that is attentive to the construction of gendered identities across multiple axes of difference (e.g., race, ethnicity, age, sexuality, religion, and nationality) and the geographies of the body.[2] Research in this strand mainly draws upon cultural, post-structural, postcolonial, and psychoanalytic theories, while turning away from objectivist epistemologies.

Although they work with different substantive foci and methods, feminist geographers tend to share some common concerns.[3] First, they hold that the material and discursive construction of gendered identities is crucial for understanding difference in the lived experiences of individuals (Women and Geography Study Group, 1997). Second, any claim to transcendent objectivity or truth is considered untenable, since all knowledge must be acquired through knowers situated in particular subject positions and social contexts (Haraway, 1991; Harding, 1991). Instead, feminist geographers recognize the partiality and situatedness of all knowledge and the importance of critical reflections on one's subject position relative to research participants, the research process, and the knowledge produced (reflexivity) (Hanson, 1992; England, 1994; Gibson-Graham, 1994; Gilbert, 1994; Staeheli & Lawson, 1995; Rose, 1997; Nast, 1998). Third, feminist geographers do not hold particular research methods as distinctively feminist (see Harding, 1987). Instead, they emphasize the need to choose research methods that are appropriate for the research questions and data (Lawson, 1995; Cope, 2002; Kwan, 2002d). Increasingly many feminist geographers advocate the use of multiple methods in a single study, since the weaknesses of each single method may be compensated for by the strengths of another (D. Rose, 1993; McLafferty, 1995; Moss, 1995; Rocheleau, 1995). Fourth, feminist geographers share a commitment to progressive social change that reduces social inequality and oppression of marginalized groups in general and gender inequality in particular. An important element of this commitment is an integration of feminist theory and practice in various forms of activism (Moss, 2002a).

Examining GIS from feminist perspectives is significant for several reasons. First, some of the most trenchant critiques of science and vision have come from feminist writings (e.g., Irigaray, 1985; Pollock, 1988; Mulvey, 1989; Haraway, 1991; G. Rose, 1993), and they have been used in the critical discourse on GIS (e.g., Bondi & Domosh, 1992; Goss, 1995). Addressing the tension between these feminist critiques and GIS methods is therefore essential before GIS can be reimagined as a method in feminist research. Second, feminist geographers have contributed to the deconstruction of binarisms in geographical discourse and methods (e.g., G. Rose, 1993; Lawson, 1995). As GIS is often considered part of quantitative/spatial analytical methods and placed as the opposite to qualitative methods/critical theories, examining GIS from feminist perspectives may help redress this kind of dualist thinking. Lastly, several feminist geographers have used GIS in their recent research (e.g., McLafferty & Tempalski, 1995; Hanson, Kominiak, & Carlin, 1997). An examination of these studies may reveal some of the ways in which GIS and feminist geographic research can enrich each other.

Feminist Critiques of Science and GIS

An important issue concerning whether GIS methods are appropriate for feminist research arises from their presumed epistemological affinity with quantitative/scientific methods and positivist modes of knowledge production. Some critics have argued that GIS is rooted in geography's quantitative revolution and thus inherits its positivism and empiricism (e.g., Taylor, 1990). They consider GIS to be basically a tool for quantitative spatial analysis and for answering sets of questions similar to those that quantitative methods answer (e.g., Dixon & Jones, 1998). They assert that the use of GIS methods in geographic research is driven by the intent to seek for universally applicable principles or to make generalizations about the world. They argue that GIS cannot be used to understand subjective differences among research participants because of its assumption of subject-object dualism (e.g., Lake, 1993). If GIS methods are inherently positivist and universalizing and cannot be used to understand difference and subjectivities, it is quite difficult to conceive any role for GIS methods in feminist geography—at least in feminist research that focuses on the geographies of difference.

Some GIS critics have drawn upon feminist critiques of science to argue that the mode of knowledge-production enabled by GIS is not only positivist but also masculinist (e.g., Curry, 1995b; Goss, 1995; Roberts & Schein, 1995). The most influential works used by critics include those by Evelyn Fox Keller (1985), Sandra Harding (1991), Donna Haraway (1991), and Judy Wajcman (1991). These feminist theorists have provided trenchant critiques of science, especially on the relationship between the social construction of science and cultures of masculinity—for example, the way scientific objectivity has been defined reflects a particular understanding closely associated with certain cultural (but contestable) attributes of maleness. For Haraway (1991, [p.] 189), scientific objectivity as conventionally understood is predicated on the positionality of a disembodied master subject with transcendent vision, which she describes as "the god-trick of seeing everything from nowhere"—where the knower is capable of achieving a detached view into a separate, completely knowable world through the use of their "optics of inquiry" (Barnes & Gregory, 1997, p. 20; see also Haraway, 1997). This kind of knowledge denies the partiality of the knower, erases subjectivities, and ignores the nexus of power-knowledge in its discursive practice. Feminist critics see this mode of knowledge production as masculinist.

Based upon these feminist critiques, Susan Roberts and Richard Schein argue that GIS is a masculinist technology. In their critiques of global imagery in the context of GIS marketing, they (1995, p. 189) assert that "A GIS is a gendered technology relying on scientific knowledge . . . The technology is socially constructed as masculine in the same way that the camera itself has been recognized as an extension of a 'redoubtable masculine will' implying (or forcing) the subject's 'surrender.'" In terms reminiscent of Haraway's (1991, p. 189) thesis of situated knowledges, Liz Bondi and Mona Domosh (1992, p. 202) argue that the Cartesian space-time grid of GIS implies the existence of an external vantage point and that the mode of knowledge production enabled by GIS is masculinist. It is important that feminist critics consider GIS methods—or, more precisely, the mode of knowledge production enabled by GIS—to be positivist and masculinist. In light of these criticisms, it is crucial to re-examine the link between GIS methods and positivist/masculinist epistemology (and ontology), and to ask whether GIS methods are inherently positivist, universalizing, and unable to be used to understand difference (without denying that particular GIS applications can be positivist).

Several issues are pertinent to this critical reflection. First, the connection between GIS methods and positivist/ masculinist epistemology is neither necessary nor inevitable. Past debates on the connection between positivism and quantitative/spatial analytical methods in geography are particularly relevant in this regard. Geographers including Robert Bennett (1985), Geraldine Pratt (1989), Victoria Lawson (1995), and Eric Sheppard (2001) have cogently argued against a necessary connection between quantitative geography and positivism. They question the essentializing characterization of all quantitative methods in geography as positivist practices. For Lawson (1995, p. 451), quantitative methods have been conflated with a particular epistemology (positivism) under the quantitative revolution and "a technique for gathering information has been conflated with a theory of what can be known." She suggests that using mixed methods in feminist research can be part of the process of separating techniques from ontological positions. For Bennett (1985, p. 219), "[T]here is not a close or one-to-one correspondence between what quantitative geography should be and positivism." He suggests that one major aspect of the confusion seems to arise from the particular representation of quantitative geography by David Harvey's (1969) *Explanation in Geography*, which depicts quantitative geography as primarily inductive, searching for universal laws and claiming to be an objective science. In a similar vein, the epistemological critiques of GIS in the early 1990s seem to be reactions to Stan Openshaw's (1991, p. 622, p. 625) representation of GIS as "data-driven and computer-based knowledge-creating technologies" that can "put geography back together again." The oppositional polemics in this debate, however, seem to have denied the possibility for GIS practices to be based upon positions other than positivism or masculinism.

Second, the connection between GIS methods and positivist/masculinist epistemology is historically and spatially contingent. It was in the particular social and political contexts within which GIS was developed and used, and through complex processes of social contest and negotiation, that GIS assumed its particular form in particular application contexts (Latour, 1987; Harris & Weiner, 1998; Chrisman, 1999; Martin, 2000; Sieber, 2000; Craig, Harris, & Weiner, 2002). Each use of GIS technology or methods represents a unique combination of technological, scientific, social, and individual perspectives. Its use as a military technology, its role as a token of positivist science, and its instrumental rationality emanate largely from such concrete and specific historical and social construction. To argue that all or any of these constitute the inherent or immutable nature of GIS is to ignore the specificity of this history—for very different kinds of GIS could have been developed under different sociopolitical interactions—and to foreclose the possibility for GIS methods to be reimagined as critical practices for feminist geographic research.

Third, the critical agency of GIS users/researchers can play an important role in reimagining and developing alternative GIS practices. Insisting that GIS technology or methods assume particular epistemologies represents a form of technological determinism—the use of a particular technology necessitates a particular mode of knowledge production—where the possibility for GIS users/researchers to assume other perspectives is entirely ruled out. This view erases the very subjectivities and agency of individual GIS practitioners, who may be willing to adopt a critical sensibility and to renegotiate GIS as a critical practice. One of the crucial tasks for feminist GIS users/researchers is to break the positivist/masculinist connection that was historically constituted and to engage in the development of critical GIS practices that are congenial to feminist epistemologies and politics. The purpose of using GIS in feminist geographic research is not to discover universal truth or law-like generalizations about the world, but to understand the gendered experience of individuals across multiple axes of difference. It aims at illuminating those aspects of everyday life that can be meaningfully depicted using GIS methods.

Feminist Critiques of Vision and GIS

The second issue concerning whether GIS methods are appropriate for feminist research is their reliance on vision and visualization as an important means of knowledge production. Much has been written about the objectifying power of an elevated vision (in both metaphorical and material sense) and the visual appropriation of the world in modern science and geography (e.g., Cosgrove, 1985; Jay, 1992, 1993; G. Rose, 1993; Gregory, 1994). Luce Irigaray, for instance, argues, "More than any other sense, the eye objectifies and it masters" (Irigaray, 1978, cited in Vasseleu, 1996, p. 129). Michel de Certeau (1984, p. 92) describes the experience of seeing an object from an elevated vantage point as "looking down like a god" where "imaginary totalizations" are produced. Roland Barthes' (1979) reflections on visitors' experience of the Eiffel Tower and Michel Foucault's (1977) analysis of panopticism are equally instructive about the power of an elevated vision and the objectifying gaze (see also: Bryson, 1983; Lefebvre, 1991; Duncan & Duncan, 1992; Grosz, 1992b; Jameson, 1992).

Feminist theorists have written trenchant critiques of the decorporealized vision in modern technoscience. Haraway (1991), for example, highlights the primacy of sight and the reliance on visual technologies in modern society for establishing truth claims and sustaining political power. As she (1991, p. 189) asserts, "Vision in this technological feast becomes unregulated gluttony; all perspective gives way to infinitely mobile vision." She argues that such a disembodied and infinite vision represents a conquering male gaze from nowhere. Drawing upon psychoanalytic theory, feminist geographers have examined the relationships between geography's visual practices and the masculine desire for and pleasure in looking. Rosalyn Deutsche (1991, p. 10), for instance, criticizes Harvey's (1989a, 1989b) "visual conceit" as a form of voyeuristic gaze. She (p. 11) describes such a disembodied gaze as "distancing, mastering, objectifying," where control is exercised "through a visualization which merges with a victimization of its object." In her cogent critique of landscape studies in geography, Gillian Rose (1993, p. 98–99) argues that the masculine gaze "sees a feminine body which requires interpreting by the cultured knowledgeable look . . . The same sense of visual power as well as pleasure is at work as the eye traverses both field and flesh: the masculine gaze is of knowledge and desire" (see also: Harding, 1991; Grosz, 1992b; and, on male gaze by cultural critics, Berger, 1972; Pollock, 1988; Mulvey, 1989).

The critique of vision, articulated largely in terms of Haraway's ocular metaphor and the Foucauldian trope of surveillance, has been applied to GIS visualizations and remotely sensed images (e.g., Goss, 1995; Pickles, 1995; Curry, 1997). Feminist geographers have also been critical of the use of vision or visualizations in GIS practices. Bondi and Domosh (1992, p. 202–3) assert that the promise of GIS to produce singular representations from a myriad of interconnected variables represents "a god's eye view" that entails "the distancing of a unitary self from the object of vision." They (p. 203) argue that GIS's "emphasis on vision as the sense that bestows on the perceiver a unitary and apparently external positions" is a specifically masculine obsession that demotes other senses more closely associated with the feminine. Reflecting on the use of satellite images, Dianne Rocheleau (1995, p. 463) argues that "[W]hen the gaze begins from space, and when the gaze-from-space is uninformed by the logic of gendered livelihoods and landscapes, then the erasure of women's place in the mapped spaces is all but certain." These criticisms not only highlight the objectifying power of GIS-based visualizations, but also call into question the suitability of GIS methods for feminist research. If the vision enabled by GIS is incorrigibly disembodied and masculinist, the use of GIS methods will only serve to perpetuate the objectifying gaze of the masculinist master subject.

In light of these critiques, the use of vision and visualization as an important means of knowledge production in GIS constitutes a major concern for feminist geographers. Before exploring how this issue may be addressed, it is, first of all, important to recognize the historical and social context of the critique of vision and to avoid "an ahistorical condemnation" (Nash, 1996, p. 151) of all visualizations as objectifying or masculinist. As Catherine Nash (1996, p. 153) argues, "There is no inherently bad or good looking." For Gillian Rose, the dominant visuality (or scopic regime) is neither inevitable nor uncontested. As she (2001, p. 9) suggests, "There are different ways of seeing the world, and the critical task is to differentiate between the social effects of those different visions." Given that objectification can also occur through other means, such as the use of language,[4] the problem is less the use of vision or GIS-based visualizations per se than the failure to recognize that vision is always partial and embodied and to acknowledge the risk of privileging sight above the other senses—or, as Haraway (1991, p. 195) puts it, "only the god-trick is forbidden."

Recent writings of feminist theorists provide critical inspiration for addressing the critique of vision when using GIS. First, the vision enabled by GIS can be reclaimed from the abstract, disembodying practice of masculinist technoscience through recorporealizing all visualizations as embodied and situated practices (Nash, 1996; Nast & Kobayashi, 1996; Rose, 2001). Haraway (1991, p. 199, p. 195) calls this appropriation of vision in modern technoscience "feminist visualizations," which are grounded in "the view from a body . . . versus the view from above, from nowhere, from simplicity." Jennifer Light (1995) also suggests a proactive redefining of technology that entails the creative act of re-envisioning its potential use. Julien Murphy (1989, p. 107) proposes a "feminist seeing" that "confronts and moves beyond the distance, destruction, and desire that permeate the look of oppression." Feminist geographers can therefore engage in the appropriation of the power of GIS's visual technologies and "participate in revisualizing worlds turned upside down in earth-transforming challenges to the views of the masters" (Haraway 1991, p. 192).

Recent works on alternative practices in critical, feminist, and postcolonial cartography provide significant insights that may help inform the development of alternative GIS visual practices (e.g., Harley, 1988, 1992; Wood, 1992; Blunt & Rose, 1994; Nash, 1994; Rocheleau, Thomas-Slayter, & Edmunds, 1995; St. Martin, 1995; Krishna, 1996; Pinder, 1996; Dorling & Fairbairn, 1997; Huffman, 1997; Seager, 1997; Sparke, 1998). The purpose of these alternative cartographic practices—variously called other maps or counter-maps—is to re-present the world in ways that question or destabilize dominant representations, which are often imbued with various silences (especially on subaltern groups) and insensitive to the effects of oppression and violence (Nash, 1994; Sparke, 1998). At the level of practice, Rose (2001) presents a helpful account of critical visual methodologies—including content analysis, discourse analysis, and psychoanalysis—that can be used to provide some guidelines for enacting critical visual practices when using GIS. A major concern in this context is how to practice reflexivity with respect to the visualization process and the images created using GIS, in addition to being attentive to one's positionality with respect to research participants, the research project, and the knowledge produced. Rose (2001, ch.1) identifies three sites that, I argue, can be the focus for practicing reflexivity when using GIS methods: (1) the site of production, where we reflect on our meaning-making visual practices; (2) the site of the image itself, where we examine the exclusions, silences, and marginalizing power of our representations; and (3) the site of audiencing, where we consider how our images encourage particular ways of looking, and how meaning may be contested or renegotiated by various audiences (Kwan, 2002c).

Second, new GIS-based visual practices can be developed for representing gendered spaces. Strong evidence exists in the writings of feminist cultural and art critics that women tend to represent spaces and construct spectator positions differently when compared to men (e.g., Doane, 1982; Pollock, 1988; Stacey, 1988; Broude & Garrard, 1994; Neumaier, 1995; Rose, 1995).[5] In an analysis of the scene location and spatial ordering in the impressionist paintings of Berthe Morisot and Mary Cassatt, Griselda Pollock (1988, p. 56) concludes that "[T]hey make visible aspects of working-class women's labour within the bourgeois home" and that their spaces are characterized by proximity and compression, instead of vast spaces in which the viewer's position is hard to infer. Rose (1995) examines how the work of three women artists (Jenny Holzer, Barbara Kruger, and Cindy Sherman) offers ways of seeing that are constructed, not through voyeurism, but through intimacy and care. Feminist geographers using GIS methods can experiment and create new visual practices, especially those that can better represent gendered spaces and help construct different spectator positions when compared to conventional GIS methods.

Third, historical studies of the experiences of women travelers hint at the possibility of a more reflexive mode of visualizing geographic data (e.g., Blunt, 1994; Morin & Guelke, 1998). In her discussion of the experiences of Victorian women explorers, for instance, Domosh (1991) alludes to the possibility of a feminine way of seeing based upon the understanding that women travelers often had different goals, routes, and destinations while traveling in foreign lands than those of men. Further, these women often spoke of the empowerment they felt when they were exploring. Thus, "even the exploitative appropriation of European exploration was not without the possibilities for developing other kinds of connections" (Bondi & Domosh, 1992, p. 211). Based on these accounts, and given that the use of GIS technologies and methods often involves the exploration of cartographic images and high-dimensional graphics in a GIS's cyberspatial environment, it seems that different kinds of interactions between the GIS user and GIS technology are possible. This hints at the contestability of the GIS user-technology relations that can be a basis for creating alternative GIS visual practices for feminist research.

My experience in viewing a three-dimensional image of the World Trade Center site on the Web after the 11 September 2001 attack may help illustrate this point. The image was created from elevation data collected by a plane flying at 5,000 feet above the site using light detection and ranging (LIDAR) technology (Barnes, 2001; Chang, 2001). The 3D topographic image shows the remains of the World Trade Center building structures and the craters that drop 30 feet below street-level at the site. Although the text accompanying the image marveled at the technological achievement and usefulness of LIDAR technology in this context (which I fully acknowledge), I was instead overwhelmed by a deep sense of grief that led me to ponder on the meaning of such a tragic incidence for the victims, for those who were affected, and for myself as a feminist geographer and GIS user/researcher. My reaction was a result not only of viewing the image but also of reading numerous chilling stories told by people from their personal experience of the calamity (including media reports, photos and news on the Web, and messages on several electronic discussion lists). These data vividly wove together a tragic story that is evocative of critical reflections and emotions.[6] This suggests that GIS users can interact with GIS-created images in a relatively embodied manner, and that GIS-based visualizations are not necessarily devoid of context or meaning. When complemented by contextual information on the ground and at microscale (e.g., stories about the lived experiences of individuals), GIS visualizations can establish important connections between large-scale phenomena (e.g., urban restructuring or land-cover change) and the everyday lives of individuals (see also: Jiang, 2001; Pavlovskaya, 2002).

Feminist Geographic Research and GIS Methods

As I argued earlier, the purpose of using GIS in feminist geographic research is not to discover universal truth or law-like generalizations about the world, but to understand the gendered experience of individuals across multiple axes of difference. It aims at illuminating those aspects of everyday life that can be meaningfully depicted using GIS methods. As major GIS data models were designed to handle digital spatial data and many of the core functionalities of GIS were developed for analyzing quantitative information, earlier debate on the role of quantitative methods in feminist geographic research is still highly relevant (e.g., Lawson, 1995; Mattingly & Falconer-Al-Hindi, 1995; McLafferty, 1995; Moss, 1995; Rocheleau, 1995). For instance, GIS methods can be used to reveal "the broad contours of difference and similarity that vary not only with gender but also with race, ethnicity, class, and place" (McLafferty, 1995, p. 438). They can be used to support arguments in political discourse for initiating progressive social and political change, and to indicate research areas that urgently require attention and suggest directions for in-depth qualitative research. GIS methods can also help discover the gender biases in conventional quantitative methods. Further, as GIS is capable of displaying and overlaying many layers of data, it can be used to reveal spatial contexts, depict spatial connections, and hint at the complex social relationships among people and places. The strength of GIS methods lies in helping the user/researcher to identify complex relationships across geographical scales.

That said, GIS methods have many limitations when used in feminist research. For instance, there are no readily available procedures in current GIS for representing gendered bodies, women's knowledges or desires, or the complex processes involved in the social construction of space (Lefebvre, 1991; Massey, 1993; G. Rose, 1993; Gregory, 1994). It is also impossible to avoid the unequal power relations between the researcher and researched when relying only on secondary data (McLafferty, 1995). It is important to acknowledge these limitations and their implications when using GIS methods. The malleability of GIS software allows some possibilities for alleviating these limitations. Specific strategies include: (1) complementing secondary data with other contextual information; (2) collecting primary quantitative and/or qualitative data from individual subjects; (3) developing dedicated algorithms instead of using inappropriate but readily available procedures in current GIS; and (4) practicing reflexivity with respect to the knowledge production process and the representational tactics (including the production and use of visual materials such as GIS-created maps and images). Using multiple methods in a particular study would also allow a more nuanced understanding of the research problem than using only GIS data and methods.

It is also crucial for feminist geographers to be attentive to ethical and privacy issues when using GIS methods (Crampton, 1995; Curry, 1995a, 1995b). This is especially true for studies of human subjects or establishments that are "hidden, secret, or concealed" (e.g., lesbian or gay venues; Brown, 2000, p. 62), since disclosing their identities or locations through GIS mapping may put them at unforeseeable risk. Procedures should therefore be taken to protect the privacy and anonymity of this kind of subject or establishment.[7] Another privacy risk in the use of GIS maps is the possibility of recovering the identities of subjects from map symbols through a process of reverse engineering called map hacking (Armstrong & Ruggles, 1999). Feminist GIS users may need to be vigilant in recognizing this kind of problem and informed by recent research on methods for hiding subjects' identities.[8]

With these caveats in mind, I describe in what follows some possibilities for using GIS methods in feminist geographic research.[9]

Linking Geographical Context and Women's Everyday Lives

The ability of GIS to incorporate information about the geographical environment across spatial scales renders it a useful tool for feminist research. As geographic data of urban environments at fine spatial scales (e.g., at the parcel or building level) can be assembled and incorporated into a GIS, it is possible to link the trajectories of women's everyday lives (including activities locations and travel routes) with their geographical context at various geographical scales. This would allow a mode of analysis that is more sensitive to scale and context than are conventional methods. Further, when individual-level data are available, GIS methods can be attentive to the diversity and differences among individuals. This mode of analysis contrasts significantly with conventional aggregate analysis and permits an understanding of women's situations "at a level that does not obfuscate their daily lives through maps and language drawn from instrumental, strategic logic" (Aitken, 2002, p. 364).

As McLafferty (2002) suggests, GIS provides a tool for representing and visualizing not only the proximate geographical context of women's lives but also environments beyond the scope of women's daily experiences (see also: Jiang, 2001). For Hanson (2002), GIS enables description and representation of context at levels of detail and scale flexibility that are difficult to achieve without using GIS. My recent studies indicate that GIS may help reveal complex links among women's experiences at various spatial scales—for example, how gender relations within the household interact with larger, urban-scale accessibility patterns through the mediation of fixity constraint (Kwan, 1999a, 1999b). In his analysis of the potential of GIS for scale-sensitive research and local activism, Stuart Aitken (2002) argues that GIS can be used to help interpret women's daily trajectories that link their experiences inside and out of the home (thus connecting the private and public spheres).

Several recent studies suggest the possibility of scale- and context-sensitive GIS-based feminist research. An example is Hanson, Kominiak, and Carlin's (1997) study on the impact of local context on women's labor-market outcome in Worcester, Massachusetts. The study examines whether the proximity to home of a large number of jobs in female-dominated occupations increases the probability that a woman will work in a gender-typed occupation. It computed the number of jobs in female-dominated occupations locally available to each woman using a person-specific spatial interpolation method and a job-search space defined by a realistic estimate of the distance traveled to work for each woman. Using this GIS method, Hanson and colleagues (1997) are able to avoid the problem of using overgeneralized census data while conducting their analysis at the individual level. The study concludes that local employment context is important for part-time workers with a college education and young children at home. It illustrates the fact that significant questions in feminist research can be addressed by developing and using innovative GIS methods that incorporate the geographical context into the analysis.

Supporting Women's Activism Through GIS-Based Research

As GIS is increasingly used in the public decision-making process, especially in the context of urban planning, an important area in which it can play a role in feminist research is empowering women's activist groups in local politics. As Hanson (2002) argues, the availability of GIS technology may strengthen activism and challenge traditional power relations and forms of governance. Feminist GIS users/researchers can play a role in supporting women's local activism in several ways. These include: (1) assembling, codifying, and coalescing women's local knowledges and experiences; (2) performing GIS analysis that women's activist groups do not have the skills or resources to undertake; (3) preparing data and analytical results to facilitate the articulation of the course of women's activist groups; and (4) disseminating results to assist the formation of a collective consciousness that enhances the effectiveness of women's activist groups in the political arena.

Few studies have documented the role of feminist GIS-based research in local politics to date. A community-initiated GIS project at Hunter College that aims at understanding the spatial tendency and potential environmental causes of breast cancer in the community of West Islip on Long Island, New York provides one good example (Timander & McLafferty, 1998; McLafferty, 2002). The project was launched on request by a group of women who were worried about a possible breast-cancer problem in their community after seeing high breast-cancer incidence among themselves. It uses individual data collected by a group of women activists through door-to-door surveys to answer specific questions arising from their fears and concerns—for example, are breast-cancer cases clustered near a hazardous site? For these women, as McLaffery (2002, p. 265) stresses, "[M]apping and GIS became important tools for acquiring knowledge outside the realm of daily experience and for connecting their personal experience of health and illness to a wider social and political agenda." As arguments and explanations that refer to "broader patterns, conditions, and relationships . . . frequently command greater legitimacy and influence" in local politics (Elwood, 2001, p. 12), GIS-based research has the potential to empower women's activist groups.

Feminist geographers, however, need to be aware of the possibility of a marginalizing effect as the scale of politics shifts up (e.g., from community groups to city or regional planning). As GIS researchers have observed, participatory politics involving the use of GIS technology can disenfranchise certain groups while empowering others (e.g., Elwood & Leitner, 1998; Harris & Weiner, 1998; Ghose, 2001; Aitken, 2002). This often happens because groups that have better command of technical and political skills (e.g., government agencies) will tend to have more power and influence in political discourse than those that do not (e.g., inner-city neighborhood groups). In the case of the Long Island project, community-based breast-cancer coalitions succeeded in capturing public attention and gaining federal funding (McLafferty, 2002). But as the grassroots-based GIS project evolved into a U.S. $27 million federal initiative, the power of the women activists dwindled, as several powerful groups (e.g., government agencies) were also on the GIS advisory board. Feminist GIS users/researchers need to be aware of this kind of problem. Conceiving strategies that assist activist groups in scaling their participatory GIS up to a higher level of politics will also be an important element in projects that seek to empower women's activist groups through GIS-based research.

Using Qualitative Data to Construct Cartographic Narratives

Although GIS can handle only digital information and has limitations in representing the diverse and complex experiences of women's everyday lives, recent development of digital technologies has greatly expanded the kind of information with which it can deal. In other words, "digital" now includes a much wider array of representational possibilities than merely numerical or quantitative data. Qualitative data such as digital photos, voice clips, and video clips can be linked or incorporated into a GIS. In studies using qualitative methods, subjects' handwriting, hand-drawn maps, and other sketches collected through ethnographic methods can also be incorporated into a GIS. The use of GIS, therefore, does not necessarily preclude the use of contextual qualitative information of subjects or locales. Indeed, a comparison of GIS software with qualitative data-analysis programs, such as NVivo or ATLAS.ti, would find many similarities (although the latter focus mainly on the coding and analysis of textual data). For instance, both types of programs adopt a highly visual approach, provide links to integrate various types of qualitative data (photos and voice clips), support a suite of query tools including Boolean operators (or, and, not), and emphasize exploratory data-analysis.

In ethnographic research, GIS has been used to incorporate qualitative data into geographic databases. For example, in an ongoing, multisite study of low-income and welfare-recipient families and their children, family ethnographic field-notes are linked with neighborhood field-notes and other contextual data in a GIS (Matthews, Burton, & Detwiler, 2001). The integration of GIS and ethnography has allowed researchers of the project to visualize and better understand the complexity of the lives of low-income families and the strategies they adopt in negotiating the welfare system. GIS has also been used in the construction of biographical narratives. An example is the Ligon history project that was initiated to preserve the history, culture, and memory of an inner-city high school (Ligon High) in Raleigh, North Carolina (Alibrandi, Thompson, & Hagevik, 2000). Besides documenting the African-American perspective of life during Ligon High School's pre- and civil-rights eras, GIS was used in the project to create a series of historical life maps that describe the biography of an alumnus.

In light of the expanded representational capabilities of current GIS, GIS methods can be used in feminist research for composing spatial stories or biographical accounts of women's lives (de Certeau, 1984). GIS may also provide a digital environment for the interactive interpretation of ethnographic data or local knowledges in which research subjects are active participants. As this mode of GIS production is more open to the articulation of different voices when compared to current GIS discursive practices, alternative GIS practices can be conceived for enhancing GIS's potential for polyvocality. For example, in a study of community integrated GIS (CiGIS) for land reform in Mpumalanga Province, South Africa, Dan Weiner and Trevor Harris (1999) incorporate views and local knowledges of different groups of subjects—in the form of sketch maps compiled through participatory mental-mapping workshops—into a multimedia GIS (see also: Rundstrom, 1995 & Ismail, 1999 for difficulties in representing knowledges of indigenous peoples).

Mapping Women's Life Paths in Space-Time

As contemporary feminist geography is particularly attentive to the construction of gendered identities and the geographies of the body, the extent to which GIS can represent gendered spaces and bodies is a major concern. Despite recent advances in GIS technology and research, current GIS data models still have serious limitations for representing entities as complex and fluid as gendered spaces and bodies. The most likely possibility is to use vector or object-oriented data models to represent the body as discrete geometric objects (e.g., stationary bodies as points and moving bodies as lines).

This representational schema, however, is problematic in light of the recent work on the geographies of the body (e.g., McDowell & Court, 1994; Duncan, 1996; Pile, 1996; Nast & Pile, 1998; Butler & Parr, 1999; Valentine, 1999; Longhurst, 2001). For instance, the lines for representing moving bodies in the Cartesian space of a GIS are clearly delimited and seem to suggest unlimited spatial freedom (G. Rose, 1993). The abstract geometry of points and lines cannot reflect many significant aspects of women's experiences (e.g., the fear of violent crime), and they are blind to the power relations that permeate public space and have impacts upon women's lives (Valentine, 1989; Pain, 1997). The representation of space and the body in current GIS therefore calls into question how GIS methods can be useful for understanding women's everyday lives.

Given these limitations, it is difficult to imagine a GIS production that can do justice to the contribution of feminist theories of corporeality and subject formation (e.g., Butler, 1990, 1993; Young, 1990; Grosz, 1992b, 1994; Bordo, 1993; Gregson & Rose, 2000). Believing that GIS methods can be a helpful visual device for illuminating certain aspects of women's everyday lives, however, I propose two directions for addressing GIS's limitations in this context. First, the lines representing women's life paths in space-time in a GIS can be re-imagined as body inscriptions—inscriptions of oppressive power relations on women's everyday spatiality and inscriptions of gendered spatiality in space-time (Laws, 1997). As Elizabeth Grosz (1992a, p. 242) argues, "[B]odies reinscribe and project themselves onto their sociocultural environment so that this environment both produces and reflects the form and interests of the body." The geometry of women's life-paths and the processes of identity formation and women's experiences of places are mutually constitutive. The movement of women's bodies in space-time is also an active element in the production of gendered spaces (Spain, 1992; Nead, 1997). Through this reimagining, the lines representing women's life paths in space-time are no longer abstract lines in the transparent Cartesian space of GIS. Instead, they are the material expressions of women's corporeality and embodied subjectivities—a mapping of their bodies onto space-time that emanates from their prediscursive practices of everyday life (Pile & Thrift, 1995). In this light, I argue that feminist geographers can appropriate GIS methods for illuminating women's spatiality, while recognizing the apparent privilege given to the physicality of the body by GIS methods.

Extending the representational capabilities of current GIS comprises another direction for overcoming some of its limitations for representing gendered spaces and bodies. For instance, I have mapped movements of women's bodies in space-time as continuous trajectories using 3D GIS in a series of studies (Kwan, 1999a, 2000a, 2000b, 2000c; Kwan & Lee, forthcoming). The body maps I have produced look like Hägerstrand's (1970) space-time aquarium, where women's body movements are portrayed as life paths in a 3D space.[10] Figure 1 shows, as an example, the daily space-time paths of the African-American women in a sample of households in Portland, Oregon (Figure 2 provides a close-up view of downtown Portland). Geovisualizations performed using this method indicate that not only do the homes and workplaces of these women concentrate in a small area of the entire metropolitan region, but their activities locations are much more spatially restricted when compared to those of all other gender/ethnic groups (Kwan, 2000c). The closeted spatiality of African-American women in the study area suggests that urban space can be racialized in a manner that goes beyond what the socioeconomic processes in the housing and job markets can fully explain.

I have extended this kind of body-mapping in subsequent studies. In a study of human extensibility in space-time (Kwan, 2000b), I developed a

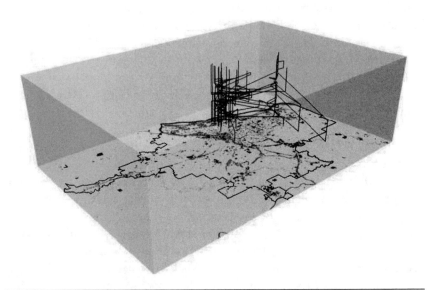

Figure 7.1   The space-time paths of a sample of African-American women in Portland, Oregon

multiscale representation of a person's extensible body boundary using 3D GIS. In another study (Kwan, 2002a), I constructed cartographic narratives with 3D GIS to tell stories about Muslim women's experience of the urban environment after 11 September 2001 using both quantitative and qualitative data collected through in-depth interviews. The study suggests that many representational possibilities of GIS remain unexplored.

Revealing the Gender Biases
of Conventional Quantitative Methods

As many quantitative methods in geography are based on the abstract logic of spatial organization and assumptions that ignore the complexities of life situations among different individuals, analytical results can deviate considerably from what people actually experience in their everyday lives. Since GIS can take into account certain complexities of an urban environment (e.g., variations in facility opening hours and the ease of travel in different locales and at different times of the day) and incorporate some behavioral attributes of individuals into dedicated geocomputational algorithms (Weber & Kwan, 2002), GIS methods can better approximate real-world behavior and can be used to reveal the gender biases in conventional quantitative methods.

In a project that examines the impact of women's space-time constraint on their employment status and access to urban opportunities in Columbus, Ohio, I argue that conventional accessibility measures are not adequate for studying women's accessibility (Kwan, 1998, 1999b). Based on locational proximity to a single reference point (e.g., home or the workplace), these measures ignore the sequential unfolding of women's daily lives in space and time and the restrictive effect of fixity constraint on their access to urban opportunities in a particular day. Instead of using conventional measures, I formulate three space-time accessibility measures that take these factors into account. I develop a geocomputational algorithm to implement these measures in a GIS environment. It uses the activity diary data I collected from a sample of individuals in Columbus, Ohio and a geographic database with parcel-level details. The results from using space-time measures reveal considerable spatial variations in women's accessibility patterns, while men's accessibility patterns mainly follow the spatial distribution of the urban opportunities in the study area. The results from using conventional measures, however, do not indicate this kind of gender difference in accessibility patterns. The study concludes that GIS-based space-time measures are more sensitive to women's life-situations when compared to conventional measures, and that conventional accessibility measures suffer from an

Figure 7.2   A detailed view of an area close to downtown Portland, Oregon

inherent gender bias and therefore are not suitable for studying women's accessibility.

As these conclusions would not have been possible without using GIS, applying GIS methods in feminist research has potential for revealing the gender biases in conventional concepts and quantitative methods in geography. In other words, GIS methods may allow feminist geographers to expose the discursive limits of certain geographical methods without invoking ontological or epistemological arguments (Derrida, 1976; Barnes, 1996).

Conclusion

Although GIS and feminist geography may have the potential to enrich each other, they have remained two separate worlds to date (Hanson, 2002; McLafferty, 2002). Despite their limitations, GIS methods can play a role in addressing certain issues in feminist geographic research. Through revisiting earlier critiques of GIS and hinting at some possibilities for alternative practices, this article calls for a different kind of critical engagement with GIS— one that seeks to re-envision and re-present GIS as a feminist practice, and one that is actively involved in the creation of GIS practices informed by feminist epistemologies and politics. Recent writings of feminist theorists and methodological debates in feminist geography provide important guidelines in grounding GIS practices in feminist epistemologies and research methodologies. They suggest that feminist GIS users/researchers need to acknowledge and deal with the limitations of GIS methods, the power relations GIS entails, the difficulty of practicing reflexivity, and the ethical or moral implications of the knowledge produced. The question is perhaps less one of the possibility of feminist GIS practices than one of how this potentiality can be realized.

At the level of practice, an urgent need exists to go beyond the conventional understanding of GIS as a largely quantitative practice and to recognize the potential of such realization for disrupting the rigid distinction between quantitative and qualitative methods in geographic research. As I have argued elsewhere (Kwan, 2002c), GIS can be a site for deconstructing the dualist understanding of geographical methods (as either quantitative or qualitative) and for enacting feminist visualization—the material practice of critical visual methods in feminist geography. Further, as Schuurman (2002) and I (Kwan, 2002c) have argued, an important element in feminist critiques of science and vision has been lost in the critical discourse on GIS in the last decade or so. Haraway (1991, p. 192) not only provides a trenchant critique of modern technoscience and visual technologies, but also emphasizes through her "cyborg manifesto" that feminists can reclaim the vision and power of modern technoscience (GIS technologies included) and participate in "earth-transforming challenges to the views of the masters." Perhaps much would be gained through teasing out the implications of her (1991, p. 4) question: "Can cyborgs, or binary oppositions, or technological vision hint at ways that the things many feminists have feared most can and must be refigured and put back to work for life and not death?"

Acknowledgments

A version of this article was first presented in a session on "Feminist Geography and GIS" I organized at the annual meeting of the Association of American Geographers, Pittsburgh, PA, April 2000. I thank Susan Hanson for her encouragement and support for the project, and Regina Hagger, Sara McLafferty, and Marianna Pavlovskaya for their stimulating presentations. I am also grateful to Nancy Ettlinger, Michael Goodchild, Vicky Lawson, Pamela Moss, Nadine Schuurman, and four anonymous reviewers for their helpful comments on earlier drafts of the article. In addition, I would like to thank Stuart Aitken, Meghan Cope, Sarah Elwood, Rina Ghose, Munira Ismail, Hong Jiang, Steve Matthews, Eric Sheppard, and Dan Weiner for sharing their thoughts in various contexts or allowing me access to their unpublished papers. All shortcomings and errors of the article remain my responsibility. I wrote this article when I held an Ameritech Fellowship (2000–2001) and was supported by a grant (BCS-0112488) from the Information Technology Research (ITR) Program of the National Science Foundation (NSF). The assistance of the Geography and Regional Science Program of the NSF is gratefully acknowledged.

Notes

1. Many perspectives can be identified within critical geographies. These include postcolonial, post-structuralist, feminist, socialist, queer, and other radical perspectives. I focus mainly on feminist geography because it is an important area of my research interests and I can draw upon my experience in writing this article. Some of my arguments (e.g., on reflexivity) in this article are perhaps also relevant to other critical perspectives.

2. A vast literature on the geographies of the body has emerged in the last decade or so. Drawing upon diverse theoretical perspectives (e.g., post-structuralist and psychoanalytic theory), this literature challenges and destabilizes much of our conventional understanding of the relations among the materiality and spatiality of the body and processes of identity and subject formation (see Longhurst, 2001, ch. 2 for a helpful introduction).

3. The common concerns identified here are necessarily overgeneralizations, as considerable difference exists among feminist geographies associated with variations in race, sexuality, class, and national context. See, for example, Janice Monk (1994) on different feminist geographies in different countries.

4. Calling or naming can also produce objectified and oppressed subjectivities. See, for instance, Louis Althusser's (1969) notion of interpellation (linguistic objectification). See also the discussions of interpellation by Kaja Silverman (1983), Stephen Melville (1996), and Heidi Nast (1998).

5. This section refers to various kinds of gender differences—the way women represent spaces, construct spectator positions, and experience travel differs from that of men. These gender differences, as reported by feminist scholars, are drawn upon as a point of departure for thinking about the possibility of alternative GIS practices. They by no means imply an essentialist understanding of women's experience, nor do they suggest that the complexities of gendered experience can be captured in terms of the binary categories of women and men.

6. See Kay Anderson and Susan Smith (2001) for the importance of recovering the role of emotions in the production of geographical knowledge. Rosalind Picard (1997) also provides an interesting perspective on the possibility of incorporating emotions in computing.

7. For instance, while Michael Brown (2000) admitted that GIS was a helpful tool in his study on sexualized urban space (with a focus on the closeted spatiality of gay venues) in downtown Christchurch, New Zealand, he was deeply concerned

about the ethical implications. To avoid disclosing the exact location of the gay venues on maps, he used their mean center to represent their spatial tendency instead of using the dot symbol to plot the location of each venue.

8. See, for example, Marc Armstrong, Gerard Rushton, and Dale L. Zimmerman (1998) on geographical masks.

9. Although each example is used to illustrate one purpose for using GIS methods, I do not mean to suggest that it is the only or the most important purpose for the study in question. Further, discussion in the following five subsections focuses largely on women's everyday lives and experiences. This, however, is more a reflection of my own research interests than a presupposition that feminist research or geography deals only with women's experiences (although women's diverse experiences constitute a major concern in feminist geography). For instance, feminist geographers have made significant contributions to the study of gendered construction of nature and space (e.g., G. Rose 1993), masculinities (e.g., Butz & Berg, 2002), and capitalism (e.g., Gibson-Graham, 1996).

10. Despite Gillian Rose's (1993) critiques on this kind of time-geographic representations, geographers have found them useful in various contexts (e.g., Hanson & Hanson, 1993; Gregory, 1994; Adams, 1995; Miller, 1995; Hannah, 1997; Laws, 1997; Dorling, 1998; Rollinson, 1998; Kwan, 2000c). Such 3D representations also seem to be helpful for illuminating the complex interactions between space and time in women's strategies for coping with their daily fixity constraint (Kwan, 1999a).

References

Adams, P. C. (1995). A reconsideration of personal boundaries in space-time. *Annals of the Association of American Geographers 85* (2): 267–85.

Aitken, S. (2002). Public participation, technological discourses and the scale of GIS. In W. J. Craig, T. M. Harris, & D. Weiner (Eds.), *Community participation and geographic information systems* (357–66). London: Taylor and Francis.

Alibrandi, M., A. Thompson, & R. Hagevik. (2000). *Documenting a culture. ArcNews 22* (3): 27.

Althusser, L. (1969). Ideology and ideological state apparatuses (notes towards an investigation). In S. Zizek (Ed.) *Mapping ideology* (100–140). London: Verso.

Anderson, K., & S. J. Smith. (2001). Emotional geographies. *Transactions of the Institute of British Geographers NS 26* (1): 7–10.

Armstrong, M. P., & A. J. Ruggles. (1999). *Map hacking: On the use of inverse address-matching to discover individual identities from point-mapped information sources.* Paper presented at the Geographic Information and Society Conference, University of Minnesota, Minneapolis, Minnesota, 20–22 June.

Armstrong, M. P., G. Rushton, & D. L. Zimmerman. (1998). Geographically masking health data to preserve confidentiality. *Statistics in Medicine 18* (5): 497–525.

ATLAS.ti. Version 4.2. Scientific Software Development, Berlin, Germany.

Barnes, S. (2001). United in purpose: Spatial help in the aftermath. *Geospatial Solutions 11* (11): 34–39.

Barnes, T. (1996). *Logics of dislocation: Models, metaphors, and meanings of economic space.* New York: Guilford.

Barnes, T., & D. Gregory (Eds.) (1997). *Reading human geography: The poetics and politics of inquiry.* London: Arnold.

Barthes, R. (1979). *The Eiffel Tower and other mythologies.* R. Howard (Transl.). New York: Hill and Wang.

Bennett, R. J. (1985). Quantification and relevance. In R. J. Johnston (Ed.), *The future of Geography* (211–24). London: Methuen.

Berger, J. (1972). *Ways of seeing.* London: Penguin.

Bondi, L., & M. Domosh. (1992). Other figures in other places: On feminism, postmodernism, and geography. *Environment and Planning D 10:* 199–213.

Bordo, S. (1993). *Unbearable weight: Feminism, Western culture, and the body.* Berkeley: University of California Press.

Blunt, A. (1994). *Travel, gender, and imperialism: Mary Kingsley and West Africa.* New York: Guilford.

Blunt, A., & G. Rose. (1994). Introduction: Women's colonial and postcolonial geographies. In A. Blunt & G. Rose (Ed.), *Writing women and space: Colonial and postcolonial geographies,* 1–25. New York: Guilford.

Broude, N., & M. D. Garrard (Eds). (1994). *The power of feminist art: The American movement of the 1970s, history and impact.* New York: Harry N. Abrams.

Brown, M. (2000). *Closet space: Geographies of metaphor from the body to the globe.* New York: Routledge.

Bryson, N. (1983). *Vision and painting: The logic of the gaze.* New Haven, CT: Yale University Press.

Burrough, P. A., & A. U. Frank (Eds.) (1996). *Geographic objects with indeterminate boundaries.* London: Taylor and Francis.

Butler, J. (1990). *Gender trouble: Feminism and the subversion of identity.* London: Routledge.

———. (1993). *Bodies that matter: On the discursive limits of sex.* New York: Routledge.

Butler, R., & H. Parr. (Eds.) (1999). *Mind and body spaces: Geographies of illness, impairment and disability.* London: Routledge.

Butz, D., & L. D. Berg. (2002). Paradoxical space: Geography, men, and duppy feminism. In P. Moss (Ed.), *Feminist geography in practice: Research and methods* (87–102). Oxford: Blackwell.

Chang, K. (2001). *From 5,000 feet up: Mapping terrain for Ground Zero workers.* The New York Times 23 September: A1.

Chrisman, N. (1999). *Full circle: More than just social implications of GIS.* Paper presented at the International Conference on Geographic Information and Society, University of Minnesota, Minneapolis, Minnesota, 20–22 June.

Cope, M. (2002). Feminist epistemology in geography. In P. Moss (Ed.), *Feminist geography in practice: Research and methods* (43–56). Oxford: Blackwell.

Cosgrove, D. (1985). Prospect, perspective and the evolution of the landscape idea. *Transactions of the Institute of British Geographers NS 10:* 45–62.

Craig, W. J., T. M. Harris, & D. Weiner. (Eds.) (2002). *Community participation and geographic information systems.* London: Taylor and Francis.

Crampton, J. (1995). The ethics of GIS. *Cartography and Geographic Information Systems 22* (1): 84–89.

Curry, M. (1995a). GIS and the inevitability of ethical inconsistency. In John Pickles (Ed.), *Ground truth: The social implications of geographic information systems,* 68–87. New York: Guildford.

————. (1995b). Rethinking rights and responsibilities in geographic information systems: Beyond the power of the image. *Cartography and Geographic Information Systems 22* (1): 58–69.

————. (1997). The digital individual and the private realm. *Annals of the Association of American Geographers 87* (4): 681–99.

de Certeau, M. (1984). *The practice of everyday life.* Steven Rendall (Trans.). Berkeley: University of California Press.

Derrida, J. (1976). *Of grammatology.* Gayatri Chakravorty Spivak (Trans.). Baltimore: Johns Hopkins University Press.

Deutsche, R. (1991). Boys town. *Environment and Planning D 9:*5–30.

Dixon, D. P., & J. P. Jones III. (1998). My dinner with Derrida, or spatial analysis and poststructuralist do lunch. *Environment and Planning A 30:* 247–60.

Doane, M. A. (1982). Film and the masquerade: Theorizing the female spectator. *Screen 23:* 74–87.

Domosh, M. (1991). Towards a feminist historiography of geography. *Transactions of the Institute of British Geographers NS 16:* 95–104.

Dorling, D. (1998). Human cartography: When it is good to map. *Environment and Planning A 30:* 277–88.

Dorling, D., & D. Fairbairn. (1997). *Mapping: Ways of representing the world.* Harlow, Essex: Longman.

Duncan, J. S., & N. G. Duncan. (1992). Ideology and bliss: Roland Barthes and the secret histories of landscape. In T. J. Barnes and J. S. Duncan (Eds.), *Writing worlds: Discourse, text, and metaphor in the representation of landscape,* 18–37. New York: Routledge.

Duncan, N. G. (Ed.). (1996). *BodySpace: Destabilizing geographies of gender and sexuality.* London: Routledge.

Egenhofer, M. J., J. Glasgow, O. Gunther, J. R. Herring, & D. Peuquet. (1999). Progress in computational methods for representing geographical concepts. *International Journal of Geographical Information Science 13* (8): 775–96.

Elwood, S. (2001). *The politics of scale: Conceptualizing the impacts of geographic information technologies in neighborhood revitalization.* Paper presented at the Digital Communities 2001 Conference, Chicago, IL, 4–7 November.

Elwood, S., & H. Leitner. (1998). GIS and community-based planning: Exploring the diversity of neighborhood perspectives and needs. *Cartography and Geographic Information Systems 25:* 77–88.

England, K. V. L. (1994). Getting personal: Reflexivity, positionality, and feminist research. *The Professional Geographer 46:* 80–89.

Foucault, M. (1977). *Discipline and punish: The birth of the prison.* Alan Sheridan (Trans). New York: Vintage Books.

Ghose, R. (2001). Use of information technology for community empowerment: Transforming geographic information systems into community information systems. *Transactions in GIS 5* (2): 141–63.

Gibson-Graham, J. K. (1994). "Stuffed if I know!" Reflections on post-modern feminist social research. *Gender, Place and Culture 1:* 205–24.

———. (1996). *The end of capitalism (as we knew it): A feminist critique of political economy.* Cambridge, MA: Blackwell.

Gilbert, M. R. (1994). The politics of location: Doing feminist research at "home." *The Professional Geographer 46:* 90–96.

Goodchild, M. F., M. J. Egenhofer, K. Kemp, D. M. Mark, & E. Sheppard. (1999). Introduction to the Varenius project. *International Journal of Geographical Information Science 13* (8): 731–45.

Goss, J. (1995). Marketing the new marketing: The strategic discourse of geodemographic information systems. In J. Pickles (Ed.), *Ground truth: The social implications of geographic information systems* (130–70). New York: Guildford.

Gregory, D. (1994). *Geographical imaginations.* Cambridge, MA: Blackwell.

Gregson, N., & G. Rose. (2000). Taking Butler elsewhere: Performativities, spatialities and subjectivities. *Environment and Planning D 18:* 433–52.

Grosz, E. (1992a). Bodies-cities. In B. Colomina (Ed.), *Sexuality and space* (241–53). New York: Princeton Architectural Press.

———. (1992b). Voyeurism/exhibitionism/the gaze. In E. Wright (Ed.), *Feminism and psychoanalysis: A critical dictionary* (447–50). Oxford: Blackwell.

———. (1994). *Volatile bodies: Toward a corporeal feminism.* Indianapolis: Indiana University Press.

Hägerstrand, T. (1970). *What about people in regional science?* Papers of the Regional Science Association 24: 7–21.

Hannah, M. (1997). Imperfect panopticism: Envisioning the construction of normal lives. In G. Benko and U. Strohmayer (Eds.), *Space and social theory: Interpreting modernity and postmodernity* (344–59). Oxford: Blackwell.

Hanson, S. (1992). Geography and feminism: Worlds in collision? *Annals of the Association of American Geographers 82* (4): 569–86.

———. (2002). Connections. In *Gender, Place and Culture 9* (3): 301–303.

Hanson, S., & P. Hanson. (1993). The geography of everyday life. In T. Garling & R. G. Golledge (Eds.), *Behavior and environment: Psychological and geographical Approaches* (249–69). Amsterdam: North-Holland.

Hanson, S., T. Kominiak, & S. Carlin. (1997). Assessing the impact of location on women's labor market outcomes: A *methodological exploration. Geographical Analysis 29* (4): 282–97.

Haraway, D. (1991). *Simians, cyborgs, and women: The reinvention of nature.* New York: Routledge.

———. (1997). *Modest_witness@Second_millennium.FemaleMan©Meets_OncoMouse™: Feminism and technoscience.* New York: Routledge.

Harding, S. (1987). Introduction: Is there a feminist method? In S. Harding (Ed.), *Feminism and methodology: Social science issues,* 1–14. Bloomington: Indiana University Press.

———. (1991). *Whose science? Whose knowledge? Thinking from women's lives.* Ithaca, NY: Cornell University Press.

Harley, J. B. (1988). Maps, knowledge, and power. In D. Cosgrove & S. Daniels (Eds.), *The iconography of landscape: Essays on the symbolic representation, design and use of past environments* (277–312). Cambridge, U.K.: Cambridge University Press.

———. (1992). Deconstructing the map. In T J. Barnes & J. S. Duncan (Eds.), *Writing worlds: Discourse, text, and metaphor in the representation of landscape* (231–47). New York: Routledge.

Harris, T., & D. Weiner. (1998). Empowerment, marginalization and community-integrated GIS. *Cartography and Geographic Information Systems* 25 (2): 67–76.

Harvey, D. (1969). *Explanation in geography.* London: Edward Arnold.

———. (1989a). *The condition of postmodernity: An enquiry into the origins of cultural change.* Oxford: Basil Blackwell.

———. (1989b.) *The urban experience.* Baltimore: Johns Hopkins University Press.

Huffman, N. H. (1997). Charting the other maps: Cartography and visual methods in feminist research. In J. P. Jones III, H. J. Nast, & S. M. Roberts (Eds.), *Thresholds in feminist geography: Difference, methodology, representation* (255–83). Lanham, MD: Rowman and Littlefield.

Irigaray, L. (1978). Interview with Luce Irigaray. In. M. F. Hans & G. Lapouge (Eds.), *Les femmes, la pornographie, et l'erotisme,* 50. Paris: Editions du Seuil.

———. (1985). *Speculum of the other women.* G. C. Gill (Trans.). Ithaca, NY: Cornell University Press.

Ismail, M. (1999). *A multi-ethnic analysis of gendered space amongst rural women in Sri Lanka.* Ph.D. diss., Graduate Group in Geography, University of California, Davis.

Jameson, F. (1992). *Signatures of the visible.* New York: Routledge.

Jay, M. (1992). Scopic regimes of modernity. In S. Lash & J. Friedman (Eds.), *Modernity and identity* (178–95). Oxford: Blackwell.

———. (1993). *Downcast eyes: The denigration of vision in twentieth-century French thought.* Berkeley: University of California Press.

Jiang, H. (2001). *Stories remote sensing images can tell: Integrating remote sensing analysis with ethnographic research in the study of cultural landscape.* Paper presented at the 97th Annual Meeting of the Association of American Geographers, New York, 27 February–3 March.

Jones, J. P., III, H. J. Nast, & S. M. Roberts. (Eds.). (1997). *Thresholds in feminist geography: Difference, methodology, representation.* Lanham, MD: Rowman and Littlefield.

Johnston, R. J. (1999). Geography and GIS. In P. Longley, M. Goodchild, D. Maguire, & D. Rhind (Eds.), *Geographical information systems: Principles, techniques, management, and applications* (39–47). New York: John Wiley and Sons.

Keller, E. Fox. (1985). *Reflections on gender and science.* New Haven, CT: Yale University Press.

Krishna, S. (1996). Cartographic anxiety: Mapping the body politic in India. In M. J. Shapiro & H. R. Alker (Eds.), *Challenging boundaries: Global flows, territorial identities* (193–214). Minneapolis: University of Minnesota Press.

Kwan, M. P. (1998). Space-time and integral measures of individual accessibility: A comparative analysis using a point-based framework. *Geographical Analysis 30* (3): 191–216.

———. (1999a). Gender, the home-work link, and space-time patterns of non-employment activities. *Economic Geography 75* (4): 370–94.

———. (1999b). Gender and individual access to urban opportunities: A study using space-time measures. *The Professional Geographer 51* (2): 210–27.

———. (2000a). *Evaluating gender differences in individual accessibility: A study using trip data collected by the global positioning system.* Final report to the Federal Highway Administration (FHWA), U.S. Department of Transportation, Washington, DC. http://www.fhwa.dot.gov/ohim/kwanreport/ kwanreport.htm (last accessed 29 August 2002).

———. (2000b). Human extensibility and individual hybrid-accessibility in space-time: A multi-scale representation using GIS. In D. G. & D. C. Hodge (Eds.), *Information, place, and cyberspace: Issues in accessibility* (241–56). Berlin: Springer-Verlag.

———. (2000c). Interactive geovisualization of activity-travel patterns using 3D GIS: A methodological exploration with a large data set. *Transportation Research C 8:* 185–203.

———. (2002a). *Constructing cartographic narratives of women's everyday lives with 3D GIS.* Paper presented at the 98th Annual Meeting of the Association of American Geographers, Los Angeles, 19–23 March.

———. (2002b). Introduction: Feminist geography and GIS. *Gender, Place and Culture 9* (3): 261–62.

———. (2002c). Is GIS for women? Reflections on the critical discourse in the 1990s. *Gender, Place and Culture 9* (3): 271–79.

———. (2002d). Quantitative methods and feminist geographic research. In P. Moss (Ed.), *Feminist Geography in Practice: Research and Methods* (160–73). Oxford: Blackwell.

Kwan, M. P., & J. Lee. (Forthcoming). Geovisualization of human activity patterns using 3D GIS. In M. F. Goodchild & D. G. Janelle (Eds.), *Spatially integrated social science: Examples in best practice.* Oxford: Oxford University Press.

Lake, R. W. (1993). Planning and applied geography: Positivism, ethics, and geographic information systems. *Progress in Human Geography 17:* 404–13.

Latour, B. (1987). *Science in action: How to follow scientists and engineers through society.* Cambridge, MA: Harvard University Press.

Laws, G. (1997). Women's life courses, spatial mobility, and state policies. In J. P. Jones III, H. J. Nast, & S. M. Roberts (Eds.), *Thresholds in feminist geography: Difference, methodology, representation* (47–64). Lanham, MD: Rowman and Littlefield.

Lawson, V. (1995). The politics of difference: Examining the quantitative/qualitative dualism in post-structuralist feminist research. *The Professional Geographer 47* (4): 449–57.

Lefebvre, H. (1991). *The production of space.* D. Nicholson-Smith (Trans.). Cambridge, MA: Blackwell.

Light, J. (1995). The digital landscape: New space for women? *Gender, Place and Culture 2* (2): 133–46.

Longhurst, R. (2001). *Bodies: Exploring fluid boundaries.* London: Routledge.

Mark, Da. M., C. Freksa, S. C. Hirtle, R. Lloyd, & B. Tversky. (1999.) Cognitive models of geographical space. *International Journal of Geographical Information Science 13* (8): 747–74.

Martin, E. W. (2000). Actor-networks and implementation: Examples from conservation GIS in Ecuador. *International Journal of Geographical Information Science 14* (8): 715–38.

Massey, D. (1993). Power-geometry and a progressive sense of place. In J. Bird, B. Curtis, T. Putnam, G. Robertson, & L. Tickner (Eds.), *Mapping the future: Local cultures, global change* (59–69). New York: Routledge.

Matthews, S., L. Burton, & J. Detwiler. (2001). *Viewing people and places: Conceptual and methodological issues in coupling geographic information analysis and ethnographic research.* Paper presented at conference on "GIS and Critical Geographic Research," Hunter College, New York, 25 February.

Mattingly, D., & K. Falconer-Al-Hindi. (1995). Should women count? A context for the debate. *The Professional Geographer 47*: 427–35.

McDowell, L. (1993a). Space, place and gender relations. Part 1: Feminist empiricism and the geography of social relations. *Progress in Human Geography 17*: 157–79.

———. (1993b). Space, place and gender relations. Part 2: Identity, difference, feminist geometries and geographies. *Progress in Human Geography 17*: 305–18.

McDowell, L., & G. Court. (1994). Performing work: Bodily representations in merchant banks. *Environment and Planning D 12*: 727–50.

McDowell, L., & J. P. Sharp. (Eds.). (1997). *Space, gender, knowledge: Feminist readings.* London: Arnold.

McLafferty, S. (1995). Counting for women. *The Professional Geographer 47* (4): 436–42.

———. (2002). Mapping women's worlds: Knowledge, power and the bounds of GIS. *Gender, Place and Culture 9* (3): 263–69.

McLafferty, S., & B. Tempalski. (1995). Restructuring and women's reproductive health: Implications for low birth weight in New York City. *Geoforum 26*: 309–23.

Melville, S. (1996). Division of the gaze: Or, remarks on the color and tenor of contemporary "theory." In T. Brennan & M. Jay (Eds.), *Vision in context: Historical and contemporary perspectives on sight,* 102–16. New York: Routledge.

Miller, R. (1995). Beyond method, beyond ethics: Integrating social theory into GIS and GIS into social theory. *Cartography and Geographic Information Systems* 22 (1): 98–103.

Monk, J. (1994). Place matters: Comparative international perspectives on feminist geography. *The Professional Geographer* 46: 277–88.

Morin, K. M., & J. K. Guelke. (1998). Strategies of representation, relationship, and resistance: British women travelers and Mormon wives, ca. 1870–1890. *Annals of the Association of American Geographers* 88 (3): 436–62.

Moss, P. (1995). Embeddedness in practice, numbers in context: The politics of knowing and doing. *The Professional Geographer* 47: 442–49.

———. (2002a). Taking on, thinking about, and doing feminist research in geography. In P. Moss (Ed.), *Feminist geography in practice: Research and methods* (1–17). Oxford: Blackwell.

———. (Ed.). (2002b). *Feminist geography in practice: Research and methods.* Oxford: Blackwell.

Mulvey, L. (1989). *Visual and other pleasures.* London: Macmillan.

Murphy, J. S. (1989). The look in Sartre and Rich. In J. Allen & I. M. Young (Eds.), *The thinking muse: Feminism and modern French philosophy* (101–12). Bloomington: Indiana University Press.

Nash, C. (1994). Remapping the body/land: New cartographies of identity, gender, and landscape in Ireland. In A. Blunt & G. Rose (Eds.), *Writing women and space: Colonial and postcolonial geographies* (227–250). New York: Guilford.

———. (1996). Reclaiming vision: Looking at landscape and the body. *Gender, Place and Culture* 3:149–69.

Nast, H. (1998). The body as "place": Reflexivity and fieldwork in Kano, Nigeria. In H. Nast & S. Pile (Eds.), *Places through the body* (93–116). London: Routledge.

Nast, H., & A. Kobayashi. (1996). Re-corporealizing vision. In N. Duncan (Ed.), *BodySpace: Destabilizing geographies of gender and sexuality* (75–93). New York: Routledge.

Nast, H., & S. Pile. (Eds.). (1998). *Places through the body.* London: Routledge.

Nead, L. (1997). Mapping the self: Gender, space and modernity in mid-Victorian London. *Environment and Planning A* 29: 659–72.

Neumaier, D. (Ed.) (1995). *Reframings: New American feminist photographies.* Philadelphia: Temple University Press.

NVivo. Version 2.0. Qualitative Solutions and Research (QSR) International Pty Ltd., Melbourne, Australia.

Obermeyer, N. J. (Ed.). (1998). Special issue on public participation GIS. *Cartography and Geographic Information Systems* 25 (2): 65–122.

Openshaw, S. (1991). A view of the GIS crisis in geography: Or, using GIS to put Humpty-Dumpty back together again. *Environment and Planning A* 23: 621–28.

Pain, R. (1997). Social geographies of women's fear of crime. *Transactions of the Institute of British Geographers NS* 22: 231–44.

Pavlovskaya, M. E. (2002). Mapping urban change and changing GIS: Other views of economic restructuring. *Gender, Place and Culture* 9 (3): 281–89.

Picard, R. W. (1997). *Affective computing.* Cambridge, MA: The MIT Press.

Pickles, J. (1995). Representations in an electronic age: Geography, GIS, and democracy. In J. Pickles (Ed.), *Ground truth: The social implications of geographic information systems* (1–30). New York: Guilford.

Pile, S. (1996). *The body and the city: Psychoanalysis, space and subjectivity.* London: Routledge.

Pile, S., & N. Thrift. (1995). Mapping the subject. In S. Pile & N. Thrift (Ed.), *Mapping the subject: Geographies of cultural transformation* (13–51). London: Routledge.

Pinder, D. (1996). Subverting cartography: The situationists and maps of the city. *Environment and Planning A 28*: 405–27.

Pollock, G. (1988). *Vision and difference: Femininity, feminism and histories of art.* London: Routledge.

Pratt, G. (1989). Quantitative techniques and humanistic-historical materialist perspectives. In A. Kobayashi & S. MacKenzie (Eds.), *Remaking human geography* (101–15). Boston: Unwin Hyman.

———. (2000). Feminist geographies. In R. J. Johnston, D. Gregory, G. Pratt, & M. Watts (Eds.), *The dictionary of human geography* (259–62). Oxford: Blackwell.

Quattrochi, D. A., & M. F. Goodchild. (Eds.). (1997). *Scale in remote sensing and GIS.* New York: Lewis Publishers.

Roberts, S. M., & R. H. Schein. (1995). Earth shattering: Global imagery and GIS. In J. Pickles (Ed.), *Ground truth: The social implications of geographic information systems* (171–95). New York: Guildford.

Rocheleau, D. (1995). Maps, numbers, text, and context: Mixing methods in feminist political ecology. *The Professional Geographer 47* (4): 458–66.

Rocheleau, D., B. Thomas-Slayter, & D. Edmunds. (1995). Gendered resource mapping: Focusing on women's spaces in the landscape. *Cultural Survival Quarterly 18* (4): 62–68.

Rollinson, P. (1998). The everyday geography of the homeless in Kansas City. *Geografiska Annaler B 80*: 101–15.

Rose, D. (1993). On feminism, method and methods in human geography: An idiosyncratic overview. *The Canadian Geographer 37* (1): 57–61.

Rose, G. (1993). *Feminism and geography: The limits of geographical knowledge.* Minneapolis: University of Minnesota Press.

———. (1995). Making space for the female subject of feminism: The spatial subversions of Holzer, Kruger and Sherman. In S. Pile & N. Thrift (Eds.), *Mapping the subject: Geographies of cultural transformation*, 332–54. London: Routledge.

———. (1997). Situating knowledges: Positionality, reflexivities and other tactics. *Progress in Human Geography 21*: 305–20.

———. (2001). *Visual methodologies: An introduction to the interpretation of visual materials.* London: Sage.

Rundstrom, R. (1995). GIS, indigenous peoples, and epistemological diversity. *Cartography and Geographic Information Systems 22* (1): 45–57.

Schuurman, N. (2000). Trouble in the heartland: GIS and its critics in the 1990s. *Progress in Human Geography 24* (4): 569–90.

————. (2002). Women and technology in geography: A cyborg manifesto for GIS. *The Canadian Geographer 46* (3): 262–65.

Schuurman, N., & G. Pratt. (2002). Care of the subject: Feminism and critiques of GIS. *Gender, Place and Culture 9* (3): 291–99.

Seager, J. (1997). *The state of women in the world atlas*. London: Penguin.

Sheppard, E. (2001). Quantitative geography: Representation, practices and possibilities. *Environment and Planning D 19*: 535–54.

Sheppard, E., H. Couclelis, S. Graham, J. W. Harrington, & O. Harlan. (1999). Geographies of the information society. *International Journal of Geographical Information Science 13* (8): 797–823.

Sheppard, E., & T. Poiker. (Eds.). (1995). Special issue on GIS and society. *Cartography and Geographic Information Systems 22* (1): 3–103.

Sieber, R. E. (2000). Conforming (to) the opposition: The social construction of geographical information systems in social movements. *International Journal of Geographical Information Science 14* (8): 775–93.

Silverman, K. (1983). *The subject of semiotics*. New York: Oxford University Press.

Spain, D. (1992). *Gendered space*. Chapel Hill: University of North Carolina Press.

Sparke, M. (1998). Mapped bodies and disembodied maps: (Dis)placing cartographic struggle in colonial Canada. In H. J. Nast & S. Pile (Eds.), *Places through the body* (305–37). New York: Routledge.

Stacey, J. (1988). Desperately seeking difference. In L. Gamman & M. Marshment (Eds.), *The female gaze* (112–200). London: The Woman's Press.

Staeheli, L., & V. Lawson. (1995). Feminism, praxis, and human geography. *Geographical Analysis 27*: 321–38.

St. Martin, K. (1995). Changing borders, changing cartography: Possibilities for intervening in the new world order. In A. Callari, S. Cullenberg, & C. Biewener (Eds.), *Marxism in the postmodern age: Confronting the new world order* (459–68). New York: Guilford.

Sui, D. Z. (1994). GIS and urban studies: Positivism, post-positivism, and beyond. *Urban Geography 15*: 258–78.

Taylor, P. (1990). Editorial comment: GKS. *Political Geography Quarterly 9*: 211–12.

Timander, L. M., & S. McLafferty. (1998). Breast cancer in West Islip, NY: A spatial clustering analysis with covariates. *Social Science and Medicine 46* (12): 1623–35.

Valentine, G. (1989). The geography of women's fear. *Area 21* (4): 385–90.

————. (1999). A corporeal geography of consumption. *Environment and Planning D 17*: 329–51.

Vasseleu, C. (1996). Illuminating passion: Irigaray's transfiguration of night. In T. Brennan & M. Jay (Eds.), *Vision in context: Historical and contemporary perspectives on sight* (128–37). New York: Routledge.

Wajcman, J. (1991). *Feminism confronts technology*. Cambridge, U.K.: Polity.

Weber, J., & M. P. Kwan. (2002). Bringing time back in: A study on the influence of travel time variations and facility opening hours on individual accessibility. *The Professional Geographer 54* (2): 226–40.

Weiner, D., & T. Harris. (1999). *Community-integrated GIS for land reform in Mpumalanga Province, South Africa.* Paper presented at the International Conference on Geographic Information and Society, University of Minnesota, Minneapolis, Minnesota, 20–22 June.

Weiner, D., T. Harris, & W. Craig. (2002). Community participation and geographic information systems. In W. J. Craig, T. M. Harris, & D. Weiner (Eds.), *Community participation and geographic information systems* (3–16). London: Taylor and Francis.

Winter, S. (2001). Ontology: Buzzword or paradigm shift in GI science? *International Journal of Geographical Information Science 15* (7): 587–90.

Women and Geography Study Group, the Royal Geographical Society with the Institute of British Geographers. (1997). *Feminist geographies: Explorations in diversity and difference.* Harlow, Essex: Addison.

Wesley, L., & Wood, D. (1992). *The power of maps.* New York: Guilford.

Yapa, L. (1998). Why GIS needs postmodern social theory, and vice versa. In D. Ruxton & F. Taylor (Eds.), *Policy issues in modern cartography* (249–69). Oxford: Elsevier Science.

Young, I. M. (1990). *Throwing like a girl and other essays in feminist philosophy and social theory.* Bloomington: Indiana University Press.

8

Practical Strategies for Combining Qualitative and Quantitative Methods

Applications to Health Research

David L. Morgan

Virtually every discussion of the reasons for combining qualitative and quantitative methods begins with the recognition that different methods have different strengths. It is tempting to believe that research projects that combine the strengths of two or more methods will produce more than those same methods could offer in isolation. This possibility is even more appealing when combining qualitative and quantitative methods because this combination maximizes the ability to bring different strengths together in the same research project.

Health researchers have been especially interested in the possibility of combining qualitative and quantitative methods (see the discussions in Carey, 1993; Goering & Steiner, 1996; McKeganey, 1995; Miller & Crabtree, 1994;

From Morgan, D., "Practical Strategies for Combining Qualitative and Quantitative Methods: Applications to Health Research," in *Qualitative Health Research*, 8(3), May 1998, pp. 362–376. Reprinted with permission of Sage Publications, Inc.

Morse, 1991; Stange, Miller, Crabtree, O'Conner, & Zyzanski, 1994; Steckler, McLeroy, Goodman, Bird, & McCormick, 1992). The most likely reason for this interest in multiple methods is the complexity of the many different factors that influence health. Given all the factors that affect virtually every aspect of health and illness, it is easy to appreciate the different strengths that different methods have to offer. Unfortunately, this appealing goal has proved elusive in practice—not just in health research but also in the many other fields that have contributed to the literature on using multiple methods. If health researchers are to succeed in combining qualitative and quantitative methods, this will require research designs that make multiple methods studies much more practical than they are now.

Currently, there are two basic explanations for why it is so difficult to combine qualitative and quantitative methods. The first asserts that combining methods is essentially a technical problem. According to these authors (e.g., Brannen, 1992; Brewer & Hunter, 1989; Bryman, 1984, 1988; Cook & Reichardt, 1979), although it may not be easy to create effective combinations of qualitative and quantitative methods, it is essentially a technical challenge that methodologists should ultimately be able to resolve. As evidence for the viability of research designs that use both qualitative and quantitative data, authors in this tradition cite a string of studies that have done so.

The second explanation argues that the underlying problem in combining comes from conflicts between different paradigms. According to these authors (e.g., Creswell, 1994; Guba & Lincoln, 1994; Smith & Heshusius, 1986), most applications of qualitative and quantitative methods rely on very different assumptions about both the nature of knowledge and the appropriate means of generating knowledge; hence, the kinds of information that they produce are often incommensurate. Authors in this tradition point out that most studies that claim to have combined qualitative and quantitative research have typically ignored paradigm concerns and thus have not addressed these deeper issues.

Reconciling these two explanations requires careful attention to the difference between choosing methods and operating within paradigms. In particular, it is important to realize that most discussions of paradigm issues are not about the practical task of creating research designs that combine qualitative and quantitative methods. Indeed, even a casual reading of those who advocate operating within a single paradigm (e.g., Creswell, 1994; Gilboe-Ford, Campbell, & Berman, 1995; Guba & Lincoln, 1994; Smith & Heshusius, 1986) shows that these authors readily acknowledge the possibility of combining qualitative and quantitative methods. Their real concern lies with any failure to understand the larger differences between qualitative and quantitative approaches to research that go well beyond technical questions about how to use different methods in the same study. Similarly, those who are interested primarily in the technical aspects of combining different methods have also concluded that this can be done without violating basic paradigmatic assumptions (see Riggin, 1997, as well as the various papers in Reichardt & Rallis, 1994).

The present approach acknowledges the importance of paradigms because there is much to be gained from recognizing the deep epistemological differences between qualitative and quantitative approaches to the pursuit of knowledge. Mixing paradigms is indeed a risky business, but this should not be confused with combining methods within a clear-headed understanding of paradigms. If a particular paradigmatic stance provides the framework for a project, then the selection of an appropriate method or combination of methods does become a largely technical task. This article will address that task by introducing a series of practical research designs that can successfully guide efforts to combine qualitative and quantitative methods. As such, it is an example of the technical approach to resolving the difficulties in combining these different methods.

The most important difference between this approach to combining qualitative and quantitative methods and previous technical treatments of this issue is the current emphasis on practical aspects of research design. Much of the existing work on technical issues consists of catalogs of studies that have combined qualitative and quantitative methods (e.g., Bryman, 1988; Sieber, 1973). There has not been enough effort to make sense of the range of options that previous researchers have used, let alone to distill this past experience into a set of guidelines that would assist future work.

In contrast, the present approach highlights a set of practical research designs with a wide range of uses. In particular, for research designs to be practical, they should be (a) reasonably certain to produce fruitful outcomes and (b) ready to be used in a relatively routine fashion. Given this emphasis on practicality, most of what follows is not truly new. What is different here is the emphasis on a small number of fundamental decisions that point directly to a well-defined set of basic research designs. Even if most of what is here amounts to old wine in new bottles, if this presentation succeeds in making this valuable content more accessible to practicing researchers, that will be a considerable achievement in and of itself.

The remainder of this article consists of three basic parts. The next section summarizes a series of different motivations for combining qualitative and quantitative methods, arguing for the practicality of approaches that rely on the complementary use of different methods with different strengths. After that follows a description of research designs along with illustrative examples from existing health research studies. Finally, the concluding section examines a series of current issues and future directions for research that combines multiple methods. This is an admittedly ambitious agenda and this article is actually a summary of a book-length version of these arguments (Morgan, in press), which will consider the uses for this approach in a variety of disciplines including health research.

Motivations for Combining Qualitative and Quantitative Methods

In a particularly systematic review of the literature on combining qualitative and quantitative methods, Greene, Caracelli, and Graham (1989; see also Caracelli & Greene, 1997, and Greene & Caracelli, 1997) point to the importance of distinguishing between broad motivations for combining different methods and specific research designs for meeting these goals. Although the present goal is to generate research designs, such designs must be matched to an appropriate set of motivations for combining qualitative and quantitative methods.

To understand the various motivations for combining methods, it helps to consider the history of this field. Like so many of the ideas that have guided social science methodology over the past several decades, the goal of combining the different strengths of different methods received its major impetus from the work of Donald Campbell and his colleagues. Campbell was especially interested in the question of how to cross-validate results on the same research question by using multiple methods. Important discussions on combining different methods occur in the work that Campbell and his colleagues did on unobtrusive measures (Webb, Campbell, Schwartz, & Sechrest, 1966) and the multitrait-multimethod matrix (Campbell & Fiske, 1959).

What distinguishes the work of Campbell and his colleagues is an emphasis on the convergence or confirmation of results across different methods. In essence, one is conducting two different studies in hopes of coming up with the same conclusions from each, thereby demonstrating that the results are not due simply to an artifact or invalidity associated with a particular method. Denzin's (1970) original work on triangulation is probably the best-known statement of this approach and it is explicitly based on arguments from Webb et al. (1966). Unfortunately, the term *triangulation* has come to have so many meanings (Mitchell, 1986; Sandelowski, 1995) that it is safer to use words like *convergence* or *confirmation* when referring to the goals of seeking cross-validation between methods.

Despite this important early history, the goal of seeking convergent findings has been a rather rare motivation for combining qualitative and quantitative methods in more recent research. One reason for this decrease in interest has been the impasse that arises when results fail to converge (Chesla, 1992; Trend, 1979). This decrease in interest has also been a response to the amount of effort that goes into the fairly limited goal of producing convergent findings. Put simply, most health researchers and others working on applied problems cannot afford to put this much effort into finding the same thing twice.

As researchers have sought alternatives to convergence, one version or another of complementarity has consistently been among the most common motivations for combining qualitative and quantitative methods. The key goal in studies that pursue complementarity is to use the strengths of one method to enhance the performance of the other method. Health researchers are particularly likely to try to connect the strengths of different methods to address the complexity of their research topics—especially when a project's goals include both pure research and applied uses in practice settings.

Unfortunately, the popularity of complementarity has been accompanied by a considerable amount of confusion. One problem has been the lack of specificity in its definition. For example, Greene et al. (1989) said the goal for complementarity is "to measure overlapping but also different facets of a phenomenon, yielding an enriched, elaborated understanding of that phenomenon," while also summarizing its purposes as seeking "elaboration, enhancement, illustration, clarification of the results from one method with the results from the other method" (p. 258–259). The broad scope of this definition makes it possible to invoke complementarity as the underlying justification for an exceedingly wide range of research goals.

Another source of confusion about complementarity has come from practical difficulties in maintaining the balance between methods in such projects. At one extreme, a smaller, complementary method may be merely tacked on to the principal study. At the other extreme, what was originally a complementary study may come to dominate the overall project. Thus, although the intrinsic goal of complementing one method with another is easily stated, specific projects that accomplish this purpose have been harder to design.

Both the popularity of complementarity as a motivation and the confusion about this actual use point to the importance of developing practical research designs based on complementarity. Such designs are the subject of the remainder of this article. It is important to underscore, however, that advancing research designs based on complementarity do not deny the value of other motivations for multimethod research. Sandelowski (1995) provides a useful discussion of different motivations for combining methods, and other discussions on this topic can also be found in Breitmayer et al. (1993), Greene et al. (1989), Morgan (in press), and Rossman and Wilson (1985, 1994).

Research Designs Based on Complementary Assistance

The emphasis in the current approach to combining qualitative and quantitative methods is on research design. The core of this approach is an effort to integrate the complementary strengths of different methods through a division of labor. This amounts to using a qualitative and quantitative method of different but well-coordinated purposes within the same overall research project. This division of labor is accomplished through two basic decisions: a priority decision that pairs a principal method with a complementary method and a sequence decision that determines whether the complementary precedes or follows the principal method.

Both the strategy of assigning priority to one method and the strategy of sequencing the two methods have been included in many of the existing statements about combining qualitative and quantitative methods (Creswell, 1994; Greene et al., 1989; Miles & Huberman, 1994; Morse, 1991; Sieber, 1973). Thus, it bears repeating that the current presentation is a practical integration and simplification of that earlier work, rather than a truly innovative approach to these issues.

The Priority Decision. The first research-design decision determines the extent to which either the qualitative or quantitative method will be the principal tool for gathering the project's data. One obvious but often impractical alternative is to give the two methods equal priority. Although this will create a fully realized data set for each method, it begs the question of how to analyze this combination of data in any coherent fashion (Morse, 1991). Making the two methods equally important leads directly to the requirement for a third effort to connect what was learned from each, along with the additional threat that the knowledge gained from the two methods may be either incommensurate or downright contradictory.

A more practical strategy is to designate one of the methods as the principal means of data collection and then to design the complementary method so that it effectively assists the principal one. This division of labor can use either a qualitative or a quantitative technique as the principal method. The choice of a complementary method then depends on what each candidate might add to the principal method. In other words, the first step in the research design process is to select a principal data collection method that has the strengths that are most important to the project's goals. The second step is to select a contrasting complementary method that offers a set of strengths that can add to the research design's overall ability to meet the project's goals.

This division of labor builds on the recognition that different methods have different strengths. Some projects that are principally quantitative can be strengthened through a well-selected set of complementary qualitative methods, whereas other qualitative projects can be supplemented by the strengths that quantitative methods offer. Of course, there is no requirement that any given project use multiple methods. For many purposes, the strengths of a single well-selected principal method will be entirely sufficient.

The Sequence Decision. The second design decision in this approach concerns the sequence or order in which the qualitative and quantitative data are used. Once again, the real question is how to connect different types of information in ways that maximize their contributions to the success of the overall research project; from a practical point of view, the most difficult design is one that uses both methods simultaneously. Part of the problem is logistical: How do you support two very different field efforts at the same time? More important, however, is the question of how to coordinate what is being learned from the two approaches. Qualitative and quantitative methods operate according to very different time lines, so creating connections between them can be a very complex problem in research design. The more practical strategy is to use the two methods in sequence so that what is learned from one adds to what is learned from the other.

A simple way to decide which method should be used first is to build on the decision about which method will be principal. At the beginning of a project, the basic goal is to optimize the effectiveness of the principal method so that one option is to use preliminary inputs from a different method to improve the main data collection strategy. Near the end of a project, the goal is to maximize the value of what is already in hand, so a second option is to follow up with a different type of information that will add new strengths to the existing data. Thus, sequence decisions depend not so much on whether a complementary method (either qualitative or quantitative) comes first, as a preliminary input to the principal method, or second, as a follow-up to the principal method.

Four Basic Designs. Taken together, the priority and sequence decisions lead to four basic families of research designs, depending on whether (a) the principal method is either qualitative or quantitative and (b) the complementary method occurs as a preliminary or a follow-up stage to the principal method. Taken together, this Priority-Sequence Model produces a 2 x 2 table. Table 8.1 summarizes these four possibilities and provides generic examples of their use in health research.

Because the two priority and sequence decisions that create Table 8.1 have been discovered several times, it is not surprising that the four basic designs

Table 8.1

	Priority Decision	
Complementary Method: *Preliminary Sequence Decision*	1. Qualitative Preliminary qual → QUANT **Purposes:** Smaller qualitative study helps guide the data collection in a principally quantitative study. → can generate hypothesis, develop content for questionnaires and interventions, etc. Example: Focus groups help develop culturally sensitive versions of a new health promotion campaign.	2. Quantitative Preliminary quant → QUAL **Purposes:** Smaller quantitative study helps guide the data collection in a principally qualitative study. → can guide purposive sampling, establish preliminary results to pursue in depth, etc. Example: A survey of different units in a hospital locates sites for more extensive ethnographic data collection.
Complementary Method: *Follow-up*	3. Qualitative Follow-up QUANT → qual **Purposes:** Smaller qualitative study helps evaluate and interpret results from a principally quantitative study. → can provide interpretations for poorly understood results, help explain outliers, etc. Example: In-depth interviews help explain why one clinic generates higher levels of patient satisfaction.	4. Quantitative Follow-u QUAL → quant **Purposes:** Smaller quantitative study helps evaluate and interpret results from a principally qualitative study. → can generalize results to different samples, test elements of emergent theories, etc. Example: A statewide survey of a school-based health program pursues earlier results from a case study.

that result have also been discussed in earlier work. Among those statements, Morse's (1991) statement is well known to health researchers; much of what is presented in this Priority-Sequence Model was already present in her work as well. One especially useful feature of Morse's article is the convenient notion that it provides for summarizing each of the four cells in Table 8.1. In her system, a study's principal method appears in capital letters (shown in Table 8.1 as QUAL and QUANT), and the complementary method is in lowercase letters (shown in Table 8.1 as qual and quant); the ordering of the two methods—joined by an arrow—shows the sequence in which they are used.

Each cell in the Priority-Sequence Model is named for the use of the complementary method associated with that cell. Thus, Cell 1 contains research designs that use a qualitative preliminary study to contribute to a study that is principally quantitative, whereas Cell 2 contains designs that use a quantitative preliminary study to enhance a study that is principally qualitative, and so forth. The remainder of this section describes the research designs represented by the four cells in Table 8.1 and provides an example of health research using each of these basic designs.

The first cell of the Priority-Sequence Model shows research designs in which a smaller, preliminary qualitative study provides complementary assistance in developing a larger quantitative study. Such studies are principally quantitative research, but they begin by using some qualitative methods to improve the effectiveness of the quantitative research that follows. The classic example would be beginning a survey / research project with a qualitative method, such as focus groups, to develop the content of the questionnaire. This would use the strengths of qualitative methods for exploratory work to help ensure that the survey not only covers the important topics but also asks about them in an appropriate fashion. By the same logic, preliminary qualitative data can also help ensure the effectiveness of experimental and quasi-experimental designs. For example, it might be possible to improve the effectiveness of an intervention program by conducting preliminary qualitative research about how to match the program's goals to the needs and preferences of people who participate in it.

A concrete, health-related example of a study using a preliminary qualitative design is O'Brien's (1993) use of focus groups to develop the content for a survey of gay and bisexual men on the topic of AIDS/HIV. O'Brien describes in some detail how she used the focus group discussions to generate questionnaire items related to such topics as safer sex and personal relationships. She also discusses how the focus groups contributed to her larger project by providing insight into recruitment issues. Because gay and bisexual individuals can be a difficult population to locate, the focus groups provided valuable information about possible routes for locating survey respondents as well as useful advice about how to conduct the recruitment for the survey in a nonthreatening way. (Other health-related examples of complementary designs that use preliminary qualitative studies include the development of survey instruments by Bauman & Adair, 1992, and Fultz & Herzog, 1993, as well as the development of intervention programs by De Vries, Weijts, Dijkstra, & Kok, 1992, and Hughes, Lawther, & Eadie, 1996.)

Moving across to the second cell, these designs use preliminary quantitative methods to contribute to a principally qualitative study. In this case, the knowledge provided by an initial small-scale use of quantitative methods helps to guide the decisions that the researcher makes in the larger qualitative research project. The classic example is a preliminary survey or census of a field setting either to guide the selection of sites and informants or to provide a context for understanding the contacts that one does make. Preliminary quantitative results can also help focus the analysis of large amounts of qualitative data. For example, if tabulations from a preliminary survey reveal interesting patterns of association, a detailed qualitative analysis can provide a much richer understanding of why these patterns exist or how they operate.

Dimond, Caserta, and Lund (1994) provide an example of a preliminary quantitative study in their investigation of factors that influenced levels of depression among older, bereaved spouses. Using a larger survey, Dimond et al. used standardized scores on an assessment to select five respondents who had a uniformly low level of depression during their first 2 years of widowhood and another five respondents who had a uniformly high level of depression in that same period. In-depth qualitative interviews revealed that the major difference between the two groups was the importance of additional life events among those who had consistently high levels of depression. Dimond et al. then discuss the implications of the impacts of further, more recent losses. (Other health-related examples of complementary designs that used preliminary quantitative studies to generate purposive samples for largely qualitative investigations are Hough, Lewis, & Woods, 1991, and Millette, 1993.)

The third cell returns to qualitative methods that complement a principally quantitative research effort, but in this case, they serve as a follow-up to the quantitative study. Here, the qualitative methods typically provide interpretive resources for understanding the results from the quantitative research. One classic example would be using qualitative methods to learn why a poorly functioning intervention program did not work as well as expected. Follow-up qualitative data can also provide insights into why strongly held hypotheses did not prove out in survey research. Weinholtz, Kacer, and Rocklin (1995) refer to such designs as using qualitative data to salvage quantitative work. For example, if the results of a survey contradict the original hypotheses, it may make sense to elicit an explanation from the respondents who provided the data rather than engage in isolated speculation about what went wrong.

An example of a follow-up qualitative design is Ornstein et al.'s (1993) use of focus groups to investigate the results of an unsuccessful intervention program that encouraged people to come in for preventive cholesterol screenings. The intervention study used patients' birthdays as a landmark event for sending out letters that suggested that they come in for a screening. As often happens with mail-out reminder programs, these letters were widely ignored. Rather than simply accepting this pessimistic outcome, Ornstein et al. conducted four follow-up focus groups among people who had not responded, with the goal of learning how the researchers could improve the effectiveness of such mailings. One problem that they uncovered was that the letter was perceived as an unexpected bill. The groups also pointed out ways to improve the content and the format of the reminder letter itself, along with the importance of providing patients with an easy way to make that appointment. (Another example of a complementary design that used a follow-up qualitative study is described in Stange et al., 1994; this involved a qualitative investigation of why a diabetes intervention program was effective for only a subset of the patients.)

The final cell consists of designs that use complementary quantitative studies to follow up on research projects that are principally qualitative. Here, the quantitative methods provide a means to expand on what was learned through the qualitative study. The classic use for this design is to explore the generalizability or transferability of conclusions from qualitative research. For example, proponents of case studies often want to know something about the relevance of their observations beyond the specific limits of that one group of people at that one point in time (i.e., the transferability of their results). Even a small quantitative follow-up can typically cover a much larger sample or range of settings than were present in the initial, in-depth qualitative research.

Borkan, Quirk, and Sullivan (1991) provide a health-related example of a follow-up quantitative study. By analyzing narrative interviews with hip-fracture patients, Borkan et al. developed an explanatory model that showed systematic differences in how patients thought about both the causes of their problem and the factors affecting their recovery. They then collected data from brief surveys on activities of daily living (ADLs) at several points after the patients' injuries. The patients' statements with regard to the key themes in the narrative analysis were consistently related to their level of ADL functioning. Borkan et al. were thus able to demonstrate that hip-fracture patients' ways of making meaning of their falls had important effects on their recovery. (Another example of a complementary design that used a follow-up qualitative study is Nichols-Casebolt & Spakes, 1995, who first used detailed qualitative interviews to discover women's perspectives on families in crisis and then located secondary quantitative data that would help convince policy makers of the importance of their finding.)

Current Issues and Future Directions

Although there are many ways to make complementary uses of qualitative and quantitative methods, the four possibilities in the Priority-Sequence Model of Table 8.1 summarize much of the existing work in this area. Some of these designs are, however, more common than others. At present, the most frequently used designs are those in Cell 1: preliminary qualitative studies to complement research that is principally quantitative. Examples of the designs in Cells 2 and 3 are less common but still relatively easy to find. Designs matching Cell 2 are used by anthropologists, especially those working in the area of health (e.g., Pelto & Pelto, 1978), who frequently begin with brief quantitative studies prior to more intensive qualitative fieldwork. Designs using Cell 3 are increasingly common among surveys researchers, who use qualitative follow-up interviews to expand on what was learned from the analysis of their questionnaires.

It is instructive that the least common and most problematic designs are those associated with Cell 4, in which follow-up quantitative research complements a principally qualitative study. One notable problem is that such designs promote the perception that qualitative results must be treated as tentative until they are confirmed by qualitative research (Morse, 1996). Arguably, this is largely a matter of perception. There is nothing about these designs that implies that qualitative research is inadequate or incomplete; instead the argument is that qualitative methods have a different set of strengths that can, in some cases and for some purposes, add to what is achieved through qualitative research alone. Yet, because qualitative researchers feel that they have been attacked in the past about the ability of their work to stand on its own, they are understandably sensitive to any implication that their work requires supplementation.

Of course, the logic of the Priority-Sequence Model in Table 8.1 also argues that quantitative projects are equally likely to benefit from a complementary use of qualitative methods, but that claim can also cause problems. For example, one might misinterpret the present framework as claiming that qualitative methods are most useful as a supplement to quantitative work, simply because the designs in Cell 1 are currently the most common. Yet from the present perspective, preliminary qualitative studies are but one of four equally useful possibilities.

The broader point here is that assertions about the value of research designs raise political as well as technical issues. Designs from both Cell 1 and Cell 4 are tied to political issues about the relative standing of qualitative and quantitative methods within the social sciences. It would be nice to believe that in an apolitical and ahistorical world, researchers would be equally likely to use all four designs from the Priority-Sequence Model. Obviously, we do not live in such a world, and political considerations make some of these designs easier to get funded and published than others. As long as this is so, qualitative researchers (and quantitative ones as well) are quite right to make sure that the value of their work is not misunderstood or denigrated.

These questions about the relative standing of qualitative and quantitative methods reflect the long-standing debate between the partisans of these two different approaches to research. Unfortunately, debates about using either qualitative or quantitative methods in isolation can easily lead to mistaken conclusions about how to use them in combination. In particular, outspoken advocacy for either qualitative or quantitative methods as the one true way almost inherently leads to a rejection of any attempt to combine them. Clearly, there is a great deal of political as well as technical work that needs to be done to pave the path for combining qualitative and quantitative methods. The efforts to address these ideological rifts are, however, quite different from the technical goals set out here.

In considering what this presentation has accomplished, it is important to reiterate that the four designs in the Priority-Sequence Model are not the only or even necessarily the best ways to combine qualitative and quantitative methods. What is best depends entirely on the goals of a given research project. These designs are specifically tailored to purposes associated with complementary combinations of methods, but as the earlier discussion indicated, there are a variety of other motivations for combining qualitative and quantitative methods. Although variations on the four designs in the Priority-Sequence Model may be useful for these other purposes, it is just as likely that other motivations will call for designs that go beyond anything discussed here.

What might some of these further designs be? One obvious limitation of the schema in Table 8.1 is that it deliberately omits the middle options of either giving qualitative and quantitative data equal priority or using them both at the same time. Using these middle options, it would be entirely possible to design a project in which neither method had priority over the other and both were used simultaneously. It may make sense to call this design true triangulation. The current emphasis on complementarity argues that true triangulation is often not the most useful design for combining quantitative and qualitative data—at least at present. Instead, designs that achieve complementarity through a division of labor, such as those in the Priority-Sequence Model, are often easier to implement and more likely to lead to productive combinations of qualitative and quantitative data. In other words, they are more practical.

Of course, one does not have to proceed all the way to true triangulation to develop further extensions of the four basic designs in the

Priority-Sequence Model of Table 8.1. There clearly can be designs that maintain a division of labor between a principal method and a complementary method while using the two together rather than in sequence. Morse (1991) offers a notation for such designs that replaces the arrow from sequencing with a plus sign; for example, QUAL+quant would indicate a smaller quantitative study that was essentially simultaneous with a larger qualitative study. Alternatively, it is quite possible to create a largely sequential division of labor between two methods that both receive relatively equal priority. These options amount to possibilities that lie somewhere between true triangulation and the present use of both priority and sequence decisions. If we learn how to design projects that effectively and routinely combine qualitative and quantitative methods without relying on either a priority decision or a sequence decision, then this may lead toward practical approaches to true triangulation.

Even if social scientists do manage to develop a set of practical and effective designs for combining qualitative and quantitative methods, there is still the question of who will do the work. How reasonable is it that one person would have the necessary expertise to direct all aspects of such a study? Within the division of labor approach presented here, it is at least possible that one person would have all the requisite skills. In particular, because one of the methods is being used only in a complementary fashion, complete mastery of that method may not be necessary.

At this point, the best way to support studies that combine methods is often to create a team that combines expertise, but the designs based on complementarity in the Priority-Sequence Model can present a distinct difficulty for teams. The problem is that these designs ask one set of professionals to subordinate their skills into a secondary role. Signs of this tension already exist in the most prevalent of the current combinations from Table 8.1—the use of qualitative methods as preliminary input into a larger quantitative project (e.g., Laurie & Sullivan, 1991). For a team-based approach to work, there have to be clear expectations about what each piece of the work consists of and why it is being done. The researchers in charge of the principal method need to be very clear about what they are asking from the other members of the team, and those in charge of the complementary method need to have a clear understanding of what they are being asked to do.

A different approach to integrating the resources that are necessary in mixed-methods studies is creating specific roles for those who have expertise in combining qualitative and quantitative methods. Rather than requiring that such boundary crossers be equally expert in both methods, this approach would emphasize a new set of skills related to coordinating combinations of qualitative and quantitative methods. As evidence that there is nothing new under the sun, it has been more than 50 years since Paul Lazarfeld (1944) explicitly called for experts such as these to shuttle back and forth between qualitative interviewing and survey research.

This discussion of whether the expertise to combine qualitative and quantitative methods should exist within individual researchers or teams is based on further presumption that is worth examining: The proper approach to combining methods lies within a specific research project. One alternative would be to achieve integration across a researcher's larger program of studies. A researcher could thus pursue a program of studies that alternated between qualitative and quantitative projects devoted to the same phenomenon (e.g., Rank, 1992). This form of integration amounts to a variation on the sequencing of different methods. Another alternative to integration at the project level would be to pursue the integration of the qualitative and quantitative research across a field of studies. In that case, experts in each method would concentrate on their own technical expertise, but they would use the knowledge produced by other methods as inputs to their own work. One example of this approach is Rotter and Frankel's (1992) integrated review of qualitative and quantitative research on the medical dialogue.

The last alternative raises questions about the extent to which we now create isolated pools of knowledge—some from qualitative research traditions and some from quantitative research traditions. Why this is so once again raises issues that go well beyond the goals of this article. Even so, it would be hard to argue in favor of a Tower of Babel approach, in which researchers pursue similar issues while purposely limiting their ability to communicate with each other. In this vein, some have claimed that the forms of knowledge produced by qualitative and quantitative approaches are so incommensurate that such communication truly is impossible. This is, however, an empirical question, and not a matter of purpose philosophy. Until we, as researchers, investigate what it takes to combine qualitative and quantitative methods, we will never know what is possible.

References

Bauman, L. J., & Adair, E. G. (1992). The use of ethnographic interviewing to inform survey construction. *Health Education Quarterly, 19,* 9–23.

Borkan, J. M., Quirk, M., & Sullivan, M. (1991). Finding meaning after the fall: Injury narratives from elderly hip fracture patients. *Social Science and Medicine, 33,* 947–957.

Brannen, J. (1992). Combining qualitative and quantitative methods: An overview. In J. Brannen (Ed.), *Mixing methods: Qualitative and quantitative research* (pp. 3–38). Brookfield, VT: Avebury.

Breitmayer, B. J., Ayres, L., & Knafl, K. A. (1993). Triangulation in qualitative research: Evaluation of completeness and confirmation purposes. *IMAGE: Journal of Nursing Scholarship, 25,* 237–243.

Brewer, J., & Hunter, A. (1989). *Multimethod research: A synthesis of styles.* Newbury Park, CA: Sage.

Bryman, A. (1984). The debate about quantitative and qualitative methods: A question of method or epistemology? *British Journal of Sociology, 35,* 75–92.

——(1988). *Quantity and quality in social research.* Boston: Unwin Hyman.

Campbell, D. T., & Fiske, D. W. (1959). Convergent and discriminant validity in the multitrait-multimethod matrix. *Psychological Bulletin, 56,* 81–105.

Caracelli, V. J., & Greene, J. C. (1997). Crafting mixed-method evaluation designs. In J. C. Greene & V. J. Caracelli (Eds.), *Advances in mixed methods evaluation: The challenges and benefits of integrating diverse paradigms* (pp. 19–32). San Francisco: Jossey-Bass.

Carey, J. (1993). Linking qualitative and quantitative methods: Integrating cultural factors into public health. *Qualitative Health Research, 3,* 298–318.

Chesla, C. A. (1992). When qualitative and quantitative findings do not converge. *Western Journal of Nursing, 14,* 681–685.

Cook, T. D., & Reichardt, C. S. (1979). *Qualitative and quantitative methods in evaluation research.* Beverly Hills, CA: Sage.

Creswell, J. W. (1994). *Research design: Qualitative and quantitative approaches.* Thousand Oaks, CA: Sage.

Denzin, N. K. (1970). *The research act: A theoretical introduction to sociological methods.* Chicago: Aldine.

DeVries, H., Weijts, W., Dijkstra, M., & Kok, G. (1992). The utilization of qualitative and quantitative data for health education program planning, implementation, and evaluation: A spiral approach. *Health Education Quarterly, 19,* 101–115.

Dimond, M., Caserta, M., & Lund, D. (1994). Understanding depression in bereaved older adults. *Clinical Nursing Research, 3,* 253–268.

Fultz, N. F., & Herzog, A. R. (1993). Measuring urinary incontinence in surveys. *The Gerontologist, 33,* 708–713.

Gilboe-Ford, M., Campbell, J., & Berman, H. (1995). Stories and numbers: Coexistence without compromise. *Advances in Nursing Science, 18,* 14–26.

Goering, P. N., & Steiner, D. L. (1996). Reconcilable differences: The marriage of qualitative and quantitative methods. *Canadian Journal of Psychiatry, 41,* 491–497.

Greene, J. C., & Caracelli, V. J. (1997). Defining and describing the paradigm issue in mixed method evaluation. In J. C. Greene & V. J. Caracelli (Eds.), *Advances in mixed methods evaluation: The challenges and benefits of integrating diverse paradigms* (pp. 5–18). San Francisco: Jossey-Bass.

Greene, J. C., Caracelli, V. J., & Graham, W. F. (1989). Toward a conceptual framework for mixed-method evaluation designs. *Educational Evaluation and Policy Analysis, 11,* 255–274.

Guba, E. G., & Lincoln, Y. S. (1994). Competing paradigms in qualitative methods. In N. Denzin & Y. Lincoln (Eds.), *Handbook of qualitative research* (pp. 105–117). Thousand Oaks, CA: Sage.

Hough, E. E., Lewis, F. M., & Woods, N. F. (1991). Family response to mother's chronic illness: Case studies of well- and poorly-adjusted families. *Western Journal of Nursing Research, 13*, 568–596.

Hughes, K., Lawther, S., & Eadie, D. (1996). Social marketing in practice: Drug culture, bridging the knowledge gap between parents and teenagers. In C. Bryant & T. Albrecth (Eds.), *Proceedings of the 5th annual conference on social marketing in public health* (pp. 174–189). Tampa: University of South Florida, Department of Community & Family Health.

Laurie, H., & Sullivan, O. (1991). Combining qualitative and quantitative methods in the longitudinal study of household allocations. *Sociological Review, 39*, 113–139.

Lazarsfeld, P. F. (1944). The controversy over detailed interviews: An offer for negotiation. *Public Opinion Quarterly, 8*, 38–60.

McKeganey, N. (1995). Editorial: Quantitative and qualitative research in the addictions: An unhelpful divide? *Addiction, 90*, 749–751.

Miles, M. B., & Huberman, A. M. (1994). *Qualitative data analysis: An expanded sourcebook* (2nd ed.). Thousand Oaks, CA: Sage.

Miller, W. L., & Crabtree, B. F. (1994). Clinical research. In N. Denzin & Y. Lincoln (Eds.), *Handbook of qualitative research* (pp. 340–352). Thousand Oaks, CA: Sage.

Millette, B. E. (1993). Client advocacy and the moral orientation of nurses. *Western Journal of Nursing Research, 15*, 607–618.

Mitchell, E. S. (1986). Multiple triangulation: A methodology for nursing science. *Advances in Nursing Science, 8*, 18–26.

Morgan, D. L. (in press). *Practical strategies for combining qualitative and quantitative methods.* Thousand Oaks, CA: Sage.

Morse, J. M. (1991). Approaches to qualitative-quantitative triangulation. *Nursing Research, 40*, 120–123.

——(1996). Editorial: Is qualitative research complete? *Qualitative Health Research, 6*, 3–5.

Nichols-Casebolt, A., & Spakes, P. (1995). Policy research and the voices of women. *Social Work Research, 19*, 49–55.

O'Brien, K. J. (1993). Using focus groups to develop health surveys: An example from research on social relationships and AIDS-preventive behavior. *Health Education Quarterly, 20*, 361–372.

Ornstein, S. M., Musham, C., Reid, A., Jerkins, R. G., Zemp, L. D., & Garr, D. R. (1993). Barriers to adherence to preventive services reminder letters: The patient's perspective. *Journal of Family Practice, 36*, 195–200.

Pelto, P. J., & Pelto, G. H. (1978). *Anthropological research: The structure of inquiry.* Cambridge, UK: Cambridge University Press.

Rank, M. R. (1992). The blending of qualitative and quantitative methods in understanding childbearing among welfare recipients. In J. F. Gilgun, K. Daly, & G. Handel (Eds.), *Qualitative methods in family research* (pp. 281–300). Newbury Park, CA: Sage.

Reichardt, C. S., & Rallis, S. F. (1994). *The qualitative quantitative debate: New perspectives.* San Francisco: Jossey-Bass.

Riggin, J. C. (1997). Advances in mixed methods evaluation: A synthesis and comment. In J. C. Greene & V. J. Caracelli (Eds.), *Advances in mixed methods evaluation: The challenges and benefits of integrating diverse paradigms* (pp. 87–94). San Francisco: Jossey-Bass.

Rossman, G. B., & Wilson, B. L. (1985). Numbers and words: Combining quantitative and qualitative methods in a single large scale evaluation. *Evaluation Review, 9,* 627–643.

———(1994). Numbers and words revisited: Being shamelessly eclectic. *Quality & Quantity, 28,* 315–327.

Rotter, D., & Frankel, R. (1992). Quantitative and qualitative approaches to the evaluation of the medical dialog. *Social Science and Medicine, 34,* 1097–1103.

Sandelowski, M. (1995). Triangles and crystals: On the geometry of qualitative research. *Research on Nursing and Health, 18,* 569–574.

Sieber, S. D. (1973). The integration of fieldwork and survey methods. *American Journal of Sociology, 78,* 1335–1359.

Smith, J. K., & Heshusius, L. (1986). Closing down the conversation: The end of the qualitative-quantitative debate among educational inquirers. *Educational Researcher, 15,* 4–12.

Stange, K. C., Miller, W. L., Crabtree, B. F., O'Conner, P. J., & Zyzanski, S. J. (1994). Multimethod research: Approaches to integrating qualitative and quantitative methods. *Archives of General Internal Medicine, 9,* 278–282.

Steckler, A., McLeroy, K. R., Goodman, R. M., Bird, S. T., & McCormick, L. (1992). Toward integrating qualitative and quantitative methods: An introduction. *Health Education Quarterly, 19,* 1–8.

Trend, M. G. (1979). On the reconciliation of qualitative and quantitative analyses: A case study. In T. D. Cook & C. S. Reichardt (Eds.), *Qualitative and quantitative methods in evaluation research* (pp. 68–86). Beverly Hills, CA: Sage.

Webb, E. J., Campbell, D. T., Schwartz, R. D., & Sechrest, L. (1966). *Unobtrusive measures: Nonreactive research in the social sciences.* Chicago: Rand McNally.

Weinholtz, D., Kacer, B., & Rocklin, T. (1995). Salvaging quantitative research with qualitative data. *Qualitative Health Research, 5,* 388–397.

9

Performing Autoethnography

An Embodied Methodological Praxis

Tami Spry

This article argues the personal/professional/political emancipatory potential of autoethnographic performance as a method of inquiry. Autoethnographic performance is the convergence of the "autobiographic impulse" and the "ethnographic moment" represented through movement and critical self-reflexive discourse in performance, articulating the intersections of peoples and culture through the inner sanctions of the always migratory identity. The article offers evaluative standards for the autoethnographic performance methodology, calling on the body as a site of scholarly awareness and corporeal literacy. Autoethnographic performance makes us acutely conscious of how we "I-witness" our own reality constructions. Interpreting culture through the self-reflections and cultural refractions of identity is a defining feature of autoethnographic performance.

From Spry, T., "Performing Autoethnography: An Embodied Methodological Praxis," in *Qualitative Inquiry*, 7(6), 2001, pp. 706–732. Reprinted with permission of Sage Publications, Inc.

In autobiographical narrative performances, the performer often speaks about acts of social transgression. In doing so, the telling of the story itself becomes a transgressive act—a revealing of what has been kept hidden, a speaking of what has been silenced—an act of reverse discourse that struggles with the preconceptions borne in the air of dominant politics. (Park-Fuller, 2000, p. 26)

 Autoethnography is a form of critique and resistance that can be found in diverse literatures such as ethnic autobiography, fiction, memoir, and texts that identify zones of contact, conquest, and the contested meanings of self and culture that accompanies the exercise of representational authority. (Neuman, 1996, p. 191)

Performance thrills me, theory does not. I would surely lose myself without performance, but I cannot live well without theory. (Madison, 1999, p. 109)

Being There

"Threshold"

Strange
right,
wrong,
odd
tensive,   dialectical,   liminal
that I am at NCA
nine days
before the trip to Chile
where I am to begin ethnographic fieldwork
with Chilean shaman.

I am not there,
but I am not here either.
NCA is a world I am expected to "report back to"
for critical evaluation,
for verisimilitude,
                    for promotion.

Clifford Geertz (1988) writes of fieldwork,
"Being There is a postcard experience.
It is Being Here, a scholar among scholars
that gets your anthropology read . . .
published, reviewed, cited, taught" (p. 130).

Trihn Mih-ha (1991) writes, "Knowledge is no knowledge
until it bears the seal
of the Master's approval" (p. 85).

I can relate to my
Sisters in the Academy
(itself a transgressive phrase),
Blair, Brown, and Baxter (1994)
when they write,
"If the professional disciplinary rules that we have specified
were to find absolute adherence, this essay would have been
    derailed by now,
for it already has revealed something of the history of its production,
hinted at a motivation grounded in anger,
and staked for itself an explicitly politicized position"
(p. 384).

There is danger here in this world,
The Academy,
as it conferences in the gilded plastic of the luxury hotel;
And in spite of myself,
my shadow selves
can still be seduced
by its empty opulence,
even when it feels like
an unkind,   disembodied,   scriptocentric,   technocratic
consumer
of knowledge.

bell hooks might call this "eating the Other,"
consuming ourselves
with monologues about what should be endorsed,
authenticated,
and marked
as scholarship.

Being Here

This autoethnography was first performed at the National Communication
Association Convention just days before I was to leave for Chile and ascend

the Andes with a Chilean shaman trained in the Mapuche traditions, to begin ethnographic research on the efficacy of performance in healing rituals. For me, autoethnographic texts express more fully the interactional textures occurring between self, other, and contexts in ethnographic research.

I have begun creating a self in and out of academe that allows expression of passion and spirit I have long suppressed. However academically heretical this performance of selves may be, I have learned that heresy is greatly maligned and, when put to good use, can begin a robust dance of agency in one's personal/political/professional life. So, in seeking to dis-(re)-cover my body and voice in all parts of my life, I began writing and performing autoethnography, concentrating on the body as the site from which the story is generated, thus beginning the methodological praxis of reintegrating my body and mind into my scholarship.

For me, performing autoethnography has been a vehicle of emancipation from cultural and familial identity scripts that have structured my identity personally and professionally. Performing autoethnography has encouraged me to dialogically look back upon my self as other, generating critical agency in the stories of my life, as the polyglot facets of self and other engage, interrogate, and embrace. The previous autoethnography, "Threshold," along with its following sections, articulates the identity fractures and acute liminality I often experience in the days before ethnographic fieldwork, or while in the threshold of Clifford Geertz's (1988) notion of "Being Here" and "Being There."

In this essay, through a weave of performative autoethnographic poetry and theoretical prose, I articulate the personally/politically emancipatory potential of autoethnographic performance, intervening, as Mary Louise Pratt (1994) notes, "on metropolitan modes of understanding" (p. 28). First, I offer a discussion of autoethnography as a methodology of scholarly praxis, including evaluative criteria for autoethnography. Second, dialogic performance and performativity in autoethnographic performance is discussed. Finally, I explore the emancipatory potential of autoethnographic performance, and its use as a method of inquiry.

This article reflects my continuing process of integrating the "doing" of autoethnography with critical reflection upon autoethnography as a methodological praxis. I believe the "doing" of autoethnography and its explication benefit by this integration. For that reason, I braid some of my autoethnographic work—subheaded "BEING THERE" as a rift off Geertz's (1988) discussions—and talk about the work of autoethnography—subheaded "BEING HERE"—throughout the article. It is interesting and not surprising that I find the authorial voice in the autoethnographic texts (BEING THERE) far more engaging due to its emotional texturing of theory and its reliance upon poetic structure to suggest a live participative embodied researcher. Though emotion and poetics constitute scholarly treason, it is heresy put to good use. And it is heresy I continue to attempt to commit in the "BEING HERE" of my own scholarly reflection.

Being There

"Threshold"

> Marianna Torgovnick (1990) says, "What is clear now
> is that the West's fascination with the primitive
> has to do with its own crisis of identity,
> with its own need to clearly demarcate   subject   and   object
> even while flirting with other ways
> of experiencing the universe" (p. 96).

> This flirting
> with the exotic "Other"
> becomes abusive
> in its objectifying

> salacious

> condescension.

> A story is *not* just a story, writes Trihn (1989).
> Once the forces have been aroused and set into motion,
> they can't simply be stopped at someone's request

Being Here

Autoethnography

Autoethnography can be defined as a self-narrative that critiques the situatedness of self with others in social contexts. Autoethnography is both a method and a text of diverse interdisciplinary praxes (Reed-Danahay, 1997). Its roots trace the postmodern "crisis of representation" in anthropological writing (Behar & Gordon, 1995; Clifford, 1988; Clifford & Marcus, 1986; Conquergood, 1985, 1991, 1998; Geertz, 1973, 1988; Marcus & Fischer, 1986; Myerhoff, 1979, 1982; Trihn, 1989, 1991; Turner, 1982, 1987) where autoethnography is a radical reaction to realist agendas in ethnography and sociology "which privilege," writes Norman K. Denzin (1992), "the researcher over the subject, method over subject matter, and maintain commitments to outmoded conceptions of validity, truth, and generalizability" (p. 20). Autoethnographic writing resists Grand Theorizing and the facade of objective research that decontextualizes subjects and searches for singular truth (Crawford, 1996; Denzin, 1997; Ellis & Bochner, 1996; Ellis & Flaherty, 1992; Goodall, 1991a, 1991b, 1998; Neuman, 1996; Reed-Danahay, 1997; Secklin, 1997). "Autoethnography synthesizes both a postmodern ethnography," writes Deborah Reed-Danahay (1997), "and a postmodern autobiography. [It] opens up new ways of writing about social life" (pp. 2–3).

Autoethnography is further informed by research on oral and personal narratives in performance and communication studies, situating the socio-politically inscribed body as a central site of meaning making (Alexander, 2000; Bauman, 1986; Dailey, 1998; Fine, 1984; Gingrich-Philbrook, 1998; Langellier, 1989, 1998, 1999; Langellier & Peterson, 1992; Madison, 1993; Minister, 1991; Park-Fuller, 2000; Pelias, 1999). Performance studies scholar Kristin Langellier's work has been foundational in the knowledge construction of personal narratives providing theoretically fecund grounding for autoethnographic performance. "Personal narrative performance gives shape to social relations, but because such relations are multiple, polysemic, complexly interconnected, and contradictory, it can do so only in unstable and destabilizing ways for narrator *and* audience . . . a story of the body told through the body which makes cultural conflict concrete" (Langellier, 1999, p. 208).

More than a decade of cultural and autobiographical studies has extensively problematized narrative representation of hegemonized voices (Anzuldua, 1990; James & Busia, 1993; Jerome & Satin, 1999; Jones, 1997; Morago & Anzuldua, 1983; Personal Narratives Group, 1989; Simpson, 1996; Smith, 1993). Mary Louis Pratt (1986) argues that autoethnography originates as a discourse from the margins of dominant culture—at which academe is central—identifying the material, political, and transformational dimensions of representational politics. Informed by recent work in autobiography, autoethnographic methods recognize the reflections and refractions of multiple selves in contexts that arguably transform the authorial "I" to an existential "we."

The dynamic and dialectical relation of the text and body emerge as a major theme in autoethnographic praxes. In the fieldwork, writing, and performing of autoethnography, text and body are redefined, their boundaries blurring dialectically (Conquergood, 1991). The living body/subjective self of the researcher is recognized as a salient part of the research process, and sociohistorical implications of the researcher are reflected upon "to study the social world from the perspective of the interacting individual" (Denzin, 1997, p. xv). Ethnographer Ruth Behar (1997), working from the writings of George Devereux, asserts, "*What happens within the observer* must be made known, Devereux insisted, if the nature of what has been observed is to be understood" (p. 6). The researcher, in context, interacting with others, becomes the subject of research, blurring distinctions of personal and social, self and other (Conquergood, 1991; Ellis & Bochner, 1996; Richardson, 1992), and reevaluating the "dialectics of self and culture" (Neuman, 1996, p. 193). "Experience, discourse, and self-understanding," writes Trihn Mihn-ha (1991), "collide against larger cultural assumptions concerning race, ethnicity, nationality, gender, class, and age" (p. 157).

The autoethnographic text emerges from the researcher's bodily stand-point as she is continually recognizing and interpreting the residue traces of culture inscribed upon her hide from interacting with others in contexts. This corporeally textual orientation rejects the notion that "lived experience can only be represented indirectly, through quotations from field notes, observa-tions or interviews" (Denzin, 1992, p. 20). In autoethnographic methods, the researcher is the epistemological and ontological nexus upon which the research process turns.

Autoethnographers argue that self-reflexive critique upon one's position-ality as researcher inspires readers to reflect critically upon their own life experience, their constructions of self, and their interactions with others within sociohistorical contexts (Ellis & Bochner, 1996; Goodall, 1998). This has certainly been the case for me in making critical, political, and personal sense of my experiences with sexual assault, grief, mental illness, and White privilege (Spry, 1995, 1997, 1998, 2000, 2001). Performing autoethnography has allowed me to position myself as active agent with narrative authority over many hegemonizing dominant cultural myths that restricted my social freedom and personal development, also causing me to realize how my Whiteness and class membership can restrict the social freedom and personal development of others.

Being There

"Threshold"

Performing artist Carlos Nakai believes that White people have forgotten their

stories.

I would say,

it's not that we have forgotten our stories,

but rather,
we don't want to hear them.
We do not believe them.
They do not constitute . . . knowledge.
They do not compute.

The kinds of stories Nakai refers to,
no matter how well written, argued, and performed,
do not
stratify,
    ratify,
        and phallosize
the study of human experience.
Rather, these "unbelievable" stories
stand in multivocal contrast
to the work of
academic colonizers
who still purport a realist agenda
for direct access to Reality.

Being Here

Autoethnographic texts reveal the fractures, sutures, and seams of self inter-acting with others in the context of researching lived experience. In interpret-ing the autoethnographic text, readers feel/sense the fractures in their own communicative lives, and like Gramsci's notion of the organic intellectual, create efficacy and healing in their own communal lives. Thirteen years after I was sexually assaulted, profound healing began when I started to rewrite that experience as a woman with strength and agency rather than accepting the victimage discourse of sexual assault embedded in our phallocentric language—and, thus, value—systems (Spry, 1995). This kind of transforma-tive and efficacious potential for researcher, researched, and reader/audience is a primary goal of effective autoethnography in print and performance.

So, what is effective autoethnography? What constitutes a good autoethnography? First, as in any evaluation of any literary genre, the writ-ing must be well crafted and "capable of being respected by critics of litera-ture as well as by social scientists" (Denzin, 1997, p. 200). Mediocre writing in any venue lacks the ability to transform readers and transport them into a place where they are motivated to look back upon their own person-ally political identity construction. Second, good autoethnography must be emotionally engaging (Behar, 1997; Ellis, 1997; Ronai, 1992) *as well as* critically self-reflexive of one's sociopolitical interactivity. Goodall (1998) argues that "good autoethnography strives to use *relational* language and styles to create purposeful *dialogue* between the reader and the author. This dialogue proceeds through close, personal identification—and recognition of difference—of the reader's experiences, thoughts, and emotions with those of the author" (p. 7).

Reflecting on the subjective self in context with others is the scholarly sagaciousness offered by autoethnography. Good autoethnography is not simply a confessional tale of self-renewal; it is a provocative weave of story and theory. "The tale being told," writes Denzin (1992), "should reflect back on, be entangled in, and critique this current historical moment and its discontents" (p. 25). The researcher and text must make a persuasive argument, tell a good story, be a convincing "I-witness." Geertz (1988) is clear on this point:

> This issue, negotiating the passage from what one has been through "out there" to what one says "back here," is not psychological in character. It is literary. It arises for anyone who adopts what one may call, in a serious pun, the I-witnessing approach to the construction of cultural descriptions. . . . [It] is to pose for yourself a distinctive sort of text-building problem: rendering your account credible through rendering your person so. . . . To become a convincing "I-witness," one must, so it seems, first become a convincing "I." (p. 78–79)

Being a "convincing I" is not simply about literary self-exposure. And here I address those who rest upon the tired relativist argument that auto-anything in scholarship is about a nonevaluative, anything-goes self-therapizing, sans theory, reason, or logic. In her book *The Vulnerable Observer,* Ruth Behar (1997) addresses this posture:

> Efforts at self-revelation flop not because the personal voice has been used, but because it has been poorly used, leaving unscrutinized the connection, intellectual and emotional, between the observer and the observed.
> Vulnerability doesn't mean that anything personal goes. The exposure of the self who is also a spectator has to take us somewhere we couldn't otherwise get to. It has to be essential to the argument, not a decorative flourish, not exposure for its own sake. (p. 13–14)

A reader of autoethnographic texts must be moved emotionally and critically. Such movement does not occur without literary craft, persuasive logic, and personal/cultural thick description. Goodall (1998) argues good autoethnography "completely dissolves any idea of distance, doesn't produce 'findings,' isn't generalizable, and only has credibility when self-reflexive, and authority when richly vulnerable. . . . When it is done well, we can *learn previously unspoken, unknown things about culture and communication* from it" (p. 2). Autoethnography is a felt-text that does not occur without rhetorical and literary discipline, as well as the courage needed to be vulnerable in rendering scholarship . . . to step out from behind the curtain and reveal the individual at the controls of academic-Oz.

Being There

"Threshold": An Ending.

Gingrich-Philbrook (1998) says,
"The story recognizes
and exploits
the ascetic quality of our faith in reality
as a place one may dwell,
a faith that demands constant avowals from [T]he [F]aithful
among us,
even though they will never come to the end of these acts,
and must live their lives always avowing

and avowing
and avowing . . ."
(p. 299,
capitalizations
mine).

Knowledge Masters
and their (post)colonizers
practice verisimilitudinal violence
when any of its "primitives"
begin to speak "unnaturally,"
not following
the Straight   -and   -Narrow
context-free universal yardstick
of Reality.

There is danger "Being Here,"
when writing of "Being There"
involves speaking in multivocal tongues
and shifting cultural shapes.

Being Here

Dialogical Performance and Performativity

As any shaman will tell you, shape shifting is a risky business, takes a lot of energy, and is enormously affected by the surroundings. When I performed "Threshold" at an academic conference, I felt I was shifting forms from scholar to primitive. The sometimes-poetic voice of performed autoethnography can surely be heard by academics as an irrational story spoken in a misbegotten tongue. But my truth is, that I am more alive with the sagacity of knowledge, and my ability to communicate it, when I shift into these shapes and speak in these tongues. "Performance helps me see," writes Madison (1999), "It illuminates like good theory. It orders the world and lets the world loose" (p. 109).

In the next section, BEING THERE constitutes "An Eating Outing: Spectacle, Desire, and Consumption," an autoethnography focusing upon my experience with anorexia. I first performed this at a communication ethnography preconference near Chicago in 1999.

Being There

An Eating Outing

In much of my early life I often felt like I was calling to myself. Speaking from subject "I" to a disembodied "you-self." Caught in the middle between Richard Schechner's (1988) not-me and not-not-me. As if I were outside my body trying to get in, homeless outside my skin.

I have often felt like I was speaking from outside of my body in my professional and personal lives. In fact, for me, academe has always been about speaking from a disembodied head. And because I often felt like I was calling out to my othered self, I never questioned the implications of a disembodying discourse. The body in academe is rather like the headless horseman galloping wildly and uncontrollably to somewhere, driven by profane and unruly emotion, while the head—holder of the Mind—is enshrined under glass in the halls of academe.

In calling to myself through the performance of autoethnography, someone, someone from inside my body, finally, gingerly, began to call back. Embodying theory about anorexia nervosa through performance allows me to enter the uninhabitable corporeal terrain of my 16-year-old body, and to problematize the context in which the anorexia thrived. Theory helps me name the experiences interred in the body, whereas performance helps me to reinhabit my body, immersing myself into those scary spaces—introducing me to myself—so that the semantic expression of autoethnographic practice reflects the somatic experience of the sociocultured body.

I want to enter the terrain of consumption, desire, and the denial of those carnivorous experiences within my own body. And I want to do it here with you in performance. Because it is here, "in performance," Ann Cooper Albright (1997) writes, that "the audience is forced to deal directly with the history of that body in conjunction with the history of their own bodies" (p. 121).

Being Here

In the process of performance, the performer engages the text of another—oral or written by self or other—dialogically, meaning the performer approaches the text/other with a *commitment* to be challenged, changed, embraced, and interrogated in the performance process (Conquergood, 1985). The purpose of dialogical performance is to embody an intimate understanding of self's engagement with another within a specific sociocultural context. In autoethnographic performance, self *is* other. Dialogical engagement in performance encourages the performer to interrogate the political and ideological contexts and power relations between self and other, and self *as* other. Ronald J. Pelias (1991) writes, "The dialogic process allows performers to present to the community others for consideration. In doing so, performers do not take the place of others. Instead they are engaged in a shared conversation in which they speak, not for, but with, the community" (p. 151). The performer asks herself, "As I seek to embody this text, how does my own cultural situatedness (i.e., standpoint theory) motivate my performance choices?" Socioculturally reflexive critique is at the heart of ethical intimate dialogical performance.

In his article "Performing as a Moral Act: Ethical Dimensions in the Ethnography of Performance," Dwight Conquergood (1985) maps the moral and ethical pitfalls possible in ethnographic performance. He articulates dialogical performance as an ethical performance approach that "struggles to bring together different voices, world views, value systems, and beliefs so that they can have a conversation with one another." Dialogical performance is a way of understanding the intersections of self, other, and context passionately and reflexively. It offers a critical methodology that emphasizes knowledge in the body, offering the researcher an enfleshed epistemology and ontology.

Anthropologist Victor Turner (1982) writes, "Through the performance process, what is normally sealed up inaccessible to everyday observation and reasoning, in the depth of social life, is drawn forth" (p. 13).

Being There

An Eating Outing

So, felt-sensing the corporeal terrains of anorexia.

I removed my virginity when I was 15. It was planned. I wanted to get rid of it. It wasn't a particularly pleasant experience. He was 16 and neither of us were very sure about how what went where. For me, it was an attempt to enter the body I was calling out to. I wanted her to know that this entering was evidence of her desirability. I wanted her to know that because she had denied her desire for food, that this boy-man's consumption of her was proof that she was a spectacle worthy of consumption and desire.

My mom was a strikingly beautiful woman. Rather a cross between Lucille Ball and Marilyn Monroe. She was crystal clear about the spectacality of femininity. She talked of facelifts, she worked hard to maintain her tiny waist, and her sense of fashion was cultivated and impeccable. Her frustration with my pre-15-year-old chubby body came from the knowledge that personally controlling the social gaze upon one's body meant having control over the inevitable spectacalization of one's body. A model of Gramsci's "organic intellectual," my mother spent much of her life intricately observing class and gender pastiche. She grew up poor in a family of 11. Her insistence on my thinness wasn't the result of some debutante-induced sensibility of maintaining social standing through my appearance. Her concern came from critical self-reflection upon her own experience of rising out of poverty and moving amongst and becoming a member of the upper-middle class.

For my mother, being thin and attractive was not about vanity, it was about achievement, it was about looking well bred, it was about maintaining one's control over cultural surveillance. Like Carol Spitzack (1993) in her article "The Spectacle of Anorexia Nervosa," my mother could have told you that "the inhabitants of poorly presented bodies were expected to take corrective action, realigning bodily aesthetics and motility with cultural images of beauty" (p. 2). She knew that "the presentation of femininity demands evidence of surveillance, beginning around the time of puberty and extending past middle age" (p. 2). She knew and wanted me to know that judgments of my attractiveness would be based, at least in part, on my "finesse in giving pleasure to those who are placed in the position of observer," Spitzack continues, "a woman embodies the positions of spectator and spectacle simultaneously" (p. 2).

Eliminating my virginity was a way for me to gain some control over my body.

I wanted there to be a tangible reason for my pleasing others by refusing food.

Upon turning 15, I began a regimented regulation of food intake. In the morning I would have half a piece of toast, at lunch I would eat half a Twinkie, and at dinner I would eat the vegetable, some meat, and a bite of the potatoes with nothing on them. Mom always said that it's not the potatoes, but what you put on them that are fattening. After dinner I would walk to the country club and work out hard for at least an hour. Depending on how much I had eaten that day, I would then sit in the sauna. I remember feeling the heat of the sauna burning the inside of my nose, and knowing that if I could stand that, I would probably lose another "good pound."

This workout occurred everyday along with dance classes and, yes, cheerleading practice, another hotbed of voluntary starvation. Kathy Davis (1997) argues that "embodied theory" must engage the relationships between the "symbolic and the material, between representations of the body and embodiment as experience or social practice in concrete social, cultural and historical contexts" (p. 15). Theory and the body are always and already integrated. Voluntary starvation is a terribly concrete social practice.

Being Here

The performance of autoethnography corporeally manifests the dialogical praxis of critical theory and the performing body. Langellier's notion of performativity plaits the theoretical grounding, ethical implications, and disciplinary rigor needed for quality autoethnographic performance. Langellier (1999) argues that the performative turn in contemporary society and scholarship "responds to twin conditions of bodiless voices, for example, in ethnographic writing; and voiceless bodies who desire to resist the colonizing powers of discourse" (p. 126). Langellier draws a distinction between *performance*, "a term used to describe a certain type of particularly involved and dramatized oral narrative" (p. 127), which "implies the transgressive desire of agency and action" (p. 129), and *performativity*, which requires the performer of personal narrative to identify and critique the power relations rooted in the sociohistorical contexts of discourse that are occurring *in the act of performing* personal stories.

The social context within which the autoethnographic performance is presented adds a further critical layer to the doing and witnessing of the performance. In "Dancing Bodies and the Stories They Tell," Ann Cooper Albright (1997) argues that the face-to-face interaction of performance "is an infinitely more intense and uncomfortable experience that demands that the audience engage with their own cultural autobiographies" (p. 121). Whether performing autoethnography at an academic conference, a community gathering on social issues, or a paid theatrical gig, audience engagement and response to these performances are intensely personal, diverse, and substantial.

Being There

In no other context is the requirement for "evidence of surveillance" and embodying cultural determinants made so manifest as in the world of dance. I began ballet at 7 years old but became serious about it around the age of 15, which is when my anorexia was peaking. Ballet and anorexia, a volatile, yet common, combination. In fact, I don't think you can have one without the other and be successful in dance. I was in the dance program at Michigan State University during my first year of college and was a member of one of their traveling repertory companies. Our ballet teacher was this tall, thin, stern and stately dancer out of New York City. She was tall and gaunt and took no crap. She was the overlord of our bodies. It was her gaze that we needed to satisfy. Maintaining the bone-jutting, taut-muscled dancer's body was right in tune with the anorexic's agenda. Spitzack (1993) writes, "A willingness to place oneself onstage voluntarily and to invite assessment are necessary elements in the preservation of [anorexia]" (p. 6). And who better to police our gendered performances than a thin, stark, professional dance drill sergeant—the body of the anorexic's dream: thin, controlled, legitimate.

See, here's how the drill went. One day—and this was typical for a company dance class—we were at the bar doing a regular ballet warm-up. Absolute concentration on controlling the body is the goal. Our teacher, who I will call Ms. Frank, walks up and down the row of black leotarded and pink-legged bodies. In one hand she holds kind of a pointing staff that she would use to tap on our bodies to indicate the need for correction in alignment, turn out, or position. In her other hand she has the pad of pink slips, better known by their grisly name: "fat slips." Our pulses would all but stop when she would bring out the fat slips.

She stopped, standing about 6 feet from the line, scribbled something on the pad, and gave it to a woman about seven bodies down the row from me. See, after you received three fat slips, you were asked to leave the class and the company. You were kicked out. Your body was analyzed and found wanting, weak, undisciplined. In ballet, one works to achieve lightness, the illusion of weightlessness, which is why I would pop at least one dexatrim every morning after dance class and no breakfast.

Being Here

This work has literally saved my life by providing me the means to claim reflexive agency in my interactions with others in contexts. In autoethnographic performance, the body is like a cultural billboard for people to read and interpret in the context of their own experience. Performing autoethnography provides a space for the emancipation of the voice and body in academic discourse through breaking the boundaries of stylistic form, and by reintroducing the body to the mind in the process of living research. For me, this emancipation is manifested in two ways. First, performing autoethnography can emancipate the scholarly voice from the monostylistic confines of academic discourse. The opening up of stylistic form in academic writing provides the opportunity for a diversity of content. Second, performing autoethnography provides space for the living, experiencing, and researching body to be seen and felt. It is not that our bodies haven't been in our work, rather, they have been shrouded in our research by dualistic separations of Mind and Body. We have been expected to accept the myth of the researcher as a detached head—the object of Thought, Rationality, and Reason—floating from research site to research site thinking and speaking, while its profane counterpart, the Body, lurks unseen, unruly, and uncontrollable in the shadows of the Great Halls of the Academy. The Body has become the hysterical and embarrassing relative, a "shut-in" in the academy's ivory tower.

Emancipating the Scholarly Voice

As a woman's feet are bound in the unnatural form of the high heel, so are her voices and the voices of "othereds" bound by the monoform of academese. Langellier (1998) writes, "The voice needs a body which personal narrative furnishes. From social life, a complementary movement applies: the body needs a voice to resist the colonizing powers of discourse. . . . Personal narrative responds to both the wreckage and the reflexivity of postmodern times when master narratives disintegrate" (p. 207). Autoethnographic performance creates a space for the detached voice and the "profane" body to dialogue reintegrating the head and the heart into academic writing, and challenging the construction of master narratives.

Being There

Dancers are experts in the theater of gender. We learn early on, as does any great female gender actor, to be acutely sensitive to the wishes of others, that our body, and its worthiness, is contingent upon external judgment. Ms. Frank, like my mom, was simply informing us of our gender performance acumen. For any lapses in training, there must be clear and swift reprimand. If one did not take corrective action of one's body after the second "slip," then clearly, there was a flaw in her internal surveillance system.

She was lax in suppressing her desire for consumption.

She was lax in her performance of desire for other's consumption.

She was lax in meeting the challenge of femininity: to regulate her body performances according to cultural dictates.

Being Here

When doing autoethnography, my voice often comes on to the page in poetic ("nonscholarly") form. Autoethnographic performance in print is often governed by how the words manifest themselves through voice and movement in performance. Movement, spatial shifts, and vocal and physical breaths somatically transmute the semantics of the performed word. The autoethnographic performance process turns the internally *somatic* into the externally *semantic*. My reading of embodied sociotextual pelts becomes the written semantic interpretation of my own somatic experience "at once asserting the somatic reality of experience while also foregrounding its discursive nature" (Albright, 1997, p. 120). Denzin (1997) adds, "Poetry, and the personal narrative, become tools for reflexive knowledge" (p. 212).

Translating the lived intersections of self, other, time, and space into autoethnographic performance has allowed me to integrate my personal, professional, and political voice. For me, the integration of selves in my life/work has resulted in what I can only term an *open agency*. Though I have always felt a good measure of agency in the world, it was a voice constrained by a power-over orientation, motivated by competitive ambition, fear, and insecurity. Success meant grafting the skins of patriarchy on my body by feeling powerful—"on top" and "in control"—in comparison to those I perceived as powerless. But the high heels pinched. The panty hose compressed. The power suits made dancing impossible.

Critically reflecting upon my place in time with others through autoethnographic performance research has made me feel power *with* rather than power *over* my self and others. I began to hear my own scholarly voice, where truth and reality are not fixed categories, where self-reflexive critique is sanctioned, and where heresy is viewed as liberatory. Trihn (1991) argues that a responsible, reflexive autoethnographic text "announces its own politics and evidences a political consciousness. It interrogates the realities it represents.

It invokes the teller's story in the history that is told" (p. 188). My voice feels powerful when it is engendering power with others. I am better able to engage the lived experience of myself with others. I am more comfortable in the often conflictual and unfamiliar spaces one inhabits in ethnographic research. I am more comfortable with my self as other.

The following autoethnography stems from the same project as "Threshold"—the continuing research project with Machi (Mapuche shaman in the Chilean Andes) focusing on the efficacious performative dimensions of Mapuche healing rituals. This passage generated from field notes illustrates my struggle to remain an open agent practicing power with my coresearchers. It also illustrates the necessity of critical reflection on power structures within any ethnographic research context. This text was first performed at the Petit Jean Performance Festival in Arkansas in 1999.

Being There

"The Camera"

I requested
and was given
a handheld videocam from the Dean's Office
specifically for this trip.
I am finding the camera very invasive generally.
It invades my participation in ritual.
It invades my relationship with the women traveling.

Yet,
Machi Luzclara and Machi Quinturay
welcome its presence
as providing a record of the Mapuche people in a time of intense transition.

The camera is operating for me as a barrier.
It is a "Master's Tool."
It is a third eye with a patriarchal gaze
that looks outward instead of in,
seeking to observe rather than immerse.

And yet, am I not sounding like the petulant privileged professor putting her own
personal and vocational process before the Machi who invited her here?
This film is

what will get us the half mil' PBS grant Machi Luzclara wants,
which will get thousands of dollars to the Machi
who live,
most of them,
in abject poverty,
not giving a damn
where they are placed on the hyphen
by the "cultural elite."
But still, I long to pitch this techno eyeball over the side of the mountain
and SEE
with *my* third eye how it becomes one with the gravel!

Clearly, I have yet to use the camera with the self-reflexive forte of Trihn.

Being Here

An autoethnographic voice can interrogate the politics that structure the
personal, yet it must still struggle within the language that represents dominant politics. "Fears of reprisal and the lack of an experimental language,"
Park-Fuller (2000) writes, "can work to inhibit the sharing of transgressive
experience" (p. 24). Speaking and embodying the politically transgressive
through experimental linguistic forms (i.e. autoethnography, sociopoetics,
performance scripts) can result in a lack of publications. Goodall (1998) continues to advocate for the multivocality of form and content in academic journals when he writes about the transgressive composition of autoethnography,
"One of the most 'disturbing' characteristics of autoethnography is that
its prose style or poetic is at odds with the clear scholarly preference for
an impersonal, nonemotional, unrhetorically charming, idiom of representation" (p. 6). The impersonal, nonemotional, and unrhetorically charming
representation of self in academia—and beyond—was something I was glad
to be rid of. The ontological and epistemological knowledge that my body
claimed would not be articulated in the rigid linguistic constructs and stylistic forms of the academic journal. My experience of "Being There" would
simply not jibe with the scholarly writing methods of "Being Here." "Ethnography . . . involve[s] owning up to the fact that, like quantum mechanics or
the Italian opera, it is a work of the imagination" (Geertz, 1988, p. 140).

Ironically, although anthropological heretics such as Clifford Geertz,
James Clifford, George Marcus, and others had boldly articulated the "crisis
of representation" in pre-Malinowskian ethnography, there had been little
recognition of the equally hegemonizing crisis of representation in the White,

male-proctored academic writing and publishing structures. "Like other cultural groups," writes Laurel Richardson (1992), "academics fail to recognize their practices as cultural/political choices, much less see how they are personally affected by those choices" (p. 126). These linguistic structures and publishing gatekeepers promote an erasure of the body from the process and product of research.

Being There

Segments from "From Goldilocks to Dreadlocks: Racializing Bodies," first performed at the Performance Studies International Conference in Tempe, AZ, 2000.

"Dreadful Beginnings"

In February of last year, my mammogram came back with some spots, some stains, some irregularities. Two of my mom's sisters died of breast cancer, and my mom died of ovarian. After 3 weeks of more and varied mammograms, Tom, Dick, and Harry decided that "my breasts were *clean*."

I trace my desire for dreadlocks to the year after my 10-year-old son was born. I had always told myself that 50, 50 years old would be the right time for dreads, an age of wisdom and sagacity, the dreads would be an earned crown of cronedom.

But the mammogram shifted something. The x-ray exposed them just
below the
surface of my skins.
Seeing that the jig was up,
having been revealed by modern radiation,
these ancient roots,
these radical risomes
began sprouting snakish saplings
these shrieking snakes of Medusa
these killing and kissing coils of Kali
these wild roots of Baba Yaga
just began growing out out out
of my head
one day.

Their time had come.
And as they emerged, they evoked many comments from many peoples.

A most interesting theme of comments emerged from White women:
"Tami, aren't you afraid of offending Black people
by wearing dreads?" "I mean, what will they think?"
"Aren't you 'taking something away' from Black people
by growing my dreads?"
As if I could
As if I were in racial drag.
As if I were   drag racing   to the finished line
of an essentialized,   homogenized   *Blackness.*

But what began to emerge for me
were essentialized, homogenized images of
Whiteness.

And I began to see the ways
that I had been living much of my life
In White   racial   drag.

Being Here

Emancipating the Body From the Shadows

When the body is erased in the process(ing) of scholarship, knowledge situated within the body is unavailable. Enfleshed knowledge is restricted by linguistic patterns of positivist dualism—mind/body, objective/subjective—that fix the body as an entity incapable of literacy. This has particular implications for women as they have been historically and culturally connected to conceptualizations of the body as an emotionally unruly and profane entity. Yet, despite decades of cogently radical critiques of positivist dualism, we still sever the body from academic scholarship. In problematizing the cultural and historical concepts and practices of the body and literacy, Carolyn Marvin (1994) writes, "A mark of literate competence is skill in disguising or erasing the contribution of one's own body to the process of textual production and practice. A mark of literate power is the freedom to command other bodies for textual display or concealment, as the occasion warrants" (p. 129).

The shadowed body common in academic discourse is of great significance to the performative ethnographic researcher. Conquergood (1991) notes, "Ethnography's distinctive research method . . . privileges the body as a site of knowing. . . . Ethnography is an *embodied practice;* it is an intensely sensuous way of knowing" (p. 180). The sociopolitics of body representation are widely articulated across disciplines. The female and/or non-White body is erased from public and political areas, thus reducing women's and/or non-White's experiences to "special interests," meaning their bodies are of marginal concern in the body politic. Moira Gatens's (1997) essay "Corporeal Representation in/and the Body Politic" cogently articulates this argument in relation to language. Gatens writes, "Women who step outside their allotted place in the body politic are frequently abused with terms like: harpy, virago, vixen, bitch, shrew; terms that make it clear that if she attempts to speak from the political body about the political body, her speech is not recognized as *human* speech" (p. 84). It is cause for hope that work like Gatens's has and continues to be published. However, when will academic discourse *reflect* the integration of the body in research rather than publishing rhetoric *about* it?

Coaxing the body from the shadows of academe and consciously integrating it into the process and production of knowledge requires that we view knowledge in the context of the body from which it is generated. I must be ready to walk the talk of my scholarship by putting my politically marked body on the lines of the printed text. This kind of embodied methodology is— and should feel—risky. Goodall's (1998) take on autoethnographic scholarship reflects this vulnerable conviction:

> It should be dangerous. It should mess with your mind. It should open locks, provide pathways, offer a language capable of inspiring personal, social, and institutional liberation. I think it should help people think and behave differently, if they choose to. Writing that doesn't do that isn't very good writing.
>
> Which is why I have such a difficult time finishing most of the essays I read in most so-called scholarly journals. (p. 5)

Whenever my work messes with my mind, I suppose that I am on to some thing, some truth among many, that others may also find useful. When my body vibrates with the gravitational pull of another body's version of reality, I know that I need to release my own gravitational hold on reality and dialogically engage this other time and space. That is not narcissism or engagement in "wannabe" participant-observation with "natives"; it is about embodying and critically evaluating the complex impulses of communication. "It is not a question of going native," states Geertz (1988), "It is a question of living a multiplex life; sailing at once in several seas" (p. 77).

The autoethnographic performance seeks to embody the polyphonic intertextuality of people in contexts. Performing autoethnography gives us what Madison (1993, 1999) might refer to as "performing theory/embodied writing." Ideologies and experiences are made manifest through performance by replacing the rigor mortis of the written with fully embodied social critique.

Such flesh-to-flesh scholarship motivates the labor of critical self-reflexivity and invigorates the concept and process(ing) of knowledge. With all our theorizing about the body, we seldom theorize body to body, a flesh-to-flesh theorizing. Madison (1999) argues for the "felt-sensing meeting between theory, writing, and performing" (p. 107). Felt-sensing is not part of the Mind over Body rational world paradigm upon which academe was founded. Felt-sensing requires vulnerability, allowing one's self to be pushed and pulled in the dialectic whirl of discursive bodies.

Representing the discursive *performing* body on the page requires an enfleshed methodology and, surely, an expansion of form in academic writing. Embodied writing must be able to reflect the corporeal and material presence of the body that generated the text in performance. Emancipating the body from its erasure in academic scholarship would, necessarily, affect stylistic form. When I performed "Ode to the Absent Phallus," dealing with being sexually assaulted, my purpose was to relocate my body as a powerful agent rather than an assaulted object. Much of that narrative agency is located in the presence of my body in performance. A print form that does not represent this materiality potentially suffocates this mode of agency. Consequently, the published version of this text is in poetic form, which seeks to reflect the critical agency of the corporeal agent, the living body in performance (Spry, 1998).

In performed autoethnography, the research artist is the existential nexus upon which the research rotates, deviates, and gyrates presenting through performance critical self-reflexive analysis of her own experiences of dissonance and discovery with others. This perspective on scholarship *requires* the researcher to access her complexity of passion and desire for living, and to articulate these *embodied* critical passions in any number of scholarly discursive forms. The embodied autoethnographic text is a story reflecting the research artist's collaboration with people, culture, and time. It is generated in the liminal spaces between experience and language, between the known and the unknown, between the somatic and semantic. The text and the body that generates it cannot be separated. Surely, they never have been. Postcolonial writing has not brought the body back, it has exposed and politicized its presence.

Like Turner's (1982, 1987) concept of flow, the polyphonic voice/body processes of cultural/identity representation activated in performance are mobile, playful, and dynamic; "Identity is more like a performance in process than a postulate, premise, or originary principle" (Conquergood, 1991, p. 185). Flesh-to-flesh methodologies stand in multifigured contrast to fixed Truth-seeking methods.

Dancing Bodies/Poetic Voices of Academic Renewal

Enacting the embodied method of autoethnography, I have learned to believe in myself when a story moves into my body and grows stronger with critical self-reflection, even if—and especially when—it causes my body to transgress into the dance of an academic heretic. Critical analysis is a tool I learned in academe; and when turning this tool back upon it, the academy can be a space filled with passionate revelation and critical polyphonic dialogue.

Human experience is chaotic and messy, requiring a pluralism of discursive and interpretive methods that critically turn texts back upon themselves in the constant emancipation of meanings. "These texts, however, are not just subjective accounts of experience," writes Denzin (1997), "they attempt to reflexively map multiple discourses that occur in a given social space" (p. xvii). Autoethnographic performance is the convergence of the "autobiographic impulse" and the "ethnographic moment" represented through movement and language in performance. A compelling performance—like a copious ethnography—does not purport to reveal the essential representation of a text, nor should it, as Wallace Bacon (1979) reminds, reveal only the performer's agenda or skill. A fine autoethnographic performance reveals a substantive, sophisticated weave of a performer's textual analysis, her contextual analysis, and her somatic acumen, thereby presenting critical self-reflexive analysis of her own experiences of dissonance and discovery with others. Autoethnographic performance can provide a space for the emancipation of the voice and body from homogenizing knowledge production and academic discourse structures, thereby articulating the intersections of peoples and culture through the inner sanctions of the always-migratory identity. Reality is always and already a social construction. Autobiographical performance makes us acutely conscious of how we I-witness our own reality constructions. Interpreting culture through the self-reflections and cultural refractions of identity is a defining feature of autoethnographic performance.

Autoethnography contributes to the burgeoning methodological possibilities of representing human action. It is one tool among many designed to work in the fields, unseating the privileged scholar from the desk in the Master's House, and de-exoticizing the non-White-male-objective scholar from the realms of the academically othered. And it is a method that calls upon the body as a site of scholarly awareness and corporeal literacy.

I end with a passage from field notes in Chile. Though I am describing embodied liminality (Turner, 1982) experienced in the Andes working with Chilean and Mapuche shaman, the passage has a haunting resonance with the researching body in academe:

Being There

December 4, 1997

We are here . . . in San Hose,' Chile—50 miles south of Santiago.
I am in the cabin that we will stay in the night before ascending the
mountain . . . on horseback . . . 17,000
feet up . . . into the Andean mountain wilderness. I have showered,
done Tai Chi,
tried to ground . . .
I am literally upside down on this side of the earth
from where I have been all of my life.
I am spinning and vibrating inside.
I am shimmering inside
as if light is trying to break through.
I am shaking and shifting inside
as if
my shape
is about to change.

Trihn (1991) helps. "A reality is not a mere crossing from one
border to another . . . Reality involves the crossing of an
indeterminate number of borderlines, one that remains multiple
in its hyphenation" (p. 107).

Indeed.
My shaking
is the liminal shifting
betwixt and between
hyphens,
Shaping
that I am
and am not in control of.
Shifting
into something
that is not me
and is not-not me.
Shaking
at the "checkpoint."
Wondering
and worrying

if here—
I will
pass
customs.

References

Albright, A. C. (1997). Dancing bodies and the stories they tell. In *Choreographing difference: The body and identity in contemporary dance* (pp. 119–149). Hanover: University Press of New England.

Alexander, B. K. (2000). Skin flint (or, The garbage man's kid): A generative autobiographical performance based on Tami Spry's *Tattoo stories. Text and Performance Quarterly, 20*: 97–114.

Anzuldua, G. (Ed.). (1990). *Making face, making soul: Creative and critical perspectives by feminists of color.* San Francisco: Aunt Lute Books.

Bacon, W. (1979). *The art of interpretation* (3rd ed.). New York: Holt, Rinehart, and Winston.

Bauman, R. (1986). *Story, performance, and event: Contextual studies of oral narratives.* Cambridge, UK: Cambridge University Press.

Behar, R. (1997). *The vulnerable observer: Anthropology that breaks your heart.* Boston: Beacon.

Behar, R., & Gordon, D. A. (1995). *Women writing culture.* Berkeley: University of California Press.

Blair, C., Brown, J. R., & Baxter, L. A. (1994). Disciplining the feminine. *Quarterly Journal of Speech, 80*: 383–409.

Clifford, J. (1988). *The predicament of culture: Twentieth century ethnography, literature, and art.* Cambridge, MA: Harvard University Press.

Clifford, J., & Marcus, G. E. (1986). *Writing culture: The poetics and politics of ethnography.* Berkeley: University of California Press.

Conquergood, D. (1985). Performing as a moral act: Ethical dimensions in the ethnography of performance. *Literature in Performance, 5*(2): 1–13.

Conquergood, D. (1991). Rethinking ethnography: Towards a critical cultural politics. *Communication Monographs, 58*: 179–194.

Conquergood, D. (1998). Beyond the text: Toward a performative cultural politics. In S. J. Dailey (Ed.), *The future of performance studies: Visions and revisions* (pp. 25–36). Annandale, VA: National Communication Association.

Crawford, L. (1996). Personal ethnography. *Communication Monographs, 63.*

Dailey, S. (Ed.). (1998). *The future of performance studies: Visions and revisions.* Annandale, VA: National Communication Association.

Davis, K. (Ed.). (1997). *Embodied practices: Feminist perspectives on the body.* London: Sage.

Denzin, N. K. (1992). The many faces of emotionality. In C. Ellis (Ed.), *Investigating subjectivity: Research on lived experience* (pp. 17–30). London: Sage.

Denzin, N. K. (1997). *Interpretive ethnography: Ethnographic practices for the 21st century*. London: Sage.

Ellis, C. (1997). Evocative autoethnography: Writing emotionally about our lives. In W. G. Tierney & Y. S. Lincoln (Eds.), *Representation and the text* (pp. 115–139). New York: State University of New York Press.

Ellis, C., & Bochner, A. P. (Eds.). (1996). *Composing ethnography: Alternative forms of qualitative writing*. Walnut Creek, CA: AltaMira Press.

Ellis, C., & Flaherty, M. G. (Eds.). (1992). *Investigating subjectivity: Research on lived experience*. London: Sage.

Fine, E. C. (1984). *The folklore text: From performance to print*. Bloomington: Indiana University Press.

Gatens, M. (1997). Corporeal representation in the body politic. In K. Conboy, N. Medina, & S. Stanbury (Eds.), *Writing on the Body: Female embodiment and feminist theory*. New York: Columbia University Press.

Geertz, C. (1973). *The interpretation of cultures*. New York: Basic Books.

Geertz, C. (1988). *Works and lives: The anthropologist as author*. Stanford, CA: Stanford University Press.

Gingrich-Philbrook, C. (1998). What I "know" about the story (for those about to tell personal narratives on stage). In S. J. Dailey (Ed.), *The future of performance studies: Visions and revisions* (pp. 298–300). Annandale, VA: National Communication Association.

Goodall, Jr., H. L. (1991a). *Living in a rock and roll mystery: Reading context, self and others as clues*. Carbondale: Southern Illinois University Press.

Goodall, Jr., H. L. (1991b). Turning within the ethnographic turn: Radical empiricism and a case for post-ethnography. *Text and Performance Quarterly, 11*: 153–157.

Goodall, Jr., H. L. (1998, November). *Notes for the autoethnography and auto-biography panel NCA*. A paper presented at the National Communication Association Convention in New York City.

James, S. M., & Busia, A. P. A. (Eds.). (1993). *Theorizing Black feminisms: The visionary pragmatism of Black women*. New York: Routledge.

Jerome, J., & Satin, L. (Eds.). (1999). Introduction. *Women and Performance: A Journal of Feminist Theory, Performing Autobiography, 19–20*: 9–19.

Jones, J. L. (1997). sista docta: Performance as critique of the academy. *The Drama Review, 41*: 51–67.

Langellier, K. (1989). Personal narratives: Perspectives on theory and research. *Text and Performance Quarterly, 9*: 243–276.

Langellier, K. (1998). Voiceless bodies, bodiless voices: The future of personal narrative performance. In S. J. Dailey (Ed.), *The future of performance studies: Visions and revisions* (pp. 207–213). Annandale, VA: National Communication Association.

Langellier, K. (1999). Personal narrative, performance, performativity: Two or three things I know for sure. *Text and Performance Quarterly, 19*: 125–144.

Langellier, K., & Peterson, E. E. (1992). Spinstorying: An analysis of women story-telling. In E. C. Fine & J. H. Speer (Eds.), *Performance, culture, and identity* (pp. 157–180). New York: Praeger.

Madison, D. (1993). "That was my occupation": Oral narrative, performance, and Black feminist thought. *Text and Performance Quarterly, 13:* 213–232.

Madison, D. S. (1999). Performing theory/embodied writing. *Text and Performance Quarterly, 19:* 107–124.

Marcus, G. E., & Fischer, M. M. J. (1986). *Anthropology as cultural critique: An experimental moment in the human sciences.* Chicago: University of Chicago Press.

Marvin, C. (1994). The body of the text: Literacy's corporeal constant. *Quarterly Journal of Speech, 80:* 129–149.

Minister, K. (1991). A feminist frame for the oral history interview. In S. B. Gluck & D. Patai (Eds.), *Women's words: The feminist practice of oral history* (pp. 27–41). New York: Routledge Kegan Paul.

Morago, C., & Anzuldua, G. (Eds.). (1983). *This bridge called my back: Writings of radical women of color.* New York: Kitchen Table.

Myerhoff, B. (1979). *Numbering our days.* New York: Dutton.

Myerhoff, B. (1982). Life history among the elderly: Performance, visibility, and remembering. In J. Ruby (Ed.), *A crack in the mirror: Reflexive perspectives in anthropology* (pp. 99–120). Philadelphia: University of Pennsylvania Press.

Neuman, M. (1996). Collecting ourselves at the end of the century. In C. Ellis & A. Bochner (Eds.), *Composing ethnography: Alternative forms of qualitative writing.* London: AltaMira Press.

Park-Fuller, L. (2000). Performing absence: The staged personal narrative as testimony. *Text and Performance Quarterly, 20:* 20–42.

Pelias, R. J. (1991). Empathy and the ethics of entitlement. *Theatre Research International, 16:* 142–152.

Pelias, R. J. (1999). *Writing performance: Poeticizing the researcher's body.* Carbondale: Southern Illinois University Press.

The Personal Narratives Group. (1989). *Interpreting women's lives: Feminist theory and personal narratives.* Bloomington: Indiana University Press.

Pratt, M. L. (1986). Fieldwork in common places. In J. Clifford & G. E. Marcus (Eds.), *Writing culture: The poetics and politics of ethnography* (pp. 27–50). Berkeley: University of California Press.

Pratt, M. L. (1994). Transculturation and autoethnography: Peru 1615/1980. In F. Barker, P. Hulme, & M. Iverson (Eds.), *Colonial discourse/postcolonial theory* (pp. 24–46). New York: Manchester University Press.

Reed-Danahay, D. E. (Ed.). (1997). Introduction. *Auto/ethnography: Rewriting the self and the social.* New York: Berg.

Richardson, L. (1992). The consequences of poetic representation. In C. Ellis & M. G. Flaherty (Eds.), *Investigating subjectivity: Research on lived experience* (pp. 125–137). Thousand Oaks, CA: Sage.

Ronai, C. R. (1992). The reflexive self through narrative: A night in the life of an erotic dancer/researcher. In C. Ellis & M. G. Flaherty (Eds.), *Investigating subjectivity: Research on lived experience* (pp. 102–124). Thousand Oaks, CA: Sage.

Schechner, R. (1988). *Performance theory.* New York: Routledge.

Secklin, P. L. (1997). Lucy's dividing family: My discovery of the person in the subject. *Journal of Personal and Interpersonal Loss, 2*: 267–275.

Simpson, J. S. (1996). Easy talk, White talk, back talk: Some reflections on the meanings of our words. *Journal of Contemporary Ethnography, 25*: 372–389.

Smith, S. (1993). *Subjectivity, identity, and the body: Women's autobiographical practices in the twentieth century.* Bloomington: Indiana University Press.

Spitzack, C. (1993). The spectacle of Anorexia Nervosa. *Text and Performance Quarterly, 13:* 1–20.

Spry, T. (1995). In the absence of word and body: Hegemonic implications of "victim" and "survivor" in women's narratives of sexual violence. *Women and Language, 18:* 27–32.

Spry, T. (1997). Skins: A daughters (re)construction of cancer. *Text and Performance Quarterly, 17:* 361–365.

Spry, T. (1998). Performative autobiography: Presence and privacy. In S. J. Dailey (Ed.), *The future of performance studies: Visions and revisions* (pp. 254–263). Annandale, VA: National Communication Association.

Spry, T. (2000). Tattoo stories: A postscript to skins. *Text and Performance Quarterly, 20:* 84–96.

Spry, T. (2001). From Goldilocks to dreadlocks: Hair-raising tales of racializing bodies. In *The green window: Proceedings of the giant city conference of performative writing* (pp. 52–65). Carbondale: Southern Illinois University.

Torgovnick, M. (1990). *Gone primitive: Savage intellects, modern lives.* Chicago: University of Chicago Press.

Trihn, M. (1989). *Woman, native, other: Writing postcoloniality and feminism.* Bloomington: Indiana University Press.

Trihn, M. (1991). *When the moon waxes red: Representation, gender, and cultural politics.* New York: Routledge.

Turner, V. (1982). *From ritual to theatre: The human seriousness of play.* New York: PAJ Publications.

Turner, V. (1987). *The anthropology of performance.* New York: PAJ Publications.

10

Exposed Methodology

The Body as a Deconstructive Practice

Wanda S. Pillow

*She had the two courages: that of going to the sources, to the
foreign parts of the self. That of torturing, to herself, almost
without self without denying the going. She slipped out of the
self, she had that severity that violent patience, she went out . . .
by laying bare the senses, it requires unclothing sight all the way
down to naked sight. (Cixous, 1994, p.91)*

*Bodies are essential to accounts of power and critiques of
knowledge. (Grosz, 1995, p. 32)*

The body has gained both attention and importance, not only in feminist
and postmodern theories but also more broadly in social theory as
a place from which to theorize, analyze, practice, and critically reconsider
the construction and reproduction of knowledge, power, class, and culture.

Michel Foucault's reformulation of the social body and feminist accounts of the gendered body have proliferated discussions concerning the absent (Moore, 1994); regulated, inscribed, and docile (Foucault, 1974); gendered (Butler, 1990, 1993; Diprose, 1994; Gaskell, 1992; Moore, 1994); classed (Allison, 1994; Davis, 1981); raced (hooks, 1990; Trinh, 1989; Walker, 1995); and sexed (Diprose, 1994; Grosz & Probyn, 1995) body. Recent works in ethnography have explored and critiqued the use and representation of the body in methodological practices and analyses (Moore, 1994; Visweswaran, 1994).

This chapter draws upon these previous works to consider how paying attention to the body, literally and figuratively, can inform and disrupt methodological practices. How does paying attention to bodies change what we look at, how we look, what we ask, and what we choose to represent? I found myself immersed in these questions and their problematics 3 years ago when I began a research project on teenage pregnancy programs. I entered field settings filled with critical, postmode[rn], feminist, and qualitative research theories and practices yet found myself unprepared for the utter *physicality* of my research experiences.

During my research, I spent almost every day in classrooms with young women whose bodies were continually changing and changed—pre- and postpregnancy swelling, stretching, widening, lactating. Our bodies provided a place and space from which we talked, shared experiences, and gained confidences. As I attempted to write stories and representations of the girls,[1] I repeatedly turned and returned to the body—to our bodies. Henrietta Moore (1994) states that feminist scholars have been "struggling with the question of how or to what degree women might be the same or similar without being identical. What is it, if anything, that we share" (p. 1)? What seemed shared, common with difference, across the girls and myself, were our bodies, their reproductive capacities, and the interests in such by the state.

However, the stories I heard from the girls, the observations I had made, were varied and complex, and I did not wish to simplify them by claiming some essentialized identity related to our female bodies. Yet I did not want to, and indeed could not, ignore the body in this research. I began to question what it would mean to pay attention to bodies, in this case, in an arena where teenage girls' bodies are simultaneously stereotyped, proliferated, ignored, and silenced. How could I, as a woman studying young women who were pregnant, use the flux of our own bodies as a site of deconstruction[2] toward an understanding of the paradox of how social structures and modes of representation simultaneously "form and *deform*" women (de Lauretis, 1984)? What kinds of strategies and commitments might a move toward the body make possible or hinder?

Elizabeth Grosz (1995) delineates what she terms "two broad kinds of approaches to theorizing the body"—one, "inscriptive," a Nietzchian, Foucauldian notion of the social body upon which "social law, morality, and values are inscribed" (p. 33). The second is the "lived body," which references the "lived experience of the body, the body's internal or psychic inscription" (Grosz, 1995). Grosz suggests that, while we are becoming adept at naming the inscriptive details of the body, we tend to shy away from the messiness of the corporal body—the lived experiences. Grosz (1995) states, "If the notion of a radical and irreducible *difference* is to be understood with respect to subjectivity, the specific modes of corporeality of bodies in their variety must be acknowledged" (p. 32).

There is, however, little research on the lived experiences—the specific physicality of the teen pregnant body (Burdell, 1993, 1995; Lesko, 1990, 1991, in press; Pillow, 1994; Tolman, 1992, 1994). Thus, in this chapter, I explore what is exposed when I pay attention to the *messiness* of bodies that exceed the boundaries of what we think we know about young women who are pregnant. After an overview of the specific corporeality of the pregnant body, I present two stories (in)formed by a specific attention to bodies. The first story considers what gets exposed when we pay attention to how teen girls experience and use their pregnant bodies as sites of resistance, specifically around issues of sex, pleasure, and power. The second story exposes the literal impact of space and architecture on teen girls' bodies and how this affects issues of self-representation, teacher pedagogy, and program implementation. I conclude by reflecting upon what these stories tell us and how the body worked in the telling of these stories.

Exposing the Pregnant Body

Bodies are not new to feminist theory. Feminist theory has utilized the specificity of the woman's body to challenge the separation of theory from experience under what has become to be known as the caveat "the personal is political." The *personal is political* highlights how the practices, representations, and knowledge of the female body are not simply innate, natural occurrences, but rather are *political*—that is, contrived, monitored, controlled, and moralized by a social system in which the female body as a collective has not had much say. The body, particularly the female body, is at best a curious and conflicting site to "go from"—a site of paradoxical social attention and avoidance. Our bodies are sites of humanist prescription, places from which binaries are structured forming polemical categories that define them: "inside/outside, subject/object, surface/depth" (p. 33). Grosz (1995) states that "bodies speak, without necessarily talking, because they become coded with and as signs. They speak social codes. They become intextuated, narrativized; simultaneously, social codes, laws, norms, and ideals become incarnated" (p. 35). These social codes we live by are complex and conditional and are further coded, often without acknowledgment, by issues of gender, race, class, physical characteristics, and sexual identity.

The pregnant female body further confounds and conflates our social codes and norms. "The significance of the maternal body differs from the public body in that it is *the site of the reproduction of the social body*" (p. 25). Tamsin Wilton (1995) states that it is "precisely because of their ability to mother that women's bodies (and their political and social selves) have been so rigidly controlled within all patriarchal political systems" (p. 182). Even in a "normal" pregnancy, what the mother does with her body—what she eats, where she goes, how and when—is open to public scrutiny. She, the mother, is a "legitimate target for moral concern" (p. 26) and thus "subject to very direct state control" (p. 183).

Pregnancy further interrupts accepted and assumed demarcations of the body and self. Questions of what is woman and fetus, woman and society, and where the locus of decision making and control lies during pregnancy have resulted in moral, ethical, and legal debates surrounding issues of birth control, abortion, and surrogacy (Diprose, 1994). Pregnancy confounds our notions of where one body ends and another begins and interrupts assumptions of a single self (p. 163). Because pregnancy exists and exhibits itself in a fluctuating, changing state, it is unclear where the pregnant body ends and the world begins (p. 116).

Teen pregnancy offers further complications and excessiveness to the already complicated issue of the state and reproduction. Teen pregnancy operates outside the norm of legitimate reproduction, marking it as a site of moral concern and state control. Teen pregnancy presents itself as a paradox to the state. While giving birth is the obligation of the female citizen, the state also has controlling interests in who gives birth. Articles promoting fear of a "browning of America" (Bane, 1986; Center for Population, 1990) feed into the concerns of the public over who gives birth, proliferating the idea that "reproduction is most certainly the obligation (and hence the right) of white, middle-class, able-bodied women" (p. 183). Teen pregnancy presents the paradox of young women fulfilling their reproductive responsibilities, but not in the way the state wishes them to (Cusick, 1989).

The paradoxical issues surrounding teen pregnancy make it difficult even to define what teen pregnancy is. Is teen pregnancy primarily a problem of "morality, fertility or poverty" (p. 1)? At what age is a woman a teen parent?

Are you a teen parent when you are 18 or 19 years of age or only if you are in public school? Is teen pregnancy as a social problem defined as only pregnancies that are carried to full term, or does it include all teen pregnancies, including those that are terminated by a miscarriage or an abortion? Are you a teen parent if you are married and/or middle class?

Correspondingly, teen pregnancy intervention and prevention programs present conflicting messages to the girls they target. On the one hand, a major purpose of teen pregnancy programs seems aimed at helping pregnant teens be good mothers, and such programs include topics related to child development, health care, enrichment, household management, and responsibility (Pillow, 1994). At the same time, these programs have the goal of preparing young mothers[3] to be independent (i.e., not on welfare) and thus concentrate upon job skills and enforce many "tough love" requirements in the interests of teaching the girls to take responsibility[4] (Lesko, 1990, 1991; Pillow, 1994). These goals—good mother and fiscal provider—and the actions they require are often conflicting and even polemical.[5]

Consistent across teen pregnancy programs, however, is an avoidance of engagement with the specific physicality of the pregnant female body. Teen pregnancy programs ignore the body outside of linear, taxonomic lists of expected changes and corresponding, acceptable, required actions (Burdell, 1995). Teen pregnancy programs thus promote and assume a clear separation of teen girls' pregnant bodies and their selves as woman, mother, student, and provider. Teen pregnancy research avidly avoids mentioning teen girls' bodies—ignoring and silencing what Nancy Lesko (in press) terms "the leaky needs" of pregnant teen girls. Research and policy aim at controlling the behavior of the teen girl's body while remaining silent about the changes and needs of the female body.

Yet, even as pregnant teen girls' bodies are silenced or even removed from some settings,[6] our society maintains a voyeuristic fascination with the sexualization of the female body as evidenced in our media, advertising, fashion, cultural practices, and myths. Research and popular media articles on teen pregnancy replicate this phenomenon, displaying visuals depicting the contrast of the young teen girl's face with her swollen belly. Such images feed our fascination and incite a moralistic response without ever acknowledging the sexual physicality of teen pregnancy (Burdell, 1995; Lesko, 1988). Ironically, teen pregnancy research and policy simultaneously ignore and proliferate the teen pregnant body (Pillow, 1977). What is made possible, then, by paying attention to the coded bodies of teen girls who are pregnant? How do the girls themselves enact, resist, and live with the increased interest and control their pregnant bodies incite in others?

Exposure I: Sex, Pleasure, and Power

While the state, policy, and research arenas may avoid the pregnant body, the teen girls I talked with, in a study conducted during 1992–1994 (Pillow, 1994), certainly could not ignore their bodies. To the contrary, I found girls who talked openly and loudly about their bodies, sex, pleasure, and their feelings on being pregnant "schoolgirls." I was drawn to these *unruly* (Rowe, 1995) girls with their strong voices and display of confidence in their bodies; however, I did not want to simply script the vocal girls' voices as victory narratives and ignore or script the "silent" girls as suffering from low self-esteem as most teen pregnancy research does.

By paying attention to bodies, I began to observe how the girls used their bodies—their changing bodies—as sites of resistance. The girls were working toward and resisting the terms of their lives as well as the requirements of the teen pregnancy program in which they participated. Whether verbally or nonverbally, I observed the girls gain an awareness of the power their bodies had over the behavior and attitude of the adults with whom they worked. For example, many girls found that adults were "uncomfortable" with their pregnant teen bodies and would use that fact to their advantage. One girl stated, "I could always get out of that teacher's class. He could not look at me without staring at my stomach. He could not get over it, y'know, he just couldn't handle me being pregnant."

One way to have power over adults, to resist, was to talk about what was forbidden or to make obvious what adults did not want to acknowledge. This was clear around issues of sex and sexuality. The program guide for the teen pregnancy program I observed had defined units to discuss sexual activity and assumed the teen girls would be silent in this process, reinforcing the gendered stereotypes of women, particularly young women, that to voice and take control of their sexual lives is not appropriate. However, during a discussion of birth control options, one girl interrupted:

> Well it['s] not like I don't know what I'm doing, I do, and I get tired of people acting like I don't. So I had sex—I got pregnant. I'm dealing with it. Y'know at some point you've gotta have sex—this isn't like the 60's—you can't wait anymore, or maybe you don't want to. But it's hard for girls to get birth control and most of the boys won't. At least while I'm pregnant I won't have to worry about getting pregnant!

This young woman's comments—that a teen girl was aware of the choices and consequences of being sexually active, that she spoke pleasure, and that she may remain sexually active during her pregnancy—exceeded the boundaries of what the teen pregnancy program (and, in this case, the teacher) was designed or prepared to address.[7] Often such comments would later be described to me as "immature" or "flippant" by the teachers—they were not to be taken seriously, except to the extent these comments spoke to how deep the girl's problem was. The girls' "silences" were coded as acquiescent and appropriate, responsible behavior, while their verbal participation was often coded as irresponsibility. In this way, presentations on birth control options that ignored factors that many women find objectionable about birth control and contribute to their nonuse—limited access, limited choice, changes in body, the idea that you are "bad" if you plan ahead for sexual activity, interruption of pleasure, and the ways to handle birth control with a guy who may not go along with it—can legitimately be continued with minimal involvement from the girls.

Fine (1988) states that, precisely because young females' discourses of desire usually occur only in marginalized settings, young teens are learning that what they, as females, feel, think, or desire is not pertinent or important enough to be discussed in a "legitimized" setting. In this way, a female discourse of desire becomes an object of regulation. However, in classrooms during discussions of sex and birth control, I observed silence both as repression and resistance. It was easy to characterize girls' silences—their lack of discussion about their own sexuality—as repression. In this way, "silence is pathologized as absence" (p. 35). But I also came to identify girls' silences as resistance,[8] resistance to a teacher's regulatory discourse, resistance to what was being left unsaid in the presentation of the lesson.

For example, after observing a teacher-presented lesson on the girls' taking responsibility for their sexual activity, during which the class had remained mostly silent and noncommittal, a girl remarked to me and her friends:

> What is that teacher talking about when she says just say "no" to sex? What if I don't wanna say no! But they'll never talk about that with us—they look down their noses at you, like you're bad. Whatta she know anyway—she's wound so tight she looks like she hasn't had any in over a year!

Nowhere were the girls' voices stronger, more independent, and resistant than when they were talking about their school experiences. Repeatedly, I heard the girls talk about how they felt they had been treated unfairly in their schools. They voiced a strong desire to learn, but because they did not "fit," they felt they were often ignored or put aside. They felt they had not been given opportunities or chances, and they were not afraid to state this fact to teachers, principals, and administrators. One girl stated:

I made him nervous. . . . I stuck my pregnant stomach out at him and said if I'm gonna be in someone's class I expect to learn something. They were harassing me for about five weeks telling me I wasn't smart enough to go to day and night school and creating problems for me. I say you're here to help me to understand—that's what you're paid for. If you can't help me then I'm getten out.

Another girl, a middle-class, white, attractive, honor roll student was a tuition-paying student at a high school out of her district when she became pregnant.

He called me into his office and he said I hear you are pregnant. And I say "yeah," so what. He says we don't have pregnant girls in this school—how it was bad for the school's reputation and would give other girls ideas. I said give me that slip right now; I'm signing and getting out of here.

"Kelley" transferred from her high school with its good reputation to "Parkside," an alternative school for students experiencing learning or behavior problems because "no other high school would let me in." She said she never felt like she fit in at Parkside—"it's not challenging; it's boring." Kelley had been on a college preparation track and felt Parkside was ill-suited to her academic needs as it focused on minimal graduation requirements and passing proficiency tests. She and her mother and the teen pregnancy teacher spent 2 months petitioning and moving through paperwork so that she could receive a variety of advanced placement courses either through home tutoring, night courses, or additional courses after her baby was born.

After the birth of her baby girl, Kelley thus shuttled across counties to attend her "old" school for academics and Parkside for her family life courses. For Kelley, this was a hard-won battle. While she felt she had lost her fight to attend her school while she was pregnant because "he [the principal] couldn't handle seeing my pregnant body in his school,"[9] she remained determined to attend her school after the birth of her baby, to show the school in her words "that having a baby didn't take away your brains." She had to repeatedly petition the administration at her home school to attend classes and functions at her school, and the decision about whether she could attend graduation and receive her diploma was not finalized until one week before graduation.[10]

Kelley was very proud of graduating "on time" and "with my class," even after the birth of her baby. She brought her graduating class sweatshirt into Parkside and showed her name on it to everyone in the school. Kelley found herself making friendships and alliances with girls at Parkside who "I never would even have talked to before," stating, "we're going through the same things, with our bodies, with our schools." These friendships were also reciprocated. Kelley had received the respect of fellow students at Parkside across marked differences of race and class because "she," as one girl said, "wore 'em down. She know now what it's like to have to fight for everything you want for your life. We all have a lot of feelings for Kelley—she deserved to graduate with her old school." Kelley commented on and summarized the events in her life over the past year by stating simply, "I never thought anyone would ever treat me this way."

Exposure II: Physically Exceeding Boundaries

What happens when pregnant schoolgirls can no longer fit into the traditional student desk? Where do school administrators decide to place the teen pregnancy classroom in their schools? How visible is the teen pregnancy classroom in the school setting? While these questions may appear simplistic and pragmatic, I believe they are questions that are vital to understanding and analyzing the lives of teen pregnant girls in schools. How do the bodies of teen girls fit into their schools? How is it that teen pregnancy and thus the teen girl's body come to be an issue to be regulated and contained?

I did not visit teen pregnancy classroom sites with these issues in mind. It was only after several visits to suburban classroom settings when I felt myself continually being led "downstairs," "around the corner," or "down and back to the left" that I began to question a classroom's physical and embodied positioning in the school as speaking and impacting on a larger discourse about teen girls who are pregnant within schools. Scheurich (1995) describes Foucault's notion of governmentality, of regulatory practices, as "a kind of governmental rationality" that is concerned with "an insatiable management of social spaces, social practices and forms" (p. 20). I began to view teen pregnancy classrooms as spaces that were the recipients of this "insatiable management."

Architecture operates as a form of disciplinary power that is exercised in its invisibility. We tend not to turn our gaze on spatial and structural practices—except, for example, the "natural" character and design of a school building. Weedon (1987) defines "space as the site for a range of possible forms of subjectivity" (p. 34) through which we define "our sense of ourselves" (p. 21). Thus, the following analysis also seeks to undo the traditional mind/body split that is prevalent in modernist discourse and stories of education. Ann Game (1991) writes that she is interested in "practices of space" in terms of the "practices a place makes possible, or closes off" (p. 83). Particularly, I am interested in how practices of surveillance, self-surveillance, and regulatory practices are reinforced through architectural discourses and how these spatial practices are written onto the bodies of students and teachers. How, then, did teen pregnancy classrooms produce their own "insatiable management" of teachers' and girls' bodies?

As I visited classroom sites, I began to notice differences in classroom location, size, accessibility, and physical set-up of the rooms. I identified two main classroom styles: first, traditional classrooms and, second, home economics classrooms. The seven teen pregnancy classrooms situated in traditional classroom settings shared several features, including their location and (in)visibility in their schools. These classrooms were all located down- or upstairs off the beaten path of main hallways. Five of the classrooms were approximately half the size of normal classrooms, and none of the seven classrooms were identified as teen pregnancy classrooms. In other words, a visitor to the school would not be able to identify the presence of a teen pregnancy classroom in the building without help. Indeed, in six of the schools I visited, I was led to the teen pregnancy classrooms because I was told, "you will not be able to find it on your own." In two of the buildings, students working in the office who were asked to take me to the teen pregnancy classroom did not know where it was, and, in one building, a student and I wandered a corridor as the student said, "I know it [the classroom] is here somewhere."

A teacher described the invisibility and obscurity of the teen pregnancy classroom in this way:

We have to keep it very quiet that we are here. I am not allowed to hang a banner or flier up saying this is a "GOALS" classroom. Some of the teachers do not even know I am here. I cannot go into other classes and talk about GOALS, so the girls really have to find me.

Another teacher stated:

The fear is that if we are too visible that the community will get upset—kids will go home talking to their parents about the pregnant girls in their school and the parents will call the principal. This hasn't occurred yet, but the principal is very clear that he does not want this to happen. So I keep it pretty quiet. That makes it hard because I don't feel like I really belong to this building.

When asked how this invisibility affects the implementation of the teen pregnancy program, the teachers responded in a similar manner:

Well, you just do what you have to do. I still feel like what I'm doing is important, and I make the agency contacts and help the girls as much as I can. But, yeah, I think I am probably missing some girls because they do not know that help is available to them in the school.

Another teacher states:

> You have to start out with a low profile, then when your principal, other teachers and school board sees results, you'll get support. It is difficult though because there is always the idea that GOALS is endorsing teen pregnancy by making it too easy for them [the girls].

While the teachers discussed the placement and invisibility of their classrooms as impacting on implementation in terms of numbers of students they served (a fact supported by other research; see Burdell, 1995), they did not mention the placement and invisibility of their classrooms as affecting program and curriculum implementation. However, the second similarity found in these seven sites, in addition to issues of location and visibility in the school at large, concerns issues of implementation, situating the physical classroom environments as important to the kinds of discourses occurring in the classrooms. Traditional classroom environments evoked similar pedagogy and also similar body discourses.

The seven traditional classroom sites operated in very traditional teacher-student relationships. The students sat in desks in rows, while the teachers stood at the front of the room and taught. The teachers in these classrooms tended to be the teachers who "followed the APRG [the program guide] closely" and developed their discourse and relations with the girls based upon the suggestions in the program guide. For example, the teachers in these classrooms, although situated in middle-class suburban communities, were more likely to describe teen parents (girls) as[12]

> hard luck kids. They are just hard luck kids. They haven't had very much go right in their life, and they've made a mistake which is now going to affect another innocent life. You have to try to help them deal with their mistakes in a mature and responsible way.

The pregnant girls at these sites were "good" girls who had [made] a mistake. When adults—teachers, administrators, parents—in these communities face the need to develop programs for teen girls who are pregnant, they do so with a sense of alarm. Comments such as "we have good girls here" and "this has never been a problem here before" incite cause for alarm and practices of containment. Lesko (in press) finds that school districts, limited by the political rhetoric of the New Right and its focus on "family values," respond to the "specific needs" of school-aged mothers with neglect and invisibility. The needs of teen mothers are excessive, "leaky," overflowing the current boundaries that attempt to contain them in the realm of "just economic" or "just family" issues (p. 190).

The pregnant girls in these settings also *seemed* to embody a similar contained view on teen pregnancy. They spoke more often of their own pregnancies as "mistakes" and were quick to classify other girls' pregnancies as "definitely a mistake." Lesko (1988) found that girls in teen pregnancy programs speak a type of reformation talk—what Lesko calls "rites of redemption" (p. 125). This discourse of redemption was also typified by the girls in the traditional classroom settings:

> I made a mistake and did some things I should not have done. I know that now. And now I need to learn how to take care of my baby and be a responsible parent and get a job . . . and yeah . . . this program will help me do that.

These discourses were embodied through the teachers' interactions with the students and the students' regulation of their own bodies in school. Seldom did the girls at these sites interact actively together in the classroom—exchanging stories or friendly gossip. In fact, I observed only one instance of this behavior during 60 visits to these classrooms. While the teachers showed warmth and jocularity with their students, there was little physical interaction. The girls also regulated their own bodies in these classrooms. While girls' bodies became relaxed in the home economics classrooms, the girls in traditional classroom settings remained proper and stiff, even as they tried to fit into traditional desks, which, by their second trimester, often became difficult to sit in and were certainly uncomfortable. By their last trimester, many of the girls had to sit on the edge of the desk seat and turn sideways to fit within the confines of the desk space.

The contrast of the girls' emerging pregnancies and the confines of the traditional classroom were not discussed in these classrooms. Sometimes, as a girl attempted to fit into a desk and made a grunt or a comment, wry smiles would pass around the room, and others stared until she was "comfortable," but there were no verbal complaints. The teachers and girls seemed to expect that the girls should adapt to their environment even if it did not suit their changing bodies. A couple of girls explained this adaptation in the following ways:

> You're just not supposed to complain in this school or act like you should be treated different because you are pregnant.

> But they treat us like we're different and you get watched twice as closely. Mrs. _____ [their teacher] says we have to set a good example, that some people think we should not even be in school.

> Yeah, it's like we shouldn't be here so you just get watched a lot, and you can't make any mistakes or let anyone know you feel sick—not when you're pregnant.

I can't wait to get home at the end of the day and relax on my couch. I think I will do home schooling for my last month—it's just too hard to be here.

While in school, these girls knew they were being watched, regulated, and expected to perform in ways that show their gratitude to be at school and demonstrate redemption for their mistakes. These girls realized they had engaged in a contract, albeit an unwritten one, with their schools that allowed them to stay in school and stay on track with their classes only if they behaved in certain ways.[13] As one girl stated:

It's like when you're pregnant and in school you have to be quiet or people think you're bad. They act like something is wrong with you anyway, and you can forget about being in clubs or anything—they won't let you. It's like you have to pay for your mistake and you better do it quietly or only say the things he [the principal] wants you to say.

In contrast, the three teen pregnancy classrooms that were housed in home economics rooms provided stories of bodies and practices different from the stories described above. The home economic rooms, although they varied in size, were situated in the main floors of their schools on a main hallway. Two of the rooms had doors opening onto two main hallways. Thus, the rooms were visible and often served as "stop-in" spots or "resting" places. These rooms had banners hanging on windows or doors acknowledging the presence of the teen pregnancy program in the building, and inside the rooms hung announcements and pictures of recent births.

The rooms were certainly more comfortable than traditional classrooms with chairs separate from large tables. Two of the rooms had couches. One room had playpens, although it did not provide on-site child care.[14] The addition of stoves, refrigerators, sinks, end tables, lamps, and rugs provided a more homey, if often crowded, feeling to the rooms. The teachers in these classrooms were more likely to "do my own thing" in implementing the teen pregnancy program and were less likely to say that the girls in their classes had made "mistakes." Rather, these teachers described the girls they worked with in the following way: "They got in trouble and society tells them [the girls] that they're the ones who have to deal with it. They just don't get a break, so I try to help them make it against everything else."

Well, I don't think they are necessarily bad. I don't think they have thought very clearly—and part of it is they get so wrapped up in boys. But now they have to stop and think of themselves and their babies, and they need help to do that.

The teachers in these settings engaged in differing pedagogical strategies to increase student participation, and the formal line between teacher and student was much less rigidly drawn. Group discussions, popular culture (for example, rap, pop music, or videos), and games were used to introduce topics of relationships, gender roles, sex, and birth control. Every time I observed in these settings, I witnessed student/student and student/teacher interactions that were friendly and informal. It was in these settings, often during "informal" times, that I heard stories of independence and "discourses of desire" (p. 48). The girls in these rooms looked forward to their times together and shared information with each other about pregnancy, boyfriends, sex, birth control, and their own sexuality. Often the teachers would let these conversations continue, interjecting only to correct misinformation or provide further information.

The most emphatic difference noted in these classroom settings, however, was the differences in bodies in the rooms. As described previously, the girls in the traditional classrooms remained "proper" in their classrooms and had to work to adapt their changing bodies to the limits of the classroom environment. The girls in the home economics classrooms claimed this space as their own—they spewed textbooks and notebooks on the tables, draped sweaters and coats on the chairs, drew on the chalkboards, admired baby pictures on the walls, and relaxed their bodies onto sofas or into chairs, putting their feet up or heads down.

Here was a space where the pregnant teen could be pregnant. Here she could put her feet up, complain about nausea or swollen ankles and get sympathy, a soda cracker, or a foot rub. Here girls loosened pants that were too tight, massaged abdomens and backs, and compared "stomachs" to "see who's biggest." Here girls shared stories and secrets. Here girls stayed in school until their ninth month and after, often sharing frank and explicit ideas on sex, sexuality, labor, and childbirth:

> You all are laughing at me, and I know this sounds gross but the nurse was telling me to do it, and I wanted to have my baby—so I'm in the room rubbing my nipples, like not to get off or something, but it can help you have your baby 'cause it makes you have, what is it?

Here the teacher intervened and answered "contractions" and confirmed to the other girls who were looking skeptical that the girl was right. And the girl continued: "You wait—you'll be so ready to have your baby you'll do anything. 'Tanya' be twisting her nipples off by 8 months."

This discussion exceeded the boundaries of what the program guide suggests should be included in the curriculum, and I never observed such a conversation in the traditional classroom settings.[15] This teacher allowed many conversations like this to occur and felt that "the girls know what they need to know about and this way gives the girls important information on pleasure and childbirth in a way they can hear it." This ease and relaxation of bodies did not mean that there were not "lessons" presented and regulatory practices in place. The teachers in these classrooms still monitored their students' diets and home lives and still had clear goals of helping the students in their programs. As described, however, these lessons took place through alternative formats and discussions and often followed the lead of the girls themselves.

"Relaxed" bodies also did not mean more easily regulated bodies. The girls in these classrooms spoke the strongest stories of independence and evoked the strongest messages of self-esteem. The girls acknowledged the importance of the classrooms in their lives in the following ways: "I can't wait to get in here and see everyone and just relax." "It's about the only place in the school where I feel comfortable—where you can just let it all hang out." "It's [the teen pregnancy room] where I come if I'm feeling depressed or sick or something—just to get away and feel okay about myself or get a hug." "I'm glad we don't have guys in our class. It's the only time you can get away from them teasing us and pulling on you and stuff. Sometimes we have to close our doors to keep 'em out too."

Thus, the teen pregnancy classes housed in home economics rooms demonstrated that space regulates practices and bodies in very different ways than in the traditional classroom setting. In the home economics classrooms, the girls reacted in more relaxed bodies and coveted their space to do so. A combination of teacher attitude and school setting provided a space where teen pregnant girls' bodies were allowed to be excessive, proliferative, leaky, and openly pregnant. These settings also provided more space for countervoices of independence and "discourses of desire" not heard in other teen pregnancy classrooms.

Concluding With Bodies and Exposures

For this research, paying attention to bodies methodologically highlights the fact that there is a physicality obvious in teen pregnancy that has for the most part been avoided. Working in a research arena that is already overexposed, such as teen pregnancy, the body as site of deconstructive practice can work to make explicit what is both overexposed and obscured elsewhere. Both of the exposures presented point to the inability of our theories, practices, and programs to deal with certain bodies, in this case, the pregnant teen body.

While school-based teen pregnancy programs assume that a separation of school and the body can be regulated and sustained (Burdell, 1995), the girls in this research demonstrated that the body is not so easily separable, nor do they desire it to be. The first exposure points to how teen girls use the tension and the discomfort that their changing, pregnant bodies invoke in others as a site of resistance. Paying attention to the bodies of teen girls who are pregnant and how they negotiate their bodies interrupts a simplistic telling of representation and resistance. Can teen girls' silence in their teen pregnancy classrooms be written simply as acquiescence or repressive practice? This research suggests it cannot. McNay (1994) points out that such a "(re)formulation of power does not deny the phenomenon of repression, but it does deny it theoretical primacy" (p. 91).

In this case, paying attention to the body methodologically seeks to acknowledge how teen girls who are pregnant take on the repressive discourse of the teen pregnancy program and speak it back, tracing how they use their bodies to this end. This move toward the body is not about celebrating what is marginalized, but an engagement in a move that interrupts a simplistic telling or a goddess worshiping of the body, moving instead toward what Elizabeth Grosz (1995) describes as

> more an enjoyment of the unsettling effects that rethinking bodies implies for those knowledges that have devoted so much conscious and unconscious effort to sweeping away all traces of the specificity, the corporeality, of their own processes of production and representation. (p. 2)

Turning the gaze upon the teen pregnancy program itself, holding a teen pregnancy program accountable for its corporeality raises many questions and exposes alternative interpretations. A view from the body sees teen pregnant girls' interruptions, silences, and/or unruliness as not simply irresponsible behavior, but as interruptive, *embodied* forms of resistance. The second exposure further explores how the *invisibility and locatedness* of teen pregnancy programs may affect the implementation of these programs. How does spatial management of teen pregnancy classrooms regulate and/or contain the bodies of teachers and girls?

Paying attention to the body and embodied practices necessitates specific and particular attention to the body as a site of information and practice, of regulation, power, and resistance. Tracing the body, its practices and exposures, is particularly important in regards to the study of gendered social issues like teen pregnancy. Brian Fay (1987) points out that "oppression leaves its traces not just in people's minds, but in their muscles and skeletons as well" (p. 146). In other words, bodies bear the marks of our culture, practices, and policies.

I have proposed a deconstructive reading of the body that calls for attention to the body deconstructively, not to build new formulations but to open possibilities for further strategies. Donna Haraway (1988) describes the view from the body as "always complex, contradictory, structuring" (p. 585). While my own research experiences have demonstrated that attention to bodies in practice and theory is complex and at times uncomfortable (Pillow, 1996b), I view this complexity as desirable in working toward social justice. Working with the complexity of our bodies—their messiness and "leakiness"—allows a thinking beyond our current boundaries, exposes what we may be too uncomfortable to portray, and works to makes what is obscured explicit.

Notes

1. I use the term *girls* here and throughout this paper to refer to the females ages 13–17 who were a part of a study I conducted during 1992–1994 (Pillow, 1994). "Girls" was the preferred term they used among themselves, and I have come to consider how the term captures the tension between their lives as girls and lives as women.

2. I am alluding here to what I see as a critical difference between reflective and deconstructive practices in ethnography. Visweswaran (1994) differentiates the two by stating that while reflexivity "says that we must confront our own processes of interpretation," deconstruction "says we must confront the plays of power in our processes of interpretation" (p. 79). See Pillow (1996b) for a discussion of the body as site of reflective and deconstructive practice.

3. While public interest has lately been focused on the fathers of teen pregnancies, intervention programs remain focused on the teen mother. Although the traditional married, two-parent family may be presented as a model, it is expected that teen mothers, in most cases, will bear full physical, developmental, and fiscal responsibility for their children.

4. Many teen pregnancy intervention programs begin with the assumption that the girls have made a mistake and must learn to make better, rational decisions in their lives. Girls who are teen parents are already viewed as having made irresponsible decisions and thus must demonstrate and prove their ability to engage in responsible decision making. Thus, programs that require girls to return to school one month after childbirth, make their own child care arrangements, excuse only three absences a year for sick children, expect girls to schedule doctor appointments for their children after school hours, and require girls to demonstrate that they are actively searching for employment justify these requirements as in the best interests of the girls (Burdell, 1995; Pillow, 1994). However, many of these practices seem aimed at the best interests of the state. Nancy Lesko (1990) in fact, refers to these practices as "rites of redemption" (p. 125).

5. Combining mothering and work is something that is difficult for any mother, regardless of age, and is certainly compounded by single-parent status and

socioeconomic class. In essence, we are asking teen parents to overcome society's own conflicting and stereotypical messages about single mothers and to do so in a responsible fashion. I have often wondered how I and the other single parents I know would hold up under the scrutiny, standards, and judgment of the teen parent programs I have studied.

6. Most programs for teen girls who are pregnant operate in separate classrooms, buildings, or campuses away from the rest of the public school setting.

7. Ironically, most teen pregnancy programs enforce and promote an asexual, neutral approach toward young women's sexuality, ignoring the fact that they have obviously already been and may continue to be sexually active (Pillow, 1994).

8. I do not want to encourage a simplistic definition of resistance (see Haney, 1996, for a discussion of the complexities of resistance between girls and the state), but rather I want to focus on how I observed girls in the teen pregnancy program become aware of the way in which their pregnant bodies were both assumed resistant and how the girls came to use this phenomenon to incite further resistance. Additionally, with the stories presented here, I am not attempting to situate a case of girls versus the program, where the girls are "right," but rather to provide a forum for a discussion of girls' bodies and resistance. I have explored and discussed elsewhere the complexities of telling teen girls' stories of resistance, where the forms of resistance may occur in ways that resist a critical or feminist telling and are stories which are uncomfortable to tell (Pillow, 1994, 1996a, 1996b).

9. Kelley also discussed how, while her mother, the teen pregnancy teacher, and she were working to arrange a continuation of her advanced placement classes, she "took pleasure" in going to every meeting "myself, with my pregnant body so that they (the school administration) would have to deal with the fact that yes, I was pregnant and that I was still a student at their school."

10. Kelley received support from the students at her old school. Against administrative wishes, the senior class included Kelley's name on a sweatshirt with signatures of the "Class of '92." The administration threatened not to let the seniors sell the sweatshirt and then later said the sweatshirt could not be worn on the school grounds—a decision that was later revoked.

11. Pseudonym for the teen pregnancy program I studied.

12. It is important to note here that the goal is not to critique these discourses or say they are "wrong"—the teachers I talked with are dedicated, caring professionals for whom I developed much respect—but to situate and attempt to understand what impact the regulatory function of architecture may have on the discourse spoken and embodied in these classrooms.

13. Similar to Fine's (1988) work on school dropouts, this research raises questions about who teen pregnancy programs do serve and perhaps, more importantly, who do they want and not want to serve? Several girls at these sites told me that they had friends who had opted not to enroll in the teen pregnancy program "because of the way you're treated in school." While the teen pregnancy program I researched claimed a high graduation rate of its students, by my closest estimations, the program served less than 35 percent of the teen pregnancies in the state. Burdell

(1995), in a review of related literature, found similar findings: programs tend to target "specific segments of students and ignore the rest" (p. 185).

14. Child care was not provided at any of the settings I observed and not condoned by the state teen pregnancy program. Girls in the suburban schools were particularly discouraged from bringing their babies to school for any reason as it was, in one teacher's view, "an inappropriate thing to do—this is a high school—a place to learn with your mind not to show off what you made with your body."

15. As discussed above, this is not to say that this type of conversation did not occur in the traditional school settings, only that these conversations were regulated out of the official space of the teen pregnancy classrooms I observed.

References

Allison, D. (1994). *Skin: Talking about sex, class and literature.* Ithaca, NY: Firebrand Books.

Bane, M. (1986). Household composition and poverty. In S. H. Danziger & D. H. Weinberg (Eds.), *Fighting poverty: What works and what doesn't* (pp. 209–31). Cambridge, MA: Harvard University Press.

Burdell, P. A. (1993). *Becoming a mother in high school: The life histories of five young women.* Unpublished doctoral dissertation. University of Wisconsin-Madison, Madison, WI.

Burdell, P. A. (1995). Teen mothers in high school: Tracking their curriculum. *Review of Research in Education, 21*(3): 163–208.

Butler, J. (1990). *Gender trouble: Feminism and the subversion of identity.* New York: Routledge.

Butler, J. (1993). *Bodies that matter: On the discursive limits of "sex."* New York: Routledge.

Center for Population Options. (1990). *Teenage pregnancy and too early childbearing: Public costs, personal consequences* (6th ed.). Washington, D.C.: The Center for Populations Options.

Cixous, H. (1994). In S. Sellers (Ed.), *The Helene Cixous reader.* London: Routledge.

Cusick, T. (1989). Sexism and early parenting: Cause and effect? *Peabody Journal of Education. 8*(4): 113–131.

Davis, A. Y. (1981). *Women, race, and class.* New York: Vintage Books.

de Lauretis, T. (1984). *Alice doesn't: Feminism, semiotics, cinema.* London: Macmillan.

Diprose, R. (1994). *The bodies of women: Ethics, embodiment and sexual difference.* London: Routledge.

Fay, B. (1987). *Critical social science.* Ithaca, NY: Cornell University Press.

Fine, M. (1988) Sexuality, schooling and adolescent females: The missing discourse of desire. *Harvard Educational Review, 58:* 29–53.

Fine, M. (1991). *Framing dropouts: Notes on the politics of an urban high school.* Albany: State University of New York Press.

Foucault, M. (1974). *The history of sexuality: An introduction, Volume L.* New York: Vintage Books.

Game, A. (1991). *Undoing the social: Towards a deconstructive sociology.* Toronto, Canada: University of Toronto Press.

Gaskell, J. (1992). *Gender matters from school to work.* Philadelphia: Open University Press.

Grosz, E. (1995). *Space, time, and perversion.* London: Routledge.

Grosz, E., & Probyn, F. (Eds.). (1995). *Sexy bodies: The strange carnalities of feminism.* London: Routledge.

Haney, L. (1996). Homeboys, babies, men in suits: The state and the reproduction of male dominance. *American Sociological Review, 61:* 759–78.

Haraway, D. J. (1988). Situated knowledges: The science question in feminism and the privilege of the partial perspective. *Feminist Studies, 14*(3): 575–99.

hooks, bell (1990). *Yearning: Race, gender, and cultural politics.* Boston: South End Press.

Lawson, A., & Rhode, D. L. (Eds.). (1993). *The politics of pregnancy: Adolescent sexuality and public policy.* New Haven, CT: Yale University Press.

Lesko, N. (1990). Curriculum differentiation as social redemption: The case of school-aged mothers. In R. Page & L. Valli (Eds.), *Curriculum differentiation: Interpretive studies in U.S. secondary schools* (pp. 113–36). Albany: State University of New York Press.

Lesko, N. (1991). Implausible endings: Teenage mothers and fictions of school success. In N. B. Wyner (Ed.), *Current perspectives on the culture of schools* (pp. 45–64). Brookline, MA: Brookline Books.

Lesko, N. (in press). The 'leaky needs' of school-aged mothers: An examination of U.S. programs and policies. *Curriculum Inquiry.*

McNay, L. (1992). *Foucault: A critical introduction.* Cambridge, MA: Polity Press.

Moore, H. L. (1994). *A passion for difference.* Bloomington: Indiana University Press.

Pillow, W. S. (1994) *Policy discourse and teenage pregnancy: The making of mothers.* Unpublished dissertation. The Ohio State University, Columbus.

Pillow, W. S. (April, 1996a). *Embodied analysis: Unthinking teen pregnancy.* Paper presented at the annual meeting of the American Educational Research Association, New York, NY.

Pillow, W. S. (April, 1996b). *Reflexivity as discomfort.* Paper presented at the annual meeting of the American Educational Research Association, New York, NY.

Pillow, W. S. (1997). Decentering silences/troubling irony: Teen pregnancy's challenge to policy analysis. In C. Marshall (Ed.), *Feminist critical policy analysis I: A primary and secondary schooling perspective.* London: Falmer Press.

Rowe, K. (1995). *The unruly woman: Gender and the genres of laughter.* Austin, TX: University of Texas Press.

Scheurich, J. J. (1995) Policy archaeology: A new policy studies methodology. *Journal of Policy Studies, 9*(4): 297–316.

Tolman, D. L. (1992). *Voicing the body: A psychological study of adolescent girls' sexual desire.* Unpublished doctoral dissertation. Harvard University, Cambridge, MA.

Tolman, D. L. (1994). Doing desire: Adolescent girls' struggles for/with sexuality. *Gender & Society, 8:* 324–42.

Trinh, T. M-H. (1989). *Woman, native, other: Writing post-coloniality and feminism.* Bloomington, IN: Indiana University Press.

Visweswaran, K. (1994). *Fictions of feminist ethnography.* Minneapolis: University of Minnesota Press.

Walker, R. (Ed.). (1995). *To be real.* New York: Anchor Books.

Walkerdine, V. (1990). *Schoolgirl fictions.* London: Verso.

Weatherly, R. A., Perlman, S. B., Levine, M., & Klerman, L. V. (1985). *Patchwork programs: Comprehensive services for pregnant and parenting adolescents.* Seattle: Center for Social Welfare Research, School of Social Work, University of Washington.

Weedon, C. (1987). *Feminist practice and poststructuralist theory.* Cambridge, UK: Basil Blackwell.

Wilton, T. (1995). *Lesbian studies: Setting an agenda.* London: Routledge.

Young, I. M. (1990). *Throwing like a girl and other essays in feminist philosophy and social theory.* Bloomington: Indiana University Press.

11

Ethnodrama

Performed Research—
Limitations and Potential

Jim Mienczakowski

D espite Victor Turner's (1986) initial call for research that also participated in performance, the worlds of theatre and research at that time
were too far apart for a viable elision between the aesthetic assumptions of
performance and the methodological and theoretical ambitions of research to
truly take place. Only recently has the full import and understanding of ethnodramatic research been given sufficient and effective credence by theatre
communities and research communities to prompt a coherent and cogent
development of theory with practice. Theoretically, these developments are
occurring because of (and paradoxically despite) the precedence established
by a raft of early documentary-style dramas involving oral history techniques
(Cheeseman, 1971; Paget, 1987) and *verbatim theatre*. There are numerous
possible reasons for this. One might be the differing interpretations of
research and its foundations and emphases within recognized *artistic performance processes and qualitative academic traditions*. Whereas the former

From Mienczakowski, J., "Ethnodrama: Performed Research—Limitations and
"Potential," in *Handbook of Ethnography,* copyright © 2001, reprinted with permission of Sage Publications, Inc.

"artistic" process is often viewed as a process of self-discovery and self-learning at an aesthetic and emotional level, the latter "research" conception is often perceived to revolve around understandings of science, theory, and methodology.

It is not my intention to enter the debate over the much-rehearsed issues distinguishing the research emphasis and critical basis of ethnodrama from earlier verbatim and oral history performance approaches. Suffice it to say that the distinctions between early oral history and verbatim theatre techniques and ethnodrama research are clear. The aforementioned verbatim theatre largely draws upon *verbatim* recordings of interviews or eyewitness accounts of historic events. Proponents of the form consider that it is the *verbatim nature* of the presentations themselves that lends meaningful authority, import, and significance to the resulting realizations. As verbatim and documentary-style performances are often about cultural reification, they frequently ignore the potential of their dramas to explore the present moment. Conversely, ethnodramas and ethnographic performances are about *the present moment* and seek to give the text back to the readers and informants in the recognition that we are all coperformers in each other's lives. In the way that ethnographic semiotics explores and decodes the meaning of culturally symbolic signs of visual and verbal communication, particularly in the realm of film (Worth, 1978), so ethnodrama is explicitly concerned with decoding and rendering accessible the culturally specific signs, symbols, aesthetics, behaviours, language, and experiences of health informants using accepted theatrical practices. It seeks to perform research findings in a language and code accessible to its wide audiences. Yet, too often, performed ethnographic narrative is associated by arts practitioners with less articulated verbatim and documentary approaches.

Ethnodramas consensually construct both their scripts and performance scenarios with informants controlling the text and representations made. The performance process is subject to continual processes of validation—including validation by expert audiences (health consumer groups) not involved as informants but otherwise familiar with the health experiences being represented. Typically, ethnodramas utilize trainee nurses and students in their research, construction, and depiction of health scenarios and consequently act as pre-professional vicarious learning opportunities for nurses about to enter the work domains being researched and performed. Performances of such researches are opened to audience comment and debate at the close of each performance and through other structured opportunities to inform the production team and cast through fax, telephone, questionnaire, or interview. Specific health agencies promote ethnodramas and most performances provide appropriate discrete counseling facilities (that is, representatives of relevant alcohol and drug services; mental health counsellors, psychiatric nurses, or sexual assault service counsellors, etc.) to assist in supporting and debriefing audiences and participants after performances. Ethnodrama performances are constantly updated according to data drawn from audience interactions. Scripts are made available to audiences prior to or at performances so that audience members may seek clarification or revisit the issues represented in the performances. Ethnodramas operate on a set of themes considered central and pertinent to understanding the experience of a particular health or social issue by relevant informants. Verbatim theatre, oral histories, and documentary theatres do not articulate their thesis beyond theatrical presentation to their audiences.

Beyond oral history and verbatim approaches, Mulkay (1985) has proposed an ethnographic dramatic narrative that uses parody as a form of social analysis. His application of humour is a deliberate ploy to portray the myriad interactions of society (which might otherwise be inaccessible or of no apparent interest) to audients using traditional comedic devices to instigate perceptual shifts in their response to ethnographic data. Similarly, Laurel Richardson's creation of a dramatized narrative "The Sea Monster: An Ethnographic Drama" (Richardson & Lockridge, 1991) enabled her to discuss those issues central to the postmodern reconstruction of ethnography through both parody and irony. Performance ethnography should be seen, in a sense, to occupy a space in ethnographic discourse that challenges traditional reporting approaches through the incorporation of genres, practices, and techniques used in "theatre, film, video, ethnography, performance, text" (Denzin, 1997). Incorporated with audience responses, this may promote wider understanding for participants. Ethnodramas differ from other forms of performance ethnographic practice because it is their overt intention not just transgressively to blur boundaries, but to be a form of public voice ethnography that has emancipatory and educational potential. Thus, the extensive validatory processes inherent in the interactionist data-gathering techniques of the ethnodrama methodology and the reflexive nature of its performance processes overcome some of the structural difficulties inevitable in the ethnographic venture.

Of particular significance in ethnodrama is the consensual nature of the validatory processes that seek to create a sense of *vraisemblance* (Todorov, 1968). Atkinson's (1990) more apt description: the creation of *plausible accounts* of the everyday world by project participants and audiences of the report, is one of the major objectives of ethnodrama. This is because both textually and, in the case of ethnodrama, physically, vraisemblance is sought in order to evoke belief by representing *perceived* social realities in terms that mask the cultural influences affecting the constructors of the report. In order to consensually agree that both the written research report and its physical interpretation on stage are in the authentic language of, and therefore recognizable to and interpretable by informants, the ethnodrama processes are extended through Bakhtinian (1984) *dialogic interactions*. These dialogic interactions may thus be interpreted as the informant group's *struggle* to create and share meaning by developing an appreciation for, and understanding of, health patients' and health professionals' experience of order and reality through formally structured group discussions that are extended via forum theatre techniques (Boal, 1979; Mienczakowski, 1994). The product or outcome of these dialogical engagements is the research report: the ethnodramatic script. This script, using the language of the informants in a lyrical, sometimes verbatim but always realistic, portrayal of informants' experiences of health practices, may then be seen as a collective endeavour to demolish or blur the barriers between health care recipients, professionals, policy-makers, and the general public.

Denzin (1997) connects the overall and rapidly expanding move towards ethnographic performance as a logical turn for a number of human disciplines in which *culture* is increasingly seen as performance and *performance texts* as being able to concretize experience. In general, the move to academically essentialize and articulate the reflexive aspects of these earlier ways of working has been limited. Denzin (1997) has clearly recognized that many forms of research performance work are bound to aesthetic conventions that need to be set aside for audiences of ethnographic performances. Thus notions of aesthetics and artistry need not subvert the potential of research narratives and their public analysis from meeting the real ethnographic goals of public explanation and cultural critique by allowing an analysis of the representations made through the "co-participatory" performance nature of postmodern ethnographic research. Consequently, ethnographic performance texts are about *speaking with* informants and audiences rather than *speaking for* or *about* them. Interactive ethnographic performances often go further still in experimenting with and disturbing the delineation between performers and audiences, texts and authors. Although Denzin (1997) opens the door to this conversation, there is still much work to be done in connecting the work of performance ethnography to the natural development of certain forms of professional/fringe theatre, which increasingly involves contesting and blurring the same aesthetic, performance, and textual boundaries. For example, the work of the *Triangle Theatre Company*[1] (Coventry, UK) exemplified the performance use of autoethnography, or critical analysis of self through autobiographical reflection, to explore and articulate personal responses to the loss of a child, then performed these ethnographic narratives in its productions.

What Has Been Done

The progression and heritage of ethnodrama has been more serendipitous and pragmatic than most theoretical turns. In 1992 academics involved in theatre, education, and health were prompted to construct a performance piece for Australia's "Mental Health Week." The brief was to construct a research performance project that sought to represent and then open for debate within the audience and cast certain key themes of schizophrenic experience. Initially, the original team of theatre practitioners and academics in psychiatric nurse education and psychology embarked upon uncovering the experience of psychosis through detailed ethnographic and phenomenological research processes which would ensure that all team members might understand the meaning of the health issues involved (Morgan & Mienczakowski, 1993). The aim was to provide accessible data in order to inform and foreground the future theatre performance. The result was the realization that, in a small way, this process had the potential to represent a new theoretical turn through finding limited grounds for Habermas' notion of human communicative consensus/competence (Mienczakowski, 1995; 1996). Furthermore, the process encouraged the development of a public voice form of research (Agger, 1991), provided significant learning opportunities for the health students involved, and, importantly, reached large, nightly audiences with ethnography.

The explanations, meanings, and insights generated by ethnodrama performances are consensually controlled and created by informant groups. As informants validate not only their own data but the scripted and performed scenarios generated by the research, the ethnodrama process represents not only an opportunity to voice informant understandings, explanations, experiences, and emotional location within the circumstances of their experiences of health or society but further gives rises to opportunities for student nurses, guidance counsellors, teachers, and health professionals to reflect, as participants or audience members, upon their own professional practices (Coffey & Atkinson, 1996).

Specifically, the ethnodrama is concerned with the recontextualization of dialogue and discourse, thus providing immediate public access to health participants including audients. This polyphonic voicing of our informants' agenda in a "public voice" (Agger, 1991) to wide audiences who might otherwise be disadvantaged or inhibited from accessing and interpreting the more traditional academic presentation of research data is not an attempt to return to a metanarrative or to lionize the worth of individual mini-narratives. If, in effect, we view the postmodern fracturing of metanarratives not in Lyotard's (1984) terms of "shattering" but more in Bernstein's (1996) terms as dislocation, specialization, and localization, then we might see postmodern stories not as a limiting rupturing of human understanding but as a tenable micro-minutia discourse on what is going on (Mienczakowski et al., 1996). That is, our performance of postmodern stories through the medium of ethn-odrama extends Bernstein's theories of giving the power of authorship back to those who live the health phenomena that is being taught or described.

The initial project in experiences of schizophrenia, *Syncing Out Loud* (Mienczakowski, 1992), was presented for a season within a university and also at Wolston Park Hospital, a large psychiatric hospital. The intent of this latter performance was twofold: first as validation of the research report (or script) and secondly as a beneficial event for the clients of the hospital, as viewed from within an emancipatory critical social framework (Mienczakowski, 1995; 1996; Morgan et al., 1993). This work, along with its successor project *Busting* (Mienczakowski & Morgan, 1993), which con-cerned itself with alcohol detoxification, has been reported fairly widely in a number of journals and disciplines (education, nursing, social sciences, and dramatic arts). Whilst this reporting has focused on the relatively innovative combination of health, drama, social research, and critical social theory, the team involved in developing the work came to understand that the implica-tions such performances held for audiences were, at times, far from being symbolic. It is this realization that has informed much of the debate presented in this chapter.

Ethnography: Contemporary Trends

The development of ethnographic narratives into a full-scale performance vehicle is clearly an elaboration and enhancement of ongoing, world-wide interest in evolving ethnographic constructions and practices (Ellis & Bochner, 1996). Ethnodrama sits within an extant school of theatre which searches for social change (Epskamp, 1989) but differs from other forms of similar theatre in that it adheres to the principles of a formal and recognizable ethnographic research methodology, above and beyond the artistic demands of aesthetics, in its attempt to produce cultural critique (Denzin, 1997). This is a route now being further explored by some high school and college practitioners (Diaz, 1997; Fox, 1997).

Contemporary ethnographic research is also written and disseminated in formats that have embraced poetry and biography (Ellis, 1995; Richardson, 1994) and interpretative interactionism (Denzin, 1989; 1997). Such moves are part of developing methodologies that attempt to use ethnographic and social science practices to question the usefulness of boundaries between literature, arts, and social science explanations of the world (Ellis & Bochner, 1996). The recognition that explanations of the world made through literature and the arts are closer to understandings gained through anthropology and the social sciences than those made via the physical sciences (Rorty, 1980) is of significance here. Turner (1986) envisaged ethnographic practice in which the *performance* of ethnography could be seen as a means of investigating channels of reception and human understanding. Critical ethnodrama seeks to meld the traditional values of textual, academic presentation and those of performance in its investigation of human understanding.

The proposition is that performed ethnography may provide more accessible and clearer public explanations of research than is frequently the case with traditional, written report texts (Mienczakowski, 1996). The public performance of ethnography in the argot of its informants may be argued to deacademize the report construction process. Significantly, ethnodrama also returns *the ownership,* and therefore the power, of the report to its informants as opposed to *possessing it* on behalf of the academy (Mienczakowski, 1996). The following script extract, largely verbatim transcription, exemplifies the potential power of this mode of research presentation to influence audiences emotionally and intellectually. Sally's monologue in this script is intentionally contrasted with the dialogue/data drawn from serving police officers who are more concerned with the unreliability of victims' testimony in court than the victim's experience of crime. It must be remembered that actors in costume perform these data and are supported with all the trappings of suspended disbelief and staging that *theatre* entails. Reading the data straight from the page might not have the same import.

Baddies, Grubs, and the Nitty-Gritty (Mienczakowski & Morgan, 1998b)

Scene 2: Rob, a new recruit to the Sexual Assault Squad, is advised by Col, the Senior Detective Inspector running the unit.

Rob: Will we use a female constable to do the interview?

Col: No. Not one available today. Look, I might as well put you straight on this. I reckon that this woman-woman stuff is all bullshit—I am a professional person and so are you, the lawyer, the doctor, even . . . I can't guarantee a jury of women only so why start now?

Strewth, if this was a rape-murder and we were looking at the naked body of a deceased female victim nobody would be expressing these sensibilities?

I want to be there when they gather evidence, if I'm allowed, to be able to direct the investigation. To be able to say photograph that bruise, what's made that scar? Take a shot of that.

Her body is a crime scene and I'm gathering evidence—to try and piece the story together and make sure it fits. Anything at all to get enough evidence for a watertight case.

And,

Scene 2 (Audio tape and slides)

Sally: Well, when I was initially sexually assaulted it was around the Christmas period and I couldn't get help. I don't think funding was very good at the time but eventually, I did speak to somebody in Brisbane, um . . . I rang as many different organizations as I could—people were either on breaks or no one was available, so in the end I was forced to ring the police.

It was very intimidating, and the police officer I saw, er, whilst he befriended me, um . . . he actually eventually crossed the line of his professional role, ah . . . Started to come around . . . —we eventually had a relationship for a while. I think he found my vulnerability and dependence, all of those things, he found them erotic.

When I went to the police . . . I wasn't . . . It wasn't offered to me to see a woman, and retelling the whole saga took eight hours. The first four hours . . . oh shit . . .

Finally I saw him, I think I saw him about a week after it had occurred. He took me into an interview room and ah . . . didn't record anything or anything the door was open. I had to come back the next day and make my statement in a public office and you could have heard a pin drop— so it was quite intimidating really. Everyone could hear and there were lots of interruptions. He very kindly came in on his day off, the next day, to take my statement 'cause he saw my genuine distress. Ah, it was still pretty intimidating I would have much preferred to talk to someone . . . a woman in an office in a sexual assault clinic.

Look, the first positive thing I did after the assault was to go to the police, well before that the first positive thing was to physically run away and hide from my assailant, the second positive thing was to go to the police. That was a really big step because it was putting all of my eggs in one basket and publicly saying "its not my fault" . . . in front of a lot of uniformed men. So I think it was a big step in the healing process . . . and going through with the stalking charges was a big step too, because it meant that I was saying that I count and have rights and the law should protect me.

And,

Rob: . . . OK. That's the baddy, so what about this woman in the interview room? What female support have we got for this woman we are about to interview?

Col: You keep banging on about support don't you? Maybe her mother—if she sits still and shuts up. She can sit there and shut up. Say nothing. Evidence just walks out of the room. Counselors give them words and language that a decent lawyer would shoot holes through. Give them ideas about dropping charges. And they are so cowardly that most of them won't go anywhere near a courtroom. But some are really good. They know the score. It's the young idealistic feminist types that are the problem. It's hard to deal with contamination of story after support service intervention.

Rob: They probably just want the person healed.

Col: Us too. We are the real bloody therapists in this.

Rob: How come?

Col: Seeing a baddy caught and sent to court to answer publicly is part of the recovery. Most victims need to hear "Yeah—you are right—he did rape you."

Transgressive or Progressive?

Peter Woods (1996) interestingly sidelines the postmodern turn in ethnographic practice as symptomatic of deliberations upon methodological trends and modes of representation. Rather than viewing postmodern approaches to qualitative research as part of an alternative or competing paradigm, he explains them simply as extensions of interactionist practices. Some may shy away from this recognition, but Woods firmly aligns meaningful and productive research with the apperception that both teaching and research have synergies as forms of art, which in turn strongly relate to Mead's (1934) concept of self and self identity. In relation to both the artistry and generalized tenets of research, Woods sees postmodern trends in qualitative approaches as opening spaces in which ethnographic research can, through a form of practitioner artistry, convincingly help the voices of participants to be heard. Some of these newly created spaces include the explanation and interpretation of ethnographic research through poetry, literary narrative, and performance.

Denzin (1997) draws clear connections between authentic expression and the transmission of validated, authentic research with the immediacy, contestability, and accessibility of performance. In essence, the potential of performance is relegated by Woods to the expression of research, and drama is limited to the status of a useful tool for prompting emotional recognition and connections between the drama's subject, participants, and audiences in general. Nevertheless, drama's potential lies in its ability to demonstrate research through the argot, codes, and symbols of its informants, thus opening research up to public discourse and informant engagement, in the same manner as research is said to be disseminated through literary and poetic channels.

As they are constructed in both a written and hybrid form of language, it might also be argued that poetic narratives represent culture-bound and inhibitory approaches for the dissemination of research. While Laurel Richardson certainly doesn't claim to produce open, public voiced texts and I emphatically imply no criticism of her lyrical poetic approach on such grounds, I do draw attention to postmodern concerns with informant and peer contestation of the written codes and stilted patriarchy of extant scientific research report writing codes. Such concern, it may be supposed, merits their replacement with more accessible written and explanatory codes. Yet by suggesting a literary, narrative, or poetic route to explanation we may be faced with an equally difficult genre for some readers to access. The use of transgressive poetic-literary writing styles undoubtedly evokes deep emotional and intellectual impacts upon those audiences *who are comfortable* with these particular expressive idioms—whilst it may perforce deny access and disenfranchise other audiences.

Denzin's (1994) uncertainty is that the construction of poetic accounts shouldn't be sanctioned simply because they provide an alternative to the many standard written approaches towards dissemination, which are often viewed as boring. He effectively insinuates that if the writer is dull, his or her attempts to create poetic interpretations of research may also be less than exciting. The call for contemporary ethnographers to heed is that intellectual coherence, insight, quality of argument, and the *appropriateness of presentation and organization* (Denzin, 1994) are the key elements of any ethnographic construction.

Another criticism of transgressive approaches I would like to include here is that of Snow and Morrill (1995) as referred to by Woods (1996). Snow and

Morrill suggest that screenwriters and playwrights may have a better eye and feel for artistry and the possibilities of constructing performance pieces than either ethnographers or academics toying with literary structures. Literature, they posit, is as hard fought for territory as is any academic discipline and *not everyone who is an ethnographer can also write decent and viable performance scripts.* It is at this point that I am obliged to argue on behalf of an emergent trend. Postmodernism has seemingly taught us to be healthily sceptical of attempts to rigidly name and compartmentalize *the other* within predetermined categories. If we distinguish literature as the domain of *literary* writers and believe that only artists *who live the life of artists* can produce art, then surely it must follow that only ethnographers can construct ethnography and only teachers can teach (Mienczakowski, 1997)?

Essentially, the arena we are in is one in which artists' *works and lives* are perceived as grounded within rigid categories and are often inseparably considered as *art*. Here also the products of the individual (books, scripts, poems, or paintings) may be considered creative, aesthetic, and "art" although the group products (scripts, performance researchers, ethnodramas, etc.) may not. With the reconstruction of ethnographic research as ethnodrama, I believe the boundaries between lived realities, art, theatre, literature, and various other eliding genres are abandoned rather than blurred or crossed. I would suggest that such artificially imposed boundaries are symbolic, largely representing the *self-interests of identity* of particular groups. Such identities are embodied within the general conception of artist, writer, poet, etc. Consequently, artists, writers, and poets seek to control both their received identities and the public judgement of what counts as an artistic or literary product. I am not for an instant suggesting that researchers, teachers, and ethnographers *per se* can all make useful and successful attempts to communicate and explain research through performance, literature, and poetry but I consider they should try. Or at the very least, they should not be disheartened or discouraged by the hypothesis that only professional writers, painters, poets, and playwrights have the skill, artistry, and aesthetic penchant to devise works of artistic worth or quality. It seems likely that such "validity claims" might functionally constrain or disenfranchise some attempts by researchers and teachers to have their artistic research works viewed on an aesthetic or artistic basis. Comparable arguments are frequently used against collaborative health theatre, which in some circumstances is inappropriately branded as purely *therapeutic* or aesthetically, artistically *compromised* as a form of theatre, in that it seemingly cannot meet the same aesthetic criteria as theatre derived from a sole professional playwright's deliberations. That may, at times, be the case but logically these suppositions have no credible or challenged theoretical foundation. It is, perhaps, a form of solipsism.

A point I have laboured elsewhere is that of Woods's acknowledgement of the potential of poetics to access audiences previously left unmoved by more traditional research approaches. This understanding is tempered by his calls for a model endorsing the supplementation of poetic-narrative interpretations with an explanatory (academic) text. Woods believes that the inclusion of such text might assist claims of veracity and confirm authority by demonstrating examples of triangulated data whilst simultaneously relating how the literary text was constructed. In his comprehension of the underlying reticence from some quarters, Woods suggests that *validity* claims might be replaced with *quality* checks to aid navigations and rigour within research. The duality of these notions makes me uneasy. On one hand, the ethnographer turned poet/playwright is forced to justify his or her research through secondary traditional academic categories that may be irrelevant to the aesthetic, semantic, and emotional construction of artistic interpretations. On the other hand, a subjective, external criterion of quality is applied to the work. Such a criterion must ponder the power of the representations to move audiences and increase understanding. Not an easy task and one that is seldom set for the authors of more traditional ethnographies! In either scenario, it seems that the transgressive arts ethnographer must produce double the work to gain the credibility and status afforded to ethnographers who chose more traditional data presentation approaches.

Happily, there are bodies of research and experimentation work that move far beyond Woods's concerns with validity and quality in performance research. Such works have attempted to seek audience understanding of and responses to ethnographically derived performance pieces and have gone a long way towards exploring the implications of constructed, *staged audience catharsis,* collective audience responses, and *emotional enlightenment* (Mienczakowski et al., 1996).

It is also possible that an entirely fictional work may receive higher aesthetic accolades, or construct stronger empathetic connections with audiences, under some criterion, than research-based performance ethnographies or transgressive literary approaches. However, Ellis and Bochner's (1992) short performance piece concerning their experience of deciding upon and undergoing an abortion may be an example of a different conception of theatre for a new kind of audience. The performance of this work is reported to have, nonetheless, still evoked high levels of emotional impact and connection with its audiences despite its nonfictional status. The piece's authoritative effectiveness most likely resided in its foundations in personal account as opposed to fictional construction or the performance abilities of the authors. Ellis and Bochner related to their academic audience by illuminating experience and emotional context in tandem. The opening of research to new and wider audiences via poetic, literary, narrative, and performance vehicles needs to be recognized too. With ethnodrama we know that we draw upon audiences specifically interested in the subject matter and intellectual location of the work. This is a new type of audience for whom aesthetics is subordinate to cogency.

Consequentially, a new conception of aesthetic understanding combined with a new consideration of audience may be required for research narratives that are not always rounded or complete in their interpretation into poetic or performance forms. Simply to adhere to and comply with a standard form of performance categorization and expectation through the insertion of dramatic plot devices or by contriving dramatic or poetic impact at the expense of research authenticity may subvert research authenticity to meet dramatic form.

I suspect that what is urgently required is a shift in the understanding and expectations of dramatic and literary form in order to acknowledge and embrace the change in form and genre that transgressive/alternative writing portends. These emergent forms—which demonstrate through performance research basis, validity, aesthetic qualities, and emotional connection combined with literary style—represent potentials yet to be realized, fully explored, and developed. The future is fraught with possibilities!

Problems in Potential

To accent some of the potentials and problems of ethnodrama, I move on to elaborate upon some of the problems of presentation. A coauthor and I have had cause (Mienczakowski, 1997; Mienczakowski & Morgan, 1998a) to divulge how we had unknowingly cast a student actor with unexpressed fundamentalist religious beliefs in a situation of personal vulnerability. Herein the student was confronted by the devil. That is, a student actor who believed schizophrenia to be the manifestation of the devil speaking through possessed persons, was happily cast as a psychiatrist for the run of a play concerning schizophrenic illness. When a group of psychiatric institution patients clambered on stage and confronted the actress as if she were *a real psychiatrist* during a performance, we (the production team) viewed the play as being rewritten and vitally enhanced through active audience participation and commentary. Simply, the subjects of our research were actively adding data. The fundamentalist actor perceived the situation altogether differently. Her religious belief system forced her towards a disturbing recognition. She believed that the psychotic patient who had confronted her and argued with her was possessed by the devil. *He was, therefore, the devil and he was trying to engage her in conversation.* She responded by taking flight and disappeared off stage and into the night.

A further demonstration of the power of plays to accurately portray events associated with health care caused us to question at what cost this was to the rehabilitative processes of our informants? An actor portraying the needle-related behaviours observed in detoxification units during rehearsals for the project performance *Busting: The Challenge of the Drought Spirit* simply discarded needles from a sharps box whilst demonstrating the routine use of multivitamin shots in detox treatment. To our special validating audience of informant detoxees from a local halfway house, this prompted recognition of "needle fixation" and associated behaviours. Several informants became agitated and excited and could not resist handling and examining the needles and further professed to be unable to concentrate on the play from that point onwards (Morgan & Mienczakowski, 1999).

Most serious of all, and it is this determination that has prompted me to recount these tales, we became aware of tendencies amongst academic and professional theatre companies in Australia to seek funding from health care sources in the name of health research theatre and health promotion specifically, to promote antisuicide awareness programmes for young people. Hooray! Hooray! Ooops! In a nation that boasts one of the highest youth suicide rates of the Western world, we should be involved in seeking resolution to such an issue. Performed ethnographic research could be an expansive and public voice method through which logical pursuit of these goals might be achieved. Wow, hold those horses—take a rain check and step right back.

From 1996 to 1999 *$AUS 31 million* in Federal government funding was committed to projects specifically related to addressing issues pertaining to youth suicide prevention strategies and programmes, research, and evaluation. We (members of our ethnodrama research team) found ourselves involved at a national level in providing some evaluation for a significant aspect of these preventative programmes relating to performances involving suicide issues. It allowed us the opportunity to assess the work of colleagues and kindred approaches and, more important, to further research the implications of performances with emancipatory intent (Morgan et al., 1998).

Instead of empowerment, we witnessed vulnerable audiences *placed at risk*. Though we can make no incontrovertible association (nor would we wish to do so), we saw health informant performers act out their own therapy to potentially vulnerable audiences. So much so, in fact, that a performed scenario concerning depression and a realistic staged suicide by hanging was echoed by the real life suicide of the cast's musical composer who hanged himself behind stage on the final night of the production. This was one of a number of suicides directly involving members of this health performance group and their health consumer network.

Notions surrounding the very real potential for drama depicting suicide to bring about copycat or clusters of suicides in real life may be traced back to similar concerns linked to the works of the writer Goethe (Phillips, 1989). Gould and Shaffer (1989) and Schmidtke and Haffner (1989) have depicted strong links between suicide scenes portrayed on German and U.S. television to cluster suicides occurring in a 2-week period after the scenes were viewed (Morgan & Mienczakowski, 1999).

I emphatically do not wish to reject the use of research performance, as it is a vital element of health education and promotion. It seems clear, however, that performance research approaches may not suit the issue of suicide. There may be other, as yet unidentified, areas best left unfathomed or treated with caution by this very public mode of research investigation and dissemination.

For some people and under some circumstances, exposure to theatre that seeks to redefine a person's relationship to a particular personal, health, or social topic may be loosely understood as entering the therapeutic realm. Transformational possibilities can also exist through observation alone, although within the context of deliberately interactive and critical ethnodrama, a participatory role for the audience may also be understood. Although substantial work is currently being undertaken in this field by a founding member of the ethnodrama project group, Steve Morgan, it has long been identified from our earlier investigations (Mienczakowski, 1995; Mienczakowski & Morgan, 1998b; Morgan et al., 1999) that research-based health performances attract a mix of health-interested persons and others who may or may not usually be attracted to theatrical presentations. Those audience members who seek a therapeutic encounter through the constructs of ethnodrama seem more likely to be affected by such strong performance themes (suicide and child abuse to name but a couple) than those who would more usually visit the theatre for the purposes of entertainment or aesthetic appeasement (Mienczakowski et al., 1996). There are reasonable grounds to explore the audience as existing cohesively as a momentary group unified in their relationship and interest in the health circumstances presented to them. In respect of audiences being in theatres for purposes of professional development and group learning, we may see ethnodrama performances as a mode of critical intervention operating within a variety of interpretative frameworks.

Note

1. Triangle Theatre Company, Coventry: *My Sister My Angel* (1997), Carran Waterfield, directed by Ian Cameron.

References

Agger, B. (1991). Theorising the decline of discourse or the decline of theoretical discourse? In P. Wexler (Ed.), *Critical theory now*. New York: Falmer Press. Ch. 5.

Atkinson, P. (1990). *The ethnographic imagination: Textual constructions of reality*. London: Routledge.

Bakhtin, M. (1984). *Problems of Dostoevsky's poetics* (Ed. and Trans., C. Emerson). Minneapolis: University of Minnesota Press.

Bernstein, B. (1996). *Official and local identities*. Marriot Seminar by Emeritus Professor Basil Bernstein, Griffith University, Gold Coast, 27–28 May.

Boal, A. (1979). *Theatre of the oppressed* (Trans., C. A. and M. L. McBride). New York: Urizen Books.

Cheeseman, P. (1971). Production casebook. *New Theatre Quarterly, 1*: 1–6.

Coffey, A., & Atkinson, P. (1996). *Making sense of qualitative data: Complementary research strategies*. Thousand Oaks, CA: Sage.

Denzin, N. (1989). *Interpretive internationalism*. Newbury Park, CA: Sage.

Denzin, N. (1994). The art and politics of interpretation. In N. K. Denzin & Y. Lincoln (Eds.), *The handbook of qualitative research*. London: Sage.

Denzin, N. K. (1997). *Interpretive ethnography: Ethnographic practices for the 21st century*. Thousand Oaks, CA: Sage.

Diaz, G. (1997). *Turned on/turned off (a clarion call)*. Qualitatives '97 OISE (Eds. L. Muzzin et al.). Toronto, ON: Desktop Publication. ISBN 0–9682062–0-4.

Ellis, C. (1995). *Final negotiations: A story of love, loss and chronic illness*. Philadelphia: Temple University Press.

Ellis, C., & Bochner, A. (1992). Telling and performing personal stories: The constraints of choice in abortion. In C. Ellis & M. G. Flaherty (Eds.), *Investigating subjectivity: Research on lived experience* (pp. 79–101). Newbury Park, CA: Sage.

Ellis, C., & Bochner, A. (1996). Talking over ethnography. In C. Ellis & A. Bochner (Eds.), *Composing ethnography: Alternative forms of qualitative writing* (pp. 13–45). Walnut Creek, CA: AltaMira.

Epskamp, K. (1989). *Theatre in search of social change: The relative significance of different theatrical approaches*. The Hague: Centre for the Study of Education in Developing Countries (CESO).

Fox, K. (1997). *First blood: Rituals of menarche*. Qualitatives '97 OISE (Eds. L. Muzzin et al.). Toronto, ON: Desktop Publication. ISBN: 0–9682062–0-4.

Gould, M. S. & Shaffer, D. (1989). The impact of suicide in television movies: Evidence of imitation. In R. F. W. Diekstra & R. Maris (Eds.), *Suicide and its prevention: The role of attitude and imitation* (pp. 331–40). (Advances in Suicidology, vol. 1). Leiden: Brill.

Lyotard, J. F. (1984). *The postmodern condition: A report on knowledge.* Minneapolis: University of Minnesota Press.

Mead, G. H. (1934). *Mind, self and society.* Chicago: University of Chicago Press.

Mienczakowski, J. (1992). *Syncing out loud: A journey into illness.* Brisbane: Griffith University Reprographies.

Mienczakowski, J. (1994). Theatrical and theoretical experimentation in ethnography and dramatic form. *ND DRAMA, Journal of National Drama, UK, 2:* 16–23.

Mienczakowski, J. (1995). The theatre of ethnography: The reconstruction of ethnography into theatre with emancipatory potential. *Qualitative Inquiry, 1*(3): 360–373.

Mienczakowski, J. (1996). An ethnographic act. In C. Ellis & A. Bochner (Eds.), *Composing ethnography: Alternative forms of writing.* Walnut Creek, CA: AltaMira Press. Ch. 10.

Mienczakowski, J. (1997). *An evening with the devil: The archaeology of emotion.* Society for the Study of Symbolic Interaction, 11–12 August, Colony Hotel, Toronto, ON.

Mienczakowski, J. (1998). Reaching wide audiences: Reflexive research and performance. *NADIE Journal, 22*(1): 75–82.

Mienczakowski, J. (1999). Ethnography in the hands of participants: Tools of discovery. In G. Walfrod & A. Massey (Eds.), *Studies in educational ethnography: Vol. 2. Explorations in methodology.* Oxford: Oxford University Institute of Education Studies/JAI Press.

Mienczakowski, J., & Morgan, S. (1993). *Busting: The challenge of the drought spirit.* Brisbane: Griffith University, Reprographics.

Mienczakowski, J., & Morgan, S. (1998a). Finding closure and moving on. *Drama, 5:* 22–29.

Mienczakowski, J., & Morgan, S. (1998b). *Stop! In the name of love and baddies, grubs and the nitty-gritty.* Society for the Study of Symbolic Interaction: Couch Stone Symposium, 22–24 February. University of Houston, University Hilton Hotel Complex, Houston, TX.

Mienczakowski, J., Smith, R., & Sinclair, M. (1996). On the road to catharsis: A theoretical framework for change. *Qualitative Inquiry, 2*(4): 439–462.

Morgan, S., & Mienczakowski, J. (1993). *Re-animation of the research report. Shaping nursing theory and practice* (Monograph No. 2). La Trobe University Press, Melbourne.

Morgan, S., & Mienczakowski, J. (1999). *Ethical dilemmas in performance ethnography: Examples from ethnodrama and theatre.* Unpublished paper presented at Couch Stone Symposium, SSSI, SSSI conference, Las Vegas, February 1999, pp. 9–15.

Morgan, S., Mienczakowski, J., & King, G. (1999). *The dramatic representation of suicide: Issues, concerns and guidelines.* Suicide Prevention Australia, Melbourne Convention Center. 25 March.

Morgan, S., Mienczakowski, J., & Rolfe, A. (1993). It's funny, I've never heard voices like that before. *Australian Journal of Mental Health Nursing, 15*(6): 244–249.

Morgan, S., Rolfe, A., & Mienczakowski, J. (1998). *Exploration! Intervention! Education! Health promotion!: A developmental set of guidelines for the presentation of dramatic performances in suicide prevention.* Mental Health Services Conferences and Proceedings, Hobart, October 1998.

Mulkay, M. J. (1985). *The word and the world: Explorations in the form of sociological analysis.* London: George Allen and Unwin.

Paget, D. (1987). Verbatim theatre: Oral history and documentary techniques. *New Theatre Quarterly, 12:* 317–336.

Phillips, D. (1989). Recent advances in suicidology: The study of imitative suicide. In R. Diekstra (Ed.), and the World Health Organization, *Suicide and its prevention: The role of attitude and imitation* (pp. 299–312). Leiden: Brill.

Richardson, L. (1994). Nine poems: Marriage and the family. *The Journal of Contemporary Ethnography, 23:* 3–13.

Richardson, L., & Lockridge, E. (1991). The sea monster: An ethnographic drama. *Symbolic Interaction, 14:* 335–340.

Rorty, R. (1980). *Philosophy and the mirror of nature.* Princeton, NJ: Princeton University Press.

Schmidtke, A., & Haffner, H. (1989). Public attitudes towards and effects of the mass media on suicidal and self-harm behaviour. In R. F. W. Diekstra (Ed.), and the World Health Organization, *Suicide and its prevention. Advances in suicidology.* Vol. 1. Leiden: Brill.

Snow, D. A., & Morrill, C. (1995). New ethnographies: Review symposium: A revolutionary handbook or a handbook for revolution? *Journal of Contemporary Ethnography, 24*(3): 341–362.

Todorov, T. (1968). Introduction: Le vraisemblable. *Communications, 11:* 1–4.

Turner, V. (1986). *The anthropology of performance.* New York: Performing Arts Journal Publications.

Woods, P. (1996). *Researching the art of teaching ethnography for educational use.* London: Routledge.

Worth, S. (1978). *Toward an ethnographic semiotic.* Unfinished paper presented at the "Utilisation de L'ethnologie par le cinema/Utilisation du Cinema par L'enthologie Conference," UNESCO: Paris URL: http://www.temple.edu/anthro/worth/sethnosem.html.

12

On the *Listening Guide*

A Voice-Centered Relational Method

Carol Gilligan, Renée Spencer,
M. Katherine Weinberg, and Tatiana Bertsch

The *Listening Guide* is a method of psychological analysis that draws on voice, resonance, and relationship as ports of entry into the human psyche. It is designed to open a way to discovery when discovery hinges on coming to know the inner world of another person. Because every person has a voice or a way of speaking or communicating that renders the silent and invisible inner world audible or visible to another, the method is universal in application. The collectivity of different voices that compose the voice of any given person—its range, its harmonies and dissonances, its distinctive tonality, key signatures, pitches, and rhythm—is always embodied, in culture, and in relationship with oneself and with others. Thus each person's voice is distinct— a footprint of the psyche, bearing the marks of the body, of that person's history, of culture in the form of language, and the myriad ways in which human society and history shape the voice and thus leave their imprints on

From Gilligan, C., et al., "On the *Listening Guide*: A Voice-Centered Relational Method," in *Qualitative Research in Psychology: Expanding Perspectives in Methodology and Design,* copyright © 2003 by the American Psychological Association. Reprinted with permission.

the human soul (Gilligan, 1993). The *Listening Guide* method comprises a series of steps, which together are intended to offer a way of tuning into the polyphonic voice of another person.

As voice depends on resonance or relationship in that speaking relies on, and is affected by, being heard, this method is intended to offer "a pathway into relationship rather than a fixed framework for interpretation" (Brown & Gilligan, 1992, p. 22) and shares a set of assumptions about the human world with what are now being called relational psychologies (e.g., Aron, 1996; Gilligan, 1982; Miller, 1976; Tronick, 1989). These assumptions include the premise that human development occurs in relationship with others and, as such, our sense of self is inextricable from our relationships with others and with the cultures within which we live (Spencer, 2000). In addition, this method draws from psychoanalytical theories that have long emphasized the layered nature of the psyche, which is expressed in a multiplicity of voices (e.g., Fairbairn, 1944; Mitchell, 1988; Winnicott, 1960). The *Listening Guide* method provides a way of systematically attending to the many voices embedded in a person's expressed experience.

The origins of the *Listening Guide* method lie in the analyses conducted in Gilligan's (1982) work on identity and moral development. The effort to render this method systematic began in 1984, and was undertaken in collaboration with graduate students—diverse in gender, race, sexual orientation, and age—over a period of about 10 years.[1] The *Listening Guide* was developed in part as a response to the uneasiness and growing dissatisfaction with the nature of the coding schemes typically being used at that time to analyze qualitative data. These techniques did not allow for multiple codings of the same text, thereby reducing the complexity of inner psychic processes to placement in single static categories. At that time, many social scientists were becoming more interested in developing methods for studying and interpreting narratives as a way of understanding meaning-making processes (e.g., Bruner, 1986; Geertz, 1983; Josselson, 1987; Mischler, 1979; Polkinghorne, 1988). This interest in, and attention to, narratives was a part of a growing awareness that the emphasis on quantitative methods in psychology was limiting what we could learn about human experience to what could be captured numerically, and many researchers were working to develop and define systematic methods for examining qualitative data in more complex ways.

The *Listening Guide* method picks up on the clinical method developed by Freud and Breuer (Breuer & Freud, 1895/1986) in *Studies on Hysteria* and that of Piaget (1929/1979) in *The Child's Conception of the World*. These works emphasize the importance of following the lead of the person being interviewed and discovering in this way the associative logic of the psyche and the constructions of the mind. The *Listening Guide* method was also inspired by literary theory, including new criticism and reader response theory, as well as by the language of music: voice, resonance, counterpoint, and fugue. It joins feminist researchers, cultural psychologists, and psychological anthropologists in their concerns about the ways in which a person's voice can be overridden by the researcher and their cautions about voicing over the truth of another (e.g., Borland, 1991; Fine & Macpherson, 1992; Scheper-Hughes, 1994).

The *Listening Guide* method has been used by many researchers interested in the psyche and in relationship, and it has been brought to bear in analyzing a range of phenomena within psychology, including girls' sexual desire (Tolman, 1994), adolescent girls' and boys' friendships (Way, 1998), girls' and women's experiences with anger (Brown, 1998; Jack, 1999), women's experiences of motherhood and postnatal depression (Mauthner, 2000), and heterosexual couples' attempts to share housework and childcare (Doucet, 1995). It has also proved useful in analyzing and interpreting U.S. Supreme Court decisions as well as a variety of literary and historical texts, including novels and diaries.

In this chapter we detail the steps involved in the *Listening Guide* method and focus specifically on the use of the guide to analyze and interpret qualitative interview data. In doing so, we demonstrate how we have been thinking about and using the *Listening Guide* method most recently, drawing on the insights of those who first developed this series of steps, the work of other researchers who have since applied the method in a wide range of projects, our own recent research, and our experiences in teaching the guide.

The *Listening Guide*

The *Listening Guide* method comprises a series of sequential listenings, each designed to bring the researcher into relationship with a person's distinct and multilayered voice by tuning in or listening to distinct aspects of a person's expression of her or his experience within a particular relational context. Each step requires the active presence of the researcher and an acute desire to engage with the unique subjectivity of each research participant. The voice of the researcher is explicitly brought into the process, making it clear who is listening and who is speaking in this analysis (Brown & Gilligan, 1991).

This approach to listening is centered on a set of basic questions about voice: Who is speaking and to whom, telling what stories about relationship, in what societal and cultural frameworks (Brown & Gilligan, 1992, p. 21)? With these larger framing questions in mind, we read the texts (in this case the interview transcripts) through multiple times, with each listening tuning into a particular aspect. Each of these steps is called a "listening" rather than a "reading," because the process of listening requires the active participation on the part of both the teller and the listener. In addition, each listening is not a simple analysis of the text but rather is intended to guide the listener in tuning into the story being told on multiple levels and to experience, note, and draw from his or her resonances to the narrative. In this sense, as Tolman (2001) has noted, the *Listening Guide* "is distinctly different from traditional methods of coding, in that one listens to, rather than categorizes or quantifies, the text of the interview" (p. 132).

Although the first two listenings are more prescribed, the later listenings are shaped by the particular question the researcher brings to the interview. No single step, or listening, is intended to stand alone, just as no single representation of a person's experience can be said to stand for that person. The listenings of each step are rendered visual through underlining the text, using different colored pencils for each listening. Each listening is also documented through notes and interpretive summaries the researcher writes during the implementation of each step. The marked interview transcript, notes, and summaries help the researcher to stay close to the text and keep track of "a trail of evidence" (Brown, Tappan, Gilligan, Miller, & Argyris, 1989), the base for later interpretations.

The need for a series of listenings arises from the assumption that the psyche, like voice, is contrapuntal (not monotonic) so that simultaneous voices are co-occurring. These voices may be in tension with one another, with the self, with the voices of others with whom the person is in relationship, and the culture or context within which the person lives. Voices are fluid and we register the continuous changes in our own and others' voices. As one young boy in the work by Chu and Gilligan noted, his mother had "a happy voice," but he also heard "a little worried voice." Each listening amplifies another aspect of a person's voice in a manner akin to listening to and following the oboe through a piece of music and then listening again, this time following the clarinet (Gilligan, Brown, & Rogers, 1990).

We describe and illustrate each step of the *Listening Guide* method by focusing on a small section of an interview conducted by Katherine Weinberg for her research with mothers who have a history of depression (e.g., Tronick & Weinberg, 1997). Weinberg extended this study in response to her observation that her quantitative work with these mothers did not fully capture the power and richness of their stories. The *Listening Guide* offered Weinberg a way of hearing what each mother was saying and of understanding the mother's experiences with depression, the ways she was coping with this illness while also coping with the demands of motherhood, and the meaning of these experiences for her. In her use of the *Listening Guide* for research with depressed women, Weinberg was guided by the work of Jack (1991) and Mauthner (1993, 1998).

The interviewee, Vanessa,[2] was 39 years old at the time of the interview. The focus of the interview was on Vanessa's history of depression and her life as a new mother. She had volunteered for Weinberg's study of the effects of depression and anxiety on maternal and infant functioning. Weinberg conducted, audiotaped, and transcribed this interview. In her verbatim transcription she maintained a respect for the spoken language by including pauses, inflections, false starts, unfinished sentences, and overlapping speech.

Step 1: Listening for the Plot

The first listening comprises two parts: (a) listening for the plot and (b) the listener's response to the interview. First, we read through the text and listen for the plot by attending to what is happening or what stories are being told, in the manner characteristic of many forms of qualitative analysis (e.g., Reissman, 1993; Strauss & Corbin, 1998; Werber, 1990). We also attend to the landscape, or the multiple contexts, within which these stories are embedded (Brown & Gilligan, 1992). We begin by first getting a sense of where we are, or what territory is by identifying the stories that are being told, what is happening, when, where, with whom, and why. Repeated images and metaphors and dominant themes are noted as are contradictions and absences, or what is not expressed. The larger social context within which these stories are experienced is identified, as is the social and cultural contexts within which the researcher and research participant come together.

In this plot listening, we also attend to our own responses to the narrative, explicitly bringing our own subjectivities into the process of interpretation from the start by identifying, exploring, and making explicit our own thoughts and feelings about, and associations with, the narrative being analyzed. Because many have pointed out that a researcher is not and can never be a "neutral" or "objective" observer (e.g., Keller, 1985; Morawski, 2001), we consciously and actively focus on and document our own response to what is being expressed and to the person speaking. Following basic principles of reflexivity (Mauthner & Doucet, 1998), we note our own social location in relation to the participant, the nature of our relationship with this person, and our emotional responses. As we go through the interview text, we notice and reflect on where we find ourselves feeling a connection with this person and where we do not, how this particular person and this interview touches us (or does not touch us), what thoughts and feelings emerge as we begin to listen and why we think we are responding in this way, and how our responses might affect our understanding of this person and the stories being told. We work to identify our own responses to this particular interview, like a clinician who identifies her countertransference, or responses to her client, in the hope that she will be better able to not confuse her own experiences with those of her client, or to not allow her own responses to the material the client brings to interfere with her ability to listen to and connect with her client.

As multiple listenings are at the heart of this method, a *Listening Guide* analysis is enhanced by work within interpretive communities (e.g., Taylor, Gilligan, & Sullivan, 1995) that provide multiple listeners. Here the goal is not necessarily agreement, but rather the exploration of the different connections, resonances and interpretations that each listener naturally brings to the analytical process. In the excerpt that follows, we listen to Vanessa's description of the effect that her own mother's depression had on her.

> And then I think you know everything kind of went underground for me and I stopped talking to people . . . Hmmm. I think when there is a mental illness in the house and it's and there . . . can be . . . and some of it can be out of control that hmmm a lot of families tend to isolate and that I think is what my family did and hmm besides I didn't have anything to talk about. What was I going to say? My mother is a raging maniac? Or or she's she's a rock and I can't talk to her. It's not something you share with people at school. Hmm and hmmm I think it made me chase my dad for for some kind of attention and of course that made him run faster. Hmmm. And so hmmm . . . and you know at that point I think that's when I stopped sleeping. And I kept worrying that one of them was going to drop dead you know. And I think that hmm some of that was behind the not sleeping.

In listening for the plot, we hear Vanessa, a 39-year-old White woman, talking about herself when she was about 10 or 11 years old. Her mother was quite depressed and Vanessa took over many of the responsibilities her mother could no longer handle, including the care of her younger siblings, two of whom were born during this time period. She portrays herself as isolated, not just from people outside the family but also from both of her parents. She attributes her isolation from people at school to not having "anything to talk about" because what was most salient for her was the fact that her mother was a "raging maniac" and that was "not something you share with people." She also states that she stopped sleeping and worried that one of her parents was "going to drop dead." Although Vanessa's family had financial resources because her father was a practicing physician, the psychological resources seem scarce.

Typically all of the people involved in the analysis of this interview would write a listener's response. Here we offer the responses of two of us for the sake of example.

Renee's response:

> I found myself filled with images of and associations with being surrounded by depression and the isolation that comes with feeling like you cannot tell anyone about it. I noticed I was tuning into the severity of her mother's depression and was both awe-struck by Vanessa's capacity to function (she continued going to school) and to take care of her younger siblings when her own needs were not being met and deeply saddened by the heavy burden she had to bear at such a young age. I also found myself a bit troubled by Vanessa seemingly taking responsibility for father's distancing as she indicates that her efforts to connect with him "made him run faster." Rather than her father's response being the natural response ("of course"), I thought there were many other ways her father could have responded to her suffering and requests for attention.

Carol's response:

> When Vanessa says she went "underground," I find myself wondering where she went and also where she is now. I think of the times I went underground and did not feel I could speak about what I was seeing. Vanessa's description of her mother's depression is so vivid ("raging maniac," "a rock"), that I found it hard to keep track of the 10-year-old girl. Listening to this interview, I know I will be listening for her.

Step 2: I Poems

The second listening focuses in on the voice of the "I" who is speaking by following the use of this first-person pronoun and constructing [what] Elizabeth Debold (1990) has called "I poems." The purpose of this step is twofold. First, it is intended to press the researcher to listen to the participant's first-person voice—to pick up its distinctive cadences and rhythms—and second, to hear how this person speaks about him- or herself. This step is a crucial component of a relational method in that tuning into another person's voice and listening to what this person knows of her- or himself before talking about him or her is a way of coming into relationship that works against distancing ourselves from that person in an objectifying way (Brown & Gilligan, 1992).

Two rules govern the construction of an I poem: (a) underline or select every first-person "I" within the passage you have chosen along with the verb and any seemingly important accompanying words and (b) maintain the sequence in which these phrases appear in the text.[3] The[n] pull out the underlined "I" phrases, keeping them in the order they appear in the text, and place each phrase on a separate line, like lines in a poem. These guidelines are intended to foster a process of following the free-fall of association. Often the I poem itself will seem to fall readily into stanzas—reflecting a shift in meaning or change in voice, the ending of a cadence or the start of a new breath. Sometimes the I poem captures something not stated directly but central to the meaning of what is being said. Other times it does not. In either case, the I poem picks up on an associative stream of consciousness carried by a first-person voice, cutting across or running through a narrative rather than being contained by the structure of full sentences. Cutting the text close and focusing in on just the I pronoun, the associated verb, and few other words moves this aspect of subjectivity to the foreground, providing the listener with the opportunity to attend just to the sounds, rhythms, and shifts in this person's usages of "I" in his or her narratives.

Constructing an "I poem" from the passage selected from Vanessa's interview would involve first underlining the I statements, as indicated in the text that follows.

> And then I think you know everything kind of went underground for me and I stopped talking to people . . . Hmmm. I think when there is a mental illness in the house and it's and there . . . can be . . . and some of it can be out of control that hmmm a lot of families tend to isolate and that I think is what my family did and hmmm besides I didn't have anything to talk about. What was I going to say? My mother is a raging maniac? Or or she's she's a rock and I can't talk to her. It's not something you share with people at school. Hmm and hmm I think it made me chase my dad for for some kind of attention and of course that made him run faster. Hmm. And so hmm . . . and you know at that point I think that's when I stopped sleeping. And I kept worrying that one of them was going to drop dead you know. And I think that hmmm some of that was behind the not sleeping.

These phrases are then lined up, like lines in a poem:

I think

I stopped talking

I think

I think

I didn't have anything to talk about

What was I going to say?

I can't talk

I think

I think

I stopped sleeping

I kept worrying

I think

Although in the full text Vanessa's isolation is apparent, by listening to this "I poem" we can hear how her description of this time is dominated by her own inner thoughts, not speaking about what was going on to anyone else, not sleeping, and worrying. Compiling several I poems from this interview highlights how much Vanessa thinks, as "I think" is repeated like a refrain.

This way of expressing herself is in contrast to her description in another section of the interview of how taking an antidepressant affected her life.

Well, <u>I think</u> that hmmm . . . well actually <u>I quit</u> a job that <u>I had been</u> in for a very long that <u>I had started</u> the program. <u>I was very good</u> but it was taking so much out of me that <u>I was exhausted</u> all of the time and one of the first things <u>I did</u> when <u>I started to feel better</u> was quit this job and shock myself. Like <u>I walked</u> into my boss's office and handed him my resignation and said "<u>I'm leaving</u> in a month. <u>I'm going. I, I</u> . . . <u>This is the end of this. I can't do this anymore.</u>"

I think

I quit

I had been

I had started

I was very good

I was exhausted

I did

I started to feel better

I walked

I'm leaving

I'm going

I

I

I can't do this anymore

In this passage, the I poem highlights how much more physical and emotional activity Vanessa became engaged in while taking antidepressants. Her reflections on this time are filled with a wider range of action on her part—walking, leaving, quitting, and going. These two I poems allow us to hear in Vanessa's own words her sense of going from feeling "very small" and "very hidden" when she was depressed to experiencing herself as "getting bigger and bigger and bigger" when she started taking the medication. Selecting several different passages throughout the interview to focus on in this step and examining them in relation to one another can facilitate hearing potential variations in the first-person voice that may include a range of themes, harmonies, dissonances, and shifts.

Step 3: Listening for Contrapuntal Voices

The next step, listening for contrapuntal voices, brings the analysis back into relationship with the research question. It offers a way of hearing and developing an understanding of several different layers of a person's expressed experience as it bears on the question posed. The logic behind this step is drawn from the musical form counterpoint, which consists of "the combination of two or more melodic lines" (Piston, 1947, p. 13). Each melodic line has its own rhythm and "melodic curve" (the shape and movement of a melody within a range of low and high notes). These melodic lines of music are played simultaneously and move in some form of relationship with each other. This third step in the *Listening Guide* method offers a way to listen for the counterpoint in the text we are analyzing, or the multiple facets of the story being told. The first two steps—establishing the plot or the story lines and the psychic landscape and bringing in the first-person expressions of the speaker—build up to, and provide a context for, the contrapuntal listenings. It is in this third step that we begin to identify, specify, and sort out the different strands in the interview that may speak to our research question. This process entails reading through the interview two or more times, each time tuning into one aspect of the story being told, or one voice within the person's expression of her or his experience. The researcher's questions shape this listening, which may be based on the theoretical framework guiding the research, or the questions raised by the previous listenings, or both.

To begin, we specify the voices we will listen for and determine what the markers of a particular contrapuntal voice are or, more simply, how we will know this voice when we hear it. The text is then read through, listening for just one voice at a time, and the appearance or evidence of this voice is underlined in a color chosen to mark it. Reading through the text a separate time for each contrapuntal voice allows for the possibility that one statement may contain multiple meanings, and therefore may be underlined multiple times, and also allows the researcher to begin to see and hear the relationship between the person's first-person voice and the contrapuntal voices. The contrapuntal voices do not have to be in opposition to one another; they may be opposing or complementary in some way. Listening for at least two contrapuntal voices takes into account that a person expresses his or her experience in a multiplicity of voices or ways. It is important to note that it also allows for the possibility that some of these voices may be in harmony with one another, in opposition to one another, or even contradictory.

Examples of contrapuntal voice analyses range widely, depending on the nature of the particular study. Building on *In a Different Voice* (Gilligan, 1982), the voices of a separate and connected self, and of justice and care, have been distinguished and followed (see Gilligan & Attanucci, 1988; Johnston, 1988; Langdale, 1983; Lyons, 1988, 1989). In the work of the Harvard Project (e.g., Brown & Gilligan, 1992; Taylor et al., 1995), the analysis of girls' development from childhood into adolescence was shaped by the counterpoint in girls' interview texts between a voice of resistance or resilience (a strong, clear, confident voice) and a voice of distress or capitulation. Rather than characterizing these girls' voices as either resistant or capitulating, the counterpoint between both of these voices was followed both within a given interview and in the interviews conducted over time (Gilligan et al., 1990). Dana Jack (1991), in her study of depressed women, followed the counterpoint between an "I" who spoke clearly and directly (I feel, I know, I want, I believe) and what she called the "over-eye," the part of the self that observed, judged, shamed the self—the voice of the depression (I should, I have to). Through her contrapuntal analysis of the relationship between these two voices, Jack observed how the voice of the over-eye came in to silence the I, and how the resistance or resilience of the I, as it was repeatedly overruled by the over-eye, contributed to the exhaustion of depression (the extraordinary effort it took to silence the self). This analysis led her to conceptualize depression as a silencing of the self.

Returning to the excerpt from the interview with Vanessa, in light of our question about motherhood and depression, we noticed in the I poems two possible contrapuntal voices; a voice of knowing and a voice of silence. In the first contrapuntal voice listening we decided to underline the places in this passage in which Vanessa, speaking about herself as a child, described her knowledge of herself and her response to her mother's depression. Here, we show these phrases in italics below.

> And then I think you know, *everything kind of went underground for me,* and I stopped talking to people . . . Hmmm. I think when *there is a mental illness in the house,* and it's, and there can be . . . and *some of it can be out of control,* that hmmm, *a lot of families tend to isolate.* And that *I think is what my family did.* And, hmmm, besides I didn't have anything to talk about. What was I going to say? *"My mother is a raging maniac?"* Or, or *"She's, she's a rock and I can't talk to her."* It's not something you share with people at school. Hmmm, hmmm, I think for, *it made me chase my Dad for some kind of attention,* and of course *that made him run faster.* Hmmm. And so, hmmm? and you know at that point, I think that's when *I stopped sleeping. And I kept worrying that one of them was going to drop dead,* you know. And *I think that hmmm, some of that was behind the not sleeping.*

Pulling out just what we have underlined in this listening, we hear how much Vanessa knew about what was going on for her, and her family, at that time:

> everything kind of went underground for me I stopped talking to people there is a mental illness in the house some if it can be out of control . . . a lot of families tend to isolate that, I think, is what my family did my mother is a raging maniac . . . she's a rock and I can't talk to her it's not something you share with people at school it made me chase my Dad for some kind of attention that made him run faster . . . I stopped sleeping I kept worrying that one of them was going to drop dead I think that hmmm, some of that was behind the not sleeping.

This listening goes to the heart of Weinberg's question about how much this mother knows about her experience with her own depressed mother. Vanessa recalls being aware of the severity of the situation with her mother ("my mother is a raging maniac") and what her own response to her mother's depression was. She began having difficulty sleeping and worried that one of her parents was going to die. Although she did try to reach out to her father, it unfortunately seemed to have contributed to her father pulling even further away ("that made him run faster"). This listening also highlights Vanessa's conflicts or uncertainties about knowing. Her repeated phrases, "you know," suggest that she wonders what others know about what she knows, and her hesitations, the "hmmms" that interrupt the flow, similarly could possibly be interpreted as a manifestation of her conflicts around speaking.

The second contrapuntal voice we listened for was a voice of not speaking. We underlined the passages in which Vanessa talked about her sense that she could not speak about what was happen[ing] to her family during this time. These passages are noted in bold text.

> And then I think you know, *everything kind of went underground for me,* and *I stopped talking* to people . . . Hmmm. I think when *there is a mental illness in the house,* and it's, and there can be and *some of it can be out of control,* that hmmm, *a lot of families tend to isolate.* And *that I think is what my family did.* And hmmm, besides, **I didn't have anything to talk about. What was I going to say?** *"My mother is a raging maniac?"* Or, or *"She's, she's a rock and I can't talk to her." It's not something you share with people at school.* Hmmm, hmmm, I think for, *it made me chase my Dad for some kind of attention,* and of course *that made him run faster.* Hmmm. And so, hmmm and you know at that point, I think that's when *I stopped sleeping.* And *I kept worrying that one of them was going to drop dead* you know. And *I think that hmmm, some of that was behind the not sleeping.*

In this listening, we hear how Vanessa became isolated by virtue of her sense that she could not talk to anyone about what was happening to her, leaving her with little to say and perhaps little around which to connect with her peers—"it's not something you share with people at school."

In the counterpoint between these two voices, we hear evidence of Vanessa's own depression and also of her resistance, her strategy of going underground. Rather than having to choose which voice best characterizes what Vanessa is expressing, we listen for the relationship between these voices as her depression might also carry some aspects of her strategies for resistance. Together, these voices convey that Vanessa went underground because of what she knew. Here she conveys that she was aware of how out of control her mother's depression was but she had the sense that saying something about it was not possible for her.

Together, these contrapuntal voice listenings raise questions about [w]hat Vanessa knows in the present that she perhaps feels she cannot talk about and whether this possible silence may be contributing to her depression. We also return to Weinberg's inquiry, which began with her observation that in our search for understanding how maternal depression affects the mother-infant relationship, the women's own experiences with depression needed to be incorporated. These observations suggest the shape of the next step, composing an analytical summary based on the series of listenings we have conducted.

Once the contrapuntal voice listenings have been completed, with each voice underlined in a different color, the transcript provides a visual way of examining how these voices move in relation to one another and to the Is. In musical counterpoint, the two or more lines of music may each develop a distinct theme, at times moving in consonance with one another and at other times in dissonance. Here too, the contrapuntal voices within one person's narrative are in some type of relationship with one another, and this relationship becomes the focus of our interest. A range of questions could be asked at this point. Does one contrapuntal voice move with particular I poems more than others, and if so how do these voices move in relationship with one another? Does one or more of the voices move completely separate from the Is? What are the relationships among the contrapuntal voices? Do some of them seem to take turns? Do they seem to be opposing one another? How do they move in and out of relationship with one another? Although we only listened for two contrapuntal voices in this example, we could have decided to listen for more, depending on the questions guiding our analysis.

The development of these listenings for contrapuntal voices is an iterative process. The researcher begins with an idea about a possible voice, creates an initial definition or description of this voice, listens for it, and then assesses whether the definition of this voice makes sense and whether it is illuminating some meaningful aspect of the text. The researcher may then fine-tune this particular contrapuntal voice and try to listen for it again. In addition, once two or more contrapuntal voices have been identified, the researcher may reflect on whether something that felt important in the other listenings is getting left out, whether something needs to be added to an already defined voice, or whether a new voice needs to be listened to. In studies that involve several interviews, the contrapuntal voices may evolve out of the analyses of many different interviews through a process of going back and revisiting this step, this time reading for voices that have been redefined or newly defined through the analysis of other interviews.

Step 4: Composing an Analysis

In the final step of the *Listening Guide* method, having gone through the text a minimum of four times (plot, I poem, and listening for two or more contrapuntal voices), leaving a trail of underlinings, notes, and summaries each time, the researcher now pulls together what has been learned about this person in relation to the research question. In essence, an interpretation of the interview or text is developed that pulls together and synthesizes what has been learned through this entire process and an essay or analysis is composed. Returning to the research question that initiated this inquiry, several questions can be considered. What have you learned about this question through this process and how have you come to know this? What is the evidence on which you are basing your interpretations? Sometimes in this step it may become apparent that the research question itself needs to be modified, or perhaps even transformed, in response to this series of listenings.

Through our analysis of Vanessa's description of her experiences as a child living with her mother who was severely depressed, we hear a tension between how much Vanessa knew about what was happening in her family and how she also felt that there was no one with whom she could talk about how out of control some things had gotten. She held on to her own knowledge by taking it with her as she went underground psychologically. We wonder whether this tension between knowing and silence highlighted in the passage is still alive for Vanessa today, though we cannot answer this question based on the evidence in this passage.

In this chapter we focused on one small passage within one interview to provide an example of how each of the steps of the *Listening Guide* can be operationalized. A full analysis of this interview would involve working with the entire transcript. Although listening for one voice at a time in the earlier steps can illuminate different aspects of a person's experience as expressed in an interview, these separate listenings must be brought back into relationship with one another to not reduce or lose the complexity of a person's expressed experience. In a study that includes multiple interviews, these *Listening Guide* analyses may be examined in relationship to one another, illuminating similarities in the themes that may begin to emerge across several interviews and also marking distinct differences between them

Conclusion

The *Listening Guide* method is a way of analyzing qualitative interviews that is best used when one's question requires listening to particular aspects of a person's expression of her or his own complex and multilayered individual experiences and the relational and cultural contexts within which they occur. It is a particularly useful tool for discovery research; to uncover new questions to pursue through focusing in on and learning from individual experiences. It is a relational method in the sense that it intentionally brings the researcher into relationship with the participant through making our responses, experiences, and interpretive lenses explicit in the process, and by listening to each participant's first-person voice before moving in to listen for answers to our own research questions. It is also relational in that the specific way the method is operationalized changes in response to, and via the process of, analysis. Through each of these steps we actively bring ourselves and our research question into relationship with the person's spoken experience to direct the analytical process, creating an opening for that person to shift our way of listening, the questions that we ask, and the ways in which we ask them.

This method requires the active engagement of the researcher throughout the analysis because it is intended to be a guide, or a set of steps that provide a basic frame, rather than a set of prescriptive rules to be followed. The researcher must make decisions with regard to how precisely to implement each step of this method in a particular research project. We have demonstrated the particular way that we have been implementing the *Listening Guide* method. As with any analytical tool, others have necessarily developed different ways of conducting the four basic steps to fit the specific needs of their various studies and sets of research questions.

Finally, although a *Listening Guide* analysis may serve as a primary method of analysis, it has also been used in conjunction with other qualitative methods of analysis such as narrative summaries (Way, 2001) and conceptually clustered matrices (Brown, 2001), as well as with a statistical analysis of thematic codes derived from interview texts (Tolman & Szalacha, 1999). These methods each offer a different pathway into and through qualitative interviews. The *Listening Guide* method offers a way of illuminating the complex and multilayered nature of the expression of human experience and the interplay between self and relationship, psyche and culture.

Notes

1. These conversations involved many people over the years, including as central participants Dianne Argyris, Jane Attanucci, Betty Bardige, Lyn Mikel Brown, Elizabeth Debold, Andrea Pamela Pleasants, Annie Rogers, Any Sullivan, Mark Tappan, Jill Taylor, Deborah Tolman, Janie Ward, Grant Wiggins, and David Wilcox.

2. Vanessa is a pseudonym.

3. We are using the same passage throughout this chapter to demonstrate how multiple readings of the same text (the heart of this method) yield different information. When working with an entire interview, the plot listening gathers information from the whole text, whereas the I poems may be constructed selectively from certain passages.

References

Aron, L. (1996). *A meeting of the minds: Mutuality in psychoanalysis*. Hillsdale, NJ: Atlantic.

Borland, K. (1991). "That's not what I said": Interpretive conflict in oral narrative research. In S. B. Gluck & D. Patai (Eds.), *Women's words: The feminist practice of oral history* (pp. 63–75). London: Routledge.

Breuer, J., & Freud, S. (1986). *Studies on hysteria* (James Strachey, Trans.). New York: Basic Books (original published 1985).

Brown, L. M. (1998). *Raising their voices: The politics of girls' anger.* Cambridge, MA: Harvard University Press.

Brown, L. M. (2001). White working-class girls, femininities, and the paradox of resistance. In D. L. Tolman & M. Brydon-Miller (Eds.), *From subjects to subjectivities: A handbook of interpretive and participatory methods* (pp. 95–110). New York: New York University Press.

Brown, L. M., & Gilligan, C. (1991). Listening for voice in narratives of relationship. In M. Tappan & M. Packer (Eds.), *Narrative and storytelling: Implications for understanding moral development. New directions for child development* (Vol. 54, pp. 43–62). San Francisco: Jossey-Bass.

Brown, L. M., & Gilligan, C. (1992). *Meeting at the crossroads: Women's psychology and girls' development.* Cambridge, MA: Harvard University Press.

Brown, L. M., Tappan, M., Gilligan, C., Miller, B., & Argyris, D. E. (1989). Reading for self and moral voice: A method for interpreting narratives of real-life moral conflict and choice. In M. Packer & R. Addison (Eds.), *Entering the circle* (pp. 141–164). Albany: State University of New York Press.

Bruner, J. (1986). *Actual minds, possible worlds.* Cambridge, MA: Harvard University Press.

Debold, E. (1990, April). *Learning in the first person: A passion to know.* Paper presented at the Laurel-Harvard conference on the psychology of women and the development of girls, Cleveland, OH.

Doucet, A. (1995) *Gender equality, gender differences, and care: Towards understanding gendered labour in British dual earner households.* Unpublished doctoral dissertation, University of Cambridge, Cambridge.

Fairbairn, W. R. D. (1944). Endopsychic structure considered in terms of object relationships. *International Journal of Psychoanalysis, 25:* 70–93.

Fine, M., & Macpherson, P. (1992). Over dinner: Feminism and adolescent female bodies. In H. Radtke & H. Stam (Eds.), *Power gender: Social relations theory in practice* (pp. 219–246). Newbury Park, CA: Sage.

Geertz, C. (1983). *Local knowledge: Further essays in interpretive anthropology.* New York: Basic Books.

Gilligan, C. (1982). *In a different voice: Psychological theory and women's development.* Cambridge, MA: Harvard University Press.

Gilligan, C. (1993). *Letter to readers, 1993, In a different voice: Psychological theory and women's development* (pp. ix–xxvii). Cambridge, MA: Harvard University Press.

Gilligan, C., & Attanucci, J. (1988). Two moral orientations: Gender differences and similarities. *Merrill-Palmer Quarterly, 43*(3): 223–237.

Gilligan, C., Brown, L. M., & Rogers, A. (1990). Psyche embedded: A place for body, relationships and culture in personality theory. In A. I. Rabin, R. A. Zucker, R. Emmons, & S. Frank (Eds.), *Studying persons and lives* (pp. 86–147). New York: Springer.

Jack, D. C. (1991). *Silencing the self: Women and depression.* Cambridge, MA: Harvard University Press.

Jack, D. C. (1999). *Behind the mask: Destruction and creativity in women's aggression.* Cambridge, MA: Harvard University Press.

Johnston, D. K. (1988). Adolescents' solutions to dilemmas in fables: Two moral orientations—Two problem solving strategies. In C. Gilligan, J. V. Ward, & J. M. Taylor (Eds.), *Mapping the moral domain: A contribution of women's thinking to psychological theory and education* (pp. 49–71). Cambridge, MA: Center for the Study of Gender, Education, and Human Development, Harvard University Graduate School of Education.

Josselson, R. (1987). *Finding herself: Pathways to identity development in women.* San Francisco: Jossey-Bass.

Keller, E. F. (1985). *Reflections on gender and science.* New Haven, CT: Yale University Press.

Langdale, C. H. (1983). *Moral orientations and moral development: The analysis of care and justice reasoning across different dilemmas in females and males from childhood through adulthood.* Unpublished doctoral dissertation, Harvard University Graduate School of Education, Cambridge, MA.

Lyons, N. P. (1988). Two perspectives: On self, relationships, and morality. In C. Gilligan, J. V. Ward, & J. M. Taylor (Eds.), *Mapping the moral domain: A contribution of women's thinking to psychological theory and education* (pp. 21–45). Cambridge, MA: Center for the Study of Gender, Education, and Human Development, Harvard University Graduate School of Education.

Lyons, N. P. (1989). Listening to voices we have not heard: Emma Willard girls' ideas about self, relationships, and morality. In C. Gilligan, N. P. Lyons, & T. J. Hammer (Eds.), *Making connections: The relational worlds of adolescent girls at Emma Willard School* (pp. 30–72). Cambridge, MA: Harvard University Press.

Mauthner, N. (1993). Towards a feminist understanding of "postnatal depression." *Feminism & Psychology,* 3(3): 350–355.

Mauthner, N. (1998). "It's a woman's cry for help": A relational perspective on postnatal depression. *Feminism & Psychology,* 8(3): 325–355.

Mauthner, N. (2000). *The darkest days of my life: Stories of postdepression.* Cambridge, MA: Harvard University Press.

Mauthner, N., & Doucet, A. (1998). Reflections on a voice-centered relational method. In J. Ribbens & R. Edwards (Eds.), *Feminist dilemmas in qualitative research: Public knowledge and private lives* (pp. 119–146). Newbury Park, CA: Sage.

Miller, J. B. (1976). *Toward a new psychology of women.* Boston: Beacon Press.

Mischler, E. G. (1979). Meaning in context: Is there any other kind? *Harvard Educational Review,* 49(1): 1–19.

Mitchell, S. A. (1988). *Relational concepts in psychoanalysis: An integration.* New York: Basic Books.

Morawski, J. (2001). Feminist research methods: Bringing culture to science. In D. L. Tolman & M. Brydon-Miller (Eds.), *From subjects to subjectivities: A handbook of interpretive and participatory methods* (pp. 57–75). New York: New York University Press.

Piaget, J. (1979). *The child's conception of the world*. Totowa, NJ: Littlefield Adams. (Original published 1929).

Piston, W. (1947). *Counterpoint*. New York: W. W. Norton.

Polkinghorne, D. (1988). *Narrative knowing and the human sciences*. Albany: State University of New York Press.

Reissman, C. K. (1993). *Narrative analysis*. Newbury Park, CA: Sage.

Scheper-Hughes, N. (1994). The violence of everyday life: In search of a critical and politically engaged psychological anthropology. In M. Suarez-Orozco, G. Spindler, & L. Spindler (Eds.), *The making of psychological anthropology II* (pp. 135–157). Fort Worth, TX: Harcourt Brace.

Spencer, R. (2000). *A comparison of relational psychologies. Project Report No. 5*. Wellesley, MA: Stone Center Working Paper Series.

Strauss, A., & Corbin, J. (1998). *Basics of qualitative research: Techniques and procedures for developing grounded theory* (2nd ed.). Thousand Oaks, CA: Sage.

Taylor, J. M., Gilligan, C., & Sullivan, A. (1995). *Between voice and silence: Women and girls, race and relationship*. Cambridge, MA: Harvard University Press.

Tolman, D. L. (1994). Doing desire: Adolescent girls' struggles for/with sexuality. *Gender and Society, 8*(3): 324–342.

Tolman, D. L. (2001). Echoes of sexual objectification: Listening for one girl's erotic voice. In D. L. Tolman & M. Brydon-Miller (Eds.), *From subjects to subjectivities: A handbook of interpretive and participatory methods* (pp. 130–144). New York: New York University Press.

Tolman, D. L., & Brydon-Miller, M. (Eds.). (2001). *From subjects to subjectivities: A handbook of interpretive and participatory methods*. New York: New York University Press.

Tolman, D. L., & Szalacha, L. (1999). Dimensions of desire: Bridging qualitative and quantitative methods in a study of female adolescent sexuality. *Psychology of Women Quarterly, 23*(1): 7–93.

Tronick, E. Z. (1989). Emotions and emotional communication in infants. *American Psychologist, 44*(2): 112–119.

Tronick, E. Z., & Weinberg, M. K. (1997). Depressed mothers and infants: Failure to form dyadic states of consciousness. In L. Murray & P. J. Cooper (Eds.), *Postpartum depression and child development* (pp. 54–81). New York: Guilford Press.

Way, N. (1998). *Everyday courage: The lives and stories of urban teenagers*. New York: New York University Press

Way, N. (2001). Using feminist research methods to explore boys' relationships. In D. L. Tolman & M. Brydon-Miller (Eds.), *From subjects to subjectivities: A handbook of interpretive and participatory methods* (pp. 111–129). New York: New York University Press.

Werber, R. P. (1990). *Basic content analysis*. Newbury Park, CA: Sage.

Winnicott, D. W. (1960). *Ego distortion in terms of true and false self, The maturational processes and the facilitating environment* (pp. 140–152). London: Hogarth.

13

Friendship as Method

Lisa M. Tillmann-Healy

Project History

In 1994, Doug Healy, whom I would marry the following year, graduated from pharmacy school and moved to Tampa, Florida. His trainer at work, David Holland, would alter the course of our lives.

For a couple weeks, Doug and I had a recurring conversation about whether David might be gay, a question David all but answered by inviting us to meet him at Tracks, a gay nightclub in nearby Ybor City. Neither Doug nor I had ever had an openly gay friend before. In fact, both of us had grown up in the rural Midwest with rather conservative ideas about sexual orientation. Despite our limited exposure to gay people and cultures, we agreed to meet David at Tracks. As it turned out, this was only the beginning.

In November 1994, David mentioned to Doug that he played softball. When Doug asked if his team needed players, David told him that the team, sponsored by a bar called the Cove, and in fact the whole Suncoast Softball league, were gay identified. If that didn't bother him, David said, Doug could join under a league provision that allowed each team to have two straight players. At the start of the next softball season, Doug became the Cove's right

From Tillmann-Healy, L., "Friendship as Method," in *Qualitative Inquiry, 9*(5), 2003, pp. 729–749, reprinted with permission of Sage Publications, Inc.

centerfielder, a position he played for 4 years, until I was hired by Rollins College and we moved to Orlando, Florida.

For more than a year, ours was an innocently personal journey: a straight couple venturing beyond the conventions of their small-town socializations. But in the fall of 1995, the journey took an unexpected turn.

That semester, I was enrolled in a graduate course on qualitative methods. After a month of class, my intended study fell through, and the softball field became my alternative fieldwork site. What started as a class project blossomed into a narrative ethnographic (see Tedlock, 1991) Ph.D. dissertation and eventually a book called *Between Gay and Straight: Understanding Friendship Across Sexual Orientation* (Tillmann-Healy, 2001a).

During the 5 years it required to research and write this book, friendship emerged not only as a subject of my research but also as its primary method. In *Between Gay and Straight* (Tillmann-Healy, 2001a), I coined the term *friendship as method*. Expanding on ideas developed there, this article discusses my project and other interpretive studies that exemplify elements of friendship as method.

I begin by defining friendship, positing friendship as a kind of fieldwork, and establishing the methodological foundations of friendship as method. Next, I propose that this mode of qualitative inquiry involves researching with the practices, at the pace, in the natural contexts, and with an ethic of friendship. Finally, I describe this approach's strengths and considerations for both researcher and participants.

Friendship Defined

In *Friendship Matters*, William K. Rawlins (1992) defined a close friend as "somebody to talk to, to depend on and rely on for help, support, and caring, and to have fun and enjoy doing things with" (p. 271). Similar to romantic and family relationships, friendship is an interpersonal bond characterized by the ongoing communicative management of dialectical tensions, such as those between idealization and realization, affection and instrumentality, and judgment and acceptance (see Rawlins, 1992).

Unlike romance and kinship, friendship in Western cultures lacks canonical status. In the United States, we tend to accord friendship second-class status. For example, we might say, "We're *just* friends," to mean, "We're neither family, nor are we lovers." On confronting the chasm between unsanctioned and sanctioned ties, Andrew Holleran (1996) reflected,

> I was always discomfited whenever I accompanied friends to hospitals, or emergency rooms, at having to answer the question of the doctor, "Who are you?"

with the words, "A friend." It sounded so flimsy—so infinitely weaker than, "His brother," "His cousin," "His brother-in-law." It sounded like a euphemism; a word that did not, could not, convey what our bond really was. (p. 34–35)

Holleran's experience supports Rawlins's (1992) claim that friendship occupies a marginal position within the matrix of interpersonal relations and has "no clear normative status" (p. 9). Kathy Werking (1997) affirmed this, calling friendship "the most fragile social bond" (p. 18).

The unstable footing of friendship in many Western societies is attributed in part to the absence of obligatory dimensions. We are not born into friendships as we are into families. Similar to marriage, friendship is a voluntary relationship (Weiss, 1998); but unlike marriage, friendship lacks religious and legal grounding, rendering the creation, maintenance, and dissolution of friendship an essentially private, negotiable endeavor (Rawlins, 1992).

Friends come and stay together primarily through common interests, a sense of alliance, and emotional affiliation (Weiss, 1998). Friendship, according to Rawlins (1992), *implies affective ties* (p. 12). In friends, we seek trust, honesty, respect, commitment, safety, support, generosity, loyalty, mutuality, constancy, understanding, and acceptance (see Rubin, 1985).

In addition to emotional resources, friendships provide identity resources. Conceptions of self and other are formed, reinforced, and altered in the context of ongoing relationships. This explains why Gary Alan Fine (1981) called friendship "a crucible for the shaping of selves" (p. 265).

Friendships tend to confirm more than contest conceptions of self because we are prone to befriend those who are similar to ourselves, those more "self" than "other." As Rawlins (1992) pointed out, this begins in early childhood, when young persons typically have more access to playmates of the same age, sex, and physical characteristics. Similarly, adolescent friends tend to be of the same race, school grade, and social standing. Throughout life, friendships have a pronounced likelihood of developing within (rather than across) lines such as culture, education, marital and career status, and socioeconomic class. One consequence of this, posited Rawlins (1992), is that friendships are more likely "to reinforce and reproduce macrolevel and palpable social differences than to challenge or transcend them" (p. 274).

When friendships do develop across social groups, the bonds take on political dimensions. Opportunities exist for dual consciousness raising and for members of dominant groups (e.g., men, Euro-Americans, Christians, and heterosexuals) to serve as advocates for friends in target groups. As a result, those who are "just friends" can become *just* friends, interpersonal and political allies who seek personal growth, meaningful relationships, and social justice.

Friendship as Fieldwork

When I began proposing friendship as a method of inquiry, I received many quizzical looks. In some cases, even those who view friendship as an important topic and who recognize that friendships sometimes arise in the context of research expressed skepticism about a methodological link between friendship and fieldwork.

In many ways, though, friendship and fieldwork are similar endeavors. Both involve being in the world with others. To friendship and fieldwork communities, we must gain entree. We negotiate roles (e.g., student, confidant, and advocate), shifting from one to another as the relational context warrants. We may experience our ties as developmental, passing through stages such as those Rawlins (as cited in Wood, 2002) described: moving from role-limited interaction to integration to stabilization. Our communication might progress, in Buber's (1988) terms, from "seeming" to "being," from I-It (impersonal and instrumental), to I-You (more personal yet role bound), to moments of I-Thou, where we are truly present, meeting one another in our full humanity.

We navigate membership, participating, observing, and observing our participation (see Tedlock, 1991). We learn insider argot and new codes for behavior. As we deepen our ties, we face challenges, conflicts, and losses. We cope with relational dialectics (see Rawlins, 1992), negotiating how private and how candid we will be, how separate and how together, how stable and how in flux. One day, finite projects—and lives—come to an end, and we must "leave the field."

Foundations

Friendship as method builds on several established approaches to qualitative research. It is based on the principles of interpretivism, which, according to Thomas Schwandt (1994), stem from the German intellectual traditions of hermeneutics (interpretation) and *verstehen* (understanding), from phenomenology, and from the critiques of positivism.

Interpretivists take reality to be both pluralistic and constructed in language and interaction. Instead of facts, we search for intersubjective meanings, what Clifford Geertz (1973), following Max Weber, called the "webs of significance" (p. 5); instead of control, we seek understanding. For interpretivists, "objectivity becomes a synonym for estrangement and neutrality a euphemism for indifference" (Jackson, 1989, p. 4). According to Norman Denzin (1997), we research and write not to capture the totality of social life but to interpret reflectively slices and glimpses of localized interaction in order to understand more fully both others and ourselves.

Additional groundwork for friendship as method has been laid by feminist researchers. Much of feminist thought combines interpretivist assumptions with political commitments to consciousness raising, empowerment, and social change (see e.g., Cook & Fonow, 1986; Lather, 1991; Reinharz, 1992; Roberts, 1990). Feminists have been instrumental in debunking the myth of value-free inquiry (Harding, 1991), in promoting communitarian ethics, and in both reflexively attending and actively resisting hierarchical separation between researcher and participants.

Standpoint theory, as articulated by Patricia Hill Collins (1991, 1998), focuses on intersecting power relations. Standpoints emerge from dominant and target group locations. Interlocking systems of individual, institutional, and cultural oppression shape and constrain what we can know and do and how we can relate. According to Collins, we must move from colonization to an "epistemology of empowerment" (1998, p. 229). Pathways toward this way of knowing include dialogue, relationships, and an ethic of caring that invites expressiveness, emotion, and empathy (Collins, 1991).

Similar to feminist research, queer methodologies call researchers to defy cultural practices of marginalization and othering (Denzin & Lincoln, 2000). A project or text is queer if it challenges heterosexism and heteronormativity (the idea that heterosexual is normal and all other sexualities deviant) and if it problematizes the binary construction of hetero- and homosexualities (Butler, 1999; Sedgwick, 1990). A key to liberation, argued Joshua Gamson (1998), is "*muddying* the categories . . . pointing out their instability and fluidity along with their social roots" (p. 222).

Also influential to friendship as method is Michelle Fine's (1994) notion of "working the hyphens." Similar to other interpretivist approaches, hers rejects scientific neutrality, universal truths, and dispassionate inquiry and works toward social justice, relational truths, and passionate inquiry. Through authentic engagement, the lines between researcher and researched blur, permitting each to explore the complex humanity of both self and other. Instead of "speaking for" or even "giving voice," researchers *get to know* others in meaningful and sustained ways.

Fine's (1994) philosophy shares much common ground with participatory action research (PAR). According to Reason (1994), this type of inquiry emerged from liberationist movements. Action researchers view truth as a product and instrument of power. PAR honors lived experience and aims to produce knowledge and action directly useful to those being studied. Research under this model can be judged by what Patti Lather (1991) and Peter Reason (1994) termed *catalytic validity*, the degree to which it empowers those researched. Central to this approach is dialogue, where the subject-object relationship of positivism becomes a subject-subject one, in which academic knowledge combines with everyday experience to reach new and profound understandings (Reason, 1994).

Closest methodologically to friendship as method is interactive interviewing (Ellis, Kiesinger, & Tillmann-Healy, 1997; Tillmann-Healy & Kiesinger, 2001). This demands more sharing of personal and social experiences on the part of the researcher than does PAR. But, similar to PAR, interactive interviewing is an interpretive practice, requires intense collaboration, and privileges lived, emotional experience.

Friendship as Method

Calling for inquiry that is open, multivoiced, and emotionally rich, friendship as method involves the practices, the pace, the contexts, and the ethics of friendship. Researching with the practices of friendship means that although we employ traditional forms of data gathering (e.g., participant observation, systematic note taking, and informal and formal interviewing), our primary procedures are those we use to build and sustain friendship: conversation, everyday involvement, compassion, giving, and vulnerability.

Practices of friendship are evident in Keith Cherry's (1996) ethnographic account of a community of people living with AIDS. To chronicle their experiences and relationships, Cherry conducted fieldwork, shot photographs, and recorded interaction, but he also played Ping-Pong and watched soap operas with residents, drove them to doctor appointments, visited them in the hospital, and helped arrange birthday parties and, eventually, funerals. These activities added emotional and relational layers to Cherry's intellectual pursuits. Responding to the changing needs of community members, his friend and researcher roles shifted from center to periphery and back again. Sometimes Cherry had the emotional space to reflect on the meanings residents assigned to everyday practices, such as gossiping and watching television; other times, he was consumed by fear and grief. The depth of his connections to this community rendered him a vulnerable observer (Behar, 1996), a compassionate witness, and a true companion.

Second, friendship as method demands that we research at the natural pace of friendship. The tempo here is that of anthropologists, who typically stay a year or more in fieldwork communities. Over the course of 18 months, Cherry (1996) spent 25 to 40 hours per week at the Tahitian Islander, an apartment complex for people living with AIDS. For 2 years, Leigh Berger (2000, 2001) volunteered, attended services, and conducted interviews at

Dalet Shalom, a Messianic Jewish congregation. Christine Kiesinger (1995, 1998a, 1998b), who wrote life histories of four women with eating disorders, devoted 3 years of academic and personal involvement to the lives of her participants. Between formal interviews, Kiesinger shared meals, transcripts, and confidences with respondents. Barbara Myerhoff's (1978) *Number Our Days* is based on 4 years of participant observation and life history interviewing within an elderly Jewish community. For 4 years, Ouyporn Khuankaew and Kathryn Norsworthy (2000) have facilitated "training of social action trainers" along the border of Thailand and Burma (also see Norsworthy, 2002). *Between Gay and Straight* (Tillmann-Healy, 2001a) required 3 years of participant observation and interviewing and 3 additional years of writing, sharing drafts with community members, and rewriting. Michael Angrosino (1998) volunteered at a group home for 3 years before even beginning his study of persons with mental retardation (which lasted another 9 years). These are serious time commitments, but in each case, both profound relationships and provocative accounts resulted.

With friendship as method, a project's issues emerge organically, in the ebb and flow of everyday life: leisurely walks, household projects, activist campaigns, separations, reconciliations, losses, recoveries. The unfolding path of the relationships becomes the path of the project.

The length of time needed may vary depending on whether the researcher and participants begin the study as strangers, acquaintances, friends, or close friends. This approach requires multiple angles of vision. Strangers tend to have keener observational eyes yet need to cultivate more intersubjective views, which develop gradually over time. Close friends already may share deeper, more intricate perspectives of self, other, and context but must continually step back from experiences and relationships and examine them analytically and critically.

Third, friendship as method situates our research in the natural contexts of friendship. Again the approach is anthropological: going where participants are. *Between Gay and Straight* (Tillmann-Healy, 2001a) takes readers into the multiple sites of my fieldwork: gay bars and clubs, softball fields, homes, restaurants, and coffee houses. In their accounts, we follow Kiesinger (1995, 1998a, 1998b), Cherry (1996), and Myerhoff (1978) to the private and public spaces where their respondents struggle to make meaning from illness and loss.

Perhaps the most important aspect of this methodology is that we research with an ethic of friendship, a stance of hope, caring, justice, even love. Friendship as method is neither a program nor a guise strategically aimed at gaining further access. It is a level of investment in participants' lives that puts fieldwork relationships on par with the project.

We sacrifice a day of writing to help someone move. We set aside our reading pile when someone drops by or calls "just to talk." When asked, we keep secrets, even if they would add compelling twists to our research report or narrative. We consider our participants an audience (see Ellis, 1995) and struggle to write both honestly and empathically for them. We lay ourselves on the line, going virtually anywhere, doing almost anything, pushing to the furthest reaches of our being. We never ask more of participants than we are willing to give. Friendship as method demands radical reciprocity, a move from studying "them" to studying *us*.

For researchers, this means that we use our speaking and writing skills and our positions as scholars and critics in ways that transform and uplift our research, local, and global communities (see Christians, 2000). Since the publication of *Between Gay and Straight* (Tillmann-Healy, 2001a), I have written three newspaper editorials, one marking the 3-year anniversary of Matthew Shepard's murder (Tillmann-Healy, 2001b), the second and third urging Orlando's city council to add sexual orientation to the classes protected by our nondiscrimination ordinance (Tillmann-Healy, 2002a, 2002b). In addition, my colleague Kathryn Norsworthy and I have given testimony on the ordinance to the Orlando Human Relations Board, spoken at a public rally, collected over a hundred faculty signatures at Rollins College, and met with three city commissioners.

After her dissertation work, Kiesinger was interviewed on National Public Radio during Eating Disorders Awareness Month. Myerhoff contributed to a film that won an Academy Award for best short documentary, bringing renewed visibility and resources to the Aliyah Center. Angrosino developed such close relationships with staff and clients at Opportunity House that he was appointed to its board of trustees, and Cherry was so transformed by his fieldwork that instead of an academic job, he accepted a position with an AIDS network. In these and many other ways, researchers can become allies with and for their research communities. Making this move, we do not deny or efface privilege associated with education or any other dominant group identity; instead, we try to use that privilege for libratory ends.

This ethic of friendship also extends to our relationships with readers. We research pressing social problems that undermine peace, equality, freedom, and democracy. We strive to ensure that our representations expose and contest oppression associated with race, gender, class, sexual orientation, religion, age, and ability. With compelling, transgressive accounts, we seek to engage readers and on multiple levels: intellectually, aesthetically, emotionally, ethically, and politically (see Bochner, 1994). Together, researchers, participants, and readers learn to practice a more active and responsible citizenship.

Strengths of Friendship as Method

For everyone involved, friendship as method can provide a unique perspective on social life. In the ethnographic dialogue (see Tedlock, 1991), we bring together personal and academic discourses, comparing, contrasting, and critiquing them.

For the Researcher

This move has much to offer qualitative researchers. Perhaps the most salient benefit is the relationships themselves. Total immersion of both our academic and personal selves can foster multifaceted bonds. Of his relationships with the men of Opportunity House, Angrosino (1998) wrote, "I didn't want to be thought of as just the guy who showed up every so often with the tape recorder. I wanted to remain someone who had connections to their lives in general" (p. 38).

Such relationships can provide what Kenneth Burke (1973) called "equipment for living." By befriending Jewish elders at the Aliyah Center, Myerhoff rediscovered her roots. Through interactive, reciprocal bonds with Abbie, Liz, Eileen, and Anna, Kiesinger added layers of meaning to her own account of bulimia; and Berger's connections with Rabbi Levinson and congregants at Dalet Shalom expanded the dimensions of her faith.

Friendship as method can bring us to a level of understanding and depth of experience we may be unable to reach using only traditional methods. In my project, by studying gay, lesbian, and queer literatures, I learn about my participants historically and politically; by observing their interactions, I get to know them interpersonally and culturally; by giving them my compassion and devotion, I experience them emotionally and spiritually.

Between Gay and Straight (Tillmann-Healy, 2001a) involved multiple cycles of conversing, sharing activities, reading about sexual orientation, exchanging what was read, writing about the group, distributing the writing, and talking about it. Throughout these cycles, my researcher and friendship roles wove together, each expanding and deepening the other. My participants became (and remain) my best friends, my family—and I theirs. Our relationships ripple through every dimension of my life.

One area profoundly affected has been my connections with women (both lesbian and heterosexual). Observing my participants' same-sex bonds, I have been prompted to seek new levels of affiliation in my own. I am better able to tap into the loving—even erotic—possibilities of female friendship, and I believe this renders me a more feminist ally to other women.

The vulnerability the Cove men and I share also has transformed my marriage. Doug and I have learned to cultivate a level of openness and risk neither of us experienced in our families of origin. Becoming immersed in a gay male community has rendered our sexual and gender identities more queer. Doug and I have developed strategies to resist binary constructions of sexuality and gender, freeing us to enact more fluid identities.

Finally, these layered connections allow me to see the many faces of oppression (Young, 2000). As a result, I work continually to infuse every aspect of my research, my pedagogy, and my institutional and community service with the values of antioppressive education (Freire, 1999). In all of these ways, this academic project has become my life project.

For Participants

Respondents can benefit from participation in such projects as well. One way is through the experience of empathic connection with the friend/ researcher, which can help participants feel heard, known, and understood (see Hutchinson, Wilson, & Wilson, 1994). Those with whom we work have unique opportunities to (co)construct meaningful accounts of troubling and painful experiences and to offer their accounts to others as gifts. Previously hospitalized for anorexia, a participant named Liz said to Kiesinger (1995), "I have been to hell and back and if I can prevent anyone from going where I've been, I will tell my story" (p. 54). Respondents also can take pride in the contributions they make to the researcher's life. About her relationship with a participant who has struggled with bulimia and obesity, Kiesinger wrote:

> Abbie took a liking to me almost instantly. She seemed very interested in my life, my story, and my bulimia. In our interactions, she played a "motherly" role and seemed eager to take me under her wing. She expressed this most strongly in the intense maternal embrace she gave me after each meeting. She would hold me close to her for a long time, patting the back of my head. I knew that she felt valued, useful, and strong when consoling me. Given that she felt unworthy, useless, and weak for most of her life, I was thrilled to let her shower me with all the advice, nurturance, and counsel she could. (p. 52)

By engaging the friend/researcher in a long-term, multifaceted relationship, participants can learn as many new ways of thinking, feeling, and relating as the researcher can. Rob Ryan, a participant in *Between Gay and Straight* (Tillmann-Healy, 2001a), reported on some specific lessons learned:

> I remember talking to you about what it meant to be gay and some of my hang-ups about it. You were the first person—whether you knew it or not—who

clarified for me that being gay related to my sexual orientation and not necessarily to being masculine or feminine. I didn't see myself as feminine, but my upbringing was that if you were gay, you were feminine, and that was a bad thing.

A year later, I asked if you saw me as "the woman" in my relationship with Tim. Your answer was: "If you're asking whether I see you as the one who tends to be more sensitive and nurturing, then yes, I see you as the woman." You turned being "the woman" from a weakness—as I unknowingly had made it out to be—to a strength. Suddenly, it dawned on me: I should value *all* my good qualities, masculine and feminine. (p. 217)

At the oral defense for my Ph.D. dissertation, Gordon Bernstein, another participant, said this:

I grew up playing baseball, played it in college for a couple years. Was very much socialized with middle-class, beer-drinking, heterosexual ideals. Socialized that way all my life. Our group has thought and talked about things since meeting Lisa that we didn't before. Our conversations were very unemotional. I don't know how often we expressed ourselves—what we thought, how we felt, how we came to terms with things. Lisa facilitated those kinds of conversations, and I don't think anyone else here could have facilitated them. I know that I couldn't have been as open, pushed the envelope that often, and really shared my views, because I was socialized not to feel pain. "Deal with it, suck it up, and move on." But Lisa made it comfortable for us, and that made it possible for her to establish the kind of friendships we have with her. (pp. 217–218)

Although it brings unusual dimensions to our relationships, my dual role of friend/researcher provides additional reasons and ways to connect. Because I study them/us, these men always can assume that I want information about their emotional and relational lives. Rob indicated that had I been "just a friend," he may not have perceived a standing invitation to share personal experiences. At the same time, because I care about them so much and embody that ethic of caring, they can trust that I will honor their disclosures and try to use them in ways that promote liberation and justice.

When we approach research as an endeavor of friendship, the emergent texts can have additional benefits for participants, including self-understanding and acceptance. Asked what he learned from the dissertation, Rob told me, "I wish I had read this before I came out. This has helped me become more comfortable with myself." On a similar note, another participant, Pat Martinez, said,

I think that I have benefited more from Lisa writing her dissertation than *she* has, or will, even by getting a Ph.D. Becoming involved with Lisa and the work she was doing . . . enabled me to deal with my coming out. It helped me combine my old athletic, fraternity-brother self and my emerging gay self. I saw that I could be a *gay* athlete, a *gay* man with gay *and straight* friends. The only "drawback" for me is that I wish the project would have started earlier. We met just as I was coming out at thirty-five. I wonder how different my twenties would have been had I crossed paths with someone like [Lisa], had I been asked to look within myself and discuss my inner struggles—as I have in my late thirties. (Tillmann-Healy, 2001a, p. 218)

What we write even can strengthen connections among members of one's research community. Rob said of the dissertation, "I wasn't involved with [my partner] Tim when many of the early events were occurring. So I felt like I got to know the group and the group's history better." David made a similar observation:

I never imagined that the dissertation would have such an impact on all of us as friends. My friendships with these guys were pretty solid before, but the project has brought us even closer. Reading the dissertation, we all learned about each other. Since then, we've talked about the events Lisa wrote about, and those discussions have reforged the bonds between us. This was a very, very unique experience that we all shared. (see Tillmann-Healy, 2001a, p. 218)

These works then can be taken outside the fieldwork community and used as sources of education. Tim Mahn said,

There are so many people I meet, or I'm friends with, or acquaintances, or family members, or people from my past that I'd like to send a copy. I think they could be enlightened. It's going to be a great tool.

Finally, our writings from friendship as method can promote social change. In Tim's words, "As a reader, I kept thinking, 'I want to do something; I *have* to do something.' It gave me energy. I feel like I'm now a bit of an activist." On a similar note, Rob told me, "You've shown us that we have a lot of responsibility, and that being out is courageous. If we can be that, I know we can help others."

Considerations of Friendship as Method

Neither every researcher nor every participant will be comfortable practicing friendship as method. The demands are high, and the implications can be daunting.

For the Researcher

First, practical issues must be considered. Our work lives are structured around and constrained by deadlines for projects, grants, tenure, and promotion. Not all researchers can afford to spend at least a year in the field and another year or more writing, revisiting, and rewriting.

Questions graduate students have asked include, "How do I get a project like this through my thesis/dissertation committee?" and "Will anyone hire this kind of researcher?" Students interested in such work must find programs that support it. Several of the projects I have discussed (my own, Cherry's, Kiesinger's, and Berger's) came out of the University of South Florida's Ph.D. program in communication. The University of Illinois at Urbana and the University of Utah also encourage critical, ethnographic, and action research. With respect to the job-seeking process, it probably is safer professionally to conduct more traditional studies. But one's passion for unconventional research—and for close relationships in the field—need not preclude academic employment. In my first year on the job market, I was invited to four campus interviews and received two offers.

On the other hand, practicing friendship as method does make it challenging to specify in advance research questions and objectives for external evaluators such as dissertation committees and institutional review boards. Our work also may be difficult to contextualize for more traditional colleagues and funding agencies. To help provide such a context, I included a detailed statement of my methodological philosophy, articulating many ideas contained in this article, in a professional assessment report for my midtenure evaluation. The statement sparked a lively discussion with the multidisciplinary evaluation committee, but I was not asked to defend my approach. Each researcher has to gauge the political and methodological climate of his or her department and institution to frame what he or she does in terms that are understandable and acceptable to peers and evaluators.

Careful consideration must be given to emotional demands as well. With friendship as method, researchers must examine, scrutinize, and critique ourselves in ways not required by traditional qualitative inquiry. During fieldwork at Dalet Shalom, Berger questioned whether her ambivalent Judaism could withstand her evangelical participants' efforts to convert her. Kiesinger's relationship with Abbie, whose account of bulimia and obesity centers on a long history of sexual exploitation, sparked a vague yet haunting sense that Kiesinger also had been sexually abused as a child. Close relationships with gay male participants/friends make it impossible to shirk my heterosexism and heterosexual privilege. Although such radical reflexivity can take us to the darkest corners of our psyche and experience, it also can enlighten our thinking, our accounts, and our humanity.

Relationally, doing fieldwork this way carries all the risks that friendship does. Because we must reveal and invest so much of ourselves, researchers are exposed and vulnerable, which means we can be profoundly disappointed, frustrated, or hurt. For 3 years, Kiesinger witnessed four women battle anorexia, bulimia, and/or obesity. Three of them followed no clear path toward recovery, and their struggles at times exacerbated Kiesinger's own struggles with body and food. By exploring the borderlands between Jewish and Christian identities, Berger learned to live with uncertainty and began to work through the conflicted feelings she had for her estranged, mentally ill father. Just as she felt ready to reconnect with him, he suddenly died. During my fieldwork, members of my research community tested positive for HIV, rendering me a fellow traveler down the emotional, medical, and political pathways of AIDS. Myerhoff and Cherry had to grieve the deaths of virtually every participant in their studies.

Another consideration involves our sometimes-conflicting obligations. On one hand, we must respect and honor our relationships with participants; on the other, we owe readers an account that is as comprehensive and complex as possible. After collecting narratives of conversion to Messianic Judaism, Berger (2000) wanted to interview participants' significant others about their reactions to the person who had changed faiths. In the end, she rejected the idea, concluding that this "would be too disruptive to the delicate truce many family members share when one member has converted" (p. 180). Although such interviews would have added a new and provocative dimension to her project, Berger privileged her ethic of friendship over her ethnographic interest.

As mentioned, due to our deep and sustained involvement, we may be told secrets that would add significant layers to our accounts. Even with nonprivileged information, the dual role of friend/researcher makes it difficult to decide what to divulge, especially regarding information that potentially discredits our participants.

Berger often was troubled by the conservative attitudes toward abortion and homosexuality her participants expressed. I frequently was disturbed by the sexism enacted by my gay male participants. In face-to-face encounters in the field, both Berger and I tended to suppress much of our disapproval. Had our participants been strangers or simply "subjects," we may have maintained a more critical distance and felt more empowered to challenge their views directly. Later, we decided to include these issues in our written accounts, hoping our portrayals would spark reflection and action both in and outside our fieldwork communities. At some level, though, even this felt like a betrayal to our friends/participants, who already are members of stigmatized and marginalized groups.

Under friendship as method, researchers must pay constant close attention to ethical issues, including informed consent, confidentiality, and beneficence. At times, we navigate their pathways in unconventional ways. Angrosino's research, for example, centered on mentally retarded adults, many of whom also have mental illness and/or a criminal history. Because his participants may have difficulty assessing the consequences of consent, Angrosino chose to write ethnographic fiction and to use composite characters.

My approach to confidentiality changed as the relationships changed. In my first class paper on the Cove, I followed social science conventions by using pseudonyms and altering other identifying details. Later, as the project became more collaborative, I asked participants to choose between having a pseudonym, using their real first names only, or using their real first and last names.[1] I explained that pseudonyms were the standard and safest approach. For the dissertation, one primary participant, Al Steel, who was not out at work or to his family, requested a pseudonym and asked that I write only generally about his occupation and hometown. The others (David, Gordon, Tim, Rob, and Pat) had me use their real first and last names. For the book, the most public document to date, two requests were made: Al wanted his real first name used, and Tim, who was embarking on a new career, asked that I alter his last name. All men consented to having photographs of them in the book, and Tim and Rob agreed to appear on the cover with Doug and me.

When Tim and Rob decided to use their real name(s), each said to me, "I want to do this for you." Although this reflects their level of investment in our relationships and the project, I had to assert my researcher role. I urged them not to base consent on their feelings for me or what they imagined I wanted. We talked at length about the personal and professional risks they would be taking. From the conversations that followed, I came to believe that although their connections with me could not be completely disentangled from their decisions, each perceived himself to be acting in his own best interest as well as the interests of other—especially younger—gay men who need role models for coming out. Had I not believed that, I would have tried to convince them to change their names.

In terms of beneficence, I clearly have profited the most professionally. This project and its publications were central to my earning a Ph.D. and getting an academic job and will be key factors in my tenure review. However, in the interest of distributing the benefits of this project, I have donated royalties from *Between Gay and Straight* (Tillmann-Healy, 2001a) to activist groups (e.g., the Human Rights Campaign, GLSEN, and PFLAG) and continually offer myself as a resource to community groups, the media, educators, and students.

When researchers become advocates for groups the dominant culture constructs as deviant (e.g., gay men, Messianic Jews, bulimics, and people with AIDS) and assign the resultant texts in their classes, not all students respond positively. Confronting this kind of work may challenge deeply held values and assumptions. I have had to answer complaints made on course evaluations and directly to my department chair, dean, provost, and president (e.g., my project as "gay propaganda"). One student had to be removed from my class before the semester even began. Seeing my book on the reading list, this student called my department chair and provost, demanded alternatives to my class (a requirement for our major), and made veiled threats, including, "This woman needs to be stopped." I am fortunate to be at an institution whose administration supports and defends my work. It would be much more difficult to continue at this time if I believed that my tenure were hanging in the balance. Nonetheless, these student complaints are both time and energy sapping.

When our projects center on oppression, our emotional and physical safety can be jeopardized as well. My participants and I have been verbally accosted by homophobic slurs. I have received packages of virulent antigay literature in response to newspaper profiles of *Between Gay and Straight* (Tillmann-Healy, 2001a). Enduring still another level of risk, Khuankaew and Norsworthy conduct workshops on violence, trauma, and HIV awareness on the Thai-Burma border, where it is illegal for them to organize. With each training session, Norsworthy, a psychologist from the United States, risks deportation and blacklist status, and her Thai collaborator, Khuankaew, faces incarceration.

Friendship as method, although potentially rewarding, comes with a new set of obligations that do not pave a smooth, comfortable road. When we engage others' humanity, struggles, and oppression, we cannot simply shut off the recorder, turn our backs, and exit the field. Anyone who takes on this sort of project must be emotionally strong and willing to face pressure, resistance, backlash, and perhaps even violence.

For Participants

When we approach research as an endeavor of friendship, and we approach participants as friends, some considerations for respondents also are heightened. As indicated, if researchers become full and trusted members of research communities, we open ourselves to disappointment and pain. Likewise, if participants take in researchers not just as visitors but also as friends, their level of risk is increased. Because I was both friend and researcher, when Tim disclosed he had tested positive for HIV (see Tillmann-Healy, 2001a, pp. 88–90), he was doubly vulnerable. When he told Lisa-the-friend, he opened himself to rejection and pain. But later, Lisa-the-researcher wrote field notes on our interaction and eventually sought his permission to include the episode in the dissertation. Although he consented, Tim remained anxious about how that evening would be portrayed. He told me that before his partner Rob brought home their copy, they had agreed to read it to each other front to back. But as soon as Tim saw it, he immediately turned to "I Have Something to Tell You." Of his reading experience, he said, "It put me right back there. It seemed so real." Later, Tim told me, "That was hard to read. I don't like revisiting that time." Having to reconfront such painful experiences might give some pause when thinking of contributing to such a project.

Because of the power imbalance between researcher and participants, field relationships always have potential for colonization and exploitation. Friendship as method seeks to undermine and disrupt this. However, if researchers do not maintain an ethic of friendship in their fieldwork practices and/or accounts, participants can sustain emotional damage. In "Emotional and Ethical Quagmires in Returning to the Field," Carolyn Ellis (1995) wrote poignantly about the anger and pain members of her fieldwork community suffered when a third party told them that she had published *Fisher Folk*, a book containing unflattering portrayals of their rural lifestyle. An extended family had taken in Carolyn as a friend, giving her years of virtually unfettered access, but as a (then) realist ethnographer, she rarely allowed herself to be similarly open. Ellis also admitted to taping conversations surreptitiously, to securing consent so early in the 12-year project that many forgot about her researcher role or assumed it had ended, and to sharing none of her published work. The honesty of "Emotional and Ethical Quagmires" helps readers become, as Ellis herself becomes, a more emotional, dialogical, and ethical researcher.

Friendship as method all but demands that writings be taken back to the community for examination, critique, and further dialogue. My central participants were given drafts of class papers, the dissertation, proposed changes for the book, and this article. All attended my dissertation defense having read the document, and many participated in the discussion. I also conducted follow-up interviews to attain additional reactions and reflections. At each stage, I incorporated their feedback and suggestions and renegotiated informed consent.

Although this process contributed to a collaborative project, it also rendered my participants vulnerable to each other and to other readers they know. Tim told me that even after giving me permission to include "I Have Something to Tell You," he worried about reactions of others in the group. Tim reported thinking, "Wow, all these people are going to read that. I wonder what they're going to say." With the publication of *Between Gay and Straight* (Tillmann-Healy, 2001a), my participants were exposed to family members, associates, and coworkers, some of whom did not know they were gay.

In some cases, our participants risk physical harm. To attend Khuankaew and Norsworthy's workshops with the women of Burma, for example, participants defy laws against organizing and risk arrest, abuse, and imprisonment. For me, few thoughts are more sobering than the possibility that one of my friends could become the victim of a hate crime as a result of his visibility in *Between Gay and Straight* (Tillmann-Healy, 2001a).

Friendship as method requires that ethics remain at the forefront of our research and our research relationships. Confidentiality and informed consent become ongoing negotiations. Researchers and participants reflexively consider and discuss power dynamics at every turn and constantly strive to balance the need to advance the social justice agenda of their projects and the need to protect one another from harm.

Conclusion

Most any study involving human "subjects" can incorporate some aspect of friendship as method. Even in the most empirical, double-blind research, we can treat participants with an ethic of friendship. We can solicit fears and concerns, listen closely and respond compassionately, and use such exchanges to refine the study and direct its implications.

The study of close relationships, including friendship, is well suited for friendship as method. In contrast to one-time, retrospective surveys, a primary means of studying relationships, friendship as method involves sustained immersion in participants' lives, offering a processual and longitudinal perspective. But most any topic could be investigated with the practices, at the pace, in the contexts, and/or with an ethic of friendship. Emotional topics, such as divorce, serious illness, or the birth of a child, probably lend themselves best to friendship as method because the more emotional and multifaceted the topic, the more appropriate it becomes for researchers and participants to share emotional and multifaceted ties.

For a mutual, close, and/or lasting friendship to develop between every researcher and all participants is unrealistic. Regardless, we can approach respondents from a stance of friendship, meaning we treat them with respect, honor their stories, and try to use their stories for humane and just purposes.

In a strange aligning of the universe, the oral defense for my Ph.D. dissertation took place the same day and time as Matthew Shepard's memorial service. Jim King, a member of my dissertation committee, posed this question: "But what if *they* are not humane and just? Would you study Matthew Shepard's killers this way?"

This was my response:

> I exhale slowly. "That would be extremely difficult. When something like this murder happens, 'we'—the non-perpetrators—often are so shocked and disheartened that we distance ourselves from 'them'—the perpetrators. We tell ourselves that they must be crazy or evil. Such explanations come quickly and easily. The hardest question to ask is this: what kinds of personal, familial, and cultural conditions have to exist for this act to make sense somehow, to seem almost *rational?* We don't ask this because it implicates us in the problem; it forces us to identify with the killers, to bring them close and see them as part of us. Russell Henderson and Aaron McKinney were unable to experience their interconnection with Matthew Shepard; that's exactly what made him so disposable. But if we dispose of them in the same way, we come no closer to creating the kind of world where such actions become less possible. It would be profoundly uncomfortable and disturbing to study Henderson and McKinney with the practices and/or with an ethic of friendship, but that may be what's most needed." (Tillmann-Healy, 2001a, pp. 212–213)

Certainly, the full scope of friendship as method is not for every qualitative project. Time, career, and interest constraints limit our ability to study social life at the natural pace of friendship. Likewise, our purposes may not best be served in the natural contexts of friendship. When doing oral history, for example, it is important to contrive an interview setting where high-quality recording can occur. Practices of friendship, moreover, such as compassion, might feel inappropriate when doing research on groups we consider dangerous or unethical.

Between Gay and Straight (Tillmann-Healy, 2001a) is unique because some of my participants already were friends or acquaintances when I began the project, and friendship was also the subject of my research. But qualitative researchers need not adopt the whole vision to benefit from friendship as method. Moving toward friendship as method may be as simple as turning off the tape recorder and cooking dinner with participants; investing more of ourselves in their emotional, relational, and political welfare; inviting respondents further into our lives than we ever dared before; hanging around longer; writing texts that are as enlightening and useful to our research, local, and global communities as to our academic careers; and/or approaching participants as we would potential or actual friends: with a desire for mutual respect, understanding, examination, and growth.

Note

1. This approach to informed consent and confidentiality may mitigate the hierarchical separation between researcher and participants. However, as long as the researcher determines the options, the differential is not eliminated. Perhaps only coauthorship has that potential.

References

Angrosino, M. V. (1998). *Opportunity House: Ethnographic stories of mental retardation.* Walnut Creek, CA: AltaMira Press.

Behar, R. (1996). *The vulnerable observer: Anthropology that breaks your heart.* Boston: Beacon Press.

Berger, L. P. (2000). *Messianic Judaism: Searching the spirit.* Unpublished doctoral dissertation, University of South Florida.

Berger, L. P. (2001). Inside out: Narrative autoethnography as a path toward rapport. *Qualitative Inquiry, 7:* 504–518.

Bochner, A. P. (1994). Perspectives on inquiry II: Theories and stories. In M. L. Knapp & G. R. Miller (Eds.), *Handbook of interpersonal communication* (2nd ed., pp. 21–41). Thousand Oaks, CA: Sage.

Buber, M. (1988). *The knowledge of man: Selected essays.* Atlantic Highlands, NJ: Humanities Press International, Inc.

Burke, K. (1973). *The philosophy of literary form: Studies in symbolic action.* Berkeley: University of California Press.

Butler, J. (1999). *Gender trouble: Feminism and the subversion of identity* (10th anniversary ed.). New York: Routledge.

Cherry, K. (1996). Ain't no grave deep enough. *Journal of Contemporary Ethnography, 25:* 22–57.

Christians, C. G. (2000). Ethics and politics in qualitative research. In N. K. Denzin & Y. S. Lincoln (Eds.), *Handbook of qualitative research* (2nd ed., pp. 133–155). Thousand Oaks, CA: Sage.

Collins, P. H. (1991). *Black feminist thought: Knowledge, consciousness, and the politics of empowerment.* New York: Routledge.

Collins, P. H. (1998). *Fighting words: Black women and the search for justice.* Minneapolis: University of Minnesota Press.

Cook, J. A., & Fonow, M. M. (1986). Knowledge and women's interests: Issues of epistemology and methodology in feminist sociological research. *Sociological Inquiry, 56:* 2–29.

Denzin, N. K. (1997). *Interpretive ethnography: Ethnographic practices for the 21st century.* Thousand Oaks, CA: Sage.

Denzin, N. K., & Lincoln, Y. S. (2000). Introduction: The discipline and practice of qualitative research. In N. K. Denzin & Y. S. Lincoln (Eds.), *Handbook of qualitative research* (2nd ed., pp. 1–28). Thousand Oaks, CA: Sage.

Ellis, C. (1995). Emotional and ethical quagmires in returning to the field. *Journal of Contemporary Ethnography, 24:* 68–98.

Ellis, C., Kiesinger, C. E., & Tillmann-Healy, L. M. (1997). Interactive interviewing: Talking about emotional experience. In R. Hertz (Ed.), *Reflexivity & voice* (pp. 119–149). Thousand Oaks, CA: Sage.

Fine, G. A. (1981). Friends, impression management, and preadolescent behavior. In G. P. Stone & H. A. Farberman (Eds.), *Social psychology through symbolic interaction* (pp. 257–272). New York: John Wiley.

Fine, M. (1994). Working the hyphens: Reinventing self and other in qualitative research. In N. K. Denzin & Y. S. Lincoln (Eds.), *Handbook of qualitative research* (pp. 70–82). Thousand Oaks, CA: Sage.

Freire, P. (1999). *Pedagogy of the oppressed.* New York: Continuum.

Gamson, J. (1998). *Freaks talk back: Tabloid talk shows and sexual nonconformity.* Chicago: University of Chicago Press.

Geertz, C. (1973). *The interpretation of cultures.* New York: Basic Books.

Hackman, W., Peters, M. L., & Zuniga, X. (Eds.), *Readings for diversity and social justice: An anthology on racism, antisemitism, sexism, heterosexism, ableism, and classism* (pp. 35–49). New York: Routledge.

Harding, S. (1991). *Whose science? Whose knowledge? Thinking from women's lives.* Ithaca, NY: Cornell University Press.

Holleran, A. (1996). Friends. In J. Preston & M. Lowenthal (Eds.), *Friends and lovers: Gay men write about the families they create* (pp. 31–37). New York: Plume.

Hutchinson, S. A., Wilson, M. E., & Wilson, H. S. (1994). Benefits of participating in research interviews. *Image: The Journal of Nursing Scholarship, 26:* 161–164.

Jackson, M. (1989). *Paths toward a clearing: Radical empiricism and ethnographic inquiry.* Bloomington: Indiana University Press.

Khuankaew, O., & Norsworthy, K. (2000). Struggles for peace, justice, unity and freedom: Stories of the women of Burma. *Seeds of Peace, 16:* 16–18.

Kiesinger, C. E. (1995). *Anorexic and bulimic lives: Making sense of food and eating.* Unpublished doctoral dissertation, University of South Florida.

Kiesinger, C. E. (1998a). From interview to story: Writing Abbie's life. *Qualitative Inquiry, 4:* 71–95.

Kiesinger, C. E. (1998b). Portrait of an anorexic life. In A. Banks & S. P. Banks (Eds.), *Fiction & social research: By ice or fire* (pp. 115–136). Walnut Creek, CA: AltaMira Press.

Lather, P. (1991). *Getting smart: Feminist research and pedagogy with/in the postmodern.* New York: Routledge.

Myerhoff, B. (1978). *Number our days.* New York: Touchstone.

Norsworthy, K. (2002). *Feminist interventions for Southeast Asian women trauma survivors: Deconstructing gender-based violence and developing structures of peace.* Greensboro, NC: ERIC CASS.

Rawlins, W. K. (1992). *Friendship matters: Communication, dialectics, and the life course.* New York: Aldine de Gruyter.

Reason, P. (1994). Three approaches to participative inquiry. In N. K. Denzin & Y. S. Lincoln (Eds.), *Handbook of qualitative research* (pp. 324–339). Thousand Oaks, CA: Sage.

Reinharz, S. (1992). *Feminist methods in social research.* New York: Oxford University Press.

Roberts, H. (Ed.). (1990). *Doing feminist research.* London: Routledge.

Rubin, L. B. (1985). *Just friends: The role of friendship in our lives.* New York: Harper & Row.

Schwandt, T. A. (1994). Constructivist, interpretivist approaches to human inquiry. In N. K. Denzin & Y. S. Lincoln (Eds.), *Handbook of qualitative research* (pp. 118–137). Thousand Oaks, CA: Sage.

Sedgwick, E. K. (1990). *Epistemology of the closet.* Berkeley: University of California Press.

Tedlock, B. (1991). From participant observation to the observation of participation: The emergence of narrative ethnography. *Journal of Anthropological Research,* 47: 69–94.

Tillmann-Healy, L. M. (2001a). *Between gay and straight: Understanding friendship across sexual orientation.* Walnut Creek, CA: AltaMira Press.

Tillmann-Healy, L. M. (2001b, October 12). Matthew Shepard: Three years later. *Orlando Sentinel,* p. A21.

Tillmann-Healy, L. M. (2002a, October 24). Coming out of homophobia's closet. *Orlando Sentinel,* p. A19.

Tillmann-Healy, L. M. (2002b, April 13). Equal rights, not special rights. *Orlando Sentinel,* p. A19.

Tillmann-Healy, L. M., & Kiesinger, C. E. (2001). Mirrors: Seeing each other and ourselves through fieldwork. In K. Gilbert (Ed.), *The emotional nature of qualitative research* (pp. 81–108). Boca Raton, FL: CRC Press.

Weiss, R. S. (1998). A taxonomy of relationships. *Journal of Social and Personal Relationships, 15:* 671–683.

Werking, K. (1997). *We're just good friends: Women and men in nonromantic relationships.* New York: Guilford.

Wood, J. T. (2002). *Interpersonal communication: Everyday encounters* (3rd ed.). Belmont, CA: Wadsworth.

Young, I. M. (2000). Five faces of oppression. In M. Adams, W. J. Blumenfeld, R. Castaneda, H. W. Hackman, M. L. Peters, & X. Zuniga (Eds.), *Readings for diversity and social justice: An anthology on racism, antisemitism, sexism, heterosexism, ableism, and classism* (pp. 35–49). New York: Routledge.

14

Gender Imago

Niza Yanay and Nitza Berkovitch

The idea of using a personal electronic correspondence as a reflexive strategy to explore ideas, theories, and personal commitments followed an invitation we received to speak before members of our department. The aim of the two lectures (delivered sequentially) was to address the psychological, cultural, and philosophical challenges of feminist and gender theories to our social thinking, knowledge, and politics. By inviting the two of us—a sociologist and a psychologist—the organizer (a feminist colleague) hoped to stage a contentious conversation on gender, self, and society to show the differences between the ways in which sociologists and psychologists frame the questions, formulate the issues, and understand the ways in which gender is constructed, experienced, and performed. Following the lecture "Gender Games, Dogma, Fixation, and Psychological Structuring," the other speaker changed her original plan. Rather than talk about the ways in which the category of gender is used (and misused) in sociology, she decided to respond directly to the previous lecture, and the title "'The Vanishing Lady': On Women, Gender, and Sociology" was replaced by "Essence, Appearance, and Identity Games."

This turning point—changing the format of two loosely connected lectures into a format in which one speaker replies directly to the other also

An abbreviated version of Yanay, N., & Berkovitch, N., "Gender Imago: Searching for New Feminist Methodologies," forthcoming in *Cultural Studies/Critical Methodologies 2005.*

triggered the beginning of a private correspondence between the two of us. This was the beginning of a responsive movement toward a correspondence that breaks the structure of serial linearity—lecture following lecture, related but separated—which established relations of exchange, contrary to the original plan. Thus, something that began as a traditional academic performance continued as an experiment of common inquiry to explore our ideas, attitudes, limits, and possibilities of gender performance. Moving from the strategy of speaking (to an audience) to "speaking-in-response" and later to "writing-in-response" was a methodological change, marking the transition from presentation to confession, from judgment to risk, and from review to translation. We thus join others who are looking for new ways to explore, understand, and write social science (Czarniawska-Joerges, 1995; Ellis & Bochner, 1999; Richardson, 1992; Rhodas, 2003; Tillmann-Healy & Kiesinger, 2001; Watson, 2000).

In this chapter, we use our personal scripts to explore the relations between experience and theory, knowledge and identity. This process of knowledge construction was formed out of an interactive process between us. Yet, our purpose is neither to "mirror" ourselves nor to focus on our experiences as such. We do not believe that experience, as some feminists claim, is a "truer" or better method to know reality. On the contrary, our aim is to problematize experience. The telling of our "stories" was a responsive construction of personal knowledge intended to evoke a social inquiry into the place of theory as a self-acting affair. We used a form of dialogue—writing-in-response—to create, negotiate, and understand the positioning of our own experiences, as well as the relations between ideas and emotions regarding sexuality, gender, desire, and fantasy.

Writing-in-response is a complex activity with no Archimedean theoretical center. In many ways, speaking and writing are—explicitly or implicitly, consciously or unconsciously—always "in response." It is always a reaction by reply, citation, or negation of previous speech. However, the specific form of writing-in-response as a genre of correspondence and dialogue is, like letters, a practice that can overcome the isolated, lonely, and distant process of academic writing and publishing, in that we send our thoughts to a specific interlocutor who is not only imagined but also an actual coperformer.

This experimental essay, then, combines three different genres: symposium, writing letters, and formal analysis. It attempts to amalgamate the spontaneity and immediacy of speaking, the intimacy of writing letters, and the rigor of scholarship. First we shall (very) briefly summarize the issues raised in our two different lectures. Then we present the electronic correspondence as it evolved during the months from April to June 2000.[1] At the end, we will discuss the letters as two texts that together translate, in different ways, the tension between theory and experiences into tentative conclusions regarding gender imago, identity, and performance.

The Seminars: Niza Speaks on "Gender Games, Dogma, Fixation, and Psychological Structuring"

At the center of my lecture stands the idea that an apparently male biological sex does not necessarily produce male desire and that female desire does not necessarily generate female identity. Furthermore, sexual fantasy is not necessarily consistent with one's biological sex. However, when the rules of the game are violated and the script becomes paradoxical, emotions as well as performance are troubled. Mainly, I wanted to illustrate how psychoanalysis deconstructs the unity of the body (male or female) and sexual identity through the treatment of personal fantasy and desire. In my lecture, I provided three anecdotes. Here I will briefly mention one. The first anecdote told the story of E., a muscular young man, aggressive and intelligent, who came to Ruth Stein (1995) for therapy, wishing to be a woman. Born male, E. fantasizes about having sex with men, but feeling like a woman. He envies big-breasted women and craves to be a woman. In his fantasy he has sex with men, as a woman. The anecdote raises the questions: Is E. a man or a woman? Why is it important? And why is E. suffering?

The examples I give in my lecture led to a discussion of drag games and their contribution to the theoretical and political understanding of sexual and gender performance and identity. Drag games explicate the nature of gender stereotypes, as well as the manner in which they crystallize and dissolve as a performance with emotional implications, at once confusing and challenging. Who, in fact, is a man dressed in women's clothing? Why are the possibilities always phrased in man/woman dualism?

Following Butler (1990b), I concluded the lecture with the idea that cross-gender appearances allow the subversive reading and parody of the common notions ascribed to the differences between women and men, by exposing their superficiality. Such dramatization does indeed recite the feminine/masculine dichotomy in society, but subverts it at the same time. Thus, a drag performance is not only a theater of identities but rather, mainly, the production of a mocking discourse that criticizes, reinforces, and deconstructs the conventional, natural, taken-for-granted notions of femininity and masculinity.

Nitza Speaks on "Essence, Appearance, and Identity Games"

Responding to the previous lecture, I argued that desires, fantasies, and blurring of identities and games must all be understood as taking place in a patriarchal context, decoding and denoting the power of ideology and social organization. One must inquire when the blurring indeed threatens the gender order and the social or biological distinctions between the sexes, and when the game is only voyeuristic.

Throughout history, there have been women who masqueraded as men in order to reach those territories that were inaccessible to them as women. Women pretended to be men in order to enter the world of study and the world of combat, or in order to escape an unwanted marriage. These figures populate the pages of the history books and the folk tales and folklore of many peoples. Some lived under this borrowed identity until their dying day. This pretense indeed undermines the biological determinism—a female does not have to live as a woman. But at the same time, it also reaffirms the social order regarding the hierarchy between categories. Most of the stories are about females living as men. Entering the category of men means aiming at a higher and better life that women are denied. Crossing the gender boundary from the other side was negatively sanctioned and punished.

Gender categories are, at times, absurd, but this does not contradict the fact that, when the politics of identity play a major role both in terms of macropolitics and in terms of the sense of belonging, these categories are highly significant. Sexual identity can become the basis for self-definition and for the formation of an explicatory community—for example, lesbianism as the basis for identity formation. However, this raises new questions. To what extent are the contents identified with the title "lesbian" fluid and diverse? Do they, too, become fixated and unifying, thus excluding alternative interpretations as well?

The significance of this discussion is that the polar, antithetical, complementary, and hierarchical normativity of gender in an andocentric society creates, mainly in women, mistrust of their femininity, and a conscious as well as unconscious quest for a different kind of femininity. At the same time, gender ideology also hails mainstream performance, forcing women to cling to, employ, and exploit patriarchal femininity. Women's struggle (their willingness and unwillingness, ability and inability) to transcend and succumb to the significatory limitations of their femininity is often revealed through the voice of literary female figures (Naveh, 1999), in the confessions of women during therapy (Friedman, 1996), and via women's political activity (Helman & Rapoport, 1997).

The E-letters

April 30, 2000

Hi Nitza,

I want to start with an experience I had yesterday at the Cinematheque: an unpleasant, albeit intellectually and emotionally intriguing experience. I went to see a film that was being shown within the framework of the Pink Movie Club called *Sex Life in Los Angeles* (Hik, 1999). It's a behind-the-scenes documentary about the "industry of male erotic fantasy" in L.A. I knew I was about to watch a film about pornographic sex between men. Five minutes before the film began, the hall was practically filled with men, young as well as older ones, and a handful of women, none of whom was unescorted. Or so I thought. I didn't really dare survey the hall too closely. I felt like a fish out of water—embarrassed, a bourgeois straight woman. In a foreign setting, all your identifying signs seem to emerge, whether pertinent or not. I had to fight off the strong urge to take paper and pen out of my bag and pretend I was there for some purpose other than a personal, voyeuristic, or freakish one. Did I feel uncomfortable as a woman (what does that mean?); would a straight man have felt as uncomfortable as I did? Or would it have been a different kind of discomfort? I still had time to think: Here you have a golden opportunity to pretend you're Butler for a moment. Fantasize you are a man who is there to watch the film. I know it was an imagined pacifying/diversionary tactic. But let's say it wasn't. What would it take for the game to work? Would I have to come dressed up as a man? Or as a drag king?

Toward the end of the workshop I teach, called "Psychoanalysis and Gender Identity," we get to Butler and the discussion of the disintegration of the binary categories of gender, the manipulation of sexual/gender boundaries, and the constitution of liminal identity, on the verge of gender. Hannah Naveh maintains that "the way out of the binary trap is by blurring this distinction, in order to eliminate its categorizing capacity and descriptive power" (1999, p. 104). However, Naveh, like Butler and others, relies on a model of combined identity comprising both sexes. For blending cannot be compared to blurring.

(Continued)

(Continued)

What is the hybridity of sexuality/gender that we have not yet come across? I sat in the Cinematheque with the sinking feeling that passion, fantasy, and visibility (body), contrary to what I've taught, are not good enough tools to allow transition, blending, and deconstruction of the patriarchal and heterosexual model of femininity and masculinity. I wanted to feel comfortable—a woman alone in an audience full of men. Is it possible? Who are the internal wardens in the postmodern era? And why is it that not every game works?

May 5, 2000

Hi Niza,

As far as I understand your story, it is a question of which specific social situations drive which of our particular identities to the foreground, transforming them from transparent to present and visible. And also, when does this awareness make us feel uncomfortable, or comfortable? Which contexts cause a fixation (if only temporary) of (one or more) identities, and which contexts allow more latitude and fluidity? In other words, we need to contextualize the dynamics Butler introduces and to ask whether and how it works in concrete social situations.[2]

I would like to respond with a story of my own. Every now and then I attend lesbian social events. At times, when they are private events, I am the only straight woman in attendance (or so I think). But otherwise, these are public events, held as part of the Pride Week events, Gay Pride Parade, and so forth, namely, events that celebrate gay sexual identity. On such occasions, I feel comfortable and powerful. Thinking about it, I believe that this sense of power stems from the presence of a multitude of women and the defiance generated by such a presence. The category "woman" in these contexts is perhaps fixated, but *not* at the expense of accentuating the many different ways of "being a woman," and *not* based on the object of sexual desire. Within such diversity I, too, find place and room to celebrate my "being a woman." As for my sexual inclination—here there is some room for play, at least insofar as my presence there puts my sexual identity in question. And this has already become a game of sorts for my close girlfriends and me. In other words, at that given moment, one binary opposition (lesbian/nonlesbian) is being blurred, but mainly because another (woman/man) is being fixated.

It was not only because of the fact that I was among women and you were among men that I felt calm and at ease. One cannot isolate gender and sexuality from other social hierarchies. Thinking back on the situation, I realized that this group of lesbians is located on the pole closest to the mainstream of *Ashkenazi* middle-class society, far from the "madding crowd" of drag queens and kings.

May 11, 2000

Hi Nitza,

I agree with you that gender identity, whether imagined, invented, stereotypical, or invisible, is indeed always transient and momentary, concurrently dependent on the specific place in which the sense of identity becomes conscious, as well as on the cultural climate in which our identity is consummated. In the seminar, you made an important point when describing periods in human history in which a certain degree of autonomy was given to both sexuality and gender. This autonomy provided greater leeway than allowed by modernity (Laqueur, 1990). Indeed, the measure of social and cultural ease (namely, ambiguity) regarding intergender transition and transformation plays an important role here. I have no doubt that my momentary desire to join the energies, tension, pleasure, thrill, and, mainly, ease of the men in the audience—as one of them and not as a woman—has to do not only with the physical unease or unconscious suspicion of the self's explicit motivations, but also with the postmodern context of our lives, which now more than ever allows expansion of the margins of thought and a split practice in the field of identity. Indeed, the sociology of gender is part of the psychology of identity.

Still, once again, I would like to stress the problematic quality inherent in the division between sexuality and identity. I challenge

(Continued)

(Continued)

this dichotomy precisely against the backdrop of postmodern deconstruction of the categories of sex and gender—through the identity of drag, for instance. In your lecture, you asserted that the blurring of the boundary between body and identity, or, in other words, the multiple implications of the affinity between body and identity, can only occur within the confines of political and sociological knowledge, where gender ambiguity generates amusement, pleasure, and social ease, but not in a culture of hatred, rejection, and fear of any behavior that implies the disintegration of the feminine/masculine dichotomy. Nonetheless, I still wonder when the game can work.

At the Cinematheque, for example, the illusion that I could manage to think of myself as a man was a priori doomed to fail, not because I don't have a penis, but because, being seen as a woman, I was not recognized as possessing one by the other participants in the event. At that moment, the desire not to be a woman only reinforced the boundaries of my female identity and the fixated, dichotomous awareness of it. On the other hand, I am very familiar with the sense of ease and empowerment that emerges from your story, generated by the (imagined) lack of division between you (or straight women) and lesbian women. The (implicit) sexual inclination of the (explicit) female body and the blurring of the boundary between them in lesbian events enable one, as you wrote, to experience feelings of defiance against the dichotomous gender regime, while making it possible to "be a woman" in a wide variety of modes and roles. It is true that (temporary) transition between the departments of passions and identities of women is more open to potential identification, identity reversals, nuances, and playfulness, because the female gaze on a woman is always mysterious, undifferentiated, inquisitive, and elusive. The female gaze on a woman does not mark the woman to whom it is directed as an inversion or antithesis, but rather as difference.

My question still remains: Can postmodern deconstruction of the woman/man binary category in philosophy, art, and writing, and in islands of subversive culture survive the disciplinary habitus of the body?

May 27, 2000

Hi Niza,

No, I'm not saying that gender identity, or any other identity, is always transient and momentary. Saying that it is time and place dependent, that it is shaped by a specific history and cultural climate, does not imply that it is short-lived, certainly not with regard to our immediate personal experience. The assertion that we "do gender"— or "perform gender"—in our everyday practice indeed implies that gender identities require routine maintenance. However, most of the time we "do the right thing," thus reinforcing the dominant identity definitions, thereby also reconcealing (from ourselves as well) the fact that it is indeed all about an act. It is an ongoing masquerade that not only looks real, but whose power results in an identity that is experienced as essential, cohesive, and stable. Niza, note that I use the term masquerade for lack of a better word. It is somewhat misleading in this context, because it presupposes the existence of a real identity hiding behind the costume, which presents itself as other than what it really is, and this is not what I mean.

Even if we consider the way in which Butler tries to avoid the fixation of language, as it were, by replacing the word "woman" with the phrase "embodied person located in the category of woman," we are well aware that such social categories have tremendous social impact, no matter how often we put the word "woman" in inverted commas. These hierarchical categories largely determine not only our feelings—whether and to what extent we are comfortable with this never-ending performance—but also our chances in life, in the most basic sense. But let's go on presenting a more intricate picture. Let's add, rather than replace it with, the deconstructive, fluid, postmodern experience. It is the combination and coexistence of these two levels that account for your experience in the Cinematheque hall, and the pleasure experienced by drag show spectators. This way we can begin to grasp the sense of discomfort, as well as the desire to play, belong, and—mainly—the ability to observe it all from a bystander's position, to ponder and ask these questions while the show goes on; add to this

(Continued)

(Continued)

the fact that you were almost the only woman in an audience of men, and the ensuing basic sense of threat. At the same time, however, there was also the somewhat confusing sense that this audience of men was mainly interested in men, rather than in you or the few other women who were present in the hall.

Drag shows, in all their variations, draw their subversive power, as well as their ability to entertain, precisely from the fact that they take place in a cultural context where there is a hierarchy between body and identity. Still, one must also bear in mind that we are concerned with a theatrical performance delineated in terms of time and space, and acted out on stage before an audience. The game takes place within boundaries that are clear and distinct. It has a starting point and a finish line in terms of time, as well as spatial boundaries. This delineation creates a clear-cut distinction between that which takes place inside the hall and the surrounding world outside, thereby also rendering and signifying that which occurs inside as "performance" and that which takes place outside as "reality." An important element that contributes to the sense of illusion transpiring "inside" is the fact that the performers use a taped soundtrack, lip-synching the words. The sound played in the background serves as yet another prop. The same applies to the performers' use of their bodies to create the performativity of gender; like dancers who employ their bodies to create lines, forms, and motion in space, so drag artists use their bodies and "voice" to illustrate the illusive quality underlying the stability of gender markers. However, the context within which this dramatization occurs—the performance—dissolves this meaning, too, defining the occurrence as an extraordinary, short-lived event based on momentary fantasy.

June 11, 2000

Hi Nitza,

It seems that our differences (how expected!) stem from our divergent disciplinary approaches. I try to trace the emotional and psychic significance of female or male identity as the fragile turning point that allows a person, albeit within the repressive dichotomous category of masculinity and femininity, to experience the gendered "other" on deep psychic levels as antithesis and semblance at one and the same time: those fleeting moments of contrastive, imagined, creative identity, which is binary yet opposed to the predominant man/woman identity.

Mundane actions, I would like to argue, provide us with numerous opportunities to experience our bodies and ourselves in all kinds of reversals and inversions, not only through the defiant drama of drag—which, to my mind, is only one political option among many. However, the experiences of inversion, interplay, and defiance can seldom be separated from the perpetual noise on the soundtrack along the continuum of binary sexual identity. Only the artist or poet can carefully unravel the antithetical coils of sexual identity through lines, words, and sounds that together generate concurrent duality and totality. Modern man's need for cohesion (or order) pushes the "sexual otherness," which is furnished ceaselessly by everyday experiences, to the realms of perversion and pathology. Had we adopted psychological and social acceptance regarding the realm of gender options, we would have experienced the everyday through alternating moments of identity, which, like emotions, create a harmony of contrasts and contradictions. In this respect, I can relate to your sociological sentiment, which perceives cultural and discursive climates as the arena of sensibility and the main source of modalities of perceptions that allow or disallow gender unruliness both in psychic terms and as a cultural and social practice.

June 20, 2000

Hi Niza,

I think it's time to wrap things up, although I'm still trying to decipher the feelings you spoke about and come up with answers to the quandaries they triggered in me. The way I chose to deal with the many question marks scattered throughout your text was to try and put the phenomena, experiences, and stories into a wider context—historical,

(Continued)

(Continued)

social, and political. However, in the course of our correspondence, I was forced to confront issues in which I am not well versed. In my scientific work, I deal with gender without sexuality, women without a body, and feminism without sexual identity. I discuss motherhood without mothers. The personal experience is not given admission. And now, all these have become the focal point of our joint discussion. Still, the division of labor created between us allowed me to re-employ the tools with which I am more familiar and more comfortable. Did I thereby fixate the reality that you insist on keeping as volatile? I feel something has happened to both of us in the transition from the seminar lectures to this dialogue: for in your lecture you sounded much more decisive about identity games than in our correspondence, and in my lecture I was more critical and reserved, whereas now, for the first time, I had to address the dimension of emotional experience and discovered its efficacy as a tool for exploration and understanding. Still, I must admit that writing was extremely difficult for me this time. A dialogue may lead to either entrenchment in one's beliefs or new insights. In my case, I think both occurred. Nevertheless, if our discussion was significant in any way, then its significance lies in the attempt to explore an explicatory framework that is open to and skeptical toward reading the gender reality around us in a manner that is relevant to our work as feminist scholars, as well as to our everyday insights about ourselves and about others.

June 24, 2000

Hi Nitza,

My thoughts and feelings keep tugging me in many directions even with the conclusion of this correspondence and under its influence. While writing, I tried to touch on the option of interplay and oscillation of gender identity in everyday life. I especially tried to explore the pragmatic meaning of "moments of gender identity" as a theoretical option. Perhaps to pursue some feeling of sexual otherness, which

I still cannot fully grasp, in order to unravel my femininity, in which the entire burden of my socialization is embedded. Our correspondence allowed me to obtain feedback in unexpected directions. When I asked you whether a woman who imagines herself as a man is a man or a woman (or is she an-other woman?), you asked me why one has to pose such a question in the first place. You always pulled me toward the normalizing social context that at one and the same time generates the fixation of my femininity as well as quandaries and quests for alternatives. Thus, perhaps unknowingly, you have rendered some of my questions both absurd and ever more real. You allowed me to examine the embarrassment in my femininity, that day in the Cinematheque, in a wider political context, when you pointed out the classifying, meaning-generating cultural forces that made me want to feel at ease among men and all too quickly waive my femininity, whose other meaning I still seek.

Reading: In This Last Section of Our Paper, We Return to Our Letters as Readers

Comment 1: Niza

In my first e-mail (April 30, 2000), I wrote, "I still had time to think: Here you have a golden opportunity to pretend you're Butler for a moment. Fantasize you are a man who is there to watch the film. I know it was an imagined pacifying/diversionary tactic. But let's say it wasn't. What would it take for the game to work? Would I have to come dressed up as a man, or as a drag king?" I read and teach Butler's theory of gender trouble. I identify with her work. However, in the cinematheque, my pretension that I could play another gender through fantasy failed. I did not have the proper masquerade or the tools to play a masculine (homosexual) other as my imagined/materialized self. I could not perform the stranger to my gender. Not even for a moment was I able to transform my hegemonic femininity, which I resist, criticize, and reject in theory, into "playing" (feeling like) a homosexual man. The power of my socialization resisted me. It is one thing to challenge the politics of gender through teaching, writing, and believing, and quite another to create a symbolic internal functioning that theatrically/psychically performs the other as oneself.

What does it take to translate theory into experience or performance? Translation, claims Derrida, is a responsibility, a debt we owe (1985). But to what "origin" do we owe our fantasies, memories, experiences, and visions? To what translation do we owe our desires or prejudices? There are memories that can only be translated as madness or hypocrisy, says Laplanche (1999). So, were my feelings of alienation, humiliation, anguish, and shame in the midst of the gay men's celebration just inevitably "normal" feelings stemming from untranslatable memories of my gender? To which knowledge do I owe my illusion, to which knowledge my failure? Regardless, I believe that I have touched the stranger in myself. I have experienced myself as a stranger who wants to know, yet all the same knows nothing. This experience, which I consider a failure, was nonetheless a moment of discovery of the foreigner as a neighbor, a different gender. The foreigner, says Kristeva (1991, p. 13), comes in when the consciousness of our difference arises. Yet it is the recognition that we are our own foreigners that counters hatred and creates "the sole support that we can attempt to live with others" (Kristeva, 1991, p. 170). The power of one's own gender, features, movements, and affects is stronger than our consciousness or ideology. Commitment to a subversive theory of gender will not bring with it peace of mind. Still, that moment in the cinematheque constituted, in Kristeva's words, "a constant quest for welcoming and going beyond the other in oneself" (Kristeva, 1990, p. 76). The success of our gender "games" is not given. It depends on powerful factors beyond our control: family bonds, language, culture, ties, social experiences, and so forth. However, the decision to worry or smile, says Kristeva, is ours. Like politics, theory is a form of translation, a responsibility. It is true that our commitment assumes too much already. Yet the phantasmal game guided by theory, even when it fails, is our debt to change.

Comment 2: Nitza

I responded with a different story about playing games (May 5, 2000). I wrote, "Every now and then I attend lesbian social events. At times . . . I am the only straight woman in attendance (or so I think). . . . On such occasions, I feel comfortable and powerful." The questions that come to mind are these: What is the difference between the two events? Why was one successful and the other a failure? And we tried to provide some tentative answers throughout our correspondence. But at this point I would like to discuss the fact that there is also a difference in the ways we formulated the stories in terms of the relations between experience and theory and among fantasy, emotions, and imagination.

At the Cinematheque, your attempt to feel more comfortable, by imagining and pretending, was theoretically inspired. But you could not carry off your gender game. Your disappointment derived from your sense that the theory failed. But what I want to point out is that you experienced the situation through and by the theory. It may not have provided satisfying answers or a means to deal with the situation, but it equipped you with the linguistic tools to verbalize the questions so that they are meaningful on both the theoretical and subjective level.

For me, on the other hand, it was not until I wrote my story in response to yours that I started to think about it in theoretical terms. Only then did it occur to me that the situation I am describing poses a wide variety of questions and requires theorizing as much as your story. Only then did I realize that my pretense and fantasy calls for answers too. In other words, for each of us, the movement to and from theory and experience shifted in different directions. Whereas you translated theory into experience, I translated experience into theory.

This difference may derive from the fact that our research, methods, and teaching shape both our subjectivity and the kind of questions we ask, not only in our academic inquiry, but also about our daily experiences. In your work, you deal with the complexity involved in the relations between subjectivity and emotions, body and sexuality, narrative and culture, whereas I examine the gendered nature of social structures and processes. As I've said before, I deal with gender without sexuality, women without a body, and feminism without sexual identity. Emotions, subjectivity, and the self do not enter into my academic work (at least not explicitly and, until now, obviously).

But it may also be the case that it is not our professional practice but, rather, the way we experienced the situation that took us down different routes. You felt uneasy. You were self-conscious. For you, the gender game failed. Thus defined and experienced, the situation called for theoretical inquiry. I, on the other hand, felt at ease. When one feels that a situation poses no challenge and no problematics surface, one is not compelled to explain it. The game was successful. This success anaesthetized the sociologist within me. It is only now that I realize that what I call "success" cannot be taken for granted and calls for theoretical investigation as well. Thus, "failure" makes one more alert theoretically and politically, whereas "success" is more likely to conceal the theoretical and political implications of the situation so defined.

Writing-in-Response (Nitza): It is common practice for academics to work jointly with colleagues (one or more) on articles and books. Many of us have been involved in such activity and find it rewarding (and at times frustrating) intellectually and socially. The ways people tend to work together can vary from a "division of labor," in which each person writes separate parts and then they blend them together into a single text, to laboring together over each sentence and paragraph. But regardless of the specific mode of work, the result is always the same: a unitary and indivisible text.

We followed another route. We kept our voices at times separate and at times fused. They are fused when the text has been produced together, and they are heard separately when indeed we spoke (in the seminars) or wrote (the correspondence and the comments) individually. But it is important to note that "separate" does not mean "isolated." One of our reasons for engaging in this project was to experience exploring and writing as a process of producing knowledge in interaction and negotiation, in dialogue and in various forms of conversation, without necessarily reaching harmony.

Also, it is likely that many use the same method we did and exchange ideas and portions of text via electronic correspondence. But once they have decided that the writing has been completed, the correspondence is trashed. It is treated as scaffolding that should be removed once the structure can stand on its own. For us, by contrast, the scaffolding is as important as what it holds. We place in broad daylight what others push to the backstage. We consider it an integral part not only of the writing process but of the end product as well. Thus, in our search for new modes of collaboration, we believe that we have found a way that did not force us to find a "common ground" that conceals our divergent standpoints. This method helped us highlight the differences in our academic training, personal experiences, and intellectual inclinations, which emerged through the process of writing-in-response. And we used them to prompt each other to think and rethink our perceptions and ideas and elicit insights that would not have come to the fore in other ways.

Theory, Performance, and Identity (Niza): In the letters, we put our feelings and ideas to the test, questioning the strength of our a priori sexual identities (our anxieties and fixations), our will to play games, and the power of our theoretical identifications. There is no one criterion or one way to cross gender cultural limits and limitations. Gender performance materializes in many illusive internal modes, including affective and psychic experiences in addition to theatrical transvestite acts. One can always fail to perform. But this is not our point. Gender performance is not only what we do but also how we feel, as well as what we know or imagine. Neither theatrical failure nor its success is the sole challenge to hegemonic gender identity. What counts, we believe, are also those brief moments of identity in which foreignness "creep(s) into the tranquility of reason itself" (Kristeva, 1991, p. 170). These moments of counteridentity, or identity in translation, form, even if only temporarily, an imagined gender-stranger-other relation, which could or would be the self in translation/transition.

This hypothetical imagined other challenges, either fearfully or playfully, our logic, fantasy, and sensations. Calling on the power of theory and imagination, we can rebut for a moment, through the wish to play or else, the one ascribed alternative of our only sex.

We claim that fantasy and theory, which invite "other" genders to stay, even for a moment, constitute a moral political standpoint that opens a space for changing the women or men that we are. These moments of pretense and identification, distance and closeness, similarity and difference, are also moments "in addition" to normative gender identity, which can challenge the history of what our socialized self usually is. In this sense, the theoretical is also personal. Imagination is an intellectual apparatus, a language, constituting consciousness and a belief of identity. Because of the power of appearance and its control over the body like a skin, imagined (sexual but also racial) identities, like communities, can be stigmatized and pathologized. At the same time, when the power of fantasy is welcomed, imagined otherness (as a political or poetic effort) can destabilize what we have always already been, becoming a better people.

Notes

1. We have edited the correspondence for this chapter.
2. It is true that the issue of situational identity has already been discussed in sociological literature, mainly as a critique of essentialist theories. However, even in that case, there was an apparent hierarchy of identities, in terms of which identities are more "natural" and which are more "social," for there was latitude only for ethnic and national identities, whereas gender identities were taken for granted.

References

Butler, J. (1990). Gender trouble, feminist theory, and psychoanalytic discourse. In L. J. Nicholson (Ed.), *Feminism/Postmodernism* (pp. 324–340). New York: Routledge.

Czarniawska-Joerges, B. (1995). Narration or science: Collapsing the division in organizational studies. *Organization, 2*(1), 11–33.

Derrida, J. (1985). Des tours de Babel. In J. Graham (Ed.), *Differences in translation.* Ithaca, NY: Cornell University Press.

Ellis, C., & Bochner, A. P. (1999). Autoethnography, personal narrative, reflexivity. In N. Denzin & Y. Lincoln (Eds.), *Handbook of qualitative research* (pp. 733–768). Thousand Oaks, CA: Sage.

Friedman, A. (1996). *Ba'ah me'ahavah: Intimiute ve'koach bazehut hanashit* [Anny Oakley won twice: Intimacy and power in female identity]. Tel-Aviv: Hakibbutz Hameuchad.

Helman, S., & Rapoport, T. (1997). Women in black: Challenging Israel's gender and socio-political orders. *British Journal of Sociology, 48*(4), 681–700.

Hik, J. (1999). *Sex life in Los Angeles* [Motion picture]. USA.

Kristeva, J. (1991). *Strangers to ourselves.* New York: Columbia University Press.

Laplanche, J. (1999). *Essays on otherness.* New York: Routledge.

Laqueur, T. (1990). *Making sex: Body and gender from the Greeks to Freud.* Cambridge, MA: Harvard University Press.

Naveh, H. (1999). Gleanings, borders and sheaves: Life outside the canon. In D. Izraeli, A. Friedman, H. Dahan Kalev, H. Herzog, M. Hassan, H. Naveh, & S. Fogiel-Bijaoui (Eds.), *Min migdar politika* [Sex gender politics] (pp. 49–106). Tel Aviv: Kav Adom, Hakibbutz Hameu'had Press.

Rhodas, A. R. (2003). Transversing the great divide: Writing the self into qualitative research and narrative. *Studies in Symbolic Interaction, 26,* 235–259.

Richardson, L. (1992). The poetic representation of lives: Writing a postmodernist sociology. *Studies in Symbolic Interaction, 13,* 19–27.

Stein, R. (1995). Analysis of a case of transsexualism. *Psychoanalytic Dialogues, 5,* 257–289.

Tillmann-Healy, L. M., & Kiesinger, C. K. (2001). Mirrors: Seeing each other and ourselves through fieldwork. In K. R. Gilbert (Ed.), *The emotional nature of qualitative research* (pp. 81–108). Boca Raton, FL: CRC Press.

Watson, T. J. (2000). Ethnographic fiction science: Making sense of managerial work and organization research process with Caroline and Terry. *Organization, 7*(3), 489–510.

15

The Personal Is Political

Using Daily Diaries to Examine Everyday Prejudice-Related Experiences

Lauri L. Hyers, Janet K. Swim, and Robyn K. Mallett

"We are trying to find ways to communicate what you know so that others may understand"

—A dedication to qualitative research participants, Morse, 1994a

M undane experiences, thoughts, feelings, and behaviors are the essential components of our daily lives. These experiences include everyday interactions with our family members, friends, and coworkers, which then influence how we think and feel about ourselves and others as well as our behaviors in other interactions. While our everyday lives are influenced by culture, politics, and social status, our *personal* experiences are typically at this more immediate level. Researchers have developed a variety of methods for assessing these experiences, including in-depth interviews, focus groups, and reactions to contrived situations in the laboratory setting. Daily diary research is an alternative method of getting a glimpse into people's daily life experiences. Diary studies use a participant-observation method of data collection in which the observers of the phenomena are members from the group of interest. On a daily basis, participants record their thoughts, feelings, behaviors, and observations in both open- and closed-ended formats. There are several types of data that can be obtained from diaries, including descriptive information about people's interactions; relationships among various aspects of the entries, accounting for effects of the immediate social context; and variations in experience due to individual differences.

In our research, we have used daily diaries to understand experiences with everyday forms of discrimination. Many people from disadvantaged groups know that prejudice is a factor in their daily lives, yet when people claim, "prejudice is no longer a problem," targets of discrimination may be left frustrated, not knowing where to begin to explain. When it comes to the pervasive, insidious nature of everyday prejudice, we have found the daily diary method to be a powerful tool for unveiling prejudice. Our participants' diaries have been a useful way to achieve one of the essential goals of qualitative research, communicating what some may know (about everyday prejudice) so that others may come to understand. (Morse, 1994b)

Before we begin our discussion of the daily diary method, it is useful to share examples from our own diary research on prejudice from the targets' perspectives in order to get a general sense of the types of information that can be revealed in daily diaries. In our research, we wanted to know how members of stigmatized groups describe their experiences with discrimination, to contribute a different perspective on the behavioral manifestations of stereotypes and prejudice, the "insiders view" (Oyserman & Swim, 2001). We also wanted to gain insights into within-group variations in these experiences and mechanisms individuals use to cope. We first explored sexism and racism, and then expanded to other prejudices, such as heterosexism, ableism, religious-based prejudices, and sizeism. Some examples of the types of experiences our participants have reported experiencing follow:

- Sexism: "A guy in my class came up to me and started complaining about how white males were constantly discriminated against in today's society. When I brought up (examples of) women's issues and sexism . . . he dismissed them saying they were unimportant and overexaggerated."
- Racism: "A woman on the bus said that African American studies was a stupid and unnecessary discipline."
- Heterosexism: "My partner and I were walking downtown and two boys shouted from a few yards away, 'lesbians, lesbians!'"
- Ableism: "I was asked by a relative how I was *feeling*. The *feeling* related to the cancer. Some people ask me how I am *feeling* instead of how I am *doing* like they used to."
- Minority group religious-based prejudice: "I was hanging out with friends and they introduced me to a guy. Initially, we talked and interacted very positively

with one another. However, as soon as he found out that I was Jewish, and born in Israel, he left the room and never talked to me again."

- Majority group religious-based prejudice: "I mentioned going out for a drink after work, and a coworker said, 'I didn't think Christians drank beer.'"
- Sizeism: "I was walking past a residence hall building, and a guy shouted out, 'Hey, Fatty!'"

The above quotes exemplify the sorts of routine experiences with prejudice participants encountered as part of their everyday lives interacting with friends, romantic partners, family, acquaintances, coworkers, and strangers. Participants encountered an array of prejudice, ranging from minor to extreme. Moreover, these encounters were not rare events, with most participants reporting at least one event per week. These incidents are a testament to one of the most important reasons for collecting these diary studies, to counter the belief that prejudice is exaggerated, unfamiliar, rare, or even obsolete.

Defining Diary Research

In common usage, a "diary" is typically a *private* (sometimes under lock and key), *unstructured narrative* of the events an individual *chooses* as important to document *at the day's end*. In research, the diary may share some of these qualities (e.g., daily recording of one's actions, thoughts, and feelings), but not all. Research diaries are not usually private as they will ultimately be shared with the researcher and perhaps a research team, and potentially with an academic audience (though anonymously). Research diaries are not always in narrative form; instead, they may partially consist of responses to structured, closed-ended items. Research diaries are rarely focused on topics of the writer's choosing. Instead, diaries include predetermined categories of events, behaviors, emotional or physical states, or thoughts, all of the researchers' choosing. Finally, research diaries are not always completed at the day's end, with researchers asking the participant to document the phenomena of interest as much as several times in a day.

Diary Research as Qualitative Research

While we have emphasized the advantages of diary methodology for obtaining qualitative information and the connotations of the word *diary* imply a qualitative methodology, some diary studies may be more qualitative than others, depending on (a) the diary structure, (b) attention to context, and

(c) the event-recording schedule. First, consider the diary structure. Diaries may solicit entirely qualitative, unstructured narrative (e.g., "write about your day") or purely quantitative measures (e.g., emotions, recorded on a quantitative scale). If narrative data are collected, and the researchers refrain from using predetermined coding schemes to make sense of the data, the study would be consistent with a more qualitative approach. With our own research, we have used both qualitative and quantitative assessment, including both a priori and bottom-up coding strategies.

A second consideration is the attention to context. "Qualitative researchers study people in their own territory, within naturally occurring settings such as the home, schools, hospitals, the street" (Willig, 2001, p. 9). One of the major benefits of the diary method is that data can be collected in a more natural, day-to-day setting than laboratory studies. The study of phenomena couched in everyday experience is more holistic and contextual than the study of isolated elements of that experience we might extract in a lab study. The greater the attention to context, the more qualitative the study will be. In the case of everyday discrimination, the target's emotional and behavioral responses are integral to the experience itself (Feagin & Sikes, 1994; Hyers, 2005; Lalonde & Cameron, 1994; Landrine, Klonoff, Gibbs, Manning, & Lund, 1995). We have found in our research that participants often describe their own behavior in response to an incident inseparably from the incident itself (e.g., in response to "Describe the incident," one might report, "He said he wanted a girl to marry that he could take care of and protect. I was shocked and disappointed and said, 'Why wouldn't you want a strong partner who can take care of herself?'"). We have also been able to get a better sense of the incidents by examining behaviors participants may have selected in anticipation of possible prejudice (Mallett & Swim, 2005) and by allowing participants to describe their motives for the response they chose (e.g., Hyers, 2005). We have also gotten a sense of the context of incidents by comparing unique qualities of experiences of everyday discrimination with experiences of nondiscriminatory daily hassles (Mallett & Swim, 2005; Swim, Hyers, Cohen, & Ferguson, 2001; Swim, Johnston, & Pearson, 2005; Swim, Pearson, & Johnston, in press).

A third aspect of a diary study concerns the schedule for making a diary entry. A more qualitative design would allow the participant to determine when an event of significance has occurred (e.g., every time you feel threatened). However, diary studies can also incorporate more quantitative schedules, with participants reporting on the phenomena at predetermined intervals (e.g., every 8 hours).

Traditional approaches of obtaining qualitative information have participants recall experiences using focus groups, structured or unstructured interviews, or perhaps surveys. Although these methods of data collection do add depth to our understanding of numerous issues—including experiences with discrimination—the diary methodology has advantages over these other methods. For instance, with regard to everyday experiences with prejudice and discrimination, compared to reports from diaries, retrospective methodologies administered to disadvantaged group members tend to capture more troublesome (and therefore more memorable) experiences, rather than experiences characteristic of daily living (Swim, Pearson, & Johnston, in press). It is also possible that given the insidious nature of discrimination and similarities of mundane experiences, it may be difficult for individuals to accurately recall the frequency of everyday experiences. Finally, when asked to recall cognitive, affective, and behavioral responses to discrimination, it is possible that coping mechanisms, including efforts at sense making, may create distortions in recall. Therefore, it could be difficult to disentangle immediate affective, cognitive, and behavioral responses from reconstructions of these responses often found in focus groups or surveys (Reis & Wheeler, 1991). By asking people from these groups to keep incident diaries as soon after they occur as possible, we obtain a different set of experiences than other methodologies, allowing us to capture characteristics and frequencies of mundane incidents and any immediate responses to those incidents, thereby better capturing some of the subtle, sometimes ambiguous, and often forgotten aspects of experience.

Diary Research as Feminist Research

Diary research by itself is not associated with any particular epistemological orientation. Testimony to this is its use in a variety of disciplines, including the social sciences (such as our work), humanities (for biographical research), creative arts (to generate material for both fictional and nonfictional creative works), and even the natural sciences (to keep logs of physiological symptoms, natural events and phenomena, experimental treatments, agricultural patterns, and a myriad of other observations that must be kept frequently and consistently). It can also be used in a manner consistent with a variety of feminist research philosophies (Denmark, Rabinowitz, & Sechzer, 2004; Gergen, 1988, 2001; Unger & Crawford, 1992).

We believe that diary methodology is particularly consistent with the feminist standpoint position that *knowing* involves the sociohistorical context, or "standpoint," of the knowers (Alcoff & Potter, 1993; Harding, 1991, 1993; Harstock, 1983, 1985; Smith, 1987). Diary research entrusts respondents (knowers) to report their experiences within the context of their daily living.

This is much different than having observers monitor the experiences of participants in the alienating setting of the lab. For diary studies with under-voiced or disenfranchised nondominant groups, feminist standpoint theory is especially relevant because it argues that stratified societies contextualize experience within dominant and subordinate subcultures, creating "situated knowledge" (Harding, 1993). For example, the targets of prejudice can be characterized as "experts" on the phenomena of prejudice, knowing, for instance, more about characteristics of both subtle and blatant forms of dis-crimination (Swim, Cohen, & Hyers, 1998). Additionally, feminist stand-point theory's rejection of nonsituated and "objective" knowledge fits well with diary designs in which participants rather than researchers decide when the phenomena of interest (e.g., sexual harassment, prejudice, positive mood) has occurred.

There are several reasons why diary methodology is consistent with femi-nist empiricism (Denmark et al., 2004; Worell & Etaugh, 1994). Similarly, diary methodology fits the themes of several related revisionist methodo-logical philosophies promoted by the radical (Brown, 1973), emancipatory (Montero, 1998), participatory action research (Borda & Ralman, 1991; Reason, 1994), multicultural (Bingham, Porche-Burke, & Sue, 1999), critical (Fox & Prilleltensky, 1997) and community (Prilleltensky & Nelson, 1997) psychology movements. First, because the qualitative nature of diary research lends itself to descriptive, inductive efforts and theory building, it is useful for informing practice and for community application. Second, diary research is ideal for providing a forum for the concerns of undervoiced subgroups. Asking targets to describe their experiences with prejudice is more empower-ing than the dominant, traditional method of learning about prejudice, which consists of studying those who endorse prejudiced beliefs (Oyserman & Swim, 2001; Unger, 1983). The diary method can be conducive to the study of agency in the midst of social constraints (Franz & Stewart, 1994; Wilkinson, 1986, 1988), as long as participants can report on their holistic experience including any active behaviors done in response to anticipated or experienced incidents (e.g., challenging, educating, or redirecting). Third, the often-exploitative researcher-participant relationship can be minimized as participants are empowered to share aspects of their daily experiences in their own words. Fourth, diary research enables the researcher to work as a change agent in undervoiced communities using cooperative inquiry; involving people's participation in the data collection and analysis; and encouraging increased consciousness, sharing of resources, dialogues, experiences, and strategy (Whyte, 1991). As long as the knowledge gathered from a diary study is analyzed in keeping with the original experiences, expressed in participants' original terminology, it can be returned to the relevant communities for their consideration. Fifth, the postmodern feminist emphasis on the use of text or narrative to reveal contextualized experience fits well with the qualitative-style diary. Finally, the feminist poststructuralist revision of the role of researcher (Henriques, Hollway, Venn, & Walkerdine, 1984; Sciarra, 1999) from "detached experimenter" to "emotionally invested learner" can be incorporated if the participants are involved as extensions of the research staff—participant observers of the phenomena alongside a research staff who also has vested interest in the well-being of the participants' social group.

Practically speaking, the types of data that can be obtained from diary studies include descriptive information about people's perceptions of their interactions, relationships among types of variables assessed such as recorded observations and resultant feelings, and the effects of individual differences and social context on everyday experiences. Ontological assumptions about the type of knowledge that can be generated using diary research will depend on the researcher's philosophy. Because diary research is often conducted with the goal of obtaining immediate and frequent measures of the phenomena of interest, there is an implication of a *reality-out-there* that will be better captured using this more targeted, immediate, and precise assessment tool. However, as diary research also represents an attempt to obtain information about experience *confounded with context*, the method may also be consistent with a more relativist stance that emphasizes uniqueness and diversity of contextualized experience. Thus, how well one captures the reality-out-there will ultimately depend on the researcher, and not just on the method itself.

Daily Diary Methodology

We will now discuss various methodological considerations when conducting diary research. For illustration, in the procedural sections that follow, we will occasionally refer to a diary study on the daily experiences with stress reported by women who are heavy (Mallett & Swim, 2005). In this study, heavy women kept a daily record for a week of situations where they anticipated that they might be a target of weight-based discrimination. We were interested in predicting the coping mechanisms these individuals use in anticipation of possible discrimination.

Participants

This section could be referred to as "Participant Observers," "Research Assistants," or "Collaborators" rather than "Participants," as their role is not to perform and be observed but to be the researcher-observer of their own experience to be monitored. The only limitation for inclusion of potential participants in a diary study, apart from being a member of the group of interest, would be with regard to their capacity to reflect on and report the phenomena of interest as well as their desire to put forth the effort required in this labor-intensive method of data collection.

Participant Recruitment. We have found it to be essential that the research staff include representatives from the group of interest in the study. These research assistants can serve as liaisons into the communities of interest for recruitment and then can make most contacts with the participants throughout the course of the study. In our heavy women diary study, we asked a mix of heavy and average-weight women to recruit participants and facilitate completion of diary entries. It is important to recognize that, because of the time commitment involved in diary research participation, it may be difficult to attract a large sample and a variety of recruitment strategies may be necessary. In the heavy women diary study, participants were recruited through flyers posted around campus and ads posted in the local and student newspapers.

Participant Attrition. The time commitment required for diary research may result in attrition of participants in the study or participants skipping days during the study. Even the most dedicated participants may have unexpected events, time constraints, or even concerns about the study that will interrupt or terminate their participation. It should be kept in mind that it is possible to do some analyses of the data even on partial data, such as analyses of relations among evaluation of events and types of affective or behavioral responses made. Nonetheless, greater confidence in the data can be obtained if strategies are used to prevent dropouts.

For those who are very busy, unable to make the time commitment, or uninterested in the topic, adequate incentives and accountability for regular writing might be beneficial. For instance, once recruited, research assistants in our heavy women diary study were in daily contact with respondents to answer questions and remind them to complete their daily diary entry.

Researchers might also use strategic participant payments at several points throughout the diary-keeping period, a bonus for completing the entire study, or lotteries where allowed. In addition, the more obvious it is that the topic of research is of interest and concern for the participants and the greater the social value of their participation, the more likely participants will be committed to the study. Attention to the length and amount of information requested and the structure and format of diaries will be important for similar reasons. Asking for too much information in each diary entry can make the act of completing an entry aversive and reduce rates of participation. This may be particularly true for those who may have difficulty keeping regular records (e.g., children, people with certain communication impairments, language barriers).

Also, if possible, it is useful to collect data on participant attrition to determine what types of participants become dropouts or complete a small proportion of the diaries. It may be possible to contact dropouts and to keep an accounting of their reasons for leaving the study. Collecting individual difference measures at the beginning of the study may also allow one to compare dropouts with participants.

Design

Diaries are typically designed to sample either events or times. If one chooses to do a study involving time sampling, a diary entry is signaled by the passing of an interval of time. Participants may be asked what they are doing or how they are feeling at random or fixed intervals during the day. In event sampling, a diary entry is signaled by an event of interest occurring. Event sampling is useful for less frequent events that might be missed with time-based sampling. For event sampling, participants make records of the phenomena of interest every time they occur. For example, in our heavy women diary study, participants made records whenever they anticipated experiencing everyday stress or stress due to discrimination. Frequency of reporting events varied from zero to three times a day per participant. When we use event-sampling procedures, we also include a time sampling component. That is, we have participants report whether nothing occurred by the end of the day to ensure that lack of reporting events is not a function of lack of attention to the study.

Regardless of whether you choose time or event sampling, consideration as to the length of time to run a diary study needs to be made. Whether you are attempting to determine the *frequency* or the *nature* of the phenomena of interest, you need an adequate sampling of events or days. If a frequency assessment is the goal, then consider what the ultimate time unit is to which you will be generalizing your results. If the nature of the phenomena is what is of interest, you need to determine the number of days needed in order to obtain an adequate sampling of the event of interest. To inform the decision, it is helpful to run a pilot study with just a few participants to determine when an adequate set of the phenomena have been acquired. In addition, during the study, it may be useful to examine the data either daily or weekly to determine when a sufficient number of events have occurred or when themes have begun repeating in the data set. Of course, staff resources, financial support, and commitment of participants are also a consideration in the decision. Because we were interested in both the frequency and nature of everyday and discriminatory stress in the heavy women diary study, we relied on our past research that suggested that members of stigmatized groups typically report on average about two to four discriminatory experiences per week (Swim et al., 2001; Swim, Hyers, Cohen, Fitzgerald, & Bylsma, 2003; Swim et al., 2005; Swim et al., in press). We therefore selected to sample for a week.

Diary studies can also be used to assess either momentary or longitudinal effects. If the data are collected as a single unit and a researcher wants to know how often a phenomenon occurs during a week, for instance, then the timing of an entry throughout the data collection period will not be a variable. Instead, each data item included for a given individual will not be assessed as a function of its placing in the diary-keeping timeframe. If, however, one is interested in change over time, diary data can provide ample repeated measures to allow for within-subject change to be assessed.

Procedure

The diary study can be divided into three periods: the introduction, the diary-keeping phase, and the closing session.

Introduction. In this phase, participants are welcomed and introduced to the study in either a group or individual session. During this time, the role of the participant should be emphasized as equal to the experimenter running the study, because the participants are the data collectors. This can be accomplished during an introductory session in which the participant receives instructions on what to do during the diary week. In these sessions, the diary-recording instrument is explained (e.g., notebook, computer, palm device), including the mode and timing of recording. The time during the session can be used to have participants complete an example diary to ensure that they understand the forms they will be completing independently. This time may also be used to provide research staff contact numbers and to distribute and collect informed consents and any background information or pretest measures.

Participants meeting in groups may feel a sense of collaboration with other participants, and this is strongly recommended for groups who have a shared experience (e.g., group membership). For groups who may not have a sense of camaraderie (e.g., participating in a study on emotion) or who may have concerns with revealing their participation (e.g., women recording diaries of sexual harassment in the workplace) or identity (e.g., lesbians who are closeted), one-on-one meetings may be more appropriate. In our heavy women diary study, we asked participants if they preferred an individual or group introductory session. In another with lesbian, gay, and bisexual individuals, although no participants took up our offer, we gave participants the opportunity to have a friend meet with researchers and convey the information to the participant in order to keep their participation anonymous (Swim, Pearson, & Johnston, in press).

Diary-Keeping Phase

During the formal part of the study, the participants may be entirely on their own or may have regular contacts with the research staff. If the participant is left unchecked during the entire study, there may be problems with correct completion of forms and, more important (for the diary methodology), there may be problems with timeliness in completing diary forms. For event sampling, we recommend dividing the diary-keeping period into segments and collecting data from participants periodically, such as every three days. For time sampling, it may be best to have participants report the time of recording on the diary sheets and to check that they are following instructions. Problems with timeliness of entries and monitoring completion of materials can be reduced if participants are asked to report their diaries via the Web or palm devices. When diaries are completed via the Web or palm devices, researchers can keep track of whether participants complete diaries on schedule. Additionally, these technologies can be used to obtain time-date stamps to ensure that participants are submitting diaries to researchers on schedule. In the heavy women diary study, participants entered diary responses using online forms. Participant awareness of the time stamp feature of the forms, in combination with daily contact from their study coordinator, ensured timely diary entries.

Closing Session. Depending on the nature of the groups involved and data collected, a group or individual closing session may be used. Again, the group session can represent a time to come together, for participants to share experiences, and for the researchers to share some initial conclusions with the group. Focus groups can also be added as part of the closing session, allowing participants to further elaborate on experiences documented in the diaries. Whether group or individual, the closing session should be used to collect any additional diary forms, debrief the participants about themes of interest or patterns found in the data, administer any postdiary measures (e.g., assessing participants' feelings about the study and how it affected their behavior, suggestions to researchers, or other concerns), and provide resources for further support. It is important to recognize that being involved in a diary study represents a large commitment from your participants, and they may need support due to often intense interpersonal surveillance to the phenomena of interest; concern about new self-knowledge gained from attending closely to their emotions, behavior, or interactions; or even attachment issues in saying farewell to the research staff or other participants. Assemble a list of resources for support and provide this to your participants at the closing. This is also a time to distribute any previously undistributed incentives to participants.

Instruments

A diary study may be conducted for purposes of description, theory building, or inferential theory testing. The goals of the research will influence the design of the diaries. Diaries can be highly structured or completely open ended or a combination of the two. We have favored the use of combining responses to be able to test a priori hypotheses as well as learn more nuanced qualitative characteristics of participants' experiences (see Appendix for an example of an open- and closed-ended diary form used in a study on anti-Black racism). A drawback of including structured response options is that such options may alter how the participants view the phenomena of interest, giving them new dimensions or components of the phenomena to attend to that they might otherwise have overlooked. Finally, as with participant-completed surveys, attention to the format of the diary is important because participants will be completing forms independently. Depending on one's sample, there may also be a need to make adjustments to font size or use oral forms for sight-impaired individuals or individuals who have difficulty with reading comprehension.

Results

Coding and analysis strategies will depend on the goals of the research. Yet, if either qualitative or quantitative descriptive information is obtained about the types of experiences individuals report from event sampling procedures, consideration about the variability in the number of events each participant records needs to be made. Although the variability of events reported is information, if one wants to get a general picture of the typical event reported, specific issues around the number of events reported must be considered. For instance, so as not to overrepresent participants who may write more or to whom an event occurs more often, researchers may wish to describe the first entry in each diary or randomly select one incident from each participant's entries to analyze. Alternatively, researchers can obtain the average probability or average tendencies that individuals report for different types of incidents.

Coding

Qualitative analyses will explore patterns in the phenomena without imposing theory or making predictions about relationships in the data. Alternatively, coding can also be achieved using a priori coding categories, informed from a previous theoretical framework. However, if the diary data you are collecting is to be used for descriptive or theory-building purposes, then a qualitative coding system such as grounded theory coding (Glaser & Strauss, 1967; Strauss & Corbin, 1990) is a popular method that complements the diary methodology. As Willig argues, "Qualitative researchers . . . do not tend to work with 'variables' that are defined by the researcher before the research process begins. This is because qualitative researchers tend to be interested in the meanings attributed to events by the research participants themselves" (Willig, 2001, p. 9).

In order to understand the phenomena in context of the everyday, it is important to keep from imposing one's own meaning on the data. Consistent with grounded theory coding, Strauss and Corbin (1990) point out that our research participants "have perspectives on and interpretations of their own and other actors' actions. As researchers, we are required to learn what we can of their interpretations and perspectives. Beyond that, grounded theory requires . . . that those interpretations and perspectives become incorporated into our own" (p. 280). Grounded theory coding involves a data-driven coding process of reading and rereading text, first generating themes that emerge from the data, next going over again and pulling examples of those themes, and eventually classifying selections into the developed coding scheme. We involved multiple coders in our analyses, ensuring that our coding group included marginal group representatives. The process should include staff who can engage in careful self-monitoring and have the ability to search for themes, create a coding procedure, and identify adjustments to the coding scheme as time goes on.

If a qualitative data analysis strategy is used, a "member check" can be conducted in which the conclusions from the study are shared with the participants themselves and other stakeholders, to ask for their evaluation of the conclusions. We have also involved participants in coding their own data.

Data Analyses

Attention to the nested nature of the data collected is important when considering statistical inferential analyses. That is, data from each diary is nested within all the diaries each individual completes. Depending on goals of the research, it is also possible to consider multiple diaries reported on a single day as being nested within days, which are then nested within the diaries the individuals report. Employing multilevel modeling becomes essential and beneficial for understanding within-person and between-person variations in the data. A full description of multilevel modeling is beyond the scope of the present chapter. It is worth noting, however, the types of analyses afforded by the use of multilevel modeling. These include examining (a) basic descriptive information about types of incidents, (b) day-to-day changes in experiences, (c) relationships between characteristics within single experiences, and (d) the role that individual differences may play.

As an example of relationships between characteristics of experiences, in our study on weight-based discrimination, we tested whether there were differences in the way that heavy women coped with stress depending on the extent to which hassles were described as discriminatory. We did so by using perceived prejudice, ranging from not at all to very much, as the predictor of the extent to which the hassles were perceived as threatening (primary appraisals), the extent to which individuals believed they had resources to cope with the hassles (secondary appraisals), and the amount of effort given to coping. Perceived prejudice was significantly positively associated with primary appraisals, showing that the more hassles were identified as discriminatory, the more harmful they were perceived to be. Perceived prejudice was not associated with secondary appraisals, showing that perceived resources did not differ depending on the extent to which the stressor was perceived to be due to prejudice. However, perceived prejudice was significantly positively related to attempts to cope with the stressor; the more hassles were identified as discriminatory, the more efforts individuals used to cope with the hassle.

Applications

Research Application. One can also consider other possible uses of daily diary methodology, including testing quasi-experimental relationships, testing the impact of experimentally manipulated experiences on daily experiences, or using the diary itself as a manipulation. One alternative use of the diary methodology involved the examination of whether participants perceived intergroup encounters differently when they anticipated these encounters verses after having actually experienced the encounters (Mallett, 2005). One group of respondents was randomly assigned to predict how they would feel and behave in upcoming intergroup interactions, whereas the other group of respondents was randomly assigned to report their actual experience. Those who predicted their intergroup experience anticipated experiencing more stress and negative emotions than those who actually experienced the encounters reported.

Diary methodology can be combined with other data collection methods. For example, other techniques such as focus group interviews or one-on-one interviews can add useful information to complement what is gathered from the diaries. Diary studies can also be used in combination with experiments in order to build or test theory. For example, we conducted an experimental counterpart of the heavy women diary study in order to ensure that all participants were thinking of the same situation when evaluating potentially threatening situations. Similar results were found across the experimental and diary study, giving us a good balance of internal and external validity in our research.

Community Application. Participants and members of their communities can benefit from knowledge gained from research. This can include consciousness rising. For instance, we have had students in classes complete daily diaries of experiences with discrimination as a teaching tool. We have also shared our findings with campus organizations. For instance, results from the heavy women diary study, along with a diary study of anti-Black racism, were shared with campus administration and were later used to aid incoming students by providing them with information on stress and coping in daily college life.

Ethical Issues

When conducting diary research, it is important to keep in mind the confidentiality of data collected across all members of the research team, both in terms of who is participating in the study and the data collected. One must also consider safekeeping of diaries and data. This includes both paper-and-pencil forms and data collected via, for instance, online Web forms. When using the Web, it is important to structure the data collection so as to maintain anonymity of participants' responses as they are sent via the Internet, such as through the use of encryption, and to utilize secure servers for data storage.

Ethical issues must also be considered when reporting results of the research. For instance, when describing information, it is important to remove names and contextual information. One should obtain participants' permissions to report about specific incidents, even when presented in this anonymous form. There is also a risk from speaking for the disadvantaged groups you study on their behalf, as if their voices are not to be viewed as credible until the diary researchers come in and validate them. Worse, some refer to this as "appropriating their stories" (Haraway, 1988; Maher & Tetreault, 1996). At the same time, the risk of underanalyzing (what Fine calls "romanticizing" the narrative) their experiences in a "retreat from analysis" and withdrawing from interpretation (Fine, 1994) is also of concern. Alcoff (1991) refers to "responsible speaking" as examining the reasons for speaking, recognizing how our personal context affects what we say, being accountable for claims, and evaluating the potential and actual effects of our speaking on the social world—to avoid objectifying, misrepresenting, or exploiting.

Limitations

There are limitations to consider if one is to conduct diary studies, including self-selection of individuals into circumstances, the effect of diaries on people's experiences, dependence on participants' commitment to the research to complete materials, and the complexity of the data analyses.

Additionally, the description of incidents reported represents the participant's view of reality. Although this view of reality can be the desired type of data obtained, it is also the case that participants may vary in their ability to communicate their perceptions and their own knowledge base for understanding their experiences. For instance, we found few reports of benevolent sexism such as paternalistic behavior (i.e., behavior that appears on the surface to be favorable to women but supports hostile sexism, Glick & Fiske, 1996). Yet, the lack of reporting may be a function of participants' lack of knowledge about this type of sexism, the difficulty in detecting it as it is masked by positivity (Swim, Mallett, Russo-DeVosa, & Stangor, in press), or the tendency for some sexist behavior to be perceived as normative and therefore to be undetected (Swim, Mallett, & Stangor, 2004).

Tennen, Suls, and Affleck (1991) point out three methodological hurdles in their diary study of personality: "the exceptional burden placed on both participants and investigator, the potential for systemic bias in how experiences are recalled, and the real possibility that our very methods influence the character of everyday life" (p. 319). Participating in a diary study has the potential to alter attention to the phenomena of interest in one's environment, making participants attend to their social interactions with more vigilance. Thus, any diary study, in part, reflects the experiences under scrutiny. You also have little control over confounds with experiences reported. For instance, some individuals may only report blatant forms of discrimination whereas others report both blatant and subtle forms of discrimination.

Individual differences in the affective consequences of experiencing discrimination may be a function of individual differences in the types of experiences people report. We also do not know the extent to which participants overreported or underreported the number of incidents they encountered during the diary-keeping phase of the study. Participants may have underreported because the diary keeping was somewhat labor intensive. On the other hand, experimenter demand may have made participants feel compelled to write about incidents (even when assured that there will be no penalty if they do not experience anything to report).

Conclusion

Mundane experiences, thoughts, emotions, and behaviors are the essential components of our daily lives. These experiences include sometimes fleeting interactions with those in our social environment, which, although brief, can influence how we think and feel about ourselves and others. As diary researchers Reis and Wheeler (1991) would concur, experience at this most basic level occupies most of our conscious attention and may be difficult to capture in lab studies or retrospective reports. The minutia of everyday experience is not easily recalled due to transience, singular insignificance, and forgetting. This is not to say that these experiences are not important. The patterned accumulation of these localized events may have global effects on mental health, personality, mood, and group identity.

Daily diary research is a useful methodological tool that is well suited to studying the minutia of life and allows researchers to study topics of interest to feminists. Although our emphasis has been on understanding everyday forms of discrimination, other feminist research philosophies can also incorporate the diary method. Daily diaries allow researchers to examine many topic areas of particular interest to feminist researchers, including (a) gender differences in thoughts, feelings, and behaviors; (b) descriptions of how gender is acted out in everyday lives; and (c) topics of special interest to women and to members of other stigmatized groups. The use of daily diaries opens possibilities in terms of access to information about people's daily lives and the ability to combine advantages of qualitative research with survey research within diary studies.

APPENDIX

Sample Open- and Closed-Ended Diary Form Used in a Study of Anti-Black Racism

Please briefly describe the stressful event:

Please explain what, if anything, you did to prepare for the event:

How far in advance did you recognize the potential for this event to become stressful?
____ weeks ____ days ____ hours ____ minutes ____ I recognized it during the event

How stressful did you anticipate this experience would be?

0	1	2	3	4	5	6
Not at all			Somewhat			Very

Please use the following scale to answer these questions: 0 = not at all, 6 = very much

1. Did you think you would *lose something* because of this event?
2. Did you think you would become *angry* because of this event?
3. Did you think you would become *anxious* because of this event?
4. Did you anticipate that this event would keep you from reaching an important goal?

1. How confident were you that you had enough *skills* to overcome the potentially negative outcome?
2. How confident were you that you had enough *resources* to overcome the potentially negative outcome?
3 How confident were you that you could overcome a potentially negative outcome?

Please use the following scale to answer these questions: 0 = not at all, 6 = very much

1. How personally threatening did you think this event was going to be?
2. How intimidated were you by this event?
3. How dangerous did you think this event might turn out to be?
4. How personally challenging did you think this event was going to be?
5. Did you feel as if your ability to deal with this incident was challenged?

---

1. I paid attention to information that told me about the nature of a potential stressor.
2. I looked for information to counteract any negative perceptions I might have had about an upcoming situation.
3. I made sure that my hair and clothing looked nice so that people knew I was a respectable person.
4. I tried to find out information about a new place (e.g., town, club) before deciding whether to go there.
5. I was aware of the race/ethnicity of the person I was interacting with.
6. I could tell whether the person I was interacting with liked people like me.

---

1. When I was not around other African Americans, I tried to change the way I normally communicated to fit what seemed to be appropriate in a particular situation (e.g., using more formal language around faculty).
2. When I was speaking to someone who was not African American, I paid close attention to what the other person was doing (e.g., eye contact, body position) because it told me more about how she or he felt than what was said.
3. When I sensed that another person did not like people like me because I am African American, I tried to educate that person about my group.
4. When I sensed that another person did not like African Americans, I tried to emphasize parts of myself that were not being called into question, but were positive (e.g., if intelligence is insulted, emphasize appearance).

Please use the following scale to answer these questions: 0 = not at all, 6 = very much

---

1. I monitored my own thoughts in a stressful situation.
2. I relied on my faith in God or a higher power in a stressful situation.
3. I tried to maintain self-control in a stressful situation.
4. I tried to remember that I was a good person in a stressful situation.
5. I paid close attention to elements of the environment when I interacted with people that were not African American (e.g., decorations, exits).
6. I paid close attention to my own behavior or performance in a stressful situation.
7. I tried to regulate my emotions when I was in a stressful situation.
8. I tried to avoid an interaction to minimize the amount of stress I might experience.
9. I tried to leave the interaction as soon as possible in order to minimize the amount of stress I might experience.

To what extent did you anticipate that it would be stressful because of possible expressions of prejudice or discrimination against a social group you belong to?

−3	−2	1	0	1	2	3
Not at all			Uncertain			Definitely

What social group did this prejudice or discrimination target (e.g., race/ethnicity, age, gender, weight)?

References

Alcoff, L. (1991). The problem of speaking for others. *Cultural Critique, 5–32.*

Alcoff, L., & Potter, E. (1993). *Feminist epistemologies.* New York: Routledge.

Bingham, R., Porche-Burke, L., & Sue, D. (1999). The diversification of psychology: A multicultural revolution. *American Psychologist, 54*(12), 1061–1069.

Borda, O. F., & Ralman, A. (1991). *Action and knowledge: Breaking the monopoly with participatory action research.* New York: Apex Press.

Brown, P. (Ed.). (1973). *Radical psychology.* New York: Harper.

Denmark, F., Rabinowitz, V., & Sechzer, J. (2004). *Engendering psychology: Bringing women into focus.* Needham Heights, MA: Allyn & Bacon.

Feagin, J. R., & Sikes, M. P. (1994). *Living with racism: The Black middle-class experience.* Boston: Beacon Press.

Fine, M. (1994). Working the hyphens: Reinventing self and other in qualitative research. In N. K. Denzin & Y. S. Lincoln (Eds.), *Handbook of qualitative research.* Thousand Oaks, CA: Sage.

Fox, D., & Prilleltensky, I. (1997). *Critical psychology: An introduction.* London: Sage.

Franz, C., & Stewart, A. (1994). *Women creating lives: Identities, resilience and resistance.* San Francisco: Westview Press.

Gergen, M. (1988). *Feminist thought and the structure of knowledge.* New York: University Press.

Gergen, M. (2001). *Feminist reconstructions in psychology: Narrative, gender & performance.* Thousand Oaks, CA, & London: Sage

Glaser, B. G., & Strauss, A. (1967). *The discovery of grounded theory: Strategies for qualitative research.* Chicago: Aldine.

Glick, P., & Fiske, S. T. (1996). The ambivalent sexism inventory: Differentiating hostile and benevolent sexism. *Journal of Personality and Social Psychology, 70,* 491–512.

Haraway, D. (1988). Situated knowledges: The science question in feminism and the privilege of partial perspective. *Feminist Studies, 14,* 575–599.

Harding, S. (1991). *Whose science? Whose knowledge? Thinking for women's lives.* Ithaca, New York: Cornell University Press.

Harding, S. (1993). Rethinking standpoint epistemology: "What is strong objectivity?" In L. Alcoff & E. Potter (Eds.), *The "racial" economy of science.* Bloomington: Indiana University Press.

Harstock, N. (1983). The feminist standpoint: Developing the ground for a specifically feminist historical materialism. In S. Harding & M. Hintikka (Eds.), *Discovering reality: Feminist perspectives on epistemology, metaphysics, and the philosophy of science.* Dordrecht, Netherlands: Reidel.

Harstock, N. (1985). *Women, sex and power.* Boston: Northeastern University Press.

Henriques, J., Hollway, C., Venn, C., & Walkerdine, V. (1984). *Changing the subject.* London: Methuen.

Hyers, L. L. (2005). *Interpersonal confrontation as a means to prejudice reduction: When oppressed group members challenge the prejudices of dominant group members.* Manuscript under review.

Lalonde, R. N., & Cameron, J. E. (1994). Behavioral responses to discrimination: A focus on action. In M. P. Zanna (Ed.), *The psychology of prejudice: The Ontario symposium, Vol. 7.* (Ontario Symposium on Personality and Social Psychology, Vol. 7, pp. 257–288). Hillsdale, NJ, & England: Lawrence Erlbaum Associates, Inc.

Landrine, H., Klonoff, E. A., Gibbs, J., Manning, V., & Lund, M. (1995). Physical and psychiatric correlates of gender discrimination: An application of the Schedule of Sexist Events. *Psychology of Women Quarterly, 19*(4), 473–492.

Maher, F. A., & Tetreault, M. K. (1996). Women's ways of knowing in women's studies, feminist pedagogies, and feminist theory. In N. Goldberger, J. Tarule, B. Clinchy, & M. Belenky (Eds.), *Knowledge, difference, and power: Essays inspired by Women's Ways of Knowing* (pp. 148–174). New York: Basic Books.

Mallett, R. K. (2005). *Cloudy crystal ball: Mis-predicting the nature of future intergroup experiences.* Manuscript in preparation.

Mallett, R. K., & Swim, J. K. (2005). Self-protective coping by targets of discrimination. *Motivation and Emotion.*

Montero, M. (1998). Psychosocial community work as an alternative mode of political action: The construction and critical transformation of society. *Community, Work and Family 1*(1), 65–78.

Morse, J. M. (1994a). *Critical issues in qualitative research methods.* Thousand Oaks, CA: Sage.

Morse, J. M. (1994b). Designing funded qualitative research. In Y. Lincoln & N. Denzin (Eds.), *Handbook of qualitative research* (pp. 220–235). Thousand Oaks, CA: Sage.

Oyserman, D., & Swim, J. K. (2001). Stigma: An insider's view. *Journal of Social Issues, 57,* 1–14.

Prilleltensky, I., & Nelson, G. (1997). Community psychology: Reclaiming social justice. In D. Fox & I. Prilleltensky (Eds.), *Critical psychology: An introduction.* London: Sage.

Reason, P. (1994). Co-operative inquiry, participatory action research & action inquiry: Three approaches to participative inquiry. In N. Denzin & Y. Lincoln (Eds.), *Handbook of qualitative research.* Thousand Oaks, CA: Sage.

Reis, H. T., & Wheeler, L. (1991). Studying social interaction with the Rochester Interaction Record. In M. P. Zanna (Ed.), *Advances in Experimental Social Psychology* (Vol. 24, pp. 270-318). San Diego: Academic Press.

Sciarra, D. (1999). The role of the qualitative researcher. In M. Kopala & L. Suzuki (Eds.), *Using qualitative methods in psychology* (pp. 37–48). Thousand Oaks, CA: Sage.

Smith, D. (1987). *The everyday world as problematic: A feminist sociology.* Milton Keynes, UK: Open University Press.

Strauss, A., & Corbin, J. (1990). *Basics of qualitative research: Grounded theory procedures and techniques.* Newbury Park, CA: Sage.

Swim, J. K., Cohen, L. L., & Hyers, L. L. (1998). Experiencing everyday prejudice and discrimination. In J. K. Swim (Ed.), *Prejudice: The target's perspective* (pp. 37–60). San Diego, CA: Academic Press.

Swim, J. K., Hyers, L. L., Cohen, L. L., & Ferguson, M. J. (2001). Everyday sexism: Evidence for its incidence, nature, and psychological impact from three daily diary studies. *Journal of Social Issues, 57*(1), 31–53.

Swim, J. K., Hyers, L. L., Cohen, L. L., Fitzgerald, D. C., & Bylsma, W. H. (2003). African American college students' experiences with everyday racism: Characteristics of and responses to these incidents. *Journal of Black Psychology, 29*(1), 38–67.

Swim, J. K., Johnston, K. E., & Pearson, N. B. (2005). *I'm coming out: Outness as a moderator of coping with heterosexist daily hassles.* Manuscript submitted for publication.

Swim, J. K., Mallett, R., Russo-Devosa, Y., & Stangor, C. (in press). Judgments of sexism: A comparison of the subtlety of sexism measures and sources of variability in judgments of sexism. *Psychology of Women Quarterly.*

Swim, J. K., Mallett, R., & Stangor, C. (2004). Understanding subtle sexism: Detection and use of sexist language. *Sex Roles, 51*(3–4), 117–128.

Swim, J. K., Pearson, N. B., & Johnston, K. E. (in press). Daily encounters with heterosexism: A week in the life of lesbian, gay, and bisexual individuals. *Journal of Homosexuality.*

Tennen, H., Suls, J., & Affleck, G. (1991). Personality and daily experience: The promise and the challenge. *Journal of Personality, 59,* 313–338.

Unger, R. K. (1983). Through the looking glass: No Wonderland yet! (The reciprocal relationship between methodology and models of reality). *Psychology of Women Quarterly, 8,* 9–32.

Unger, R. K., & Crawford, M. E. (1992). *Women and gender: A feminist psychology.* Philadelphia: Temple University Press.

Whyte, W. F. (1991). Introduction. In W. F. Whyte (Ed.), *Participatory action research.* Newbury Park, CA: Sage.

Wilkinson, S. (1986). *Feminist social psychology.* Philadelphia: Open University Press.

Wilkinson, S. (1988). The role of reflexivity in feminist psychology. *Women's Studies International Forum, 11,* 493–502.

Willig, C. (2001). *Introducing qualitative research in psychology.* Buckingham, UK: Open University Press.

Worell, J., & Etaugh, C. (1994). Transforming theory and research with women: Themes and variations. *Psychology of Women Quarterly, 18*(4), 443–450.

16

Feminist Media Ethnography in India

Exploring Power, Gender, and Culture in the Field

Radhika Parameswaran

This article is a self-reflexive account of one postcolonial feminist media scholar's research among young middle-class women in urban India who read Western romance fiction. Urging feminist scholars to pay attention to the politics of representation of audiences in media studies, the article explores power imbalances in the field that arise due to social constructions of gender, ethnic, class, and sexual identities. The article reflects on failures, successes, and dilemmas experienced during the research process to show that feminist media ethnographies are embedded within discourses of power. By examining the multiple positionalities occupied by the researcher in relation to people encountered in the field, this account challenges binary distinctions

From Parameswaran, R., "Feminist Media Ethnography in India: Exploring Power, Gender, and Culture in the Field," in *Qualitative Inquiry*, 7(1), 2001, pp. 69–103, reprinted with permission of Sage Publications, Inc.

between categories such as Self/Other, native/Westerner, and insider/outsider. In concluding, the article underscores the implications of research by non-Western feminist scholars in their own cultures for postcolonial feminist ethnography, feminist media ethnographies, and media reception research on globalization in the cultural studies tradition.

In the past two decades, claims to universal and objective knowledge production in the academy have been challenged by postmodernist and feminist scholars. In particular, postmodern and feminist anthropologists have drawn our attention to the politics of location that shapes knowledge production and argued that ethnographic representations are necessarily partial, constructed, and situated (Abu-Lughod, 1990a; Behar, 1993; Clifford, 1986; Gordon, 1988; Visweswaran, 1994; M. Wolf, 1992). In ethnographic fieldwork, the process of conducting fieldwork involves the cultural biography of researchers and calls for negotiations of power relationships between researchers and people they encounter in the field. For feminist ethnographers especially, rigorous self-reflexivity has become an important channel to interrogate the research process and reveal power inequalities that arise in the field due to social constructions of gender, class, racial, sexual, and ethnic identities. It is within the context of arguments for located and positioned knowledge that I anchor this self-reflexive account of the fieldwork I carried out in a south Indian city among young women readers of Western romance novels.

This article is based on a project that explored the significance of romance reading for young middle- and upper-class women in an urban setting in postcolonial India. The English-language romance novels that Indian women read are commonly referred to as "Mills & Boons" after the British firm Harlequin Mills & Boon, which produces and exports these novels to India. The primary research questions that formed the basis of my project were as follows: How does reading as a leisure activity fit into the social context of Indian women's everyday routines? How do Indian women make sense of their own sexual identity in the process of reading Western romance fiction? How do readers interpret the cultural expectations of women in India when they read narratives from another culture? How does the historical context of colonialism influence middle-class readers' perceptions of their romance reading? How does the concept of the West as the symbol of material success shape readers' perceptions of Western romance fiction?

Broadly speaking, the findings of my ethnographic research indicate that romance reading by elite women in a Third World setting is a complex activity that allowed readers to assert simultaneously the moral superiority of Indian culture, resist cultural expectations of women in India, and enjoy the material aspects of Western culture. My analysis of fieldwork data showed that leisure reading that is pursued in the private sphere is a gendered activity for Indian women who face considerable restrictions on their mobility in public spaces. My project demonstrated the contradictory character of women's interpretations of sexuality in Western romance novels; that is, they identified with the sexual awakening of virginal White heroines, yet they also expressed cultural superiority when they discussed the "real" morals of Western women. Women's interpretations of these novels, I argued, can be traced to visions of ideal Hindu femininity in 19th-century Indian nationalist discourse, which was primarily elite and male. I explained women's defensive construction of their romance reading in the English language as a "high-culture" activity by tracing links among class, language, and British colonial history in India. Middle-class urban women experienced proximity to Western culture when they read romance fiction, a proximity that enabled them to feel modern and cosmopolitan. A part of women's reading pleasure, I found, arose out of their unquestioned belief in the truth and reality of Western material lifestyles represented in these narratives. I do not discuss or analyze the results of my research in further detail in this article because I focus here on my experience of conducting fieldwork in a metropolitan context in India. My emphasis on methodological rather than substantive issues in this account shows that although I was interested in studying the embeddedness of romance reading in India within discourses of patriarchy, nationalism, and modernity, these discourses were starkly inscribed onto the research process itself.

As a feminist academic who teaches and conducts interdisciplinary research in media studies, particularly ethnographic audience studies, I encountered self-reflexive fieldwork accounts of feminists in anthropology, sociology, geography, literary studies, and women's studies.[1] These feminists' fieldwork accounts demystified the "finished" product of ethnographic research and foregrounded ethical problems that can arise in research relationships for beginning ethnographers. With the exception of a few scholars (Lengel, 1998; Seiter, 1990), feminist media ethnographers have not engaged in similar self-reflexive discussions about the politics of studying and representing audiences, the problems they negotiated in the field, and the experience of power differences between and among researchers and audience members. Leveling similar kinds of critiques about the lack of self-reflexivity in audience reception research in general, Patrick Murphy (1999) writes that "even the most celebrated researchers of media reception" (p. 481) are reluctant to analyze methodological problems or debate the merits of different qualitative techniques in the field. Murphy's article on his research experiences in Queretaro, Mexico, represents one of the first lengthy accounts of a media ethnographer's efforts to establish authority, carry out the intrusive task of observation, and analyze the "productive discomfort" (p. 482) generated through interactions with people in the field. Focusing on the impact of his identity as an outsider, a "gringo" American, in his relationships with Mexican community members of Queretaro, Murphy demonstrates the boundedness of the research process within national, race, and class boundaries.[2]

In responding to Murphy's (1999) call for greater self-reflexivity in audience research, my article similarly engages the subjective process of qualitative research and highlights issues of identity and power in field research. In contrast to his description and analysis of gaining entry and acceptance among informants as an outsider, I reflect on the implications of my identity as an insider (urban, middle-class Indian woman from Hyderabad, India) and outsider (stranger, postcolonial feminist academic from the United States) for ethnography among cosmopolitan audiences in the Third World. By explicitly drawing on the writings of feminist ethnographers, I build on Murphy's contributions to cultural studies by engaging with issues relevant to feminist empirical research such as negotiating solidarity with women informants, challenging limited representations of women, and reconceptualizing women's identities. In addition, rather than providing a chronological account, I emphasize difficult and challenging moments in the field to show that the knowledge I wanted to produce about the popularity of Western romance fiction among young Indian women (audience consumption of popular culture) was shaped by the larger discursive construction of romance reading (audience activity) itself among a range of social mediators—parents, library owners, peers, and teachers—in women's lives.

Inviting cultural studies scholars to address the politics of representation in audience research, Vamsee Juluri (1998) draws our attention to the possibilities of audience studies in the Third World that are carried out by postcolonial scholars who "share the burden and privilege of certain kinds of colonized and racialized subjectivities that allow us to speak as both insiders and outsiders, as transnational intellectuals and as representatives of specific national and/or local constituencies" (p. 86). As one among a recent generation of non-Western and bicultural feminist scholars who were trained in the Western academy and returned "home" to carry out fieldwork (Abu-Lughod, 1988; Bolak, 1996; Mankekar, 1993; Visweswaran, 1994), I was aware of being part of a historical moment in the social sciences where most knowledge of the non-West has been produced by Western scholars. The return of "natives" in anthropology as scholars studying their own societies has prompted discussions about ethnography and its troubled historical alliance with colonialism, the authenticity of insider versus outsider accounts of cultures, and the hybrid identities of "native" scholars. These debates have important implications for audience studies in non-Western, postcolonial contexts, which are rapidly entering the realm of global audiencehood over the past few years. Self-reflexive research on the reception of Western media among postcolonial audiences can address concerns of location, knowledge, and power that are central to the spread of global media and Western modernity.

Given the history of Orientalist representations of the non-West in the Western academy, what are the political implications of insider/native ethnographic audience research by postcolonial feminist scholars? How do concepts of Self and Other emerging from experiences with colonialism and nationalism influence fieldwork encounters in postcolonial contexts? What positions does the postcolonial feminist ethnographer occupy in a Third World setting in relation to his or her age, class, gender, and cultural capital as an academic trained in the West? How can researchers' reflections and analysis of dilemmas and difficulties in fieldwork contribute to feminist media ethnography? What are the implications of self-reflexivity in audience ethnography for cultural studies? In addressing these questions in this article, I argue that the multiple positions I occupied as a middle-class postcolonial feminist working among elites in her own culture disrupts notions of power and difference that are typical of debates about Self and Other in traditional ethnographies wherein the Self is the White, Western academic and the Other is the Third World, poor informant.

Using "narrative, interpretive, and reflexive modes of writing," I examine the "research process as a hierarchical social interaction" and analyze the implications of my different positionalities in the field (Lal, 1996, p. 186). Although I emphasize multiple locations that shape fieldwork, I do not endorse a free-floating "hybrid identity" (Narayan, 1993) for the postcolonial feminist, because notions of hybridity can often ignore the effects of historical and political processes on identities and imply that the researcher is *"free"* to choose among many plural identities (Visweswaran, 1994, p. 132). I begin with a brief discussion of political and personal goals that guided my research and provide details about my fieldwork. My analysis of "failed" interviews and my critique of interactions with young Indian women, which follows, challenges binary distinctions between insiders and outsiders and demonstrates the instability of identities such as Third World woman, native, Self, and Other that cannot be predetermined. In the concluding section, I consider the implications of self-reflexivity for the work of postcolonial feminist ethnographers in their own cultures and dwell on the contributions of self-reflexive audience research to feminist media ethnography and media reception research in the cultural studies tradition.

Reflections Before Fieldwork:
South Asian Women as Subjects

My decision to study urban middle- and upper-class Indian women's culture, a relatively elite culture, was prompted in part as a reaction to my encounters with two naturalized images of South Asian women as oppressed women and as village women with problems. These two images have formed an important part of the Western gaze on South Asian women both inside and outside the academy. The image of the South Asian woman as passive, oppressed, and as only a victim of patriarchy has persisted in popular consciousness and in scholarship on South Asian women. Since the publication of Edward Said's (1978) book *Orientalism*, which criticized colonial representations for producing the "passive Oriental," Third World feminists have joined his project to critique the dominant representation of Third World women as always being passive victims of male domination (Kumar, 1994; Mohanty, 1991; Spivak, 1988). A second, more recent image of South Asian women is the monolithic representation of "The South Asian Woman" as the "authentic village woman" found in development research, anthropological accounts, and United Nations documents (Mankekar, 1993, p. 58). In development discourse that has dominated research on the Third World, the rural South Asian woman constantly battles poverty, famine, and the trials of mothering numerous children. The obsessive academic focus on rural women as oppressed Third World subjects has limited the scope of study of South Asia by ignoring the complexities of class, caste, and colonial history and women's subtle forms of agency. In addition, the vibrant growth of popular culture in urban areas and the changing landscape of rural India, which is gaining access to urban culture in the form of global television, have also been ignored. Seeking an understanding of romance reading among young urban, cosmopolitan Indian women was thus, for me, a vehicle for challenging simplistic and problematic visions of South Asian female subjectivity.

Other compelling reasons to study urban Indian women's reading of Western romance novels were located in the lessons about gender that I learned growing up as an urban middle-class woman in India. Since my childhood, my parents and extended family members encouraged me to excel academically and to seek out intellectual challenges. As a third-generation woman of the Indian nationalist and independence movement, I, along with my peers, benefited from social reforms that abolished some traditional practices that oppressed women and facilitated the entry of middle-class women into the public sphere of education and paid employment. In the specific upper-caste Indian context in which I was raised, elders and parents viewed education as a good thing for young women. However, I also learned from my social environment that women's education was not about autonomy or independence. Education would render women more attractive in the urban middle-class marriage market and ultimately would be a mere instrument to allow women to support themselves economically if that became necessary.

Like South Asian feminist Uma Narayan (1997), who writes that her childhood perceptions of gender inequalities in India predated her "explicit acquisition of a feminist politics" (p. 9), I too learned about the limits of questioning social norms in my early teens. Unlike my brother, who was free to go wherever he wished, I found that my mobility and freedom were curtailed. I began hearing lectures from my mother about not doing anything that would bring dishonor to my family. My mother's list of anything included staying out late, dressing immodestly, refusing to learn domestic chores, engaging in interactions with men who were not part of our social circle, and becoming sexually active before marriage. Also included in this list of forbidden activities was reading Mills & Boon romance novels. In my late teens, I noticed some of my girlfriends at school and in college reading romance novels voraciously. A few women read these novels openly at home, and others, who feared their parents' disapproval, did it surreptitiously during breaks at college. When I began borrowing these books from friends and brought them home to read, my mother, who was an English teacher, banned romance novels as trash that would ruin my English. Although I partially believed my mother, I also knew that she was concerned about these novels because they were about love, sexuality, and romance, often in very explicit ways. I did not pursue this conflict with her partly because I strategically decided to focus on other battles and moved on, but still remained curious about my young peers' voracious romance reading. My memories of my girlfriends' Mills & Boon romance reading in India were thus linked to larger social discourses about female sexuality, modesty, honor, and respectability.

In addition, before I, went to India for fieldwork, colleagues and friends in the United States posed interesting questions about class, gender, and colonial history that I, as a privileged insider to middle-class urban Indian culture, took for granted. Why do women in certain parts of the postcolonial world such as India read romance novels in the English language and not in translation, as women in China, Japan, and Eastern Europe do? Why do middle- and upper-class women in India read these romance novels, unlike readers in the United States, who belong to a wider range of socioeconomic categories? Wary of generalizing about all Indian women based on my research among elite women, I conducted research to show that leisure reading in English among urban middle- and upper-class Indians had become possible due to the literacy project in the English language that was initiated during British colonialism in the 19th century. My interest in romance reading among women in India was thus a process of the familiar becoming strange, of envisioning larger questions about an ordinary everyday leisure practice, and of rethinking and reconnecting the personal with the political.

Fieldwork at "Home": Returning to India as a Feminist

These questions about gender, class, postcolonialism, and romance reading led me to Hyderabad, a city in south India, which is one of several places that I call home. I conducted my fieldwork in Hyderabad during the four summer months of May through September 1996. I had lived in Hyderabad, where most of my immediate family still lives, until I was 22 years old, when I left to pursue graduate education in the United States. After having read studies of romance readers in the United States before I left for India, I wanted to read as many Mills & Boon romance novels as I could and conduct intensive individual and group interviews with young women to find out why Western romances were pleasurable for them. The 42 young Indian women I interviewed were all middle and upper class, single, college-going women between the ages of 17 to 21 years.

Heeding the advice of Angela McRobbie (1990), who has urged feminist scholars to contextualize audiences' engagement with the media by analyzing other activities that surround media consumption, I sought active involvement in my informants' lives beyond their romance reading. I ate snacks and lunch at cafes with groups of women, went to the movies, dined with them at their homes, and accompanied them on shopping trips. I joined women's routine conversations during break times and interviewed informants at a range of everyday sites, such as college grounds, homes, and restaurants. I visited used-book vendors, bookstores, and lending libraries with several readers and observed social interactions between library owners and young women. To gain insight into the multidimensional relationship between women's romance reading and their experiences with everyday social discourse about romance readers, I interviewed young women's parents, siblings, teachers, bookstore managers, and owners of the lending libraries they frequented.

I was returning to India for my fieldwork after a 6-year stay in the United States as a graduate student in my late 20s. One among the many social positions available to me is the "subjective construction of my identity as an Indian woman" (Lal, 1996, p. 190). I grew up in a rather sheltered university-town setting in Hyderabad, India, for most of my life. As the daughter of two teachers—my father was a university professor and my mother a schoolteacher—I benefited from all the privileges of a solid middle-class background. I attended an elite convent school where English was the medium of instruction and took for granted class privileges such as a good college education, a career, and the cultural capital I possessed as someone who was raised in a family where education was highly valued. Because my parents were fairly liberal compared to many of my friends' parents, I grew up with a little more awareness than many middle- and upper-class Indians of the differences between my life and that of the vast majority of Indians. Although I questioned some restrictions that were specific to women of my class, I did not have the language to engage in a systematic feminist critique of patriarchy or nationalism. Feminism for me had been unfortunately constructed as an illness that struck highly Westernized intellectual Indian women who were out of touch with reality. As other South Asian feminists have reported (John, 1988; Lal, 1996), it was my dislocation from India to the relatively racialized context of the United States that prompted my political development as a feminist and a woman of color.

Reflections on Fieldwork: Failures, Successes, and Dilemmas

What are the challenges of doing research for feminist media ethnographers who interview elites in their cultures?[3] How do kinship roles assigned to native scholars shape social interactions in the field? How can commitments to sisterhood make it difficult for feminist ethnographers to achieve critical distance and discuss female informants' prejudiced views? Using these questions to guide my analysis, I now discuss the implication of my identity as a feminist researcher within the very social discourses of patriarchy, class, and nationalism that I wanted to make the objects of my work.

Failed Interviews: Gender, Sexuality, and Class in Fieldwork

Feminist ethnographers in the past decade have begun to record and theorize their failures in the field, although for different reasons (Gluck & Patai, 1991; Kumar, 1994; Visweswaran; 1994; M. Wolf, 1992). Kamala Visweswaran (1994) suggests that feminists should write about failures in ethnography not just to add to the feminist manual on methodology but because "failures are as much a part of the process of knowledge constitution as are our oft-heralded 'successes'" (p. 99). Visweswaran argues that failures in the field should be discussed not only to point to possible problems with our interviewing techniques but also to theorize failures as moments that are shaped by history as well as by accountable positionings. Furthermore, analysis of difficult and challenging moments in the field can contribute to a richer understanding of the phenomena we hope to study.

During my fieldwork in India, I found myself often justifying and explaining my interest in studying romance reading. The social construction of sexuality as a taboo subject, rarely discussed with strangers, affected my professional interactions with people. A few older men not only found the topic of my research offensive but also thought it was inappropriate for a "respectable woman" to want to study and discuss romance novels. One such interview was my tense and troubled interaction with Raja Rao, the manager of the Hyderabad branch of India Book House, an old and reputable Indian publishing firm that distributes imported Mills & Boon romance novels in India. When I phoned India Book House, a secretary took a message, but I never heard back from Raja Rao. After repeated phone calls and numerous messages that elicited no response, I decided to go in person to his office. As I always did when I lived in India, I was dressed in a *shalwar kameez* (loose pants and a long shirt), and I wore my long hair braided. When I was shown into his spacious office, the manager, a man in his 50s, was on the phone. He motioned me to sit down and handed me a few brochures about India Book House. In a few minutes, he ended his phone call and then asked me rather curtly, "What do you want?" After I finished my usual explanation, he demanded that I show him a letter to prove that I was indeed working on an official project. Then, after he read my letter, instead of letting me begin my interview, he began interrogating me and spent more than 15 minutes delving into my personal background.

In the course of his interrogation, we found out that he had actually met my father several years before when he had visited him for some advice about his nephew's career. Raja Rao (RR) expressed his disappointment because I had not brought my father along to the interview. Beginning to act more and more avuncular, he expressed his dissatisfaction with my choice of a topic for my dissertation:

RR: Do *you* read Mills & Boons?

Me: I have been reading them for the past few months.

RR: So, you have been reading them for your research. You should know by now why you did not read them before. Your father must have told you better. Why did you choose this strange topic? Those Mills & Boons are worthless, and you should not be wasting your time and money.

Me: I wonder why you call them worthless.

RR: Those stupid girls who think they are so modern with—it is those girls who read these books. They hold those books and walk around the college shamelessly. Have you seen the covers of the new books? They are very bad. Young girls should be doing more useful things. Parents should discourage their daughters from reading these books. Those books will encourage them to misbehave. Maybe reading these English books is better than those cheap roadside Telugu novels, but doing research on Mills & Boons is not good. Research should be done on things that are good about our culture. Did you talk to your father about your topic? I am sure he would say the same thing.

Me: But if fewer women read these books, you could not sell as many books to bookstores and libraries. Does that concern you?

RR: No! Not at all. The decision to distribute these books was made in Bombay, and I had nothing to do with it. I wish India Book House would stop selling these books. I don't want my company to be associated with Mills & Boons. The same is true for your thesis too. You will be writing this in the United States, and they will read about India Book House and associate it with Mills & Boons.

Me: [Trying to steer the conversation back] Could you give me some information about the distributing relationship India Book House has with the Mills & Boon company?

RR: No. I cannot waste time on your project. I am telling you this for your own good. Let me suggest something. India Book House is the proud publisher of the *Amar Chitra Katha* comics. I'm sure you read those as a child. [I nodded my head.] Those comics have stories about our culture and our history. We try to educate children about the rich culture of India. Many children no longer can hear our mythological stories from their parents, who are too busy working. Write about those comics. If you want, I can write you a reference letter to show to your Ph.D. guide or what did you say, Ph.D. adviser?

Me: So, I cannot expect any help or information from you at all?

RR: [Looking a little apologetic but still stubborn] No, you can talk to my secretary about whatever you want. As long as he gets permission from me to spend time with you, I don't mind. But I hope you will change your mind. Please share my suggestion with your father.

As an older, urban, English-educated professional man who knew my father, Rao adopted a condescending and critical tone toward me. His position as an older man from the same class milieu also meant that he could boldly tell me what I should or should not study. This familiarity enabled him to openly criticize women who read Mills & Boons as "shameless," thus seeking my alliance and creating a distance between me (not a habitual romance reader and thus a good woman) and young women who read romance novels. I heard similar labels—"stupid," "senseless," "useless"—used by other older middle-class men with reference to romance readers. My inability to challenge such language about young women reminded me of Jayati Lal's (1996) acute discomfort when managers she contacted in and around Delhi insulted factory women she wanted to interview by explicitly objectifying their bodies. Commenting on the "deeply implicated" process of conducting research, Lal (1996) writes, "Moreover, if the men one is researching have power . . . then they act to undermine and subvert a researcher's goal of non-hierarchical and non-objectifying relationships" (p. 196).

Expressing his dissatisfaction with my research agenda, Rao also indicated that my work on Indian women's pleasure in reading about sexuality would not represent his organization or Indian culture appropriately in the eyes of Western audiences. I encountered similar responses among some fathers of young women; whereas a few men openly displayed their skepticism when I explained my research, others pointed out that there were many more worthy ideas for research I could have pursued. Among the range of possible ideas suggested were the success of the televised Hindu epics *Ramayana* and *Mahabharata,* classical dance forms, Hindu texts, and "great" English-language Indian newspapers such as *The Hindu.* One man told me within minutes into our meeting that studying "dirty" books such as Mills & Boons for my dissertation was a "complete waste" of the "wonderful" academic opportunities I had. Displaying remarkable cultural self-consciousness about how India should be represented in the West, a few men implied that it was my duty to provide Westerners insights into the spiritual greatness of India.

In short, through my work as a responsible insider on useful and worthy projects about India, I was to play what feminist Uma Narayan (1997) has called the role of an "Emissary" (p. 128). Deconstructing the role Third World scholars can play as "Authentic Emissaries" in representing their cultures, Narayan writes that Emissaries focus on providing knowledge about the Third World through the lens of a "cultural riches approach" to their cultures:

What I am calling the "cultural riches" approach has a significant tendency to focus on the texts and artifacts of "High Culture," the cultural products of privileged sections of a society, whose social position not only gave them privileged access to the domains of cultural achievement, but also gave them power to constitute these achievements as "definitive," "emblematic," and "monumental" aspects of the culture in question. (p. 128)

Narayan argues that these representations of "High Culture" that become universalized marginalize the culture of minority groups within the Third World and obstruct understanding of the place of these cultural achievements within the political fabric of their social contexts. In addition, the sermons I received on studying and teaching the spiritual greatness of India in the United States relied on "cliched oppositions" between "materialist" Western culture and "spiritual" Indian culture (Narayan, 1997, p. 130). Ironically, the emotional investment I noticed among these people in constituting such binary oppositions between spiritual India and the material West have also been a part of Orientalism, a colonial, Western enterprise that constructed India as the essential, spiritual opposite Other of the rational Self of Western culture (Prakash, 1990; Ram, 1992). As Narayan (1997) points out in her critique of Ananda Coomaraswamy's book *The Dance of Shiva,* efforts to emphasize the greatness of India that draw on Orientalism can also be made by Third World "Orientalist" subjects seeking to validate their culture in the eyes of Westerners by reinforcing these binary oppositions.

Although my interview with manager Rao exemplified efforts to position me as an emissary, one interview that did not take place at all provided insight into compromises that had to be negotiated between romance readers as transgressive women on one hand and lucrative consumers on the other. The owner of an old and well-known bookstore in a busy part of the city refused to grant me an interview, saying, "I do not want to speak about these books. Yes, they sell a lot, a lot more than any other kind of books and bring in money, but I would not allow my own daughter to read these books." When I returned to the store later to try to talk to him again, I could not see the bookstore owner anywhere. Pretending to be a customer, I walked up to a young man who seemed to be in charge. Friendly and courteous, the young man offered to help me. Feeling reassured, I described my work and informed him that the manager had refused to speak to me. Looking a little embarrassed, the young man softly said, "That's my uncle. He did not want to sell Mills & Boons, but I persuaded him because all these girls from Stanley Junior's College, which is next door, read these books. He likes the money, but he has never been comfortable with his decision."

Failed/difficult interviews also included challenges to my professional identity that highlighted the marginal location of mass communication as a field of study in postcolonial India. A few fathers and mothers of young women expressed disbelief when I solicited opinions about their daughters' romance reading. These responses were usually followed by discussions about their own relatives who lived in the United States. Reeling off names of sons, daughters, nephews, and uncles who were very "well settled" in the United States as scientists, doctors, or computer professionals, I was asked what the point of my research was, what problem I really hoped to solve, and what my chances of success were in a nonscientific field such as mass communication in the United States. One parent who interrogated me about the value of my project implied that my lack of interest in computer science was the fault of my irresponsible parents. As a scholar in a nonscientific field, I had to field questions from several parents about media research and the possibilities for this research to be transformed into something of practical value. Ashis Nandy (1987), who has written extensively about postcolonial psychology, writes about the legacy left behind by Jawaharlal Nehru, first prime minister of independent India, in whose modern, rationalistic, and European-influenced worldview, Western science, scientific rationality, and technology presented the solutions to India's problems. Discussing the celebration of Western science among Asian intellectuals, government officials, and elite Indians in the postcolonial era, Nandy despairs of their "uncritical acceptance of science as the absolute standard of validation [which] is now more common than the Asian flu" (p. 106).

In some failed interviews, I encountered open hostility because parents and elders assumed I was supporting and encouraging young women to read romance novels. Two men who had agreed to my requests for interviews readily on the phone quickly and curtly recanted their offer when I met them in person. Speaking about his ongoing problems with his daughter who continued to disobey him, one of the two men abruptly said to me, "Why are you creating more problems for us? God knows what she will do when her head gets filled with all that nonsense." One woman, an aunt of one of my informants, responded angrily with a "no" when I asked her for her views on her niece's romance reading. In seeking out interviews with parents, I always sought the permission of my primary informants and only contacted their parents after they gave me their consent. Anticipating such hostility perhaps and fearing their parents' anger at being "found out," 8 out of my 30 primary informants told me that they did not want me to contact their parents or interview them at their homes because they were afraid their parents might overhear our discussions about Mills & Boons.

In reflecting on my difficult experiences in interviewing certain men and in gaining access to a few women's parents, I realized that these methodological problems explained in part young women's resentment about the silent and vocal disapproval of romance reading they encountered from parents and other elders in their extended families. Underlying some women's expressions of resistance and protest to cultural expectations of docile, asexual femininity was a feeling of betrayal and regret about their parents' lack of trust in them. These women suggested that romance reading was a "harmless" manifestation of youthful interest in sexuality, a rite of passage that would disappear in a few years. Other women's resistance took the form of a rather sophisticated critique of parents' simplistic assumption that romance novels could have a "magic bullet" effect, that is, an instantaneous impact on young women's sexual behaviors. Articulating their preferred construction of romance novels as manuals on sexuality in a culture where they had few sources to go to for information about sex, these women argued that romance reading was a form of healthy and "sensible" sex education. A third set of women spoke about romance reading as a "right" that they deserved because it was an appropriate practice for modern, cosmopolitan women who were exploring new identities unlike their traditional mothers and grandmothers.

The difficulties I experienced in interviewing some middle-class people were a contrast to my warm and friendly interactions with lending library owners and used-book vendors, who were eager to spend time with me. They offered to introduce me to their customers and readily permitted me to "hang out" at their libraries. Differences in class, cultural capital, and my affiliation with America were responsible for my pleasant experiences with library owners, most of whom were lower middle class and did not have any formal education beyond high school. My position as an "America-returned" academic, which provoked many questions about material life in the United States, brought home to me the mythic aura of America that now surrounded me: I represented someone who had escaped all the chaos, dirt, inconveniences, and poverty of India. However, as I spent more and more time at lending libraries, I learned about other reasons for the relative ease with which I was accepted. One day, during an informal conversation, Nagaraj, a chatty library owner, expressed his surprise and pleasure that I had not become very "Americanized." On probing further, he said, "If you had not told me that you were now studying in the States and that you had lived there 6 years, I would never have guessed. Your dress and your behavior . . . Nowadays, I have noticed that girls who even live here think they are movie stars—wearing all kinds of clothing, makeup, etc." My Indian clothes; the lack of makeup; my spoken English, which still retained an Indian accent; my ease with Hindi and Telugu; and the details I had divulged about staying with my family in Hyderabad had all combined to code me as a modest and respectable woman. I had achieved the success of going to America yet had managed to resist the corrupting influences of Western culture.

Continuing our conversation, Nagaraj said in a conspiratorial tone, "One of my customers, an older lady with a son, a computer engineer in the United States, said that some young Indian women who live in America do not make the best brides because they become 'fast' girls. They begin staying out late, start enjoying life [with a wink], and don't know how to respect husbands." His tone and manner indicated to me that had he any suspicion that I could be one of these immodest women, he would not have revealed this tidbit to me. Like non-Western feminist ethnographers Lila Abu-Lughod (1988), Hale Bolak (1996), and Soraiya Altorki (1988), who attributed certain successful moments in the field to others' approval of their modesty, my appearance of being a modest woman may also have prevented "failure" with men who were not from my social class.[4]

Negotiating Sisterhood: Empathy and Dilemmas in Interviewing Women

Having grown up in India, I knew that as a middle-class woman I would have easier access to young college women than would most male researchers. The milieu for my research in India was similar to the fieldwork environment of feminist scholars who have described how being women allowed them easier access to non-Western women's culture (Altorki, 1988; Abu-Lughod, 1988; Bolak, 1996). The urban Indian middle-class female world I was reentering was by no means a strictly gender-segregated world; that is, the segregation did not imply that women and men lived and worked in completely different spheres. Sex segregation in modern India means a "less stringent bifurcation of social life, whereby women venture into public space and participate in numerous male spheres but must nevertheless observe real or decorous distance from men" (Altorki & Fawzi El-Solh, 1988, p. 5).

When I first visited women's colleges, I could easily enter the gates of two colleges without being stopped or interrogated by the guards who stood outside. When I asked principals of the four colleges I visited for permission to interview their students, I could see that they perceived me as harmless. With every request for permission, I was asked to divulge personal details about my family and my parents. At three of the four colleges I visited, the principals seemed visibly relieved and happy when they found out that I was the daughter of two academics. One woman recalled that she had heard my father speak at a professional meeting. During these principals' inquiries about my personal background, it became apparent that my affiliation with the local academic community in Hyderabad assured these women that I presented no danger to their female students' safety.

Once I obtained written permissions, I was free to walk on the campus grounds to seek out and interview students. I could be fairly inconspicuous because I did not look much older than the students and was dressed like many of them. I asked women for interviews during their lunch breaks when they were sitting in circles eating their lunch. When I approached groups of women, introduced myself, and spoke about my research, I could see the surprise on many of their faces. In contrast to the skepticism and hostility of some older authority figures I had interviewed, these young women seemed amused and curious about my interest in talking to them. Unlike the lending library owners, who had questioned me about wealth and prosperity in a fantasy America, these women, many of whom had relatives abroad, were more interested in my everyday life, academic experiences, and the details of admission and financial aid to go to school in the United States. Given the "brain drain" from India, that is, the continued migration of educated urban Indians to the United States, many of these young women wanted to go to America themselves. They barraged me with questions about my work and my interest in their romance reading because most of them had never been questioned before by strangers about the popular culture they enjoyed. When some women found out about my local roots and the schools and colleges I had been to, they animatedly inquired if I knew their friends and acquaintances who had attended the same institutions.

Informants' feelings of shame and anxieties about the pleasure they experienced in reading romance novels, which arose from their reactions to patriarchal constructions of women as pure and asexual, was an integral part of the research process. When I shared the informed consent process and explained that I would be using pseudonyms in all my writing, I noticed that some women who initially appeared tense and unwilling to participate in my study looked relieved. Concerned about being identified in my research, these women asked me probing questions: Who will be reading this dissertation? Are you going to publish anything in the local newspapers or magazines in Hyderabad? Are you going to share transcripts of interviews with anyone in Hyderabad? Can you promise us that you will keep using pseudonyms wherever you publish your research?

To my amazement, with one group of young women, my requests for their pseudonym preferences turned into a social event that raised provocative questions of identity and authenticity that are implicated in the naming process in ethnographic research. Several women in this group, in response to my request, began talking, laughing loudly, and sharing ideas for names. Two women looked at me, winked, got down on their knees in front of two other seated women, and in elaborate courtship style, asked for their hands and begged for the privilege of using one another's names. This game got picked up by others, who soon began enacting similar courtship rituals and asked their friends' permission to use their names. Just as nostalgic memories of my own fun-filled college days began hitting me, one woman interrupted my thoughts and asked, "Should we choose only Indian names? Why can't I be

Janet, Jennifer, Carolyn, Nancy, or Katy, names that women have in the romance novels we're reading?" I remember feeling at a complete loss for an answer to this question, and thankfully at that point, our conversations turned to other things. In the end, all of them chose Indian Hindu names for pseudonyms, and I was relieved because, at the end of my fieldwork, I still did not have an answer except that I knew Indian names would make my dissertation more "authentic" (Visweswaran, 1994, pp. 60–61).[5]

Doing fieldwork among elites can be a challenging process where informants can question our intrusion into the routines of their everyday lives. Such challenges to the researcher's authority can surprise even those who are insiders to the culture and prompt unanticipated changes in methodology. After I had completed the informed-consent process, I began requesting one-on-one interviews with women who read Mills & Boon romance novels. I intended to follow up individual interviews with collective sessions where I would facilitate discussions among women about their romance reading. Assuming that the process of scheduling these interviews would go smoothly, I had carefully budgeted my time over the next month. My confidence about how these individual interviews would proceed was partly based on my assumptions about my insiderness—the trust I could earn quickly—and partly on my impatience to get my work underway. To my surprise, several young women did not seem happy or willing to spend time with me alone right away. When I requested the first group of women to meet me on an individual basis and asked if they could meet me during their breaks from classes, I was surprised and uncomfortable with the loud silence that ensued. Looking flustered, one woman said, "I don't know . . . College break times are fun for us. We see each other, we go to the cafe to drink soda, we go to the library to get books, and we plan what we want to do with our friends on Sunday." Immediately, another woman continued, "Why can't you talk to us when we're together? After all, our friends know everything about us."

When I faced similar questions from another group of women who also appeared to resent my appeals to meet with them alone, I realized that I had arrogantly encroached into their intimate, everyday rituals of friendship. It dawned on me slowly that break times in college were sacred for these women. Knowing well that without collecting data from these possibly recalcitrant subjects, I had no project, I reluctantly changed my plans and agreed to accept their demands. I began talking to them in groups first, and gradually, more than 30 women willingly agreed to meet me in individual sessions. Later, I discovered that they preferred to respond to me as a group first because they were wary about the kinds of questions I planned to ask about their sexuality and romance reading. The more public nature of group discussions meant that it was a safe space where I might hesitate to ask intrusive and personal questions. This situation of resistance from women illustrates Margery Wolf's (1992) cautionary words about reversals in power relationships between fieldworkers and their informants:

> Even the most arrogant neocolonialist soon discovers that one cannot order rural people to reveal important thoughts about their culture . . . Those who carry the culture and those who desperately want to understand it may participate in a minuet of unspoken negotiations that totally reverses the apparent balance of power. (p. 134)

Women's resistance to my efforts to separate them for the purpose of my research suggests that relationships within interpretive communities of readers or viewers can have surprising and unanticipated implications for our research practices. The notion of interpretive communities discussed in reader response theory (Fish, 1980; Radway, 1984) proposes that meanings of cultural texts are not inherent within texts themselves because meanings are created by communities of readers who interpret texts based on common social and individual experiences as women, Asians, Blacks, and so forth. Feminist media scholars have widely applied this notion of interpretive community to studies of audiences in the United States. However, some scholars have been criticized for imposing the concept of community on audiences through their research practices, when in reality, the viewers or readers they interviewed consumed media texts in isolation. Critiquing Janice Radway's ethnographic study of romance readers for its reliance on a realist epistemology, which leads her to deny the "construction of culture," Ien Ang (1996, p. 101) writes that Radway may have created an interpretive community of female romance readers for the first time when she brought women together for collective interviews. In contrast to Radway's research, romance reading for the young women I talked to was already embedded within friendships and a strong sense of community. Far from having to bring women together as an artificially created collective for my research, I was challenged to earn the right to become a part of their peer communities.

Group interviews in which women spoke about love, courtship, and heterosexual relations in Western romance fiction became opportunities to debate, contradict, and affirm their opinions about a range of gendered social issues in India such as sexual harassment of women in public spaces, stigmas associated with single women, expectations of women to be domestic, pressures on married women to obey elders in husbands' families, and the merits of arranged versus choice/love marriages. The backdrop and starting point for many of these discussions was women's explicit comparison between values held in Indian and Euramerican culture about love, family, parenting, and gender relations. Other than some references to class differences in India, social difference as constructed in group interviews stayed mostly at the level of nation, gender, and culture and rarely addressed religious or caste differences. Furthermore, although many women had been discussing gender restrictions casually with their friends prior to my arrival, the group interviews I facilitated, as some informants reported, appeared to be the first time such discussions took on a very emotional and intense quality. Although it is tempting for "undercover" feminist scholars to label such group interviews as consciousness-raising sessions and to cast themselves as feminist missionaries, the lack of long-term contact on my part with these women, the novelty of my presence, and the more abstract nature of these conversations in a public setting mitigate against such an interpretation. What did strike me, however, was the regret and sadness that many young women expressed about leaving behind this community—their world of relatively carefree womanly bonding—for future lives as professionals, wives, and mothers. Also, romance reading was not a practice that all women in these female communities shared; in an interesting and unexpected outcome, I listened to two women's passionate attempts during group interviews to persuade their friends who did not read romance novels to begin reading Mills & Boons.

In contrast to these collective sessions where young women's discussions primarily revolved around gender discrimination toward women as a group, in individual interviews, many women were much more talkative about restrictions on their sexuality, and several women shared their frustrations with immediate, everyday problems pertaining to family members' control over their movements. Women's candid responses in private, one-on-one interviews could relate to cultural taboos against criticizing family members in public settings such as group interviews and in my "safe" outsider status as someone who no longer lived in the local community of Hyderabad. For some women, the privacy of individual interviews and my own insider identity as a Hindu, upper-caste, and middle-class woman allowed them to discuss more freely their opinions about caste and religious differences perhaps because these identities have become sensitive and highly politicized categories in the public sphere of news and politics in India.

In my interactions with young women, I was gradually assigned the role of a *"didi"*—an older sister. Other feminist ethnographers have also written about how their assigned kinship roles as honorary mothers, daughters, wives, or sisters created solidarity and empathy, caused conflicts, or posed threats to ethnographic authority (Abu-Lughod, 1988; MacIntyre, 1993; Raheja & Gold, 1994). Although this insider kinship role facilitated data gathering among young women, being an older sister also put me in the uncomfortable position of having authority over my informants, which parents and relatives wanted to manipulate for their own ends. The role of didi proved ideal because had I been a mother figure, I could not have encouraged these women to speak to me about pleasure, romance reading, love, or sexuality. The 8 to 12 years' difference in age meant that I did not belong to the young women's peer group; however, I could still participate in their group activities without intimidating them. The role of older sister also allowed me to blend in and participate in many of these young women's everyday rituals, such as shopping, eating out, visiting lending libraries, and going to the movies. Some women asked me to interview them at their homes, two groups of women invited me to watch videos at home on Sundays, and several women set up interviews for me with their parents at their homes. For ethnographers, even those who are native scholars, becoming an insider in the community one hopes to study is thus a moment in the personal histories and biographies of both researcher and researched—a fleeting discourse that may well be difficult to recapture in the same way again.

In my role as an older sister, I gradually earned the friendship, trust, and affection of many young women. A few informants with whom I developed closer relationships invited me home several times to share meals with their families. Some of the more extroverted women eagerly offered to help me with my research. Three women proudly introduced me to their library owners as their friend from the United States and set up interviews for me. Several women sought out and urged their friends to call me or talk to me in person. Some women brought me articles from newspapers and magazines they thought were relevant for my research. At one college, one young woman spoke to the college librarian and convinced her to allow me to use the library and its resources despite policies that restricted use of the library to students only.

However, being an older sister also meant that I had to constantly negotiate the delicate boundary between being a confidante and being comfortable with authority. In the role of confidante, I found myself listening to stories about secret rebellions, resentment against parents, and tales about friends who had lovers and boyfriends. During these times, a few women explicitly asked me to turn off my tape recorder and to confirm my promises of anonymity and confidentiality. Despite the comfort and familiarity of the older sister figure to which I became accustomed, these anxieties among young romance readers revealed the uneasy and tense relationship between my professional life as researcher and the insider kinship role conferred upon me in fieldwork. Most accounts I listened to about "friends" were later revealed as events and circumstances in the lives of my informants themselves. Despite their eventual willingness to share their fears and complaints about gendered social pressures, I still wonder whether these young women would have been more open about their sexuality with a Westerner who might be seen as less likely to judge them based on cultural expectations of women's behavior in Indian society. The well-known word *rapport*, which is often used to signify acceptance and warm relationships between informants and researchers, was thus something I could not take for granted despite being an insider; all I could claim was an imperfect rapport.

Although the didi role allowed me entry into young Indian women's emotional worlds, this role also meant that I became privy to active attempts by parents to recruit me as a spy and a channel to exert control over their daughters. During interviews, a few working mothers anxiously inquired if their daughters were indeed in college when I visited because they were worried about bringing up good daughters. One mother was particularly concerned because her daughter's college had two movie theaters within walking distance, and she had heard from her colleagues at work that many young women skipped classes to watch movies. Two mothers wanted to know more about a nearby college for men, which had a reputation for unruly male students: "Did you see these men hanging around outside the gates? Did my daughter hint to you that she had a boyfriend from that college? Did you see her riding on any men's scooters?" One father wanted to know how often his daughter visited the lending library and blamed her for being stubborn about enrolling in a college far away from home: "She wanted to be with her friends from school so she insisted on going to this college. Now we don't know anything she does after she leaves home." Several parents assumed that I was conducting a survey about reading habits to pinpoint problems with rebellious young women who were ambivalent about conforming to idealized notions of Hindu middle- and upper-class femininity—dutiful, docile, educated, cultured, and domestic. I was told by a few parents that as an older "sensible" Indian woman who had achieved success (going to the United States), I could dissuade these young women from reading romance novels and instead urge them to spend time on more productive intellectual or domestic pursuits. My perceived insiderness, which arose not only because I was Indian but also because of my local connections, age, cultural capital, and class, thus led parents to invest me with the cultural authority attributed to the didi role.

Resisting parents' attempts to recruit me as a disciplining authority figure was not the only difficult situation I had to negotiate. A thornier dilemma I experienced was in thinking and writing about my informants' responses that revealed prejudice toward marginalized others: working-class and poor Indian men, minority Indian women of other religions, and racial minorities in the United States. In their talk about the sexual harassment of women in public spaces in urban India, many of my informants bitterly complained about their feelings of humiliation in city buses and on busy streets in Hyderabad, where they were frequently subject to verbal and physical abuse by men. Attributing the problem of women's harassment in public spaces to poor and working-class men who "were cheap," "had no culture," "were uneducated," "drunk," or "had no control," many women were silent about and resistant to discussing the less visible participation of middle- and upper-class educated men in these forms of harassment. Some women called for more police control over their harassers, and others wondered why these men found pleasure in inviting the unwilling attention of women like them, that is, women who were clearly unattainable by men from the lower classes.

By recounting middle- and upper-class women's criticisms of male harassers in Hyderabad, I do not imply that sexual harassment is similar in all Indian cities or that class hierarchy in India falls into the sharply polarized binary system of privileged versus poor classes, when in fact, class in India is enormously complicated by religion, language, regional differences in caste, colonial history, gender, urban versus rural locations, occupations, income, education, and land ownership (Ahmad, 1992; Basu, 1996; Beteille, 1965; Hancock, 1995; Liddle & Joshi, 1986; Lieten, 1996; Seymour, 1995; Varma, 1998).[6] Most of the upper-caste Indian women I interviewed in Hyderabad belonged to the professional English-speaking class, which is an elite group not solely in terms of wealth, but also in its ability to harness cultural capital through access to education and skilled jobs (Joshi, 1991; Sridhar, 1977; Varma, 1998). Unlike larger cities such as New Delhi or Bombay, where men from the newly rich classes are also likely to harass women, in Hyderabad, a smaller south Indian city, class mobility through entrepreneurship is less likely, and therefore, street harassment can be more easily attributed to working-class and poor men.[7]

In individual interviews, informants struggling to discuss their pleasure in reading sexually explicit material explained their sexual identity as a contrast to dominant discursive representations of minority Indian women's sexuality. Emphasizing their differences from Muslim and Anglo-Indian women, these Hindu women expressed their understanding of their own sexuality as being in the "middle." By "middle," they implied that they were not, on one hand, as sexually repressed as working-class and poor Muslim women and not, on the other hand, as sexually immoral or "easy" as women from the Anglo-Indian community, a community formed of children born to Indian women who were mistresses or concubines of British men during colonialism. Distancing themselves from Muslim and Anglo-Indian women, these romance readers constructed their own gender identity as being the perfect compromise between tradition and modernity: cosmopolitan yet modest, career oriented yet domestic.

Similarly, I also learned that part of the pleasure in reading romance novels as expressed by some informants lay in the ability of these novels to transport them into the world of predominantly White, affluent, First World citizens. My questions about their possible interest in recent and newer romance novels featuring men and women of color—mostly African Americans—were received with indifference, confusion, and annoyance. I learned from two women that my questions had displayed my ignorance of what defined a good Mills & Boon romance: courtship between White men and women or between White women and exotic aristocratic men such as Arab Sheiks or Egyptian princes. Expressing racist opinions about African Americans as criminals, poor, and underachieving and other Asians such as Chinese and Japanese as unemotional and passive, these romance readers argued that a "great Mills & Boon" had to be a romantic story set within the context of White middle- and upper-class life. Paradoxically, these readers even rejected the idea of a romance novel set in India with Indian men and women. Reading a favorite Mills & Boon romance novel was thus a vicarious experience located within specific dominant class and race formations.

Although I was comfortable with explaining women's gender oppression, I found myself denying, resisting, and avoiding writing about women's elitist views about class, religion, and race partly out of loyalty and partly out of my own difficulties in achieving critical distance. Given previous Western scholarship on India as the model example of a highly hierarchical society, I also feared that my representation of these negative views of Indian women in my work after publication in the United States would fuel ethnocentric views of Indian culture.[8] The political goal of my project, which was to write about Indian women's experiences with and resistance to patriarchal control over their sexuality, was thus complicated by strong and unexpected scripts of privilege and prejudice. These scripts did not neatly fit into images of women's subversive resistance to patriarchy that I had repeatedly encountered in the work of feminist media scholars.

Writing about hierarchical views of elite women raises new issues about feminist scholars' ethics, particularly, researchers' potential to use women informants' words to represent their lives and identities in ways that they may not endorse. In charting the future course of feminist research in its earlier stages, pioneering feminist scholars in different disciplines have debated and outlined the politics and ethics of feminist work (research goals, topics for research, and methods) in the academy. Expressing concerns about androcentrism and the silencing of women's voices in the academy, Sandra Harding (1987) wrote that feminist research should be "for women"; that is, feminist scholars must be committed to recovering women's everyday experiences to write about the world from women's perspective. Renate Duelli Klein (1983),

Ann Oakley (1981), and Shulamit Reinharz (1983) viewed qualitative field research methods that involved lived interaction with women as egalitarian and ethical methods to produce knowledge about women's everyday lives. In her frequently cited essay "U.S. Academics and Third World Women: Is Ethical Research Possible?" which dwells on the ethical issues generated by material inequalities between poor Third World women and Western/North American feminist ethnographers, Daphne Patai (1991) urged feminist scholars who "study down" to commit themselves to political action. How is it possible to retain Harding's (1987) vision of feminist research if women themselves are doing the silencing? How are these ethical issues related to the politics of research different when we "study up" and have to take into account elite, not poor, Third World women's experiences of privilege within dominant class, caste, and religious structures?

In considering the ethics of how we represent elite women's discourses of "othering," it is perhaps easier for feminist scholars to study and narrate disturbing responses of male rather than female informants due to fears of betraying the sisterhood and of distracting from the overall goal of redistributing power between the sexes (Sanday, 1990; Seiter, 1990; Weis, 1990). Some feminist ethnographers, including Judith Stacey (1991) and Sondra Hale (1991), have written about how strongly ingrained assumptions of empathy and solidarity with women's gender oppression can create emotional and intellectual conflict when female subjects express racist, classist, homophobic, and other elitist views. Criticizing feminist notions about ethnography as a less exploitative and more respectful research method because it is based on personal interactions with real women, Judith Stacey (1991) suggests that feminists can diminish the "inequality and potential treacherousness" (p. 113) inherent in ethnography by looking to critical and postmodern ethnographers. She writes that an uneasy fusion of feminist and postmodern/critical ethnography that rigorously questions power relationships in the field and within the academy can temper feminist celebrations of ethnography. However, relying on the insights of postmodern and critical ethnography could not mitigate the anxieties I experienced in deciding how, where, and if I should include my informants' problematic opinions about marginalized others. Although I had theoretical knowledge about intersections among race, gender, and class identities in feminist theory, applying this theory to real women with whom I had developed friendships was difficult.

Ultimately, I decided to include and integrate Indian women's denigration of other social groups within my analysis of the complex ways in which audiences in non-Western contexts appropriate global media to reinforce local meanings of power—meanings that may not have been envisioned by the original producers of transnational culture. My decision to include women's problematic views in the written product of my fieldwork was inspired by scholars who advise against a retreat from analyses of privilege and power in the real world. Grappling with the political project of cultural studies, Stuart Hall (1991) asks cultural studies scholars to return to the "worldliness of cultural studies":

> I want to go back to that moment of "staking out a wager" in cultural studies, to those moments in which positions begin to matter. This is a way of opening the question of the "worldliness" of cultural studies, to borrow a term from Edward Said . . . I'm trying to return the project of cultural studies from the clean air of meaning and textuality and theory to the something nasty down below. (p. 278)

Urging qualitative researchers to resist the romanticizing of fieldwork narratives, Michelle Fine (1994) writes that one way of interrupting the binaries of Self/Other and identifying possibilities for change is to productively engage the contradictions that litter texts and fieldwork experiences. Fine suggests that exploring the structures and practices of othering by individuals living in spaces of privilege (class, gender, or race) can disrupt the taken-for-granted fixedness of social categories and point to the multiple and interchangeable roles of Self and Other that we all occupy. One strength of qualitative, ethnographic research, after all, lies in the access it promises to the ways in which power and privilege get articulated at the level of people's everyday lives. In writing about how elite South Asian women constructed the other, I had to, however, resist creating simple and *"flat* caricatures" (Fine, 1994, p. 79) of dominant versus powerless groups and instead map out the "overlapping, conflicting, and de-centered circles of . . . identities" (Denzin, quoted in Fine, 1994, p. 79).

Recent definitions of feminist ethnography also allowed me to analyze women's multiple subjectivities as including experiences of power as well as powerlessness. Sally Cole and Lynne Philips (1996) define feminist ethnography as a project not only of giving voice but also of "documentation and presentation of the conflicting, contradictory, and heterogeneous experiences of women cross-culturally" (p. 4). My efforts to explain Hindu middle- and upper-class women's negative views toward other minority Indian women resonated with Kamala Visweswaran's (1994) arguments for going beyond binary analyses of White/Black, Western/Third World, and colonized/colonizer in ethnography. Urging women-centered feminist ethnography to explore and theorize "relationality," she writes, "But rather than foreground men's relationships to one another [which classical ethnography does quite well] . . . perhaps a feminist ethnography could also focus on women's relationships to other women, and the power differentials between them" (p. 20).

Acknowledging her difficulties with writing about multiple hierarchies among women in Burkina Faso, Marie Andree Couillard (1996) describes the power differences she witnessed between urban, educated women and rural women:

> Women's solidarity, rather than being taken for granted, must be problematized and investigated in specific contexts . . . Moreover some "sisters" manage better than others vis-à-vis "brothers" who hold powerful positions. And some "sisters" will not hesitate to manipulate "brothers" to their own ends while preventing other sisters from having access to knowledge, skills, and resources. (pp. 65–66)

Influenced by Foucault, feminist ethnographers have also reconceptualized women's subjectivities as complex, that is, as including agency and passivity, oppression and power, as well as resistance and accommodation to power structures (Abu-Lughod, 1990b; Kumar, 1994; Mankekar, 1993). These new perspectives on women as actors who devise complex strategies allowed me to go beyond binary constructions of power along the lone axis of gender and instead explore the articulation of power as a complex process that includes multiple social identities.

Conclusion

Engaging in a critique of our research practices reveals the troubled and power-laden circumstances that underlie the production of knowledge within the academy. In returning to the questions I raised in the introduction about qualitative media research carried out by postcolonial feminist scholars in their own cultures, my analysis of methodological concerns has implications for postcolonial feminist ethnography, feminist media ethnography, and finally, for audience ethnographies of media reception in a global context.

The entry of postcolonial scholars from the Third World in the U.S. academy as scholars and ethnographers studying their own cultures rather than as the traditional "objects" of research has been heralded as a major transformation in the history of Euramerican academic knowledge production (Escobar, 1993, p. 364; Tedlock, 1991, p. 81; M. Wolf, 1992, pp. 137–138). Postcolonial feminist ethnographers carrying out research in their own cultures could claim that, as authentic insiders, they have the capability of producing knowledge that is closer to the truth or reality of people's lives in the Third World. However, as some postcolonial feminists have cautioned, such claims about the authenticity of knowledge produced by insiders can be problematic because they confer authority based on biological essentialism and attribute representational power to insiders in the political sense of "speaking for" silenced subjects (Ganguly, 1992; Narayan, 1997; Spivak, 1988), that is, of claiming authority to be a transparent medium through which native informants' voices become heard. In exploring the impact of my age, gender, class, and cultural capital on my research relationships in Hyderabad, including my interactions with Indian women of a similar background, my analysis demonstrates that rather than experiencing neatly categorized states of insiders or outsiders, postcolonial feminist ethnographers will find themselves negotiating insider/outsider and Self/Other positions depending on the dialogical and interactive process of identity constitution in the field (Tedlock, 1991).

Given the history of Orientalist representations inside and outside the academy, postcolonial feminists have taken on the task of challenging limited Western representations of Third World women as a homogenous group of women who are typically represented as passive victims of indigenous patriarchal systems (Kumar, 1994; Mani, 1991; Mohanty, 1991; Ong, 1988; Visweswaran, 1994). Conducting ethnographies in their own cultures to show the diversity of people's lives in the Third World and highlight non-Western women's resistive discourses can therefore be politically empowering experiences for postcolonial feminist ethnographers. In building on the challenge to Orientalism that postcolonial feminists have initiated, my project on Indian women's romance reading questioned the monolithic representation of Third World women as the rural, poor woman of development and mainstream news discourses that usually ignore urban, cosmopolitan cultures in the Third World. My project also suggested that far from passively accepting patriarchal constructions of ideal middle-class femininity, young Indian women were actively questioning the control and regulation of their sexuality and mobility, even if these expressions of resistance appeared to partially accommodate existing norms rather than advocate a complete transformation of patriarchy. In writing about Third World women's agency to contest Orientalist representations, postcolonial feminist ethnographers must, however, resist the desire to minimize the power of traditional patriarchy on women's lives merely because such a representation might weaken Western notions of cultural superiority. Based on my fieldwork experience, I also argue that despite pressure from community members to produce celebratory accounts of glorious traditions in their cultures, postcolonial feminist ethnographers must resist the role of emissary because, as feminists, they have a stake in "calling attention to norms, unfair, and oppressive to many within their societies, including women" (Narayan, 1997, p. 133).

In seeking South Asian women's abilities to fashion their own hidden discourses even as they are part of a repressive social order, postcolonial feminist ethnographers should also examine the darker side of women's agency, that is, how women themselves can call upon dominant, hegemonic meanings to construct their identities in opposition to those who are marginalized. Given the "extreme heterogeneity of the people called women, unified not by class or region, history or culture, only tenuously by biology, and not at all by age" (Kumar, 1994, p. 22) in South Asia, postcolonial feminists must be prepared to engage in multidimensional analyses of power that cannot always be attributed to sources such as colonialism, the "Big, Bad, West," or "those traditional men." To circulate representations of South Asian women as agents who can participate in the reproduction of dominant discourses might present challenges for postcolonial feminists who work within the Euramerican academy because of their feminist politics and loyalty toward their community. Avoiding critiques of female subjects, however, only implies that postcolonial feminist ethnographers are abdicating responsibility to a vision of transnational feminism that is committed to critiquing all systems of power, including the rising tide of religious fundamentalism (Grewal & Kaplan, 1994; Hancock, 1995; Mankekar, 1993; Mazumdar, 1994; Moghadam, 1994). The increasing power of Hindu fundamentalist discourses in India that demonize Muslims as foreign, uncivilized, barbaric, and so forth forms the larger context within which Hindu women readers in my study denigrated Muslim women, a context that demands attention to the politics of religious identity. Encouraging transnational feminists to go beyond the "holy trinity" of race, class, and gender because it limits the range of discussion around women's lives, Indrepal Grewal and Caren Kaplan (1994) write,

What is often left out of these U.S. focused debates are other complex categories of identity and affiliation that apply to non-U.S. cultures and situations. U.S. feminists often have to be reminded that . . . other categories also enter into the issues of subject formation both within and outside the borders of the United States, requiring more nuanced and complex theories of social relations. (p. 19)[9]

Feminist media ethnography would benefit greatly from an increased sense of self-reflexivity about the research we do among readers and viewers of popular culture. Warning feminist scholars about the dangers of a self-reflexivity that could turn into a narcissistic focus on the researcher herself, a "hidden form of self indulgence," Ien Ang (1989, p. 28) cautions us against promoting struggles over writing and representation within the academy rather than engaging with the external realities of people's lives. As my article demonstrates, far from ignoring the power of dominant discourses or suggesting that representational power can be disrupted through a "politics of textuality" (Said, 1989, p. 209), self-reflexivity on the part of feminist media ethnographers can enrich our work and productively explore tensions between the politics of the world and the experiences we have with research subjects. Methodological problems, such as difficult interactions with book managers, parents' reneging on interviews, and failures to gain access to some parents, only served to reinforce the strength of young Indian women's loud and vocal defense of their romance reading. In addition, writing about and reflecting on troubled relationships in the field has enhanced my understanding of why romance readers' expressions of resistance were ridden with contradictory feelings, such as pleasure/guilt, resistance/accommodation, and superiority/inferiority.

Interrogating unexpected moments and ethical dilemmas in the field could also provide feminist media ethnographers opportunities to put into practice a politics of pedagogy that can be more effective in deconstructing authority and power than theoretical disavowals of objectivity, realism, or equality in relationships between researchers and researched. For many feminist researchers, as Lal (1996) writes, the academy can be a site of politics because our reflexive methodologies have great "potential for the pedagogical empowerment of a new generation of feminist scholars" (p. 205). To enable future feminist media ethnographers to become aware of the significance of fieldwork experiences for the knowledge we produce about gender and the politics of pleasure, it is important that we begin to reflect on dilemmas, silences, failures, and successes in doing qualitative research. My students' enthusiastic reactions to a recent book, *Speaking of Abortion: Television and Authority in Women's Lives*, one of the first publications in feminist audience studies to include an insightful opening chapter and methodological appendix about authors Andrea Press and Elizabeth Cole's interactions with women during focus groups, suggests that situating ourselves in the field can enable feminist media ethnographers to reach out to one of our most important constituents within the academy (Press & Cole, 1999).

With regard to the contributions of self-reflexive audience ethnographies in postcolonial settings to cultural studies, I argue that analyzing how we gain access to audience members, negotiate representational dilemmas, and contend with silences and opposition during fieldwork can richly illustrate the contradictory reception to global culture within a range of social groups. Reflecting on parents' hostility and anxieties about their daughters' romance reading; mothers' coercive efforts to enlist me in the role of spy and role model; older, educated middle-class Indians' disdain for my discipline and research topic; and informants' momentary desire for pseudonyms drawn from Western culture provided insights into the context of global media consumption within which postcolonial scholars often work. Global Western media, as my account reveals, are an integral part of the ways in which power and hierarchy get mapped out across transnational borders, within national boundaries, and through the trajectories of colonial history.

Self-reflexive research on media reception can also promote cultural studies' ongoing interest in interdisciplinary dialogue and facilitate a politics of methodology that is different from the capitalist media industry's interest in audiences. Emphasizing the value of reflective writing for enabling a richer understanding of context in audience studies, media scholar Murphy (1999) points out that "narrative development, questions of power, reflexivity, and concerns over voice" (p. 501) remain neglected in ethnographic research. The absence of analysis about research and fieldwork as sites of cultural politics is a symptom of cultural studies' limited vision of interdisciplinarity because audience ethnographers have liberally borrowed theoretical and methodological approaches from anthropology; however, unlike feminist, postmodern, and critical ethnographers in anthropology, they have neglected to historicize and examine the politics of audience research. Lack of sensitivity to the histories of methodologies and the politics of knowledge production about audience activity can lead to ethnocentric assessments about the future course of research in cultural studies. As Vamsee Juluri (1998) notes, recent nostalgia about audience research and arguments to abandon ethnographic studies of audiences so we can return to political economies of media industries fail to be reflective about the kinds of audiences we have heard from during the past two decades—mostly White audiences in the Euramerican world. In fact, extending Juluri's argument to questions of culture and postcoloniality, it is only recently that cultural studies in the United States has begun to contemplate questions of postcolonial identity, despite the prominence of postcolonial theory in allied fields such as anthropology, literature, and women's studies.[10] Furthermore, anthropologists have recently begun acknowledging the "profoundly influencing" challenge that the mass media pose to "orthodox notions of culture" because the media allow us to transgress cultural, national, and regional boundaries (Gupta & Ferguson, 1992, p. 18–19). Audience ethnographies in the Third World could speak to anthropology's current interest in seeking a better understanding of the role transnational popular culture plays in human experiences of cross-cultural modernity. Finally, audience research by postcolonial media scholars among elite, cosmopolitan audiences in the Third World has tremendous potential to challenge troublesome relationships in the paradigm of "Powerful Self (Western academic)/Oppressed Other (Third World, poor informant)" (Radway, 1989, p. 5) that is ever present in traditional notions of ethnography in anthropology.[11]

Criticizing audience ethnographer David Morley for not reflecting on his position as a researcher in his book *Family Television,* Ang (1996) asks,

Why examine audiences empirically at all? After all, some critical scholars still dismiss the idea of doing empirical audience research altogether, because, so they argue, it would necessarily implicate the researcher with the strategies and aims of the capitalist culture industry. (p. 51)

She argues that this troubling question should not imply a retreat from empirical audience research because ethnographies of media reception, unlike the neat and manageable data generated from market research, remind us that reality is always more complicated and diversified than our theories can represent. This article's emphasis on problems, failures, and unexpected events in fieldwork rather than successful moments alone shows us that it is futile to objectify audiences or treat audience activity as slices of reality because media ethnographers' access to audience interpretations are always bound by our identities and the contexts in which we carry out our research.

Notes

1. For examples of self-reflexive essays of feminists in anthropology and folklore, see Abu-Lughod (1988); Behar (1993); Gordon (1988); MacIntyre (1993); Narayan (1993); Stoeltje, Fox, and Obrys (1999); Visweswaran (1994); and M. Wolf (1992); in sociology, see Bolak (1996); Naples (1996); and Stacey (1991); in geography, see England (1994); Gilbert (1994); and Kobayashi (1994); in literary studies, see Radway (1986); and in women's studies, see Altorki and El-Solh (1988); Cole and Philips (1996); Patai (1991); and D. Wolf (1996).

2. I thank the coeditor of *Qualitative Inquiry*, Norman Denzin, for drawing my attention to Patrick Murphy's (1999) research.

3. Most self-reflexive accounts of non-Western feminists discuss the rupturing of their feelings of "insiderness" when they were interviewing poor and working-class women from their own cultures (Bolak, 1996; El-Solh, 1988; Lal, 1996; Ram, 1992b). These feminists have written that their middle- and upper-class backgrounds rendered them as much outsider to the working-class people they were talking to as Western scholars who do research among the poor in the Third World.

4. For example, in her article about becoming a dutiful "modest" daughter, Lila Abu-Lughod (1988, pp. 139–162) discusses her identity as an Arab-American among the Bedouin in the Egyptian Western Desert and writes that to be accepted, she had to distance her American self with its connotations of immodesty. She reveals that her father's background, the fact that he accompanied her on her trip and introduced her to prominent families, and her willingness to do domestic chores endeared her to the Bedouin community.

5. Rereading my notes later, I recalled Kamala Visweswaran's (1994, pp. 60–61) discussions about the naming process in research. Raising a series of questions about the naming process, Visweswaran asks us to pay more attention to our naming practices and to think about the relationship between naming, identity, and authenticity.

Asking her readers why names such as Francoise, Ghislane, or Jennifer would not satisfy audiences because her informants were all Indian women, she writes, "The pseudonym is a false name that stands for a real person. As such it marks a key site between the real and fictitious in anthropological writing. Yet some fictions are expected, indeed required, to figure both ethnography and authority" (p. 61). To move away from realist narratives that feed audiences' needs for authenticity, she resorts to calling her subject "M" in the tradition of the cheap detective novel.

6. For research that explores linkages among gender, caste, and class, see Liddle and Joshi (1986) and Seymour (1995). Basu (1996) and Hancock (1995) examine the ways in which the recent upsurge in Hindu fundamentalism affects class, gender, and caste identities. Ahmad (1992) considers the rise of the English language and English-language publishing for the consolidation of elite postcolonial urban culture in India. Lieten (1996) and Beteille (1965) examine the changing relationship between caste and class structures and conclude that, for the most part, upper-caste people continue to belong to the economically higher strata of middle- and upper-class groups. Pavan Varma's (1998) recent book *The Great Indian Middle-Class* provides good background information and a cogent analysis of the origins and growth of the elite, English-educated Indian middle class in urban areas. Varma describes the rise of the urban middle class during British colonialism; explains the involvement of members of this class in the nationalist, anticolonial movement; and analyzes the current, pervasive interpellation of urban middle-class Indians as ideal consumers in a global economy.

7. I am grateful to an anonymous reviewer of *Qualitative Inquiry* for pointing out the range of social categories that mediate experiences of class in India and for drawing my attention to different kinds of street harassment in larger Indian cities such as New Delhi.

8. For an excellent critique of Western fascination for collectivism and caste hierarchy in India, see Ram (1992a).

9. Discussing Hinduism or Islam and non-Western women's religious identities raises the issue of how postcolonial feminist ethnographers' research might be received in Euramerican contexts. To write and speak about the patriarchal control over Indian women's sexuality, I must discuss Hinduism, arranged marriage, and sexuality as configured in Hindu religious texts and scriptures. Given the glaring absence of feminist ethnographies in the West, which take into account the impact of Christianity on the social construction of sexuality, such discussions of Hinduism and Indian women can become an exotic discourse drifting in and out of conference rooms for the "facile consumption of cultural Otherness" (Salazar, 1991, p.100). Thus, it may be even more challenging for a postcolonial feminist ethnographer to deconstruct Self/Other distinctions that are produced by her research.

10. For debates on the implications of postcolonial studies for global communication studies, see Juluri (1998), Kavoori (1998), and Shome (1998).

11. Another way of challenging the classic paradigm of Western Self/non-Western Other would be to reverse the relationship whereby Third World scholars would study First World cultures. For an excellent discussion of such reversals in fieldwork relationships, see Stoeltje et al. (1999, pp. 174–176).

References

Abu-Lughod, L. (1988). Fieldwork of a dutiful daughter. In S. Altorki & C. Fawzi El-Solh (Eds.), *Arab women in the field: Studying your own society* (pp. 139–162). New York: Syracuse University Press.

Abu-Lughod, L. (1990a). Can there be a feminist ethnography? *Women and Performance: Journal of Feminist Theory, 5*(1), 7–27.

Abu-Lughod, L. (1990b). The romance of resistance: Tracing transformations of power through Bedouin women. *American Ethnologist, 27*(1), 41–55.

Ahmad, A. (1992). *In theory: Classes, nations, literatures.* London: New York: Verso.

Altorki, S. (1988). At home in the field. In S. Altorki & C. Fawzi El-Solh (Eds.), *Arab women in the field: Studying your own society* (pp. 25–48). New York: Syracuse University Press.

Altorki, S., & Fawzi El-Solh, C. (1988). *Arab women in the field: Studying your own society.* New York: Syracuse University Press.

Ang, I. (1989). Beyond self-reflexivity. *Journal of Communication Inquiry, 13*(2), 27–29.

Ang, I. (1996). *Living room wars: Rethinking media audiences for a postmodern world.* New York: Routledge.

Basu, A. (1996, Summer). Caste and class: The rise of Hindu nationalism in India. *Harvard International Review,* pp. 28–31.

Behar, R. (1993). *Translated woman: Crossing the border with Esparanza's story.* Boston: Beacon Press.

Beteille, A. (1965). *Caste, class, and power: Changing patterns of stratification in a Tanjore village.* Berkeley: University of California Press.

Bolak, H. (1996). Studying one's own in the Middle East: Negotiating gender and self-other dynamics in the field. *Qualitative Sociology, 19*(1), 107–130.

Clifford, J. (1986). Introduction: Partial truths. In J. Clifford & G. Marcus (Eds.), *Writing culture: The poetics and politics of ethnography* (pp. 1–26). Berkeley: University of California Press.

Cole, S., & Philips, L. (1996). The work and politics of feminist ethnography. In S. Cole & L. Philips (Eds.), *Ethnographic feminisms: Essays in anthropology* (pp. 1–19). Ottawa, Canada: Carleton University Press.

Couillard, M. (1996). From women's point of view: Practising feminist anthropology in a world of differences. In S. Cole & L. Philips (Eds.), *Ethnographic feminisms: Essays in anthropology* (pp. 1–19). Ottawa, Canada: Carleton University Press.

El-Solh, C. (1988). Gender, class, and origin. In S. Altorki & C. Fawzi El-Solh (Eds.), *Arab women in the field: Studying your own society* (pp. 91–114). New York: Syracuse University Press.

England, K. (1994). Getting personal: Reflexivity, positionality, and feminist research. *Professional Geographer, 46*(1), 80–89.

Escobar, A. (1993). The limits of reflexivity: Politics in anthropology's post-writing culture era. *Journal of Anthropological Research, 49*(4), 377–391.

Fine, M. (1994). Working the hyphens: Reinventing self and other in qualitative research. In N. Denzin & Y. Lincoln (Eds.), *Handbook of qualitative research* (pp. 70–82). Thousand Oaks, CA: Sage.

Fish, S. (1980). *Is there a text in this class? The authority of interpretive communities.* Cambridge, MA: Harvard University Press.

Ganguly, K. (1992). Accounting for others: Feminism and representation. In L. Rakow (Ed.), *Women making meaning: New feminist directions in communication* (pp. 60–79). New York: Routledge.

Gilbert, M. (1994). The politics of location: Doing feminist research at "home." *Professional Geographer, 46*(1), 90–96.

Gluck, S. B., & Patai, D. (1991). *Women's words: The feminist practice of oral history.* New York: Routledge.

Gordon, D. (1988). Writing culture, writing feminism: The poetics and politics of experimental ethnography. *Inscriptions, 3/4*, 1–7.

Grewal, I., & Kaplan, C. (1994). Introduction: Transnational feminist practices. In I. Grewal & C. Kaplan (Eds.), *Scattered hegemonies: Postmodernity and transnational feminist practices* (pp. 3–33). Minneapolis: University of Minnesota Press.

Gupta, A., & Ferguson, J. (1992). Beyond "culture": Space, identity, and the politics of difference. *Cultural Anthropology, 7*(1), 7–23.

Hale, S. (1991). Feminist method, process, and self-criticism: Interviewing Sudanese women. In S. Gluck & D. Patai (Eds.), *Women's words* (pp. 121–136). New York: Routledge.

Hall, S. (1991). Cultural studies and its theoretical legacies. In L. Grossberg, C. Nelson, & R. Treicher (Eds.), *Cultural studies* (pp. 277–294). New York: Routledge.

Hancock, M. (1995). Hindu culture for an Indian nation: Gender, politics, and elite identity in urban south India. *American Ethnologist, 22*(4), 907–926.

Harding, S. (1987). *Feminism and methodology.* Bloomington: Indiana University Press.

John, M. (1988). Postcolonial feminists in the Western intellectual field: Anthropologists and native informants? *Inscriptions, 5*, 49–73.

Joshi, S. (Ed.). (1991). *Rethinking English: Essays in literature, language, history.* New Delhi, India: Trianka.

Juluri, V. (1998). Globalizing audience studies: The audience and its landscape and living room wars. *Critical Studies in Mass Communication, 15*, 85–90.

Kavoori, A. (1998). Getting past the latest "post": Assessing the term "post-colonial." *Critical Studies in Mass Communication, 15*, 195–202.

Klein, R. (1983). How to do what we want to do: Thoughts about feminist methodology. In G. Bowles & R. Klein (Ed.), *Theories of women's studies.* London: Routledge & Kegan Paul.

Kobayashi, A. (1994). Coloring the field: Gender, "race," and the politics of fieldwork. *Professional Geographer, 46*(1), 73–80.

Kumar, N. (Ed). (1994). Introduction. In N. Kumar (Ed.), *Women as subjects: South Asian histories.* Charlottesville: University of Virginia Press.

Lal, J. (1996). Situating locations: The politics of self, identity, and "other" in living and writing the text. In D. Wolf (Ed.), *Feminist dilemmas in field work* (pp. 185–214). Boulder, CO: Westview.

Lengel, L. (1998). Researching the "other," transforming ourselves: Methodological considerations of feminist ethnography. *Journal of Communication Inquiry*, 22(3), 229–250.

Liddle, J., & Joshi, R. (1986). *Daughters of independence: Gender, caste, and class in India.* New Brunswick, NJ: Rutgers University Press.

Lieten, G. K. (1996). Hindu communalism: Between caste and class. *Journal of Contemporary Asia*, 26(2), 236–252.

MacIntyre, M. (1993). Fictive kinship or mistaken identity? In D. Bell, P. Caplan, & W. Jahan (Eds.), *Gendered fields: Women, men, and ethnography* (pp. 44–62). New York: Routledge.

Mani, L. (1991). Cultural theory and colonial texts: Reading eyewitness accounts of widow burning. In L. Grossberg, C. Nelson, & P. Treichler (Eds.), *Cultural studies* (pp. 392–408). New York: Routledge.

Mankekar, P. (1993). Reconstituting "Indian womanhood": An ethnography of television viewers in a North Indian city (Doctoral dissertation, University of Washington, 1993). *Dissertation Abstracts International*, 54(12), 4498.

Mazumdar, S. (1994). Moving away from a secular vision? Women, nation, and the cultural construction of Hindu India. In V. Moghadam (Ed.), *Identity politics and women: Cultural reassertions and feminisms in international perspective* (pp. 243–272). Boulder, CO: Westview.

McRobbie, A. (1990). *Feminism and youth culture.* Boston: Unwin Hyman.

Moghadam, V. (Ed.). (1994). *Identity politics and women: Cultural reassertions and feminisms in international perspective.* Boulder, CO: Westview.

Mohanty, C. (1991). Under Western eyes: Feminist scholarship and colonial discourses. In A. Russo & L. Torres (Eds.), *Third World women and the politics of feminism* (pp. 51–80). Bloomington: Indiana University Press.

Murphy, P. (1999). Doing audience ethnography: A narrative account of establishing ethnographic identity and locating interpretive communities in fieldwork. *Qualitative Inquiry*, 5(4), 479–504.

Nandy, A. (1987). *Traditions, tyranny, and utopias.* Delhi, India: Oxford University Press.

Naples, N. (1996). A feminist revisiting of the insider/outsider debate: The outsider phenomenon in rural Iowa. *Qualitative Sociology*, 19(1), 83–106.

Narayan, K. (1993). How native is a "native" anthropologist? *American Anthropologist*, 95, 671–686.

Narayan, U. (1997). *Dislocating cultures: Identities, traditions, and third world feminism.* New York: Routledge.

Oakley, A. (1981). Interviewing women: A contradiction in terms. In H. Roberts (Ed.), *Doing feminist research* (pp. 30–61). London: Routledge & Kegan Paul.

Ong, A. (1988). Colonialism and modernity: Feminist re-presentation of women in non-Western societies. *Inscriptions*, 3/4, 79–93.

Patai, D. (1991). U.S. academics and Third World women: Is ethical research possible? In S. Cluck & D. Patai (Eds.), *Women's words* (pp. 137–153). New York: Routledge.

Philips, L. (1996). Difference, indifference, and making a difference: Reflexivity in the time of cholera. In S. Cole & L. Philips (Eds.), *Ethnographic feminisms: Essays in anthropology* (pp. 1–19). Ottawa, Canada: Carleton University Press.

Prakash, G. (1990). Writing post-Orientalist histories of the Third World: Perspectives from Indian historiography. *Comparative Studies in Society and History, 32*(2), 383–408.

Press, A., & Cole, E. (1999). *Speaking of abortion: Television and authority in women's lives.* Chicago: University of Chicago Press.

Radway, J. (1984). *Reading the romance: Women, patriarchy and popular literature.* Chapel Hill: University of North Carolina Press.

Radway, J. (1986). Identifying ideological seams: Mass culture, analytic method and political practice. *Communication, 9*(1), 93–124.

Radway, J. (1989). Ethnography among elites: Comparing discourses of power. *Journal of Communication Inquiry, 13*(2), 4–11.

Raheja, G., & Gold, A. (1994). *Listen to the heron's words: Reimagining gender and kinship in North India.* Berkeley: University of California Press.

Ram, K. (1992a). Modernist anthropology and the construction of Indian identity. *Meanjin, 51*(3), 589–614.

Ram, K. (1992b). *Mukkuvar women: Gender, hegemony, and capitalist transformation in a South Indian fishing community.* New Delhi, India: Kali for Women.

Reinharz, S. (1983). Experiential analysis: A contribution to feminist research. In G. Bowles & R. Klein (Ed.), *Theories of women's studies* (pp. 168–172). London: Routledge & Kegan Paul.

Said, E. (1978). *Orientalism.* London: Routledge & Kegan Paul.

Said, E. (1989). Representing the colonized: Anthropology's interlocutors. *Critical Inquiry, 15,* 205–225.

Salazar, C. (1991). A Third World woman's text: Between the politics of criticism and cultural politics. In S. Cluck & D. Patai (Eds.), *Women's words: The feminist practice of oral history* (pp. 93–106). New York: Routledge.

Sanday, P. (1990). *Fraternity gang rape: Sex, brotherhood, and privilege on campus.* New York: New York University Press.

Seiter, E. (1990). Making distinctions in audience research: Case study of a troubling interview. *Cultural Studies, 4*(1), 61–71.

Seymour, S. (1995). Family structure, marriage, caste, and class: Exploring the linkages in an Indian town. *Indian Journal of Gender Studies, 2*(1), 67–85.

Shome, R. (1998). Caught in the term "post colonial": Why the "post-colonial" still matters. *Critical Studies in Mass Communication, 15,* 203–212.

Spivak, G. (1988). Can the subaltern speak? In C. Nelson & L. Grossberg (Eds.), *Marxism and the interpretation of culture* (pp. 271–313). Urbana: University of Illinois Press.

Sridhar, K. (1977). *The development of English as an elite language in the multilingual context of India.* Unpublished doctoral dissertation, University of Illinois at Urbana-Champaign.

Stacey, J. (1991). Can there be a feminist ethnography? In S. Gluck & D. Patai (Eds.), *Women's words* (pp. 111–119). New York: Routledge.

Stoeltje, B., Fox, C., & Obrys, S. (1999). The self in "fieldwork": A methodological concern. *Journal of American Folklore, 112*(44), 158–182.

Tedlock, B. (1991). From participant observation to the observation of participation: The emergence of narrative ethnography. *Journal of Anthropological Research, 47*(1), 69–94.

Varma, P. (1998). *The great Indian middle-class.* New Delhi, India: Viking Penguin India.

Visweswaran, K. (1994). *Fictions of feminist ethnography.* Minneapolis: University of Minnesota Press.

Weis, L. (1990). *Working class without work.* New York: Routledge.

Wolf, D. (1996). Situating feminist dilemmas in fieldwork. In D. Wolf (Ed.), *Feminist dilemmas in fieldwork* (pp. 1–55). Boulder, CO: Westview.

Wolf, M. (1992). *A thrice told tale: Feminism, postmodernism, and ethnographic responsibility.* Stanford, CA: Stanford University Press.

Conclusion

"Coming at Things Differently":
The Need for Emergent Methods

Our story begins at a small drug rehabilitation center for troubled teenage girls located in Miami, Florida. The number of girls who enter Florida's juvenile justice system because they have committed a violent crime is up 24% from 1992 to 2003, compared with a 2% increase for their male counterparts for this same location and time period (Sheets, 2005, p. B1). Ashley, a Haitian immigrant housed at this center, notes the following:

> A lot of times when you come to a different country you are ashamed of the way people observe you and talk about you—so you say you're from somewhere else. . . . They actually call Haitians "boats."

An innovative arts workshop program sponsored by the Museum of Contemporary Art in Miami has museum researchers and educators going on-site to detention centers where troubled girls like Ashley are housed. The program, known as "Girls Rise!" provides girls with a *new* perspective and set of tools to express their identity issues in a way that is not physically or emotionally destructive to them. At Ashley's detention center, the girls attend four 2-hour workshops that introduce them to the work of contemporary female artists "who have had blows dealt to them and have struggled just to be able to practice art" (Sheets, 2005, p. B7). These artists' personal narratives and artistic expression provide troubled teens with role models and artistic skills as a way to come to terms with their own feelings of oppression, concerns about body image, and ethnic identity as well as their own sexuality. One workshop leader notes, "I don't know if it will change anything they do, but at least they have tools to come at it differently" (Sheets, 2005, p. B7).

Coming at Things Differently

Researchers and practitioners can glean important lessons from this story by thinking outside their traditional "methods/practice box." Emergent methods facilitate coming at things differently. In this case, through the medium of photography and the creation of collages, girls learn to articulate their issues and concerns so they can begin to change their current life situations.

Ashley's remarks at the beginning of this chapter remind us how emergent methods are often driven by necessity. The rates of detention for young girls are climbing, and there is pressure to find new approaches to stem this growth. We can, in fact, think of some emergent methods as forged "on the fly," as a response to an external crisis or concern.

We have also witnessed within many readings in this volume how new research problems require methods that reach across traditional disciplinary boundaries. The trauma that causes girls like Ashley to wind up in a juvenile detention center may only be the beginning of a longer delinquent career in the juvenile and adult justice systems. Traditional forms of data gathering such as a quantitative interview at *one point in time* may not provide researcher and those researched with any insights into understanding Ashley's experiences—her life as a poor female Haitian migrant. Instead, a multidimensional methods approach that crosses traditional disciplinary borders by using methods from the arts and humanities may enable researchers to "get at" Ashley's subjugated experiences. These methods that, in Denzin's words, "trouble[s] the traditional distinctions between science, the humanities, rhetoric, literature, facts, and fictions" (Denzin, 2003, p. 244).

If we were interested in understanding the long-term outcome of the museum-sponsored program in Miami, Florida, on Ashley's life chances and those of other troubled youth, how might we proceed with this research problem? The types of questions we might begin to ask may look something like this:

- In what sense (if any) does the new art program impact the short-term outcome for rehabilitation of troubled youth who attend this program?
- What is the long-term outcome in terms of girls' recidivism rates? Rates of violent crimes after leaving the program?
- What, if any, impact does the program have on troubled girls' sense of empowerment? Do these girls use the tools they are provided with to deal with life issues, such as relationships with their family? Their peers? Their significant others?

Answering the questions we raise here may, in fact, require the use of a variety of methods that are practiced across time: methods that allow us to track, in real time, the experiences of girls over the course of their teenage years and into young adulthood. A *longitudinal research design* consisting of a range of traditional and emergent methods may be needed. Perhaps we might wind up selecting a mix of both qualitative (interviewing) and artistic (use of diaries and drawings), as well as quantitative (to capture rates of detention over time), designs. David Morgan's article (Chapter 8, this volume) provides us with a good beginning for creating mixed models for doing this type of research. It presents *four mixed-methods research designs* based on the sequencing (time ordering) and relative importance (priority) of each method.

The Practice and Writing Up of Emergent Methods: A Methods Lag

Another aspect of emergent methods is that when a breakthrough method is discovered and practiced by researchers, they may not report their use of this method in a formal way—in a research publication, for example. Newly emergent methods may then pass under the radar of mainstream researchers until they are rediscovered. Platt (1996) notes, for example,

> Beatrice Webb used participant observation before "participant observation" had been "invented" as a recognized technique. . . . Selvin . . . showed how Durkheim used analytic strategies which no one had formalized at the time. Lazarsfeld pointed out how Stouffer did novel things which he did not himself label as such, and for which Lazarsfeld received credit. (p. 32)

Some emergent methods quickly disappear, only to be rediscovered decades later emerging in a new discipline and even taking on a different conceptualization. Such is the case of "participant observation":

> "Participant observation" was done in the 1920s but . . . it was not then called that, or given the full significance it later acquired until the 1940s; nor was it seen as clearly distinct from modes of data collection now regarded as quite different. (Platt, 1996, p. 44)

Platt goes on to point out that the early use of the method we know today as *survey research* stressed the social reform aspects and "local community self-improvement" goals of this method. It was not seen primarily as a data collection tool with which to gather large amounts of data to generalize to a large population:

> Surveys were carried out in a limited geographical area; the typical early "survey" collected facts about a town by whatever means came to hand. It had in

common with the later "survey" that it often employed a schedule, though usually one completed by an enumerator, and without questions with a fixed wording to be addressed to individual subjects. It had nothing to do with attitudes, and the jokingly pejorative reference to this sort of activity as "outhouse-counting" was not without foundation. (p. 45)

Methods Are Flexible and Fluid

What we have also learned from looking at the range of emergent methods discussed in this volume is the idea that research methods are not fixed entities but, instead, are flexible and fluid, adaptable and ever changing. Jennifer Platt's (1996) research into the history of American sociological research methods from 1920 to 1960 is one of the few monographs that recognizes the importance of paying attention to the changing character of methods, not viewing them as only derivative of sociological theory. She argues for a shift in the balance of attention from the focus on the *history of sociological theory* to the *history of research methods:*

> The history of sociology has most commonly been written as the history of theoretical ideas. This has sometimes included methodological ideas, treated at an abstract and philosophical level, but has seldom given attention to practical research methods or, indeed, to empirical research. The history of theoretical ideas is an interesting and important area, but there has been proportionately too much of it for justice to be done to sociology as a whole. . . . The time has come to shift the balance of historical concern further in the direction of empirical research and ideas about its methods. (Platt, 1996, p.1)

Problems and Resistance to Emergent Methods

The Experience Gap

The range of innovative methods presented in this volume raises concerns about an experience gap in a researcher's understanding and practice of emergent methods. Many researchers were trained in the use of one primary method. Using an innovative method may require them to reach out across their own "methods comfort zone," to think outside their normal everyday methods routine. In this sense, the practice of emergent methods may upend their philosophical, methodological standpoint (see Hesse-Biber & Leavy, 2006). A qualitative researcher who decides to employ experience sampling, for example (see Chapter 6 by Conner & Bliss-Moreau in this volume), may not fully subscribe to positivism and the assumption that there is a "reality" out there waiting to be discovered. Instead, he or she may be more comfortable with an interpretative approach, one that privileges multiple realities. Practicing experience sampling may create a type of philosophical dissonance on the part of this researcher. Can a researcher trained in qualitative methods, with an interpretative philosophy, practice positivism? Can a positivist practice an interpretive method?

Conducting research across disciplinary borders or tweaking or significantly changing one's methods practices also highlights how important it is for researchers to reflect on their own *standpoint* within the research process. *Reflexivity* helps break down the idea that research is the "view from nowhere." Reflecting on the many ways our own agendas impact the research process at all points in our research—from the selection of the research problem to the selection of method and the ways in which we analyze and interpret our findings—is crucial for creating authenticity in the research process.

Funding Gap

It has been argued that funding agencies, both private and governmental, can influence how research methods are practiced and which methods become "the standard" within a given field. Funding agencies may operate within their own "methods funding comfort zone." Alvin Gouldner, in his classic work *The Coming Crisis in Western Sociology* (1971), argues that funding agencies are unduly influencing the types of methods and research problems within the field of sociology toward applied research and what he terms "theoryless" theories (Gouldner, 1971, p. 444).

Yet, an examination of research studies to determine the influence funding of research has on research outcomes is mixed. Platt's (1996) thorough review of much of the research on this topic notes that whereas funding agencies "may tip the balance" somewhat, there remains a series of *additional factors* that contribute to our understanding of what types of projects do get funding beyond the intellectual and economic interests of these agencies (see Platt, 1996).

When one examines the history of sociological methods in America, for example, one can appreciate how much the *practice of methods* is influenced by academic context. Sociology departmental culture is also a factor in determining what research practices come to dominate publications and teaching of methods at the departmental level, especially when faculty involve their students in research projects using specific methods. In fact, within some departments, the practice of certain methods and theoretical points of view comes to label a department as being of a certain school of thought with a specific set of methods practices. For example, the Chicago School of Sociology in the 1920s came to be defined as a place where the practice of qualitative methods dominated and where newly emergent qualitative methods took hold. Yet, as Platt (1996) notes, during this time as well, there were significant quantitative emergent practices carried out by quantitative researchers from the Chicago school. Yet, these innovations were rendered invisible. How so? Platt (1996) argues that quantitative work tends to cross over disciplinary boundaries and therefore may become invisible in departmental history. Citing work by Martin Blumer and Joan Blumer (1981), she notes that

> Blumer and Blumer suggest that one reason is that those committed to quantitative work are much less interested in their history. They see the development of their field as cumulative advance, and so do not legitimate their activities by reference to ancestors. (p. 265)

While it is not the intention of this conclusion to go into depth concerning the social structure within which social research methods emerge and are practiced, it is clear that there are a range of factors within and outside the academy that need to also be considered in our understanding of why some methods emerge and become routinized, whereas others remain on the periphery. What is not often talked about as well is the particular work style that emergent methods may require of the social researcher, especially when the practice of methods crosses disciplinary boundaries, as is the case with many of the articles in this volume.

Work Style and Structure
in the Practice of Emergent Methods

The chapters in this book suggest that the practice of emergent methods may require a restructuring in how researchers go about practicing their trade. Increasingly, "team" projects involving several researchers from across disciplines may become the norm. The readings in this volume underscore the importance of looking beyond our own disciplines to imagine how we might expand our disciplinary visions in order to rerevision, a process that Laurel Richardson calls "de-disciplining" ourselves as researchers.

Many of the chapters in this book also reveal the "personal" side of working with an emergent method. Laurel Richardson provides perhaps the most vivid account of the personal costs and triumphs of working with unconventional methods within a discipline that is at times hostile to new ways of thinking and practicing one's trade. As these chapters attest, working with emergent tools means working sometimes at the margins of our disciplines, sometimes working between disciplines, and sometimes even bridging the qualitative-quantitative divide. There is sometimes a personal cost of practicing emergent methods, yet the potential rewards to our research and ourselves are vast.

We end this volume by offering some tips from those who have worked at the borders of multiple disciplines and who have sought to integrate ideas from multiple disciplinary sites. Klein's (1990) research into the personality characteristics associated with interdisciplinarians suggests that they are high on "reliability, flexibility, patience, resilience, sensitivity to others, risk- taking, a thick skin, and a preference for diversity and new social roles" (p. 182). Interdisciplinarity requires good communication skills (good teamwork) among colleagues from different disciplines and, within the classroom setting, between faculty and students. Klein notes that the wider the gap between disciplines and the number of disciplines involved, the wider the potential communication gaps (p. 183).

The authors of this volume push on the boundaries of traditional knowledge building by venturing out of their methods routine and using their creativity, intellect, and social skills to create new tools or refashion old ones in the service of answering complex questions that arise from a range of newly emerging theoretical perspectives as well as responding to immediate problems within their environment. We hope that this volume will encourage other researchers to begin to create accounts of their own emergent methods practices and histories, so we can make visible and build on the range of emergent methods that reside within and across the disciplines.

References

Blumer, M., & Blumer, J. (1981). Philanthropy and social science in the 1920s: Beardsley Ruml and the Laura Spelman Rockefeller Memorial, 1922–29. *Minerva, 19,* 347–407.

Denzin, N. (2003). Reading and writing performance. *Qualitative Research, 3*(2), 243–268.

Gouldner, A. W. (1971). *The coming crisis in Western sociology.* London: Heinemann.

Hesse-Biber, S., & Leavy, P. (2006). *The practice of qualitative research.* Thousand Oaks, CA: Sage.

Klein, J. T. (1990). *Interdisciplinarity: History, theory and practice.* Detroit, MI: Wayne State University Press.

Platt, J. (1996). *A history of sociological research methods in America: 1920–1960.* Cambridge, UK: Cambridge University Press.

Sheets, H. M. (2005, June). Using art to build pride: Artists become role models in a program for troubled girls. *New York Times,* B1, B7.

Index

Aaker, D. A., 17
Abu-Lughod, L., 338, 339, 340, 352,
    356, 363
Access, 17
    face-to-face negotiation, 18
    research ethics and, 18
    to documents, 15
    to materials, 15
    to people, 15
    to settings, 15
    See also Access work; Élite
        settings, accessing
Access work, 15–16, 17
    high-tech élite and, 21
    inside knowledge and, 15
    reflexive approach, 21
    STS, 15
    studying-up and, 16
    See also Élite settings, accessing
Action researchers, 277
Active qualitative research methods,
    xvi. See also Creative qualitative
    research methods
Activity, collecting data to analyze,
    59–60, 83
Actor-networks, construction of, 14
Adair, E. G., 173
Adams, P. C., 148
Affleck, G., 112, 328
Agger, B., 239
Ahmad, A., 359
Aitken, S., 132, 143, 145
Albright, A. C., 194, 196, 199
Alcoff, L., 317, 328
Alexander, B. K., 188
Alibrandi, M., 146

Allison, D., 214
Almeida, D. M., 113
Alonso Quecuty, M. L., 28
Althusser, L., 139
Altorki, S., 339, 352
Analytic control, 61, 64–65, 71, 76
Andersen, T., 25
Anderson, E., 62
Anderson, H., 25
Anderson, K., 21, 25, 141
Ang, I., 355, 365, 367
Anggal, W., 99, 103
Angrosino, M. V., 279, 281
Anzuldua, G., 188
Argyris, D. E., 256
Armeli, S., 112
Armstrong, M. P., 143
Aron, L., 254
Atkinson, J. M., 64
Atkinson, P., 16, 17, 61, 237, 239
ATLAS.ti, 146
Attanucci, J., 263
Audience catharsis, staged, 246
Audience responses, collective, 246
Audio capture, 55
Autobiographical writing:
    as feminist practice, 10
Autoethnographic performance, xxi,
    xxii, xxiii, 183–184, 186, 198, 206
    dialogic performance in,
        186, 193, 194
    performativity in, 186, 193, 196
    personally/politically emancipatory
        potential of, 186, 198–200
    possible moral/ethical pitfalls, 194
    shadowed body in, 203–204

Autoethnographic texts, xxii-xxiii,
    186, 189, 190
  interpreting, 190
Autoethnographic writing, 188
Autoethnography, xxii, xxiii, xxvii,
    187–189, 201, 238
  as method of scholarly
    praxis, 186, 187
  effective, 190–192
Ayres, L., 169

Babb, S., 43
Bacon, W., 206
Bad news, analysis of reactions to, 81
Bakhtin, M., 238
Balabanis, M., 115
Bane, M., 216
Baol, A., 238
Barnes, S., 141
Barnes, T., 135, 150
Barrett, D. J., 116, 121
Barrett, L. F., 113, 116, 120, 121
Barthes, R., 137
Basu, A., 359
Baugh, J., 66
Bauman, L. J., 173
Bauman, R., 188
Baxter, L. A., 185
Beach, W. A., 71
Beal, D. J., 112
Beck, A. L., 111
Becker, H. S., 19
Behar, R., 187, 189, 191, 278,
    338, 339
Bennett, R. J., 136
Berg, L. D., 143
Berger, C. F., 110
Berger, J., 138
Berger, L. P., 278, 286
Berglund, P., 111
Bergmann, J. R., 78
Berkhof, H., 112
Berman, H., 166, 167
Bernstein, B., 239
Beteille, A., 359
Bias, 49
Billig, M., 75
Bingham, R., 318
Bird, S. T., 166, 167

Blair, C., 185
Blatner, A., 104
Bliss-Moreau, E., 116, 120
Blumer, H., 64
Blumer, J., 380
Blumer, M., 380
Blunt, A., 139, 140
Bluntness strategy, 56, 57, 81–82
Bochner, A. P., 188, 189, 240,
    241, 246, 280, 296
Boden, D., 64
Body, deconstructive reading of,
    xix-xxi, xxix
  exposing pregnant, 215–217
  inscriptive theory, 215
  lived body theory, 215
  social codes and, 216
  See also Gendered body; Pregnant
    teenagers, body and; Social
    body; Teen pregnancy; Teen
    pregnancy intervention
    programs
Boedy, D. L., 100
Bogdan, R., 19
Bolak, H., 339, 340, 345, 352
Bolger, N., 110, 113, 116,
    117, 122, 124
Bondi, L., 134, 135, 138, 140
Booth, T., 21
Booth, W., 21
Borda, O. F., 318
Bordo, S., xix, 147
Borkan, J. M., 175
Borland, K., 255
Bosk, C. L., 18
Bosker, R., 120
Boucher, C., xxii, xxiii
Bourdieu, P., 63, 65
Boyd, E., 66
Bradburn, N. M., 13, 17, 19
Brannen, J., 166, 167
Brannen, P., 18, 35
Breakwell, G. M., 13, 17, 21
Breathing, 66
Breitmayer, B. J., 169
Brenner, M. C., 13, 17, 20
Breuer, J., 254
Brewer, J., 166, 167
Broadhead, R., 17

Brochmann, J., 21
Broderick, J. E., 112, 117
Broude, N., 140
Brown, J., 13, 17, 20
Brown, J. R., 185
Brown, K. W., 111
Brown, L. M., 255, 257, 254, 255,
    256, 259, 263, 268
Brown, M., 142
Brown, P., 318
Bruner, J., 254
Bryk, A. S., 124
Bryman, A., 166, 167
Bryson, N., 137
Buber, M., 276
Burawoy, M., 63
Burdell, P. A., 215, 217, 223, 225, 227
Burgess, R. G., 13
Burke, K., 281
Burrough, P. A., 132
Burton, L., 146
Busia, A. P. A., 188
Butler, J., 147, 214, 277, 297
Butler, R., 147
Butz, D., 143
Bylsma, W. H., 322

Cade, B. W., 101
Calvin, T., ix
Cameron, J. E., 317
Campbell, D. T., 168
Campbell, J., 166, 167
Campos, L., 28
Cannel, C., 17, 19, 26, 35
Canter, D., 13, 17, 20
Caracelli, V. J., 168, 169, 170
Carey, J., 165
Carlin, S., 134, 143, 144
Carney, M. A., 112
Carruthers, B., 45
Cartographic narratives,
    using qualitative data to
    construct, 145–146
Caserta, M., 174
Case studies, 175
    creative research methods in, 106
Cash, Jr., W. B., 13, 17
Cassell, J., 14, 18
Castells, M., 16, 21, 23, 36

Catalytic validity, 277–278
Center for Population, 216
Chandler, J., 17
Chang, K., 141
Charmaz, K., 71, 80
Cheeseman, P., 235
Cherry, K., 278, 279
Chesla, C. A., 169
Chibber, V., 45
Chicago School of Sociology,
    19, 22, 379–380
Chrisman, N., 136
Christians, C. G., 280
Cicourel, A. V., 63, 64, 68
Cixous, H., 213
Clark, L. A., 111
Clark, R. E., 73, 74, 75
Clayman, S. E., 63, 66
Clifford, J., 16, 187, 338
Clore, G. L., 113
Clough, P. T., 61
Coding, 55
Coffey, A., 239
Cognitive interviews, 28–29
Cohen, L. L., 317, 318, 322
Cohn, C., 18
Cole, E., 366
Cole, S., 339, 362
Coleman, S., 13, 17, 18, 25
Collins, P. H., 277
Collins, R. L., 116
Communities of practice, 63
Complementarity, 169, 177.
    See also Complementary
    assistance, research designs
    based on
Complementary assistance, research
    designs based on, 170–175
    follow-up qualitative, 172,
        174–175, 176
    follow-up quantitative,
        172, 175, 176
    preliminary qualitative,
        172, 173, 176
    preliminary quantitative,
        172, 174, 176
    priority decision, 170–171
    sequence decision, 170, 171
    See also Priority-Sequence Model

Computerized sampling methods, 116–117
Confer, W. N., 101
Confidentiality, friendship as method and, 290
Congdon, R., 124
Conner, T., 116, 120
Conquergood, D., 187, 188, 189, 194, 203, 205
Consciousness raising, daily diary research and, 327
Constantine, L. L., 98, 99
Content analysis, 44, 46–47, 140
coding schemes, 47
Contextualization cues, 63
Conversation analysis, 55, 56, 58, 59, 61, 62, 83
building additional affinities between ethnography and, 69–71
constraining use of ethnography, 71–73
ethnographer critique of, 61
ethnography and, 61, 67, 81–82, 83
repair, 65
See also Conversation analysis, contextual critique of
Conversation analysis, contextual critique of, 62–64
response to, 64–67
See also Analytic control; Data loss
Conversation analysts, ethnographers and, xv-xvi
Cook, J. A., 277
Cook, T. D., 166, 167
Cooney, N. L., 115
Cope, M., 134
Coppersmith, E., 99
Corbin, J., 257, 325
Corporeality theory, ix, xiii, xix
feminist, 147
inscribed body, xix-xx
lived body, xix, xx, 215
pregnant body and, 215, 228
Corsaro, W. A., 61, 62, 64, 71
Cosgrove, D., 137
Cotterill, P., 21
Couclelis, H., 132
Couillard, M., 363
Coulthard, M., 63

Court, G., 147
Covert research ethics, 19
Crabtree, B. F., 13, 17, 165, 166, 167, 175
Craig, W. J., 132, 136
Crampton, J., 142
Crawford, L., 188
Crawford, M. E., 317
Creative qualitative research methods, 95–106
art and drawing, 95, 96, 99–101, 105
limitations, 105
metaphors, 95, 96, 101
participatory research philosophy and, 97
photography and videography, 95, 96, 97, 103, 105
role-playing, 95, 104
sculpting, 95, 96, 98–99, 105
timelines, 95, 96, 102–103
writing exercises, 95, 96, 101–102
Creswell, J. W., 166, 167, 170
Critical cartography, 139
Critical discourse analysis, 75
Critical ethnodrama, 241. See also Ethnodrama
Critical theory, ix, 196
Csikszentmihalyi, I. S., 111
Csikszentmihalyi, M., 110, 111, 116, 117
Cultural stories, 2
Cultural theories, 133
Curry, M., 135, 138, 142
Cusick, T., 216
Cyberpower, 14
Czarniawska-Joerges, B., 296

Dailey, S., 188
Daily diary research, xxvii-xxviii, 313–315, 329
analysis strategies, 324, 325–326
as feminist research, 317–319, 329
as qualitative research, 315–317
coding strategies, 324–325
community application, 327
defining, 315
descriptive, 324, 325

diary attention to context and, 316–317
diary entry schedule and, 317
diary format, 324
diary structure and, 316
ethical issues, 327–328
event sampling, 321
inferential theory testing, 324, 325–326, 327
limitations, 328–329
purposes, 324
research application, 326–327
sample for African Americans, 330–332
theory building, 324, 325, 327
time sampling, 321
See also Daily diary research methodology; Daily diary research procedure; Diary studies
Daily diary research methodology, 316, 319–321
design, 321–322
participant attrition, 320–321
participant recruitment, 320
participants, 319–321
See also Daily diary research procedure
Daily diary research procedure, 322–324
closing session, 322, 323–324
diary-keeping phase, 322, 323
introduction, 322–323
Darling, R. B., 57, 73
Data loss, 61, 65–67, 71, 76
Daus, C. S., 112
Davis, A., 110, 116, 117, 124
Davis, A. Y., 214
Davis, K., 196
Debold, E., 259
de Certeau, M., 137, 146
De-disciplining, researchers, xxx, 2–3, 10. *See also* Pleated text; Writing-stories
de Lauretis, T., 214
Delespaul, P., 111, 117, 120
Denmark, F., 317, 318
Denzin, N. K., x, xi, 16, 61, 168, 187, 188, 189, 190, 191, 199, 206, 237, 238, 240, 244, 276, 277, 376

Derrida, J., 150, 308
Detwiler, J., 146
Deutsche, R., 138
Devereux, 189
DeVries, H., 174
de Vries, M. W., 111, 112, 116, 117
Dexter, L. A., 14, 18
Diaries, research. *See* Daily diary research
Diary methods, 110
Diary studies, 313–314, 316
type of data attained from, 319
See also Daily diary research
Diaz, G., 240
Diener, E., 111, 115
Digerati, 21
Dijkman-Caes, C., 117
Dijkstra, M., 174
Dimond, M., 174
Dingwall, R., 59
Diprose, R., 214, 216
Discourse analysis, 140
Discovery research, 267. *See also* *Listening Guide* method
Discrimination experiences, daily diary research and:
ableism, 314
heterosexism, 314
majority-group religious-based prejudice, 315
minority-group religious-based prejudice, 314–315
racism, 314
sexism, 314
sizeism, 314, 315
Dixon, D. P., 134
Doane, M. A., 140
Documentary theatres, 237
Domosh, M., 134, 135, 138, 140
Dorling, D., 139, 148
Doucet, A., 255, 257
Douglas, J. D., 22
Downey, G., 113
Drew, P., 58, 64, 68
Duhl, B., 98
Duhl, F., 98, 103
Dumont, J., xxii
Duncan, J. S., 137
Duncan, N. G., 137, 147

Duneier, M., 70
Duranti, A., 61, 62, 63, 67

Eadie, D., 174
Ecological momentary
    assessment, 110–111
Economists, sociologist among. *See*
    Historical methods, negotiating;
    Historical sociologists; Historical
    sociology; Positionality;
    Subjectivity
Edmunds, D., 139
Egenhofer, M. J., 132
Eid, M., 111
Élite, high-tech, xiv, 16, 21, 35
Élite, sociologists accessing high tech.
    See Élite, high-tech; Élite interview
    process; Élite interviews; Élite oral
    history; Élites; Élite settings,
    accessing; Élite studies
Élite interview process, 13, 16,
    17–21, 50
Élite interviews, 13, 17–21. *See also*
    Interview process; Interviews
Élite oral history, 17, 20
Élites, xiv, 14
    economic, xiv-xv
    influence on society, 16
    online, 14
    typology, 17–18
    versus experts, 29
    See also Élite interview process;
        Élite interviews; Élite studies
Élite settings, accessing, 29–31
    borrowing power from powerful,
        31–33
    interview preparation, 29
Élite studies, 13, 15, 18, 19
    altruism issues, 15
    authority issues, 15
    domination issues, 15
    exchange issues, 15
    power issues, 15
    reciprocity issues, 15
Élite women:
    discourses of othering, 361
    doing fieldwork among, 354, 360
Ellis, C., xxii, 188, 189, 191, 240, 241,
    246, 278, 280, 289, 296

El-Solh, C., 345
Elwood, S., 132, 145
Embodied methodological praxis. *See*
    Autoethnographic performance;
    Autoethnographic texts;
    Autoethnographic writing;
    Autoethnography; Embodied
    practice; Embodied theory;
    Embodied writing
Embodied practice, 203
Embodied theory, 196
Embodied writing, 204, 205
Emergent research methods, xi-xiii,
    xv-xix, xxx, 124
    experience gap as problem
        with, 378–379
    funding gap as problem
        with, 379–380
    lag between writing up of and
        practice of, 377–378
    need for, 375–381
    work style/structure in practice
        of, 380–381
    *See also specific emergent research
        methods;* Ethnographic research,
        emergent methods in
Emerson, R. M., 59, 62, 76
Emotional enlightenment, 246
Empiricism, 134
Enfleshed knowledge, xx, 194, 203
Enfleshed methodology, 205
Engberg, J. B., 112
England, K., 339
England, K. V. L., 133
Episodic knowledge, 113–114
Epskamp, K., 240
Epston, D., 25
Erickson, F., 61
Escobar, A., 363
Etaugh, C., 318
Ethnodrama, xxiii-xxiv, xxix, 5–7,
    236, 241, 245, 247
    dialogic interactions, 238
    examples, 239–240
    problems, 247–249
    vraisemblance, 237
    See also Ethnodramas;
        Ethnodramatic research;
        Ethnographic performances

Ethnodramas, 236
  health agencies and,
    236–237, 239–240
  See also Ethnodrama; Ethnographic
    performances
Ethnodramatic research, xxiii–xiv, 235
Ethnodramatic script, 238
Ethnographers, 49
Ethnographic abstraction, 74–76
Ethnographic audience studies, 339
  politics of representation in, 340
Ethnographic data, 83
Ethnographic dialogue, 281
Ethnographic dramatic narrative, 240
  parody as social analysis in, 237
Ethnographic naturalism, 62
Ethnographic performances,
    236, 238, 241
  interactive, 238
  research-based, 246
Ethnographic semiotics, 236
Ethnography, xiii–xv, xxiii, xxv,
    xxix, 49, 55–56, 58, 59, 61,
    62–63, 66, 83
  building additional affinities
    between conversation analysis
    and, 69–71
  conversation analysis and,
    61, 67, 81–82, 83
  GIS use in, 146
  See also Ethnography, contemporary
    trends in; Ethnography,
    conversation analyst uses of
Ethnography, contemporary trends
    in, 240–243
  biography, 240
  interpretive interactionism, 240, 241
  literary narrative, 244
  performance, 244
  poetry, 240, 244, 246
Ethnography, conversation analyst
    uses of, 67–69
  describing settings and identities, 67
  explaining "curious" patterns prior
    sequential analysis may reveal,
    67, 68–69
  explicating unfamiliar
    terms/phrases/courses of
    action, 67–68

See also Limited affinity,
    conversation analysis-
    ethnography
Ethnography of speaking tradition, 64
Ethnomethodological social
    constructionism, 62
Ethnomethodology, 20, 58, 70
Event-sampling methods, 110
Example questions for illustration, 33
Experience questions, 33
Experience sampling methods, xvi–xvii,
    109–110, 124, 378–379
  correlational nature, 114
  disadvantages in using, xvii, 114–116
  for study of emotional
    experience, 111
  history of, 110–111
  in business-related fields, 112
  in clinical research, 111
  in health-related research, 112
  in natural settings, 109, 112–113
  in real time, 110, 113–114
  in sociology, 112
  measurement reactivity, 114–115
  on repeated time occasions, 110
  resource-intensive, 114, 124
  rationale for using, 112–114, 124
  use of, 111–112
  See also Experience sampling
    methods study, designing;
    Naturalistic sampling methods
Experience sampling methods data:
  analyzing, 124
  cleaning, 123–124
  preparing, 123
Experience sampling methods
    study, designing, 116–122
  assessing resources, 116
  choosing software and
    equipment, 120–121
  determining sampling protocol/
    parameters, 118–120
Experience sampling methods
    study, implementing,
    122–124
  ensuring compliance with study
    protocol, 122, 123
  maintaining integrity of equipment,
    122, 123

maintaining participant motivation,
122–123
recruiting participants, 122
Experience Sampling Program, 121
Experimental designs, 173
Eyssell, K. M., 113

Faimberg, H., 21, 26, 35
Fairbairn, D., 139
Fairbairn, W. R. D., 254
Fairclough, N., 75
Falconer-Al-Hindi, K., 133, 142
False starts, 66
Families, qualitative research on.
See Creative qualitative research
methods
Fawzi El-Solh, C., 339, 352
Fay, B., 228
Feagin, J. R., 317
Feldman, L. A., 111
Felt-sensing, 205
Feminism, xiii, xxvi, xxvii, 306,
309, 345, 365
Feminist cartography, 139
contemporary, 146
Feminist empiricism, daily diary
research and, 318–319
Feminist ethnography, xxix
recent definitions of, 362–363
See also Postcolonial feminist
ethnography
Feminist geographers, common
concerns of, 133–134
Feminist geographies of
difference, 133, 135
Feminist geography/geographic
research, xvii–xix, 133, 135
countermaps in, xviii
ethical/privacy issues with
GIS methods,
142–143, 151
GIS and, 133–134, 141–143
supporting women's activism
through, 144–145
women's everyday lives and,
143–144
See also Geographic information
systems (GIS)

Feminist media ethnography, xviii–xvix,
338, 363, 365–366. See also
Feminist media ethnography in
India, postcolonial
Feminist media ethnography in India,
postcolonial, 337–342, 363–368
empathy/dilemmas interviewing
women, 337, 352–363
failed interviews, 337, 345–352
findings, 338–339
pre-fieldwork reflections, 342–344
primary research questions, 338
researcher returning home as
feminist, 344–345
See also Self-reflexivity
Feminist methodology, 20
Feminist poststructuralism, xiv, 4
Feminist research:
daily diary research as, 317–319, 329
emergent practices, xxvi–xxx
See also Daily diary research,
Feminist media ethnography;
Feminist media ethnography in
India, postcolonial; Writing-in-
response
Feminist standpoint theory, ix, 277
daily diary research and, 317–318
Feminist theory, xxix, 134
body in, xix, 213, 215
class identities in, 361
friendship as method and, 277
See also Feminist standpoint theory
Feminist visualization, xvii–xviii, 133,
139, 151. See also Feminist
geographic research; Feminist
geographies of difference; Feminist
geography/geographic research;
Geographic information systems
(GIS)
Ferguson, J., 367
Ferguson, M. J., 317, 322
Field study, 59, 60, 68
Fieldwork, xxv, xxvi, 18, 35, 176, 186,
274, 278, 280, 285–286, 289
autoethnography, 188
friendship as, 276
informant relationship, 26
relationships, 279

Fife-Schaw, C., 13, 17, 21
Finch, J., 20
Fine, E. C., 188
Fine, G. A., 275
Fine, M., 219, 225, 255, 277, 328, 362
Fischer, M. M. J., 187
Fish, S., 355
Fiske, D. W., 168
Fiske, S. T., 328
Fitzgerald, D. C., 322
Flaherty, M. G., 188
Fleeson, W., 111
Flexibility in data analysis, 114
Flow, 111, 205
Focus groups, 173, 174, 175
  creative research methods in, 106
  daily diary research and,
    313, 315, 323, 327
Fog, J., 13, 17, 25
Fonow, M. M., 277
Forecasting strategy, 56, 57
Foucault, M., xix, 137, 214
Fowler, Jr., F. J., 13, 17
Fox, C., 339, 367
Fox, D., 318
Fox, K., 240
Frank, A. U., 132
Frankel, R., 179
Franz, C., 318
Fredrickson, B. L., 113
Freire, P., 282
Freksa, C., 132
Fretz, R. I., 59, 62, 76
Freud, S., xxv, 254
Friedman, A., 298
Friedman, N. L., 18
Friendship:
  definition, 274–275
  emotional resources, 275
  identity resources, 275
  See also Friendship as research
    method
Friendship as research method,
  xxv-xxvi, xxix, 274, 278–280,
  290–291
  contexts of friendship, 278, 279
  ethics of friendship, xxvi, 278,
    279–280

friendship as fieldwork and, 276
issues for participants to consider,
  288–290
issues for researcher to consider,
  285–288, 291
pace of friendship, 278–279
practices of friendship, 278
qualitative research foundations,
  276–278
strengths for participants, 282–284
strengths for researcher, 281–282
Fritzsche, B. A., 111
Fultz, N. F., 173

Gable, S. L., 110, 113, 114,
  116, 118, 120, 122, 124
Galaskiewicz, J., 18, 35
Game, A., 221
Gamson, J., 277
Gamson, W. A., 47
Ganguly, K., 364
Gardner, H., 35
Garfinkel, H., 16, 20, 58, 67
Garr, D. R., 174, 175
Garrard, M. D., 140
Gaskell, J., 214
Gatekeepers, 17, 202
Gatens, M., 204
Gaylord, J., 115
Geertz, C., 184, 186, 187, 191,
  201, 204, 254, 276
Gehring, T. M., 98
Gendered body, 214
Gender performance. See Personal
  electronic correspondence as
  reflexive strategy; Writing-in-
  response
Geographic information systems
  (GIS), 131–151
  alternate practices, 137
  feminist critiques of science
    and, 134–137
  feminist critiques of vision
    and, 137–141
  limitations, 132
  limitations in feminist research,
    142, 147, 150, 151
  negative impacts on society, 132

practicing reflexivity when using,
140, 151
software, 142
view as masculinist technology, 135
See also Feminist
geography/geographic research
Geographies of the body, 133
Gergen, M., 317
Getting in, 17
Ghose, R., 132, 145
Gibbs, J., 317
Gibson-Graham, J. K., 133, 143
Giddens, A., 16
Gilbert, M., 339
Gilbert, M. R., 133
Gilbert, N., 102
Gilboe-Ford, M., 166, 167
Gill, V. T., 59
Gilligan, C., 254, 255, 256, 257,
258, 259, 263, 254
Gillmore, M. R., 115
Gingrich-Philbrook, C., 188, 192
Girls Rise! Program, 375
Gladwell, M., 21
Glaser, B. G., 19, 60, 74, 75, 81, 325
Glasgow, J., 132
Glick, P., 328
Gluck, S. B., 345
Goering, P. N., 165
Goffman, E., 16, 20, 63
Gold, A., 356
Goldman, L., 96
Goldstein, I. B., 112
Goleman, D., 35
Gollnisch, G., 116
Goodall, Jr., H. L., 188, 189,
191, 201, 204
Goodchild, M. F., 132
Goodman, R. M., 166, 167
Goodwin, C., 63, 78
Goodwin, M. H., 61, 71
Gordon, D., 338, 339
Gordon, D. A., 187
Goss, J., 134, 135, 138
Gould, M. S., 249
Gouldner, A. W., 379
Graef, R., 111
Graham, S., 132

Graham, W. F., 168, 169, 170
Grand-tour questions, 26, 33
Granovetter, M., 21
Greatbatch, D., 64
Green, A. S., 117, 122
Greenberg, I. A., 104
Greene, J. C., 168, 169, 170
Gregory, D., 135, 137, 142, 148
Gregson, N., 147
Grewal, I., 365
Grimshaw, A., 61, 63, 65
Grønning, T., 18
Grosz, E., xix, xx, 137, 138, 147,
213, 214, 215, 228
Grounded theory, 19–20, 325
coding, 325
Guba, E. G., 29, 97, 98, 166, 167
Gubrium, J. F., 17, 61, 62, 69, 70, 71
Guelke, J. K., 140
Gumperz, J. J., 61, 63, 66
Gunther, O., 132
Gupta, A., 367
Gusterson, H., 18

Haffner, H., 249
Hägerstrand, T., 148
Hagevik, R., 146
Hale, S., 361
Hall, S., 362
Hammersley, M., 16, 17
Hammond, S., 13, 17, 21
Hancock, M., 359, 365
Haney, L., 219
Hanks, W. F., 63
Hannah, M., 148
Hannerz, U., 16
Hanson, P., 148
Hanson, S., 132, 133, 134, 143, 144,
148, 150
Haraway, D., 131, 133, 134, 135,
137, 138, 139, 151, 328
Haraway, D. J., 229
Harding, S., ix, 133, 134, 135, 138,
277, 317, 318, 360, 361
Harlan, O. 132
Harley, J. B., 139
Harrington, J. W., 132
Harris, T., 132, 136, 145, 146

Harstock, N., 317
Hartway, J., 115
Harvey, D., 136, 138
Hatfield, E., 80
Health research, mixed-method,
    165–166, 173, 175. *See also*
    Qualitative research methods,
    combining quantitative methods
    and
Heath, C., 71
Heilbrun, C., 2
Hektner, J., 116
Helman, S., 298
Henriques, J., 319
Hepworth, J. T., 114
Heritage, J., 58, 62, 64, 66, 68, 70
Hermeneutics, 276
Herring, J. R., 132
Hertz, R., 13, 17
Herzog, A. R., 173
Heshusius, L., 166, 167
Hesitations, 66
Hess, D., 15
Hesse-Biber, S., 378
Hik, J., 299
Hindmarsh, J., 71
Hiromi, O., 112
Hirtle, S. C., 132
Historical methods, negotiating, 44–49.
    See also Positionality; Subjectivity
Historical sociologists, 45, 52. *See also*
    Historical methods, negotiating;
    Positionality
Historical sociology, 44–45
Hoffmann, J. E., 18, 25, 31, 36
Holleran, A., 274
Hollway, C., 319
Holstein, J. A., 17, 61, 62, 69, 70
hooks, b., 214
Hoppe, M. J., 115
Hopper, R., 61
Hormuth, S. E., 110
Hough, E. E., 174
Houtkoop-Steenstra, H., 63
Hromi, A., 112
Huberman, A. M., 170
Huffman, N. H., 139
Hufford, M. R., 115, 117

Hug, R., 112
Hughes, K., 174
Human communicative
    consensus/competence, 239
Human experience, sampling in
    naturalistic settings. *See* Experience
    sampling methods; Experience
    sampling methods data;
    Experience sampling methods
    study, designing; Experience
    sampling methods study,
    implementing; Experience
    Sampling Program
Hunter, A., 166, 167
Hurewitz, A., 112
Hurlburt, R. T., 110
Hutchinson, S. A., 282
Hyers, L. L., 317, 318, 322
Hymes, D., 64

Idiographic analyses, 114
iESP, 121
Imber, J. B., 13, 17
In-depth interviews, xxv, xxvi,
    20, 21, 313
Indexical expressions, 58, 69, 83
Informed consent, friendship as method
    and, 290
Informing interview, 71, 72–73
Interaction analysis, 20
Interactive interviewing, friendship as
    method and, 278
Interpretive communities, 355
Interpretivism, 276, 277
Intersubjectivity, xxvi, 67
Interview error, 19
Interview guide, 19
Interview methods, qualitative, 20
Interview process, 33–35
    follow-up, 33, 34
    grand tour, 33, 35
    opening, 33, 34
Interviews, 55, 58, 59, 81, 83, 327
    creative research methods in, 106
    with key insiders, 43
    See also specific types of interviews;
        Interviews as social science
        methodology

Interviews as social science
    methodology, 16–21
    empiricist survey research, 19
    qualitative research, 19
    See also Élite interview process; Élite
        interviews; Interviews
Investigative inquiry, 14, 22, 27–29,
    30, 33, 36
    detailed inquiry, 28
    sociologist as inquiry, 27
    See also Cognitive interviews
I poems, 259–262, 263, 266. See also
    Listening Guide method
Irigaray, L., 134, 137
Ismail, M., 146

Jack, D. C., 21, 25, 255, 257, 263
Jackall, R., 18
Jackson, M., 276
James, S. M., 188
Jameson, F., 137
Jamner, L. D., 112
Jay, M., 137
Jefferson, G., 60, 65, 75
Jerkins, R. G., 174, 175
Jerome, J., 188
Jiang, H., 141, 143
Jimerson, J. B., 61
John, M., 345
Johnson, J., 15, 17, 25, 35, 36
Johnston, D. K., 263
Johnston, K. E., 316, 317, 322, 323
Johnston, R. J., 132
Jones, J. L., 188
Jones, J. P., III, 133
Jones III, J. P., 134
Jordan, T., 14
Jorgensen, D. L., 17, 33
Joshi, R., 359
Josselson, R., 254
Journalistic inquiry, 14, 22–25,
    29, 30, 33, 34, 36
    key informant approach, 23
Juluri, V., 340, 367
Juster, F. T., 112

Kacer, B., 174
Kaell, A. T., 112
Kahn, R. L., 17, 19, 26, 35

Kahneman, D., 113, 115
Kamarck, T. W., 112
Kantor, D., 98
Kaplan, C., 365
Kaschub, C., 116, 120
Kashdan, T. B., 116
Kashy, D. A., 124
Kasimatis, M., 111
Katz, J., 81, 115
Kaufmann, F., 64
Kaul, H., 21, 25
Kavoori, A., 367
Kebbel, M. R., 29
Keller, E. F., 135, 257
Kemp, K. D., 132
Kenny, D. A., 124
Key informants, 23
Khuankaew, O., 279
Kiesinger, C. E., 278, 279, 282
Kiesinger, C. K., 296
King, G., 249
Kinnell, A. M. K., 68
Kirschbaum, C., 112
Klein, J. T., 381
Klein, R., 360
Kliment, A., 112
Klinger, E., 110
Klonoff, E. A., 317
Knafl, K. A., 169
Knorr-Cetina, K., 15, 16, 18
Knowledge building, ix, xiii, xiv,
    xxiv, xxx, 381
    in diary research, xxviii
    in geographic research, xvii
    political nature of, xii
    "speaking-in-response" method
        of, xxvii
Kobayashi, A., 139, 339
Kok, G., 174
Kominiak, T., 134, 143, 144
Kopp, R. R., 101
Krishna, S., 139
Kristeva, J., 308, 310
Kruger, J., 115
Kuhn, T., xi
Kumar, N., 342, 345, 363, 364, 365
Kwan, M. P., 132, 134, 140, 143, 148,
    149, 151
Kwiatkowska, H. Y., 100

LaBeff, E. E., 73, 74, 75
Labov, W., 66
Lake, R. W., 135
Lal, J., 341, 344, 345, 348, 366
Lalonde, R. N., 317
Landrine, H., 317
Langdale, C. H., 263
Langellier, K., 188, 196, 198
Laplanche, J., 308
Laqueur, T., 301
Larsen, R. J., 111, 113
Larson, R. W., 110, 111, 113, 117
Lather, P., 277
Latour, B., 25, 32, 136
Laurenceau, J. P., 113
Laurie, H., 178
Lave, J., 63
Lavin, D., 66, 71
Laws, G., 147, 148
Lawson, V., 133, 134, 136, 142
Lawther, S., 174
Lazarsfeld, P. F., 19, 179
Leavy, P., 378
Lebo, K., 116, 120
Lee, J., 148
Lee, R. M., 17, 18, 19, 20, 25
Leeka, J., 111
Lefebvre, H., 137, 142
Leigh, B. C., 115
Leitner, H., 132, 145
Lengel, L., 339
Lesko, N., 215, 217, 223, 224
Leveton, E., 104
Levinson, S. C., 58, 61
Lewis, F. M., 174
Liddle, J., 359
Lie, M., 35
Liebow, E., 62
Lieten, G. K., 359
Light, J., 139
Limited affinity, conversation
     analysis-ethnography, 62, 66,
     67–69, 71, 81–82, 83
Limited ethnographic descriptions, 76
Lincoln, Y. S., xi, 16, 97, 98, 166, 167,
     277
Lindner, R., 22
Lindström, A., 70
Lipton, H. L., 59, 74

Listening Guide method, xxiv-xxv,
     253–257, 267–268
  composing analysis, 266–267
  conceptually clustered matrices
     and, 268
  discovery research and, 267
  I poems, 259–262, 266
  listening for contrapuntal voices,
     262–266
  listening for plot, 257–259, 266
  narrative summaries and, 268
  origins of, 254–255
Literature reviews, 20
Litotes, 78
Litt, M. D., 115
Lloyd, R., 132
Lockridge, E., 237
Lofland, J., 17, 19, 20, 31, 74
Lofland, L. H., 17, 19, 20, 31
Longhurst, R., 133, 147
Longitudinal ethnography, 71
Longitudinal research design, 377
Luff, P., 71
Lund, D., 174
Lund, M., 317
Lutfey, K., 69, 71
Lyons, N. P., 263
Lyotard, J. F., 239

Maaløe, E., 34, 35
MacIntyre, M., 339, 356
Macpherson, P., 255
Macro-level conclusions:
  from micro-level data, 45, 47
Madison, D., 184, 188, 193, 204, 205
Maher, F. A., 328
Mallett, R. K., 317, 319, 326, 328
Mangione, T. W., 13, 17
Mani, L., 364
Mankekar, P., 340, 342, 363, 365
Manning, V., 317
Manzo, J., 64, 70
Map hacking, 143
Marcus, G. E., 16, 187
Marcus, S., 28
Mark, D. M., 132
Mark, M., 132
Markoff, J., 45
Marlaire, C. L., 59

Marshall, C., 16
Martin, E. W., 136
Marvin, C., 203
Massey, D., 142
Matthews, S., 146
Mattingly, D., 133, 142
Mauthner, N., 255, 257
Maynard, D. W., 56, 57, 59, 63, 64,
    65, 66, 68, 69, 70, 74, 78, 81, 82
Mazumdar, S., 365
McClenahen, L., 74
McCormick, L., 166, 167
McCracken, G., 13, 17, 20, 26, 34
McDowell, L., 133, 147
McKeganey, N., 165
McKenas, D. K., 111
McLafferty, S., 132, 134, 142, 143,
    144, 145, 150
McLeroy, K. R., 166, 167
McNay, L., 228
McRobbie, A., 344
Mead, G. H., 243
Meaning making, xviii, xx,
    xxv, 188, 254
Media reception research on
    globalization, 338, 363. See also
    Feminist media ethnography in
    India, postcolonial
Mehan, H., 63
Melville, S., 139
Memory biases, 113
Merleau-Ponty, M., xx
Merton, R. K., x, 19
Meulenberg-Buskens, I., 102
Mexican Miracle, técnicos and, 52
Michalowski, R. J., 51
Micro-level data, 45, 47
Mienczakowski, J., 238, 239, 240,
    241, 245, 246, 247, 248, 249
Miles, M. B., 170
Miller, B., 256
Miller, G., 61, 63, 75
Miller, J. B., 254
Miller, R., 132, 148
Miller, W. L., 13, 17, 165,
    166, 167, 175
Millette, B. E., 174
Mills, C. W., 18, 24, 31
Milne, R., 29

Mindfulness, 111
Minh-ha, T. T., xii
Minister, K., 188
Mini-tour questions, 33
Mischler, E. G., 254
Mishler, E. G., 17, 20
Mitchell, E. S., 168
Mitchell, S. A., 254
Modes of inquiry, 14, 22–29. See also
    Investigative inquiry; Journalistic
    inquiry; Therapeutic inquiry
Moelino, L., 99, 103
Moerman, M., 63, 69
Moghadam, V., 365
Mohanty, C., ix, 342, 364
Mohr, C. D., 112
Molotch, H., 70
Monk, J., 133
Montero, M., 318
Moon, S., 96
Moore, B., 44
Moore, H. L., 214
Moore, R. J., 65
Morago, C., 188
Morawski, J., 257
Moreno, J., 104
Morgan, D. L., 168, 169
Morgan, S., 239, 240, 241,
    247, 248, 249
Morin, K. M., 140
Morril, C., 244, 245
Morrison, D. M., 115
Morse, J. M., 166, 167, 170,
    172, 176, 178, 313, 314
Morse, P., 115
Moss, P., 133, 134, 142
Moyser, G., 14, 18, 31
Mulkay, M. J., 237
Multilevel modeling, daily diary
    research and, 326
Multiple research methods, 166
    convergence, 168–169
    See also Complementarity;
        Complementary assistance,
        research designs based
        on; Qualitative research
        methods, combining quantitative
        methods and
Multiple selves, 50, 52

Multiple subjectivities, xii, 362
Mulvey, L., 134, 138
Murphy, J., 139
Murphy, P., 339, 340, 367
Musham, C., 174, 175
Mutual affinity, conversation
    analysis-ethnography,
    61–62, 71
Myerhoff, B., 187, 279
Myin-Germeys, I., 111
Mykhalovsky, E., 7

Nader, L., 16, 17
Nakai, Carlos, 189
Nandy, A., 350
Naples, N., 339
Narayan, K., 339, 341
Narayan, U., 343, 348, 349, 364
Narrative summaries, 268
Narrative tradition:
    pattern makers, 20
Nash, C., 139
Nast, H., 133, 139, 147
Native-language questions, 33
Naturalistic sampling methods,
    109–110. *See also* Experience
    sampling methods; Experience
    sampling methods data;
    Experience sampling methods
    study, designing; Experience
    sampling methods study,
    implementing; Experience
    Sampling Program
Nave, H., 298, 299
Nead, L., 147
Neale, J. M., 111
Needs assessments, 98
Negotiating entry, 17
Nelson, C. K., 61
Nelson, G., 318
Network élite, 21
    switchers, 21
Neuendorf, K. A., 47
Neumaier, D., 140
Neuman, M., 184, 188, 189
Nezlek, J. B., 114, 117, 124
Nicholas, J. P., 112
Nichols-Casebolt, A., 175
Nicholson, L., ix

Nicolson, N., 112
Noetic crisis, 59, 80
Norsworthy, K., 279
Nvivo, 146
Nye, J., 14

Oakley, A., 20, 25, 34, 361
Obermeyer, N. J., 132
O'Brien, K. J., 173
Obrys, S., 339, 367
Observation, 58, 59, 81, 83, 97
Ockenfels, M. C., 112
O'Conner, P. J., 166, 167, 175
Oishi, S., 114
Olshansky, S., 80
Ong, A., 364
Open-ended interviews, 19, 61
Openshaw, S., 136
Optics of inquiry, 135
Oral histories, xxii, xxiii, xxiv,
    49, 52, 235, 236, 237
Ornstein, S. M., 174, 175
Oskowitz, B., 102
Ostrander, S. A., 17, 18, 23
Oyserman, D., 314, 318

Paget, D., 235
Pain, R., 147
Paper-and-pencil sampling
    methods, 117
Pappworth, J., 17, 20
Paradigms, xi-xii, 166, 167
    mixing, 167
Paradigm shifts, xi
Park, Robert, 22
Park-Fuller, L., 184, 188, 201
Parr, H., 147
Participant observation, 17, 55, 61, 377
Participation frameworks, 63
Participatory action research,
    xxvi, 318
    friendship as method
        and, 277–278
Patai, D., 339, 345, 361
Patton, M. Q., 96, 97
Paty, J. A., 111, 112, 115
Pavlovskaya, M. E., 141
Pearson, N. B., 316, 317, 322, 323
Pelias, R. J., 188, 194

Pelto, G. H., 176
Pelto, P. J., 176
Penner, L. A., 111
Peräkylä, A., 71, 78
Perez, E., ix
Performance texts, 238
Performed research. *See* Ethnodrama;
    Ethnodramas; Ethnodramatic
    research; Ethnographic dramatic
    narrative; Ethnographic
    performances
Personal electronic correspondence as
    reflexive strategy, 295–297
    e-letters, 299–307
    e-letters as readers, 307–311
    seminars/lectures, 297–298
    See also Writing-in-response
Personal Narratives Group, 188
Perz, W. G., 112
Peterman, A. H., 112
Peterson, E. E., 188
Peuquet, D., 132
Phenomenology, xxvi, 276
Philips, L., 339, 362
Phillips, D., 249
Piaget, J., xxv, 254
Picard, R. W., 141
Pickles, J., 138
Piercy, F., 97, 99, 103
Pietromonaco, P. R., 113
Pile, S., 147
Pillow, W. S., 214, 215, 217,
    218, 219, 229
Pinder, D., 139
Piston, W., 262
Platt, J., 377, 378, 379, 380
Pleated text, xiii-xiv, 2
Poiker, T., 132
Polkinghorne, D., 254
Pollock, G., 134, 138, 140
Pomerantz, A., 63
Porche-Burke, L., 318
Porter, L. S., 112
Positionality:
    dilemmas of, 49
    negotiating subjectivity and, 49–52
Positivism, xxvi, 134, 276
    subject-object relationship, 278

Positivist/masculinist epistemology, GIS
    methods and, 136–137
Postcolonial cartography, 139
Postcolonial feminist ethnography,
    338, 363, 364–365. *See also*
    Feminist media ethnography
    in India, postcolonial
Postcolonial theory, ix, xiii, xxix, 367
Postcolonial writing, 205
Postmodernism, ix, xxix, 245
    qualitative research and, 243–244
Postmodern theory, xxi
    body and, xix, 213
Poststructuralism, xiii, 133
Potter, E., 317
Potter, J., 61, 63
Power imbalances in field, 337
Prakash, G., 349
Pratt, G., 132, 133, 136
Pratt, M. L., 186, 188
Pregnant teenagers, body and, 218–221
    discourses of desire, 226, 227
    discourses of redemption, 224
    physically exceeding boundaries,
        221–227, 228
    relaxed bodies, 226–227
    sites of resistance, 218–219, 228
    See also Teen pregnancy intervention
        programs
Prescott, S., 110
Press, A., 366
Prilleltensky, I., 318
Primary historical sources, 43, 45
    analysis problems, 44
    finding, 45
Priority-Sequence Model, 171–175,
    176–178
Probyn, F., 214
Program evaluations, 98
Pronk, N. P., 111
Prosodic manipulations, 66–67
Prospective indexical, 78
Psychoanalysis, 140
Psychoanalytic theories, 133
Public voice, 239
Purdue Momentary Assessment
    Tool, 121
Puwar, N., 18, 22, 27, 34

Qualitative research, 19, 380
  daily diary research as, 315–317
  See also Creative qualitative research
    methods; Qualitative research
    methods
Qualitative research methods, xii xxv,
    10, 19, 134, 145, 151, 171, 173,
    174, 176, 178, 268, 274, 379, 380
  versus quantitative research
    methods, xi, 96
  See also Creative qualitative research
    methods; Qualitative research
    methods, combining quantitative
    methods and
Qualitative research methods,
  combining quantitative
    methods and, 165–179, 377
  motivations for, 168–169
  paradigm-conflict problems,
    166, 167
  political issues, 176–177
  team-based approach, 178
  technical problems, 166, 167, 176
  See also Health research, mixed-
    method
Quantitative research methods, xii,
    134, 136, 142, 174, 175, 177, 254
  gender biases of conventional,
    149–150
  versus qualitative research
    methods, xi, 96
Quasi-experimental designs, 173
Quattrochi, D. A., 132
Queer studies, ix, xxvii, 8, 9
Queer theory, xxvi, xxvii, 281
  friendship as method and, 277
Questionnaires, 109, 173
Quirk, M., 175

Rabinowitz, V., 317, 318
Radway, J., 339, 355, 367
Rafaeli, E., 110, 116, 117, 122, 124
Raheja, G., 356
Rainbird, H., 16
Rallis, S. F., 17, 167
Ralman, A., 318
Ram, K., 345, 349, 360
Rank, M. R., 179

Rapoport, T., 298
Raudenbush, S. W., 124
Rawlins, W. K., 274, 275, 276
Raynor, D. A., 112
Reader response theory, 355
Reason, P., 277, 278, 318
Reciprocity, 17
Redelmeier, D. A., 115
Reed-Danahay, D. E., 187, 188
Reflexive practice, xxii, xxvi
Reflexive writing, xxvii
Reflexivity, xviii, 379
Reichardt, C. S., 166, 167
Reid, A., 174, 175
Reinharz, S., 50, 52, 277, 361
Reis, H. T., 110, 113, 114, 116, 117,
    118, 120, 122, 124, 316, 329
Reissman, C. K., 257
Relational psychologies, 254
Research:
  applied, 98
  basic, 98
Research designs:
  complementary assistance-based,
    170–175
  practical, 167
Researching sensitive topics, 17
Resources, experience sampling
    method, 116–118
  assessing, 116–117
  platform implementation, 116–117
  research team strength, 116, 118
  subject remuneration, 116, 117–118
Retrospective self-reports, 115–116
  accuracy of, 113
Rhodas, A. R., 296
Richardson, L., xiv, 1, 4, 9, 61,
    189, 202, 237, 240, 296
Ricks, D. F., 110, 111
Riggin, J. C., 167
Rist, R., 17
Roberts, H., 277
Roberts, S. M., 133, 135
Robin, L., 113
Robinson, M. D., 113
Rocheleau, D., 134, 138, 139, 142
Rocklin, T., 174
Rogers, A., 256, 263

Rolfe, A., 240, 248
Rollinson, P., 148
Ronal, C. R., 191
Rorty, R., 241
Rose, D., 133, 134, 138, 140
Rose, G., xviii, 134, 137, 139, 140,
    142, 143, 147, 148
Rosenblatt, P., 97
Rossman, G. B., 16, 17, 169
Rotter, D., 179
Rowe, K., 218
Rubin, L. B., 275
Ruggles, A. J., 143
Rundstrom, R., 146
Rushton, G., 143
Russo-Devosa, Y., 328
Ryan, R. M., 111

Sacks, H., 60, 61, 62, 65
Said, E., 342, 362, 365
Salazar, C., 365
Sampling, 17
Sampling period, 118, 119–120
Sampling protocols, 118
  event-contingent sampling,
      119, 120, 121
  interval-contingent sampling,
      119, 120
  signal-contingent sampling,
      118–119, 120
Sanday, P., 361
Sandelowski, M., 168, 169
Sanders, W. B., 27
Satin, L., 188
Schechner, R., 193
Schegloff, E. A., 60, 62, 64, 65,
    66, 67, 75
Schein, R. H., 135
Scheper-Hughes, N., 255
Scheurich, J. J., 221
Schmidt, J., 116
Schmidtke, A., 249
Schultheiss, R. B., 98
Schulz, J., 61
Schuurman, N., 132, 151
Schwandt, T. A., 276
Schwartz, J. E., 111, 117
Schwartz, R. D., 168
Sciarra, D., 319

Science and technology studies (STS)
    community, 13, 14, 30, 35
  access issues, 15
  See also Interview as social science
      methodology; Social science
      methodology, interview in
Scollon, C. N., 115
Seager, J., 139
Sechrest, L., 168
Sechzer, J., 317, 318
Secklin, P. L., 188
Secondary historical sources,
    43, 45, 47–48
Sedgwick, E. K., 277
Sefi, S., 68
Seidman, S., ix
Seidmann, I. E., 17
Seiler, M., ix
Seiter, E., 339, 361
Seldon, A., 17, 20
Self-reflexive research, 341, 367.
    See also Feminist media
    ethnography in India,
    postcolonial; Self-reflexivity
Self-reflexivity:
  critical, 205
  in audience ethnography, 341
  in audience research, 340
  lack of in audience reception, 339
  of postcolonial feminist
      ethnographers, 341, 365
  rigorous, 338
  See also Feminist media ethnography
      in India, postcolonial
Semantic knowledge, 113
Seo, M. G., 112
Sequential analysis, 62, 63, 67, 68, 69
Seymour, S., 359
Shaffer, D., 249
Shapiro, D., 112
Sharp, J. P., 133
Shaw, C. R., 19
Shaw, G. B., 15
Shaw, L. L., 59, 62, 76
Sheets, H. M., 375
Sheppard, E., 132, 136
Shields, A. L., 115
Shiffman, S. S., 110, 111, 112,
    115, 116, 117

Shome, R., 367
Shrout, P. E., 117, 122
Sieber, R. E., 132, 136
Sieber, S. D., 170
Sikes, M. P., 317
Silences, 66
Silverman, D., 61, 75
Silverman, K., 139
Simon, G. E., 111
Simpson, J. S., 188
Sinclair, M., 240, 246, 249
Smith, D., ix, 19, 44, 317
Smith, J. K., 166, 167
Smith, N. L., 29
Smith, R., 240, 246, 249
Smith, S., 188
Smith, S. J., 141
Smith, V., 18
Smyth, A., xxii, xxiii
Smyth, J. M., 112
Snijders, T., 120
Snow, D. A., 244, 245
Social body, 214
Social science methodology,
    interview in, 16–21
Social scientific writing:
    enlarging, 5
    examining, 5
    story lines, 2
Sociological imagination, 24
Soefer, M. H., 112
Sorokin, P. A., 110
Souhami, R. L., 82
Spain, D., 147
Spakes, P., 175
Sparke, M., 139
Speaking-in-response, xxvii, 296.
    See also Personal electronic
    correspondence as reflexive
    strategy
Speech tokens, 66
Spector, M., 14, 18, 19
Spencer, G., 17, 18, 31
Spencer, J. W., 61
Spencer, R., 254
Spitzack, C., 195, 197
Spivak, G. C., ix, 342, 364
Spradley, J. P., 17
Sprenkle, D., 96

Spry, T., 189, 190, 205
Sridhar, K., 359
St. Martin, K., 139
Stacey, J., 140, 339, 361
Staeheli, L., 133
Stafford, F. P., 112
Stalling strategy, 56–57
Standpoint theory, 277. See also
    Feminist standpoint theory
Stange, K. C., 166, 167, 175
Stangor, C., 328
Steckler, A., 166, 167
Stein, R., 297
Steiner, D. L., 165
Stewart, A., 318, 325
Stewart, C. J., 13, 17
Stivers, T., 66
Stoeltje, B., 339, 367
Stone, A. A., 110, 111, 112, 116, 117
Story lines, social scientific
    disciplines,' 2
Strauss, A. L., 19, 60, 74, 75, 81, 257
Structured interviews, 97, 315
Stubbs, M., 63
Studying-up, 17, 50
    as strategy of inquiry, 16
Subjective experience, access to, 109
Subjectivity, 49
    negotiating positionality and, 49–52
Sudman, S., 13, 17, 19
Sue, D., 318
Sui, D. Z., 132
Sullivan, A., 258
Sullivan, M., 175
Sullivan, O., 178
Sulon, J., 112
Suls, J., 328
Survey research, 377–378
Surveys, 55, 173, 174
Svarstad, B. L., 59, 74
Swendsen, J. D., 111
Swim, J. K., 314, 316, 317, 318,
    319, 322, 323, 328
Symon, G., 102
Szalacha, L., 268

Tappan, M., 256
Tashakkori, A., xi
Taylor, J. M., 258

Taylor, P., 134
Taylor, S. J., 19
Technological determinism, 14
Teddlie, C., xi
Tedlock, B., 274, 276, 281, 363, 364
Teen pregnancy, 216, 227
  defining, 216–217
  See also Pregnant teenagers, body
    and; Teen pregnancy
    intervention programs
Teen pregnancy intervention
    programs, 217
  classroom styles, 222–227, 228
  view of body, 217
  See also Pregnant teenagers,
    body and
Teen pregnancy prevention
    programs, 217
Tempalski, B., 134
ten Have, P., 85
Tennen, H., 112, 328
Tenni, C., xxii, xxiii
Tetreault, M. K., 328
Therapeutic inquiry, 14, 22, 25–27,
    29, 30, 33, 36
  listening to listening, 26
  trust and, 25
Thick description, 49
Thomas, R. J., 14, 18, 36
Thomas, V., 97
Thomas-Slayter, B., 139
Thompson, A., 113, 146
Thorvik, K., 14, 26, 30
Thought sampling, 110
Thrift, N., 147
Tillmann-Healy, L. M., xxv, 274,
    278, 279, 280, 281, 282, 284,
    287, 288, 289, 290, 291, 296
Tilly, C., 45
Tilly, L., 45
Tilly, R., 45
Timander, L. M., 144
Todorov, T., 237
Tolman, D. L., 215, 255, 256, 268
Torgovnick, M., 187
Transcribing conventions, 86–87
Traweek, S., 13, 15, 16, 18, 24
Trend, M. G., 169
Triangle Theatre Company, 238

Triangulation, 52, 97, 168, 177
Trinh, T. M-H., 185, 187, 189,
    199, 201, 207, 214
Tronick, E. Z., 254, 256
Trust relations, 17
Trustworthiness in research, 98
Turner, V., 187, 194, 205,
    206, 235, 241
Tversky, B., 132

Undheim, T. A., 13, 14, 26, 30
Unger, R. K., 317, 318
Unstructured interviews, 315
Urquidi, Victor, 48–49, 50, 52
Utterances, 55, 57, 58, 66. *See also*
    Conversation analysis;
    Ethnography; Limited affinity,
    conversation analysis-ethnography

Valentine, G., 147
van Dijk, T., 61, 75
van Eck, M. M., 112
Van Maanen, J., 16, 61
van Os, J., 111
Varma, P., 359
Vasseleu, C., 137
Venn, C., 319
Verbatim theater, xxiv, 235, 236, 237
Vernon, R., 52
Verstehen, 276
Video capture, 55
Villella, O., x
Visweswaran, K., xxix, 214, 338, 339,
    340, 341, 345, 354, 362, 364
Voice-centered relational method. *See*
    Listening Guide method

Wadeson, H., 100
Wagstaff, G. F., 29
Wagstaffe, M., 18
Wajcman, J., 135
Walford, G., 13
Walker, R., 214
Walkerdine, V., 319
Wang, P. S., 111
Wasow, M., 80
Watson, D., 111
Watson, T. J., 296
Way, N., 255, 268

Webb, E. J., 168
Weber, J., 149
Weber, Max, 276
Weedon, C., 221
Weijts, W., 174
Weinberg, M. K., 256
Weiner, D., 132, 136, 145, 146
Weinholtz, D., 174
Weis, L., 361
Weiss, H. M., 112
Weiss, R. S., 13, 17, 275
Wenger, E., 63
Werber, R. P., 257
Werking, K., 275
Wessman, A. E., 110, 111
West, S. G., 114
Wetherell, M., 75
Whalen, M. R., 64
Wheeler, L., 110, 116, 117, 316, 329
White, M., 25
Whitmore, E., 96
Whyte, W. F., 19, 26, 62, 318
Wikler, L., 80
Wilkinson, S., 318
Williams, P. M., 22
Willig, C., 316, 325
Willmuth, M., 100
Wilson, B. L., 169
Wilson, H. S., 282
Wilson, M. E., 282
Wilson, T., 64, 216
Wing, A. K., ix
Winkler, J., 18, 33, 36
Winnicott, D. W., 254
Winter, S., 132
Wirtz, D., 115
Wodak, R., 75
Wolf, D., 339
Wolf, M., 338, 339, 345, 355, 363
Women, everyday lives of:
   linking geographical context
      and, 143–144

Women and Geography Study
   Group, 133
Women's activism:
   supporting through GIS-based
      research, 144–145
Women's life paths, mapping in
   space-time, 146–149
Wood, J. T., 139, 276
Woods, N. F., 174
Woods, P., 243, 244, 246
Worell, J., 318
"Working the hyphens," friendship as
   method and, 277
Worth, S., 236
Writing:
   as practical process, 1
   as theoretical process, 1
   content, 4
   frame, 4
   power relationships in, 3
   textual form, 4
   voice, 4
   See also Autobiographical writing;
      Social scientific writing; Writing
      as method; Writing-in-response;
      Writing-stories
Writing as method, xxvii
Writing-in-response, xxvii, 296,
   309–310. See also Personal
   electronic correspondence as
   reflexive strategy
Writing-stories, xiii, 2, 3–5

Yapa, L., 132
Young, I. M., 147, 282

Zapata, Francisco, 46
Zelizer, V., 45
Zemp, L. D., 174, 175
Zimmerman, D. H., 62
Zimmerman, D. L., 143
Zyzanski, S. J., 166, 167, 175

About the Editors

Sharlene Nagy Hesse-Biber is Professor of Sociology at Boston College. She is also the founder and director of The National Association of Women in Catholic Higher Education. She is coeditor of several books, including *Feminist Perspectives on Social Research* (Oxford University Press, 2003), *Women in Catholic Higher Education* (OUP, 2003), and *Feminist Approaches to Theory and Methodology* (OUP, 1999). She is also the coauthor of *The Practice of Qualitative Research* (Sage Publications, 2006) and *Working Women in America* (OUP, 2000), and the author of *Am I Thin Enough Yet?* (OUP, 1996). She is general editor of *The Handbook of Feminist Research: Theory and Praxis* (forthcoming, Sage Publications, 2006) and coeditor of *When Methods Meets Technology* (forthcoming, Sage Publications, 2006). She has written numerous articles in the fields of body image, qualitative methods, feminism, and computer approaches to data analysis.

Patricia Leavy is Assistant Professor of Sociology and Director of Gender Studies at Stonehill College in Easton, Massachusetts. She is coeditor of *Approaches to Qualitative Research: A Reader on Theory and Practice* (Oxford University Press, 2004). She is also the coauthor of *The Practice of Qualitative Research* (Sage Publications, 2006) and *A Feminist Research Primer* (forthcoming, Sage Publications). She has published articles in the fields of popular culture, research methods, body image, and collective memory.

About the Contributors

Sarah Babb is Associate Professor of Sociology at Boston College. Her recent book *Managing Mexico: Economists from Nationalism to Neoliberalism* (Princeton, 2001) examines the evolution of the Mexican economics profession over the course of the twentieth century. Her more recent research interests include mission creep at the International Monetary Fund, economic policy fads and fashions in Washington, DC, and the fate of indigenous capitalists in Latin America in the age of globalization.

Nitza Berkovitch is a Senior Lecturer in Sociology at the Department of Behavioral Science in Ben Gurion University in Israel. She works in the areas of gender, citizenship, women's movements, human rights, and globalization.

Her book *From Motherhood to Citizenship: Women's Rights and International Organizations* (1999, Johns Hopkins University Press) explores the history of global struggles for equality and rights of international women's movements. She is a member of the editorial boards of *Social Politics* and *Israeli Sociology*.

Tatiana Bertsch completed her J.D. from New York University School of Law in 2005. She now works at the Public Defender's office in Palm Beach County, Florida.

Eliza Bliss-Moreau is currently a Ph.D. student in psychology at Boston College. Her research interests lie in the areas of affective reactivity, affective induction, poverty and affect, language and experience, functional neuroscience of emotion processes, and sex differences in emotion knowledge.

Tamlin Conner is currently a Visiting Assistant Professor at Boston College in the Department of Psychology. She received her Ph.D. in psychology from Boston College in 2003.

Her research interests lie in the fields of social cognition, implicit cognition and links to conscious experience, self-report process, emotional experience, and experience sampling procedures.

She is the coauthor of the article "Ecological Momentary Assessment" in *Encyclopedia of Health and Behavior* with M. M. Tugade and L. Feldman Barrett (Sage Publications, 2004).

Sharon A. Deacon, M.S., is a family therapist who focuses on using experiential techniques and the creative arts with families in therapy. She graduated from USC in 1969. She is a doctoral candidate in the Marriage and Family Therapy Program, Department of Child Development and Family Studies, at Purdue University in West Lafayette, Indiana.

She has published a handful of articles on creative strategies for qualitative research and program evaluation. She is the coauthor (with Fred Piercy) of the manual *Qualitative Evaluation of Human Service Programs*. This manual takes readers step by step through the process of program evaluation using a participatory research approach. She is the coauthor (with Lorna L. Hecker) of *The Therapist's Notebook: Homework, Handouts, and Activities for Use in Psychotherapy (Haworth Marriage and the Family)*.

Carol Gilligan is a Professor at New York University. She received her Ph.D. in social psychology from Harvard University.

She is the author of *Mapping the Moral Domain* (1988), *Making Connections* (1990), *Between Voice and Silence: Women and Girls, Race and Relationship* (1995), and *The Birth of Pleasure* (2002), among others.

Lauri L. Hyers earned her Ph.D. in social psychology from Pennsylvania State University. She is currently Assistant Professor of Psychology at West Chester University of Pennsylvania.

Her teaching and research interests lie in the fields of experience of prejudice from the target's perspective, intergroup relations, group identity, qualitative research methodology, and gender/ethnicity-specific rites of passage.

Mei-Po Kwan is currently a Professor in the Department of Geography at Ohio State University. She received her Ph.D. in geography from the University of California, Santa Barbara, in 1984.

Her research interests are in the theoretical and substantive questions in urban, transportation, and economic geography through the application of GIS methods. She focuses primarily on the geographical and temporal characteristics of people's daily activities, and the impact of recent social, economic, and political changes on their everyday lives as manifested through changes in the geographies of their daily activities. She also researches the development of new analytical methods for geographical research, specifically, GIS-based 3D geovisualization and geocomputation.

She is the author of *Gender, Race and Homeland Security: Negotiating Muslim Identities in the U.S. After 9/11* with Cara Aitchison and Peter Hopkins (Aldershot: Ashgate, 2005).

Robyn K. Mallett earned her Ph.D. in social psychology from Pennsylvania State University. She is currently a Postdoctoral Fellow at the University of Virginia.

Her research interests lie in the areas of psychology of prejudice and intergroup relations from the perspective of members of both stigmatized and nonstigmatized social groups.

Douglas W. Maynard is currently a Professor at the University of Wisconsin–Madison in the Sociology Department. He is the author of *Bad News, Good News: Conversational Order in Everyday Talk and Clinical Settings* (University of Chicago Press, 2003). He is the coauthor of *Ethnomethodology and Conversation Analysis* with Steven E. Clayman (AltaMira Press, 2003).

Jim Mienczakowski is currently Deputy Vice-Chancellor (Academic & Research) at CQU. He was the Dean of Education and Creative Arts at CQU. He has taught in the UK, the West Indies, and Australia. He is also internationally acknowledged for his scholarship and contribution to the field of ethnography.

He has theoretical and practical research experience. He is interested in research areas of significant social and emotional impact expressed through his construct: the discourse of performed ethnography, or *ethnodrama*.

He is especially interested in areas such as road trauma and legal processes, suicide prevention and educative awareness programs, prevention strategies for alcohol and substance abuse, trajectories of recovery from sexual assault, experiences of cosmetic and plastic surgery, health education, and beginning teacher preparation.

David L. Morgan received his Ph.D. in sociology from the University of Michigan and is currently a Professor in the School of Community Health at Portland State University. In addition to his work on focus groups, he also has done work on broad social science research methods. He is currently working on a book that describes practical approaches to combining qualitative and quantitative methods.

Radhika Parameswaran received her Ph.D. in mass communication from the University of Iowa in 1997. She is an Assistant Professor in the School of Journalism, Indiana University, Bloomington.

Her research interests include gender and the media, ethnographic research, postcolonial studies, and audience studies. Her recent research has been published in the *Journal of Communication, Gazette: The International Journal of Communication Studies, Frontiers: A Journal of Women's Studies,* and the *Journal of Communication Inquiry.* Her chapter is based on the author's dissertation "Public Images, Private Pleasures: Romance Reading at the

Intersection of Gender, Class, and National Identities in Postcolonial India," directed by Professor Carolyn Dyer.

Wanda S. Pillow is an Associate Professor of Educational Policy Studies at the University of Illinois at Urbana-Champaign. She received her Ph.D. in educational policy and leadership at Ohio State University in 1994.

Dr. Pillow's research interests include the intersections of gender, race, class, and sexuality as they impact issues of representation, access, voice, and equality. She explores these issues through thinking and writing about the doing of qualitative research and the methodologies that guide our analyses.

She is the author of *Unfit Subjects: Education Policy and the Teen Mother: 1972–2002*. This book builds from the aforementioned interests and further develops her thinking about doing critical, race-based feminist policy analysis. This book uses qualitative, historical, legal, and policy research to analyze how the purpose of education for teen mothers has been and is currently defined and how the purposes of education are often defined differentially based on the race of the teen mother. She also coauthored (with Elizabeth St. Pierre) *Working the Ruins: Feminist Poststructural Theory and Methods in Education*.

Laurel Richardson is Professor Emeritus of Sociology and Visiting Professor of Cultural Studies in the College of Education at Ohio State University. She received her undergraduate degrees from the University of Chicago and her Ph.D. from the University of Colorado.

She is the author of *Fields of Play: Constructing an Academic Life* and *Travels with Ernest: The Literary-Ethnographic Divide*.

Renée Spencer, Ed.D., LICSW, is an Assistant Professor at the Boston University School of Social Work. She received her master's in social work from the University of Texas at Austin and her doctorate in human development and psychology from the Harvard Graduate School of Education. Her research focuses on youth mentoring relationships, adolescent development, and gender. Recent publications include "Growth-Promoting Relationships Between Youth and Adults: A Focus Group Study," published in *Families in Society* (2004); "Studying Relationships in Psychotherapy: An Untapped Resource for Youth Mentoring," published in *New Directions in Youth Development: Theory, Practice and Research*, edited by G. Noam (2004); and "Understanding the Mentoring Process Between Adolescents and Adults," to be published in *Youth and Society*.

Tami Spry is an Associate Professor in the Department of Speech Communication and Communication Studies at St. Cloud State University in Minnesota. She is a performing theorist, teacher, and director in performance studies.

Janet K. Swim obtained her Ph.D. in social psychology at the University of Minnesota. She is now Professor of Psychology at the Pennsylvania State University.

Her research deals with how people come to decide when they or others have been targets of everyday prejudice or discrimination; the affective, motivational, and behavioral consequences of being a target of discrimination and recognizing others' experiences with discrimination; and how people cope with being a target of prejudice and discrimination. Her work primarily addresses everyday forms of sexism, racism, and heterosexism.

Lisa M. Tillmann-Healy is an Assistant Professor of Communication at Rollins College in Winter Park, Florida. She is a graduate of Marquette University (B.A.) and the University of South Florida (Ph.D.).

She is the author of the book *Between Gay and Straight: Understanding Friendship Across Sexual Orientation* (AltaMira Press, 2001), and she also has written and contributed to several articles and book chapters on relationships, qualitative methods, and narrative inquiry.

Trond Arne Undheim is a Senior Research Fellow at the Norwegian University of Science and Technology, Department of Interdisciplinary Studies of Culture, at the Center for Technology and Society. His research interests are within science and technology studies, organizational studies, and policy making in the areas of ICT, biotechnology, and sustainability. Currently, he works as a Project Manager in the Norwegian Board of Technology doing parliamentary technology assessment in technology foresight, software policy, sustainability, and innovation. In the spring of 2002, he was awarded a Ph.D. of sociology for his work "What the Net Can't Do: The Everyday Practice of Internet, Globalization and Mobility, a Study of High Tech Knowledge Workers and Organizational Practices in Norway, Italy and Silicon Valley."

Dr. Undheim has been a Visiting Fellow to the University of California, Berkeley, and is currently a Visiting Fellow at the European Commission's Joint Research Center, the Institute of Prospective Technologies (IPTS) in Seville.

M. Katherine Weinberg received her Ph.D. in Developmental Psychology from the University of Massachusetts at Amherst in 1992. She is currently an Assistant Professor of Psychiatry at the Harvard Medical School and a Research Associate at Boston's Children's Hospital. She is also on the research staff at the T. B. Brazelton Child Development Unit at Children's Hospital.

Dr. Weinberg's research focuses on the effects of maternal depression and anxiety on maternal and infant socio-emotional development. She is particularly interested in the differential effects of maternal depression and panic disorder on infant and maternal functioning, on the stability of maternal depressive illness over the course of the first year postpartum, and on the differences in compromises observed in mothers with diagnosed clinical depression or subclinical depressive symptomatology. Dr. Weinberg also studies emotion development, with a particular emphasis on emotion regulation, during infancy and early childhood. Her work focuses on how boys and girls differentially regulate emotion and cope with stress and how these abilities change with age.

Dr. Weinberg has received support from the National Science Foundation, the National Institute of Mental Health, and the National Institute of Child Health and Development. She is on the Editorial Board of the Infant Mental Health Journal and an Ad Hoc Reviewer for several national and international journals. She has served as a reviewer for the National Institute of Mental Health and the Israel Science Foundation. Her work has been published in leading peer-reviewed journals including *Pediatrics*, *Developmental Psychology*, and *Child Development*.

Niza Yanay is a Senior Lecturer of social psychology in the Department of Behavioral Sciences at Ben Gurion University in Israel. She is interested in the areas of social psychology and feminist theory.

She has published articles on the relations between emotions, discourse, and culture. She is now writing on the construction of hatred as a personal experience and national discourse. She is an associate editor of *HAGAR: Studies in Culture, Polity and Identities*.